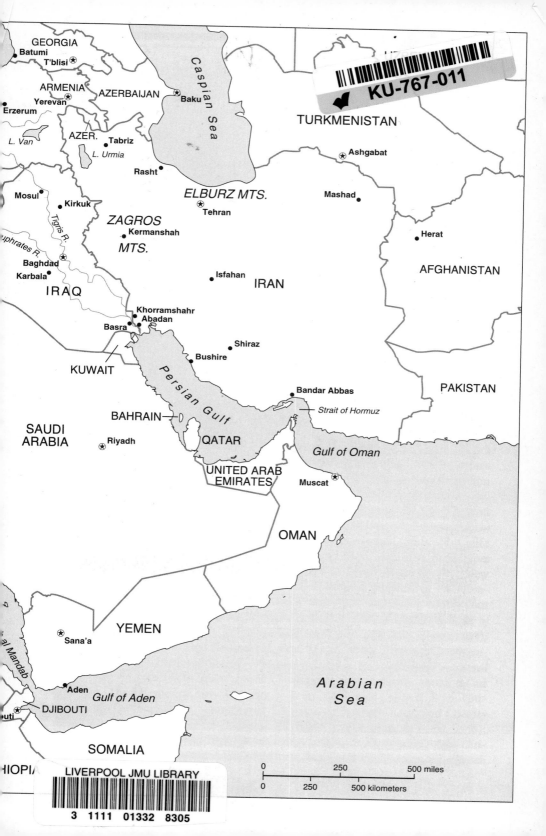

GEORGIA
Batumi
T'blisi ✪
ARMENIA
Yerevan ✪
Erzerum
AZERBAIJAN
Baku ✪
Caspian Sea
TURKMENISTAN
Ashgabat ✪
L. Van
AZER.
Tabriz
L. Urmia
Rasht
ELBURZ MTS.
Mashad
Mosul
Kirkuk
ZAGROS
Tehran ✪
Kermanshah
MTS.
Herat
Tigris R.
Euphrates R.
Baghdad ✪
Karbala
IRAQ
Isfahan
IRAN
AFGHANISTAN
Khorramshahr
Abadan
Basra
Bushire
Shiraz
KUWAIT
Bandar Abbas
Persian Gulf
Strait of Hormuz
PAKISTAN
BAHRAIN
QATAR
Gulf of Oman
SAUDI
ARABIA
Riyadh ✪
UNITED ARAB
EMIRATES
Muscat ✪
OMAN
YEMEN
Sana'a ✪
al Mandab
Aden
Gulf of Aden
Arabian
Sea
DJIBOUTI
uti ✪
SOMALIA
HIOPIA

0		250		500 miles
0	250		500 kilometers	

PALESTINE AND THE ARAB-ISRAELI CONFLICT

Seventh Edition

CHARLES D. SMITH
University of Arizona

BEDFORD/ST. MARTIN'S
Boston • New York

For Bedford/St. Martin's

Publisher for History: Mary V. Dougherty
Executive Editor: Traci Mueller
Director of Development for History: Jane Knetzger
Senior Editor: Heidi L. Hood
Developmental Editor: Marilea Polk Fried
Editorial Assistant: Jennifer Jovin
Production Assistant: Ashley Chalmers
Executive Marketing Manager: Jenna Bookin Barry
Project Management: Books By Design, Inc.
Cover Design: Billy Boardman
Cover Photo: *Dome of the Rock and Western Wall, Israel.* © Gary Cralle/Getty Images
Composition: Books By Design, Inc.
Printing and Binding: RR Donnelley & Sons Company

President: Joan E. Feinberg
Editorial Director: Denise B. Wydra
Director of Marketing: Karen R. Soeltz
Director of Editing, Design, and Production: Marcia Cohen
Assistant Director of Editing, Design, and Production: Elise S. Kaiser
Manager, Publishing Services: Emily Berleth

Library of Congress Control Number: 2009928649

Manufactured in the United States of America.

4 3 2 1 0 9
f e d c b a

For information, write: Bedford/St. Martin's, 75 Arlington Street, Boston, MA 02116
(617-399-4000)

ISBN-10: 0-312-53501-5
ISBN-13: 978-0-312-53501-8

Acknowledgments
Acknowledgments and copyrights are contin[ued at the] [back of the book on] pages 559–62, which constitute an extension [of the copyright page.]

PREFACE

THE 1967 ARAB-ISRAELI WAR, which led to Israel's occupation of the Sinai Peninsula, the West Bank, and the Golan Heights, thrust the Middle East into global consciousness as never before. General as well as scholarly interest in the Middle East, along with more polemical analyses, has increased over the years—and especially over the last decade. A series of events—the collapse of the Israeli-Palestinian Camp David talks in 2000 and eruption of the second intifada that year, the al-Qaida–sponsored attacks on the United States on September 11, 2001, the American-led attack on Iraq in 2003, the 2006 Israeli-Hizbollah conflict, and the 2008 clash between Israel and Hamas in Gaza—often resulted in the American public being offered polarizing images that led to claims of a clash of civilizations and occasional stereotyping of the peoples involved. To fully understand the Arab-Israeli conflict, it is necessary to study the history behind the headlines.

When I introduced my own course on the conflict, I could not find a satisfactory text for the college student or the general reader. As a historian, I envisaged a book that, in addition to comprehensive coverage of recent history, gave equal weight to the period before Israeli independence in 1948, because it was during this earlier period that Zionism claimed Palestine and Palestinian resistance began. An understanding of the pre-1948 history of Arab-Zionist relations reveals the foundations of subsequent Arab and Israeli attitudes and suggests how crises today can be evaluated with reference to events that extend back to World War I and earlier. I decided to write such a book, which resulted in the publication of the first edition of *Palestine and the Arab-Israeli Conflict* in 1988. From its inception, this book has given equal emphasis to the modern histories of both Palestine and Israel, beginning with extended treatment of the nineteenth century, the critical era of World War I, and the period of British mandatory rule down to 1947 as points of departure for the era since Israel's independence. Later, as it became clear that students would benefit from reading primary sources from the conflict for themselves, I added documents throughout the book as well.

Because this book is intended primarily for college students and the general reader, and also because I believe that readers should have easy access to my sources, I cite only works published in English and do not claim to have exhausted that material. Depending on the topic, this may mean that I sometimes refer to more works by Israeli scholars than by Arab. On the other hand, much of this Israeli scholarship offers insights and critical perspectives unknown to many Americans.

Inevitably, the question of balance or fairness arises when we deal with subjects that are controversial and that arouse intense emotions. As a historian I believe it necessary to examine other peoples and eras in light of the values and historical processes that produced them. This means that opinions and claims abhorrent to observers removed from the scene may become entirely comprehensible when viewed as part of a people's history and experience in interaction with others. I consider Zionist and Palestinian attitudes to be equally comprehensible in the context of their respective histories and cultures. Moreover, there is no one Zionist/Israeli or Palestinian/Arab view of events or each other, contrary to the polarized perspectives that have gained acceptance in some quarters.

NEW TO THE SEVENTH EDITION

I have extended the book's coverage up to spring 2009, including the significance of the American and Israeli elections that installed Barack Obama and Binyamin Netanyahu as president and prime minister, respectively. Equally important is the population data released in May 2009 by Israel's Central Bureau of Statistics (see the Epilogue) which reveals that Jews are no longer a clear majority in Israel and the occupied territories. The expectation that population parity between Jews and Arabs would occur by the year 2020 has been preempted by a decade and increases the urgency of Israel's deliberation over whether to create a two-state solution to maintain Israel's identity as a Jewish state.

There are several features new to this edition. I have added a prologue to provide a concise overview of the pre-Christian and early Islamic periods, noting major scholarly developments regarding the archaeology of ancient Israel. I have also added an epilogue that examines recent developments in the Arab-Israeli conflict and evaluates future prospects for the region. New end-of-chapter Questions for Consideration reinforce chapter themes and offer opportunities for classroom discussions and assignments. Two new maps in Chapter 11 show the West Bank separation barrier in 2007 and West Bank aquifers.

As in previous editions, I have updated documents and photos for various chapters to illustrate developments and social processes. Among the new documents is a report of an assurance of nonaggression given by Jordan's King Abdullah to the Zionist leadership in May 1948, excerpts from the 2002 Arab League peace proposal to Israel, and an interview with U.S. Secretary of State Hillary Clinton. The seventh edition now includes forty-one photos—an increase of more than one-third—eighteen of which are new. I have made a special effort to include more photographs of everyday people and to illustrate issues of gender by adding photographs that portray women at particular points of historical significance.

Likewise, I have updated the Selected Bibliography to highlight recent scholarship, with emphasis on works published since the year 2000. I have sought to identify research on topics beyond the scope of the text, especially studies on social history and gender that examine Israeli and Palestinian experiences. Here I have added a new section on Ethnicity and Identity to account for the numerous scholarly works that have recently appeared. Students should examine these books and also their bibliographies as guides to further study.

As in the sixth edition, I have used Internet sources extensively, particularly in the notes for Chapter 11. I again include a special section in the Selected Bibliography listing Web sites of particular value for the range of sources and information they provide. The companion Web resource Make History, at bedfordstmartins.com/makehistory, provides students and instructors with links to many additional Web sites and primary documents—indexed by course, topic, and date range—plus all the maps from the book for download or presentation. Also included at the Make History site are research and writing aids, including documentation guidelines and advice on avoiding plagiarism.

A NOTE ON USAGE AND TRANSLITERATION

I have been generally consistent in my spelling of Arab names but have catered to general usage on occasion. For example, I refer to Gamal Abd al-Nasser, not Jamal Abd al-Nasir. I use the al- prefix consistently for names from the mandate period, such as al-Husayni, but for more familiar figures of the recent past I drop the prefix after the first use of the name; al-Nasser thus becomes Nasser and al-Sadat becomes Sadat. Although the prefix is included in index listings, it is not a factor in the alphabetization of entries.

ACKNOWLEDGMENTS

I wish to acknowledge the assistance of those at Bedford/St. Martin's who contributed to the development and expansion of this new edition, especially Mary Dougherty, Jane Knetzger, Heidi Hood, and Jennifer Jovin; my developmental editor, Marilea Polk Fried; copyeditor Joan Flaherty; and Nancy Benjamin and Emily Berleth, who managed the book's production. I wish also to thank the following reviewers who made many valuable suggestions, not all of which could be incorporated into the text: Farid M. Al-Salim, Kansas State University; Corinne Blake, Rowan University; Michael Bracy, Oklahoma State University; Martin Bunton, University of Victoria; John Calvert, Creighton University; Nancy Gallagher, University of California, Santa Barbara; Toby Jones, Rutgers University, New Brunswick; Jon Mandaville, Portland State University; Kent Schull, University of Memphis; Peter Sluglett, University of Utah; Nancy L. Stockdale, University of North Texas; and Susan L. Tananbaum, Bowdoin College. I again end with thanks to Julia and Elisabeth, who have shared in the development of this book since its inception, but whose hopes for a concluding chapter noting a peaceful resolution of the conflict have yet to be rewarded.

Charles D. Smith

CONTENTS

11. IS THE TWO-STATE SOLUTION DEAD?
Camp David 2000, Palestinian Rebellion, and Israeli Unilateralism, 1999–2009 **480**

PHOTOS AND MAPS

Photos

Maps

PROLOGUE

The Arab-Israeli Conflict in Historical Perspective: The Middle East and Palestine to 1517

THE PALESTINIAN and Arab-Israeli conflicts are modern and secular in origin. They first appeared at the end of the nineteenth century as a response to the emergence of Zionism in Eastern Europe. Zionism, the Jewish national movement, strove to establish a Jewish presence in Palestine as the forerunner to an ultimate Jewish state. Palestinian and other Arabs, Christian as well as Muslim, opposed this movement not because of Jewish immigration per se, but because by 1914 the political goals of Zionists clearly included removal of Arabs from Palestine.

To be sure, Palestine, especially Jerusalem, was and is sacred to all three monotheistic religions—Judaism, Christianity, and Islam. For Jews, Palestine was "Eretz Israel," the ancient land of Israel, the land they hoped to redeem as a modern Jewish state, a goal that was finally accomplished in 1948. The Western Wall in Jerusalem, a remnant of the Temple of the Herodian era, recalls the Jewish presence and intermittent independence in the area over a millennium and buttresses the Temple Mount, the holiest site in Judaism. For Christians, Palestine is the region where their religion first emerged; Jerusalem's Church of the Holy Sepulchre is believed to be the site of Jesus' crucifixion. For Muslims, Jerusalem is the third holiest city in Islam, after Mecca and Medina. Muslims first prayed toward Jerusalem before turning to Mecca. Muslims believe that on the Prophet Muhammad's night journey to be in God's presence, he ascended from the Temple Mount. The Dome of the Rock, a Muslim shrine on the Temple Mount, surrounds a large stone with an imprint believed to be that of the Muhammad's foot. Thus the Jewish Temple Mount is for Muslims the *Haram al-Sharif*, the Noble Sanctuary, whose area commemorates Muhammad's visit, and Israel represents land that was ruled by Muslim dynasties for thirteen centuries before Israeli independence in 1948.

ANCIENT ISRAEL AND PALESTINE TO THE COMING OF ISLAM

The past twenty years have seen a revolution in scholarship on ancient Israel. Biblical tradition dates the Kingdom of Israel to around 1000 BCE, the supposed era of the kingships of Saul and David that presaged the rise of a far-flung but brief empire under Solomon (c. 970–931), who built the first temple to Yahweh in Jerusalem. Following Solomon's death, this unified kingdom split in two, Israel in the north and Judah in the south. Both succumbed eventually to imperial conquest, Israel to the Assyrians in 722 BCE and Judah to the Babylonians in 586 BCE; the latter defeat resulted in the Babylonian exile, during which many of the Judean elite were transferred to Mesopotamia, present-day Iraq.

Recent scholarship, based on extensive archaeological excavations, has challenged many of these assumptions. One school, the "minimalist," goes so far as to claim there is no evidence that David or Solomon ever existed, let alone that they founded kingdoms. The mainstream of this new scholarship rejects extreme minimalist claims. It notes inscriptional evidence referring to a "house of David," but it dates that "house" to a later period and disputes biblical lore regarding what it considers to be the legends of David's and Solomon's kingdoms and their influence, accounts produced centuries later.

Mainstream scholars now argue that the Canaanite period of the third and second millennia BCE lasted longer than the Bible suggests. There was an Israelite tribal presence in the hill country of Palestine that gradually expanded to take over the coastal area. But this expansion occurred later than believed, as did the brief emergence of a unified Jewish state in all of Palestine, founded by Israel, the kingdom in the north. The southern kingdom of Judah, centered around Jerusalem, did not appear as a real state power until the late eighth century BCE, long after the supposed eleventh-century kingdoms of David and Solomon. And it was Judah's ruling house that then strove to centralize religious belief on Yahweh; until this time polytheism had retained its hold on many Jews. Though Judah was eventually destroyed by the Babylonians, the power of the monotheistic tradition retained its influence, preserved and reinforced by religious leaders in exile.

The archaeological evidence thus summarized verifies the existence of Jewish settlements in Palestine prior to the appearance of Saul and David but views them as local tribal chiefs with little regional influence. The same can be said for Solomon, and no trace of his palace or temple has been found. Their mythical attainments were developed in later versions of the Old Testament, most of them composed during the sixth and fifth centuries BCE.[1]

Political Fragmentation and Rebellion to the Roman Period

Following the conquest of Babylon by the Persian dynasty of the Archaemenids in 539 BCE, Jews who had been sent into exile were allowed to return to Palestine, though most remained in Mesopotamia. In Palestine Jews built a temple in

Jerusalem and were allowed to observe their religious traditions, but they remained subject to outside rule for over three hundred and fifty years. When they rebelled it was because their Seleucid overlords, based in Syria, decided to implant Greek culture throughout their domain. One ruler dedicated the temple in Jerusalem, the holiest site in Judaism, to the Greek god, Zeus. This ignited the Revolt of the Maccabees in 165, during which Jews took control of Jerusalem; by 140 BCE, they had restored Jewish independence through the Hasmonean dynasty that lasted for eighty years. Imbued with religious zeal, the Maccabees forcibly converted much of the by then mostly non-Jewish populations in the north, but their achievements proved to be temporary. By 63 BCE, Judea had been incorporated as an autonomous unit within the Roman Empire, henceforth to be known as Palestine.

Palestine under Roman and Byzantine Rule

As subjects of the Roman Empire, Jews in Palestine were allowed political and religious autonomy as long as their rulers acknowledged Roman suzerainty. The best known of these kings, a continuance of the Hasmonean line, was Herod the Great (37–4 BCE), who reconstructed and expanded the temple in Jerusalem (the complex known as the Temple Mount, or Haram al-Sharif, follows the Herodian foundation). The emperor Augustus granted Herod mastery over much of southern Syria, extending almost to Damascus, to facilitate Jewish control of pilgrimage routes between Babylon and Jerusalem. Still, many Jews saw their rulers' collaboration with the Romans as a corruption of Jewish values. Disputes arose between those Jews who counseled moderation and cooperation with Rome as a means of preserving their autonomy and those, often known as the Zealots, who considered their subjection to Roman rule to be intolerable.

The Zealots rebelled in 66 CE and held out until 73, when their fortress at Masada was taken. Roman retaliation had been fierce; Jerusalem was razed in 70 and the Temple destroyed. All that remained of the Temple was the Western (Wailing) Wall, the remnant of their central place of worship. Autonomy was restored under stricter Roman surveillance, but Jewish unrest persisted and led to a more carefully planned rebellion, the Bar Kokhba revolt, that lasted from 132 to 135 CE. Although initially successful, the revolt ended in disaster. The Romans retaliated by systematically destroying villages throughout Palestine, killing and enslaving thousands of Jews. Palestine/Judea lost its autonomous status and became a Roman colony known as Syria Palestina. Although many Jews remained in Palestine, they were concentrated in the Galilee and, as punishment for their rebellion, they were forbidden to enter Jerusalem, now in ruins. Jews outside Palestine far outnumbered those within it. Jewish communities had sprung up in the Greco-Roman world prior to the Roman conquest, but their numbers were small compared with those that resulted from the dispersions following the failed rebellions of 66 and 132 CE. Nevertheless, Jews still considered Palestine to be Eretz Israel, the land promised them by God, and Jerusalem remained the focal point of their religious observances.

Though banned from entering Jerusalem and forced to pay special taxes, Jews "were allowed practical self-government in all their internal affairs and were able to set up their own administrative machinery."[2] They were also permitted freedom of religious observance and teaching so long as they did not seek to convert Gentiles (i.e., anyone who was not Jewish). In practice, these regulatory laws were not strictly enforced, and Palestinian Jews were relatively free to direct their own affairs, especially during the decline of Roman power in the first half of the third century. But the efforts of the emperor Diocletian to restore imperial authority and stabilize the empire at the end of the century had severe repercussions. He imposed harsh tax measures throughout the empire; their application in Palestine led to a significant decline in the Jewish population. By 300 CE, Jews made up one-half of the total population in the Galilee and less than one-fourth in the rest of the region. Once Christianity became the official religion of the Eastern Roman Empire, a new era dawned and Palestine became as important to Christian rulers as it was to Jews.

Palestine, as the home of Jesus, was sacred to Christians. When the rulers of the Eastern Roman (Byzantine) Empire, based in Constantinople, accepted Christianity, Palestine—and Jerusalem in particular—acquired a significance totally lacking in the traditional Roman attitude toward the area. Christians considered Jews to be rivals in Palestine, as well as a people who had rejected Jesus as the savior sent by God. As a result, the Byzantines applied existing Roman laws limiting Jewish activities more rigorously and created new ordinances aimed at isolating the Jews. In the fifth century, Byzantine emperors passed laws forbidding the construction of new synagogues in Jerusalem and its hinterland and specifying what types of repairs could be made to those then in use. These laws were not always applied to the letter, however, as had also been the case under pagan Rome. New synagogues were built in the early sixth century, when the Jews and the Christian majority in Palestine prospered. But the reign of the emperor Justinian saw new laws imposed that interfered with the internal affairs of the Jewish community such as marriage contracts, something previously unknown. The articles applying to the building of synagogues were enforced, and hostile mobs destroyed many places of worship. Jews returned the favor when they were briefly permitted to rule Jerusalem after the Persian Sassanid dynasty took Palestine during its extended war with Byzantium in the early seventh century: they burned churches and killed many Christians. But Byzantine authority was soon restored and remained in force for the next twenty years until Palestine and the rest of the Middle East fell to Arab invaders from the desert. They brought with them a new religion, Islam.

THE ARABS AND THE SPREAD OF ISLAM

The Arab invasion of the urbanized areas of the Near East shattered the balance of power that had existed, with interruptions, for over two millennia. The region had usually been controlled and fought over by empires situated initially in Egypt and Mesopotamia and later in the northern Mediterranean and southern Mesopotamia/Iran. The last series of wars between Byzantium and the Sassanids, which included the brief Persian occupation of Jerusalem, exhausted the military capacities of both camps and facilitated the Arab conquest.

The Arabs are a Semitic people, ethnically and linguistically related to the northern Semitic tribes that included the Canaanites and the Hebrews. The term Arab first occurs in Assyrian texts of the eighth century BCE, referring to camel herders of the desert. Those who could settled in fertile oases with stable supplies of water and food, but most had to pursue the wandering life of the bedouin. Arab contacts with the peoples of the settled areas were frequent, through booty raids and tribes who served as auxiliary fighters during campaigns. The Arabs' inclination and ability to invade the central Middle East in 632–633 CE indicated that major changes had occurred in their social and political organization. These changes reflected the impact of the personality of the Prophet Muhammad and the revelation from God (Allah) that he delivered to the Arabs, the origins of the religion of Islam.

Muhammad (c. 570–632 CE) was born in Mecca, a trading community and religious sanctuary situated near the Red Sea in the region known as the Hijaz, along the caravan routes between Yemen and the central Near East. He was a member of the clan of the Hashim, a subgroup of the Quraysh tribe that controlled Mecca. Mecca's prosperity was derived in part from the caravan trade, but also from its possession of a black meteorite that had become the focal point of worship for the tribes of the Hijaz. According to Islamic tradition, Muhammad was visited by the angel Gabriel, who informed him that he had been selected by God to deliver a revelation to his people. Believing he had been chosen to preach God's word, Muhammad gave up a secure livelihood and place within Meccan society to challenge the existing religious practices of Mecca and the Hijaz, which formed the basis of the prosperity of the Quraysh.

Muhammad began preaching about the year 610. In 622, Meccan opposition forced him and his followers to flee northward to the oasis of Yathrib (known henceforth as Medina). Once there, Muhammad took advantage of his prestige and Medinian factionalism to establish himself among the Arab tribes as the recognized leader of the oasis. In 630 he gained Mecca's submission, and by the time of his death in 632, Muhammad had been accepted as the prophet of Allah in much of central and southern Arabia.

Scholars differ over whether Muhammad intended to expand Islam beyond the Arabian peninsula, but such an expansion did occur. By 637, Muslim forces took the Sassanian capital of Ctesiphon, enabling the conquest of Mesopotamia and western Iran. In Syria and Palestine, Damascus was captured in 635, Jerusalem fell in 638, and Muslim armies conquered Egypt in 640. Expansion eastward and westward continued intermittently over the next ninety years. By 730, approximately a century after Muhammad's death, the boundaries of Islam extended from the Pyrenees in southwestern Europe to beyond the Oxus River in Central Asia and to the Indus River Basin in India.

This growth occurred under the direction of the first four caliphs of Islam, those who succeeded Muhammad as heads of the community, and the caliphs of the Umayyad dynasty (661–750). Their successors founded the Abbasid caliphate (750–1258) and moved the capital from Damascus to Baghdad in Iraq. Baghdad became the center of a sophisticated culture, but the Abbasids were unable to maintain control over their vast empire. By the tenth century, political life in Islam was characterized by instability and fragmentation, even though Islamic civilization continued to flourish.

In addition, the religion had broken into two major segments, Sunni and Shi'i Islam. The split originated during the first century of Islam in a dispute over the legitimacy of the claim of Ali, the fourth caliph, to retain his position as leader of the Muslim community. Those who backed the claims of Ali and his descendants to assume the leadership of the Islamic community were (and still are) called Shi'ites. They challenged the formation of the Umayyad caliphate and its successors, which the Sunni Muslims had accepted. Differences in religious interpretation followed from this rift. The Umayyad and Abbasid caliphates were Sunni, as were many of the provincial governors who broke with the Abbasids; but a major Shi'i dynasty, the Fatimids, established itself in Egypt in 969 and lasted until 1171. For a time it even threatened the continuance of the Abbasid caliphate as head of Sunni Islam in Baghdad. We shall return to our discussion of political authority in Islam in our treatment of Palestine under Muslim rule.

Islam and Its Relationship to Judaism and Christianity

The word *Islam* means "submission" (to the will of Allah); those who profess faith in Allah as the only God are called Muslims, "those who submit." As noted, Muhammad was selected by Allah to be His messenger. Muhammad was a human being who became a prophet—to Muslims a messenger of God analogous, though not identical, to the selection of Abraham by Yahweh to deliver a covenant to the Jews. Allah's covenant was the Quran, the revelations that Allah delivered to the Arabs of the Hijaz through the mouth of Muhammad. These recitations were written down after Muhammad's death and, as the Quran, have been the basis of Muslim life to this day. Along with the compilation of Muhammad's own sayings and examples, the Quran became the basis of Muslim law, the *sharia*. The sharia also contains later interpretations and elaborations by Muslim legal scholars, similar to the Jewish Talmud with its body of legal commentary reflecting the divine wisdom found in the commandments and the Torah.

Muslims consider Islam the culmination and perfection of the Jewish and Christian traditions; Allah is also the God of the Jews and Christians. According to Islam, Allah gave His revelation to prophets He selected to establish Judaism and Christianity (in Islam, Jesus is revered but not considered divine), but in each case the believers failed to adhere to His commands; this resulted in the fragmentation of the Jewish and the Christian communities. Allah then sent a final revelation to Muhammad. Muslims believe that the black meteorite in Mecca, which Muhammad designated as the place of pilgrimage for Muslims, was initially a shrine of Abraham, thus establishing a link between earliest Judaism and Islam.

To Muslims, Jews and Christians were "People of the Book of Revelation," recipients of a divine message that they corrupted. As such, they were to be tolerated because of their place in the lineage of Islam, but they were nevertheless deemed inferior to Muslims because of their treatment of God's messages to them. Islam was the perfection of that revelation, meaning that Muslims were superior to Jews and Christians, who, though permitted to retain their religious beliefs were to be kept in a humble status appropriate to their denial of God's gift. At the heart of the relationship was Islam's award of protection to non-Muslims, including their right to worship, in return for payment of the *jizya*, a poll tax paid by non-Muslims, and the *kharaj*, a property tax that was later paid by Muslims as well. Jews and Christians became known as *dhimmis*, those who were granted protection in return for their submission to Muslim rule and their payment of the jizya.

Muslim treatment of non-Muslims was consistent with, and in some ways an improvement upon, the policies of Byzantium and the Sassanids toward Jews and Christians, respectively. Byzantine laws prohibited the construction of new synagogues, required the destruction rather than the repair of unsafe ones, interfered in Jewish doctrinal matters at times, and in general aimed at relegating Jews to eternal subordination in the probable hope that they would disappear; intermarriage with Christians was forbidden. Schismatic Christian groups (and "pagans") were also treated harshly. Sassanian rulers permitted Jews to regulate their own affairs but watched Christian sects more closely and banned the construction of new churches.

These rules, with modifications, were incorporated into Islam's policies toward Christians and Jews. Islam denied them the right to build new churches and synagogues, and the repair of existing houses of worship required official permission. Dhimmis were forbidden to wear clothing identical to that worn by Muslims, in order to preserve visible signs of differentiation, or to build houses that overlooked the inner areas of Muslim dwellings. Later rules decreed that dhimmis could not ride animals as large as those ridden by Muslims. The enforcement of these regulations varied considerably according to place and historical circumstances. Under Islam, Jews experienced a lessening of control in certain aspects of their lives. Unlike the Byzantines, Muslim authorities did not interfere in doctrinal matters and allowed Jews to visit and inhabit Jerusalem. Indeed, Christians felt more debased by Muslim policies because they were now equated with Jews, after having ruled them and discriminated against them for more than two centuries.[3]

As a rule, dhimmi security or insecurity reflected the historical circumstances in which Muslims found themselves. The Christian Crusades and the later European economic and political penetration of the Islamic world, especially during the nineteenth century, threatened the ongoing stability of Muslim society. In these situations tolerance declined, and regulations affecting Jews and Christians were enforced more harshly. In general, Muslims discriminated against non-Muslims but did not persecute them, although persecution was not unknown. Intolerant by modern Western standards of racial and religious equality, Muslim policies were consistent with—and often an improvement on—the prevailing treatment of Jews and Christians as subject peoples in an age when religious equality was unknown and inconceivable. Similar legal protection for religious minorities in Europe did not appear for another millennium. Official tolerance and protection of dhimmis in a pluralistic society survived numerous dynastic changes from the seventh century onward to confront, ultimately in the eighteenth and nineteenth centuries, European claims for dhimmi equality with Muslims backed by Western military might.

Palestine under Muslim Rule to 1517

The place of Palestine in Islamic history down to the modern era was generally a minor one, the exception being the period of the European Crusades (1097–1291), which sought to replace Islamic rule with that of Latin Christianity. But Palestine was not unimportant to Islam. As noted, Jerusalem, a city holy to both Jews and Christians, was sacred to Muslims as the heirs and perfecters of the Judeo-Christian tradition. Surpassed only by Mecca and Medina, it became the third holiest city in Islam, owing to the Islamic tradition that Muhammad had set foot on the Temple Mount prior to his night journey to heaven. The Dome of the Rock, built by an Umayyad caliph to commemorate that event and completed in 691, was the first major Muslim edifice constructed outside of Mecca.

The Umayyad caliphs situated in Damascus showed concern for Jerusalem and endowed several buildings in the city in addition to the Dome of the Rock. But Umayyad rule lasted less than a century (661–750). Once the Abbasids shifted the capital to Baghdad, official attention waned, although during the ninth century Harun al-Rashid did permit the Frankish emperor Charlemagne and his son Louis to endow several hostelries for Latin pilgrims. Caliphs were frequently unable to retain control of provinces adjacent to Iraq, let alone those more distant. Palestine fell under the sphere of those who controlled Egypt, whether Sunni Muslims such as Ahmad ibn Tulun (868–883) or the Shi'i Fatimid dynasty, which held Palestine from 969 to 1099 when the Crusaders took Jerusalem.

The inhabitants of Palestine seem to have prospered during much of the period from the Muslim conquest to the onslaught of the Crusaders. A majority of the population was now Muslim, but there were many Christians and Jews. Palestine, especially Jerusalem, remained a center of pilgrimage for members of all three faiths. Muslim rule was generally unobtrusive, to the point that construction of new churches and synagogues was permitted. Friction among the religious communities and the official sanction of violence against one group or another were infrequent.

The Crusaders took Jerusalem in 1099, subjecting much of its citizenry—Muslim, Jewish, and Eastern Christian—to a bloodbath. The Crusaders saw themselves as wresting the most sacred city in Christianity from heathen Muslim rule. Jerusalem became for a time "a Christian city where no Muslim or Jewish cult was permitted and no non-Christian could take residence permanently."⁴ Several more years passed before Muslims and Jews were allowed to pray in the city. But effective Christian control of Jerusalem lasted less than a century. Saladin recaptured the city for Islam in 1187, and it resumed its Muslim character, interrupted by a struggle between rival Ayyubid princes in Cairo and Damascus that permitted the return of Jerusalem to Christian governance between 1229 and 1244.

From 1250 onward, for nearly 300 years, Palestine was ruled by the Mamluks, a Muslim military elite centered in Cairo and in Damascus. Although Damascus oversaw Palestine's administration, the Mamluks considered Jerusalem a separate entity under the authority of Cairo, where the Mamluk sultan resided, in order to protect the holy places of the three religions. When Mamluk authority declined in both Cairo and Damascus in the early sixteenth century, bedouin raids disrupted the stability of the area, a situation that persisted until the Ottoman Turks took Palestine in 1516–1517. The Ottomans ruled Palestine almost continuously until 1918.

CHRONOLOGY

c. 3000–900 BCE	Canaanites inhabit Palestine west of Jordan River, coastal Lebanon, and southern Syria.
c. 1200–1100 BCE	Philistines and Jews settle in Palestine region of Canaan.
c. 8th century BCE	Kingdom of Israel established in northern Palestine.
722 BCE	Assyria conquers northern Kingdom of Israel.
c. 7th century BCE	Kingdom of Judah established in southern Palestine; Jerusalem becomes major political and religious center.
586 BCE	Babylonian Empire conquers Judah; temple destroyed and many Jews exiled to Babylon.
539–140 BCE	Persians conquer Babylon, permit Jews to return to southern Palestine; temple rebuilt; Palestine ruled by Persian and Greek dynasties until revolt of the Maccabees in 140 BCE.
140–63 BCE	Maccabee revolt creates Hasmonean dynasty and restores Jewish independence until Roman conquest in 63 BCE when Palestine is incorporated into province of Judea.
63 BCE–638 CE	Palestine nearly continuously under Roman or Byzantine rule.
66–73 CE	Jewish Zealots rebel, hold out at Masada to 73 CE. Romans destroy Jerusalem and temple in restoring Roman rule.
132–135 CE	Bar Kokhba revolt against Romans. Roman retaliation results in dispersal of many Jews, ending Palestine's autonomy.
c. 570 CE	Muhammad, messenger of Islam, born in Mecca.
622–632 CE	Emigration of Muhammad to Medina and beginning of Muslim calendar (622); forming of community and subjugation of Mecca to Muhammad's death in 632.
c. 630–730 CE	Islamic expansion results in control of regions stretching from Spain in the west across North Africa and the Middle East to Central Asia and borders of India in the east.
638 CE	Jerusalem and Palestine incorporated into Islamic rule.
661–750 CE	Umayyad caliphate rules Islamic empire from Damascus.
750–1258 CE	Abbasid caliphate rules Islamic empire from Baghdad.
1097–1291 CE	Crusader presence in Middle East.
1099–1187, 1229–1244 CE	Crusader control of Jerusalem.
1250–1516/17 CE	Period of Mamluk dynasties, centered in Damascus and Cairo, ruling Greater Syria, including Palestine, and Egypt.
1453 CE	Ottoman Turks conquer Constantinople; end of Byzantine Empire.

Notes

1. I rely here on the scholarly but more popular accounts of Israel Finkelstein and Neil Asher Silberman in *The Bible Unearthed: Archaeology's New Version of Ancient Israel and the Origin of Its Sacred Texts* (New York, 2002) and in *David and Solomon: In Search of the Bible's Sacred Kings and the Roots of the Western Tradition* (New York, 2006). More scholarly analysis giving evidence of clashing interpretations can be seen in Finkelstein's "The Archaeology of the United Monarchy: An Alternative View," *Levant* 28 (1996): 177–87, and the response by Amihai Mazar "Iron Age Archaeology: A Reply to I. Finkelstein," *Levant* 30 (1998): 157–67, with Finkelstein's reply "Biblical Archaeology or Archaeology of Palestine in the Iron Age? A Rejoinder," *Levant* 30 (1998): 167–73. Compare their revisionism to the classic biblical treatment in John Bright, *A History of Israel*, 3rd ed. (Philadelphia, 1981). Bright's approach, while rejected by scholars, retains wide currency among Christian fundamentalists and evangelical Christians who back Israeli retention of the occupied territories. The political nature of archaeology regarding Israel/Palestine is well analyzed in two books: Neil Asher Silberman, *Between Past and Present: Archaeology, Ideology, and Nationalism in the Modern Middle East* (New York, 1989), and Nadia Abu el-Haj, *Facts on the Ground: Archaeological Practice and Territorial Self-Fashioning in Israeli Society* (Chicago, 2002).

2. Michael Avi-Yonah, *The Jews of Palestine: A Political History from the Bar Kokhba War to the Arab Conquest* (New York, 1976), 83.

3. C. E. Bosworth, "The Concept of Dhimma in Early Islam," in *Christians and Jews in the Ottoman Empire: The Functioning of a Plural Society*, ed. Benjamin Braude and Bernard Lewis, vol. 2, *The Arabic-Speaking Lands* (New York, 1982), 37–54.

4. S. D. Goitein, "al-Kuds," *Encyclopedia of Islam*, vol. 5 (Leiden, 1980), 330.

1

OTTOMAN SOCIETY, PALESTINE, AND THE ORIGINS OF ZIONISM

1516–1914

I N 1453, the Ottoman Turks conquered Constantinople and ended the existence of the Byzantine Empire. Descendants of tribal warriors who established themselves in western Anatolia after the Mongol invasions of the thirteenth century, the Ottoman sultans inherited an imperial legacy they sought to expand for Islam. By the end of the sixteenth century, vast areas of Eastern Christendom fell under Muslim authority. Ottoman rule reached westward in Europe to Budapest and beyond; Vienna was nearly taken twice, in 1529 and 1683. Ottoman power also extended along the southern rim of the Mediterranean into Algeria. By taking greater Syria (including Palestine), Egypt, and the Hijaz in 1516–1517, the Ottomans inherited the responsibility of protecting pilgrims traveling to Mecca, thus assuming more directly the mantle of authority held by Muslim rulers.

Ottoman society was pluralistic, similar to its Byzantine and Arab predecessors in its inclusion of different peoples and faiths, but on a larger scale. As one study noted:

> Remarkably this polyethnic and multireligious society worked. Muslims, Christians, and Jews worshipped and studied side by side. . . . The legal traditions and practices of each community, particularly in matters of personal status — death, marriage, and inheritance — were respected and enforced throughout the empire. . . . Opportunities for advancement and prosperity were open in varying degrees to all the empire's subjects. . . . For all their shortcomings, plural societies did allow diverse groups of peoples to live together with a minimum of bloodshed. In comparison with the nation-states which succeeded them, theirs is a remarkable record.[1]

As Sunni Muslims, the Ottomans viewed the dhimmis as inferiors, but accepted responsibility for their protection and usually acted swiftly when mobs threatened their safety. The status of the dhimmis was far better than that of the Jews in medieval and early modern Europe. Indeed, the Ottoman Empire became a haven for Iberian Jews who fled the persecution of Jews as well as Muslims that followed the Spanish reconquest that was completed in 1492. Ottoman Jews prospered during the sixteenth and seventeenth centuries, in part due to their economic contributions, such as the textile industry at Salonica, and in part because the Ottomans permitted non-Muslims to hold certain positions that involved contact with foreigners.

But this situation began to change in the eighteenth century. Jews were replaced by Christian rivals, not because of a shift in Ottoman policy but because of increasing European influence. European patronage of Christian minorities was an extension of efforts by European powers to expand their commercial and political influence in the Ottoman Empire and to undermine Ottoman authority. Ottoman attempts to resist these pressures failed and led to a redressing of the nature of Muslim–non-Muslim relations in the middle of the nineteenth century, with serious repercussions for the empire and for the attitudes of Muslims toward their former subjects. Still, Jewish communities retained their strength in many areas of the empire, not least in Salonica, where they were the largest single community at the end of the nineteenth century.[2]

By this time, however, Zionist migration to Palestine had become a factor in Ottoman affairs with Ottoman officials unable to stem the influx of European Jews who called for the restoration of a Jewish state in that region. The resultant clash of Zionist and Palestinian Arab national movements, coupled with Western imperial rivalries for control of Ottoman lands, would ultimately challenge the very existence of the empire.

COMMERCIAL RELATIONS AND MILITARY DECLINE, 1500–1800

The treaties that ultimately weakened Ottoman sovereignty originated in agreements undertaken at the height of Ottoman power. During the sixteenth century, the sultans had granted to several European states privileges that permitted their agents to trade within Ottoman lands under protection of legal immunity. Negotiated from a position of strength, these arrangements posed no threat to Ottoman authority until the balance of power shifted in the middle of the eighteenth century. By this time, European countries had made tremendous strides in developing their domestic economies and their military technology, with Western European commercial expansion in particular largely the result of overseas conquests and the exploitation of foreign markets.

Hampered by internal disarray and court intrigue, Ottoman rulers failed to respond effectively to these challenges, which first appeared at the end of the seventeenth century when various European rivals initiated campaigns to recover lands and trade routes lost two centuries earlier. The Treaty of Karlowitz in 1699 was the first in which the Ottomans were forced to deal with Europeans as equals and cede territory to them. From that time onward, the sultans were continually faced with the territorial ambitions of Austria and the newly emerging power of Russia to the north. And, henceforth, military reverses were often accompanied by European demands for greater influence in the affairs of the Ottomans' Christian subjects as a means of expanding their own authority at the Ottomans' expense.

The first treaty exhibiting these tendencies was that between the French and the Ottomans in 1740. It granted the French the right to protect Roman Catholics in the empire and to represent their interests before the sultans. In addition, French priests were given privileges that included the right to build new churches in Palestine. To further extend their influence, the French arranged for the Christian Maronites of Lebanon to recognize papal authority and thus be designated as Roman Catholics; in return, Rome allowed the Maronites to retain their own language for the Mass, their rites, and their priestly orders. As Roman Catholics, the Maronites qualified for French tutelage in Lebanon, where the French had extensive commercial interests. Finally, the French acquired the right to grant special status (the *barat*) to Ottoman subjects employed by French companies and officials, giving them trading privileges and legal immunity formerly reserved for foreigners. This set in motion a process that allowed dhimmis to escape Ottoman control by gaining the protection of a European power. Naturally, the French, and later other powers, awarded this status to Christians who represented their interests, often at the expense of other minorities. This precedent of giving Christians a privileged status was actually set prior to the French-Ottoman Treaty of 1740. For example, in the seventeenth century, an Armenian replaced a Jew as a customs official in Aleppo at the behest of the French consul there.

Equally significant was the Treaty of Kuchuk Kanarji of 1774, signed after the Russians had driven the Ottomans out of the Crimea and gained access to the Black Sea. The treaty acknowledged Russian control of the north coast of the Black Sea and Russian rights of commercial navigation on it, but it also included clauses that affected non-Muslim subjects of the Ottomans. The Russians demanded and received the right to build a Greek Orthodox church under their protection in Istanbul, rights allowing them to intercede on behalf of the clergy and patrons of that church and, by inference, all Greek Orthodox in the city. Russian pilgrims gained greater access to Palestine, and Russian Orthodox clergy were allowed to build hostels and churches there. These considerations, similar to those given to the French in 1740, led to an acrimonious rivalry among clergy of different faiths for possession of certain Christian holy places in Palestine. One such clash between Roman Catholic and Russian Orthodox monks, backed by their respective government sponsors, France and Russia, was the catalyst for the Crimean War of 1854–1856.

As a corollary of these developments, trade came increasingly under European control during the nineteenth century, often handled by non-Muslim Ottoman subjects who gained the protection of the countries they represented and thus became free of Muslim-imposed restrictions. As a result, the Ottoman Empire became a focal point for larger imperial rivalries, with the European powers eager to use trading rights and control of non-Muslims as tools to wield influence against their competitors as well as against the Turks. For much of the period, the major protagonists were Great Britain, France, and Russia.

REGIONAL STRIFE, IMPERIAL INTERVENTIONS, AND OTTOMAN RETRACTION, 1800–1914

In contrast with France and Russia, Great Britain did not seek initially to use protection of non-Muslim minorities as a wedge to expand its influence and weaken Ottoman power. The British wished to maintain the political stability of the region and, if possible, the territorial integrity of the Ottoman Empire to ensure the safety of their routes across Ottoman lands to India, the centerpiece of their own empire. Consequently, they strove for most of the nineteenth century to prop up the Ottomans in order to block the ambitions of their European rivals and to keep open their lines of communication to the East. As part of that policy, they joined the Ottomans in successfully opposing Napoleon Bonaparte when he landed with a French army in Egypt in 1798, seeking to interdict those routes and weaken British power in Europe as well as Asia. Likewise, the British challenged the ambitions of the Ottoman governor of Egypt, Muhammad Ali, when, with French backing, he took over Greater Syria, including Palestine, in 1831 and threatened to overthrow the Ottoman sultan. They were finally successful in 1840, following a new international crisis in which Muhammad Ali's son and deputy, Ibrahim, seemed on the verge of taking Istanbul.

Britain's policy was an aspect of what has been called "The Great Game in Asia," a contest in which Russia posed the main threat because its southward expansion threatened the security of India's frontiers. Britain's actions in the Middle East were designed to keep the Russians out of Istanbul in order to forestall the prospect that a Russian fleet stationed there with access to the Mediterranean could cut Britain's imperial lifeline to India.

Britain's success in achieving its goals depended on European cooperation, which was generally forthcoming following the Congress of Vienna in 1815. British diplomats encouraged Ottoman officials to undertake administrative and legal reforms intended to stabilize the regime and forestall further European inroads. But Ottoman reform efforts, though relatively successful, were hampered by internal opposition and rising nationalist sentiment that fostered separatist movements backed by European nations. The Greek Rebellion of 1821 ultimately succeeded because of joint Anglo-Russian intervention.

The Crimean War of 1854–1856, itself sparked by religious rivalries in Palestine between Catholic and Orthodox monks backed by France and Russia, respectively, resulted in a major Russian defeat at the hands of France and Great Britain. From this time onward, the tsars encouraged Balkan separatist movements in order to acquire influence against both the Ottomans and Russia's major European rival in Eastern Europe, Austria-Hungary, which itself strove to

dampen nationalist ardor. Even Russian setbacks contributed to regional instability. Russian victories in the Russo-Turkish War of 1877–1878 led to concerted
European diplomacy at the Congress of Berlin (1878) that reduced the extent
of Moscow's territorial gains, but at Istanbul's expense as well. The congress
granted independence to Serbia, Romania, and Montenegro and allotted the
Austrians Bosnia-Herzegovina, all former Ottoman possessions. Mutual dissat-
isfaction at this dividing of the spoils contributed to further conflict: Austro-
Hungarian–Serbian enmity over the status of Bosnia-Herzegovina resulted ultimately in the assassination of the Austrian Archduke Ferdinand on June 28, 1914,
in the Bosnian capital of Sarajevo, setting in motion the diplomatic exchanges
and ultimatums that led to the outbreak of World War I.

Elsewhere, in their Arab lands, the Ottoman Turks also lost extensive territory as Britain abandoned its former policy of discouraging outside threats to
Ottoman territorial integrity. In 1869, the Suez Canal had opened, creating a
direct sea route to India through the Mediterranean. Alarmed initially because
construction of the canal was a joint French-Egyptian venture, London soon
decided to become involved in the Suez Canal Company and in 1875 bought the
shares of the Egyptian ruler, the Khedive Ismail. For most British diplomats and
politicians, the security of the canal was now vital to their imperial interests, an
association that created greater interest in Egypt's financial and internal stability. As part of this concern, Britain acquired the island of Cyprus from the
Ottomans at the Congress of Berlin, viewing it as a potential naval base able to
protect the Suez Canal if the Ottomans crumbled. Then, when Egyptian anger
at European interference in its financial affairs threatened to topple Ismail's successor, the British invaded Egypt in 1882; they remained until 1956.

The British absorption of Egypt, though not decided on for several years,
contributed to a scramble for African territories by the French and the Germans,
who hoped to establish a balance of power abroad commensurate with their
ambitions in Europe. In North Africa the French, who had invaded Algeria in
1830, took Tunisia in 1881 and gained control of Morocco in 1912 following a series
of crises with Germany. The Italians landed in Libya in 1911. Ottoman efforts
to oust the Italians were stymied by the outbreak of further Balkan wars in
1912–1913. By 1914, Istanbul controlled only a small strip of land in Europe. What
remained secure were the Turkish heartland, Anatolia, and the Arab provinces of
the Middle East down to the Sinai Peninsula. The Germans were now the
Ottomans' major ally as a result of British and French involvement in the carving
up of the empire that occurred in the aftermath of the Congress of Berlin.

OTTOMAN SOCIETY IN AN AGE OF REFORM

The progressive diminution of Ottoman power in the nineteenth century
affected the stability of Muslim society, especially Muslim-Christian relations,
as a result of European intervention and Ottoman responses to these incursions. The customary Muslim view of a world in which dhimmis remained in

inferior positions befitting their status began to be shaken. The improved position of the Christian dhimmis seemed to many Muslims to be the result of a loss of Ottoman power at the hands of hostile forces that sought to weaken Muslim control over lands they had ruled for centuries. The situation in Palestine remained relatively stable—more so than in areas of Syria and Lebanon—as did Muslim attitudes toward Jews, until the appearance of Zionists, who claimed that Palestine was inherently Jewish and should revert to Jewish rule.

EUROPEAN INROADS AND COMMUNAL TENSIONS TO MID-CENTURY

Ironically, the impact of European claims of rights of protection over Christian sects was made known to many Arab Muslims by a Muslim ruler, Ibrahim, the son of Muhammad Ali of Egypt. Ibrahim governed Syria, Palestine, and parts of Lebanon from 1831 to 1840. Eager to exploit the local populace in order to finance the costs of occupation, he enforced tax policies that had been ignored for generations. Faced with the opposition of the area's Muslim population, Ibrahim turned to dhimmis, usually Christians, whom he placed in high administrative posts. It was not uncommon for a Christian official to assess taxes on well-to-do Muslim families in cities such as Damascus and Aleppo. Moreover, Ibrahim encouraged European trade and the influx of Christian missionaries into Lebanon and Syria as a means of gaining European backing against Ottoman demands for Egyptian withdrawal. As part of these tactics, Ibrahim granted Christians and Jews effective political and religious equality with Muslims, thus overturning the foundations of the structure on which intercommunal relations had been based for centuries. The Muslim masses, traditionally exploited by Ottoman officials, suddenly found themselves subject not merely to harsher taxes but also to military conscription from which non-Muslims, their supposed equals, were exempt.

Muslim resentment against Christians intensified because European consuls and traders hired Arab Christians to represent them in the selling of European goods, which were cheaper, being mass-produced, than the indigenous products sold by Muslim merchants. This influx of foreign goods followed the Balta Liman Convention of 1838, which the British forced on the Ottomans; it lowered protective tariffs, thereby opening Ottoman lands to the products of the industrial revolution and affecting the livelihood of many. (See Document 1.1.) The local market on which Muslims relied was thus undermined to the benefit of Europeans and their Arab Christian protégés, who usually acquired protective status (barat) and became exempt from Muslim authority, being protected, as were Europeans, by capitulations. To make matters worse some Christian clergy flaunted their newfound equality by holding public processions in elaborate vestments and having church bells rung, practices forbidden for centuries under Muslim ordinances. In contrast to the Christian ostentation, Jews accepted their official equality cautiously and without fanfare. This contributed to the greater stability of Muslim-Jewish relations during a period of Muslim-Christian enmity. Indeed, the major threat to Jewish communities during much of the century came from Christians who were their rivals in trade. The blood libel against the Jews in Damascus in 1840 was inspired by the Christians, although they tried to enlist Muslim mobs in their cause. Conversely, when the Muslims rioted against the Christians in Damascus in 1860, the Jews were reported to have encouraged them.[3]

Muslim self-regard was further undermined when edicts issued by the Ottoman sultans reaffirmed the hated practices initially instituted by the Egyptians, the result of the great power pressures just noted. Following Sultan Mahmud II's disastrous attempt to drive Ibrahim out of Syria in 1839, only British intervention had kept Ibrahim from marching on Istanbul. Mahmud died that same year. Four months after his death, his young successor, Sultan Abdul Medjid, issued the Hatti Sharif of Gulhane (1839), an imperial edict proclaiming principles derived from Western liberalism that called for equal rights for all Ottoman subjects, reform to the justice system, and the like. In part this declaration was the work of Ottoman statesmen who believed that reforms in education, the economy, and military technology should be based on these principles. In this sense, the Hatti Sharif was the beginning of the *Tanzimat,* or the reordering of society, the creation of a new system intended to enable the Ottomans to strengthen themselves internally and resist further threats to their frontiers. But the Hatti Sharif was also the work of the British ambassador in Istanbul, Stratford de Redcliffe, who believed that these reforms were necessary if the Ottomans were to prevent the Russians from gaining control of the Bosporus Strait. He saw the document as an appeal to British and broader European opinion meant to justify a concerted anti-Russian effort on behalf of the Ottomans. Moreover, de Redcliffe and Ottoman officials hoped that the offer of equality would encourage Eastern European areas under Ottoman rule to embrace Ottoman citizenship rather than pursue separation, which offered pretexts for outside intervention.

Likewise, the conclusion of the Crimean War saw British efforts to draft a document reaffirming Ottoman adherence to the Hatti Sharif before the convening of the Congress of Paris in 1856 where penalties against the Russians would be imposed. The new declaration, the Hatti Humayun (see Document 1.2), proclaimed unequivocally the equality of Ottoman dhimmis with Muslims in access to education and in the administration of justice, and it guaranteed freedom and openness of worship. Officials ordered to implement these policies in the provinces often encountered popular resentment, with the anger directed mostly at the European powers who were seen as forcing the sultans to issue the decrees. As a consequence, Muslim animosity toward Ottoman Christians flared, the most explosive example being the massacre of thousands in Damascus in 1860 as a result of Maronite Catholic-Druze tensions in Mount Lebanon. There had also been anti-Christian riots in Aleppo in 1850 and in Nablus in northern

Palestine in 1856, the latter instigated by the accidental killing of a Muslim by an English missionary.[4] The interrelationship of local sectarian rivalries and outside interference would take a new turn in Palestine once Arab Christians and Muslims joined in opposing European Jewish claims to the region.

PALESTINE IN THE NINETEENTH CENTURY

The Ottomans had divided Palestine into districts known as *sanjaks*, incorporated within the province of greater Syria and governed from Damascus since the seventeenth century. These were the sanjaks of Gaza, Jerusalem, Nablus, Lajun, and Safad. Jerusalem was granted as a source of income to the governor in Damascus, who sometimes imposed excessive taxes. In general, life in the towns and villages of the hill country was secure, but the bedouin were a constant threat to travelers and farmers in the coastal areas. Urban inhabitants and peasants often suffered more from the exorbitant revenue demands of local Ottoman officials left unsupervised by a faltering imperial government in Istanbul than from bedouin encroachments. Over time the Ottomans came to rely on leading Arab clans to carry out local governmental functions. During the late seventeenth and eighteenth centuries, a number of prominent Palestinian families emerged as tax collectors, guardians of charitable endowments, and the like; among them were the Khalidis, Nusaybas, Alamis, Husaynis, and Nashashibis.

Still divided into several administrative entities in 1800, Palestine underwent various transformations as the century progressed. The officials primarily responsible for the area were the pashas of Sidon and Damascus. The pashas of Sidon resided in Acre, within Palestine; on occasion they controlled areas of Lebanon up to and including Beirut, the Galilee in northern Palestine, and parts of the northern Palestinian coastal region. The pashas of Damascus, in addition to their responsibilities in Syria, were concerned with the administration of central Palestine on a north-south axis, including Jerusalem.

These *pashaliks* of Sidon and Damascus were divided into sanjaks, or districts, where local notables appointed by the Ottomans were responsible to them for security and the collection of taxes. Further subdivisions extended down to the village level, where the small area known as a *nahiya*, made up of several villages, was represented by a dominant local family.

The most heavily populated region was the central mountain terrain, which was more easily defended against bedouin incursion and invasion by outside powers. The area was dotted with villages and several large towns. Political authority lay in the hands of notables or chiefs, heads of prominent families who became the tax collectors of their regions. In some areas one or two families might dominate; in others, such as Nablus, there were eight or nine families vying for power whose fortunes waxed and waned according to their willingness to serve Ottoman interests and the strength of their opponents. Village coalitions grouped by clan loyalties dominated the countryside. The situation was different around Jerusalem because Jerusalem notables did not control land

and the collection of land revenues at this time. Their authority rested on their possession of religious offices, as the Muslim hierarchy in Jerusalem appointed functionaries in the Palestinian towns. Nonetheless, these functionaries could derive a good deal of wealth from these offices. In addition, they profited from their control of the many charitable endowments (*waqfs*) in the area; their collection of taxes and security payments from the dhimmis; and the constant flow of pilgrims, most of them Christian, to holy places in the city and its environs. As in rural areas, there existed intense competition among Jerusalem families for these posts.

Changing Patterns: Trade, Land, Agriculture, and Population

Palestine, like the rest of Syria, had felt the impact of Ottoman agreements that opened the Levant to European trade using local agents. The British-Ottoman Commercial Convention of 1838 in particular drew the region more directly into the world economy. At the same time, local merchant communities, already part of regional trading networks reaching to Damascus and Cairo, were able to take advantage of these developments, as Beshara Doumani's study of Nablus during this period illustrates. Nonetheless, this dynamism had its price: "Regional trade networks lost much of their autonomy as they were subordinated—or more accurately as Nabulsi merchants were integrated—into the larger regional or world economies."[5] The margin between subordination to these larger economies and profitable integration into them could be a narrow one; workers in certain industries in Greater Syria were severely affected as the century wore on. The local monetary/trading networks of the interior of Palestine responded creatively to the dual impact of competition from European trade and Ottoman centralization policies in the first half of the century. But Nablus merchants were gradually forced to focus their attention more on the centers of importation of European goods, Beirut notably but also Jaffa and Haifa. And with greater European religious interest in Palestine, Jerusalem gradually became an object of Ottoman attention as well, giving it a political and administrative status it had not held previously.

The question of land ownership and the impact of the Ottoman land reform laws passed in 1858 and 1867 seriously affected social relations and power in the latter half of the century. As we have seen, the Ottomans issued the Hatti Humayun in 1856 in the hope that a guarantee of equal rights for all Ottoman subjects would reduce the separatist tendencies of non-Muslim minorities and thus promote stability within the empire. Equally important to this process of stabilization in Ottoman eyes was their reassertion of authority over Anatolia and the Arab provinces whose tax revenues had been lost to Istanbul because of inefficient administration and the Egyptian occupation of Syria. Ottoman officials began applying Tanzimat principles in earnest in Syria and Palestine. The goal of the land laws was to regularize the structure of land ownership and the cultivation of land throughout the empire. By establishing clear proof of title to possession or use of land, the Ottomans could make the holders of these titles liable for taxes and thus increase state revenues. The law of 1867 had granted foreigners the right to own land but only if they agreed to pay taxes on it to the Ottoman government. This law was intended to lessen the scope of the capitulations and to force foreigners, mainly Europeans, to submit to Ottoman jurisdiction in return for their investment in land in the empire.

The implementation of these laws and their impact varied widely. Traditionally, there were three categories of land: state land (*miri*), privately owned land (*mulk*), and land cultivated by peasants who practiced a form of communal ownership of the soil they tilled (*musha'a*); for this last category, shares of land would be rotated. According to the new legislation, peasants, in addition to mulk land, could buy title to parcels of state land, miri, so long as they could pay taxes on their shares. Women also could participate and they could designate heirs to their property. Recent research indicates that in areas of southern Syria and present-day Jordan, many peasant villages saw inhabitants taking title to both state and private lands, while extensive use of musha'a, or collective land, also prevailed.[6]

Similar studies are lacking for Palestine, but it appears that the inconsistent application of these laws, coupled with peasant indebtedness, opened the way for extensive outside investment with little Ottoman success in controlling the tax revenues. A great deal of land in Palestine had been state land (miri), some of it uncultivated for decades because of the insecurity of life in the area. Some had been taken over by landowners, including peasants, who exploited it as private property (mulk) without the Ottoman government's benefiting from either the revenues paid for the use of state land or from the taxes they could assess on private landholders.

Palestinian peasants had often been victimized by Ottoman functionaries and peasant resistance to the imposition of taxes was well known; officials in Damascus had on occasion destroyed whole villages that had openly defied attempts to collect revenues from them.[7] Many peasants were in debt to larger landholders and could not pay the fees to establish title, let alone pay taxes on the land. In addition, many peasants who were able to pay were afraid to do so because they or their sons would become subject to military recruitment once their names appeared on the tax rolls. Consequently, they, as well as the indebted peasants, were quite willing to have their lands registered in the names of individuals who assumed the tax burdens and became large landholders in the process. As a result, title deeds to extensive areas of land were acquired by relatively few people or families while the peasants on much of that land continued to farm it as before and still assumed that they had customary rights to its use.

Palestinian Notables and Absentee Landowners.   Among those who purchased land in this manner were Palestinian notables, many of whom served as tax collectors for the Ottomans. Among these were families from Jerusalem who had not previously owned land. Others were merchants, local Christian, Lebanese, or European, who began to invest in land in Palestine. Among these were Christian merchants from Beirut. The most prominent was the Sursuq family, Greek Catholics who owned a silk factory there and exported textiles. The Sursuqs bought land from peasants or acquired uncultivated state land that the Ottoman government offered for sale. They acquired a total of 230,000 *dunams*, approximately 57,500 acres (one dunam equals a quarter acre), in the Galilee, mostly in the Marj ibn Amir (Plain of Esdraelon) and near Nazareth, where much of the land they bought had belonged to nearby villages. This latter sale violated a provision of the 1858 land law that forbade the possession of village (musha'a) lands by an individual, but the Ottoman desire for revenue prevailed. Extensive Jewish investment and colonization did not begin until after 1882.

It is clear that a major transformation of landholding patterns had occurred in Palestine prior to Zionist immigration. One estimate from the turn of the twentieth century is that "only 20 percent of the land in Galilee and 50 percent in Judea was in the hands of the peasants."[8] Nevertheless, peasant and village holders retained possession of two-thirds of the cultivable land, nine million dunams, with other large tracts owned by tribes who cultivated the coastal plains of Gaza and Beersheba. This left one million dunams for the Sursuqs, the Sultans, and other great families. What had changed was the increase in the amount of Palestinian land under cultivation. Much of the property bought by the Sursuqs in the Marj ibn Amir had not been tilled for years because of local strife.

Palestinian Agricultural Productivity.   What then of the land's productivity? Palestine experienced major economic growth following the Crimean War, when the restoration of Ottoman authority brought greater regional security. More land was cultivated, by peasants and tribes as well as by large cultivators, in response mainly to world market developments. Gaza became an important grain-producing region, initially because Russian grain exports declined during the Crimean War. During the 1860s, cotton production exploded to meet increased European demand owing to the loss of American cotton during the Civil War, but this market did not last beyond the mid-1870s.

More successful and better known was the vast expansion of citrus cultivation, especially of oranges: "The garden area of Jaffa (orange plantations and vegetable gardens) was quadrupled between 1850 and 1880 . . . [with] the annual yield of the orange harvest . . . cited as 20 million in 1856 and 36 million in 1882."[9] Similar expansion in wheat production and exports was matched by "a doubling of the soap factories at Nablus from 15 in 1860 to 30 in 1882 [which] corresponded to the expansion of olive cultivation and the doubling of soap export via Jaffa."[10] Production continued to increase after 1880 in response to European demand and also because growers introduced European agricultural techniques. From the 1880s to 1914, the orchard area for oranges around Jaffa multiplied by seven times, and exports nearly quintupled. By 1913, Jewish colonists at Petah Tikva near Jaffa were exporting about 15 percent of Palestine's crop.[11]

As these figures indicate, a major expansion of Palestinian agricultural and industrial productivity occurred before Zionist colonization. But they also reflect a phenomenon occurring in other colonial contexts, namely, the relative inefficiency of indigenous production methods compared to those introduced by European colonists, in this case the Jews and others, such as the German Templars, from the 1880s onward. Palestinian per capita agricultural output would be lower than that of colonists who had access to imported technology and external capital (see Figures 1.1 and 1.2). A similar contrast can be seen in industries such as soap and olive oil manufacturing, where Arabs continued to use traditional methods of production and exported to regional markets, including Egypt, while European immigrants built factories that used imported machinery.

Tourists and Immigrants. Tourist and pilgrim traffic to the Holy Land grew rapidly during the latter half of the nineteenth century, as conditions for travel improved, and Muslim hostility to foreigners, frequently noted by travelers during the first half of the century, seemed to abate. Various European Christian groups organized tours from the 1850s, and travel agents began touting excursions from the 1870s. During the 1870s between ten and twenty thousand pilgrims visited Jerusalem annually, the largest contingent from Russia. These

Figure 1.1 ■ **Arab Farmers in the Jezreel Plain, circa 1900**

Arab agriculture continued to rely on camels and donkeys as well as cattle long after the Zionists had begun importing tractors from Europe. Note also the traditional one-handled wooden plow, which continued to be used, whereas Zionists, aided by Rothschild funding, introduced a heavy metal plow ultimately powered by steam (see also Figure 1.2).

Figure 1.2 ■ A Zionist Settler with a Manufactured Reaper Imported from Europe

This horse-drawn reaper, being used at Petah Tikva, replaced the Arab sickle, probably in the mid-1890s. Its use illustrates the Zionist importation of advanced European devices set against traditional Palestinian agriculture.

visitors provided an important source of revenue for several cities in Palestine, especially Jerusalem, Bethlehem, and the ports of Jaffa and Haifa. This tourist influx also reflected a growing European interest in antiquities, leading to various archaeological expeditions. Most surveys of Palestine during the century "were concerned with the geography of the region in relation to its past" and in identifying biblical sites.[12]

Other visitors to Palestine intended to establish a presence there. French Catholics participated in what they called "the peaceful crusade," visiting holy places and donating sums to build religious institutions. The German Templars established agricultural colonies with the idea of settling in Palestine and Christianizing it if possible. Finally, Protestant missionaries from England and America came to Palestine. They sought converts among members of other Christian sects and encouraged Jewish migration. As evangelical Christians who considered the end of the world to be at hand, they hoped to bring Jews to Palestine and convert them to Christianity in the Holy Land before the Day of Judgment. Similar aspirations can be found today among Christian fundamentalists in the United States and form one component of their support for Israel.

But during most of the century, the Jews who came to Palestine did so for their own religious motives. They were making their pilgrimage to the land of ancient Israel, many in order to die there. They settled in several cities, but especially in Jerusalem where Jews comprised the majority of the population by

1890. Another town where Muslims lost their majority was the port of Haifa, which expanded greatly from the 1850s onward. Christians made up the largest single group, many of them Lebanese traders who came to take advantage of the commerce and pilgrim traffic that passed through Haifa. And between 1895 and 1914, forty thousand Jews entered Palestine, often not for religious reasons but to colonize it and establish a base for the future restoration of Palestine as Israel. As Zionists they were more interested in establishing agricultural colonies than in settling in the cities.

Population and Identity.   Our discussion of immigration raises the question of the nature of the population of Palestine during this period and the reasons for its increase to about 650,000 by 1914. Was this due to natural causes or immigration, including Arabs from outside Palestine? Israeli and other scholars of the question have concluded that a natural increase in the overwhelmingly Arab population of Palestine from the 1840s would account for an Arab component of the 1914 estimate (650,000) of between 555,000 and 585,000. Taking the lower figure of 555,000 and adding a Jewish population of about 80,000 in 1914 still allows for an additional 25,000 to 40,000 settlers, whether other Europeans or Arabs. Arabs undoubtedly did migrate to Palestine or were settled by Ottoman officials there during this seventy-year period, but they probably comprised no more than 8 percent of the Arab population of Palestine in 1914.[13]

Nevertheless, a predominantly Palestinian Arab population does not necessarily indicate the widespread existence of a Palestinian Arab national consciousness at this time. The concept of nationalism was a recent European phenomenon, just beginning to be known in the Arab world, that often collided with the family and village loyalties that predominated along with one's religious identity. On the other hand, as Haim Gerber has shown, sources dating from the seventeenth century, and possibly earlier, indicate that educated Palestinians were conscious of living in a region called "Palestine" that was distinct from, even if a part of, a larger territory called "Syria."[14] This awareness cannot be called nationalism in the European sense of the term, which defined the bonds linking a people to a specific piece of land as the source of their primary identity. Nationalism was a secular concept, although it could be justified by a religious legacy as Zionism did for secular Jewish nationalism. Nationalism would not have defined a Palestinian's primary awareness of himself as an Ottoman subject of Muslim, Christian, or Jewish religious persuasion, who nonetheless lived in that part of the empire known as Palestine. This new scholarship does suggest, however, that educated Palestinian Arabs considered themselves to live in Palestine, establishing an identity with a region defined by boundaries. This identification was not simply the result of their encounter with Jewish nationalism in the form of Zionism, as has often been assumed.[15]

Nationalism in the European sense was, however, part of Zionism and would be used to justify Zionist claims to Palestine, where a Jewish kingdom had existed two thousand years earlier. Zionists comprised about 25,000, or 31 percent, of the Jewish population of Palestine in 1914. They planned to reclaim Palestine as Eretz Israel, the land of the Jewish people.

ZIONISM: ITS ORIGINS AND DEVELOPMENT TO 1914

The modern Zionist movement dates from the second half of the nineteenth century, inspired by secular nationalism and anti-Jewish prejudice in Western and especially Eastern Europe. Underlying modern Zionism was the wish to establish an independent Jewish existence in Palestine, the ancient land of Israel. Modern Zionism differed from the traditional Jewish yearning to return to Zion, Eretz Israel, in that religious Jews viewed the matter as one to be decided by God. Just as their exile reflected Yahweh's punishment of Jews for their transgressions of His laws, so would their return indicate that He had granted them redemption, a redemption that many believed could occur only when the end of the world was at hand. In contrast, modern or political Zionism was activist and predominantly secular. It was a movement of Jews who were disenchanted with their religious culture but who rejected the idea of assimilation into European society where hostility toward Jews persisted despite the passage of laws in Western Europe granting them equality. The situation was much worse in Eastern Europe, where the persecution of Jews intensified as the century drew to a close.

The Jews of Western Europe

Until the Crusades, Western European Jews had suffered sporadic persecution offset by long periods of relative tolerance. Under Christianity, as in pagan Rome, Jews were the only religious community allowed to retain their religious autonomy. While Christian laws prohibited Jewish proselytization or expansion, including the building of new synagogues, existing structures were protected. With the Crusades, the haphazard expression of Christian hostility toward Jews became more focused. Intended to seize Jerusalem from Islam, the Crusades aroused intense feelings of hostility toward all who denied the divinity of Jesus and gradually established a climate of hysteria in which the Jews were cast as a people seeking to subvert Christian security.

Latent religious hostility was reinforced by the competition that the Jews presented to a newly emerging Christian bourgeoisie, who were often allied with monarchs eager to acquire wealth to bolster their power. As a result, Jews were expelled from England in 1290, not to return until the end of the seventeenth century, and from France in 1306, although small communities remained. Protestantism was no less hostile to Jews in regions under its control. The most extreme example of Christian fear of subversion occurred in Spain, where the Spanish reconquest led to the expulsion laws of 1492, causing, as noted, an exodus of Spanish Arab Muslims to North Africa and of Jews into the Mediterranean world, especially the Ottoman Empire. During the eighteenth century, Jews were readmitted to the northern European countries of England

and France under state sponsorship, initiating a process of assimilation at the higher levels of society in France, England, and some German states even before the French Revolution. This served as a catalyst for the legal emancipation of Western European Jewry during the nineteenth century.

The French Revolution of 1789 and its Declaration of the Rights of Man proclaimed the equality of all people as the basis for true citizenship. Jews were specifically offered the opportunity to assimilate as individuals into French society. Assimilation meant that Jews would presumably give up their commitment to retain their distinctiveness as a separate community adhering to Jewish laws and, with that, their commitment to the idea of a return to Eretz Israel, a hope that had bound them together for centuries. The majority of Western European Jewry opted for assimilation during the nineteenth century as barriers gradually broke down in Germany, Austria, England, Hungary, and later in Italy and France. By midcentury, Jews were permitted to stand as candidates for Parliament in England. In France, and especially in Germany, assimilation proceeded rapidly. Intermarriage and a declining birthrate led to a sharp decrease in the original German-Jewish community, but the Jewish population there remained distinctive because of the influx of Jews from Eastern Europe.

The Jews had made great strides toward legal and social equality by the end of the nineteenth century, but latent and sporadic open hostility toward them remained. It was during this period, the 1880s, that the term "anti-Semitism" was coined by an anti-Jewish German author to emphasize the nature of his antipathy as racial and thus "modern," as opposed to the traditional religious antagonism toward Jews. Although anti-Semitism went hand in hand with Jewish efforts to assimilate, most Western European Jews continued in their efforts to merge more fully into society. When an active Zionist movement emerged, its initial impulse and its main support came from Eastern Europe, where legal equality, let alone assimilation, seemed increasingly unattainable.

Eastern European Jewry and the Rise of Zionism

At approximately the same time that Jewish equality with non-Jews was declared in Western Europe through the French Revolution, Eastern European Jewry was entering a century-long phase of increased hostility and segmentation within Polish and Russian society. The future of Eastern European Jewry was decided by the partition of Poland, which occurred in three stages in 1772, 1793, and 1795. Portions of the country went to Russia, Prussia, and Austria. As a result, Russian Jewry, heretofore a small community, expanded significantly and created in Russian eyes a question they had to deal with in a decisive manner. The Russians' response was both harsh and contradictory. They attacked Jews for their separatism but usually imposed laws forbidding them to participate freely in Russian society unless they converted. Laws passed in 1790 and 1791 created the Pale of Settlement. These decrees stipulated that Jews could not live in the major Russian cities of the interior. They were confined to the former Polish territories and certain other areas of southwest Russia where they were supposed to live in the larger cities. Even here they were later barred from cities such as Kiev and Sebastopol. Although these laws were not always strictly enforced, they reflected an official attitude of suspicion and hostility that led to repeated attempts to isolate Jews from Russians, whether inside or outside the Pale.

The Origins of Zionism.   Eastern European Jewry's isolation and forced concentration of populations during the nineteenth century ensured the continuity of its strong religious and communal bonds at a time when adherence to those traditions was fading in the West. Thus it "was the Jew whose attachment to tradition was loosening who found the condition of Jews intolerable," whereas the leadership of Eastern Jewry sought to preserve the strength of the community that lay in its adherence to traditional values and practices.[16] Modern Zionism found its roots among Russian Jews who had already broken with communal life in the Pale, many of whom had hoped briefly for the opportunity to assimilate into Russian society. The bases of these aspirations lay in the modernist Russian Jewish movement called the *haskala*, which arose in the 1850s. Their members were attracted to Western European literary models and the idea of legal equality with non-Jews that was occurring there. The reign of Tsar Alexander II inspired optimism among the modernists because many restrictive laws were relaxed; Jewish students, for example, were allowed to attend universities in Moscow and elsewhere. But the tsar's assassination in 1881 reimposed a conservative regime hostile to modernization and Jewish integration. Equally alarming to Alexander III and his chief adviser, Pobedonostsev, was the specter of peasant unrest, especially in southern Russia. A means of diverting peasant hostility from the government lay in tolerating, if not encouraging, attacks on Jewish communities, the catalyst for the decision of some Jews to seek a haven in Palestine.

The first series of attacks, or *pogroms*, erupted in 1881 and continued until 1884. They consisted of peasant assaults on Jewish quarters accompanied by rape, looting, and some killing. Although rioters were brought to court and some were punished by exile, the peasants believed they had the tsar's approval. The pogroms continued, encouraged by the tacit support of local officials. The impact of these pogroms has lasted to the present day. To many Jews they were proof that Russia would never grant legal emancipation. The result was the beginning of a vast emigration movement, in which 1.5 million Jews left Russia between 1900 and 1914. The great majority headed for the United States, but some, especially Jewish students whose hopes for greater equality had been raised during the reign of Alexander II and who had broken with their communal traditions, directed their attention toward Palestine.

BILU and Hibbat Zion.   This movement became known as BILU, an acronym taken from the Hebrew initials in Isaiah 2:5, "O House of Jacob, come and let us go." Its founders were students from Kharkov who decided to establish agricultural settlements in Palestine. Their success was meager. Most who actually settled there soon left. But the ideals of the members of BILU were to leave a lasting impression on later Zionists. They envisaged a Jewish state in Palestine founded on the principles of Jewish agriculture and Jewish labor. And they were quite specific about the need to return to Palestine, the ancient home of the Jews, rather than to seek a haven elsewhere. All these factors would later be part of Zionist labor ideology. Their vision of agricultural communes led ultimately to the forming of the *kibbutzim*, which many saw as the embodiment of Zionist principles.

A more diffuse but longer-lived organization that emerged in 1881–1882 would later be known as Hibbat Zion (The Love of Zion). Circles whose members called themselves Hovevei Zion (Lovers of Zion) began to meet in various cities, including St. Petersburg. Viewing themselves as the custodians of the Hebrew language and Jewish culture, they found life in Russia intolerable and saw emigration to Palestine as the only answer. Unlike the BILU, the Lovers of Zion did not immediately strive to establish agricultural settlements in Palestine, but they did expand greatly in Russia so that by 1895 they had approximately 10,000 members. The Hovevei Zion attracted diverse types who envisaged the restoration of Eretz Israel, including Y. L. Pinsker, whose book *Auto-emancipation* was published in 1881.

Pinsker believed that Jews had to acquire territory somewhere in order to escape the persecution they experienced in Europe, but he was not committed to a Jewish return to Palestine. Although Pinsker wrote his book in response to the Russian pogroms and the plight of Eastern European Jewry, he had little faith in the assimilation process under way in the West. To him Jewish security in Europe was a mirage. A key to his thesis was that Jews had to emancipate themselves rather than rely on non-Jews, an argument that had great appeal to the Lovers of Zion even though they disagreed with Pinsker's lack of specific commitment to Palestine. Pinsker had written his book as an appeal to German Jews in the West to save their Russian brethren, but he found his audience only in the East. He agreed in 1883 to become head of the Lovers of Zion in Odessa and ultimately became leader of the Hibbat Zion movement until his death in 1891.

In Palestine itself the expansion of Jewish settlements owed little to the Hibbat Zion movement. Indeed, the majority of the Jewish immigrants in the first wave following the pogroms of 1881–1884 were not technically Zionists. Inspired by religious more than nationalist motives, they settled in urban areas. Whereas between twenty and thirty thousand Jews entered Palestine as part of this first wave of immigrants (*aliya*), fewer than three thousand settled in the new villages that were established. These agricultural enterprises survived not because of funds from Russian Jews but primarily because of the philanthropy of wealthy Western Jews, such as Sir Moses Montefiore and particularly Baron Edmond de Rothschild of the great banking family, who between 1883 and 1889 gave the settlers 1.6 million pounds sterling.[17] But whatever Rothschild's role was in preventing the collapse of Zionist efforts during this period, he was not a leader of a movement. That task fell to Theodor Herzl, an assimilated Viennese Jew, whose efforts produced the formation of the World Zionist Organization in 1897.

Theodor Herzl and the Zionist Movement to 1914

Theodor Herzl's contributions to the development of Zionism were seminal, as many scholars have noted, but they have also stressed that Herzl (see Figure 1.3) did not instigate the idea of Zionism itself. Indeed, for years he was unfamiliar with the strands of Zionist thought and activity current in Eastern Europe. In many ways his decision to seek a solution to the question of the Jews in Europe was self-inspired. He had dreamed of being the leader who would liberate them even while, as a journalist for a prestigious Viennese paper, he appeared to be well integrated into European culture. The catalyst for his decision to commit himself to the cause of European Jewry was the trial of Alfred Dreyfus, a French-Jewish officer falsely accused of treason and sentenced to Devil's Island. The trial aroused the vengeance of the French right at what they saw as the undermining of the nation by the liberalization of its laws, which included the granting of equality of Jews. It became a cause célèbre, with violent anti-Semitic overtones that caused the French left to take up Dreyfus's defense. Herzl had lived in Paris from 1891 to 1895 and was aware of the depth of French anti-Semitism before the Dreyfus case, but it was the Dreyfus trial that led him to write *Der Judenstaat* (The State of the Jews), which established him as the principal leader of world Zionism.

Figure 1.3 ■ Theodor Herzl, circa 1895

In this photograph, Herzl's intensity and self-confidence are evident on the eve of his achieving prominence as leader of the fledgling Zionist movement.

Herzl and the World Zionist Organization.   In *Der Judenstaat* (1896), Herzl called for the creation of a Jewish state that would absorb European Jewry and thus end the anti-Semitism that still prevailed even in Western Europe and proved that assimilation was impossible (see Document 1.3). Though he was vaguely aware of the plight of Eastern European Jewry and of the intellectual currents then prevalent there (he read Pinsker's *Autoemancipation* after completing *Der Judenstaat*), he directed his appeal to European statesmen and wealthy Jews in the West. He hoped that those Jews would provide financial assistance for the formation of an organization, perhaps a company, that would arrange the transference of Jews to their new home. They could also help persuade European leaders of the validity and feasibility of the idea. Herzl saw Jewish migration to Palestine (or possibly elsewhere) as a movement of colonization similar to that being undertaken by European countries at the time, and thus something with which they would sympathize[18] (see Document 1.4). Like Pinsker, Herzl was not committed to Palestine as the prospective Jewish homeland, although he did not discount it as the ideal solution. Rather, he preferred to accept empty territory that might be offered, such as sections of Argentina. In this, as in his eagerness to seek the aid of prominent Europeans, Herzl's aspirations were quite different from those of the Lovers of Zion, who emphasized self-help within the Jewish community and stressed the need to reestablish the Jewish state in Palestine.

These differences proved to be crucial to the ultimate direction of the Zionist movement. When Herzl called a congress to meet in Basel in 1897 to establish a Zionist organization, he expected to gain the support of leading Western Jews. But most stayed away, fearful that his efforts would endanger their status as newly assimilated citizens of their countries. The majority of delegates to the congress were from the East, Lovers of Zion who were attracted to Herzl's ideas if not in total agreement with them. At Basel, they formed the World Zionist Organization with Herzl as its president. Its program declared that the goal of Zionism was "the creation of a home for the Jewish people in Palestine to be secured by public law"[19] (see Document 1.5). The real objective was a Jewish state, but it was deemed advisable not to declare that openly because of Ottoman objections to the idea of a new nationality seeking self-rule within its territory. Likewise, the term "public law" rather than "international law" was used to allay Ottoman fears that European powers sought to carve up the empire.[20]

The question before this and later congresses was how best to pursue Zionist objectives. Herzl favored diplomacy. He continued to seek Ottoman approval for Jewish settlement and the idea of a Jewish state in return for Jewish repayment of the by-then substantial Ottoman national debt. He wanted official recognition of the Jewish right to Palestine as a prelude to extensive settlement there; consequently, Herzl opposed the efforts of Eastern European Zionists to create a de facto Jewish presence in the area because he feared they would undermine his diplomatic endeavors. The Ottomans had passed laws forbidding Jews from purchasing land in Palestine, but Zionists evaded them with the aid of foreign consuls and Ottoman Jews sympathetic to their cause. Ottoman officials informed Herzl that Jews could settle in designated areas of Syria and Iraq but not in Palestine and that they could enter Ottoman territory only as individuals, not as a distinct community with political ambitions.

Herzl devoted himself to diplomacy. He visited Istanbul on several occasions and met Sultan Abdul Hamid in 1901. Herzl turned to the British in 1902, seeking the al-Arish area in the Sinai Peninsula because it was adjacent to Palestine and could serve as an opening for future demands for expanded migration to the area. Joseph Chamberlain, then British colonial secretary, replied by suggesting land in British-controlled East Africa, now part of Kenya. Though initially hostile to this idea, Herzl later saw it as granting a temporary haven that might give the Zionists leverage in their demands for Palestine. This led to a major clash with the representatives of Eastern European Jewry who remained steadfast in their commitment to Palestine. They suspected Herzl of being willing to abandon Zionism, a suspicion encouraged by Herzl's secretiveness in diplomacy and his aloof personal style. Herzl's death in 1904 ensured the failure of the project. The leadership of world Zionism passed to the Russian Lovers of Zion, who stressed the need for practical achievements in Palestine as the prerequisite to political recognition.

Herzl had been unable to gain international recognition of the Jewish right to a state of their own. Toward the end he had encountered strong opposition from Eastern European Zionists who, unconcerned with international approval, stressed the need for continual settlement in Palestine. But the success of their efforts in coming years was to a large degree the result of his endeavors. With his encouragement, the World Zionist Organization created its own bank in 1899, and in 1901 the Jewish National Fund was established for the express purpose of purchasing and developing land for Jewish settlements in Palestine. The fund played a major role in the acquisition of land that became inalienably Jewish, never to be sold to or worked by non-Jews, as part of the program to establish a dominant Jewish presence in the area.

Militant Zionism: The Second Aliya.   Equally important, however, was the ideological commitment of the second wave of immigrants, those who came to Palestine between 1904 and 1914, among them David Ben-Gurion (né Green), who later became Israel's first prime minister. Many were socialists nurtured in the revolutionary atmosphere then prevalent in Russian intellectual circles. But they were also Zionists who were determined to achieve their socialist ideals within a separate Jewish environment rather than as part of a world movement. Their vision of a new Jewish society entailed a commitment to the land and to the creation of a socialist agricultural basis for the future Israel. In this they fused their socialist ideals with the agricultural vision found in the writings of David Gordon (d. 1922), an educator and activist who extolled the "religion of labor" by which Jews would redeem the land of Israel.

This new society was to be based on Jewish labor alone, a principle that caused these new immigrants to look down on the earlier generation of Jewish settlers whose farms employed Arabs: to rely on Arab labor violated Jewish socialist ideals. For the Zionists of the second wave, Jewish socialism meant an egalitarian Jewish society that excluded Arabs. They formed two groups, Poale Zion (Workers of Zion) and Hapoel Hatzair (The Young Worker), both of which devoted themselves to creating new settlements that reclaimed the land for cultivation by Jewish labor and communal living based on socialist principles. They were helped in their efforts by the Jewish National Fund. By 1914, of the forty-four Jewish agricultural settlements, fourteen had been sponsored by the World Zionist Organization, the nucleus of Zionist efforts in Palestine from that time onward. Jews owned over 400,000 dunams of land (about 100,000 acres), of which slightly more than half was under cultivation.

Out of the approximately 85,000 Jews then in Palestine, 12,000 lived on the land. Most Palestinian Jews were in their dress and appearance not dissimilar from Arabs, part of a Middle Eastern society quite different from the vision imparted by the European Jews who now appeared. (See Figure 1.4.) Nevertheless, despite their small numbers, the Zionist drive to purchase land and the openness of their commitment to a separate Jewish entity in Palestine had, by 1914, already aroused Arab fears, which were well known to Zionist leaders in Palestine but were ignored or downplayed by Zionist leaders in the West.

THE ARAB RESPONSE TO ZIONISM

At the turn of the twentieth century, Palestine was divided into two principal administrative districts: the northern sector, the sanjaks of Acre and Nablus, was part of the vilayet (Arabic: *wilaya*) of Beirut; to the south, the independent governorate of Jerusalem, overseen directly by the Ministry of the Interior in Istanbul, encompassed most of central Palestine (see Map 1.1). The direct link between Jerusalem and the Ottoman capital probably reflected the increased pace of tourism and immigration into southern and central Palestine during the latter half of the nineteenth century, which prompted Ottoman authorities to keep closer surveillance on Jerusalem and the surrounding areas.

The Arab population of Palestine was overwhelmingly Sunni Muslim. Eleven percent were Christian, primarily Greek Orthodox. Despite local rivalries, a sense of community prevailed, especially among the Muslims, because of the religious festivals that brought them together from various parts of Palestine and also because of the influence of the highest religious official, the mufti of Jerusalem, whose authority extended into the northern vilayet. The al-Husayni family controlled the post of mufti from the mid-nineteenth century and consequently attained national prominence, which was buttressed by their hold over various administrative posts in Jerusalem as well.[21] Their longevity in office led to British recognition of the then mufti, Hajj Amin al-Husayni, as the leading Arab representative during the Mandate following World War I, but it also contributed to resentment among rival Jerusalem families and in prominent clans in other areas.

Figure 1.4 ■ The Western (Wailing) Wall in Jerusalem, circa 1900

This photograph illustrates the narrow passage giving access to the Western Wall and the clothing and appearance of Palestinian Jews, which did not differ greatly from that of Arabs; nor, apparently, did men and women segregate themselves when praying as rigorously as they would later.

Map 1.1 ■ Ottoman Palestine and Syria, 1910   ▶

This map indicates the separate status of the Sanjak of Jerusalem, which was directly under Istanbul's control. It also shows the Hijaz Railroad, then reaching to Medina, which the sultan intended to extend to Mecca. The Sharif Husayn perceived this plan as a threat to his freedom of action, and it influenced his alignment with the British in World War I.

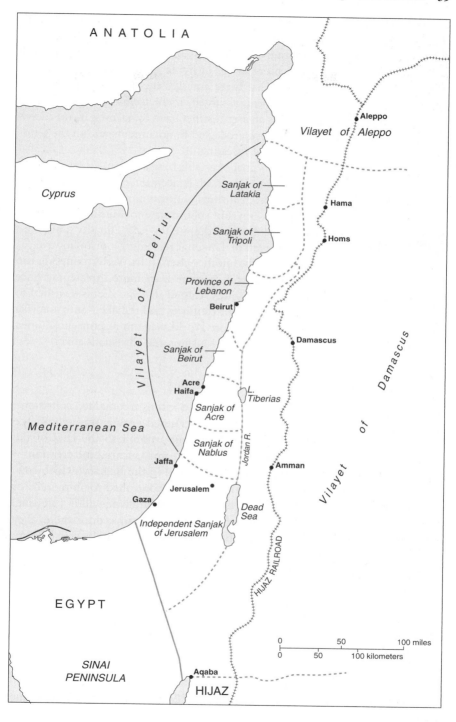

ANATOLIA

Aleppo

Vilayet of Aleppo

Cyprus

Sanjak of
Latakia

Hama

Sanjak of
Tripoli

Homs

Province of
Lebanon

Beirut

Damascus

Sanjak of
Beirut

Acre
Haifa

L.
Tiberias

Sanjak of
Acre

Sanjak of
Nablus

Vilayet

of

Jordan R.

Damascus

Jaffa

Amman

Vilayet

of

Jerusalem

Gaza

Dead
Sea

Mediterranean Sea

Independent Sanjak
of Jerusalem

EGYPT

HIJAZ RAILROAD

| 0 | | 50 | | 100 miles |
| 0 | 50 | | 100 kilometers | |

SINAI
PENINSULA

Aqaba

HIJAZ

Arab conceptions of identity varied. Beyond local and family ties, Muslims considered themselves to be Ottoman subjects and gave allegiance to the sultan/caliph as head of the Islamic community. Christians, especially the Greek Orthodox, seem to have been more aware of living in a specific region called Palestine, and it is among them that there emerges the dominant journalistic opposition to Zionism. Nevertheless, as noted, there seems to have existed a general conception of Palestine as an area distinct from Syria, even if considered part of it for administrative purposes, reflected in documents and in the Ottoman government's term "the land of Palestine."[22]

It is clear that Zionism, with its goal of establishing a dominant Jewish presence in Palestine, revised significantly the Arab conception of the Jews and their place in a Muslim society. As noted, Muslims had traditionally viewed Jews as occupying dhimmi status, protected by, but subordinate to, Muslims, a role that most Ottoman Jews had continued to play despite the legal equality granted to them along with Christians as a result of Tanzimat reforms. Zionism however, as a European movement, appeared to be another attempt by Western imperialism to subordinate Muslims to Europeans. It became even more threatening once Palestinians, Christians as well as Muslims, realized that the Zionists wished to take part of what had been Arab lands for centuries and remake it into a Jewish homeland. Arab opposition emerged before World War I in response to Zionist immigration and land purchase, shared by Muslims and Christians alike.

Ottoman Policies and Jewish Land Purchases

As we have seen, official Ottoman policy toward Zionism remained consistent: "Jewish immigrants will be able to settle as scattered groups throughout the Ottoman Empire, excluding Palestine. They must submit to the laws of the empire and become Ottoman subjects."[23] The Ottomans feared the creation of another "national" problem similar to those found in the Balkans, which continued to erode their hold on territories they had controlled for hundreds of years. But official Ottoman policy was not effectively implemented in Palestine. Jewish immigrants entered the area as tourists or pilgrims; once there, they acquired the protection of foreign consuls as the European powers were eager to protect their own rights under capitulations laws. Restrictions on land sales to foreigners were circumvented by having Ottoman Jews or foreign consuls buy the land for them. As a result, concern about Jewish immigration and land purchases existed in certain circles in Palestine before the World Zionist Organization was created in 1897. In that year, an Arab commission was formed in Jerusalem, headed by the mufti, to examine the issue of land sales to Jews, and its protests led to the cessation of such sales for several years. Jewish agents discovered that it was much easier to buy land in the northern vilayet, and in 1900 the Jewish Colonization Association opened an office in Beirut. Purchases were facilitated both by the fact that many large landholders in northern Palestine resided in Beirut and by the willingness of the Ottoman officials there to ignore

Figure 1.5 ■ Turkish Troops Marching in Jerusalem, 1898

This parade would have served to stress Ottoman control of the city, but the European banks and hotels lining the street and the dress of many onlookers call attention to the growing Western presence in the city. The procession has attracted many hotel guests to hotel windows and the roof of the Central Hotel in the distance.

regulations. Similar practices occurred in and around Jerusalem from 1901 onward as the appointed Ottoman governors permitted Jews to buy land in return for financial favors. For example, the Anglo-Palestine Company, the first Zionist organization to be established in Palestine, found that despite Ottoman laws, local Ottoman authorities would permit land sales in return for loans from the company to the governor.

Although Ottoman regulations and protests by Arab officials were often ineffective in blocking Jewish purchases of land, general Arab opposition did not arise immediately. Arab peasants initially opposed Jewish land purchases, and in cases where they were ousted from their homes, violence and armed resistance resulted. Most peasants, however, gradually accepted Jewish landowners through the 1890s because the latter usually permitted them to work the soil and receive income from it, a practice that was condemned by labor Zionists.[24]

Growing Apprehension: Palestine and the Arab World

Alarm appeared more frequently among Arabs by the end of the decade, including those Arabs outside Palestine who were also aware of Zionism. Thus the

Syrian Christian–owned journal *al-Muqtataf*, based in Cairo, published an article in 1898 warning against Jewish hopes to control trade in Palestine. The next year Yusuf al-Khalidi, a prominent Jerusalemite, wrote to the chief rabbi of France, telling him that although "historically it is your country" and Zionism could be understood in theory, in practice its implementation would require "brute force"; he pleaded with the rabbi to "let Palestine be left in peace." Herzl replied by reassuring al-Khalidi that Zionism meant no harm and that the Arabs' wealth and well-being would increase through Zionist investments.[25] Rashid Rida, a Muslim reformer born in the Beirut vilayet but living in Cairo, published an article in 1902 in his journal, *al-Manar*, stating that Jews entering Palestine sought national sovereignty, not simply a haven from persecution. Finally, in a book published in Paris in 1905 (*Le Reveil de la Nation Arabe*, The Awakening of the Arab Nation), Naguib Azoury, a Maronite Catholic, called for the separation of Arab provinces from Ottoman rule; Azoury also predicted violent clashes in Palestine between the Arabs and Jews for control of the area with neither side willing to compromise. Azoury's demand for Arab independence reflected a Christian's, as opposed to a Muslim's, concern for the future of the region. Muslim opinion was still loyal to Ottoman authority even though some circles were becoming increasingly critical of it. His remarks on Arab-Jewish tensions, though exaggerated, appear prophetic with hindsight:

> Two important phenomena of the same nature but opposed . . . are emerging . . . in Asiatic Turkey. They are the awakening of the Arab nation and the latent effect of the Jews to reconstitute on a very large scale the ancient kingdom of Israel. Both these movements are destined to fight each other continually until one of them wins. The fate of the entire world will depend on the final result of this struggle between these two peoples representing two contrary principles.[26]

These Arab protests, with the exception of that of the Jerusalem commission of 1897, were the work of individuals, but they presumably reached a receptive audience. *Al-Muqtataf* and *al-Manar*, although totally different in character, circulated throughout the Arab world and were read in Christian and Muslim circles, respectively. More significant was the nature of the opposition that emerged from 1908 onward, presumably in response to the more strident calls of labor Zionism, which openly opposed Jewish employment of Arabs and called for the establishment of a separate Jewish entity in Palestine. These arguments, espoused in the Zionist press and translated into Arabic, became known to increasing numbers of Palestinian Arabs, especially once a Palestinian Arab press appeared in 1908.

The editors of the papers most emphatically opposed to Zionism were Greek Orthodox Christians. The papers were *al-Karmil*, created in 1908, and, significantly, *Filastin* (Palestine), founded in 1911; the former was published in Haifa, the latter in Jaffa. *Al-Karmil* was openly pro-Ottoman in its loyalties, although following the Young Turk Revolt of 1908 it became increasingly critical of the Committee of Union and Progress for failing to protect Palestinian interests. *Filastin* backed the Committee of Union and Progress, but as its name indicates, it stressed local nationalism rather than Ottoman allegiance; it referred to Palestine as an entity and to its readers as "Palestinians."[27] The importance of the press is indicated by the fact that when *Filastin* was first founded, Jews (under Arab pseudonyms) submitted articles to it supporting Zionism.

While most Palestinian Muslims remained loyal to Ottoman authority, they usually agreed with those Palestinian Christians who led the public opposition to Zionist immigration, land purchases, and, in a general way, Jewish exclusiveness. Debates in the Ottoman parliament in Istanbul, where Arab Muslim representatives from Palestine called for greater Ottoman vigilance against Zionist activities, echoed editorials in *Filastin* and *al-Karmil*. A key issue was the fact that the Zionists, as European Jews, were protected by the capitulations while bringing in wealth lacking to the Arabs: "they [rely] on the special rights accorded to foreign powers in the Ottoman Empire and on the corruption and treachery of the local administration. Moreover, they are free of most of the taxes . . . on Ottoman subjects."[28] For one Palestinian candidate for elections to the Ottoman parliament in 1914, Jews would be welcome if they were willing as individuals "to accept Ottoman nationality and [to] learn the language of the country. . . . [B]ut if the foreign subject comes to fight us with the weapons of his foreign nationality and despises our sons and brethren and breaks our statutes and laws, then it is our duty not to pass over this in silence."[29]

CONCLUSION

Zionism thus contributed to a growing sense, among educated Muslims and Christians in Palestine, of a common identity as Palestinians at a time when Muslim suspicion of Christians, because of Ottoman territorial losses in the Balkans, was increasing elsewhere in the empire. The rising tensions in Palestine led to outbursts against foreign Christians and Jews that usually reflected socioeconomic circumstances in which Muslims found themselves progressively at a disadvantage with respect to outsiders. Most urban disturbances from 1860 onward "broke out in towns where Muslims had originally been in the majority [especially Haifa and Jaffa], but where their majority status either had been obliterated or was seriously threatened by the influx of foreigners and non-Muslims, . . . [and where] poverty, disappointment, jealousy, and exposure to new and unfamiliar ways of life, all combined to produce social instability."[30] By 1914 and the outbreak of World War I, Zionist officials in Palestine were well aware of Arab fears and their opposition to Zionist goals. The coming of the war presaged new developments of the utmost importance to the expectations of both Arabs and Jews as to the ultimate fate of Palestine.

QUESTIONS FOR CONSIDERATION

1. The Tanzimat reforms were intended to strengthen Ottoman society. How did the reforms affect Muslim-Christian relations in the Arab lands ruled by the Ottomans?

2. Great Britain was not an early participant in the development of the Suez Canal. Why did Britain come to consider the Suez Canal important to its imperial interests? How did its involvement change the balance of power in the region?

3. Why did the modern Zionist movement emerge in Eastern Europe? What goals did Eastern European Zionists share with Theodor Herzl? In what ways did they disagree?

4. How did Palestinian Arabs react to Zionist settlement in Palestine before 1914? What was Zionist policy regarding land use and ownership?

CHRONOLOGY

1453	Ottoman Turks take Constantinople; end of Byzantine Empire.
1516–1918	Palestine under Ottoman rule.
1740	French-Ottoman treaty granting France the right to protect Roman Catholics in the empire.
1774	Russian-Ottoman treaty allowing Russia to protect Eastern Orthodox residents of Istanbul.
1789	French Revolution begins.
1790–1791	Russia passes laws restricting Jews to Pale of Settlement.
1798	Napoleon invades Egypt.
1831–1840	Egyptian ruler Muhammad Ali controls Syria and Palestine.
1838	Ottoman-British Balta Liman Convention.
1839	Hatti Sharif of Gulhane reforms Ottoman justice system.
1854–1856	Crimean War.
1856	Hatti Humayun proclaims equality of dhimmis with Muslims.
1858, 1867	Ottoman land reform laws passed.
1869	Suez Canal opens.
1875	Britain buys Egyptian ruler's shares of Suez Canal Company.
1881	Y. L. Pinsker's *Autoemancipation* published.
1882	Founding of BILU and Hibbat Zion. Britain occupies Egypt, remains to 1956.
1896	Theodor Herzl's *Der Judenstaat* published.
1897	Founding of World Zionist Organization.
1900	Jewish Colonization Association opens office in Beirut.
1901	Jewish National Fund established.
1905	Naguib Azoury's *Le Reveil de la Nation Arabe* published.
1908	Young Turk Revolution. Ottoman Parliament reopens.
1908, 1911	*Al-Karmil* and *Filastin* Palestinian Arab newspapers founded.

Notes

1. Benjamin Braude and Bernard Lewis, eds., *Christians and Jews in the Ottoman Empire: The Functioning of a Plural Society*, vol. 1, The Central Lands (New York, 1982), 1.

2. Mark Mazower, *Salonica, City of Ghosts: Christians, Muslims and Jews, 1430–1950* (London, 2004).

3. Discussion of these matters can be found in two works by Moshe Ma'oz, *Ottoman Reform in Syria and Palestine* (Oxford, 1968) and "Changes in the Position of the Jewish Communities of Palestine and Syria in the Mid-Nineteenth Century," in *Studies on Palestine during the Ottoman Period*, ed. Moshe Ma'oz (Jerusalem, 1975), 142–63.

4. David Kushner, "Intercommunal Strife in Palestine during the Late Ottoman Period," *Asian and African Studies* 18 (1984): 197. For Maronite-Druze clashes and the Damascus riots, see Leila Fawaz, *An Occasion for War: Civil Conflict in Lebanon and Damascus in 1860* (New York, 1994).

5. Beshara Doumani, *Rediscovering Palestine: Merchants and Peasants in Jabal Nablus, 1700–1900* (Berkeley, 1995), 94. Doumani's study is an important source for this period.

6. See the recent study by Martha Mundy and Richard Saumarez Smith, *Governing Property, Making the Modern State: Law, Administration, and Production in Ottoman Syria* (London and New York, 2007).

7. Two travelers' accounts mentioning the destruction of villages are Henry Light, *Travels in Egypt, Nubia, Holy Land, Lebanon and Cyprus in the Year 1814* (London, 1818), 158–59; and William C. Prime, *Tent Life in the Holy Land* (New York, 1857), 220.

8. Alexander Schölch, "European Penetration and the Economic Development of Palestine, 1856–82," in *Studies in the Economic and Social History of Palestine in the Nineteenth and Twentieth Centuries*, ed. Roger Owen (Carbondale, Ill., 1982), 23–24. My discussion of economic development and land transfers in Palestine is drawn primarily from Schölch and from E. R. J. Owen, *The Middle East in the World Economy, 1800-1914* (New York, 1981), 153–79, 264–72.

9. Alexander Schölch, *Palestine in Transformation, 1856–1882: Studies in Social, Economic, and Political Development*, trans. William C. Young and Michael C. Gerrity (Washington, D.C., 1993), 285. This collection of Schölch's articles is an important source for the period.

10. Ibid.

11. Owen, *The Middle East*, 271.

12. C. Gordon Smith, "The Geography and Natural Resources of Palestine as Seen by British Writers in the Nineteenth and Early Twentieth Century," in Ma'oz, ed., *Studies on Palestine*, 90.

13. Haim Gerber, "The Population of Syria and Palestine in the Nineteenth Century," *Asian and African Studies* 13 (1979): 58–80; Yehoshua Ben-Arieh, "The Population of the Large Towns in Palestine during the First Eighty Years of the Nineteenth Century according to Western Sources," in Ma'oz, ed., *Studies on Palestine*, 49–69; Alexander Schölch, "The Demographic Development of Palestine, 1850–1882," *International Journal of Middle East Studies* 17 (November 1985): 485–505, an excellent overview; and Justin McCarthy, *The Population of Palestine: Population Statistics of the Late Ottoman Period and the Mandate* (New York, 1990). The question of population has been the subject of sensationalist studies claiming that the numbers of Arab immigrants equaled that of Jewish immigrants, claims rejected by scholars. The best—or worst—example of this effort is Joan Peters, *From Time Immemorial* (New York, 1984).

14. Haim Gerber, "'Palestine' and Other Territorial Concepts in the 17th Century," *International Journal of Middle East Studies* 30 (November 1998): 563–72. See also Gerber's important new book, *Remembering and Imagining Palestine: Identity and Nationalism from the Crusades to the Present* (New York, 2008).

15. There is a vast literature on nationalism generally. Summary analyses, with reference to the sources and to the Arab world, can be found in Roger Owen, *State, Power and Politics in the*

Making of the Modern Middle East (London, 1992); Charles D. Smith, "Imagined Identities, Imagined Nationalisms: Print Culture and Egyptian Nationalism in Light of Recent Scholarship," *International Journal of Middle East Studies* 29 (1997): 607–22. James Jankowski and Israeli Gershoni, eds., *Rethinking Nationalism in the Arab Middle East* (New York, 1997) has several articles of interest with occasionally conflicting views of what constitutes nationalism. For Palestinian nationalism, see Rashid Khalidi, *Palestinian Identity: The Construction of a Modern National Consciousness* (New York, 1997).

16. David Vital, *The Origins of Zionism* (Oxford, 1975), 74. I rely mainly on Vital for my discussion of Zionism.

17. Ibid., 214.

18. Amos Elon, *Herzl* (New York, 1975), 312; Elon also notes the assumption that the takeover of Palestine by European Jews would benefit the Arabs, a reflection of the "pious hopes and pious delusions" of that age.

19. Vital, *Origins of Zionism*, 368.

20. Elon, *Herzl*, 242.

21. Y. Porath, *The Emergence of the Palestinian Arab National Movement, 1918–1929* (London, 1974), 14.

22. Neville J. Mandel, *The Arabs and Zionism before World War I* (Berkeley and Los Angeles, 1976), xix. Schölch (*Palestine in Transformation*, 13–14) notes that the Ottomans proposed unifying Palestine into a single province in 1872 but rescinded the measure out of fear that it would facilitate European inroads into the area. The boundaries envisaged approximated those established for mandatory Palestine.

23. Mandel, *The Arabs*, 2.

24. For early Zionist colonization of Palestine and Arab resistance, see two studies: Gershon Shafir, *Land, Labor, and the Origins of the Israeli-Palestinian Conflict, 1882–1914* (Cambridge and New York, 1989); and Khalidi, *Palestinian Identity*, 89–117.

25. Elon, *Herzl*, 311–12. For the full text of Herzl's response, see Walid Khalidi, ed., *From Haven to Conquest: Readings in Zionism and the Palestine Problem until 1948* (Washington, D.C., 1987), 91–93.

26. Naguib Azoury, *Le Reveil de la Nation Arabe dans l'Asie Turque* (Paris, 1905), 245–47, quoted in *Arab Nationalism: An Anthology*, ed., Sylvia G. Haim (Berkeley, 1964), 81–82; and Azoury, v, quoted in Neville J. Mandel, *The Arabs and Zionism before World War I* (Berkeley, 1976), 52. Azoury's discussion of Palestine also reflected the intrusion of French anti-Semitic arguments into the discussion of Jewish aims in Palestine, the result of the Dreyfus affair and French Catholic propaganda.

27. Mandel, *The Arabs*, 128; and Porath, *Emergence*, 7–8. An excellent discussion of these and other issues pertaining to Ottoman Palestine at the turn of the century can be found in Khalidi, *Palestinian Identity*, chapters 3 and 4.

28. Mandel, *The Arabs*, 81.

29. Ibid, 185.

30. Kushner, "Intercommunal Strife," 199.

DOCUMENT 1.1

WORKING-CLASS CONDITIONS, 1838 AND 1873 — GREATER SYRIA

Compare the reports for 1838 and 1873. In the former, written by a British observer, conditions appear to compare favorably with those in England. In the latter, written by an American consul in Damascus unaware of conditions thirty-five years earlier, the workers no longer eat meat frequently and the bazaars contain items from Europe, the result in part of the Balta Liman Convention (Document 1.2), which was issued in 1838, the year of the first report. The American assumes the much poorer Syrians are happy with their lot. Note the information in footnote 1. The decline in silk looms owed in part to the opening of the Suez Canal in 1869. This enabled Europeans easier access to the better quality Chinese and Japanese silk.

Conditions in 1838

(From John Bowring, *Report on the Commercial Statistics of Syria*, reprint, New York, 1973, 49–50 [originally published, London, 1840].)

The condition of the labouring classes is, comparatively with those in England, easy and good. They feed on mutton, at 3 piastres per oke, several times a week, bread daily, sometimes rice pillaus, and always bulgur pillaus: bulgur is a preparation of wheat, husked and bruised, or half ground, after having been moistened and dried; their pillaus are made either with butter, olive or sesame oil; leben or joghuourt, cheese, eggs, olives, various dried fruits and abundance of vegetables, beet-roots, turnips, and radishes preserved in brine or vinegar, and for winter use. Their clothing is not very coarse; the fine climate permits them to wear light cotton and other similar apparel, and in the short winter they are generally well covered. Their lodging is good; generally each family has a separate house. The prices of lodging vary according to locality; lodging generally in Syria for all classes is cheap comparatively with most other countries. . . .

In Syria a great portion of the labour is done by females. They are constantly seen carrying heavy burthens, and, as in Egypt, a large portion of their time is employed in fetching water from the wells for domestic use. They bring home the timber and brushwood from the forests, and assist much in the cultivation of the fields. The Christian women of Palestine go unveiled.

They are a robust, and generally speaking a very handsome race. Many of them wear ornaments on their foreheads, consisting of wires or round plates of silver overwrapping one another like a coat of mail or the fins of fish.

Source: Charles Issawi, ed., *The Fertile Crescent, 1800–1914: A Documentary Economic History* (New York, 1988), 55–56.

Conditions in 1873

(From US GR 84, Miscellaneous Correspondence, T 367 11.)

The bazaars are filled with poor articles from Birmingham and Sheffield; with the merchandise of Manchester, and the cheap manufactures of France and Germany; but little is seen of Syrian manufactures, which are used only by natives and are no longer exported.*

The wages of a Damascene workman average 45 to 60 cents per day, according to the nature of his work. He lives on bread, rice, fruit and vegetables. He consumes a great quantity of olive oil. Meat is a luxury which he can rarely afford. The cheapness and abundance of fruits and vegetables enable him to obtain them at a low price and save from his wages enough to purchase his clothes and for other expenses.

He can hire a house containing four or five rooms for $1.25 to $1.50 per month, such as it is, built of mud and stone. The streets where he lives are narrow and filthy. He is exposed to the heat during summer and to the cold during winter, he is also exposed, for want of all sanitary precautions, to every kind of epidemic that prevails.

Thus it will seem that the life of the Damascene working man is not better than that of his countrymen dwelling in the other purely oriental cities. There is a more numerous class of laborers worthy of mention, the assistant-workmen, the carriers of stone, mortar etc., their wages vary from 20 to 37 cents per diem. They lead a life necessarily lower than that of their master-workmen in all that regards food, clothing and lodging. If the laborer is unmarried, he occupies a room with comrades similarly circumstanced; if he is married he hires a room for himself and family at about 3 to 4 cents per day, or $1 per month, sometimes for less. The furniture consists of an "abba" or coarse cloak, a carpet rug, a mat and a few kitchen utensils. The bed is a blanket in winter and a mat during summer.

A mussulman of this class, if a bachelor, lodges in the Khans, which costs him from 1 to 2 cents a night. He takes his meals at one of the numerous "bakals," eating houses for the lower classes, with which the city abounds. If married, he hires a room, and cooks in the open air. The working men of Damascus are simple-minded, contented with their lot, without ambition, happy when they have earned a few piastres to go and spend them at the coffee shops. . . .

---

*Earlier in the report the consul had stated that before 1860 there had been 3,000 looms in Damascus, whereas now they were said barely to reach 1,300. — Ed.

THE ISLAHAT FERMANI [HATTI HUMAYOUN] OF FEBRUARY 1856

As part of the Tanzimat reforms, Sultan Abdul Majid issued this proclamation reaffirming more specifically principles declared in 1839. In addition, edicts were proclaimed decreeing the equality of all religions in the empire, granting all Ottoman citizens equal access to educational institutions and equal treatment before the law. The product of British pressure for reform, this decree was also a serious effort to reform Ottoman policies and make all within the empire "citizens" rather than "subjects" defined by their religious adherence. But the sultan was forced to accept existing privileges and immunities previously granted to non-Muslims within the empire.

Let it be done as herein set forth. . . .

It being now my desire to renew and enlarge still more the new institutions ordained with a view of establishing a state of things conformable with the dignity of my empire and the position which it occupies among civilized nations, and the rights of my empire having, by the fidelity and praiseworthy efforts of all my subjects, and by the kind and friendly assistance of the great powers, my noble allies, received from abroad a confirmation which will be the commencement of a new era, it is my desire . . . to effect the happiness of all my subjects, who in my sight are all equal, and equally dear to me, and who are united to each other by the cordial ties of patriotism, and to insure the means of daily increasing the prosperity of my empire.

I have therefore resolved upon, and I order the execution of the following measures:

The guarantees promised on our part . . . and in conformity with the Tanzimat, to all the subjects of my empire, without distinction of classes or of religion, for the security of their persons and property, and the preservation of their honor, are to-day confirmed and consolidated, and efficacious measures shall be taken in order that they may have their full entire effect.

All the privileges and spiritual immunities granted by my ancestors *ab antiquo*, and at subsequent dates, to all Christian communities or other non-Mussulman persuasions established in my empire, under my protection, shall be confirmed and maintained.

Every Christian or other non-Mussulman community shall be bound within a fixed period, and with the concurrence of a commission composed *ad hoc* of

Source: J. C. Hurewitz, *The Middle East and North Africa in World Politics* (New Haven, Conn., 1975), 315–18.

members of its own body, . . . to examine into its actual immunities and privileges, and to discuss and submit to my Sublime Porte the reforms required by the progress of civilization and of the age. The powers conceded to the Christian patriarchs and bishops by the Sultan Mahomet II and to his successors shall be made to harmonize with the new position which my generous and beneficent intentions insure to these communities. . . .

The patriarchs, metropolitans, archbishops, and [rabbis] shall take an oath, on their entrance into office, according to a form agreed upon in common by my Sublime Porte and the spiritual heads of the different religious communities. The ecclesiastical dues, of whatever sort or nature they be, shall be abolished and replaced by fixed revenues of the patriarchs and heads of communities, and by the allocation of allowances and salaries . . . [to] the different members of the clergy.

The property, real or personal, of the different Christian ecclesiastics shall remain intact; the temporal administration of the Christian or other non-Mussulman communities shall, however, be placed under the safeguard of an assembly to be chosen from among the members, both ecclesiastics and laymen, of the said communities.

In the towns, small boroughs, and villages where the whole population is of the same religion, no obstacle shall be offered to the repair, according to their original plan, of buildings set apart for religious worship, for schools, for hospitals, and for cemeteries. . . .

My Sublime Porte will take energetic measures to insure to each sect, whatever be the number of its adherents, entire freedom in the exercise of its religion. Every distinction or designation pending to make any class whatever of the subjects of my empire inferior to another class, on account of their religion, language, or race, shall be forever effaced from administrative protocol. . . .

. . . All the subjects of my empire, without distinction of nationality, shall be admissible to public employments, and qualified to fill them according to their capacity and merit, and conformably with rules to be generally applied.

All the subjects of my empire, without distinction, shall be received into the civil and military schools of the government, if they otherwise satisfy the conditions as to age and examination which are specified in the organic regulations of the said schools. Moreover, every community is authorized to establish public schools of science, art, and industry. Only the method of instructions and the choice of professors in schools of this class shall be under the control of a mixed council of public instruction, the members of which shall be named by my sovereign command.

All commercial, correctional, and criminal suits between Mussulmans and Christians, or other non-Mussulman subjects, or between Christian or other non-Mussulmans of different sects, shall be referred to mixed tribunals. The proceedings of these tribunals shall be public; the parties shall be confronted and shall produce their witnesses, whose testimony shall be received without distinction, upon an oath taken according to the religious law of each sect. . . .

The equality of taxes entailing equality of burdens, as equality of duties entails that of rights, Christian subjects, and those of other non-Mussulman sects, as it has been already decided, shall, as well as Mussulmans, be subject to the obligations of the law of recruitment.

The principle of obtaining substitutes, or of purchasing exemption, shall be admitted. A complete law shall be published, with as little delay as possible, respecting the admission into and service in the army of Christian and other non-Mussulman subjects. . . .

As the laws regulating the purchase, sale, and disposal of real property are common to all the subjects of my empire, it shall be lawful for foreigners to possess landed property in my dominions, conforming themselves to the laws and police regulations, and bearing the same charges as the native inhabitants, and after arrangements have been come to with foreign powers.

The taxes are to be levied under the same denomination from all the subjects of my empire, without distinction of class or of religion. The most prompt and energetic means for remedying the abuses in collecting the taxes, and especially the tithes, shall be considered. . . .

The heads of each community and a delegate, designated by my Sublime Porte, shall be summoned to take part in the deliberations of the supreme council of justice on all occasions which might interest the generality of the subjects of my empire. They shall be summoned specially for this purpose by my grand vizier. The delegates shall hold office for one year; they shall be sworn on entering upon their duties. All the members of the council, at the ordinary and extraordinary meetings, shall freely give their opinions and their votes, and no one shall ever annoy them on this account. . . .

Steps shall be taken for the formation of banks and other similar institutions, so as to effect a reform in the monetary and financial system, as well as to create funds to be employed in augmenting the sources of the material wealth of my empire. Steps shall also be taken for the formation of roads and canals to increase the facilities of communication and increase the sources of the wealth of the country.

Everything that can impede commerce or agriculture shall be abolished. To accomplish these objects means shall be sought to profit by the science, the art, and the funds of Europe, and thus gradually to execute them.

Such being my wishes and my commands, you, who are my grand vizier, will, according to custom, cause this imperial firman to be published in my capital and in all parts of my empire; and you will watch attentively and take all the necessary measures that all the orders which it contains be henceforth carried out with the most rigorous punctuality.

THEODOR HERZL

DER JUDENSTAAT (THE JEWISH STATE)

1896

Herzl called for the creation of a Jewish state to resolve the question of anti-Semitism, which threatened Jews in Europe. His book is striking both for its calm definition of the problems facing European Jews and for its optimism that the goal can be achieved.

The idea which I have developed in this pamphlet is an ancient one: It is the restoration of the Jewish State. . . .

I therefore state, clearly and emphatically, that I believe in the achievement of the idea, though I do not profess to have discovered the shape it may ultimately take. The world needs the Jewish State; therefore it will arise. . . .

The Jewish question still exists. It would be foolish to deny it. It is a misplaced piece of medievalism which civilized nations do not even yet seem able to shake off, try as they will. They proved they had this high-minded desire when they emancipated us. The Jewish question persists wherever Jews live in appreciable numbers. Wherever it does not exist, it is brought in together with Jewish immigrants. We are naturally drawn into those places where we are not persecuted, and our appearance there gives rise to persecution. This is the case, and will inevitably be so, everywhere, even in highly civilized countries—see, for instance, France—so long as the Jewish question is not solved on the political level. The unfortunate Jews are now carrying the seeds of anti-Semitism into England; they have already introduced it into America.

Anti-Semitism is a highly complex movement, which I think I understand. . . . I consider the Jewish question neither a social nor a religious one, even though it sometimes takes these and other forms. It is a national question, and to solve it we must first of all establish it as an international political problem to be discussed and settled by the civilized nations of the world in council.

We are a people—*one* people. . . .

No one can deny the gravity of the Jewish situation. Wherever they live in appreciable number, Jews are persecuted in greater or lesser measure. Their equality before the law, granted by statute, has become practically a dead letter. They are debarred from filling even moderately high offices in the army, or in any public or private institutions. And attempts are being made to thrust them out of business also: "Don't buy from Jews!" . . .

Source: The Zionist Idea: A Historical Analysis and Reader, ed. Arthur Hertzberg (New York, 1960), 204–9, 215–23.

Modern anti-Semitism is not to be confused with the persecution of the Jews in former times, though it does still have a religious aspect in some countries. The main current of Jew-hatred is today a different one. In the principal centers of anti-Semitism, it is an outgrowth of the emancipation of the Jews. When civilized nations awoke to the inhumanity of discriminatory legislation and enfranchised us, our enfranchisement came too late. . . .

The very impossibility of getting at the Jews nourishes and deepens hatred of them. Anti-Semitism increases day by day and hour by hour among the nations; indeed, it is bound to increase, because the causes of its growth continue to exist and are ineradicable. Its remote cause is the loss of our assimilability during the Middle Ages; its immediate cause is our excessive production of mediocre intellectuals, who have no outlet downward or upward—or rather, no wholesome outlet in either direction. When we sink, we become a revolutionary proletariat, the corporals of every revolutionary party; and when we rise, there rises also our terrifying financial power. . . .

The whole plan is essentially quite simple, as it must necessarily be if it is to be comprehensible to all.

Let sovereignty be granted us over a portion of the globe adequate to meet our rightful national requirements; we will attend to the rest.

To create a new State is neither ridiculous nor impossible. Haven't we witnessed the process in our own day, among nations which were not largely middle class as we are, but poorer, less educated, and consequently weaker than ourselves? . . .

The scientific plan and political policies which the Society of Jews will establish will be carried out by the Jewish Company.

The Jewish Company will be the liquidating agent for the business interests of departing Jews, and will organize trade and commerce in the new country. . . .

Is Palestine or Argentina preferable? The Society will take whatever it is given and whatever Jewish public opinion favors. The Society will determine both these points. . . .

Palestine is our unforgettable historic homeland. The very name would be a marvelously effective rallying cry. If His Majesty the Sultan were to give us Palestine, we could in return undertake the complete management of the finances of Turkey. We should there form a part of a wall of defense for Europe in Asia, an outpost of civilization against barbarism. We should as a neutral state remain in contact with all Europe, which would have to guarantee our existence.

The holy places of Christendom could be placed under some form of international exterritoriality. We should form a guard of honor about these holy places, answering for the fulfillment of this duty with our existence. The guard of honor would be the great symbol of the solution of the Jewish question after what were for us eighteen centuries of affliction.

DOCUMENT 1.4

THEODOR HERZL

"WHO FEARS A STATE?" FROM *DIE WELT*

February 18, 1898

Addressing a German-Jewish audience of over 1,000 in Berlin, Herzl challenged those who doubted the likelihood of Zionist success in creating a state. He also sought to calm the fears of Jews who wished to remain in Europe but saw statehood as a possible threat to their assimilated status. These factors would reappear in British discussions of Zionism in 1917. An accomplished orator, Herzl employed arguments that reflected the assumptions of an imperial age when settlement of non-Western lands was the norm: Zionism was emulating Britain and Germany in creating a colony. The audience to whom he addressed his remarks opposed Palestine as the Jewish homeland.

Since I am speaking to you as a foreigner [not a German citizen], I am not permitted to go into the very delicate area of your views of citizenship. I shall merely tell you that I cannot quite see how an attempt to create a homeland for a part of a people that feels superfluous, how the acquisition of a territory by means of a public discussion, could have a harmful effect on the rights of those who want to remain where they are. Don't you know what a colonial age we are living in? As a consequence of overpopulation, and of the resultant ever more acute social question, many nations are endeavoring to found overseas colonies in order to channel the flow of emigration there. This is the policy which England has been pursuing for decades, and which has been regarded as exemplary by many nations. I believe that Germany, too, has taken steps to become a Greater Germany, since it has looked across the seas and has striven to found colonies everywhere. . . .

I think that . . . Mr. Klausner . . . will find places suited for settlement in the territory of Palestine—and there *is* a Palestine; it is located on the Mediterranean. . . .

Both speakers seem to recoil from the word "state." Well, what is a state? A big colony. What is a colony? A small state. Mankind seems never to have seen anything terrible in that. . . .

Look upon this movement as one which is committed to the general welfare, which wishes to serve the poor, is inimical to no one, and can bring a measure of relief to all mankind.

Source: Theodor Herzl, *Zionist Writings: Essays and Addresses*, vol. 1, January 1896–June 1898, trans. Harry Zohn (New York, 1973), 211–15.

THE BASEL PROGRAM

1897

Approved at the first Zionist congress in 1897 in Basel, Switzerland, the program defined Zionist goals in a manner designed to appeal to non-Jews as well as Jews. The word "homeland" was substituted for "state" and "public law" for "international law" so as not to alarm the Ottoman sultan.

The aim of Zionism is to create for the Jewish people a homeland [homestead] in Palestine secured by public law.

[This would be achieved by:]

1. The settlement in Palestine of farmers, artisans and laborers in such a manner as serves the purpose [of creating a national home].

2. The organization and union of the whole of Jewry in suitable local and general bodies, in accordance with the laws of their respective countries.

3. The strengthening of Jewish national feeling and national consciousness.

4. Preparatory steps to obtain governmental consent necessary to achieve the goals of Zionism.

Source: Amos Elon, *Herzl* (New York, 1975), 242–43.

2

WORLD WAR I, GREAT BRITAIN, AND THE PEACE SETTLEMENTS

1914–1921

THE OUTBREAK of World War I on August 1, 1914, ended an extended period during which the European powers had avoided outright conflict. Following the Franco-Prussian War of 1870 and the Russo-Turkish War of 1877–1878, potential great-power clashes had been settled by diplomacy, but past grievances and resentments remained strong. The French still hoped to avenge their defeat at Prussian hands and remained deeply suspicious of British imperial ambitions. Russia continued to view Constantinople and the Bosporus Strait as its chief prize. Britain strove to maintain the status quo and hence the territorial integrity of the Ottoman Empire, if only because this situation permitted it to guard areas of great strategic importance to Britain, such as southern Iraq and the Suez Canal area, without challenge from other European powers.

Despite their mistrust of one another's motives, Britain, France, and Russia were allies in 1914, having created the Triple Entente that reflected fear of a common enemy more than sincere friendship. The foe was Germany, whose industrial and military expansion since the 1880s, coupled with its aggressive involvement in the race for colonies in the 1890s, aroused general alarm. The British were also wary of Germany's intentions in Ottoman lands. Germany had gained many concessions from the Ottomans, the most significant in British eyes being that for a railway from Constantinople through Baghdad to Basra and the Persian Gulf. British officials considered southern Iraq a sphere of military and commercial influence, as well as part of a defense perimeter protecting allies in the Gulf and the oil fields discovered in southwest Iran in 1907. Britain controlled these fields, which were vital to its military position in Europe as well as in Asia: the British navy had gone over to oil in 1912, and the Iranian reserves were the source of its supply. In addition, British agents were investigating potential oil deposits in northern Iraq around Mosul.

These matters, plus the growing number of Indian Shi'i Muslims undertaking the pilgrimage to the shrine at Karbala, near Baghdad, made the British extremely sensitive to the threat of German incursion. Any incitement of India's

Muslims against British rule would threaten the stability of Britain's position in India and divert British troops from the war in Europe. It might also lead Indian Muslims to refuse to serve in the British-led Indian army, which saw extensive service on the western front during the war as well as in the Middle East. The specter of a recurrence of the 1857 Indian Mutiny was always a factor in British thinking.

Defense of Ottoman territorial integrity was not absolute, however. It served as a means of maintaining a European power balance that might otherwise collapse. Thus, the British ambassador in Constantinople wrote to the foreign secretary, Sir Edward Grey, in 1913 that "all the powers including ourselves are trying hard to get what they can out of Turkey. They all profess to the maintenance of Turkey's integrity but no one ever thinks of this in practice."[1] The European powers worried about being omitted from the future division of the spoils. If European stability depended for the moment on maintaining Ottoman territory intact, so did future harmony rely on guaranteeing an equitable parceling of Turkish-controlled land according to recognized geopolitical interests. These diplomatic criteria, well grounded in the traditions of nineteenth-century diplomacy, were the bases of British actions in the Middle East once war broke out. They were later altered to meet demands advanced by politicians and British officials in the field who sought to further Britain's strategic interests at the expense of its allies. It is in this context that one can analyze the nature of the promises and pledges made to the Arabs and Jews during the war that radically transformed the nature and future of the region.

WORLD WAR I: THE OTTOMAN EMPIRE AND THE EUROPEAN POWERS

Germany's declaration of war on Russia on August 1, 1914, obligated the Turks to enter the hostilities on Germany's side in keeping with an alliance they had concluded that same day. Instead, the ruling officers of the Committee of Union and Progress declared neutrality, which they maintained until November 2. During this interval the Entente powers tried to persuade the Ottomans to remain neutral. Turkish neutrality would be necessary if the straits were to remain open to commercial shipping; this was Russia's lifeline, through which it could receive military equipment and export grain, a major source of Russian foreign exchange.

The Entente countries were hampered in their wooing of the Turks by their long-standing policies regarding Ottoman territorial integrity. Their commercial and political involvement in Ottoman lands required that they support the continuation of the capitulations whereby foreigners were free of Turkish law in Ottoman territory. In contrast, the Germans backed the Ottomans when they abolished the capitulations unilaterally on September 9, an act that drew the muted ire of all three Entente members. British efforts to ensure Ottoman neutrality were further weakened when the government canceled delivery of two cruisers that had been contracted for construction in Britain by the Ottoman government; instead they were diverted to duty with the British fleet to confront the Germans. The Germans seized the opportunity to enhance their status with the Turks by presenting them with two German cruisers, the *Goeben* and the *Breslau*, which were ostensibly handed over to the Turkish navy, although they retained their German officers and crews. Russia declared war on the Ottomans on November 2, following an incident in which the *Goeben* shelled Russian installations along the Black Sea while accompanied by Turkish destroyers. The British and French followed suit, and the Ottomans closed the straits to foreign shipping. By the end of the year, Russian munitions supplies had become seriously depleted, and the British and the French expressed concern about their ally's ability to maintain a formidable presence on the eastern front.

British Imperial Objectives

With the Ottoman Empire officially in the war, the British took swift action to ratify their existing occupation of Ottoman territory. In December, they declared Egypt a British protectorate and annexed Cyprus. These actions pleased the Russians as they established a precedent for acquiring Ottoman lands that could be used by Britain's allies as well. British forces sent from India had already landed in southern Iraq in November, taking Basra by the end of the month. Their immediate goal was to secure the oil fields and adjacent territory in southwest Iran. British officials in India, commanding the operation, also hoped to establish a British presence at least as far north as Baghdad, with a view to its incorporation into the empire after the war. Security arrangements were also made with tribes in eastern Arabia to secure their cooperation against Turkish forces.

Here, India Office officials anticipated future strategic arrangements that London had not yet considered in any specific terms. British statesmen had declared as early as November that the Ottoman Empire should be dismembered because of its entry on the side of Germany, but just how that would be done was unclear, along with what would be claimed by the Entente allies. Grey, the foreign secretary, believed that the Muslim holy places of Mecca and Medina should be independent under an Arab sovereign after the war. Otherwise he was inclined to postpone consideration of the disposition of territories. Thus when Herbert Samuel, later the first British high commissioner in Palestine, submitted a memorandum in November 1914 suggesting that Palestine be considered as the home of the Jewish people, he received little sympathy. Palestine seemed of little strategic importance when compared with British interests in Iraq and their concern for the security of the Suez Canal. These attitudes changed, however, as the war progressed and as conditions for harmony among the Entente demanded recognition of individual spheres of interest.

Gallipoli and Imperial Bargaining.   Of particular importance to the fate of Ottoman territorial holdings in Asia was the conduct of the Gallipoli campaign that was approved by Britain and France in January 1915. The idea was to have the fleet storm the Ottoman defenses guarding the Dardanelles and break through to Istanbul. The seizure of the Ottoman capital, ending its involvement in the war, would open the Bosporus Strait to Allied shipping that could bring badly needed supplies to Russia. The British cabinet already feared that Russia might withdraw, thereby enabling Germany to divert all its forces to the western front against the British and French armies. Keeping Russia in the war was of the utmost importance both in 1915 and with respect to the motives behind the Balfour Declaration of 1917.

In addition, the Foreign Office saw the plan's potential for enhancing Britain's postwar bargaining position with Russia because the British would control Istanbul and the straits. This idea occurred to Russian officials also. In early March, they demanded that London acknowledge Russia's right, at the end of the war, to gain control of the straits, Istanbul, and the adjacent territory surrounding both. The British were forced to concede the issue, given the war needs of the moment, in the Constantinople Agreement of March 1915, which gave Russia what it had requested. In return, Russia recognized Asiatic Turkey and the Arab lands under Ottoman rule as the special sphere of British and French interests. The following month the Treaty of London was signed whereby the Allies, in return for Italy's entrance into the war, recognized its claims to Libya and to the Dodecanese Islands off the Turkish coast and promised Italy a portion of southern Anatolia to be specified after the war.

The de Bunsen Committee.   In light of these agreements and the obvious disarray within the British war cabinet as to what course it should take, the cabinet in April 1915 appointed a special committee chaired by Maurice de Bunsen to explore a range of options defining potential areas of interest to Great Britain in the Middle East. The de Bunsen Committee delivered its report on June 30. It identified four possible dispositions of Ottoman territory. They ranged from outright partition of the empire into areas controlled by the European powers to a decentralized Ottoman state containing the autonomous provinces of Anatolia, Armenia, Syria, Palestine, and Iraq, all under nominal Ottoman sovereignty. The committee's preference for the latter has led some scholars to present the British as essentially uninterested in annexing Ottoman territory.[2] Nevertheless, even the decentralization scheme provided for the Russian annexation of Constantinople and the straits, as established in the Constantinople Agreement, and for the British annexation of Basra. The decentralization alternative also advocated the designation of the supposedly autonomous provinces of Iraq and Palestine as special zones subject to British influence exclusively, a recommendation that took account of British wishes to build a railway from Haifa in Palestine to Baghdad and Basra in Iraq. This would create a direct link between the Mediterranean and the Persian Gulf across British-controlled territory and bolster the security of both the empire in India and the Iranian oil fields. Two other proposals offered by the committee reproduced this plan for Britain to control Palestine and Iraq, either outright or as a sphere of exclusive influence; France would be given Syria, including Lebanon, from just south of Damascus into southern Anatolia.[3]

The de Bunsen Committee's alternative recommendations were intended to clarify future discussions on the subject of partition. Its suggestions formed the basis of British policy for the rest of the war, especially with respect to French claims. The committee's schemes stipulated that Mosul and its oil fields be included within Iraq, under direct British control or subject to its influence. The French were to be permitted extensive holdings in central and northern Syria, including Lebanon and southern Anatolia, to compensate them for losing Palestine which, as the committee was well aware, the French considered part of their rightful claim within Greater Syria. Palestine, with its holy places, was to be internationalized to avoid complications arising from great-power competition and conflicting Christian claims to the area. International status would also block French efforts to incorporate Palestine into its sphere. At this point de Bunsen, and British officials in general, showed little interest in controlling Palestine, but the committee did recommend that Haifa and Acre be recognized as British enclaves to ensure the linkage of imperial communications from Haifa to Iraq. In the words of a British imperial historian, "Britain had thus, only a few short months after the outbreak of the war with Turkey, completely changed its views on the desirability of maintaining Ottoman territorial integrity. Considerable areas of Asiatic Turkey were to be completely detached from Turkish rule and the rest retained only under stringent terms. Even Grey accepted the inevitability of dissection however long he might prefer to delay it."[4]

With the de Bunsen Committee proposals in hand, Sir Edward Grey could now turn to the demands of the French, whose interests in Syria, including Palestine, had been made clear to him in March 1915 when he discussed the matter with the French ambassador in London. But before official talks with France began, Arab claims came to the fore, transmitted by British officials in Cairo acting with some degree of independence from London. Arab aspirations and the need to reconcile them with French interests, or to appear to do so, dominated British discussion of the Middle East for nearly a year. Indeed, the consequences of British promises to both remain the basis of Arab grievances to the present.

BRITAIN, THE ARABS, AND THE HUSAYN-McMAHON CORRESPONDENCE, 1915–1916

In February 1914, Sharif Husayn of Mecca sent his second son, Abdullah, to Cairo to request British aid against the Turks. Sharif Husayn, a member of the Hashim clan to which the Prophet Muhammad had belonged, was the official guardian of the holy places of Mecca and Medina. As an Ottoman official, he held his post subject to Istanbul's approval, but he sought to retain the greatest autonomy possible. Alarmed by Ottoman intentions to extend the Hijaz railway to Mecca, Husayn deputized Abdullah to seek British support to block the Turkish plan. The British response was negative. Lord H. H. Kitchener, then consul general in Cairo, informed Abdullah that Great Britain would not supply arms to be used against a friendly power. But ten months later when Britain declared war on Turkey, Kitchener, now secretary of war in the British cabinet, cabled Ronald Storrs, oriental secretary at the British Agency in Cairo, with instructions concerning Husayn. Storrs was to inform Husayn that in return for any assistance the "Arab nation" might give to the British, they would defend the Arabs against external aggression, protect Husayn against internal threats, and support the principle that an "Arab of true race" might become caliph in Mecca. This message, with embellishments by Storrs, was delivered to Husayn and created the basis for a relationship that lasted throughout the war.

The Lure of an Arab Revolt

The reasons for the British interest in Husayn and the Hijaz were clear. They believed that Husayn might inspire an Arab revolt that at the least could divert the Ottoman troops from positions threatening the Suez Canal. At the most, as envisaged a year later, such a revolt might entail a massive uprising throughout the Arab Middle East that would completely undermine Ottoman security in the area. In return, Kitchener and Storrs promised British protection and the installation of the caliphate in Mecca, with Husayn presumably as caliph. The British did not make these promises out of regard for Husayn alone. Indeed, they were endowing him with prestige well beyond his position within the Arab Middle East. His power was confined to the Hijaz; in addition, he was challenged by Arab tribes in eastern Arabia, especially by the Wahabbi reform movement identified with Ibn Saud, who himself was being funded by British officials based in India.

Nevertheless, the British were eager to spur Arab aspirations for freedom from Turkish rule. They were aware of separatist sentiments among Arab officers in the Ottoman army, many of whom were members of Arab societies that, on the eve of the war, sought at least autonomy for the Arab lands under Ottoman sway.[5] They hoped to encourage them to look to the British for fulfillment of their hopes. As a result, British officials in Cairo, apparently without consulting London, sent a letter to Abdullah in December 1914, the contents of which were also distributed in the Arab world generally. In the letter, Storrs addressed the "natives of Arabia, Palestine, Syria, and Mesopotamia" and promised them that Great Britain had no designs on their territories after the war. He then stated that if the Arabs rebelled and drove out the Turks, the British would recognize and help establish Arab independence "without any intervention in your internal affairs."[6]

The sincerity of such statements was clearly questionable. British officials in Cairo as well as in London were uncertain as to what form or extent any independent Arab entity should have after the war. All accepted Grey's conception of an independent Arabia, meaning the peninsula, with the caliphate in Mecca. Kitchener and Storrs apparently hoped that this caliphate could rule a British-protected Syria despite their knowledge of French ambitions, which they hoped to reward elsewhere. Their wartime alliance notwithstanding, British officials viewed French territorial claims in the Middle East as threats to their legitimate spheres of interest; the feeling was mutual. Grey might consider a division of the spoils to be necessary and proper, but Kitchener saw France as a potential post-war enemy that should be thwarted in its demands for any territory adjacent to the Suez Canal and Arabia. He and others saw Palestine as occupying the crucial position of a buffer between potential French-held areas and Egypt. Initially, an internationalized Palestine with British enclaves would suit British imperial needs; later, a Palestine promised to the Zionists seemed to do the same.

The Husayn-McMahon Correspondence: Defining the Terms

Once under way, the Husayn-McMahon correspondence embraced issues that went well beyond the reservations and contingencies London believed necessary. The exchanges began with a July 14, 1915, letter from Sharif Husayn (see Figure 2.1) to Ronald Storrs in Cairo (see Document 2.1). Husayn demanded a great deal, namely, that Great Britain recognize the "independence of the Arab countries" whose boundaries encompassed all of Greater Syria, including Palestine, Lebanon, Iraq, and the Arabian Peninsula. The only exclusion would be Aden, to which Britain's rights were acknowledged. The British would proclaim an Arab caliphate as well. In return, the sharif would grant the British "preference in all economic enterprises in the Arab countries."[7] Husayn requested an answer within thirty days or he would consider himself released from all obligations suggested in his letter.

The British were annoyed by Husayn's claims but were unwilling to reject them out of hand. Henry McMahon, now high commissioner in Cairo, seems to have acted with some latitude despite suggestions sent to him by the Foreign Office and by officials at the India Office. The latter were backing Ibn Saud and questioned whether Husayn had support in Arabia for his claims to the caliphate. McMahon sent a response to Husayn, dated August 30, which was far more encouraging than London intended. He affirmed with pleasure Husayn's view that British and Arab interests were the same. He then declared that "we hereby confirm to you the declaration of Lord Kitchener [November 1914] . . . in which was manifested our desire for the independence of the Arab countries and their inhabitants and our readiness to approve an Arab Caliphate upon its proclamation." McMahon also noted British willingness to have the caliphate in the hands of "a true Arab born of the blessed stock of the Prophet."[8] Beyond this, however, he deferred consideration of specific boundaries on the advice of

Figure 2.1 ■ The Sharif Husayn of Mecca at Jidda, December 12, 1916

This photo was taken six months after the outbreak of the Arab Revolt during a visit by Ronald Storrs, oriental secretary at the British Agency in Cairo. The visit marked the first time Storrs had met Husayn, although it was his fourth trip to Jidda to discuss the revolt's progress and Arab requests for supplies.

London, arguing that the war and Arab passivity under Turkish rule precluded a discussion of details. Nevertheless, McMahon had gone beyond London's instructions and even what Kitchener had written to Abdullah in November 1914. Kitchener had never promised "the independence of the Arab countries" but had referred instead to the "freedom of the Arabs." McMahon's reference to this independence, which is omitted from some studies of the correspondence, and its implications, seemed to acknowledge Husayn's demands in language almost identical to his, while avoiding mention of the boundaries in question.[9]

Husayn replied on September 9, 1915. He stressed his unhappiness at British hesitancy to acknowledge the "essential clause" in his first letter, namely, the matter of boundaries. Nevertheless, he indicated his eagerness to have Britain's response, intimating that an Arab revolt in Turkish-occupied territory awaited a favorable reply. Although Husayn had dispatched his elder son, Faysal, to contact Arab nationalist circles in Damascus, his ability to instigate a rebellion seemed exaggerated. Then, coincidentally, his promises seemed to be supported by a Syrian officer in the Ottoman army who defected to the British and arrived in Cairo in September 1915. Muhammad Sharif al-Faruqi impressed British officials there with his knowledge of Husayn's demands; apparently members of his circle had been in contact with Husayn and probably inspired his first letter to Storrs in July.[10]

Al-Faruqi's appearance, coupled with Husayn's letters, created a sense of urgency among British officials in Cairo, perhaps augmented by the disasters of the Gallipoli campaign. There, Britain and France suffered a major defeat at the hands of the Ottomans, causing British officials to worry about a loss of face in Arab eyes. At the same time, al-Faruqi intimated that Husayn's requests might be modified. In imparting their alarm to London, British officials noted that the Arabs apparently wished for autonomy in Palestine and Iraq under British guidance and that they would resist the French occupation of Syria.[11] What emerged, as McMahon cabled Grey, was the idea of including the "districts of Aleppo, Damascus, Hama, and Homs" — Syrian cities regarded as purely Arab — in the area to be promised to the Arabs. Grey instructed McMahon to tell Husayn that the Arabian Peninsula and the Muslim holy places would be independent. But he cautioned that the British would probably want to control most of Iraq, a sphere in which Husayn and al-Faruqi proposed British guidance, not total authority. Grey did not refer to Syria except to warn against any general encouragements that might alarm the French. Still, Grey emphasized the need to "prevent the Arabs from being alienated" and left McMahon to decide the exact phrasing of his response.

McMahon's Deception: The Roots of Arab Bitterness

Given this leeway, and feeling the need to encourage the Arabs to side with the British, McMahon wrote to Husayn on October 24, 1915 (see Document 2.1), with promises that became the basis of Arab claims that Great Britain betrayed them after the war. McMahon acknowledged Husayn's concern regarding the definition of boundaries and he outlined British recognition of Arab areas of independence subject to reservations, which he left in some cases deliberately vague. He argued that northwest Syria (Mersin and Alexandretta) and "portions of Syria lying to the west of the districts of Damascus, Homs, Hama, and Aleppo" were not "purely Arab" and would be exempted from Arab areas of postwar self-rule. The provinces of Baghdad and Basra in Iraq were to be placed under British administrative supervision, presumably with Arab autonomy, in order to safeguard British interests, and Britain's arrangements with shaykhs along the coast of the Persian Gulf would remain in force. Other than that, and with the stipulation that the Arabs seek only British assistance to establish their government(s), McMahon stated that in the areas "where Great Britain is free to act without detriment to the interests of her ally France," it pledged "to recognize and uphold the independence of the Arabs in all the regions lying within the frontiers proposed by the Sharif of Mecca" and to protect the holy places against external aggression. These areas appeared to include, at the least, central Syria, including Damascus, Homs, Hama, and Aleppo, northern Iraq, and Arabia.

This declaration, although apparently specific in certain instances, was intended to promise more than it would fulfill. A bone of scholarly contention has been the use of the word "district" to refer to Damascus, Homs, Hama, and Aleppo. The Arabic word used was *wilaya* (in Turkish *vilayet*), which usually meant "province," and was employed in that sense with respect to Basra and Baghdad in the same letter. But when referring to the four Syrian cities, it signified to McMahon "cities and adjacent environs," a meaning clear in McMahon's own references to the term and the areas involved.[12] The importance of this distinction rests in what was intended to lie west of these "districts." If "districts" meant cities, as McMahon felt at the time, then the areas west of them would incorporate an area from Lebanon, including Beirut, in the south extending north beyond Alexandretta, already omitted from the region that Husayn had demanded. In this interpretation, Palestine, unmentioned in the letter, was not specifically excluded from the Arab territory to be independent after the war. The British later claimed, however, that the term "wilaya" signified an administrative district when applied to Damascus. According to this interpretation, the wilaya of Damascus included eastern Palestine, the land across the Jordan River, and omitted western Palestine, which by this time had been promised to the Zionists by the Balfour Declaration. As subsequent developments demonstrate, the British never intended to cede Palestine to the Arabs, even though some officials acknowledged privately that McMahon's letter seemed to include it.

Later confusion over the place of Palestine in the Husayn-McMahon correspondence can be attributed to oversight and incompetence, but no such excuse can explain McMahon's evasiveness when referring to French interests in the October 24 letter. As he explained to Grey, McMahon was careful not to be precise regarding areas France might seek: "While recognising the towns of Damascus, Homs, Hama, and Aleppo as being within the circle of Arab countries, I have endeavoured to provide for possible French pretensions to those places" by simply referring vaguely to areas "where French interests might exist."[13] In other words, whatever the apparent specificity of McMahon's pledges to Husayn concerning Damascus, Homs, Hama, and Aleppo, he deliberately left their disposition open to future French claims. British officials in Cairo did not feel bound by the promises implicit, and even apparently explicit, in McMahon's first two letters to Husayn; they felt that terms like "statehood" and "independence" were meaningless to the Arabs. At the same time, they used these terms to attract the Arabs to the British side. McMahon's letters of August 30 and October 24, 1915, seemed to promise independence, subject to an Arab rebellion, whatever the interpretations he and his aides preferred to place on them. Such independence, when applied in light of the proclamation sent to Abdullah in December 1914, included Palestine, Syria, and Iraq.

In the remaining letters of the exchange, McMahon was careful to emphasize the closeness of French-British relations and the need for Britain to accommodate French interests at the end of the war, although he mentioned only Beirut and Aleppo specifically. Husayn reiterated his belief that the two cities were Arab and emphasized his opposition to French control of any Arab land. The correspondence ended on a note of agreeing to disagree about Lebanon and northern Syria until the end of the war. Husayn acknowledged British interests in Iraq and accepted their temporary occupation of it in return for their assistance in Arab development there. Left outstanding was the issue of French demands, which by that time—January 1916—British diplomats in London knew they had to curtail, not out of concern for Husayn but to protect their own interests in the region.

ANGLO-FRENCH INTERESTS AND THE SYKES-PICOT AGREEMENT

British diplomats had long known of French aspirations in Syria and Palestine and had discussed the matter informally with their French counterparts in the spring of 1915. On October 21, one day after he had advised McMahon to give Husayn sufficient assurances to bind him to the British side, Grey proposed to the French that they appoint a representative to discuss the prospective partition of Ottoman lands. He did so not out of concern about Britain's potential obligations to the Arabs but because he believed, mistakenly, that British troops were about to enter Baghdad. Assuming that Iraq, considered vital to postwar British interests, had been effectively secured, Grey felt able to discuss with France the disposition of other areas.

The principal negotiators were Georges Picot, a diplomat with wide experience in the Middle East, and Sir Mark Sykes, a member of Parliament seconded to military service, an Arabist who had no official diplomatic experience but whose closeness to Kitchener enabled him to gain access to policymaking circles. Picot initially insisted on all of Syria, Lebanon, and Palestine, from the Egyptian border in the Sinai to the Taurus Mountains in Anatolia. Sykes, influenced by the de Bunsen Committee report, was determined to create a belt of English-controlled territory from the Mediterranean to Iraq and the Persian Gulf. He also wished to block French ambitions in Palestine by having it granted international status, again in keeping with the de Bunsen recommendations. But to accomplish this, Sykes decided to cede Mosul to the French sphere of influence to be created in Syria and northern Iraq, contrary to the de Bunsen report. Finally he gained Picot's agreement to have Damascus, Homs, Hama, and Aleppo "included in the territories administered by the Arabs under French influence."[14] Here Sykes operated on the basis of the assurances given to him by al-Faruqi during their conversation in Cairo in November 1915, ignoring Husayn's known opposition to French advisers.

Spheres of Control and Influence

The Sykes-Picot Agreement, officially ratified in May 1916, defined areas of direct and indirect British and French control in Arab lands and southeast Turkey. The British would occupy Iraq from Baghdad south to the Gulf; they would have indirect authority in a region designated as their exclusive sphere of influence that ran from the Egyptian border through eastern Palestine into northern and southern Iraq, thus protecting the Baghdad-Basra axis and establishing the linkage to the Mediterranean recommended by the de Bunsen Committee. The French were allotted Lebanon and coastal Syria as their areas of direct control, along with southeastern Turkey (Cilicia). Their sphere of indirect influence included the rest of Syria from just west of the "districts" of Damascus, Homs, Hama, and Aleppo through northern Iraq, including Mosul, to the Iranian border. In the areas of direct authority, both countries would have the right "to establish such direct or indirect administration or control as they desire and as they may think fit to arrange with the Arab State or Confederation of Arab States." In the spheres of indirect influence, each would "have priority of right of enterprise and local loans . . . and shall alone supply advisers or foreign functionaries at the request of the Arab State or Confederation of Arab States."[15] The terminology indicates the degree of control presumably assigned: to be imposed as each power should "think fit" in the areas of direct authority but to be asserted "at the request" of the Arab state(s) in areas of indirect influence. Palestine was internationalized, the type of administration to be determined after discussions with Russia, other allies, and Sharif Husayn. The British were given the ports of Haifa and Acre as enclaves under their authority and gained the right to build and control a railway from Haifa to Baghdad (see Map 2.1).

For the most part, the Sykes-Picot Agreement met British more than French territorial objectives. Sykes's willingness to grant the French a sphere of influence across Iraq to the Iranian border reflected Kitchener's desire, based on nineteenth-century strategic principles, that Britain should never share a frontier with Russia; the French thus served as a buffer in that Russia had been granted land in northeastern Turkey.

British Evaluation of Their Commitments

Some scholars view the agreement as compatible with McMahon's pledges to Sharif Husayn, reached "in order to obtain international recognition for and confirmation of McMahon's promises to the Sharif."[16] This seems doubtful. Both British and French officials appear to have assumed that they would have what amounted to protectorates throughout their respective territories, whatever the Arabs' expectations. McMahon could promise Husayn in his letter of December 13, 1915, that "Great Britain does not intend to conclude any peace whatsoever, of which the freedom of the Arab peoples and their liberation from German and Turkish domination do not form an essential condition."[17] But he

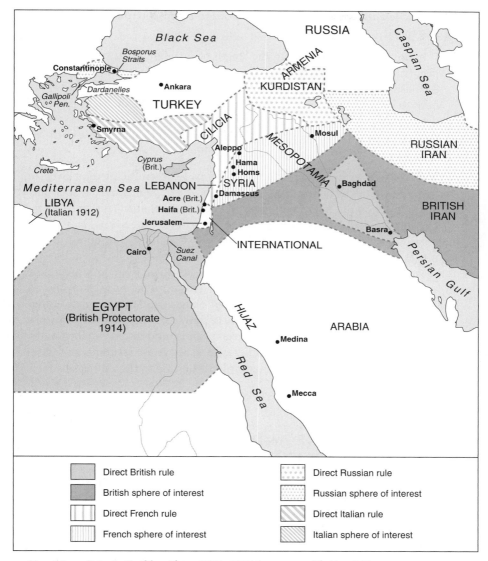

Map 2.1 ■ Entente Partition Plans, 1915–1917 (compare with Map 2.2)

Mutually suspicious of one another's imperial designs, Britain, France, and Russia sought to guarantee satisfaction of their own ambitions and those of their allies to sustain the war effort. British intent to link Egypt and the Suez Canal zone to southern Mesopotamia and the Persian Gulf is clear, as is their desire to have the French between them and the Russians.

could also defend himself against charges of promising too much to Husayn by arguing that

> I do not for one minute go to the length of imagining that the present negotiations will go far to shape the future form of Arabia or to either establish our rights or to bind our hands in that country. . . . What we have to arrive at now is to tempt the Arab peoples into the right path, detach them from the enemy and bring them over to our side. This on our part is at present largely a matter of words and to succeed we must use persuasive terms and abstain from haggling over conditions.[18]

In short, if there were no specific contradictions between the pledges given to Husayn and the areas demarcated in the Sykes-Picot Agreement, it was only because McMahon did not intend to be precise in his letters to Husayn.

On the other hand, British officials soon came to view the Sykes-Picot Agreement itself as a temporary wartime collusion. As we shall see, they hoped to take advantage of their superior military presence in the Arab Middle East at the end of the war to gain total control of the area, either through direct occupation or through sponsorship of an Arab state in Damascus. At this time, the pledges to Husayn became a means of blocking British obligations to the French under Sykes-Picot, and vice versa; neither European power saw the two sets of promises as compatible. The discrepancy between promise and intent widened as the war progressed, and Great Britain and France issued more assurances of independence to the Arabs while Britain awarded Palestine to the Zionists as their national home.

BRITAIN, PALESTINE, AND THE BALFOUR DECLARATION

For the first two years of the war, Palestine was of little strategic interest to British policymakers in London. Its primary value was as a potential buffer between French-controlled territory in Syria and Lebanon and British-held Egypt. Hence Mark Sykes advocated the internationalization of Palestine while reserving Haifa and Acre for British suzerainty. Even when British statesmen began to pay more attention to Zionist urgings for a Jewish state in Palestine, they did not necessarily consider Britain the logical protector of Palestine. Some, including the foreign secretary, Arthur Balfour, wished to hand over authority in Palestine to the United States if internationalization were no longer the accepted procedure.

British interest in Zionism and Palestine increased as 1916 drew to a close. The Asquith government fell, and David Lloyd George, long sympathetic to Zionism, became prime minister. He was eager to involve himself in all aspects of foreign policy, much to the alarm of the Foreign Office. In Russia, 1917 saw the beginning of revolutionary ferment that soon toppled the tsarist regime and ultimately brought the Bolsheviks to power. Concern that Russia might withdraw from the war, permitting the Germans to concentrate all their forces against France and Britain in the West, led to efforts to promote Zionism as a means of persuading Russian Jews—believed to be influential in revolutionary circles—to support Russia's war effort. London Zionists encouraged this idea in order to foster official British sentiment for a pro-Zionist declaration, even though they knew that no such Russian Jewish backing for the war effort existed.[19] Finally, the British hoped to gain specific American commitments of aid and troops to assist them in Europe, and they believed that their support of Zionism would lead American Jews to encourage President Woodrow Wilson to enter the war on the side of the Entente. All these factors, added to a concern for the fate of European Jewry, led to the Balfour Declaration of November 2, 1917, which promised the Jews a national home in Palestine. Although it did not meet all Zionist requirements, the declaration went a long way toward recognition of a future Jewish state in Palestine and was recognized as such by those in London who supported its proclamation.

Chaim Weizmann and British Politics

The issuing of the Balfour Declaration was the product of intense activity and lobbying by several leading Zionists, the most persuasive of whom was Chaim Weizmann, who later became the first president of the state of Israel. Weizmann was born in the Pale of Settlement in southern Russia to a relatively prosperous family, whose wealth, combined with his intelligence, enabled him to leave Russia for Switzerland, where in 1904 he received his doctorate in chemistry from the University of Geneva. In 1908, he left Switzerland for England and a post at the University of Manchester, where he remained until 1916 when he took up special work in the employ of the British government: he was engaged in experiments leading to advances in munitions manufacture.

An ardent Zionist, Weizmann had been deeply involved in World Zionist Organization activities in Europe from the turn of the century. Once in England, he soon acquired prominence inside and outside Jewish circles. A persuasive public speaker and conversationalist, he converted several prominent Manchesterites to his cause, most notably C. P. Scott, editor of the *Manchester Guardian*. In one sense, British willingness to issue the Balfour Declaration was largely due to Weizmann's efforts. During the war he established ties with important personalities within the British government, including Mark Sykes, who supported Zionism. But the Balfour Declaration would not have come about without the blending of Weizmann's arguments regarding the value of Zionism to British interests with the emergence of events that seemed to prove him right and that caused British officials to decide that they wished to control Palestine rather than permit it to be internationalized.

Before the change of governments in London in December 1916, British policy toward the Middle East had been formulated in accordance with the idea of an equitable division of the spoils among the allies. British control of Palestine did not suit such a division balancing Russian and French interests, whereas internationalization of the region and its holy places did. Nevertheless, Weizmann and others were active in their lobbying efforts for British sponsorship of a Jewish Palestine during this period, and various British officials pursued the idea, especially because of its potential value to the war effort. Thus Lord Crewe, personally sympathetic to Jewish aspirations, instructed the British ambassadors in Paris and Petrograd on March 11, 1916, to discuss with host government representatives the idea of an appeal to world Jewry to support the Entente war effort in return for Britain's backing of Zionism. In his view, the "Zionist idea has in it the most far-reaching political possibilities, for we might hope to use it in such a way as to bring over to our side the Jewish forces in America, the East and elsewhere which are now largely, if not preponderantly hostile to us."[20] British sympathy at this time did not indicate a willingness to assume control of Palestine as the Zionists wished; rather, the British still favored an international administration of the area.

British War Aims and Palestine

Lloyd George's accession to the prime ministership in December 1916 coincided with a reassessment of Britain's war objectives by the British military command. As trench warfare dragged on, with appalling casualties on the western front during the spring and summer of 1916, British statesmen and generals began once more to look favorably upon a campaign in the East. The General Staff proposed a campaign into Palestine, to be undertaken in the autumn of 1917, a plan approved by Lloyd George and his cabinet in January 1917. Along with the military criteria, however, there was now a political one associated with U.S. policy. President Woodrow Wilson, in a speech on December 18, 1916, had called for "peace without victory," an end to the conflict in order to stop the carnage. Lloyd George and his cabinet opposed the idea, but their situation was complicated by Britain's increasing reliance on American goods and their eagerness to bring the United States into the war militarily on the side of the Entente. Aware that Wilson would oppose a British occupation of Palestine in principle as suggesting imperialist intent, the cabinet decided to link their attack with support for Zionism, hoping that American Jews close to Wilson might persuade him to support the occupation. The advocate of this idea was C. P. Scott, not only a confidant of Weizmann but very close to Lloyd George as well. Sympathetic to Zionist aspirations, he also saw a British-controlled Palestine as a vital strategic asset in guarding the Suez Canal, Britain's imperial lifeline. Linking support of the Jews to Britain's interests was thus a means of furthering Britain's immediate wartime needs while ensuring its long-range imperial goals.

Also eager to assist the Zionists was Mark Sykes. He too sympathized with Zionist hopes to regain Palestine and was now converted to the idea that Palestine—rather than be internationalized as stipulated in the Sykes-Picot Agreement—should be taken over by the British. Sykes was in a key position in that

Figure 2.2 ■ Ottoman *Kankaleh* Stretchers near the Suez Canal, February 1915

Ottoman troops had attacked British positions along the Suez Canal in January 1915, one of the factors encouraging the British approach to the Sharif Husayn of Mecca (Figure 2.1) in the hope that his alliance with them would divert Ottoman forces from Egypt. This photo shows how the Turkish wounded were removed from the battlefield, by placing stretchers on camels. Supplies could also be transported in this manner. The British would use this method to supply troops and to evacuate wounded in their Sinai campaigns of 1916 and 1917.

Lloyd George had appointed him assistant secretary to the war cabinet to oversee Middle Eastern affairs. He was aware that to occupy Palestine would require that the French be finessed. Sykes thus hoped to amend the Sykes-Picot Agreement to gain Palestine for Great Britain. An alliance with British Zionism "provided a way to outmanoeuvre the French without breaking faith [*sic*], and a useful card at the future peace conference to play against any move by Germany to rally the German-oriented and Turcophile Jews to buttress her claim" for a role in the region.[21] But the Foreign Office was still wedded to the idea of the Entente and the Sykes-Picot Agreement, whatever Balfour's personal sympathy for Zionism. Sykes thus undertook his own diplomacy without consulting the Foreign Office but with Lloyd George's blessing.

Sykes's efforts bore fruit because of new developments that threatened the war effort. In March 1917, the first Russian Revolution produced developments that foreshadowed Russia's possible withdrawal from the war. At the same time, the new Russian government denounced imperial schemes for dividing up territories after the war. In addition, there was Woodrow Wilson's campaign against further annexation of nonwestern lands and his known sympathy for the principle of self-determination, to be officially promulgated with his declaration of the "fourteen points" in January 1918. Zionism now seemed even more attractive, for to support it was to back the idea of Jewish self-determination in Palestine. It thus "provided a cloak under which Britain could appear free from any annexationist taint" while ensuring its own control of the area.[22] Sykes also felt pressured by rumors that the Germans were considering a pro-Zionist declaration. This was particularly threatening because most American Jews were inclined toward Germany rather than Great Britain, if only because of the latter's alliance with Russia; whereas American Jews of German origin retained affection for Germany, Jewish immigrants from Russia recalled the pogroms and felt sympathy for Russia's opponents, not her allies. Nevertheless, Weizmann and Sykes were aware of Wilson's interest in Zionist aspirations, communicated to them by Louis Brandeis, a Supreme Court Justice, who headed the Zionist organization in the United States and who was close to the American president.

The immediate problem was France. Sykes, in consultation with British Zionists, pressed for French recognition of Zionist aims. In June, Jules Cambon, the French foreign minister, gave assurances that the French supported "the renaissance of Jewish nationality" in Palestine, in part because they saw it as a means of encouraging Russian Jews to press the provisional government to stay in the war. Nevertheless, the French statement permitted the British, in their view, to proceed with the formulation of a statement acknowledging Jewish claims to Palestine without going into the question of their own planned control of the area, a goal the French strongly opposed. Lord Walter Rothschild, titular leader of the British Jewish community, was invited in June 1917 to submit a draft proposal outlining Jewish goals for consideration by the government.

Negotiating the Text

The process that resulted in the Balfour Declaration reflected disagreements within the British Zionist community as well as opposition to the idea in the cabinet (see Document 2.2). Weizmann favored a version that declared British support for "the reconstitution of Palestine as a Jewish State and as the National Home of the Jewish People." This draft contained the phrase "reconstitution *of* Palestine as a Jewish State" rather than "*in* Palestine" because the latter might enable the Arabs in Palestine to control the state administration: "give the Arabs all the guarantees they like for cultural autonomy; but the State must be Jewish."[23] The London Zionists disagreed. They saw this proposal as demanding too much too soon, although a state was certainly the Zionist objective. Hence Lord Rothschild submitted a draft that requested British recognition of Palestine "as the National Home of the Jewish People" and acceptance of the Zionist Organization *in* Palestine as an autonomous, self-governing body representing the Jews there until they achieved a majority. By early August, a statement incorporating Rothschild's criteria was prepared for Balfour's signature. British and French leaders now feared even more acutely that Russia might withdraw from hostilities, and British officials sought more American aid, both economic and military. Although the United States had declared war on Germany in April 1917, only a token military force had been sent; large military detachments would not arrive until January 1918. The temporary mutiny of French troops in the spring of 1917 had presented the specter of Britain's being forced to fight the Germans alone, bereft of French as well as Russian aid. A favorable response to the Zionist request could be used as the basis of a propaganda push in both Russia and the United States. But no decision was immediately forthcoming, in part because of substitutions made by cabinet members and in part because of the concerted effort by the secretary of state for India, Edwin Montagu, the only Jew in the cabinet, to block the declaration altogether.

Montagu's objections stemmed mostly from his feeling that a declaration in support of a Jewish state in Palestine, defining the Jews as a separate nation, would threaten the position of assimilated Jews in countries where they had established themselves as citizens. It would raise the question of loyalties and might well result in demands that English Jews, for example, renounce their citizenship and go to the new Jewish state. For Montagu, Jews and Judaism comprised a culture but not a nation, and he believed that granting national status to Jews would arouse European anti-Semitism by emphasizing Jewish distinctiveness. Montagu's campaign, though disruptive, alone did not delay the declaration. Bureaucratic inertia also played a part, along with the time taken to consider drafts from cabinet officials that modified the proposed August statement accepting Rothschild's letter. Of vital importance to the final version of the Balfour Declaration were the modifications made by Lord Milner, a member of the war cabinet. He favored a statement supporting "the establishment of a home for the Jewish people in Palestine," a version that omitted the idea of nationhood and the concept that such a nation or a home should possess all of Palestine. He did so out of concern for the fate of the Arab population and for the security of British interests, notably in India and Egypt.

Finally, renewed alarm about Russian intentions and rumors that the Germans were considering a pro-Zionist proclamation in order to persuade the Russians to withdraw from the war led to cabinet debate over the Zionist request. On October 31 the war cabinet met, with Balfour speaking in favor of a declaration. He argued that

> from a purely diplomatic and political point of view, it was desirable that some declaration favorable to the aspirations of the Jewish nationalists should now be made. The vast majority of Jews in Russia and America, as indeed all over the world, now appeared to be favorable to Zionism. If we could make a declaration favorable to such an ideal, we should be able to carry on extremely useful propaganda both in Russia and in America.

In Balfour's view, the term "national home" was acceptable, but he clearly envisaged it as signifying the ultimate accomplishment of "an independent Jewish State." The cabinet approved a draft known as the Balfour Declaration, issued as a letter to Lord Rothschild on November 2, 1917. It stated:

> His Majesty's Government view with favour the establishment in Palestine
> of a national home for the Jewish people, and will use its best endeavours

to facilitate the achievement of this object, it being clearly understood that nothing shall be done which may prejudice the civil and religious rights of existing non-Jewish communities in Palestine, or the rights and political status enjoyed by Jews in any other country.

The last clause took account of Montagu's fears concerning the place of Jews in Western society. The preceding clause incorporated Milner's concern for the future of the then Arab majority of 90 percent in Palestine, but it was modified to specify that only their civil and religious rights would be respected. This ensured that political rights would be reserved for the prospective Jewish community once it attained a majority.[24]

Once the Balfour Declaration had been announced, the propaganda commenced. Leaflets were dropped over German and Austrian troops, urging the Jews to look to the Entente powers because they supported Jewish self-determination. American Jewish groups undertook publicity designed to encourage greater commitment to the war effort. Great celebrations erupted in Russia, although they had little effect on events. The Bolsheviks, who had gained power on November 7, 1917, denounced wartime treaties and entered into peace negotiations with the Germans in December. Without the Russian contribution, Britain and France might well have lost the war if the United States had not decided to commit itself more fully to the Entente and to send large detachments of troops, beginning in January 1918.

The Balfour Declaration was not based solely on British evaluations of self-interest and immediate war aims. Key British statesmen had a deep sympathy for Zionism, inspired by a Christian interest in the land of the Old Testament and by a sense of guilt at Europe's treatment of the Jews. Balfour, Lloyd George, and Sykes all were Zionists in part because of these feelings, sentiments that Weizmann exploited masterfully in private interviews in which he addressed the question of Zionism in light of his listener's concerns, religious fulfillment, or strategic interests.[25] These innate affinities with Zionism played an important role in that the Jews, unlike other "small nationalities" seeking self-determination, were not a majority in the land they claimed. Rather, they had to win recognition of their right to the land based on history, namely, their possession of it two thousand years before. Once this right was recognized, Palestinian Arabs were automatically denied the same right, a conclusion based on sympathy for the Jews and, in Britain's case, on an evaluation of which group would better suit its imperial desiderata. Sympathy alone would not have produced the Balfour Declaration.

GOALS VERSUS PROMISES: THE EUROPEAN POWERS, ZIONISM, AND THE ARABS, 1917–1918

British Middle East policy continued to be shaped by individuals eager to extend British power in the region despite the apparent contradictions in their promises to different parties. Many pledges already made had been given with an eye to postwar negotiations. Mark Sykes backed Arab, Jewish, and Armenian claims for independence. He apparently assumed that conflicts among them could be ironed out after the war; the important thing was to have Britain appear to back self-determination in order to negate attempts by rival European powers to extend their own influence in the area. Impulsive by nature, Sykes wrote several more statements that promised independence to various Arab groups even though they were in direct contradiction to other arrangements he had previously helped formulate. Nevertheless, his ideas were backed by the war cabinet, at times over the objections of officers in the field.[26]

In March 1917, British forces took Baghdad. The cabinet issued a declaration, written by Sykes, that told the Iraqis they should look to Sharif Husayn of the Hijaz, who had "expelled the Turks and Germans," and concluded by encouraging them to collaborate with "the Political Representatives of Great Britain . . . so that you may unite with your kinsmen in the North, South, East, and West in realizing the aspirations of your race."[27] British representatives in Iraq thought the statement went beyond the political awareness of most Iraqis, but it was designed to encourage the Iraqi officers with Faysal (Husayn's son) to look to the British, apparently to ensure their cooperation after the war. Intentionally vague, the statement suggested a future independent status quite different from that intended by the British.

Reassuring Sharif Husayn

Such visions of independence were significant when the Arab Revolt, declared by Sharif Husayn in June 1916, had yet to show much military promise. Lavishly funded by Britain, the Arab tribal armies were commanded by Husayn's sons, but military plans and supplies were organized by a select group of British advisers, notably T. E. Lawrence. Mecca and the coastal Hijaz had been quickly secured, but Medina would hold out under Turkish control until the war's end. The Arab conquest of Aqaba would not occur until July 1917. Although the tribal contingents had served to divert and tie down Turkish troops and to disrupt the Hijaz Railway, their real military contributions awaited the campaigns into Palestine (1917) and into Syria (1918), when the army led by Faysal played an important role in cutting supply lines and in threatening the Ottoman/German eastern flanks.[28]

In May 1917, Sykes and Picot went to the Hijaz to discuss the Sykes-Picot Agreement with Sharif Husayn. There Husayn rejected French claims to inner Syria as a sphere of influence along with control of Lebanon. He changed his mind only after being falsely informed by Sykes that the French role in Lebanon would be the same as that of the British in Baghdad, that is, as advisers only. This was the basis of Husayn's acceptance of the Sykes-Picot Agreement, even though his understanding of it in terms of Baghdad as well as Lebanon was wrong. That is, Baghdad was within the zone of direct British control, not that of influence dependent on consultation with the sharif.[29]

Once the Balfour Declaration had been issued, instructions were sent to the Arab Bureau in Cairo to transmit further "assurances" to Husayn. Sykes again wrote a declaration that referred to the Arabs' achievement of independence as a nation and proclaimed the British government's support for Jewish aspirations to return to Palestine only "in as far as is compatible with the freedom of the existing population, both economic and political. . . ."[30] This statement, with assurances of political freedom for Palestinian Arabs that were clearly not contained in the Balfour Declaration, led Husayn to indicate his unconcern. David Hogarth, the British agent delivering the message, reported that Husayn "left me in little doubt that he secretly regards this (Palestine) as a point to be reconsidered after the Peace, in spite of my assurance that it was to be a definitive arrangement."[31] Husayn welcomed Jews to Arab lands, said Hogarth, a formula recalling previous Ottoman policy. But as Hogarth noted, "the King would not accept an independent Jewish State in Palestine, nor was I instructed to warn him that such a State was contemplated by Great Britain. He probably knows little or nothing of the actual or possible economy of Palestine and his ready assent to Jewish settlement there is not worth very much."[32] Husayn's acceptance of Jewish immigration in Palestine was thus of a piece with Jewish immigration into Arab lands in general, but he opposed a Jewish state, a Zionist goal that Hogarth refrained from imparting to him. It seems that Husayn, having been informed—with deliberate omissions—of the various arrangements made by the British, assumed that they would amount to nothing: "He has real trust in the honour of Great Britain . . . and is more assured than ever both of our power to help him and the Arabs, and of our intention to do so, and . . . he leaves himself confidently in our hands."[33] This, of course, was unwise.

To a degree Husayn was deluding himself. He had initially claimed rulership over the entire Arab Middle East, had left areas still subject to dispute in his exchanges with McMahon, and had been informed of various agreements undertaken by the British with France and the Zionists. His awareness of these agreements bolstered later British arguments that they had been open with him and that he and Faysal had no right to claim that they had been deceived by the British. Yet whatever Husayn's delusions of grandeur, he had been deliberately misled about France's goals in the Husayn-McMahon correspondence; he had been intentionally misinformed by Sykes as to the exact terms of the Sykes-Picot Agreement; and he had been falsely assured by Sykes, through Hogarth, that Zionist immigration would not compromise the political and economic freedom of the Arab population of Palestine. This had happened because the British needed Husayn and the continuance of the Arab revolt, even though they realized that Husayn's position in the Arabian Peninsula was shaky and that his appeal to Arabs in Syria, Iraq, and Palestine was doubtful. In return, Husayn needed the British to facilitate creation of his kingdom in these areas, which made him more than willing to accept British explanations of the meaning of their arrangements. British actions were in keeping with Reginald Wingate's analysis of the overtures made to Husayn in 1915: "After all what harm can our acceptance of his proposals do? If the embryonic Arab state comes to nothing all our promises vanish and we are absolved from them — if the Arab state becomes a reality we have quite sufficient safeguards to control it."[34]

Syria and "Self-Determination"

British reassurances to Husayn became particularly important during 1918, when the Ottomans launched a propaganda offensive against them in the first half of the year. The Bolsheviks' publication of the secret agreements dividing up the Middle East had given most Arabs their first news of them. The Ottomans seized the opportunity to publicize the treaties, advising the Arabs that British promises were meaningless. In addition, President Woodrow Wilson proclaimed his Fourteen Points in January 1918: their advocacy of self-determination received immense publicity in the Middle East as elsewhere. Finally, these developments occurred at that moment when British forces had occupied most of Palestine and were planning their assault on Syria, where they hoped to meet a receptive populace. Jerusalem had been taken in December 1917, at which time General Edmund Allenby had announced that in the East, Great Britain sought "the complete and final liberation of all peoples formerly oppressed by the Turks and the establishment of national governments and administrations in those countries deriving authority from the initiative and free will of those peoples themselves."[35] (See Figure 2.3.) These promises were repeated in June 1918 in a statement issued by British officials in Cairo to a delegation of Syrians, then residing in Cairo, who asked about British intentions toward Arab territories. The British responded with the "Declaration to the Seven," which promised the following: in Arab territories independent before the war or liberated by Arab forces, Great Britain recognized the "complete and sovereign independence of the Arabs." In regard to those areas freed from Turkish rule by Allied military action, the British called the Syrians' attention to the Baghdad proclamation of March 1917 and Allenby's Jerusalem declaration of December: the future government of such lands should be based on the consent of the governed. This condition presumably applied to the southern half of Palestine, includ-ing Jerusalem and Jaffa, and Iraq from Baghdad south. As for regions still under Turkish domination, namely, northern Palestine, Syria, and northern Iraq, the British promised to work for the "freedom and independence" of their inhabitants.[36]

The expectations aroused by these promises were considerable once they became known. The French, on the other hand, strongly suspected the British of trying through such proclamations to justify excluding them from Syria. Their fears were confirmed when Damascus was taken in the autumn of 1918. Allied troops destroyed Turkish resistance, but Faysal and his Arab forces were permitted to be the first detachment into the city. Damascus was thus "liberated" by

Figure 2.3 ■ **British Proclamation of Martial Law in Jerusalem, December 11, 1917**

Once the British captured Jerusalem in December 1917, General Edmund Allenby issued a proclamation securing the city. This photo depicts the reading of the announcement in English, but it was read in Arabic, Hebrew, and French also. Allenby assured residents that Britain would maintain the status quo regarding the established religious rights and practices of all groups represented in the city. Jewish attempts to alter such practices with respect to men and women praying together at the Western Wall would result in major Arab-Jewish clashes in 1929 (see Chapter 3).

the Arabs, presumably ensuring that it would be independent according to the terms of the "Declaration to the Seven." Allenby allowed Faysal to establish himself in Damascus, where he proceeded to set up an Arab administrative system and government. Allenby interpreted the Sykes-Picot Agreement to mean that French military officials could occupy only Lebanon west of the districts of Damascus, Homs, Hama, and Aleppo. Though correct in the strict interpretation of the accord, Allenby's decision did not fulfill French expectations of their rights to inner Syria, especially when Faysal's creation of an Arab government led the British to try to undermine Sykes-Picot by a fait accompli. An independent Arab state under British sponsorship would preclude French occupation of the area and would align the British with Arab nationalist aspirations. Lloyd George pursued this tack until August 1919, when he finally acceded to French insistence on their right to Syria.

In the meantime British and French officials made one final pledge of freedom to the Arabs following the Armistice of Mudros, signed on October 30, 1918, when the Ottomans capitulated. In that announcement, dated November 7 and posted throughout Palestine, Syria, and Iraq, the two powers promised once more to support the creation of national governments in Syria and Iraq derived from "the initiative and choice of the indigenous populations" and elected by their free will. This statement, which contradicted British and French true intentions, was intended to calm the inhabitants and facilitate occupation of the region.[37]

Zionist-Arab Fears: The Faysal-Weizmann Agreement

The war was now over in the East, and the armistice in the West was imminent. The Arabs had been promised much more explicitly and publicly in 1918 what had been only implied to Sharif Husayn. Anticipation ran high in Damascus, but there was already unease in Palestine, where British statements seemed to conflict with Zionist aspirations as embodied in the Balfour Declaration. Reports of Arab unrest from officials in Palestine inspired the British to send a Zionist delegation led by Weizmann in the spring of 1918. Once there, he met with Palestinian notables and later with Faysal. In both instances, he told his opposites that the Zionists did not intend to create a Jewish government in Palestine or "to get hold of the supreme power and administration."[38] Though untrue, this declaration served to allay Arab fears and protests about Zionist goals, which had been inspired largely by Zionists in Palestine; with the Balfour Declaration they had immediately begun to proclaim statehood as the Jewish dream. But if the Arabs in Palestine were alarmed about Zionist intentions, Weizmann was himself fearful of what the British might do, when confronted with Arab protests, to undermine the Balfour Declaration. As he saw it, British administrators in Palestine were "distinctly hostile to Jews" because in trying to be fair to both sides, they threatened to undermine Jewish prospects. The

British were acting according to "the democratic principle, which reckons with the relative numerical strength, and the brutal numbers operate against us, for there are five Arabs to one Jew."[39] Indeed, Weizmann believed that British fairness played into the hands of "the treacherous nature of the [Palestinian] Arab" who exploited it to gain the advantage.

Insofar as Palestinian Arab and Zionist feelings were concerned, the lines were drawn, although Weizmann hoped to gain Faysal's recognition of Zionist aims in Palestine in return for Weizmann's support of Faysal against the French; both opposed implementation of the Sykes-Picot Agreement, which had been made known to Faysal only at the end of the war. Accord seemed a possibility on the eve of the Peace Conference in January 1919 when Faysal and Weizmann signed an agreement embodying these principles, but Faysal then appended a statement repudiating his support of Zionist immigration into Palestine unless he gained his independent Arab state in Syria (see Document 2.3). Subsequent claims by both Arab nationalists and Zionists that Faysal, as the main Arab leader, had abandoned Palestine, must be balanced, as noted above, with the awareness that Weizmann had assured Faysal in their first meeting in June 1918 that "the Jews did not propose to set up a government of their own but wished to work under British protection, to colonize and develop Palestine without encroaching on any legitimate interests." Weizmann and Faysal had mutual interests. Weizmann was eager to deal with non-Palestinian Arabs willing to consider Jewish interests in Palestine. Faysal anticipated Jewish support for Arab aspirations in Syria, having in mind the image of worldwide Jewish financial power impressed upon him by Mark Sykes and on the British as well as Faysal by Weizmann himself.[40]

However expedient the Faysal-Weizmann Agreement may have been, it did symbolize, if only for a moment, the potential for accord, leaving open the question of Faysal's full awareness of Zionist political goals in Palestine. At this point, both men entered the Peace Conference, in which the British abandoned Faysal, and Weizmann and the Zionists gained further confirmation of their right to Palestine (see Figure 2.4).

THE PEACE SETTLEMENTS AND THE MANDATE SYSTEM

The British found themselves at the end of the war in a far more advantageous position than the French in regard to their respective Middle East objectives. British forces had occupied Palestine, Syria, and Iraq. French efforts to guarantee recognition of Palestine's international status had failed. In Syria, Faysal had been installed as head of what became a Syrian Arab government, and French officials had been denied access to Damascus. The French were infuriated, believing that the British had recognized their claims to Syria in December 1918.

Figure 2.4 ■ Emir Faysal with His Aides and Advisers at the 1919 Peace Conference

Left to right: Rustum Haydar, Faysal's secretary; Nuri al-Said, later prime minister of Iraq; Capitaine Pisani, French liaison to the delegation; T. E. Lawrence, upon whom Faysal relied heavily; and Captain Hassan Qadri, who later wrote a memoir of the period. Although Faysal sought British protection, Pisani's presence indicates French determination to assert their claims in Syria. Lawrence championed Faysal out of a desire to block the French as much as from sympathy for the Arab cause.

Faysal and the British-French Struggle for Syria

As noted earlier, the British were eager to revise, if not abrogate, the Sykes-Picot Agreement. On December 1, 1918, Georges Clemenceau, the French prime minister, and Lloyd George met in London to seek to reconcile potential areas of dispute before the Peace Conference began. When Clemenceau asked what the British sought from France, Lloyd George responded that he wanted Mosul incorporated into Iraq plus British control of Palestine. Both points significantly changed the status of the affected areas as established in the Sykes-Picot Agreement. Clemenceau agreed immediately but the understanding was made orally and in private, apparently so that neither party could be held accountable for opposing self-determination when they met with Woodrow Wilson. France did not come away empty-handed. In return, Lloyd George apparently agreed to Clemenceau's demands that the remaining portions of the Sykes-Picot Agreement be upheld, with the important proviso that Aleppo and Damascus be included with Lebanon in the area under direct French control. And it is certain that the French were promised a share of Middle East oil in return for ceding Mosul to the British zone.[41] Lloyd George had gained Palestine, but apparently at Faysal's expense, perhaps another factor explaining why the British encouraged Faysal to reach an accord with Weizmann.

Having made this private agreement with Clemenceau, Lloyd George, with the encouragement of Lord George Curzon at the Foreign Office, tried to break it with respect to Syria. The idea, approved during December 1918, was to establish exclusive British sway in the French sphere of influence as delineated in the Sykes-Picot Agreement. This meant backing Faysal in Damascus by invoking self-determination for the Arabs while giving the French only Lebanon and the Syrian coast, including the much-desired port of Alexandretta. This policy seemed to have a chance of success, given the predominance of British forces in the region, but British explanations enraged the French during the ensuing negotiations, which occupied much of 1919. On at least one occasion Clemenceau and Lloyd George nearly came to blows.

In the meantime, British support for Faysal was further weakened by their backing of Zionist claims to Palestine that were rejected by the General Syrian Congress in Damascus (see Document 2.4). This in turn caused Faysal to repudiate outright his tentative agreement with Weizmann of January 1919 and to claim that Palestine had been promised to the Arabs in the Husayn-McMahon correspondence. Faysal's arguments were seen to have some validity, especially by Curzon, but only in the sense that there seemed to be contradictions in the promises made to Arabs and to Jews throughout the war.

On the other hand, the Zionist delegation to the Peace Conference had submitted a memorandum to the British before the conference began, asking that Palestine be acknowledged as the Jewish National Home under the aegis of Great Britain during a period in which immigration would permit its development "into a Jewish commonwealth . . . in accordance with the principles of democracy."[42] The delegation also defined the boundaries of Palestine to include southern Lebanon up to and including the Litani River, the east bank of the Jordan, and the Sinai Peninsula to al-Arish. The Jewish communities in Palestine were to be allowed as much self-government as possible, presumably meaning that the British administration sought by the Zionists was to oversee the Arab community alone. These demands were later scaled down significantly.

The dilemma faced by the British government during the first half of 1919 was one that its members recognized clearly. They approved in principle the idea of self-determination, if only to mollify Wilson's suspicions about European ambitions in conquered lands. They were now backing Faysal's call for an Arab state in Damascus, based on self-determination, in order to block French claims that the British had supposedly acknowledged as valid. But when faced with Palestinian Arab demands for the right to self-determination, Britain rejected them in favor of Jewish proposals. This, according to Balfour, was morally right: "Our justification . . . is that we regard Palestine as being absolutely exceptional; that we consider the question of the Jews outside Palestine as one of world importance and that we conceive the Jews to have an historic claim to a home in their ancient land; provided that home can be given them without either dispossessing or oppressing the present inhabitants."[43]

Wilson, the League of Nations, and the Mandate System

These arguments were made in the context of discussions of the type of rule that the powers would impose on the territories given to them. Woodrow Wilson had consistently opposed the annexation of land as spoils of war; he had also advocated the creation of a League of Nations after the war to provide a forum for settling international disputes peacefully. The Covenant of the League of Nations, reluctantly accepted by the British and French, included Wilson's Fourteen Points and provided a formula whereby former German or Ottoman territories could be taken over temporarily by the victors. This was the mandate system. The country awarded a mandate over a given area accepted it with the understanding that it would encourage the development of political, economic, and social institutions to the point that self-government would result and that the mandatory power would withdraw. It was thus a system of tutelage, although British and French officials viewed it principally as a means of legitimizing their control of desired territories while satisfying Wilson's concerns for the application of the principle of self-determination. In theory, however, the opinions of the region's inhabitants should be ascertained. The Arab lands were designated class A mandates, meaning that they were judged to have "reached a stage of development where their existence as independent nations can be provisionally recognized subject to the rendering of administrative advice and assistance by a mandatory power until such time as they are able to stand alone. The wishes of these communities must be a principal consideration in the selection of a mandatory power."[44]

It was the last sentence that created the problem. The United States proposed forming a commission to ascertain the desires of the inhabitants of Syria, Iraq, and Palestine as to the power that should guide them to independence. The French and the British, already at odds over Syria, attempted to block any delegation from going to the Middle East. In the end, American envoys, designated as the King-Crane Commission, set out for the Middle East to ask the preferences of the inhabitants, while the British and French continued their acrimonious discussions in Paris and London. The commission interviewed Arabs and Jews in Palestine as well as inhabitants of Syria and Lebanon but did not go to Iraq. It concluded that one Arab state of Greater Syria, including Lebanon and Palestine, should be created, with Faysal as its king and the United States as the mandatory power; the second choice was Great Britain. A majority of the commission favored a drastic curtailment of the Zionist program, which should be limited to an expanded Jewish community within the Arab state. The report was submitted to the Peace Conference in August 1919 but was not published for consideration by the diplomats there because it threatened British and French objectives. With President Wilson in the United States futilely seeking the Senate's support for a League of Nations and weakened by his ultimately fatal illness, there was no American pressure to counter Anglo-French inclinations. There is little doubt, however, that the commission's findings accurately reflected both Zionist hopes and Palestinian Arab fears and opposition to Zionism, as well as the Syrians' anti-French sentiments.[45]

As the summer wore on, Balfour reviewed Britain's apparent obligations set against the wishes of the resident populations in the Arab world. The Sykes-Picot Agreement bound the British, rightly thought Balfour, to give Syria to the French despite Faysal's and the Syrian Arabs' obvious preference for either independence or the United States or Great Britain as the mandatory power. The Anglo-French Declaration of November 1918 had promised to build governments in accordance with the inhabitants' wishes, principles found also in the criteria for mandates enshrined in the Covenant of the League of Nations. But in Balfour's view, these promises could not be reconciled with others: Palestine was a "unique situation" in which "we are dealing not with the wishes of an existing community but are consciously seeking to re-constitute a new community and definitely building for a numerical majority in the future." In this light, the opinions of the Palestinian Arabs were not important, however understandable they might be. The Allies were violating the principles of the covenant because the powers (including the United States) were "committed to Zionism. And Zionism, be it right or wrong, good or bad, is rooted in age-long traditions, in present needs, in future hopes, of far profounder import than the desires and prejudices of the 700,000 Arabs who now inhabit that ancient land." That, in Balfour's view, was also "right," although he recognized that "so far as Palestine is concerned, the Powers have made no statement of fact which is not admittedly wrong, and no declaration of policy which, at least in the letter, they have not always intended to violate."[46]

Confronted with domestic problems resulting from demobilization and from the cost of maintaining troops in postwar ventures, Lloyd George decided in September to withdraw from Syria and let Faysal deal directly with the French. This in essence meant giving the French a free hand there once they had sufficient troops. In the meantime, the Allies agreed to distribute the mandates, as decided upon in the Lloyd George–Clemenceau conversation of December 1918. This occurred at the San Remo Conference in April 1920, where the French were given mandatory rights in Syria and Lebanon, the British in Palestine and Iraq (see Map 2.2). The Balfour Declaration was included in the obligations for the mandatory power in Palestine, thus binding Great Britain to establish conditions whereby the incoming Jewish population would be assisted in their path toward ultimate dominance in Palestine. The mandates were ratified by the League of Nations in July (see Documents 2.5 and 2.6). French-Arab skirmishing had begun in May. Determined to oust Faysal, whose presence symbolized

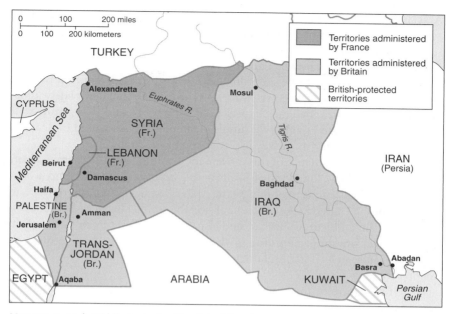

Map 2.2 ■ Arab Middle East after Mandate Allocation at San Remo, 1920

With Russian claims withdrawn after the Bolshevik Revolution and the fate of Turkey unresolved, Anglo-French disposition of the Arab lands differed from the partition plans indicated in Map 2.1. The French mandate for Syria gave Paris direct control rather than the sphere of influence defined in Sykes-Picot but without the Mosul region of Mesopotamia (now Iraq), which France had ceded to Britain. France also agreed to a British mandate for Palestine rather than its proposed international status. Transjordan was a special case. Initially assigned to the British sphere of influence in the Sykes-Picot Agreement, the area was claimed by the Zionists as part of Palestine promised in the Balfour Declaration, an issue never resolved to their satisfaction. In July 1920 (after San Remo) the French ousted Faysal from Syria, causing his brother, Amir Abdullah, to establish himself near Amman as a potential threat to the French position. Fearing French intrusion into its sphere of influence, Britain added the area, designated as Transjordan, to its Palestine mandate but as an Arab province not subject to Zionist claims. Though technically under mandatory authority from 1922 onward, Transjordan developed as a separate principality ruled by Abdullah with its own British resident while also answering to the British High Commissioner in Palestine.

Arab nationalist aspirations, the French commander in Beirut presented him with a series of ultimatums and then marched on Damascus even though Faysal had accepted them. Damascus fell to the French on July 24, and Faysal was escorted to British Palestine. The British later installed him as the king of Iraq, to the consternation of the French, since his prominence reminded Arabs of the short-lived independent Arab kingdom in Syria.

Postwar Crises and the Creation of Transjordan

However brief Faysal's rule in Syria might have been and however unstable his reign as an outsider buffeted by Anglo-French intrigues, he left a memory of

Arab independence and the potential for Arab unity that has resonated to the present day. Nationalism in the Arab world might emerge in the context of a specific country, such as Syria, Palestine, or Iraq, but Arabs did not—and would not—forget the idea of a broader Arab identity as a nation in which specific state identities might be subordinated if not subsumed. Pan Arabism, the call for Arab unity, was particularly strong in the central Arab lands lately under Ottoman rule, which had not experienced autonomy and a separate state administration as had Egypt, for example. Arab politicians focused on Damascus and control of Syria as the key to leadership of the Arab cause.

Struggles for dominance of this movement would pit rival Hashemite rulers in Iraq and the new kingdom of Transjordan against each other and would involve Egypt in attempts to dominate the Arab cause from the 1950s onward, to the alarm of the United States. As we shall see, the conflict between particularistic nationalism and Pan Arabism would also appear in Palestinian factionalism from the 1960s onward, where groups who identified with pan-Arab ideals challenged al-Fatah under Yasir Arafat, that instead insisted on a focus on Palestinian objectives.[47]

The ratification of the mandates by the League of Nations confirmed the agreements finally reached by Great Britain and France after bitter recriminations. Yet the Allies, especially the British, found themselves still mired in the Middle East while trying to restore a semblance of normalcy to life at home. In Turkey, the British backed the Greeks, whom they had permitted to land in Asia Minor in the summer of 1919. But the Greek occupation of Asia Minor and subsequent invasion of Anatolia spurred Turkish resistance culminating in the complete collapse of the Greek offensive in August and September 1922. The Greeks were driven into the sea by Turkish national forces who occupied most of Anatolia and precipitated a near confrontation with Allied troops in Constantinople. The British were forced to back down, and Turkish independence in Anatolia was acknowledged in the Treaty of Lausanne, signed on July 24, 1923.

The British also found themselves facing armed resistance in the Arab Middle East. A rebellion broke out in Iraq in May 1920 and lasted through the summer. There were many casualties, and reinforcements had to be sent from India. British officials, civil and military, were concerned about the financial expenditures these commitments required at a time when British citizens were demanding a return to peacetime standards of living. Winston Churchill had a particular interest in the issue. He had been appointed secretary of state for war in 1919 and became colonial secretary in January 1921 with responsibility for Palestinian and Iraqi affairs and authority over a specific Middle East department.

Churchill was determined to stabilize the British position in the Middle East while drastically cutting expenditures. He and his advisers, who included T. E. Lawrence, arranged the Cairo Conference of March 1921 to pursue these goals. It was here that they agreed to install Faysal in Baghdad, "the best and cheapest solution," and to grant to his brother Abdullah eastern Palestine, which became Transjordan.[48] This was done over Zionist objections, although they were made privately. Churchill acted on the advice of Lawrence, who declared that the Damascus wilaya included eastern Palestine. While this permitted western Palestine to be allotted to the Zionists according to the Husayn-McMahon correspondence, it also legitimized the awarding of eastern Palestine to the Arabs. Neither the Arabs nor the Jews were entirely satisfied with this arrangement, but it remained in force. It permitted the British to withdraw troops from eastern Palestine and cut expenses. With the Cairo Conference, the British distribution of land and titles ended. Then began the process of striving to lower imperial costs while maintaining a strong presence in the face of growing Arab nationalism, a tightrope act that did not end until 1954.

CONCLUSION

Our focus on the Middle East must be balanced by the awareness that many of the decisions affecting it were made during the war with a view to their European and worldwide impact, not to their implications for the region's inhabitants. The Gallipoli campaign, designed to save Russia, led to the Constantinople Convention of 1915. That accord set in motion events resulting in the Sykes-Picot Agreement, itself intended to harmonize Allied relations by satisfying mutual aspirations in the region. Promises of independence, and later of governments based on the consent of the governed, were products of wartime expediency and, in the latter case, the desire to show conformity with Wilsonian principles and ensure U.S. support and cooperation. The Balfour Declaration, whatever the Old Testament inspiration of Lloyd George, was essentially granted because of its long-term promise of a stable bastion governed by a people friendly to British imperialism and a short-term advantage believed to be the attraction of world Jewry to the side of the Entente.

What emerges most clearly is the nature of the great powers' decision-making process which, in the words of one scholar, was "exceedingly informal, flexible, and by design almost, amateurish." Individuals rather than governments or united cabinets made decisions and "where senior statesmen floundered, the influence of pressure groups or unofficial grey-eminence confidants could sometimes be decisive."[49] This was less so in Britain and France than among the Central European powers, but it clearly existed, especially as evidenced in the waning role of the British Foreign Office under Grey during 1915–1916, when the initiative passed to men in the field and it appeared "that Grey felt totally out of his depth."[50] With the accession of the Lloyd George government at the end of 1916, the influence of the Foreign Office lessened further as the prime minister took an active and decisive part in Middle East policy. Here the personal access enjoyed by Weizmann was crucial to convincing British officials that Zionism was in the interests of the British and did not challenge their imperial aspirations, a benefit that was less sure to be derived from support of the Arabs.

Finally, there was the natural assumption of European statesmen that they had the right to dispose of foreign lands as they wished, conditional on the agreement of their rivals rather than the wishes of the lands' inhabitants. Imperialism and the security of imperial interests were the crux of nineteenth-century great-power relations, based on the economic as well as military and political advantages to be derived from direct or indirect control of territory. Here Zionism melded with British assumptions of their right to deal with territories as they saw fit. Zionism was also "right" because it was part of a European experience — the persecution of the Jews — that had to be redressed. That it was admittedly a unique situation was part of its appeal, and this in turn meant, at least in the beginning, that Palestinian Arab opposition was of little import.

But to Jews and to Palestinian Arabs, the struggle was really just beginning. Each rejected the idea that the British had an obligation to the other. The idea of fairness under the mandate, of encouraging the development of self-governing institutions, could apply only to themselves, not to their rivals. For the British to attempt to balance the scales was to the Arabs a denial of their basic rights; to the Jews, the same; and to some, evidence of the anti-Semitism of the British administrators in the bargain. There was to be no harmonizing of these conflicting conceptions of "right," a gap reflected also in the vastly disparate circumstances and habits of an incoming population schooled in Europe and a native Eastern people living in a nearly traditional society. If the Palestinian Arabs believed that their right to the land stemmed from historical precedent acknowledged by the great powers for other peoples and found in Allied promises made during the war, the Jews believed that they had a right because of history, both Middle Eastern and European. They had lived in Palestine as a majority two thousand years before, and their pariah experience in Europe justified their achievement of independence and normalcy in the land of their distant origins. This too had been recognized during the war, by a power that was able and willing to impose its will in favor of Zionism. That will would be tested severely as the mandate took shape.

QUESTIONS FOR CONSIDERATION

1. What were British goals in the Middle East during World War I? How did a change in Britain's leadership affect those objectives?

2. Both the Husayn-McMahon correspondence and the Sykes-Picot Agreement addressed the partition of Ottoman lands. What were the similarities and differences in these agreements? How did they affect French-Anglo relations?

3. What political, diplomatic, and military pressures led Great Britain to issue the Balfour Declaration?

4. Did the inclusion of the Balfour Declaration in the Palestine Mandate adhere to or violate the terms of the Covenant of the League of Nations? In formulating your response, address the ways in which historical precedent and conflicting views of morality influence diplomacy and geopolitics.

CHRONOLOGY

August 1, 1914–November 11, 1918	World War I.
1914	**November 2.** Ottomans enter war on German side. **December.** British declare protectorate over Egypt.
1915	**February–December.** Gallipoli campaign. **March.** Constantinople Agreement negotiated by Allies. **April.** Treaty of London signed by Allies. **June.** De Bunsen Committee report issued.
July 1915–January 1916	Husayn-McMahon correspondence.
1916	**May.** Great Britain and France ratify the Sykes-Picot Agreement. **June.** Sharif Husayn declares Arab Revolt against Ottomans.
1917	**March.** First Russian Revolution. British forces take Baghdad. **November 2.** Balfour Declaration issued by British. **November 7.** Bolshevik Revolution. **December.** British forces capture Jerusalem.
1918	**January.** U.S. President Woodrow Wilson proclaims Fourteen Points. **June.** British issue promises to Arabs in "Declaration to the Seven." **October 30.** Ottomans surrender; Armistice of Mudros signed. **November 7.** Anglo-French Declaration to Arabs. **November 11.** Armistice signed in Europe; World War I ends.
1919	**January.** Paris Peace Conference opens. Weizmann-Faysal agreement.
1920	**March.** Kingdom of Syria declared. **April.** San Remo Conference: Mandates approved. **July.** French occupy Damascus.
1921	**March.** Cairo Conference: British install Faysal as king of Iraq, Abdullah as king of Transjordan.

Notes

1. Marian Kent, "Constantinople and Asiatic Turkey, 1905–1914," in *British Foreign Policy under Sir Edward Grey*, ed. F. H. Hinsley (Cambridge, 1977), 155.

2. Isaiah Friedman, *The Question of Palestine, 1914–1918: British-Jewish-Arab Relations* (New York, 1973), 21.

3. This division recognized French wishes to possess the port of Alexandretta in northern Syria. The fourth proposal placed Alexandretta in a British zone, giving direct access to Iraq.

4. Marian Kent, "Asiatic Turkey, 1914–1916," in Hinsley, ed., *British Foreign Policy*, 444.

5. For the emergence of Arab nationalism before and during World War I, see the detailed discussions of Eliezer Tauber, *The Emergence of the Arab Movements* (London, 1993) and *The Arab Movements in World War I* (London, 1993); Rashid Khalidi et al., eds., *The Origins of Arab Nationalism* (New York, 1991) and Philip Khoury, *Urban Notables and Arab Nationalism: The Politics of Damascus, 1880–1920* (Cambridge, 1983).

6. Elie Kedourie, *In the Anglo-Arab Labyrinth: The McMahon-Husayn Correspondence and Its Interpretations, 1914–1939* (Cambridge, 1976), 21.

7. The complete correspondence can be found in George Antonius, *The Arab Awakening* (New York, 1965), 413–27.

8. Ibid., 415–16.

9. Kedourie, *Labyrinth*, 69–70, omits the reference to "the independence of the Arab countries" from his quotation of the passage and from his discussion of it, focusing his attention on the promise of the caliphate to Husayn.

10. Ibid., 74–75.

11. Ibid., 81. But al-Faruqi told Mark Sykes in November that the Arabs might accept French advisers.

12. Ibid., 99–103.

13. Ibid., 98–99.

14. Jukka Nevakivi, *Britain, France, and the Arab Middle East, 1914–1920* (London, 1969), 33.

15. Ibid., 261.

16. Kedourie, *Labyrinth*, 198. See also Friedman, *Palestine*, 112.

17. Antonius, *Arab Awakening*, 424.

18. Quoted in Kedourie, *Labyrinth*, 120.

19. Steven J. Zipperstein, *Elusive Prophet: Ahad Ha'am and the Origins of Zionism* (Berkeley, 1993), 301.

20. Friedman, *Palestine*, 57.

21. Ibid., 126.

22. Ibid., 175.

23. Ibid., 252–53.

24. Ibid., 275–80, traces the final stages of approval of the Balfour Declaration.

25. Friedman, *Palestine*, 283, quotes from Sir Charles Webster, *The Art and Practice of Diplomacy* (London, 1961), 5–6, in which Webster recalls how Weizmann "with unerring skill . . . adapted his arguments to the special circumstances of each statesman."

26. Elizabeth Monroe, *Britain's Moment in the Middle East, 1914–1956* (London, 1963), 40–41. For the Foreign Office's and Chaim Weizmann's impressions of Sykes, see Zara Steiner, "The Foreign Office and the War," in Hinsley, ed., *British Foreign Policy*, 526; and Weizmann, *Trial and Error* (New York, 1966), 181.

27. Quoted in Monroe, *Britain's Moment*, 41.

28. There were other British advisers with the Arab Revolt who had as much responsibility as Lawrence, but none had the fortune to be promoted by the American journalist Lowell Thomas. An excellent biography is Jeremy Wilson, *Lawrence of Arabia: The Authorized Biography of T. E. Lawrence* (London, 1989), but see also B. H. Liddell Hart, *T. E. Lawrence* (London, 1934). For the campaigns, Lawrence's own *Seven Pillars of Wisdom* (1926 and numerous later editions), to be used with caution; Hubert Young, *The Independent Arab* (London, 1933); and Liddell Hart. A study of the appeal of Lawrence and the mythology surrounding him and his representation is Steven C. Caton, *Lawrence of Arabia: A Film's Autobiography* (Berkeley, 1999). See also Randall Baker, *King Husain and the Kingdom of the Hijaz* (Cambridge, Mass., 1979); and William Ochsenwald, *The Hijaz Railroad* (Charlottesville, Va., 1980).

29. Kedourie, *Labyrinth*, 165–77, has a long discussion of this meeting and Sykes's maneuvers.

30. Quoted in Kedourie, *Labyrinth*, 189–90. Kedourie disputes as "worthless" Antonius's claim that Hogarth's message was a significant reduction of the commitments made by the British to the Zionists in the Balfour Declaration because it recognized the political rights of the Palestinian Arabs, not simply their civil and economic rights as stated in the declaration; he argues that the paragraph in question "is no more than a reiteration of the Balfour Declaration" (282–84). Given the evidence we have on the British intent to grant political rights in Palestine only to the Jews, Hogarth's message was clearly not "a reiteration of the Balfour Declaration," and Kedourie's contemptuous dismissal of Antonius can be applied more justly to his own conclusions. On the other hand, Antonius's claim that Hogarth was reducing the scope of the Balfour Declaration (*Arab Awakening*, 267–68) is probably not true. Hogarth, following Sykes's lead, was stringing Husayn along. As shown below, he refrained from telling Husayn, in the same conversation, that the Zionists intended to form a state. Nevertheless, Antonius is correct to argue that what Husayn could have understood about the Balfour Declaration from Hogarth's version was indeed a significant misrepresentation of what the declaration actually entailed. Friedman, *Palestine*, 328, follows Kedourie's argument.

31. Kedourie, *Labyrinth*, 189–90.

32. Quoted in Leonard Stein, *The Balfour Declaration* (London, 1961), 633.

33. Quoted in Kedourie, *Labyrinth*, 191.

34. Quoted in ibid., 46.

35. Quoted in Doreen Ingrams, *Palestine Papers, 1917–1922: Seeds of Conflict* (London, 1972), 20.

36. The text is in Antonius, *Arab Awakening*, 433–34.

37. Ibid., 435–36. Palestine was mistakenly included in the distribution of the leaflets.

38. Ingrams, *Palestine Papers*, 30.

39. Ibid., 32.

40. Jehuda Reinharz, *Chaim Weizmann: The Making of a Statesman* (New York, 1993), 255–56. Reinharz believes that Faysal knew of Zionist plans for a Jewish state.

41. Nevakivi, *Arab Middle East*, 89–93. Equally if not more important was Lloyd George's pledge to come to French aid if the Germans attacked.

42. Ingrams, *Palestine Papers*, 53.

43. Written on February 19, 1919, and quoted in Ingrams, 61.

44. Paul C. Helmreich, *From Paris to Sèvres: The Partition of the Ottoman Empire at the Peace Conference of 1919–1920* (Columbus, 1974), 27.

45. The standard source for the history of the commission is Harry N. Howard, *The King-Crane Commission: An American Inquiry in the Middle East* (Beirut, 1963).

46. All quotations are from Ingrams, *Palestine Papers*, 73.

47. An excellent discussion of Arab nationalism and politics is Michael N. Barnett, *Dialogues in Arab Politics: Negotiations in Regional Order* (New York, 1998). For Faysal and Syria, see Malcolm

Russell, *The First Modern Arab State: Syria under Faysal, 1918–1920* (Minneapolis, 1985); and James Gelvin, *Divided Loyalties: Nationalism and Mass Politics in Syria at the Close of Empire* (Berkeley, 1998), which has a good analysis of Syrian society and Faysal's interaction with it but virtually no explanation of the international circumstances in which Faysal found himself. The standard source for Syria after the war is Philip Khoury, *Syria and the French Mandate* (Princeton, 1987). For the question of national identities among Palestinians and other Arabs, see Rashid Khalidi, *Palestinian Identity: The Construction of Modern National Consciousness* (New York, 1997).

48. Martin Gilbert, *Winston S. Churchill*, vol. 4, *The Stricken World 1916–1922* (Boston, 1975), 546. For more extended discussion of the Cairo Conference and British concern about expenditures, see Aaron S. Klieman, *Foundations of British Policy in the Arab World: The Cairo Conference of 1921* (Baltimore, 1970).

49. Both quotations are from G. D. Clayton, *Britain and the Eastern Question: Missolonghi to Gallipoli*, London History Studies, no. 8 (London, 1971), 245.

50. Steiner, "The Foreign Office and the War," 528. See also Marian Kent, "Great Britain and the End of the Ottoman Empire, 1900–1923," in *The Great Powers and the End of the Ottoman Empire*, ed. Marian Kent (London, 1984), 188–89.

DOCUMENT 2.1

THE HUSAYN-McMAHON CORRESPONDENCE
July 1915–January 1916

These selections from the correspondence between Sharif Husayn of Mecca and Henry McMahon, British high commissioner in Cairo, illustrate Arab requests for independence, to be backed by Britain, and Arab opposition to French territorial claims after the war. On the British side, McMahon strives to leave room for French interests in his October 24 letter while appearing to grant Arab control of most of Syria, and to gain Arab agreement to take action against the Turks. The covering letter from Husayn's son Abdullah to British Agency Oriental Secretary Ronald Storrs (excerpted here) makes reference to previous British propaganda efforts.

(Cover Letter to the Sharif Husain's First Note)
The Amir 'Abdullah to Mr. Ronald Storrs

Mecca, Ramadan 2, 1333
[July 14, 1915]

Complimentary titles.

I send my affectionate regard and respects to your esteemed self, and trust that you will ensure, as you know how to, the acceptance of the enclosed note which contains our proposals and conditions.

In this connexion, I wish to give you and your Government my assurance that you need have no anxiety about the intentions of our people, for they realise how closely their interests are bound to those of your Government. Do not trouble to send aeroplanes or warships to distribute news and reports as in the past: our minds are now made up. . . .

The Sharif Husain's First Note to Sir Henry McMahon

Mecca, Ramadan 2, 1333
[July 14, 1915]

Complimentary titles.

Whereas the entire Arab nation without exception is determined to assert its right to live, gain its freedom and administer its own affairs in name and in fact;

And whereas the Arabs believe it to be in Great Britain's interest to lend them assistance and support in the fulfilment of their steadfast and legitimate aims to the exclusion of all other aims;

Source: George Antonius, *The Arab Awakening* (New York, 1965), 413–27.

And whereas it is similarly to the advantage of the Arabs, in view of their geographical position and their economic interests, and in view of the well-known attitude of the Government of Great Britain, to prefer British assistance to any other;

For these reasons, the Arab nation has decided to approach the Government of Great Britain with a request for the approval, through one of their representatives if they think fit, of the following basic provisions...

1. Great Britain recognises the independence of the Arab countries which are bounded: on the north, by the line Mersin-Adana to parallel 37° N. and thence along the line Birejik-Urfa-Mardin-Midiat-Jazirat (ibn 'Umar)-Amadia to the Persian frontier; on the east, by the Persian frontier down to the Persian Gulf; on the south, by the Indian Ocean (with the exclusion of Aden whose status will remain as at present); on the west by the Red Sea and the Mediterranean Sea back to Mersin.

2. Great Britain will agree to the proclamation of an Arab Caliphate for Islam.

3. The Sharifian Arab Government undertakes, other things being equal, to grant Great Britain preference in all economic enterprises in the Arab countries.

...

5. Great Britain agrees to the abolition of Capitulations in the Arab countries, and undertakes to assist the Sharifian Government in summoning an international congress to decree their abolition. ....

Sir Henry McMahon's First Note to the Sharif Husain

Cairo, August 30, 1915

Complimentary titles.

... It pleases us ... to learn that Your Lordship and your people are at one in believing that Arab interests are in harmony with British interests, and vice-versa.

In earnest of this, we hereby confirm to you the declaration of Lord Kitchener as communicated to you through 'Ali Efendi, in which was manifested our desire for the independence of the Arab countries and their inhabitants, and our readiness to approve an Arab caliphate upon its proclamation.

We now declare once more that the Government of Great Britain would welcome the reversion of the caliphate to a true Arab born of the blessed stock of the Prophet.

As for the question of frontiers and boundaries, negotiations would appear to be premature and a waste of time on details at this stage, with the War in progress and the Turks in effective occupation of the greater part of those regions. All the more so as a party of Arabs inhabiting those very regions have, to our amazement and sorrow, overlooked and neglected this valuable and incomparable opportunity; and, instead of coming to our aid, have lent their assistance to the Germans and the Turks; ...

The Sharif Husain's Second Note to Sir Henry McMahon

Mecca, Shawwal 29, 1333
[September 9, 1915]

Complimentary titles.

We received your note of the 19th Shawwal, [August 30,] with gratification, . . . notwithstanding the obscurity and the signs of lukewarmth and hesitancy . . . in regard to our essential clause. . . .

Your Excellency will suffer me to say . . . that your statements in regard to the question of frontiers and boundaries — namely that to discuss them at this stage were unprofitable and could only result in a waste of time since those regions are still occupied by their sovereign government, and so forth — reflect what I might almost describe as reluctance or something akin to reluctance, on your part.

The fact is that the proposed frontiers and boundaries represent not the suggestions of one individual whose claim might well await the conclusion of the War, but the demands of our people who believe that those frontiers form the minimum necessary to the establishment of the new order for which they are striving. This they are determined to obtain; and they have decided to discuss the matter, in the first resort, with that Power in whom they place their greatest confidence and reliance, and whom they regard as the pivot of justice, namely Great Britain. . . .

Sir Henry McMahon's Second Note to the Sharif Husain

Cairo, October 24, 1915

Complimentary titles.

. . . Your note of the 29th Shawwal, 1333, and its tokens of sincere friendship have filled me with satisfaction and contentment.

I regret to find that you inferred from my last note that my attitude towards the question of frontiers and boundaries was one of hesitancy and lukewarmth. . . . All I meant was that I considered that the time had not yet come in which that question could be discussed in a conclusive manner.

But, having realised from your last note that you considered the question important, vital and urgent, I hastened to communicate to the Government of Great Britain the purport of your note. It gives me the greatest pleasure to convey to you, on their behalf, the following declarations which, I have no doubt, you will receive with satisfaction and acceptance.

The districts of Mersin and Alexandretta, and portions of Syria lying to the west of the districts of Damascus, Homs, Hama and Aleppo cannot be said to be purely Arab, and must on that account be excepted from the proposed delimitation.

Subject to that modification, and without prejudice to the treaties concluded between us and certain Arab Chiefs, we accept that delimitation.

As for the regions lying within the proposed frontiers, in which Great Britain is free to act without detriment to the interests of her ally France, I am authorised to give you the following pledges on behalf of the Government of Great Britain, and to reply as follows to your note:

(1) That, subject to the modifications stated above, Great Britain is prepared to recognise and uphold the independence of the Arabs in all the regions lying within the frontiers proposed by the Sharif of Mecca;

(2) That Great Britain will guarantee the Holy Places against all external aggression, and will recognise the obligation of preserving them from aggression;

(3) That, when circumstances permit, Great Britain will help the Arabs with her advice and assist them in the establishment of governments to suit those diverse regions;

(4) That it is understood that the Arabs have already decided to seek the counsels and advice of Great Britain exclusively; and that such European advisers and officials as may be needed to establish a sound system of administration shall be British;

(5) That, as regards the two vilayets of Baghdad and of Basra, the Arabs recognise that the fact of Great Britain's established position and interests there will call for the setting up of special administrative arrangements to protect those regions from foreign aggression, to promote the welfare of their inhabitants, and to safeguard our mutual economic interests.

I am confident that this declaration will convince you, beyond all doubt, of Great Britain's sympathy with the aspirations of her friends the Arabs; and that it will result in . . . the liberation of the Arab peoples from the Turkish yoke which has weighed on them all these long years. . .

The Sharif Husain's Third Note to Sir Henry McMahon

Mecca, Zul-Hejja 27, 1333
[November 5, 1915]

Complimentary titles.

With great gratification have we received your note of the 15th Zul-Hejja [October 24] to which we would reply as follows.

First, in order to facilitate agreement and serve the cause of Islam . . . we no longer insist on the inclusion of the districts of Mersin and Adana in the Arab Kingdom. As for the vilayets of Aleppo and Bairut and their western maritime coasts, these are purely Arab provinces in which the Moslem is indistinguishable from the Christian, for they are both the descendants of one forefather. . . .

Since the provinces of Iraq were part of the former Arab Empire, . . . we should find it impossible to . . . renounce that honourable association . . . [but] we should be willing, in our desire to facilitate agreement, to allow those parts which are now occupied by British troops to remain so occupied for a period to be determined by negotiation. . . .

Your advocacy of speedy action seems to us to entail risks as well as advantages . . . [but] the moment the Arabs feel confident that, when the time comes for the conclusion of peace in Europe, Great Britain and her allies will not leave them in the lurch face to face with Turkey and Germany, but that they intend to help them and advocate their case effectively in the peace negotiations, from that moment will Arab participation in the War undoubtedly serve the general Arab interest. . . .

Sir Henry McMahon's Third Note to the Sharif Husain

Cairo, December 13, 1915

Complimentary titles.

. . . I was glad to find that you consent to the exclusion of the vilayets of Mersin and Adana from the boundaries of the Arab countries. . . .

As for the two vilayets of Aleppo and Bairut, the Government of Great Britain have fully understood your statement in that respect and noted it with the greatest care. But as the interests of their ally France are involved in those two provinces, the question calls for careful consideration. We shall communicate again with you on this subject, at the appropriate time.

We fully approve your desire to proceed warily [in preparing to revolt], and do not wish to impel you to hasty action which might obstruct the success of your objectives. But, at the same time, we deem it imperative that you should turn your endeavours to uniting the Arab peoples to our joint cause. . . . On the success of your endeavours, and on the efficacy of the measures which, when the time comes, the Arabs will find it possible to take in aid of our cause, will the strength and permanence of our agreement depend.

In these circumstances, the Government of Great Britain have authorised me to declare to your Lordship that you may rest confident that Great Britain does not intend to conclude any peace whatsoever, of which the freedom of the Arab peoples and their liberation from German and Turkish domination do not form an essential condition.

The Sharif Husain's Fourth Note to Sir Henry McMahon

Mecca, Safar 25, 1334
[January 1, 1916]

Complimentary titles.

. . . . With regard to the northern parts and their coastal regions, . . . we have felt bound to steer clear of that which might have impaired the alliance between Great Britain and France and their concord during the calamities of the present war. On the other hand—and this Your Excellency must clearly understand—we shall deem it our duty, at the earliest opportunity after the conclusion of the War, to claim from you Bairut and its coastal regions which we will overlook for the moment on account of France. . . .

Any concession designed to give France or any other Power possession of a single square foot of territory in those parts is quite out of the question. In proclaiming this, I place all my reliance on the declarations which concluded your note. . . .

Sir Henry McMahon's Fourth Note to the Sharif Husain

Cairo, January 30, 1916

Complimentary titles.

. . . We . . . do not question the fact that you are working for the good of the Arab nation without any ulterior motive whatsoever. . . .

As for the northern regions, we note with great satisfaction your desire to avoid anything that might impair the alliance between Great Britain and France. It has not escaped you that it is our firm determination not to allow anything, however small, to stand in the way of our ending this war in complete victory. Moreover, when victory is attained, the friendship between Great Britain and France will be stronger and closer than ever, cemented as it will have been by the shedding of British and French blood—the blood of those who have fallen fighting side by side in the cause of right and freedom.

The Arab countries are now associated in that noble aim which can be attained by uniting our forces and acting in unison. We pray God that success may bind us to each other in a lasting friendship which shall bring profit and contentment to us all. . . .

DOCUMENT 2.2

DRAFTS AND FINAL TEXT OF THE BALFOUR DECLARATION

These drafts trace the initial expectations behind Zionist proposals and the evolution of the Balfour Declaration to its final form. Zionist claims to all of Palestine were modified to "a national home in Palestine" although both sides expected that a state would be the result. The objections of the only Jew in the cabinet, Sir Edwin Montagu, produced the clause that rights of Jews in other countries would be protected—he feared that Jews would be forced to leave their homes and go to the new Jewish state. And a clause was added protecting the civil and religious right of the "non-Jewish" communities, the Arabs, who were 90 percent of the population; political rights were reserved for Jews once they attained a majority.

Source: Leonard Stein, *The Balfour Declaration* (London, 1961), 664.

Zionist Draft, July 1917

1. His Majesty's Government accepts the principle that Palestine should be reconstituted as the national home of the Jewish people.

2. His Majesty's Government will use its best endeavours to secure the achievement of this object and will discuss the necessary methods and means with the Zionist Organisation.

Balfour Draft, August 1917

His Majesty's Government accepts the principle that Palestine should be reconstituted as the national home of the Jewish people and will use their best endeavours to secure the achievement of this object and will be ready to consider any suggestions on the subject which the Zionist Organisation may desire to lay before them.

Milner Draft, August 1917

His Majesty's Government accepts the principle that every opportunity should be afforded for the establishment of a home for the Jewish people in Palestine and will use its best endeavours to facilitate the achievement of this object and will be ready to consider any suggestions on the subject which the Zionist organisations may desire to lay before them.

Milner-Amery Draft, 4 October 1917

His Majesty's Government views with favour the establishment in Palestine of a national home for the Jewish race and will use its best endeavours to facilitate the achievement of this object, it being clearly understood that nothing shall be done which may prejudice the civil and religious rights of existing non-Jewish communities in Palestine or the rights and political status enjoyed in any other country by such Jews who are fully contented with their existing nationality (and citizenship).

(*Note*: words in parentheses added subsequently)

Final Text, 31 October 1917

His Majesty's Government view with favour the establishment in Palestine of a national home for the Jewish people and will use their best endeavours to facilitate the achievement of this object, it being clearly understood that nothing shall be done which may prejudice the civil and religious rights of existing non-Jewish communities in Palestine or the rights and political status enjoyed by Jews in any other country.

DOCUMENT 2.3

THE FAYSAL-WEIZMANN AGREEMENT
January 3, 1919

On the eve of the Paris Peace Conference of 1919, Emir Faysal and Chaim Weiz-mann signed the following agreement, which reflects their mutual interests in achiev-ing their own distinct goals in Syria and Palestine. No Palestinian Arab view was consulted.

Text of the Faisal-Weizmann Agreement

His Royal Highness the Amir FAISAL, representing and acting on behalf of the Arab Kingdom of HEJAZ, and Dr. CHAIM WEIZMANN, representing and act-ing on behalf of the Zionist Organisation, mindful of the racial kinship and ancient bonds existing between the Arabs and the Jewish people, and realising that the surest means of working out the consummation of their national aspira-tions, is through the closest possible collaboration in the development of the Arab State and Palestine, and being desirous further of confirming the good un-derstanding which exists between them, have agreed upon the following Articles:

Article I

The Arab State and Palestine in all their relations and undertakings shall be controlled by the most cordial goodwill and understanding and to this end Arab and Jewish duly accredited agents shall be established and maintained in their respective territories.

Article II

Immediately following the completion of the deliberations of the Peace Confer-ence, the definite boundaries between the Arab State and Palestine shall be determined by a Commission to be agreed upon by the parties hereto.

Article III

In the establishment of the Constitution and Administration of Palestine all such measures shall be adopted as will afford the fullest guarantees for carrying into effect the British Government's Declaration of the 2nd of November, 1917.

Source: George Antonius, *The Arab Awakening* (New York, 1965), 437–39.

Article IV

All necessary measures shall be taken to encourage and stimulate immigration of Jews into Palestine on a large scale, and as quickly as possible to settle Jewish immigrants upon the land through closer settlement and intensive cultivation of the soil. In taking such measures the Arab peasant and tenant farmers shall be protected in their rights, and shall be assisted in forwarding their economic development.

Article V

No regulation nor law shall be made prohibiting or interfering in any way with the free exercise of religion; and . . . No religious test shall ever be required for the exercise of civil or political rights.

Article VI

The Mohammedan Holy Places shall be under Mohammedan control.

Article VII

The Zionist Organisation proposes to send to Palestine a Commission of experts to make a survey of the economic possibilities of the country, and to report upon the best means for its development. The Zionist Organisation will place the aforementioned Commission at the disposal of the Arab State for the purpose of a survey of the economic possibilities of the Arab State and to report upon the best means for its development. The Zionist Organisation will use its best efforts to assist the Arab State in providing the means for developing the natural resources and economic possibilities thereof.

Article VIII

The parties hereto agree to act in complete accord and harmony in all matters embraced herein before the Peace Congress.

Article IX

Any matters of dispute which may arise between the contracting parties shall be referred to the British Government for arbitration.

Given under our hand at LONDON, ENGLAND, the THIRD day of JANU-ARY, ONE THOUSAND NINE HUNDRED AND NINETEEN.

[Translation]

Provided the Arabs obtain their independence as demanded in my Memorandum dated the 4th of January, 1919, to the Foreign Office of the Government of

Great Britain, I shall concur in the above articles. But if the slightest modification or departure were to be made [*sc.* in relation to the demands in the Memorandum] I shall not then be bound by a single word of the present Agreement which shall be deemed void and of no account or validity, and I shall not be answerable in any way whatsoever.

Faisal Ibn Husain (*in Arabic*)
Chaim Weizmann

DOCUMENT 2.4

RESOLUTIONS OF THE GENERAL SYRIAN CONGRESS

July 2, 1919

These resolutions were presented by the General Syrian Congress to the King-Crane Commission, which was then touring Syria and Palestine. Aware of President Woodrow Wilson's previous declarations on the principle of self-determination, the congress implicitly repudiates the Faysal-Weizmann Agreement by requesting Arab independence within the areas originally defined by Sharif Husayn. French and Zionist claims are rejected.

We, the undersigned, members of the General Syrian Congress assembled in Damascus on the 2nd of July 1919 . . . have resolved to submit the following as defining the aspirations of the people who have chosen us to place them before the American Section of the Inter-Allied Commission. With the exception of the fifth clause, which was passed by a large majority, the Resolutions which follow were all adopted unanimously:—

1. We desire full and absolute political independence for Syria within the following boundaries: on the north, the Taurus Range; on the south, a line running from Rafah to al-Jauf and following the Syria-Hejaz border below 'Aqaba; on the east, the boundary formed by the Euphrates and Khabur rivers and a line stretching from some distance east of Abu-Kamal to some distance east of al-Jauf; on the west, the Mediterranean Sea.

2. We desire the Government of Syria to be a constitutional monarchy based on principles of democratic and broadly decentralised rule which shall safeguard the rights of minorities, and we wish that the Amir Faisal who has striven so nobly for our liberation and enjoys our full confidence and trust be our King.

3. In view of the fact that the Arab inhabitants of Syria are not less fitted or gifted than were certain other nations (such as the Bulgarians, Serbs, Greeks

Source: George Antonius, *The Arab Awakening* (New York, 1965), 440–42.

and Rumanians) when granted independence, we protest against Article XXII of the Covenant of the League of Nations which relegates us to the standing of insufficiently developed races requiring the tutelage of a mandatory power. [See Document 2.5.]

4. If . . . the Peace Conference were to ignore this legitimate protest, we shall regard the mandate mentioned in the Covenant of the League of Nations as implying no more than the rendering of assistance in the technical and economic fields without impairment of our absolute independence. We rely on President Wilson's declarations that his object in entering the War was to put an end to acquisitive designs for imperialistic purposes. In our desire that our country should not be made a field for colonisation, and in the belief that the American nation is devoid of colonial ambitions and has no political designs on our country, we resolve to seek assistance in the technical and economic fields from the United States of America on the understanding that the duration of such assistance shall not exceed twenty years.

5. In the event of the United States finding herself unable to accede to our request for assistance, we would seek it from Great Britain, provided . . . that its duration shall not exceed the period mentioned in the preceding clause.

6. We do not recognise to the French Government any right to any part of Syria, and we reject all proposals that France should give us assistance or exercise authority in any portion of the country.

7. We reject the claims of the Zionists for the establishment of a Jewish commonwealth in that part of southern Syria which is known as Palestine, and we are opposed to Jewish immigration into any part of the country. We . . . regard their claims as a grave menace to our national, political and economic life. Our Jewish fellow citizens shall continue to enjoy the rights and to bear the responsibilities which are ours in common.

8. We desire that there should be no dismemberment of Syria, and no separation of Palestine or the coastal regions in the west or the Lebanon from the mother country; . . . .

9. We desire that Iraq should enjoy complete independence, and that no economic barriers be placed between the two countries.

10. The basic principles proclaimed by President Wilson in condemnation of secret treaties cause us to enter an emphatic protest against any agreement providing for the dismemberment of Syria and against any undertaking envisaging the recognition of Zionism in southern Syria; and we ask for the explicit annulment of all such agreements and undertakings.

The lofty principles proclaimed by President Wilson encourage us to believe that . . . we may look to President Wilson and the liberal American nation, who are known for their sincere and generous sympathy with the aspirations of weak nations, for help in the fulfilment of our hopes.

We . . . would not have risen against Turkish rule under which we enjoyed civic and political privileges, as well as rights of representation, had it not been that the Turks denied us our right to a national existence. We believe that the Peace Conference will meet our desires in full, if only to ensure that our political privileges may not be less, . . . than they were before the War.

We desire to be allowed to send a delegation to represent us at the Peace Conference, advocate our claims and secure the fulfilment of our aspirations.

DOCUMENT 2.5

ARTICLE 22 OF THE COVENANT OF THE LEAGUE OF NATIONS

January 1920

Ratified in January 1920, the covenant served as the basis for allocating mandates and defining their terms. Concern for the "wishes of communities" in selecting mandatory powers is expressed only for areas of the former Ottoman Empire. It does not appear in the actual mandate for Palestine.

1. To those colonies and territories which as a consequence of the late War have ceased to be under the sovereignty of the States which formerly governed them and which are inhabited by peoples not yet able to stand by themselves under the strenuous conditions of the modern world, there should be applied the principle that the well-being and development of such peoples form a sacred trust of civilization and that securities for the performance of this trust should be embodied in this Covenant.

2. . . . The tutelage of such peoples should be entrusted to advanced nations who by reason of their resources, their experience or their geographical position can best undertake this responsibility, and who are willing to accept it, and that this tutelage should be exercised by them as Mandatories on behalf of the League.

3. The character of the Mandate must differ according to the stage of the development of the people, the geographical situation of the territory, its economic conditions and other similar circumstances.

4. Certain communities formerly belonging to the Turkish Empire have reached a stage of development where their existence as independent nations can be provisionally recognized subject to the rendering of administrative advice and assistance by a Mandatory until such time as they are able to stand alone. The wishes of these communities must be a principal consideration in the selection of the Mandatory.

Source: The League of Nations Covenant (London: The League of Nations Union, 1919).

5. Other peoples, especially those of Central Africa, are at such a stage that the Mandatory must be responsible for the administration of the territory under conditions which will guarantee freedom of conscience and religion, subject only to the maintenance of public order and morals, . . . and will also secure equal opportunities for the trade and commerce of other Members of the League.

6. There are territories, such as South-West Africa and certain of the South Pacific Islands, which, owing to the sparseness of their population, or their small size, or their remoteness from the centres of civilization, or their geographical contiguity to the territory of the Mandatory, and other circumstances, can be best administered under the laws of the Mandatory as integral portions of its territory, subject to the safeguards above-mentioned in the interests of the indigenous population.

7. . . . The Mandatory shall render to the Council an annual report in reference to the territory committed to its charge. . . .

DOCUMENT 2.6

THE MANDATE FOR PALESTINE

July 24, 1922

The Mandate incorporates the Balfour Declaration and obligates Britain to encourage the growth of the Jewish national home in Palestine. Although the British were awarded the Palestine Mandate in April 1920, the League of Nations did not ratify it until July 1922. During the interim Britain successfully proposed the addition of Article 25, which accounted for the British decision in March 1921 to separate Palestine east of the Jordan River and award it to the Emir Abdullah as the Emirate of Transjordan. The articles selected here also illustrate Britain's dual commitment to support Jewish efforts to build a national home while protecting the rights of "other sections of the population." British officials would return to these articles in the 1939 White Paper (Document 3.3), which withdrew Britain's commitment to a Jewish state in Palestine.

The Council of the League of Nations:

Whereas the Principal Allied Powers have agreed, for the purpose of giving effect to the provisions of Article 22 of the Covenant of the League of Nations, to entrust to a Mandatory selected by the said Powers the administration of the

Source: League of Nations Council, *Mandate for Palestine, together with a note by the Secretary-General relating to its application to the territory known as Transjordan, under the provisions of Article 25* (London: H.M. Stationary Office, 1922).

territory of Palestine, which formerly belonged to the Turkish Empire, within such boundaries as may be fixed by them; and

Whereas the Principal Allied Powers have also agreed that the Mandatory should be responsible for putting into effect the declaration originally made on November 2, 1917, by the Government of His Britannic Majesty, and adopted by the said Powers, in favour of the establishment in Palestine of a National Home for the Jewish people, it being clearly understood that nothing should be done which might prejudice the civil and religious rights of existing non-Jewish communities in Palestine, or the rights and political status enjoyed by Jews in any other country; and

Whereas recognition has thereby been given to the historical connection of the Jewish people with Palestine and to the grounds for reconstituting their National Home in that country . . .

Whereas His Britannic Majesty has accepted the Mandate in respect of Palestine and undertaken to exercise it on behalf of the League of Nations in conformity with the following provisions . . .

Article 1. The Mandatory shall have full powers of legislation and of administration, save as they may be limited by the terms of this Mandate.

Article 2. The Mandatory shall be responsible for placing the country under such political, administrative, and economic conditions as will secure the establishment of the Jewish National Home, as laid down in the preamble, and the development of self-governing institutions, and also for safeguarding the civil and religious rights of all the inhabitants of Palestine, irrespective of race and religion.

Article 3. The Mandatory shall, so far as circumstances permit, encourage local autonomy.

Article 4. An appropriate Jewish Agency shall be recognized as a public body for the purpose of advising and co-operating with the Administration of Palestine in such economic, social and other matters as may affect the establishment of the Jewish National Home and the interests of the Jewish population in Palestine, and, subject always to the control of the Administration, to assist and take part in the development of the country.

The Zionist organization, so long as its organization and constitution are in the opinion of the Mandatory appropriate, shall be recognized as such agency. It shall take steps in consultation with His Britannic Majesty's Government to secure the co-operation of all Jews who are willing to assist in the establishment of the Jewish National Home.

Article 5. The Mandatory shall be responsible for seeing that no Palestine territory shall be ceded or leased to, or in any way placed under the control of, the Government of any foreign Power.

Article 6. The Administration of Palestine, while ensuring that the rights and position of other sections of the population are not prejudiced, shall facilitate Jewish immigration under suitable conditions and shall encourage, in co-operation with the Jewish Agency referred to in Article 4, close settlement by

Jews on the land, including State lands and waste lands not required for public purposes. . . .

Article 25. In the territories lying between the Jordan and the eastern boundary of Palestine as ultimately determined, the Mandatory shall be entitled, with the consent of the Council of the League of Nations, to postpone or withhold application of such provisions of this Mandate as he may consider inapplicable to the existing local conditions, and to make such provision for the administration of the territories as he may consider suitable to those conditions, provided that no action shall be taken which is inconsistent with the provisions of Articles 15, 16 and 18.

3

PALESTINE BETWEEN THE WARS
Zionism, the Palestinian Arabs, and the British Mandate

1920–1939

HE PALESTINE that British forces entered in December 1917 was quite different from what had existed in 1914. It had served as a staging area for Ottoman troops throughout much of the war and finally as a battleground. Many foreign residents and recent immigrants had left or were forcibly deported at the outbreak of war. The Turks conscripted thousands of Arab peasants, confiscated their crops, and caused extensive deforestation as the occupation progressed and wood was needed for fuel. These actions, coupled with locust plagues and poor crop yields, impoverished whole sectors of the Arab peasantry. Malnourishment, disease, and finally famine appeared in parts of Palestine as well as in Syria and Lebanon, afflicting the less fortunate, Christian and Jewish as well as Muslim. The immediate task of the British government was to provide food and medical supplies to the destitute and to restore social and economic order to the region.[1]

In the midst of these efforts, British officials encountered Arab hostility toward Zionism, inspired both by awareness of the Balfour Declaration and by the actions of many Jews in Palestine who believed that the achievement of a Jewish state was imminent. The Zionist Commission arrived in April 1918 to act as the representative of the Zionist movement. Granted status as a semi-independent body by the Foreign Office, the commission could either request concessions from British military and civilian authorities in Palestine or intervene in London to countermand decisions made by these authorities if it thought them unfavorable. Soon after their arrival, members of the commission asked military officials to grant the Hebrew language equal status with Arabic in all official proclamations, to appoint Jews as government officials, to appoint a Jew as mayor of Jerusalem, and to move to ensure that half of the municipal council of Jerusalem would be Jewish. British officials complied with the first two demands and acceded to the Zionist Commission's request that Jewish government employees be granted higher pay than Arabs because, the commission argued, as Europeans they needed higher salaries to live on. Zionists were also permitted to fly the Zionist flag, the symbol of their aspiration to sovereignty, but Arabs were prohibited by government order from flying theirs.

These actions had a devastating effect on the Palestinian Arabs still recovering from the war. As we have seen, traditional Ottoman society had defined the places of Christians and Jews vis-à-vis Muslims. Prewar Zionist activities had not disrupted the traditional political and social order. Now that was threatened by the appearance of militant Jews demanding and receiving equal status with Arabs, granted by a British government apparently fulfilling Zionist wishes. Knowledge that during 1919 certain Jewish papers were calling for the forced emigration of Palestinian Arabs to Faysal's Arab state in Syria also roused alarm.[2] Arab fears were only partially tempered by British reassurances. Zionist celebrations on November 2, 1918, the first anniversary of the Balfour Declaration, led to several clashes between Arabs and Jews, followed by an Arab petition to the British authorities that protested Zionist immigration and the idea that Palestine was to belong to the incoming Jews and not to the resident Arab population. The Anglo-French Declaration of November 7, inadvertently publicized in Palestine, temporarily mollified Arab unrest, but such unintended assurances were soon countered by Zionist activity. As a result, joint Muslim-Christian groups, initially formed in early 1918, now coalesced into the Muslim-Christian Association that first appeared in Jaffa and then Jerusalem in November of that year. Made up of leading notables among the Muslim and Christian Arab communities, the association became for a while the leading Palestinian nationalist forum and, as such, was encouraged by the British military authorities who wished to balance Zionist activities.[3]

British military officials in Palestine were clearly sympathetic to the Palestinian Arabs. They resented Zionist appeals to London if their demands were not met, but they also regarded Zionist calls for statehood as fomenting unrest and possibly threatening the stability of the British imperial presence in Palestine. In this they were at odds with British politicians in London, many of whom considered Zionism the primary cause of Britain's presence in Palestine that enabled it to justify its occupation of the region.[4] A pattern emerged that continued throughout the 1920s. Most local British authorities and those who came to investigate the disturbances invariably began to sympathize with Arab views, whereas the British government, out of concern for its imperial presence as well as sympathy for Jewish needs and awareness of domestic political considerations, sided with the Zionists.

Senior British officials continued to back Zionism until Britain's imperial position seemed threatened by the resentment of other Arab countries at the onset of World War II. These officials then issued a White Paper in 1939 that essentially repudiated the Balfour Declaration and seemed to ensure Arab domination of a future Palestinian state. This shift, even more than the Balfour Declaration, was dictated by expediency and resulted in armed conflict between the British and Zionist forces, the subject of the next chapter.

THE FIRST PHASE: HOPES FULFILLED
AND DASHED, 1918–1920

During this period, the Zionist leadership, headed by Chaim Weizmann, was concerned principally with acquiring recognition by the great powers of the Zionists' right to Palestine. Although Weizmann told the delegates to the Peace Conference that he envisioned Palestine becoming as Jewish as England is English—a statement that added to Arab alarm in the country—he was himself disturbed by local Zionist enthusiasm and claims of immediate statehood and sought to downplay their "undue exuberance," referring to demands that included the possible deportation of Palestinian Arabs to Syria.[5]

The Palestinian Arabs, on the other hand, had fewer options and less scope for their pursuit. The end of 1918 found Palestine united under a single administration for the first time in centuries. But unity brought with it the potential for rivalries among different families and groups, whose traditional bases of power and prestige might not be recognized at a national level. Disagreement arose as to what policy to pursue with respect to the British and Zionism, with differences often reflecting the status of one's family before the war. The al-Husayni family, for example, controlled in 1918 the two most important posts in the Jerusalem administration: Musa Kazim al-Husayni was mayor and Kamil al-Husayni was mufti, the chief legal official of the Muslim community. Both, but especially Kamil, welcomed British rule and cooperated with the administration in its early stages. Both opposed Zionism but recognized that their own positions of prominence were not threatened by the British assumption of power. It was through them and members of other notable families that the Muslim-Christian Association was founded in November 1918.

Younger Arabs, though not unsympathetic to the British as potential administrators of Palestine, looked to Faysal in Syria and the hope of union with him as the best means to foil Zionist goals. There emerged the idea of Palestine as "southern Syria," with Palestinian Arabs among the most ardent pan-Arab nationalists in Damascus during the heyday of Faysal's rule in 1918 and 1919. Among these young Palestinians was Hajj Amin al-Husayni, younger brother of Kamil al-Husayni, who headed a society called the al-Nadi al-Arabi. A rival society, the al-Muntada al-Adabi, was dominated by members of the al-Nashashibi family. Nationalist fervor reached its height in March 1920 when the Syrian National Congress, which included Palestinians such as Hajj Amin, proclaimed Faysal the king of a united Syria. These developments, reported by Zionist intelligence, had profound repercussions in Palestine. The image of an independent Syria that included Palestine within the Arab nation offered hope of undermining Zionist goals that would deny Palestinian Arab aspirations. Nonetheless, Palestinians were suspicious of Faysal's apparent collaboration with Weizmann as a means to gain British backing against the French, and they identified more with the congress than with the king.

The Syrian National Congress, which had always been anti-Zionist, had actually forced Faysal to back away from his tentative support of Zionist goals. Once the congress crowned Faysal, demonstrations broke out in Palestine in which Musa Kazim al-Husayni, the mayor of Jerusalem, played a role. Tensions escalated as the festival of Nebi Musa (Prophet Moses) was scheduled for April 4–5. A celebration that traditionally brought Muslims together from throughout Palestine, the festival was also an occasional source of religious friction, since it often coincided with both Passover and Easter. Nationalist fervor led to anti-Zionist riots during the Nebi Musa observances, encouraged in part by Hajj Amin al-Husayni, recently returned from Damascus, who declared that the British would support the idea of Faysal's rule over Palestine.[6] Muslims attacked the Jewish quarter in old Jerusalem. In the melee prior to the intervention of British forces, 5 Jews were killed and 211 wounded, whereas Arab casualties were 4 killed and 32 wounded.

British reaction was swift. Ronald Storrs, governor of Jerusalem, summarily dismissed Musa Kazim al-Husayni as mayor for having ignored his directive to stay out of politics. He replaced him with Raghib al-Nashashibi, head of the less-prominent but ambitious Jerusalem family that hoped to acquire power at the al-Husaynis' expense. Al-Nashashibi's willing accession to the mayoralty was to encourage a growing split within Palestinian Arab ranks that dominated and fragmented nationalist activity throughout the mandate. As the al-Nashashibis moved closer to the British, the al-Husaynis distanced themselves somewhat, although they were always careful during this period to maintain ties with the mandatory power. Their rivalry became all the more significant when pan-Arab hopes were dashed soon after the Nebi Musa riots. The mandate, including the Balfour Declaration, was confirmed on April 24 at San Remo, and a declaration to that effect was read in Palestine on April 28. The British military administration was summarily dismissed, and the first High Commissioner of Palestine, Herbert Samuel, inaugurated civilian rule as of July 1. On July 20, Faysal's government collapsed, and with it Arab hopes of independence. The Palestinian Arabs would now have to turn inward to deal with a high commissioner determined to fulfill British responsibilities toward both Arabs and Jews under the terms of the mandate.

POLITICAL LEADERSHIP IN PALESTINIAN ARAB AND ZIONIST COMMUNITIES

Though a dedicated Zionist, Herbert Samuel believed that he should take account of Arab grievances while not reversing Britain's basic obligation to assist the fulfillment of Zionist aims. He hoped to gain Arab participation in mandate affairs and to guard their civil and economic rights while simultaneously refusing them any authority that could be used to stop Jewish immigration and purchase of land in Palestine. His efforts were "subtly designed to reconcile Arabs to the . . . pro-Zionist policy" of the civil administration.[7] To this end, Samuel felt that Great Britain should establish conditions in which Zionist activity could flourish but that he should not intervene directly on their behalf. His tactics ultimately led to recriminations from both sides.

Palestinian Arabs and British Policies

Samuel tried to establish contacts with the Arab Executive (AE) and was usually conciliatory toward those who represented Arab nationalist feelings. When the mufti, Kamil al-Husayni, died in the spring of 1921, Samuel recommended Hajj Amin al-Husayni for the post, even though he had lost the elections to the candidate backed by the al-Nashashibis. Hajj Amin al-Husayni would ultimately emerge as the unquestioned leader of the Palestinian Arab movement. In January 1922, he became head of the Supreme Muslim Council (SMC), which oversaw all appointments to religious offices in Palestine's Islamic community.

Conciliation could not repress Arab dislike of Zionism, however. With the end of the war, Jewish immigration had resumed in what became the Third Aliya (1919–1923). These new immigrants were "young, enthusiastic, penniless workers," socialists for the most part, who were eager to contribute to the building of a Zionist society.[8] In their manners and their ideology, they were the antithesis of the norms of Arab culture, and many Arabs, and others also, saw them as signifying the introduction of communism into Palestine. (See Figure 3.1.) Over 10,000 Jewish immigrants entered Palestine in 1919–1920, most of them part of this worker influx; another 8,294 entered in 1921.[9] Rivalries among factions of these workers led to renewed outbreaks of Arab-Jewish strife. On May Day 1921, riots erupted in Tel Aviv between Jewish communists, parading in support of a Soviet Palestine, and socialists who opposed them. The fighting spread into adjacent areas of Arab Jaffa and led to Arab attacks on Jews and Jewish reprisals. One of the main targets of the Arab attacks was the Jaffa Immigrants Hotel, where many incoming Zionists stayed.[10] In this fighting, 14 Arabs and 43 Jews were killed and 49 Arabs and 143 Jews were wounded. Further violence occurred almost immediately as the Nebi Musa celebrations began. Arabs attacked Jewish settlements, which were armed, and the British responded with air attacks on the Arab rioters. In these clashes, 47 Jews and 48 Arabs were killed and 146 Jews and 73 Arabs were wounded.

The May Day riots had a profound impact on Samuel, who halted Jewish immigration, if only temporarily, and assured the Arabs that the British government "would never impose on [the people of Palestine] a policy that people had reason to think was contrary to their religious, their political, and their economic interests."[11] This speech led many Zionists in Palestine to view Samuel as having betrayed his official obligations. It encouraged the Arab leaders to believe that British concessions might be forthcoming. An Arab delegation composed of members of notable families went to London in July 1921, where

Figure 3.1 ■ Zionist Immigration Camp near Tel Aviv, circa 1919–1923

In the aftermath of World War I, different Zionist socialist parties encouraged immigration into Palestine under the umbrella of the World Zionist Organization. The vast majority were young, unemployed workers, usually ardent adherents of often competing socialist doctrines. Some could be placed in hotels but others were assigned to tent camps until assigned to projects, as shown here.

they demanded that the Balfour Declaration be repudiated and that Britain agree to build an Arab national government. Their claims were rejected by British officials, including Winston Churchill, who offered them a representative assembly with an Arab majority but denied it effective power to block British support of the Zionist cause. Eager to mollify Arab feelings, the British government issued a White Paper in June 1922. It declared that Britain did "not contemplate that Palestine as a whole should be converted into a Jewish National Home, but that such a home should be founded *in Palestine*" (see Document 3.1). This statement departed not so much from the letter of the Balfour Declaration as from its spirit, which to Zionists and their British allies meant ultimate Jewish statehood in all of Palestine. Although not pleased by this modification of previous statements, the Zionists accepted it, if only to appear cooperative with the mandatory power. And with official approval of the mandate by the League of Nations in July 1922, they could feel they had the right to pursue their objectives to the utmost.

The Legislative Council Plans.   With these documents in hand, Samuel now turned to the task of trying to create a legislative body in Palestine that would incorporate the different segments of the community. Britain had drafted a constitution for Palestine that was officially promulgated on August 10, 1922. It provided for a consultative body that would advise the high commissioner and his subordinates on matters of concern to them. The council would be composed of twenty-three members, eleven selected from the government (the high commissioner and ten government officials) and twelve to be elected from the population in proportion to the size of the respective communities (eight Muslims, two Christians, and two Jews). This was an improvement over the advisory council that Samuel had created in October 1920, which had included four Muslims, three Christians, and three Jews, a ratio that significantly underrepresented the Muslim community, given its share of the population of Palestine. Nevertheless, both Muslims and Christians, through the Arab Executive, decided to boycott the elections for the new council because the AE was specifically denied the right to discuss matters pertaining to British obligations to the Zionists. The al-Nashashibi camp had quietly favored the idea of the legislative council but would not say so publicly out of fear of reprisals.

Samuel tried again in the spring of 1923, this time to create a council with the same proportion of representatives but with all its members appointed by the high commissioner. Failing in this effort, Samuel sought Arab agreement for creation of an Arab Agency that would presumably represent Arab interests in the same manner as the Zionist Executive did for the Zionists. But there were differences. The Zionist Executive was a self-selecting institution whose membership was outside British control, whereas members of the Arab Agency would be chosen by the high commissioner. And by restricting the Arab Agency's concerns to the affairs of the Arab community, which precluded consideration of Zionist policies, the British isolated the agency's proposed scope of responsibility from matters that were of greatest concern to the Arabs. This too failed to gain Arab backing and ended British efforts to bring Arab leaders into official contact with the government. Later Arab willingness to participate in such institutions in the 1930s would be foiled by the course of events and Zionist opposition.

The Arabs' refusal to cooperate with the mandatory regime by participating in these councils prohibited them from presenting their views from within the administration of Palestine. But for Arab leaders to have done so would have meant recognition of the mandate and the Balfour Declaration, and thus acceptance of the right of the Jews to immigrate freely into Palestine. Such acknowledgment would have undermined the foundation of their claim that they should be granted the right of self-determination in Palestine.

Palestinian Arab Rivalries.   On the other hand, the Arabs' rejection of Samuel's proposal did not mean that all segments of the community opposed it. As noted, the al-Nashashibi faction privately favored participation, presumably hoping to establish rapport with the high commissioner by displaying a cooperative attitude. As mayor of Jerusalem, Raghib al-Nashashibi needed and sought a close relationship with Samuel, but it was also known that he would generally approve what the al-Husaynis opposed and vice versa, often as a matter of principle rather than in support of a specific policy.[12] Here the al-Nashashibis benefited, as the 1920s progressed, from the growing Muslim resentment at the al-Husayni family's control over the Arab Executive and the Supreme Muslim Council. Some Arab Christians, though opposed to Zionism, were wary of Hajj Amin al-Husayni's prominence as a Muslim leader, although he, unlike some more radical associates, always strove to maintain Muslim-Christian ties as the basis of a national Arab coalition opposing Zionism. These factors enabled the al-Nashashibi party to gain a majority of the seats in the 1927 municipal elections held throughout Palestine. Its success was encouraged by Zionist donations, as several members of the Jewish Executive were eager to promote opposition to the al-Husaynis. Some funding went also to the two major independent newspapers, *Filastin* and *al-Karmil*, which in 1926 switched their backing to the al-Nashashibis.[13] The extent of the opposition was such that the AE, headed by Musa Kazim al-Husayni, closed its offices in 1927, a step that indicated also the AE's inability to secure any concessions from the British that might weaken their commitment to Zionism.

In fact, hopes of achieving such concessions were unrealistic: "no British cabinet would have sanctioned the establishment . . . of a government really representative of the Arab majority and possessing effective powers."[14] Arab leaders thus turned inward during the mid-1920s to seek to expand their influence against one another, encouraged perhaps by a sharp decrease in Jewish immigration that lessened their sense of urgency regarding the likelihood of Zionist success: Jewish emigration was higher than immigration in 1927. The moderate al-Nashashibi party felt secure enough from 1925 onward to espouse openly the idea of Arab participation on a legislative council, especially after the arrival in midyear of the new high commissioner, Lord Plumer, to replace Herbert Samuel. Aware of its declining influence, the AE decided to back the project in 1927, but it was not until June 1928, when the Palestine Arab Congress met for the first time in five years, that the two coalitions agreed to push for representative institutions. Talks were begun with both Raghib al-Nashashibi and Musa Kazim al-Husayni once Plumer's successor, Sir John Chancellor, announced in January 1929 that he would consider proposals for a legislative assembly.

These discussions were interrupted, however, by the outbreak of new riots in August 1929, the outgrowth of Muslim-Jewish tensions stemming from the question of access to—and control of—the Western Wall in old Jerusalem. These riots, and the ensuing furor over British policy recommendations, ultimately reinforced British commitments to Zionist policies and undermined the possibility of creating legislative bodies on the lines that had been considered likely to succeed a few months earlier. They were the product of ongoing as well as immediate points of conflict, the result of Arab-Jewish interactions that we will consider before turning to the riots.

Zionist Leadership in Palestine and Abroad

Zionist leadership in Palestine existed at several levels, reflecting the concerns of international Zionism and the struggles for control of Palestinian Jews by local Zionist leaders. Zionism in Palestine was represented initially by the Zionist Commission. It had been sent out in 1918 by the World Zionist Organization (WZO), now based in London and headed by Chaim Weizmann, to act as a semi-independent authority in dealing with British officials. In 1921, the Zionist Commission was replaced by the Palestine Zionist Executive (PZE), meaning those members of the WZO Executive residing in Palestine who acted in accordance with directives from London. The PZE oversaw the activities of the major organizations that had been created to secure a Zionist presence, such as the Keren Hayesod, the key financial institution for financing projects in Palestine, and the Jewish National Fund, which sought to purchase land that would then become inalienably Jewish.

Weizmann and the Jewish Agency.   Weizmann hoped to broaden world Jewish support for the Zionist cause by creating a commission that would include non-Zionist as well as Zionist Jews. His major incentive was financial: to increase donations for use in Palestine that would be controlled by official Zionist groups. Throughout the 1920s, contributions funneled through Zionist channels made up only a small portion of the infusion of Jewish capital into Palestine; between 1919 and 1926, 22 out of 28 million English pounds brought into Palestine were capital investments for corporations abroad or money devoted to private enterprises.[15] This type of funding sought profit and immediate results, as opposed to serving long-term Zionist or socialist goals; managers speculated in land and hired cheaper Arab labor, not Jewish workers. Differences over the philosophy of such funding had led a bloc of American Zionists, represented by U.S. Supreme Court Justice Louis Brandeis, to withdraw from the World Zionist Organization in the mid-1920s. Brandeis wanted immigrants with sufficient capital to be productive on arrival, whereas Weizmann and the European members of the WZO believed it necessary to encourage anyone to settle in Palestine, if only to increase the Jewish population. If Jews of independent means were unwilling to go to Palestine through Zionist auspices, then poor workers should be encouraged, sponsored by Zionist funds. But this approach required a good deal of money. Weizmann spent six years, between 1923 and 1929, seeking commitments from wealthy European and American Jews who were not necessarily committed personally to Zionism. Inevitably, prospective donors wanted a say in how their contributions were distributed.

In 1929, Weizmann succeeded in gaining agreement for the creation of a new governing body for the Zionist movement in Palestine, the Jewish Agency, which supplanted the Palestine Zionist Executive. The agency's headquarters were located in Jerusalem, with a branch office in London directed by its president, Chaim Weizmann, who took the post by virtue of his leadership of the

World Zionist Organization. The bylaws granted non-Zionists equal representation with Zionists on the agency's major committees, an arrangement designed to give non-Zionists financial oversight of Zionist projects. Also, the agency's partnership with Weizmann and the WZO would help coordinate the pursuit of Zionist objectives in Palestine and the representation of their interests before the British government in London and the League of Nations, which supervised the mandate.

The new arrangement, however, set the stage for future rivalries between Weizmann and the leadership of the Zionist movement in Palestine, which resented outside control. The latter decided to increase their influence in world Zionist circles through elections to the newly created Jewish Agency, where they took over the seats on the major committees, including the Executive Council, that were allotted to non-Zionists. This proved simple to do, as technically a non-Zionist was anyone not nominated for a post by Weizmann and the WZO. Palestinian Zionists' success in this effort would eventually provoke confrontations between the leadership of the Yishuv, the Jewish community in Palestine represented by David Ben-Gurion, and the world Zionist leadership centered in Weizmann, as to the nature of the policy to be pursued in the area.

Palestinian Jews and Labor Zionism.   The manner in which the Palestinian Zionists gained influence in world Zionist councils illustrates the nature of intra-Jewish relationships in Palestine as well as Jewish assumptions about the Arab community. The Jewish community in Palestine on the eve of World War I was divided into three main sectors. First there were the Orthodox Jews, still a majority, who rejected Zionist pretensions because they clashed with their own vision of a universe controlled by divine will. Second, there was the private Jewish sector, predominantly landowners, which was the offshoot of the early colonizing efforts of Hibbat Zion and the later donations of Baron de Rothschild. These landlords used Arab labor and had in many ways become part of the Palestinian landscape rather than identifying themselves solely with a separatist Jewish cause. Finally, there were the labor Zionists, the offspring of the Second Aliya in the first decade of the twentieth century. They were ardent socialists as well as Jewish nationalists, reared in the revolutionary fervor of Russian collectivism and committed to establishing a singular Jewish presence in the land of ancient Israel. They attacked Jewish landlords for using Arab labor, both as socialists on the grounds of exploitation and as Zionists on the grounds that these actions undermined the Zionist goal of a self-governing Jewish community devoted to restoring Palestine to Jewish control.

There were two main factions among the labor Zionists during this period and later. Poale Zion (Workers of Zion) retained ties with its parent labor-Zionist organization in Europe and for years identified with European revolutionary socialism in principle, even though its own nationalist views contradicted basic socialist ideology. Although leaders of Poale Zion, including David

Ben-Gurion, supported the idea of Jewish settlement on the land, they focused their attention on Palestine's cities because it was there that most Jewish immigrants settled. In contrast, Hapoel Hatzair (The Young Worker), inspired by the writings of David Gordon, stressed the need for collective settlement of the land as the foundation for the building of a Jewish nation. Both groups adopted the idea of the "conquest of labor," which signified the victory of Jewish labor in creating a new society. This in turn meant that Jewish investment and capital were meaningful only when Jewish labor was used. For many years, however, neither group controlled a majority of the workers. When construction of Tel Aviv, the first all-Jewish city, began in 1909, financed by the Jewish National Fund, Arab labor predominated.[16]

Both Poale Zion and Hapoel Hatzair were to a degree political as well as labor groups, Poale Zion especially, since it seemed to encourage class conflict. In 1919, Poale Zion reconstituted itself as a new party, the Ahdut Ha'Avodah, which incorporated many unaffiliated unionists and a small number of Hapoel Hatzair members. Both Ahdut Ha'Avodah and Hapoel Hatzair encouraged postwar worker immigration, which reached over 10,000 by the end of 1920. The socialist commitment of these immigrants pushed the Ahdut Ha'Avodah to agree with Hapoel Hatzair to form a single workers' organization to control Jewish labor. This was the Histadrut, created in December 1920 and destined to become the dominant force in Jewish affairs in Palestine. Both parties retained their separate identities within the organization and competed to control the Histadrut executive, a contest eventually won by Ben-Gurion and the Ahdut Ha'Avodah.

Ben-Gurion Triumphs: Mapai and the Histadrut. As the dominant party in the Histadrut, Ben-Gurion and his colleagues eventually came to control the fortunes not only of Jewish labor but of world Zionism as well. Histadrut funds had been dispensed initially by the World Zionist Organization, which designated areas for their use. By the mid-1920s, the WZO granted the Histadrut the right to allocate these funds, thus aiding Ahdut Ha'Avodah fortunes. Incoming workers were assigned jobs through labor exchanges sponsored by the Histadrut but actually controlled by the party. Nevertheless, political and organizational strife throughout the 1920s led Ben-Gurion to strive to merge Ahdut Ha'Avodah and Hapoel Hatzair into one party, called Mapai, accomplished in 1930.

Several factors led to Maipai's creation. After the first wave of worker immigrants at the start of the decade, most newcomers during the 1920s were from the middle class, mainly from Poland. They settled in cities and became part of the private economy outside Histadrut control. Then an economic crisis in 1927–1928 caused massive unemployment among the workers sponsored by the organization.[17] These problems led the Histadrut to push its attacks on Jewish enterprises that employed Arabs, actions many Jewish merchants considered a threat to their livelihood. For Ben-Gurion, unifying the labor movement politically would increase the Histadrut's effectiveness in dealing with its opponents within the Jewish community in Palestine. But the creation of the Mapai Party in December 1930 had other goals as well — to forestall further capitalist inroads into Palestine by increasing labor's influence in world Zionist councils.

Labor Zionists in Palestine saw Weizmann's success in gaining non-Zionist membership in the new Jewish Agency as a threat to their authority. Most of the new members were wealthy capitalists who would presumably encourage the agency to back private projects outside Histadrut's control. Consequently, once the Ahdut Ha'Avodah and Hapoel Hatzair had merged to become the Mapai, the new party's leadership undertook an energetic campaign in Europe and America to gain support for representation on world Zionist councils. They gained 40 percent of the votes for delegates to the 1931 Zionist Congress and 44 percent in 1933. The Mapai also gained access to the Jewish Agency through election to the "non-Zionist" seats, and by 1933 its members had become the most powerful bloc within the agency. The merger of the labor factions thus enabled the Histadrut and the Mapai, under Ben-Gurion's direction, to increase their influence over Zionist politics in Palestine and to gain a major voice in world Zionist policymaking.

Revisionist Zionism Challenges Labor.   Still, the ascendance of labor Zionism did not go unchallenged. Its main opponents inside and outside Palestine were followers of Vladimir Jabotinsky, who in 1925 founded the Revisionist Party. A forceful writer and speaker, Jabotinsky believed that Zionism should focus solely on the creation of a Jewish state, ideally in conjunction with Great Britain. But if Britain were unwilling to act decisively, Jewish forces should be mobilized to attain statehood by military action against the British. The immediate achievement of a state outweighed all other considerations. Consequently, Jabotinsky viewed the Histadrut, and labor Zionism in general, "as a cancer on the national body politic."[18] Arguments about social goals and class structures weakened the Zionist effort. Furthermore, the Zionist experience showed that private investment and middle-class immigration were the true foundations of Zionist state formation; the Histadrut's emphasis on socialism and collectivity threatened rather than contributed to the likelihood of Zionist success.

The directness of Jabotinsky's appeal had a major impact on young Jews, especially in Europe where he formed youth groups (Betar) whose practices, patterned after the tactics and symbols of fascism, included wearing brown shirts and using special salutes.[19] These exercises were intended to emphasize the idea of strength and unity in contrast to the weakness and factionalism of the Zionist leadership and labor Zionism. Jabotinsky demanded the union of Palestine both east and west of the Jordan, thus incorporating into the prospective Jewish state the region of Transjordan. According to Jabotinsky, the fact that Weizmann had accepted Transjordan's separation from Palestine indicated his willingness to bow before British demands. During the latter half of the 1920s, Betar groups were formed in Palestine, while Revisionist Zionism gained increasing strength in Europe, from four delegates to the Zionist Congress in 1925 to twenty-one in 1929 and fifty-two in 1931.

In the process, antagonism and hatred developed between the labor Zionists and the Revisionists, memorialized by the murder in 1933 of perhaps the leading labor Zionist of his day, Chaim Arlosoroff. Revisionists were arrested and charged with the crime. Although they were ultimately released for lack of evidence, labor Zionists continued to believe that Revisionists were responsible for Arlosoroff's murder, enshrining a bitterness that has continued to the present. (Indeed, Menachem Begin, the self-styled inheritor of Jabotinsky's mantle of leadership, tried to reopen the trial in 1982 to prove that the Revisionists were innocent of the crime.) In general, labor Zionist and Revisionist rivalry persisted. The Histadrut's efforts to force Jewish employers to use only union members and its incitement of strikes were countered by Revisionist strike-breaking tactics and offers to supply their own workers to the Jewish bourgeoisie of Palestine, who often backed them against the Histadrut. These rivalries led Jabotinsky to break with the World Zionist Organization in 1935. He formed his "New Zionist Organization" which, at its first congress in Vienna, welcomed delegates who had been elected by 713,000 Revisionist voters, compared with the 635,000 voters for the WZO's nineteenth congress.[20]

Agudat Israel.   Another group of some significance, the Agudat Israel, was composed of Orthodox Jews who believed political Zionism to be heretical. During the 1920s it was quite active in its anti-Zionist activity, which included contacts with Palestinian Arabs and with anti-Zionist British parliamentarians, and it sent messages to the League of Nations attacking the British mandate's obligation to fulfill the Balfour Declaration. To the Zionists, the Agudat Israel's actions gave the "impression of treacherous fraternization with the greatest enemies of Zionism," and hostility to the Agudat Israel culminated in the assassination of its most ardent opponent of Zionism, Dr. Israel DeHahn.[21] The 1929 Western Wall riots, in which Arab assaults were mostly against Orthodox Jews who were unarmed, pushed the Agudat Israel to affiliate itself with the Zionist movement by 1931.

JEWS AND ARABS UNDER THE MANDATE: THE CLASH OF CONFLICTING ASPIRATIONS

Unlike the Arabs, the Zionists, with their organizations in Europe and the United States, were not isolated in a direct interaction with the mandate officials in Palestine. And whereas the Arabs were primarily concerned about the Zionist component in Britain's mandatory role, the Jews were much less concerned about an Arab threat to their position for most of this period. From the Zionist perspective, the Arabs would naturally object to Zionism—that was understood—but it was a problem for the British, not the Jews. Jews should be able to proceed with the building of the Jewish state while the British kept the Arabs at bay and ensured that they did not become a military or, more important, a political threat to the development of the Zionist program. Zionist leaders such as Weizmann were thus far more interested in British than in Arab policy, while Palestinian Zionist leaders such as Ben-Gurion were far more involved in internal matters regarding power within the Zionist community than with Jewish-Arab problems.

This did not mean that Zionists were unaware of Arab opposition. Ben-Gurion told fellow Zionists in 1918 that "there is no solution to the question of relations between Arabs and Jews. . . . And we must recognize this situation. . . . We as a nation want this country to be ours; the Arabs, as a nation, want this country to be theirs. . . ."[22] Resistance was to be expected. When arguing for a Jewish military force at the Zionist Congress in Prague in 1921, Jabotinsky declared succinctly that "I don't know of a single example in history where a country was colonised with the courteous consent of the population."[23] It was necessary that the British keep the Arabs in check so that the Jewish community could expand. This meant also keeping the Arab economy as separate as possible from the Jewish. That goal had been expressed as early as 1913 by Arthur Ruppin, a Zionist economic adviser, who foresaw the "creation of a Jewish milieu and of a closed Jewish economy in which producers, consumers, and middlemen will all be Jewish."[24] The Zionists did not intend to create a joint society with the indigenous Arabs nor to give them access to the modern Jewish economy that would emerge. The fact that this goal could not be easily achieved did not undermine its currency as a basic tenet of Zionist ideology.

For Ben-Gurion, any agreement with Palestinian Arabs on the nature of Palestine would be possible only when Arabs accepted Zionist hegemony. That would result from Arab recognition of the absolute nature of Zionist power and Arab weakness, a relationship that should be continually impressed on the Arabs, as Ben-Gurion did in talks with prominent Arabs in the 1930s. By 1936 he, like Jabotinsky, called for a Jewish state including Transjordan in conversations with Arabs who sought his opinion. Ben-Gurion viewed the Palestinian Arabs as part of a broader Arab nation deserving independence, but not in Palestine.[25] Thus, British paternalism toward the Arabs and attempts to assist them to develop political resources were viewed with concern but not outright alarm so long as the nature of Arab institutions did not threaten the basic Zionist interests, especially immigration but also land purchases. It was precisely here that the Palestinian Zionists had a great advantage over the Arab community because of their influence in the British mandatory government and the sympathetic ear they could generally rely on, especially in London.

Both communities in Palestine served the British with divided loyalties, their primary allegiance being to their own groups, but there were differences. The Arabs were a majority, but the percentage of their representation in government posts was less than their percentage of the total population, reflecting their more traditional educational experience. Furthermore, their inclusion was designed to "emasculate Arab nationalist opposition to the mandatory system" while excluding them from positions in which they might be able to exert influence against that system.[26] No Arab was nominated to be head of a government department. This policy was backed by many British officials in subordinate posts who, to many Jews, were pro-Arab because they were critical of Zionist policies. But British paternalism toward the Arabs contained an implicit assump-tion of their own superiority and an open unwillingness to deal with the Arabs in government on an equal basis. For example, one qualified Arab was given a responsible position only because British officials could pay him a lower salary than they would have had to pay an Englishman.[27]

The Jews, on the other hand, did not experience either the psychological or the economic disadvantages felt by the Arabs in the mandatory government. Their salaries were higher, and their participation was a means of furthering Zionist objectives that they themselves espoused. And in situations requiring major decisions by the mandatory power, the Jews could often rely on an offi-cial who was at least sympathetic to Zionism if not a committed member of the movement. Norman Bentwich, for example, was deeply involved in Zionist activities; he was also the senior judicial officer during the military administra-tion and retained his high legal status as attorney general in the mandatory gov-ernment. As such, he pushed successfully for the assignment of supervision of the Land Registry Department to the chief legal adviser and "enjoyed unparal-leled influence over land matters until High Commissioner Chancellor included these offices under his purview in 1929."[28] Leopold Amery, colonial secretary from 1924 to 1929, was an ardent Zionist, as was William Ormsby-Gore, colonial secretary from 1936 to 1938. And when the foundation stone for the Hebrew University of Jerusalem was laid in an elaborate ceremony in 1925, Arthur Bal-four gave the invocation; key dignitaries in attendance included Weizmann and Herbert Samuel (see Figure 3.2).

In addition, Zionist organizing was far superior to the rudimentary and fac-tionalized Arab efforts to influence British opinion. Both Arabs and Jews in the mandatory government passed information, but "Jewish intelligence gathering was more systematic, pervasive, and centralised."[29] Zionist officials had access to nearly all secret documents drawn up both in Jerusalem and in the Colonial Office in London, either through their own spies or through British officials sympathetic to their cause. When British policies were formulated in 1930 to restrict Zionist activity in Palestine, leading Zionists wrote the rebuttal that the British prime minister issued to counter that policy. In the Palestine gen-darmerie, only Jews were allowed to serve along with British soldiers; Arabs were excluded because of their anti-Zionist attitudes. Jews used their positions in the force to steal arms, which they transferred to the Hagana, the Jewish defense force under Histadrut control. By these means and by extensive arms smuggling, aided by Jewish customs officials, the Yishuv became fairly well armed, especially compared with the Arabs who had few weapons.

From the Zionist perspective, this was and should have been the natural order of things. Palestine was their country, and the role of the British was to fa-cilitate their acquisition of it. In such circumstances, concern for legality focused on British adherence to the terms of the mandate, not on the means by which the Yishuv could be consolidated. From the Arab perspective, the expansion of the Yishuv posed a recognized threat they should try to resist but many real-ized they could not do so through legal processes. Adherence to administrative

Figure 3.2 ■ **Laying the Cornerstone of the Hebrew University of Jerusalem, April 1925**

The founding of the Hebrew University of Jerusalem was seen by Zionists as a major step in the formation of a Jewish state, with the ceremony having a semi-official air with the presence of Arthur Balfour and High Commissioner Herbert Samuel. Those in the foreground from left to right are: Sir Arthur Balfour, issuer of the Balfour Declaration; Herbert Samuel; Judah Magnes, first chancellor and then first president of the Hebrew University and a backer of the idea of a bi-national Jewish-Arab state; and Chaim Weizmann.

procedures established under the mandate guaranteed the progressive loss of Arab Palestine. Eventually, violence became the only recourse.

In the meantime, the efforts of Arab notables to oppose Zionist strategy were undermined by their own rivalries and by British policies that undercut their economic position. As we have seen, intra-Arab antagonisms encouraged the al-Husayni–al-Nashashibi split and the rival parties that developed from them. During the mid-1920s, some members of the Palestine Zionist Executive exploited these differences and paid stipends to the moderates to encourage their opposition to the al-Husayni party. In some cases, they approached the Arabs, and in others, the Arabs approached the Zionists. On occasion Musa Kazim al-Husayni, president of the Arab Executive, received funds from H. Kalvarisky, head of the PZE's Arab Department.[30] By this method Zionist leaders could hope to influence those Arab leaders who were regarded as being in the forefront of opposition to Zionism. The most important area where Arabs seemed willing to undermine their own proclaimed hostility to Zionism was land sales to Jews, a process that reflects the complexity of intra-Arab as well as Arab-Jewish interaction.

The Land Question

To both Arabs and Jews, land was crucial to either the retention or the attainment of their respective national existences. Palestinian Arab society—especially its Muslim component, which was 90 percent of the total—worked on the land. In contrast, only a relatively small percentage of Jews in Palestine ever farmed, but Zionists considered the possession of land to be essential to the foundation of the future Jewish state. Zionists had recognized this issue from the beginning. They established the Jewish National Fund at the fifth Zionist Congress in 1901 to coordinate and centralize Jewish land purchases and to ensure that land thus bought would never again be available for sale; once bought, only Jews could work the land. This conception of the inalienable nature of the land purchased by the Jewish National Fund became central to official Zionist policy even though the actual amount bought by the fund—as opposed to other sources of Jewish land capital investment—remained relatively small. By 1914, for example, Jews owned slightly over 420,000 dunams, 20 percent of the land registered as owned by Jews in 1948, but only 4 percent of this amount belonged to the Jewish National Fund. The remainder, slightly over 400,000 dunams, was in private hands, 275,000 dunams of which had been settled and developed through Baron Edmond Rothschild's financial assistance, which amounted to some forty million francs by 1900 when he turned over his properties to the Jewish Colonisation Association. Private Jewish capital continued to play the major role in land purchase and development as well as in industry down to Israel's independence in 1948. Without this massive infusion of private capital and the assistance of Western specialists in modern agricultural techniques, Jewish settlements would have failed. It was precisely this access to outside funds that distinguished Jewish from Arab land practices following World War I.[31]

Patterns of Arab Land Ownership.   Arab landholdings varied considerably in size and in the nature of ownership or the assumption of right to the land. The most common form of holdings for village peasants was called *musha'a*, or collective village ownership. Each shareholder was allotted a fixed share of the total property for cultivation, and fields were redistributed periodically to give all shareholders equal access to the best land held under common ownership. Musha'a-owned land, or land worked according to musha'a principles, which amounted to between four and five million dunams after the war, was situated primarily in the plains and valley regions; individual ownership was the norm in the hill country.[32] Yet by 1923, approximately 75 percent of musha'a lands were owned by absentee landlords living in towns. This was due to the escalation of peasant indebtedness, which was always endemic but had increased during the war because of the devastation that Palestine suffered. As a rule, the former peasant shareholders remained on the land as tenants of those owning the right to the land in the village. Most musha'a land was deliberately unregistered in order to avoid taxes, a practice that continued under the British mandate.

In short, peasant society predominated in Arab Palestine, but many farmers did not own the land they tilled, although they might originally have "owned" it through the musha'a system. They had rights of cultivation only, but they often assumed it was a legal right, as opposed to one of sufferance. As a result,

> the Zionist ability to create a national home was significantly aided by the poor economic status of the Palestinian peasant during the Ottoman and Mandatory periods. Insufficient rainfall and draft animals, inefficient management of agricultural lands, small parcel size, lack of investment capital, indebtedness, and a general disillusionment with government aided Jewish nation building. Lack of interest in the majority of the fella-heen agricultural population by a socially distanced Palestinian Arab landowning elite also aided the development of the Jewish national home. The Palestinian Arab community was unquestionably a numerical majority throughout the Mandate, but its own financial distress gave the Zionist minority a distinct advantage in the struggle to control Palestine.[33]

This was particularly the case in the 1930s, when the peasants' sale of land to Zionists increased sharply. Until then the majority of sales were made by non-resident absentee landlords and resident large landholders.

As discussed in Chapter 1, changes in land laws in the second half of the nineteenth century had led peasants to transfer their titles of ownership to avoid conscription and tax assessments. This encouraged land purchases by Arabs residing outside Palestine and by leading urban families in the area. The number of large landholders is not known, but it is clear that they controlled directly or indirectly a significant amount of the cultivable land in Palestine. Excluding the Gaza and Beersheba districts in the south, where large tribal holdings were concentrated in family units, 116 families owned a total of 1.131 million dunams as of 1915. The size of these family holdings varied widely: the Sursuq properties, for example, amounted to 230,000 dunams and were concentrated principally in the Esdraelon Plain. Lands belonging to resident families might be distributed in various sectors of the region. The al-Husayni family was reputed to own about 50,000 dunams, the Abd al-Hadi family in the realm of 60,000.[34]

The disparities in land ownership can be shown by the following statistics for 1936, although they are incomplete and account for only about two-fifths of all property holdings. One hundred and fifty families owned 1,000 or more dunams. These properties were only 0.2 percent of all individual plots listed, but they took up 27.5 percent of the land area. Within this category, there were some immense land holdings; thirteen of these 150 families had holdings that incorporated 19.2 percent of the land area evaluated for all properties.[35] In contrast, property holdings under 100 dunams were 91.8 percent of the total but comprised 36.7 percent of the area.

In sum, plots larger than one hundred dunams were only 8.2 percent of all plots but encompassed 63.3 percent of the cultivable land. The situation of the peasants was even more precarious in view of the fact that a majority of those owning plots smaller than one hundred dunams actually had forty or fewer, when eighty to ninety was considered necessary for subsistence. But these contrasts in land holdings conceal the fact that the great landowners were land rich but cash poor. With nearly all their wealth in land, and barred from receiving outside capital, unlike the Zionists, some landowners would eventually sell land to the Zionists to gain money needed to maintain their prominence in Arab society, discussed in detail below.

Zionist Land Purchases.   The Zionists were well versed in the intricacies of Arab land ownership even before World War I, and British officials relied on them for information as they began to draft land laws in 1918–1919. By that time nonresident owners held significant portions of Palestinian land, about 500,000 dunams. Zionist land agents focused on them, especially the Sursuqs with whom they had been negotiating since before the war. In general the Zionists hoped to buy large properties, both for reasons of efficiency in terms of integrating Jewish-held lands and for political reasons. Norman Bentwich, when drafting the first Land Transfer Ordinance, issued in 1920, calculated that Zionist purchases from the Palestinian notables would weaken the latter's political and social prestige and thus undermine Arab opposition to Zionism by discrediting its leadership.

Zionists were immediately successful in arranging for the purchase of approximately 240,000 dunams in the Esdraelon Plain (to be called the Jezreel), primarily from the Sursuq family, between 1921 and 1925. The buyers were the Jewish National Fund and the American Zion Commonwealth, a private company. The cost was £800,000, compared with an initial cost to the Sursuqs of £20,000.[36] But Zionists also succeeded in buying land from Palestinian Arab notables, some of whom were prominent in the nationalist movement, especially after 1927. Tables listing Zionist land purchases from 1878 to 1936, admittedly restricted to 55.4 percent of total acquisitions, indicate that during this period 90.6 percent was bought from large landowners and only 9.4 percent from peasants. When broken down further, the statistics indicate that although nonresident landowners sold 80 percent of the land bought by Jews between 1920 and 1927, they sold only about 30 percent of the land bought between 1928 and 1936. The difference in the latter period was made up by Palestinian Arab landlords, who sold about 50 percent of the properties bought by Jews, and by peasants, who sold about 20 percent.[37]

The reasons for the increasing willingness of the Palestinians, whether large or small landholders, to sell land to Zionists were primarily economic. As the Muslim-Christian Association recognized in 1920, "the Jewish population was the only financially viable segment of Palestine's population at the conclusion of World War I."[38] Zionist organizations, though registered in Palestine and staffed by Jews living there, had access to external sources of capital, the only source of their financing. In contrast, Palestinian Arab families lacked capital and had no ready access to outside funds. Their wealth was in land, and the major means of maintaining or seeking to increase it was through land speculation. This ultimately meant the sale of land to Jews to gain cash that enabled the notables to preserve their economic and political status in the Arab community. As a consequence, only Zionist organizations could afford to buy large land areas owned by nonresident Arabs who themselves, at least initially, were forbidden by the Land Transfer Ordinance of 1920 from purchasing more land in Palestine. Arab notables retained possession of most of their land, but the fact that they might sell portions of it to the very Zionists they condemned fueled Zionist optimism about the success of their endeavors.

The procedures followed in the sale of such lands varied and often required the circumvention of existing regulations. There was, however, an ongoing problem for both sides, the question of the fate of those who worked the land, whether tenants—peasants who often assumed customary rights to work the land—or a larger class of agricultural laborers. Stipulations in the Land Transfer Ordinance of 1920 required that the peasants (tenants) be left an area sufficient for their sustenance in case the land changed hands. But the Jewish purchasers linked to Labor Zionism wanted land without tenants when they took possession, so that it could automatically revert to inalienable Jewish ownership. They thus frequently had clauses inserted in the sales agreements stating that properties would be free of tenants when handed over to them. The Arab sellers, whether the actual owners or agents, were often eager to comply, and the tenants usually had little leverage, being indebted to their landlords or to money lenders. Thus they usually accepted monetary compensation from buyers, either willingly or under compulsion, meaning that the right of these tenants to maintenance areas was ignored despite their supposed protection. The status of a "tenant in occupation" was not legally defined until 1929. The much larger sectors of agricultural laborers and small landowners who lived on their properties had no protection under the law.[39]

The Landless Arab Problem.   As a result, thousands of Arabs who worked the land for their livelihood were forced to leave, many without compensation because they did not qualify as tenants; the compensation itself averaged an estimated one year's wages. In some cases, when the land area sold was extremely large and affected many tenants, they were given the option to stay on a portion of the property. For example, 688 tenant families lived on the Sursuq lands. Each family could accept compensation of £39, about $195 per family, or opt to accept land instead of money, with the option to purchase it after six years; purchase was highly unlikely because they had no capital. Most left, a displacement of about 3,000 people among the tenant families, although many estimate that the total displacement was closer to 8,000.[40] When efforts were made in 1930–1931 to determine the extent of the landless Arab problem, the British government accepted in essence the Jewish Agency's definition of what constituted a "landless Arab," one that referred to tenant cultivators only. Consequently, a much larger category of persons who were actually landless as a result of Jewish land purchases was automatically excluded, especially "owners who habitually let their lands, ploughmen and persons who, from debt or bad seasons or other causes, had ceased to be cultivators and had become laborers, etc."[41] In consequence, the Landless Arab Inquiry of 1931–1933 accepted fewer than 900 claims of displacement out of a total of nearly 4,000, a major propaganda victory for the Jewish Agency.

The Landless Arab Inquiry was itself the outgrowth of a major investigation of conditions in Palestine ordered by London following the riots in August 1929 that had left many Jews and Arabs dead. This explosion of Arab hatred and frustration against the Jews, the first since 1921, stemmed from both the Arab fear of Jewish infringement on their territory in general and specific resentment over what they saw as a threat to the most sacred Muslim site in Jerusalem, an area also holy to Jews. The pressures brought to bear on the leaders of both camps indicate the complexity of the relationships within each community and between them. Because of the riots, the Arab community lost its chance to be represented politically in the mandate structure, a goal that had seemed within reach in early 1929.

The Conflict over the Western Wall, 1928–1929

To the Jews, the Western Wall (Wailing Wall) was the last remnant of the outer wall that had surrounded Herod's temple, which had been built on the presumed site of Solomon's temple. It was thus a relic of the sanctuary of ancient Israel, the most holy place in Judaism and a focal point of religious and national pride. To the Muslims, the wall was the outer perimeter of the Haram al-Sharif, the third-holiest site in Islam, the Temple Mount on which they had built the al-Aqsa Mosque and the Dome of the Rock. As we have seen, the latter commemorated the place from which, according to Muslim belief, the Prophet Muhammad had ascended to heaven on his night journey. The wall was itself holy to the Muslims because Muhammad had tethered his horse, al-Buraq, to it before his ascension; the Muslims gave the wall the horse's name. The wall was administered by funds from a charitable estate, which made it part of a religious foundation, the Maghrebi waqf, named after the Moroccans who inhabited the area.

Jews had always prayed at the wall, which abutted a narrow lane separating it from the houses of the Muslims of that quarter. During the nineteenth century, as the Jewish population of Jerusalem increased and Jews began to acquire protection from foreign consuls, they attempted to change longstanding practices by bringing chairs to the wall on which the elderly could rest and a screen to divide male and female worshippers. Muslim leaders opposed such amendments, fearful that any alteration of the status quo could be then used to argue for further changes, with Jewish demands backed in Istanbul by foreign influence, a natural response in an environment in which different Christian groups sought to gain control of certain holy places at the expense of rivals.

With the British assumption of power, matters became increasingly politicized. The terms of the mandate called for maintaining the status quo in practices related to religious sites. However, various Zionist leaders, including Weizmann in 1919, proposed buying the wall from the Maghrebi waqf. One such suggestion in 1926, by Colonel Frederick Kisch of the PZE, had the intent to force the Moroccans out of their houses in the area adjacent to the wall and to demolish the buildings in order to create a broader area for the worshippers (this was finally done after the 1967 war). In his memo, Kisch added that the "political effect would be very great," meaning that Palestinian Muslims would be forced to recognize Zionist power.[42] Muslims viewed Jewish attempts to buy the wall as an example of the Zionist wish to take over Palestine. Once the Supreme Muslim Council was established in 1922, Hajj Amin al-Husayni stressed the sacred Muslim character of the property and challenged Zionist attempts to modify the conditions of prayer permitted to Jews. British officials backed Muslim claims to supervision of the entire area, but in an atmosphere of increasing tension. Al-Husayni sent emissaries to seek financial aid from other Muslim countries, helped by the discovery of a painting done in the latter part of the nineteenth century which showed the Dome of the Rock crowned by the Star of David, the symbol of Jewish nationalism. Meanwhile, Weizmann pursued efforts to buy the wall and had collected £61,000 by December 1928. By then the friction had intensified.

On the Jewish Day of Atonement (Yom Kippur), September 24, 1928, Jews brought a screen to the wall to divide male and female worshippers. The screen blocked the eleven-foot-wide alley along which the inhabitants of the quarter passed daily. The incident was not unique in the history of contention for greater Jewish access to the wall and Arab resistance to it. Arab protests to the British authorities brought from them a request that the screen be removed to preserve the status quo. When it remained there into the next day, September 25, further Arab complaints led the police to remove the screen, which had to be done forcibly because of some resistance by the worshippers. From here matters escalated. Jewish reaction was swift, not only inside Palestine but outside as well. Leading Zionist officials and the chief rabbi protested to the British government in London and the League of Nations. Claims of police brutality were spread about, and one Jewish paper compared the Muslims with the Russians who participated in pogroms, even though no Muslims had taken part in the events at the wall. The matter had suddenly become a conflict beyond the scope of earlier protests and had taken on political as well as religious significance.[43]

The Muslim response came at the beginning of October, when Hajj Amin al-Husayni, as head of the Supreme Muslim Council, reacted to Jewish demands that the wall be turned over to them. His official defense of the Muslim position to British administrators was accompanied by public calls to the Muslim community to be alert to the threat to al-Buraq, and a committee to defend the wall was formed, presumably with his encouragement. Although the crisis enabled him to enhance his position within the Arab community, Jewish threats and political and religious propaganda sparked Muslim concern and seemed to validate his claims. Weizmann wrote in an open letter to the Yishuv, published in November 1928, that the only feasible solution to the problem of access to the wall was to "pour Jews into Palestine" and gain control of their ancient homeland, thus implicitly resolving the wall issue because Jewish sovereignty would have been established. The linkage of the wall question with Jewish sovereignty was to Muslims proof of their initial suspicions. For both communities the matter was now thoroughly politicized.[44]

No major incidents occurred for nearly a year. Then, in July 1929, the mufti resumed building activities around the wall, apparently hoping to pressure the British government to issue a statement supporting Muslim ownership of the property. The Zionists raised the alarm, especially Jabotinsky's Revisionist Party, which formed a committee for a defense of the wall to match the Muslims'. One rightist paper called for rebuilding the temple, and Rabbi Kook, spiritual leader of the Jewish community, lauded young Jews "willing to sacrifice their lives in the cause of their Holy Place."[45] On August 15, members of Betar, the Revisionist Party's youth organization, marched to the wall, raised the Zionist flag, and sang the Zionist anthem. The next day, a Friday, the Muslim Sabbath saw thousands of Arabs march to the wall and burn the slips of paper inscribed with prayers inserted by Jews. Sermons calling on Muslims to defend the wall aroused strong emotions.

Matters came to a head on Friday, August 23, as rumors spread that Jews were planning an attack on the al-Aqsa mosque. Militants poured in from outlying areas and, inspired by radical speakers, prepared to defend the Haram al-Sharif. When the mufti tried to calm the mob, some accused him of betraying Islam. Arabs then poured out to attack Jewish quarters, initially in Jerusalem and later in other towns. Orthodox Jews suffered the most, as they were unarmed; sixty-four were killed in Hebron and others in Safad. Zionist groups retaliated, at one point invading a mosque in Jaffa to kill a religious official and six others. The rampage lasted nearly a week, with 133 Jews and 116 Arabs killed and many more wounded. Most Arab casualties were inflicted by British reinforcements called in to bolster the undermanned British police force. The ancient Jewish community of Hebron was evacuated, even though many of its inhabitants had been saved by Arab neighbors and the bravery of the one British policeman there.

Attribution of responsibility for the outbreak has varied, some accusing the mufti of direct responsibility and others considering the Betar demonstration of August 15 as the catalyst for what followed. What seems clear is that the struggle for control of the Western Wall evolved from a purely religious matter of long standing into a political confrontation in which both the hopes and the

Figure 3.3 ■ Palestinian Delegation Protesting British Policy following the Western Wall Riots, 1929

Among this group of Palestinian dignitaries are from left to right, foreground: Raghib al-Nashashibi (light suit); Alfred Roch, a Palestinian Catholic; Hajj Amin al-Husayni in Arab dress; and Musa Kazim al-Husayni, former mayor of Jerusalem whom the British had ousted and replaced with al-Nashashibi.

fears of the respective populations were fused. Rumors fueled alarm on both sides, a classic response in quarters where each sector felt threatened by the other. Ironically, the ultimate result of the outbreak was to entrench Hajj Amin al-Husayni as leader of the Palestinian Arabs while at the same time weakening Arab ability to influence British policy (see Figure 3.3).

Investigations and Retractions: The Passfield White Paper

The British appointed a commission, led by Sir Walter Shaw, to investigate the 1929 riots and to propose policies to prevent their recurrence. A majority of the commission absolved Hajj Amin al-Husayni of direct responsibility and went on to present what they considered to be the underlying causes of Arab unrest. The Shaw Report, published in March 1930, identified Zionist immigration and land practices as the reasons for the 1929 riots. The report declared that "a landless and discontented class is being created" and it called for limitations on the transfer of land to non-Arabs. It concluded that

> the fundamental cause [of the outbreak] is the Arab feeling of animosity and hostility towards the Jews consequent on the disappointment of their political and national aspirations and fear for their economic future. . . .

> The feeling as it exists today is based on the two-fold fear of the Arabs that by Jewish immigration and land purchases they may be deprived of their livelihood and placed under the economic domination of the Jews.[46]

The report called for a more explicit British policy regulating land transfers and immigration, one that would, if implemented, sharply curtail the Jews' ability to pursue their national goals.

These recommendations challenged the economic underpinnings of the mandate and thereby posed a domestic political threat to the British government, the minority cabinet of Ramsey MacDonald. The curtailment of land transfers to Jews would mean the loss of tax revenues and a reduction in the influx of Jewish capital brought by immigrants. These revenues and tax payments helped fund social services and administrative costs, allowing the British to allot a comparatively small amount of their own money to military needs. The financial cost of administering Palestine would rise, placing a greater economic burden on the British taxpayers. One of the ironies of the dilemma was that Jewish immigration and the capital generated by it permitted the British to maintain their imperial presence at comparatively little expense, whereas this same immigration aroused Arab alarm and violence, which threatened the security of the British position there.

The MacDonald cabinet now confronted calls for the formation of a new commission to reverse the Shaw findings, led by the authors of Britain's Palestine policy, who were now in the conservative opposition and in close contact with the Zionist leadership in London. MacDonald compromised by creating an investigatory committee to examine the economic issues pertaining to land and immigration, headed by Sir John Hope-Simpson. This step enabled MacDonald to defer his decision until Hope-Simpson completed his inquiry. Nevertheless, Jewish immigration was suspended temporarily, leading the Zionists to prepare for a struggle to confront MacDonald if Hope-Simpson's conclusions ratified those already expressed in the Shaw Report.

In the meantime, Zionist officials in Palestine tried to persuade Hope-Simpson that the landless Arab question was insignificant; some hoped also that he might consider the unilateral transfer of Arabs to Transjordan, since he had directed Greek-Turkish population exchanges following the Treaty of Lausanne in 1923.[47] He, however, became increasingly sympathetic to the Arab case and reached conclusions as threatening to Zionist hopes as were those of the Shaw Report. Hope-Simpson attacked Jewish exclusionary labor policies and viewed them as contributing to Arab unemployment. He pointed out that although Article 6 of the mandate required British permission for "close settlement of the Jews on the land," it also demanded that "ensuring the rights and positions of other sections of the population" not be "prejudiced by Jewish immigration and settlement."[48] According to Hope-Simpson, Jewish labor policies and the practice of making Jewish-bought land inalienable violated the second clause of the article, which should have been given equal if not more weight than that referring to Jewish settlement.

Hope-Simpson's analysis and recommendations were incorporated into the Passfield White Paper of October 1930. In it, Lord Passfield, the colonial secretary, criticized Jewish colonization policies and the immigration practices of the Histadrut that focused on Jewish labor, arguing that consideration must be given to all the unemployed in Palestine. The White Paper called on Jewish leaders to make "concessions . . . in regard to the independent and separatist ideas which have developed in some quarters in respect of the Jewish National Home." It asked the Arabs to recognize "the facts of the situation," which presumably meant accepting the Jews then living in Palestine.[49]

The Passfield White Paper aroused a furor that seemed to threaten the stability of the MacDonald government. Weizmann resigned as head of the World Zionist Organization and the Jewish Agency. Other leading Zionists followed suit, and conservative parliamentarians attacked the White Paper and called for its repudiation. Politically weak and alarmed at the threat of Jewish pressure on the U.S. government to bring economic sanctions against Great Britain, MacDonald entered into discussions with Weizmann, the intermediary being MacDonald's son, Malcolm, an ardent Zionist himself. MacDonald then issued a letter to Weizmann, in effect dictated by Weizmann and his colleagues, that repudiated the Passfield White Paper after talks during which Weizmann told the prime minister: "We want it made clear that the letter to me containing the authoritative interpretation of the White Paper shall be the basis of the law in Palestine."[50] The British government's capitulation ensured that the Jewish community would expand, aided during the 1930s by European events — most specifically the rise of Adolf Hitler in Germany and the ensuing exodus of many German Jews to Palestine.

EUROPEAN CRISES AND THEIR REPERCUSSIONS: YISHUV EXPANSION AND ARAB REBELLION

Adolf Hitler was sworn in as chancellor of Germany on January 30, 1933. He quickly had laws passed that barred Jewish participation in many professional and commercial activities. The Nuremberg laws of July 1935 that restricted citizenship to Aryans and banned marriage or any type of sexual relationship between Germans and Jews triggered German Jewish emigration, although a majority of those leaving did not go to Palestine. Those who did were able to transfer much of their money, thanks to agreements reached between Zionist leaders and the Nazi government.[51] Indeed, the Nazis were so eager to get rid of the German Jews that they permitted the Zionist organization to establish vocational training camps in Germany to train future immigrants. The SS officer in charge of facilitating these arrangements was Adolf Eichmann, later to be placed on trial in Israel for Holocaust crimes.[52]

German Jewish immigration to Palestine coincided with increased Jewish immigration from Eastern Europe, especially Poland. Between 1933 and 1935 the Jewish population of Palestine doubled: nearly one-half of these immigrants were Polish and about one-fifth were German. This influx, far more middle class than working class in its composition, brought a major infusion of capital into Palestine, whose urban and Jewish sectors underwent an economic boom in the mid-1930s, despite the worldwide Depression. Most immigrants settled in the cities, which grew rapidly. Tel Aviv, including Jaffa, expanded from 46,000 inhabitants in 1931 to 135,000 in 1935; Haifa's Jewish population went from 16,000 to 40,000 during the same period. Encouraged by the influx of German Jewish funds, industry expanded: the number of industrial firms increased from 6,000 in 1930 to 14,000 in 1937.[53] The Yishuv was thus able to consolidate itself during the mid-1930s to a point that it was much more stable than it had been in 1931 and in a stronger position to argue against continuing Arab requests for a legislative council on which they would be represented.

The question of a legislative council had been mentioned in the Passfield White Paper but was not considered until 1933, at which time it became clear that Zionist opposition remained, especially that of the Yishuv in Palestine. Arab leaders favored the idea, al-Nashashibi openly and the al-Husayni faction privately. In return Arab leaders hoped that the British would declare the Jewish National Home to have been achieved, thus freezing immigration and the scope of the Jewish community in Palestine. The new high commissioner, Sir Arthur Wauchope, finally presented a specific proposal in December 1935, albeit in the face of the opposition of the Zionist Congress; its delegates had rejected the idea two months earlier and had called for the resettlement of Palestinian Arabs elsewhere, especially to Transjordan. With Jewish opposition in the open, the British government invited Arab leaders to London to discuss the matter. But before they left Palestine, the matter was taken up in both the House of Lords and the House of Commons on the initiative of British parliamentarians favorable to the Zionist cause. They scuttled the proposals, leaving the British government with nothing to present to the Arabs once they reached London.

British parliamentary rejection of the council idea, at a time when Arab leaders were leaning toward participation and recognition of the mandate as it then existed, confirmed to the Arabs the scope of Zionist power and influence in the British government, even though Zionist officials had neither initiated nor requested the action. Nevertheless, the motions put forth by British legislators sympathetic to the Zionist cause reflected Weizmann's wish to delay discussion of the matter to enable continuing Jewish immigration and land purchases, which would further consolidate the Jewish presence in Palestine. It was precisely these concerns that had led Arab leaders to move toward acceptance of the legislative council idea. They hoped to stem the tide of immigrants. But British legislators were concerned with conditions in Germany and Eastern Europe that caused Jews to flee, not the impact of the Jewish plight and emigration on Arabs in Palestine. For the Arabs, however, this was one final rejection, coming at a time when the surrounding Arab populations in Egypt and Syria seemed to be moving toward greater self-rule under either British or French sway. More radical Arabs had already been advocating armed resistance. Now it erupted into what became known as the Arab Revolt, which began in April 1936.

The Arab Revolt: Its Roots and Impact on Palestine

If the early 1930s were a time of triumph for the Zionists, they marked a continuation of divisiveness and economic disarray for the Palestinian Arabs. Not only had the Zionists thwarted the Passfield White Paper through the MacDonald letter, they had also written the terms of the Landless Arab Inquiry so that fewer than 900 claims were deemed valid, permitting them to argue that Zionist settlement efforts had little or no impact on Arab peasant society. Initially eager to resolve the landless Arab question because unrest would require further expenditures to maintain public order, the British government had backed down in 1933 in the face of carefully orchestrated Zionist efforts to respond to any and all charges brought before British officials investigating the issue. Arab leaders failed to respond decisively to British findings because Lewis French, the head of the Landless Arab Inquiry, revealed that a number of leading Arab families had been involved in selling land to Jews. This disclosure intensified antagonism between Hajj Amin al-Husayni and the more moderate faction led by the al-Nashashibis and Musa Kazim al-Husayni, head of the Arab Executive until his death in 1934. As head of the Supreme Muslim Council and leader of the fight to preserve the Western Wall under Muslim control, Hajj Amin had gained a great deal of prestige during 1929 and had used it to enhance his political stature and influence. His followers publicized the news of Arab land sales to Jews and castigated the Arab Executive for its apathy in confronting this situation. At the same time, Hajj Amin retained correct relations with British officials to preserve his status as mufti and to be in a position to deal with the British in trying to stop Zionist gains in Palestine.

Zionism and the Arab Economy.   Yet despite increasing Arab concern about land sales to Jews, economic conditions during the 1930s were forcing more Arabs, often of the smaller landholding class, to sell portions of their land just to survive. Indeed, "in the early 1930s, Arab land sales and Jewish land purchases contributed to the evolution of an Arab landless class"[54] during the very period when the Landless Arab Inquiry concluded that the problem was negligible. As we have noted, Palestine experienced something of an economic boom during the 1930s, but it was due to the influx of Jewish capital and it benefited the Jewish economy almost exclusively, although there was some spin-off to the Arab urban economy and to Arabs who left the land to work in construction trades in the rapidly expanding cities. Many of these workers became part of an expanding Arab proletariat surviving on the edge of Jewish urban centers. One report stated that in Haifa in the mid-1930s, 11,160 Arab workers were living in 2,500 gasoline-can huts.[55] Arab access to certain jobs was restricted by British policies. In the public works sector, the Jewish Agency gained British agreement to employ Arabs and Jews on a fifty-fifty basis rather than on that of population ratios, which would have been approximately 70 percent Arab to 30 percent Jewish. The justification was that Jews provided 50 percent of the tax revenues in Palestine. This reflected the modern European economy installed by the Jews, but the rationale contributed to Arab unemployment.

As noted, the majority of the Arab population, and nearly 90 percent of the Muslims, lived on the land. As peasants and small landholders, their economic situation had deteriorated continually since the end of World War I. In addition, Palestine's status as a mandate under European control placed it in a disadvantageous economic position, able to be exploited in classic colonial fashion. Article 18 of the mandate established that Palestine could not create discriminatory tariffs against members of the League of Nations. It thus became an open market into which countries with surpluses could dump both agricultural and industrial goods, a frequent practice after the onset of the Depression.[56] This worked totally to the disadvantage of the Arab economy in Palestine. Wheat production dropped in the early 1930s as imports increased, driving peasants further into debt to Arab moneylenders, often doubling as grain merchants, who demanded cash rather than kind.[57] As a result, many peasants seem to have left the land for possible work in the cities or for Jewish citrus-grove owners, themselves under attack by the Histadrut for using non-Jewish labor. Equally significant from 1931 onward was the increasing number of land sales to Jews by smaller landholders in need of capital who were willing to sell portions of their land to try to survive in adverse times. This pattern, fueled by the weakening economic condition of much of the Arab peasantry, continued throughout the 1930s and explains why the peasants formed the basis of support for the Arab Revolt when it erupted in 1936.

Arab Factions Emerge.   Equally important to the growth of more overt Arab resistance was the emergence of a younger generation of Arabs, educated under the mandate and advocating more open defiance of British authority (see Figure 3.4). Many had ties to Hajj Amin al-Husayni and backed his more hostile stance against Zionist policies, which increasingly incorporated Islamic themes. Some were influenced by the example of organized youth in Italy and Germany, as were Jabotinsky's Betar members. They encouraged the formation of Boy Scout troops and branches of the Young Men's Muslim Association as a means of creating cadres ready to confront Zionist immigration or British authority. A Congress of Arab Youth met for the first time in January 1932, but it could not escape the imprint of the al-Husayni–al-Nashashibi rift. The formation of the Istiqlal (Independence) Party in August 1932 marked a new phase in Palestinian politics. It advocated pan-Arab unity as the only solution to the Arab plight in Palestine and harked back to the Greater Syria themes prominent during Faysal's rule in Damascus from 1918 to 1920.

Figure 3.4 ■ Arabs Protesting Zionist Immigration, Jerusalem, 1933

With Hitler's rise to power, Jewish immigration began to increase, leading to more determined Arab protests, which were met with a forceful British response, as indicated here.

The Istiqlalists, primarily from northern Palestine, especially Nablus, shared an aversion to the factionalism rampant among the leading Jerusalem families in the early 1930s. Raghib al-Nashashibi had established the National Defense Party in December 1934 to represent his opposition to the al-Husayni bloc, which in turn created the Palestine Arab Party in March 1935. In June, Husayn al-Khalidi, scion of another leading Jerusalem family and victor over Raghib al-Nashashibi in elections for mayor of Jerusalem in late 1934, formed the Reform Party. Although both al-Khalidi and al-Nashashibi opposed the power of Hajj Amin al-Husayni, they were rivals themselves, and al-Nashashibi sought to undermine al-Khalidi at every opportunity.[58] But both agreed in their preference for political rather than militant opposition to British policies whereas Hajj Amin, though considering the Istiqlal a challenge to his authority, seems to have sympathized with its call for active armed resistance to Zionism. And his use of Muslim ideology to seek external Islamic assistance to confront Zionism blended at times with the pan-Arab ideas of the Istiqlal.

Al-Qassam and the Outbreak of Violence.   Several secret societies were formed during the early 1930s, one led by Abd al-Qadir al-Husayni, the son of Musa Kazim, who himself preferred al-Nashashibi moderation and sought an accommodation with the mandatory authorities; generational cleavages were beginning to appear. The younger al-Husayni founded an organization called Holy War and began buying arms in preparation for open resistance. Finally, there was a group led by a Muslim shaykh, Izz al-Din al-Qassam, and two founding members of the Istiqlal. Al-Qassam called for rejection of the influences of modern culture as a precursor to open resistance against the British. He preached for years in Haifa and its environs, calling for strict adherence to Muslim principles and finding an audience among a population becoming progressively impoverished in the face of an influx of Jewish immigrants and the great expansion of Haifa itself under their impact. Al-Qassam and two followers were killed in November 1935 after they had killed a Jewish policeman whom they had encountered while preparing for open resistance.

Al-Qassam's death occurred shortly after a major Jewish arms smuggling operation had been discovered at the Jaffa port. This, and the inability of British officials to locate the addressee, aroused Arab alarm; their arms purchases were rudimentary compared with Jewish efforts, which had resulted, according to a 1937 official British estimate, in a stockpiling of weapons and ammunition sufficient to arm an army of 10,000.[59] These developments, coupled with increasing Arab unemployment, led to calls for a strike and demands for greater vigilance by the mandatory authorities over Jewish arms smuggling. Although concerned, High Commissioner Wauchope felt that the granting of a legislative council would satisfy Arab grievances because he knew that Hajj Amin al-Husayni, along with the al-Nashashibis, was willing to accept the proposal. Palestinian Arab expectations of greater representation had been encouraged by developments in Egypt and Syria where popular demonstrations in late 1935 had led to

British and French willingness to negotiate new treaties with Egyptian and Syrian nationalists in early 1936. In this atmosphere, Zionist opposition and the council proposal's rejection by the British Parliament provided the spark for open revolt.

With the outbreak of Arab attacks on Jews in April 1936, the feuding Arab factions joined forces in a temporary display of unity to form the Arab Higher Committee. The committee called for a general strike by all Arab workers and government employees, a boycott of Jewish goods and sales to Jews, and attacks on Jews, Jewish settlements, and British forces. This first stage of the revolt lasted from mid-April to early November 1936. In many ways it was unsuccessful. For example, Arab workers in major Jewish enterprises often could not strike effectively because they would simply be replaced by Jewish workers. For Arab government employees to strike would mean the loss of any ability to influence government policies; they pledged a tenth of their salary instead. And where a strike was sustained, as in the closing of the port of Jaffa, then the only large port for Palestine, the Jewish Agency leadership petitioned successfully to have Tel Aviv developed as a port for Jewish goods. Here, as in other instances, the strike simply encouraged further Zionist self-reliance.

Fighting shifted gradually to the countryside, where armed bands mined roads and sought to disrupt transportation. Palestinian groups were aided by other Arabs, most notably Fawzi al-Qawuqji, a Lebanese-born officer in the Iraqi army who led occasional attacks on British forces. By early fall, almost 20,000 British troops had arrived and quickly quelled Arab resistance. In early November, the leaders of the Arab Higher Committee were willing to call off the strike, in part because of its relative failure and in part thanks to mediation by the ministers of surrounding Arab states, who tried to achieve a peaceful settlement of the matter, albeit one favorable to the Palestinian Arab cause.[60] In an apparent reward for Arab efforts, the Colonial Office approved only 1,800 Jewish entry permits for the period of October to March 1937, 17 percent of the 11,200 requested by the Jewish Agency.[61]

The Peel Commission and Partition.   With hostilities ended, the Peel Commission—appointed in May to investigate the motives for Arab resistance—arrived and received testimony from Jews and Arabs regarding the underlying causes of unrest. The Zionists called for unlimited immigration and the purchase of land as a matter of right, whereas Hajj Amin demanded that Palestine be declared an Arab state in which there would be no place for the nearly 400,000 Jews who had immigrated since World War I; his stance signaled a major reversal of the statement he had issued in 1935, accepting the mandate and its existing Jewish community. The commission published its findings in July 1937 (see Document 3.2) and concluded that the Palestine Mandate was not viable. Its terms were impossible to sustain in themselves but especially in the face of the unyielding mutual hostility found in the conflicting demands for statehood made by the Arabs and the Jews. According to the stipulations of the mandate, Arab objections to Jewish immigration and land purchases were unwarranted, but since Jewish statehood could come about only by imposing it on a hostile Arab population, it too was contrary to the mandate, which was supposed to guard Arab as well as Jewish interests. It was, in the end, a case of "right against right," a situation that the Peel Report believed could be resolved only through the partition of Palestine into separate independent Arab and Jewish states. Great Britain would remain as a mandatory power in a zone including the holy places (see Map 3.1). The Peel Commission awarded to the proposed Jewish state about 20 percent of Palestine, comprising the northern region of the Galilee and the Jezreel Plain (Esdraelon) south of Nazareth and the coastal plain from the Lebanese border to a point south of Jaffa, which itself would remain Arab. The Arabs were granted the remainder of the area, which meant central Palestine from slightly below Nazareth and the Negev. The commission envisaged Arab Palestine being united with Transjordan, presumably under the rule of Amir Abdullah. Jerusalem and Bethlehem would be under British mandatory control, with access to the sea.[62]

Arab opposition to partition was swift. Though the Arab state would comprise about 80 percent of post-1922 Palestine, the most fertile land had been granted to the Jews, and 250,000 Arabs living in the Galilee would have to be evacuated. The area awarded to the Jews contained a nearly equal number of Arabs, whereas the Arab area was 90 percent Arab in composition. Palestinian Jews would achieve an independent state but the Arab state might be under Hashemite rule, not Palestinian. Neighboring Arab governments joined the Arab Higher Committee in condemning the proposals, and an Arab congress met in Bludan, Syria, in September 1937 and called for united Arab resistance to world Jewry and its efforts to establish a state in Palestine. Palestine was becoming an Arab, as opposed to a purely Palestinian Arab, issue (see Figure 3.5).

The Zionist response to the partition proposal was mixed, if cautiously favorable. In the face of strong opposition, Ben-Gurion and Weizmann found themselves united in tentatively accepting partition in principle but demanding larger, if unspecified, borders. For them the issue was one of sovereignty. They would have an independent state with rights to unlimited immigration, a crucial point at a time when more and more Jews were beginning to flee anti-Semitism in Central and Eastern Europe. Whatever the original applicability of the Zionist claim that Palestine would be a haven for world Jewry, it now seemed justified. Furthermore, Weizmann and Ben-Gurion did not feel they had to be bound by the borders proposed. These could be considered temporary boundaries to be expanded in the future. As one British member of Parliament favorable to the

Map 3.1 ■ Peel Commission Partition Plan, 1937   ▶

The proposed Arab state, to be linked to Transjordan, was much larger in territory than the proposed Jewish state but much poorer in wealth and agricultural land, leading the commission to propose subsidies from the wealthier Jewish sector.

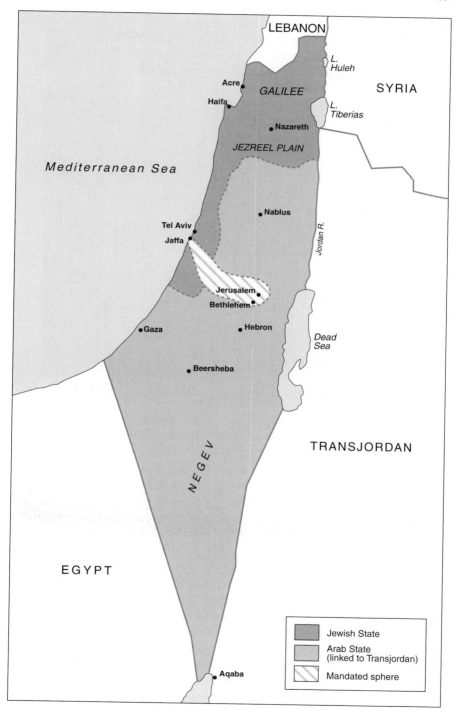

LEBANON

L.
Huleh

SYRIA

Acre

GALILEE

Haifa

L.
Tiberias

Nazareth

JEZREEL PLAIN

Mediterranean Sea

Nablus

Tel Aviv

Jaffa

Jordan R.

Jerusalem

Bethlehem

Gaza

Hebron

Dead
Sea

Beersheba

N E G E V

TRANSJORDAN

EGYPT

Aqaba

Jewish State

Arab State
(linked to Transjordan)

Mandated sphere

Figure 3.5 ■ **Palestinian Christian Women Wear Keffiyeh as the Arab Revolt Erupts, August 1937**

These Palestinian Christian women, faces unveiled, have adopted the keffiyeh head-dress to signify Palestinian national unity in the midst of Arab protests and rebellion.

Zionists declared, "I hope that the Jews will treat it merely as a stepping-off ground for further advance." And Ben-Gurion announced at the World Zionist Congress in August that although "there could be no question . . . of giving up any part of the Land of Israel, . . . it was arguable that the ultimate goal would be achieved most quickly by accepting the Peel proposals."[63] The congress authorized Zionist leaders to negotiate for more territory.

The Second Stage of the Revolt.   Aware of Zionist tactics and totally opposed to the initial partition plan, Arab leaders despaired of retaining control of Palestine. The ensuing tensions led to the second and much more violent stage of the Arab Revolt, from September 1937 to January 1939. For the first time, British officials became targets; the acting district commissioner for Galilee was murdered on September 26. The violence continued even though the Arab Higher Committee had disbanded after Hajj Amin al-Husayni fled to Lebanon and then to Iraq, barely escaping British efforts to capture him in the belief that he had inspired the resistance. The al-Nashashibis initially favored the partition plan but reversed themselves when faced with assaults from opponents. They then discovered that their patron, Amir Abdullah of Transjordan, backed partition; he viewed it as an opportunity to take over Arab Palestine, the strategy he later followed in 1948.

With the Arab Higher Committee in disarray, leadership of the revolt devolved to individual commanders in the field. Peasant despair at their lot and hatred of the great landowners caused the revolt to last a year and a half and to include retaliatory attacks on leading Arab families, not just on Jews and British troops. Armed bands roamed much of central Palestine during 1938 and for a time controlled most major lines of communication and many towns: "By September 'the situation was such that civil administration and control of the country was to all practical purposes nonexistent.'"[64] Raghib al-Nashashibi fled to exile in Egypt following assassination attempts ordered by the mufti.

Attacks on Jews led to Jewish reprisals. The Hagana, the Jewish defense organization linked to the Histadrut, counseled self-restraint, but from 1936 onward this meant selective retaliation rather than purely defensive measures. Once the Arab Revolt became widespread, in 1938 the Hagana and British forces cooperated. The Hagana was permitted to arm itself legally and special Jewish units, formed under the direction of a British officer, Orde Wingate, carried out night attacks on "guerrilla" bases. Indeed, the British used women members of Hagana to search Palestinian peasant women suspected of concealing arms. In addition, in 1937 a Revisionist splinter group known as the Irgun Zvai Leumi began its own operations. The Irgun advocated terrorist tactics in response to those used by Arabs who attacked individual Jews. In three weeks in 1937, Irgun bombs planted in Arab marketplaces killed seventy-seven Arabs.

British forces were harsh in their treatment of the Arabs. Between 1937 and 1939 over one hundred were hanged, and many more were killed by British troops in acts of unofficial retribution. The houses of families suspected of harboring guerrillas were dynamited, a practice adopted by the Hagana and after 1948 by the Israeli government. But when the British tried to curb Irgun acts by hanging a member of Betar for an attack on an Arab bus, it seemed to the Jews to be discriminatory, an attempt to demonstrate fairness to the Arabs rather than a penalty consonant with the supposed crime. This in turn appears to have encouraged the Irgun to undertake more intensive actions against Arabs and to prepare for resistance to the British.[65]

In such a conflict, many Arab villagers were caught between guerrillas demanding assistance and British forces seeking information. They might be tortured by Arab resistance groups or have their houses blown up by British troops on suspicion of aid to the resistance. Consequently, some villages were willing to respond to Fakhri al-Nashashibi's efforts to organize counterrevolutionary squads, which fought the rebels and gave information to the British and the Zionists.[66] During 1938, nearly 1,700 Arabs were killed, 1,138 officially defined as rebels and 486 as civilians. In addition, 292 Jews were killed and over 600 wounded, along with 69 British troops killed and over 200 wounded. British forces "presumably killed a great many more rebels than officially listed."[67] By the end of the year, British reinforcements had again reached 20,000. Divisions had been freed from European duty following the Munich agreement between Hitler and Neville Chamberlain in early October, which appeared to have resolved the Nazi threat to Czechoslovakia. By 1939, organized Arab resistance had collapsed, reduced to acts of retribution against other Arabs considered to be traitors.

The Legacy of the Revolt.   Despite its failure, the Arab Revolt left a lasting imprint on both Palestinian Arabs and British officials. Many of its most devoted participants had belonged to the Istiqlal Party or were followers of the late Shaykh Izz al-Din al-Qassam. Others were led by Abd al-Qadir al-Husayni. All had emerged as leaders during the early 1930s, and many would fight during the war of early 1948. Equally important, however, was the lack of central authority over the Arab resistance, a vacuum created by the departure of the mufti that would never be filled. Palestinian Arabs, whether moderates or militants, were essentially leaderless at a time when the Zionists under Ben-Gurion's leadership seemed to be stronger than ever and when Zionist terror squads had established themselves as an independent force with which the British as well as the Arabs would have to contend.

To the British, however, the Arab Revolt signified a rebellion that had to be crushed, not simply to preserve Britain's own position in Palestine as the mandatory power but also to consolidate that position by appealing for Arab support both within and outside Palestine once the revolt had ended. This stance emerged once a new European war seemed imminent. Nazi and Fascist propaganda encouraging Arabs in other areas of the Middle East to revolt against the British endangered their strategic position in Egypt athwart the Suez Canal. Any such rebellion would require large numbers of troops to be tied down in the Middle East when they would be desperately needed in Europe. These considerations led to the issuing of the 1939 White Paper, which, in a stunning reversal of policy, called for severe restrictions on Jewish immigration and seemed to guarantee achievement of an Arab Palestine within ten years.

BRITAIN RETHINKS ITS OBLIGATIONS: THE 1939 WHITE PAPER

Throughout the period of the Arab Revolt, 1936 to 1939, British attempts to resolve the crisis in Palestine occurred against a backdrop of developing tensions in Europe and the Mediterranean that ultimately had a major impact on Britain's Palestine policy. Since the Italian invasion of Abyssinia (Ethiopia) in October 1935, British diplomats and military officials had been deeply concerned about the potential Italian threat to Egypt and to British naval power in the eastern Mediterranean. The chiefs of staff argued that if war broke out, Britain's eastern Mediterranean fleet would have to proceed to the Far East, essentially conceding the region to the Italians. At best, the British could hope to defend Egypt and the Suez Canal. In such circumstances, British military planners—and diplomats—now began to view Palestine in light of envisaged wartime needs. Peace in Palestine appeared essential to British military security, as any troops there would have to be transferred to the canal and Egypt in time of war. Also, assuming Italian control of the Red Sea entrance to Suez by virtue of its Abyssinian position, reinforcements from India would have to be sent overland from Iraq through Palestine to Egypt.

Palestine in British Strategy

These considerations further emphasized Palestine's strategic importance to the British. In 1933 they had completed construction of a modern harbor at Haifa and in 1935 had finished laying pipe that linked their oil fields in northern Iraq to Haifa, thus bypassing the Suez Canal. France had a similar pipeline that ended at the port of Tripoli in Lebanon. Finally, Palestine was a crucial link in Britain's system of imperial air defense and communications, serving as a major way station, along with Egypt, for flights to Africa, Iraq, India, and the Far East. The potential for nationalist unrest in Egypt and Iraq threatened British security there, despite treaties ensuring British use of military installations and airfields in both countries. Britain's bases in Palestine, under direct control, thus assumed added significance.[68]

But control of Palestine could not by itself ensure British security in the region. Equally important was British assurance of the tacit, if not open, support of the neighboring Arab countries. To be forced to confront Arab hostility in states such as Syria, Iraq, or Egypt, encouraged by German and Italian propaganda, would place too great a burden on British resources. Here the situation in Palestine was crucial, given the increasing involvement of Arab leaders in Palestinian affairs as the revolt progressed. Resolving the Palestinian crisis in a manner favorable to its Arab population came to be seen as a means of acquiring the cooperation of the wider Arab world once war began. British strategists on the subcommittee of the Committee of Imperial Defence declared in January 1939,

> we feel it is necessary to point out . . . the strong feeling . . . in all Arab states in connection with British policy in Palestine. . . . We assume that, immediately on the outbreak of war, the necessary measures would be taken . . . in order to bring about a complete appeasement of Arab opinion in Palestine and in neighboring countries. . . . If we fail thus to retain Arab goodwill at the outset of a war, no other measures which we can recommend will serve to influence the Arab states in favor of this country.[69]

Partition Foiled: The Woodhead Commission

These ideas were not new in early 1939, but they served to emphasize that it was only through British retention of its mandatory role in Palestine that Britain could rely on it as a strategic base, a role that had been challenged by the Peel

Commission's recommendation of partition: if the Jews were recognized as having national status in part of Palestine, what further justification would there be for Britain's staying there as mandatory authority? The cabinet had approved the Peel recommendations and had been startled by the force of Zionist opposition to the plan, even though Weizmann argued that partition would be acceptable if Jewish borders were expanded. When Zionist complaints caused opponents of the government, led by Churchill, to call for a new commission to investigate the ramifications of partition, the proposal played into the hands of the Foreign Office, which, unlike the Colonial Office, strongly opposed partition. Fearing Arab hostility to British policy, the Foreign Office was able to have the new committee, the Woodhead Commission, reopen the question of the practicability of partition, not just its scope. Colonial Office objections were rebuffed as the Foreign Office argued that "the European implications of a hostile Middle East aligned with Britain's enemies must override the arguments in favour of partition."[70]

The Woodhead Commission, formed in January 1938, did not submit its report until November, after a period that had witnessed the more severe aspects of the Arab Revolt that temporarily paralyzed much of Palestine. It concluded that there were no feasible boundaries for "self-supporting Arab and Jewish states."[71] Nevertheless, the four commissioners recommended three different partition plans among them. Plan C, supported by two members, reduced the proposed Jewish state to about 400 square miles along the coast, leaving northern Palestine in British hands. The other two plans outlined even smaller areas for a Jewish state. The Zionists naturally rejected these proposals, enabling the government to issue a White Paper on November 9, 1938, that discarded the entire notion of partition as "impracticable." This left the British with "responsibility for the government of the whole of Palestine" but with the need to confront the fact of Arab-Jewish irreconcilability as portrayed in the Peel Commission Report. The White Paper thus called for a conference of Arabs and Jews in London to discuss "future policy, including the question of immigration into Palestine." The document concluded that if the talks did not end in agreement, the British would "take their own decision in the light of their examination of the problem," an intimation of their willingness to consider the likelihood of a reevaluation of their mandatory obligations.[72]

The St. James Conference

The new colonial secretary, Malcolm MacDonald, who had been the 1931 liaison between his father, Ramsay, and Weizmann, opened the St. James Conference in February 1939. He accepted his government's rejection of partition, and thence his relations with Zionist leaders deteriorated swiftly. Members of the Arab Higher Committee, other than the mufti, were permitted to attend along with Fakhri al-Nashashibi. Also present were representatives of Egypt, Iraq, Saudi Arabia, Transjordan, and Yemen. On the Jewish side were members of the Jewish Agency and leaders of the American and English Jewish communities. The

British conducted separate meetings because the Arabs refused to sit with the Jewish delegates. There was no common ground.

Jamal al-Husayni, cousin of the mufti, demanded the creation of an independent Arab state and the dismantling of the Jewish National Home. Weizmann called for a continuation of the mandate and British sponsorship of unlimited immigration. British officials bowed to al-Husayni's request that the Husayn-McMahon correspondence be reexamined, but a joint British-Arab committee could not agree on its findings. The Arabs argued that McMahon had promised to support Arab independence in Palestine. British members, though concluding that the entire correspondence showed that Palestine was intended to be excluded from Arab territory, admitted that the language was not as precise as formerly assumed and declared it to be evident from the correspondence that "His Majesty's Government were not free to dispose of Palestine without regard for the wishes and interests of the inhabitants of Palestine." This conclusion tacitly backed the Arabs' assertions that they had a right to oppose the establishment of a Jewish state.[73]

The conference quickly reached an impasse. MacDonald presented various proposals to the Arab and Jewish delegations. For the Arabs he was willing to consider a unitary state, enshrining an Arab majority if they allowed Jewish immigration to continue on a restricted basis for a limited period. But the Palestinian Arabs rejected this and demanded an independent state immediately, something Britain would not concede. To the Zionists, MacDonald proposed that they acknowledge that their presence in Palestine should be based on Arab consent, a matter stated also in the British report on the Husayn-McMahon correspondence but never mentioned in the Balfour Declaration. The Zionists scorned this proposal and demanded continued immigration and a guaranteed position in Palestine, not one subject to Arab veto. The conference fell apart despite the Arab states' willingness to accept the government proposals. But the negotiations continued with representatives of the Arab states who requested a specific transitional period of ten years, after which Palestine could become independent. These discussions took place from mid-March to May 1939, against a backdrop of the German absorption of part of Czechoslovakia, Italy's invasion of Albania, and, on May 7, the creation of a formal German-Italian military alliance. The British finally agreed to the Arab state overtures and on May 17 published the White Paper, which reinterpreted their mandatory obligation and seemed to guarantee an independent Palestine with an Arab majority (see Document 3.3).

The 1939 White Paper

The 1939 White Paper declared that "His Majesty's Government believe that the framers of the Mandate in which the Balfour Declaration was embodied could not have intended that Palestine should be converted into a Jewish State against the will of the Arab population of the country."[74] It called for the creation of a Jewish National Home in an independent Palestinian state. Jewish immigration would be permitted to continue at a maximum pace of 15,000 yearly for five years, after which it could occur only with Arab agreement. In addition, 25,000 refugees would be admitted. Unlimited land transfers to Jews would be restricted to designated coastal areas. The White Paper foresaw an independent Palestine within ten years, at which time the Jews would comprise no more than one-third of the population. The British government would develop self-governing institutions incorporating both Arabs and Jews during this period, even if both sides rejected the idea. If there were no cooperation and Palestine seemed unsuitable for independence after ten years, then Great Britain would consult with Palestinian Arabs and Jews, Arab states, and the League of Nations to determine the course it should take.

Both Arabs and Jews rejected the 1939 White Paper. The Jewish Agency declared that the system envisaged was contrary to international law and a violation of the promises made to the Jews in and since the Balfour Declaration. It warned that Jews would resist implementation of the White Paper, and Ben-Gurion declared that although Jews necessarily would "fight with Great Britain in this war as if there was no White Paper," they would subsequently "fight the White Paper as if there was no war" (see Figure 3.6). This reflected the Jewish dilemma well recognized by the British. The Zionists had no choice but to fight with the British against the Nazi threat. On the other hand, the Palestinian Arabs, through the Arab Higher Committee, repudiated the White Paper because it did not promise them immediate independence with a halt to Jewish immigration.

GREAT BRITAIN AND PALESTINE ON THE EVE OF WORLD WAR II

In the midst of the abortive St. James Conference in early 1939, British officials, as we have seen, attempted to persuade Zionist leaders to acknowledge the principle of Arab agreement to future Jewish immigration into Palestine, thereby tacitly granting that this was not an absolute right to be undertaken despite Arab opposition. The Zionists objected, not simply because they had always considered Jewish immigration a matter for their control but also because they foresaw the need for increased immigration given the attempts of European Jews to escape persecution in Germany and Eastern Europe. At one point Chaim Weizmann responded angrily to Malcolm MacDonald, "Are the British in Palestine with the consent of the Arabs?"[75] Clearly they were not. The partnership between British imperialism and the Zionist colonizing effort since World War I had been predicated on the assumption that Arab consent was unnecessary precisely because it was unattainable. Now, however, circumstances had changed. The Zionists were more willing to consider taking in all Jews who wished to enter, in contrast to their selective immigration quotas of the interwar period that targeted the young and the wealthy. The spread of Fascism confirmed to Jews their original assumptions regarding the irrelevance of Arab consent. But their stance clashed with the increasing British concern for their

Figure 3.6 ■ Organized Zionist Protest to 1939 White Paper

Zionist riots could be as spontaneous as that of the Palestinians seen in Figure 3.4. Here we see a carefully organized demonstration/parade of labor Zionists on a main Jerusalem street near the Jewish Agency executive complex (see Figure 4.1).

imperial security that, in the latter's view, required greater interest in Arab than in Jewish goodwill.

In this light, the White Paper of 1939 was an even greater act of expediency than the Balfour Declaration in 1917. Both were motivated by strategic concerns related to war efforts, either existing, as in 1917, or imminent, as in 1939. But the Balfour Declaration did reflect some genuine interest in the future of European Jewry, whereas the White Paper exhibited no corresponding concern for either Palestinian Arabs or Jews. The Balfour Declaration had not provided for a British obligation to take into account Arab opinion regarding Jewish immigration and the building of a national home. Knowing what that opinion was, British officials strove to placate it throughout most of the interwar period while ensuring that no concessions were made that would seriously endanger Zionist efforts. In consequence, Britain's newfound regard for Arab objections to Zionism, coming on the heels of a revolt that British forces had suppressed with scant restraint toward their opponents, had little to do with morality. Arab opinion in the wider Middle East now seemed more important to British interests than was Jewish opinion in Palestine or Jewish political influence in London. In addition, the abandonment of partition permitted the British to retain control over all of Palestine; the creation of separate entities might have required their abdication of sovereignty over those areas.

For the Arabs and the Jews of Palestine, the White Paper was a disappointment of differing magnitudes. The Arab community in Palestine was essentially leaderless, riven with more factions than ever before. The moderate Arabs of the al-Khalidi and al-Nashashibi camps found it hopeful, as did the leaders of the Arab governments, but the Arab Higher Committee retained its authority and its intransigence, even though many of its members had now repudiated Hajj Amin al-Husayni. The example of the Arab Revolt and its presumed success in forcing Britain to deal with the Arabs, whatever its military failure, apparently gave optimism to those who counseled defiance. The Arab Higher Committee's disavowal of the White Paper was based on arguments first presented in 1918 and indicated a consistent refusal to admit that any part of Palestine should be given to the Zionists.

The shock of the White Paper forced the Zionist leadership to reconsider their ties to Great Britain. For Ben-Gurion, the events of the later 1930s and the White Paper proved that the Jews would have to look for the support of another great power and large Jewish community, namely, the United States. Above all, Ben-Gurion insisted on the right of Jews to determine their own course regardless of British policies. While cooperating with the British militarily to stem the Axis tide in the Middle East in the early years of the war, he oversaw a concerted effort to steal weapons and munitions from them to prepare Jews for a likely armed conflict with Great Britain once the war ended.

CONCLUSION

The Arab and Jewish communities in Palestine, both greatly expanded since 1919, were much more separate than they had been previously. From approximately 10 percent of the population, Jews had become nearly 30 percent in 1939–1940, about 467,000 out of a total population of about 1.528 million. Nearly 300,000 of these were immigrants who had arrived during the 1930s, an increase of 64 percent, not counting the number of illegal immigrants estimated at between 30,000 and 40,000. From the first census in 1922 to 1940, the Arab population increased from 660,641 to about 1,060,750, a rate of nearly 27 percent, very little of which was due to illegal immigration. The entrance of Arabs from neighboring countries was principally seasonal, temporary labor, as opposed to Jewish illegal immigrants who sought to remain permanently.[76] The increase in the Arab population was due primarily to a very high birthrate among Arab women, averaging about seven children per mother during the period, and a significant decline in infant mortality.[77]

Yet despite important transformations in Arab patterns of living—the Arab urban population increased 111 percent between 1922 and 1944—there were still major gaps between the traditional Arab and the more modern Jewish economies; the latter was much more closely integrated into the world economic system. The only area in which Arab capital had held its own through further development was in citrus cultivation. As of 1943, Arabs (including other non-Jews) held 145,572 dunams in citrus, as opposed to 141,188 held by Jews, with a similar ratio in the valuation of the land. But in industry, for example, although in 1943 Arabs and other non-Jews owned 1,558 industrial "establishments," as opposed to 1,907 Jewish, there was no comparison in terms of capital invested, slightly over £2 million (Arab) versus nearly £12.1 million (Jewish); and persons employed in industry, 8,804 (Arab) versus 37,773 (Jewish), about 0.7 percent of the Arab population as opposed to about 8.5 percent of the Jewish.[78]

As for land, Jews owned nearly 1.3 million dunams in 1939 as opposed to 456,000 in 1920, an increase of about 185 percent. This equaled nearly one-seventh of the cultivable land in Palestine, about 9 million dunams, out of a total land area of 26 million. Given the fact that Arabs owned nearly 17 million dunams of uncultivable land, that meant that they owned about 7.75 million dunams of cultivable land in 1939, leaving an Arab-Jewish ratio of six to one.[79] Despite this disparity in favor of the Arabs, they paid £351,000 in rural and urban property taxes, whereas the Jews paid £448,000, another index of the valuation gap reflecting the divergent natures of both productivity and size of landholdings. Jewish holdings were far more integrated for both political and economic reasons, the result of planning undertaken by the Jewish Agency during the 1930s.

The Arab and Jewish communities in Palestine continued to diverge with respect to both their economic growth and the quality of their leadership. The British entered the maelstrom of World War II aware that their Palestine policy reversal in the 1939 White Paper had outraged the Zionists without satisfying the Arabs. They accepted this as the price for temporarily stabilizing their military and strategic positions in Palestine and the Arab world at large, important in themselves and as a means of securing communications with India and the Far East. It was a short-term strategy of expediency and calculated appeasement designed to serve Britain's immediate wartime and possibly long-range imperial designs, which assumed a British presence in Palestine for the foreseeable future.[80]

QUESTIONS FOR CONSIDERATION

1. During the interwar period, what were the major political divisions within the Palestinian Arab and the Zionist communities? How significant were the divisions to each community's attainment of its goals?

2. How did Hitler's rise to power in Germany affect the Arab and Jewish communities in Palestine?

3. What were the causes of the Arab Revolt? How did the Arab and Jewish communities in Palestine react to the Peel Commission recommendations?

4. Why did Britain issue the 1939 White Paper? Did it confirm or contradict statements found in the Balfour Declaration and the Peel Commission Report?

CHRONOLOGY

1920	**April.** Arab anti-Zionist riots break out.
	July. British military administration in Palestine ends; civil administration begins.
	December. Histadrut created. Hagana founded.
1921	**April.** Hajj Amin al-Husayni appointed mufti of Jerusalem.
1922	**January.** Supreme Muslim Council established.
	June. British White Paper (Churchill Memorandum) issued.
	July. League of Nations ratifies draft of British Mandate.
1925	Vladimir Jabotinsky founds Revisionist Party.
1929	**August.** Western (Wailing) Wall riots.
1930	**October.** Passfield White Paper.
	December. Mapai Party founded.
1931–1933	Landless Arab Inquiry.
1932	**August.** Istiqlal (Independence) Party founded.
1933	**January.** Adolf Hitler becomes German Chancellor.
1935	**July.** Hitler issues Nuremburg Laws.
	November. Izz al-Din al-Qassam killed.
1936	**April–November.** Arab Revolt, first stage.
1937	**June.** Peel Commission inquiry and partition report.
	September. Second stage of Arab Revolt begins.
	September–October. Irgun Zvai Leumi founded.
1938	**October.** German-British Munich Pact on Czechoslovakia.
1939	**February–March.** St. James Conference.
	Mid-March. Nazi takeover of Czechoslovakia.
	May 17. British White Paper.
	August 23. Nazi-Soviet Pact.
	September 1. Nazi invasion of Poland.
	September 3. Britain and France declare war on Germany, start of World War II.

Notes

1. Bernard Wasserstein, *The British in Palestine: The Mandatory Government and the Arab-Jewish Conflict, 1917–1929* (London, 1978), 1–2; and Ronald Storrs, *The Memoirs of Sir Ronald Storrs* (New York, 1937), 301–11. On the issue of famine, see Linda Schatkowski Schilcher, "The Famine of 1915–1918 in Greater Syria," in *Problems of the Modern Middle East in Historical Perspective: Essays in Honour of Albert Hourani*, ed. John Spagnolo (Reading, U.K., 1992), 229–58.

2. Simha Flapan, *Zionism and the Palestinians* (London, 1979), 57.

3. Y. Porath, *The Emergence of the Palestinian-Arab National Movement, 1918–1929* (London, 1974), 33–34; and Muhammad Y. Muslih, *The Origins of Palestinian Nationalism* (New York, 1988).

4. Wasserstein, *British in Palestine*, 15.

5. Jehuda Reinharz, "Chaim Weizmann as Political Strategist: The Initial Years, 1918–1920," in *Essays in Modern Jewish History: A Tribute to Ben Halpern*, ed. Frances Malino and Phylis Cohen Albert (Rutherford, N.J., 1982), 273–74.

6. The highest British officials in Palestine, Generals Allenby and Bols, supported this idea; see Wasserstein, *British in Palestine*, 60–61. See also Porath, *Emergence*, 69–105, and Muslih, *Origins*, 177–204, for a detailed treatment of these issues.

7. Wasserstein, *British in Palestine*, 92.

8. Ibid., 72–73.

9. Ibid., 160, Table.

10. Porath, *Emergence*, 60.

11. Wasserstein, *British in Palestine*, 109.

12. Philip Mattar, "The Role of the Mufti of Jerusalem in the Political Struggle over the Western Wall, 1928–1929," *Middle Eastern Studies* 19 (January 1983): 113. See also Mattar's book, *The Mufti of Jerusalem: Al-Hajj Amin al-Husayni and the Palestinian National Movement* (New York, 1988), for a broader treatment of the mufti's career.

13. Porath, *Emergence*, 276.

14. Wasserstein, *British in Palestine*, 157.

15. Yonathan Shapiro, *The Formative Years of the Israeli Labour Party: The Organization of Power, 1919–1930*, Sage Studies in Twentieth-Century History, vol. 4 (Beverly Hills, 1976), 12–13. The following draws on Shapiro and on Noah Lucas, *The Modern History of Israel* (New York, 1975), 76–93.

16. Lucas, *Modern History*, 59.

17. Shapiro, *Formative Years*, 205.

18. Lucas, *Modern History*, 131–32.

19. Shlomo Avineri, *The Making of Modern Zionism: The Intellectual Origins of the Jewish State* (New York, 1981), 159–86, has a good overview of Jabotinsky's intellectual development, with a brief mention of his attraction to Fascism (171–76). More detailed treatment of this issue is found in Lenni Brenner, *Zionism in the Age of the Dictators* (London, 1983), 116–34; and Yonathan Shapiro, *The Road to Power: The Herut Party in Israel* (Albany, N.Y., 1991), 9–42.

20. Howard M. Sachar, *A History of Israel: From the Rise of Zionism to Our Time* (New York, 1976), 186.

21. A. Revusky, *Jews in Palestine* (New York, 1936), 200–201.

22. Neil Caplan, *Palestine Jewry and the Arab Question, 1917–1925* (London, 1978), 42.

23. Ibid., 113.

24. Ibid., 13. See also the excellent study of 1920s Palestine, Barbara J. Smith, *The Roots of Separatism in Palestine: British Economic Policy, 1920–1929* (Syracuse, N.Y., 1993).

25. Ben-Gurion could speak of Arab-Jewish cooperation and Arab economic development but only within the context of absolute Jewish political sovereignty, precisely the issue that the Arab leaders could not accept: see Shabtai Teveth, *Ben-Gurion and the Palestinian Arabs: From Peace to War* (Oxford, 1985).

26. Wasserstein, *British in Palestine*, 194.

27. Ibid., 173.

28. Kenneth Stein, *The Land Question in Palestine, 1917–1939* (Chapel Hill, N.C., 1984), 46.

29. Wasserstein, *British in Palestine*, 201.

30. Porath, *Emergence*, 67–68.

31. Stein, *Land Question*, 38. Still a very important source used by students of the land issue is A. Granott, *The Land System in Palestine* (London, 1952).

32. Granott, *Land System*, 221–27; and Stein, *Land Question*, 14–15.

33. Stein, *Land Question*, 34.

34. Granott, *Land System*, 81–82.

35. Ibid., 41.

36. See Stein, *Land Question*, 59ff; and Granott, *Land System*, 80.

37. Stein, *Land Question*, Chapter 6. A good summary discussion of these issues is in Y. Porath, *The Palestinian Arab National Movement, 1929–1939: From Riots to Rebellion* (London, 1977), 80–108.

38. Stein, *Land Question*, 48.

39. Ibid., 51.

40. A good overview is by John Ruedy, "Dynamics of Land Alienation," in *The Transformation of Palestine: Essays on the Origin and Development of the Arab-Israeli Conflict*, ed. Ibrahim Abu-Lughod (Evanston, Ill., 1971), 119–38. In seeking to redress the balance, Stein seems to err in arguing that comparatively few Arabs were displaced: *Land Question*, 56–59.

41. Government of Palestine, *Survey of Palestine: Prepared in December 1945 and January 1946 for the Information of the Anglo-American Committee of Inquiry*, 2 vols. (Jerusalem, 1946), 1: 296.

42. Mattar, "Role of the Mufti," 109; Wasserstein, *British in Palestine*, 224.

43. Quoted in Mattar, "Role of the Mufti," 106.

44. Porath, *Emergence*, 266; and Mattar, "Role of the Mufti," 107.

45. Wasserstein, *British in Palestine*, 227; and Mattar, "Role of the Mufti," 113.

46. Quoted in John Marlowe, *The Seat of Pilate: An Account of the Palestine Mandate* (London, 1959), 117. See also Stein, *Land Question*, 88ff.

47. See Stein, *Land Question*, 91, 110–12, for a discussion of the issues.

48. The text of the mandate is in Walter Laqueur and Barry Rubin, eds., *The Israel-Arab Reader: A Documentary History of the Middle East Conflict*, 5th rev. ed. (New York, 1995), 30–36.

49. Quoted in Marlowe, *Seat of Pilate*, 123.

50. Quoted in Norman Rose, *The Gentile Zionists: A Study in Anglo-Zionist Diplomacy, 1929–1939* (London, 1973), 26. Rose has a good treatment of the British-Zionist interactions on this crisis; see 1–40. The text of the MacDonald letter is in Laqueur and Rubin, eds., *Israel-Arab Reader*, 50–55.

51. Revusky, *Jews in Palestine*, 224. The 1935 edition, unlike that of 1936, does not contain this information. The German laws barring the export of capital predated the Nazi regime, having been passed in 1931 to stem capital outflows during financial panics related to the world Depression. Zionist and Nazi officials reached an accord whereby emigrant German Jews would enter an agreement with the Reichsbank. Their money would be transferred to Palestine in the form of German goods, and they would receive compensatory payment for the value of these goods,

minus taxes, in Palestinian pounds. German Jews thus transferred most of their money, and German commerce benefited from the influx of German goods into Palestine.

52. Sachar, *History of Israel*, 197. See Brenner, *Zionism in the Age of Dictators*, 79–90; Brenner's style is occasionally more condemnatory than analytical.

53. Statistics from Sachar, *History of Israel*, 189–90; compare 201 and n. 94. Immigration figures vary widely.

54. Stein, *Land Question*, 142.

55. Joel S. Migdal, ed., *Palestinian Society and Politics* (Princeton, N.J., 1980), 26; and Pamela Ann Smith, *Palestine and the Palestinians, 1876–1983* (London, 1984), 54.

56. Said B. Himadeh, "Industry," in *Economic Organization of Palestine*, ed. Said B. Himadeh (Beirut, 1938), 297. Text in Laqueur and Rubin, eds., *Israel-Arab Reader*, 39–40.

57. Stein, *Land Question*, 131, 143–44; and Montague Brown, "Agriculture," in Himadeh, ed., *Economic Organization*, 121–33.

58. Porath, *Emergence*, 63–79.

59. See the discussion in Pamela Ann Smith, *Palestine and the Palestinians*, 63 and n. 105, drawing on Nevill Barbour, *Nisi Dominus: A Survey of the Palestine Controversy* (London, 1946; reprinted Beirut, 1969), 161.

60. In particular, Nuri Said, the Iraqi prime minister, asked Moshe Shertok (later Sharett), then political officer for the Jewish Agency, to agree to restrict immigration as a sign of willingness to cooperate with the Arabs in seeking to resolve the tensions. Shertok refused on the grounds that it was a concession to violence and because immigration was "an absolute Jewish right" that would not be subject to concessions. Jacob Hurewitz, *The Struggle for Palestine, 1936–48*, 2nd ed. (New York, 1976), 70.

61. Ibid., 72. See also Porath, *Emergence*, 162–216, for a detailed treatment of this period; and Michael Cohen, *Palestine, Retreat from the Mandate: The Making of British Policy, 1936–1945* (London, 1978), 15–31, for an analysis of the revolt and British policymaking.

62. This discussion is drawn from Hurewitz, *Struggle*, 72–76; Marlowe, *Seat of Pilate*, 140–45; and Cohen, *Retreat*, 32–38.

63. Quoted in Nicholas Bethell, *The Palestine Triangle: The Struggle for the Holy Land, 1935–1948* (New York, 1979), 32.

64. Porath, *Emergence*, 237–38; and Cohen, *Retreat*, 52–61.

65. J. Bowyer Bell, *Terror out of Zion: Irgun Zvai Leumi, LEHI, and the Palestinian Underground, 1929–1949* (New York, 1977), 39–42; Porath, *Emergence*, 238; Dan Kurzman, *Ben-Gurion, Prophet of Fire* (New York, 1983), 218; Yehuda Bauer, *From Diplomacy to Resistance: A History of Jewish Palestine, 1939–1945* (Philadelphia, 1970), 11–15; and Munya M. Mardor, *Haganah* (New York, 1964), 3–16.

66. Smith, *Palestinians*, 66–68; and Porath, *Emergence*, 249–56.

67. Bell, *Terror*, 46.

68. This material relies on Cohen, *Retreat*, 1–9; and Hurewitz, *Struggle*, 25–26.

69. Quoted in Cohen, *Retreat*, 4.

70. Ibid., 42. See also Rose, *Gentile Zionists*, 165–73.

71. Cohen, *Retreat*, 72.

72. All quotations are from Laqueur and Rubin, eds., *Israel-Arab Reader*, 62–63.

73. Quoted in Hurewitz, *Struggle*, 99.

74. Laqueur and Rubin, eds., *Israel-Arab Reader*, 66. For the European backdrop, see Hurewitz, *Struggle*, 101.

75. Bauer, *Diplomacy*, 28.

76. *Survey of Palestine*, 1: 210–11. Many Jewish women immigrants circumvented legal restrictions by arranging marriages of convenience with Palestinian Jews to qualify them to enter as dependents. Once there and awarded citizenship, they divorced their husbands: the divorce rate among Jews in Palestine in 1936 was 509 per 1,000 marriages: Lister G. Hopkins, "Population," in Himadeh, ed., *Economic Organization*, 29. My statistics are extrapolated from Porath, *Emergence*, 129; and Rachelle Taqqu, "Peasants into Workmen: Internal Labor Migration and the Arab Village Community under the Mandate," in Migdal, ed., *Palestinian Society*, 266.

77. *Survey of Palestine*, 2: 704–13.

78. Ibid., 566–67, Tables 2 and 3, and 719. There is a major discrepancy between this estimate of Jewish industrial enterprises and Sachar's tabulation of 14,000 in 1937; see n. 53. It may be explained by the fact that the estimate in 1943 excluded small businesses such as printing presses and laundries.

79. *Survey of Palestine*, 2: 566, Table 2; and Stein, *Land Question*, 226.

80. See the evaluation of Gabriel Sheffer, "Appeasement and the Problems of Palestine," *International Journal of Middle East Studies* 11 (May 1980): 377–99.

THE CHURCHILL WHITE PAPER

July 1, 1922

As Great Britain's colonial secretary, Winston Churchill sought to balance Jewish and Arab interests. In this policy statement, he rejected Arab pleas to repudiate the Balfour Declaration but criticized statements suggesting that Palestine would become "as Jewish as England is English." Churchill also disputed the Arab interpretation of Henry McMahon's letter to Sharif Husayn of October 24, 1915 (see Document 2.1), arguing that Palestine was deliberately excluded from areas promised to the Arabs.

The Secretary of State for the Colonies has given renewed consideration to the existing political situation in Palestine, with a very earnest desire to arrive at a settlement of the outstanding questions which have given rise to uncertainty and unrest among certain sections of the population. After consultation with the High Commissioner for Palestine the following statement has been drawn up. . . .

The tension which has prevailed from time to time in Palestine is mainly due to apprehensions, which are entertained both by sections of the Arab and by sections of the Jewish population. These apprehensions, so far as the Arabs are concerned, are partly based upon exaggerated interpretations of the meaning of the Declaration favouring the establishment of a Jewish National Home in Palestine, made on behalf of His Majesty's Government on 2nd November, 1917. Unauthorised statements have been made to the effect that the purpose in view is to create a wholly Jewish Palestine. Phrases have been used such as that Palestine is to become "as Jewish as England is English." His Majesty's Government regard any such expectation as impracticable and have no such aim in view. Nor have they at any time contemplated, as appears to be feared by the Arab Delegation, the disappearance or the subordination of the Arabic population, language or culture in Palestine. . . . The terms of the Declaration referred to do not contemplate that Palestine as a whole should be converted into a Jewish National Home, but that such a Home should be founded *in Palestine*. In this connection it has been observed with satisfaction that at the meeting of the Zionist Congress, the supreme governing body of the Zionist Organisation, held at Carlsbad in September, 1921, a resolution was passed expressing as the official statement of Zionist aims "the determination of the Jewish people to live with

Source: J. C. Hurewitz, *The Middle East and North Africa in World Politics, vol. 2, British-French Supremacy, 1914–1945* (New Haven and London, 1979), 302–40.

the Arab people on terms of unity and mutual respect, and together with them to make the common home into a flourishing community, the upbuilding of which may assure to each of its peoples an undisturbed national development."

It is also necessary to point out that the Zionist Commission in Palestine, now termed the Palestine Zionist Executive, has not desired to possess, and does not possess, any share in the general administration of the country. Nor does the special position assigned to the Zionist Organisation in Article IV of the Draft Mandate for Palestine imply any such functions. That special position relates to the measures to be taken in Palestine affecting the Jewish population, and contemplates that the Organisation may assist in the general development of the country, but does not entitle it to share in any degree in its Government.

Further, it is contemplated that the status of all citizens of Palestine in the eyes of the law shall be Palestinian, and it has never been intended that they, or any section of them, should possess any other juridical status.

So far as the Jewish population of Palestine [is] concerned, it appears that some among them are apprehensive that His Majesty's Government may depart from the policy embodied in the Declaration of 1917. It is necessary, therefore, once more to affirm that these fears are unfounded, and that that Declaration . . . is not susceptible of change. . . . When it is asked what is meant by the development of the Jewish National Home in Palestine, it may be answered that it is not the imposition of a Jewish nationality upon the inhabitants of Palestine as a whole, but the further development of the existing Jewish community, with the assistance of Jews in other parts of the world, in order that it may become a centre in which the Jewish people as a whole may take, on grounds of religion and race, an interest and a pride. But this community . . . should know that it is in Palestine as of right and not on sufferance. That is the reason why it is necessary that the existence of a Jewish National Home in Palestine should be internationally guaranteed, and that it should be formally recognised to rest upon ancient historic connection.

This, then, is the interpretation which His Majesty's Government place upon the Declaration of 1917, and, so understood, the Secretary of State is of [the] opinion that it does not contain or imply anything which need cause either alarm to the Arab population of Palestine or disappointment to the Jews.

For the fulfilment of this policy it is necessary that the Jewish community in Palestine should be able to increase its numbers by immigration. This immigration cannot be so great in volume as to exceed whatever may be the economic capacity of the country at the time to absorb new arrivals. . . .

With reference to the Constitution . . . , the draft of which has already been published, it is desirable to make certain points clear. In the first place, it is not the case, as has been represented by the Arab Delegation, that during the war His Majesty's Government gave an undertaking that an independent national government should be at once established in Palestine. This representation mainly rests upon a letter dated the 24th October, 1915, from Sir Henry McMahon, then His Majesty's High Commissioner in Egypt, to the Sherif of Mecca, now King

Hussein of the Kingdom of the Hejaz. That letter is quoted as conveying the promise to the Sherif of Mecca to recognise and support the independence of the Arabs within the territories proposed by him. But this promise was given subject to a reservation made in the same letter, which excluded from its scope, among other territories, the portions of Syria lying to the west of the district of Damascus. This reservation has always been regarded by His Majesty's Government as covering the vilayet of Beirut and the independent Sanjak of Jerusalem. The whole of Palestine west of the Jordan was thus excluded from Sir H. McMahon's pledge.

DOCUMENT 3.2

PALESTINE ROYAL (PEEL) COMMISSION REPORT
July 1937

The Peel Commission concluded that partition was the only possible solution to Arab-Jewish strife and to the conflicting promises the British had made to both sides "under the stress of the World War . . . in order to obtain their support." The selections define the reasons behind the decision and the type of partition recommended.

The Force of Circumstances

1. Before submitting the proposals we have to offer for its drastic treatment we will briefly restate the problem of Palestine.

2. Under the stress of the World War the British Government made promises to Arabs and Jews in order to obtain their support. On the strength of those promises both parties formed certain expectations.

3. The application to Palestine of the Mandate System in general and of the specific Mandate in particular implied the belief that the obligations thus undertaken towards the Arabs and the Jews respectively would prove in course of time to be mutually compatible owing to the conciliatory effect on the Palestinian Arabs of the material prosperity which Jewish immigration would bring to Palestine as a whole. That belief has not been justified, and we see no hope of its being justified in the future. . . .

5. What are the existing circumstances?

An irrepressible conflict has arisen between two national communities within the narrow bounds of one small country. About 1,000,000 Arabs are in strife, open or latent, with some 400,000 Jews. There is no common ground between them. The Arab community is predominantly Asiatic in character, the Jewish community predominantly European. They differ in religion and in

Source: Palestine Royal Commission Report, CMD 5479 (London, 1946), 278–96.

language. Their cultural and social life, their ways of thought and conduct, are as incompatible as their national aspirations. These last are the greatest bar to peace. Arabs and Jews might possibly learn to live and work together in Palestine if they would make a genuine effort to reconcile and combine their national ideals and so build up in time a joint or dual nationality. But this they cannot do. The War and its sequel have inspired all Arabs with the hope of reviving in a free and united Arab world the traditions of the Arab golden age.

The Jews similarly are inspired by their historic past. They mean to show what the Jewish nation can achieve when restored to the land of its birth. National assimilation between Arabs and Jews is thus ruled out. In the Arab picture the Jews could only occupy the place they occupied in Arab Egypt or Arab Spain. The Arabs would be as much outside the Jewish picture as the Canaanites in the old land of Israel. The National Home, as we have said before, cannot be half-national. In these circumstances to maintain that Palestinian citizenship has any moral meaning is a mischievous pretence. Neither Arab nor Jew has any sense of service to a single State.

6. This conflict was inherent in the situation from the outset. The terms of the Mandate tended to confirm it. . . .

7. The conflict has grown steadily more bitter. It has been marked by a series of five Arab outbreaks, culminating in the rebellion of last year. In the earlier period hostility to the Jews was not widespread among the *fellaheen*.* It is now general. The first three outbreaks, again, were directed only against the Jews. The last two were directed against the Government as well.

8. This intensification of the conflict will continue. . . . The educational systems, Arab and Jewish, are schools of nationalism, and they have only existed for a short time. Their full effect on the rising generation has yet to be felt. And patriotic "youth-movements," so familiar a feature of present-day politics in other countries of Europe or Asia, are afoot in Palestine. As each community grows, moreover, the rivalry between them deepens. The more numerous and prosperous and better-educated the Arabs become, the more insistent will be their demand for national independence and the more bitter their hatred of the obstacle that bars the way to it. As the Jewish National Home grows older and more firmly rooted, so will grow its self-confidence and political ambition.

9. The conflict is primarily political, though the fear of economic subjection to the Jews is also in Arab minds. The Mandate, it is supposed, will terminate sooner or later. . . . Every intelligent Arab and Jew is forced to ask the question "Who in the end will govern Palestine?" This uncertainty is doubtless aggravated by the fact that Palestine is a mandated territory; but, in the light of nationalist movements elsewhere, we do not think the situation would be very different if Palestine had been a British Colony.

10. Meantime the "external factors" will continue to play the part they have played with steadily increasing force from the beginning. On the one hand,

---

*fellaheen: Arab peasants. — Ed.

Saudi Arabia, the Yemen, Iraq and Egypt are already recognised as sovereign states, and Trans-Jordan as an "independent government." In less than three years' time Syria and the Lebanon will attain their national sovereignty. The claim of the Palestine Arabs to share in the freedom of all Asiatic Arabia will thus be reinforced. . . . That they are as well qualified for self-government as the Arabs of neighbouring countries has been admitted.

11. On the other hand, the hardships and anxieties of the Jews in Europe are not likely to grow less in the near future. The pressure on Palestine will continue and might at any time be accentuated. . . . The Mandatory will be urged unceasingly to admit as many Jews into Palestine as the National Home can provide with a livelihood and to protect them when admitted from Arab attacks.

12. Thus, for internal and external reasons, it seems probable that the situation, bad as it now is, will grow worse. The conflict will go on, the gulf between Arabs and Jews will widen. . . .

14. . . . To put it in one sentence, we cannot—in Palestine as it now is—both concede the Arab claim to self-government and secure the establishment of the Jewish National Home. And this conflict between the two obligations is the more unfortunate because each of them, taken separately, accords with British sentiment and British interest. On the one hand, the application of the Mandate System to Arab Palestine as a means of advancement to self-government was in harmony with British principles—the same principles as have been put into practice since the War in different circumstances in India, Iraq and Egypt. British public opinion is wholly sympathetic with Arab aspirations towards a new age of unity and prosperity in the Arab world. Conversely, the task of governing without the consent or even the acquiescence of the governed is one for which, we believe, the British people have little heart. On the other hand, there is a strong British tradition of friendship with the Jewish people. Nowhere have Jews found it easier to live and prosper than in Britain. Nowhere is there a more genuine desire to do what can be done to help them in their present difficulties. Nowhere, again, was Zionism better understood before the War or given such practical proofs of sympathy. And British interest coincides with British sentiment. From the earliest days of the British connexion with India and beyond, the peace of the Middle East has been a cardinal principle of our foreign policy; and for the maintenance of that peace British statesmanship can show an almost unbroken record of friendship with the Arabs. . . .

A continuance or rather an aggravation . . . of the present situation . . . will mean constant unrest, . . . disturbance in peace and potential danger in the event of war . . . [and] a steady decline in our prestige. . . .

19. Manifestly the problem cannot be solved by giving either the Arabs or the Jews all they want. . . . now that the hope of harmony between the races has proved untenable. . . . But while neither race can justly rule all of Palestine, we see no reason why . . . each race should not rule part of it. . . . Partition seems to offer at least a chance of ultimate peace. We can see none in any other plan.

1. A Treaty System

6. Treaties of Alliance should be negotiated by the Mandatory with the Government of Trans-Jordan and representatives of the Arabs of Palestine on the one hand and with the Zionist Organisation on the other. These Treaties would declare that, within as short a period as may be convenient, two sovereign independent States would be established—the one an Arab State, consisting of Trans-Jordan united with that part of Palestine which lies to the east and south of a frontier [see original document and Map 3.1]; the other a Jewish State consisting of that part of Palestine which lies to the north and west of that frontier. . . .

2. The Holy Places

12. We regard the protection of the Holy Places as a permanent trust, unique in its character and purpose, and not contemplated by Article 22 of the Covenant of the League of Nations. We submit for consideration that, in order to avoid misunderstanding, it might frankly be stated that this trust will only terminate if and when the League of Nations and the United States desire it to do so, and that, while it would be the trustee's duty to promote the well-being and development of the local population concerned, it is not intended that in course of time they should stand by themselves as a wholly self-governing community. . . .

10. Exchange of Land and Population

35. We have left to the last the two-fold question which, after that of the Frontier, is the most important and most difficult of all the questions which Partition in any shape involves.

36. If Partition is to be effective in promoting a final settlement it must mean more than drawing a frontier and establishing two States. Sooner or later there should be a transfer of land and, as far as possible, an exchange of population. . . .

Conclusion

1. "Half a loaf is better than no bread" is a peculiarly English proverb; and, considering the attitude which both the Arab and the Jewish representatives adopted in giving evidence before us, we think it improbable that either party will be satisfied at first sight with the proposals we have submitted for the adjustment of their rival claims. For Partition means that neither will get all it wants. It means that the Arabs must acquiesce in the exclusion from their sovereignty of a piece of territory, long occupied and once ruled by them. It means that the Jews must be content with less than the Land of Israel they once ruled and have hoped to rule again. But it seems to us possible that on reflection both parties will come to realise that the drawbacks of Partition are outweighed by its advantages. For, if it offers neither party all it wants, it offers each what it wants most, namely freedom and security. . . .

DOCUMENT 3.3

THE 1939 WHITE PAPER

This British policy statement, issued on May 17, 1939, challenged the idea that Palestine could become a Jewish state in spite of Arab opposition to the very idea. It recognized the need for Jewish immigration into Palestine to accommodate refugees fleeing Europe, but it specified that Arab needs and Arab agreement were basic to the continuance of such immigration. The White Paper stipulated that Jewish immigration was to be permitted during the next five years (1939–1943) at a rate that would bring the Jewish population in Palestine to a level of approximately one-third that of the total population. After this five-year period had elapsed, further Jewish immigration was not to be permitted "unless the Arabs of Palestine acquiesce to it." By contrast to the relative freedom of Jewish immigration, land sales to Jews were to be placed under immediate regulation and restriction. The High Commissioner was to be given the power to regulate or prohibit transfers of land from Arab to Jewish ownership in areas where such transfers could be deemed detrimental to the living standards of Arab farmers already in the area or where they could lead to the creation of "a considerable landless Arab population." These powers were to remain in effect throughout the transitional period. Zionist leaders viewed this document as a betrayal of the intentions behind the Balfour Declaration.

2. The Mandate for Palestine, the terms of which were confirmed by the Council of the League of Nations in 1922, has governed the policy of successive British Governments for nearly 20 years. It embodies the Balfour Declaration and imposes on the Mandatory four main obligations. These obligations are set out in Articles 2, 6 and 13 of the Mandate. . . .

3. The Royal Commission [Peel Commission] and previous Commissions of Enquiry have drawn attention to the ambiguity of certain expressions in the Mandate, such as the expression "a national home for the Jewish people," and they have found in this ambiguity and the resulting uncertainty as to the objectives of policy a fundamental cause of unrest and hostility between Arabs and Jews. His Majesty's Government are convinced that . . . a clear definition of policy and objectives is essential. The proposal of partition recommended by the Royal Commission would have afforded such clarity, but the establishment of self-supporting independent Arab and Jewish States within Palestine has been found to be impracticable. It has therefore been necessary for His Majesty's Government to devise an alternative policy which will, consistently with their obligations to Arabs and Jews, meet the needs of the situation in Palestine. Their views and proposals are set forth below under the three heads, (I) The Constitution, (II) Immigration, and (III) Land.

Source: J. C. Hurewitz, *The Middle East and North Africa in World Politics, vol. 2, British-French Supremacy, 1914–1945* (New Haven and London, 1979), 532–38.

I. — The Constitution

4. It has been urged that the expression "a national home for the Jewish people" offered a prospect that Palestine might in due course become a Jewish State or Commonwealth. His Majesty's Government do not wish to contest the view, which was expressed by the Royal Commission, that the Zionist leaders at the time of the issue of the Balfour Declaration recognised that an ultimate Jewish State was not precluded by the terms of the Declaration. But, with the Royal Commission, His Majesty's Government believe that the framers of the Mandate in which the Balfour Declaration was embodied could not have intended that Palestine should be converted into a Jewish State against the will of the Arab population of the country. That Palestine was not to be converted into a Jewish State might be held to be implied in the passage from the Command Paper of 1922 which reads as follows: —

> Unauthorised statements have been made to the effect that the purpose in view is to create a wholly Jewish Palestine. Phrases have been used such as that Palestine is to become "as Jewish as England is English." His Majesty's Government regard any such expectation as impracticable and have no such aim in view. Nor have they at any time contemplated . . . the disappearance or the subordination of the Arabic population, language or culture in Palestine. They would draw attention to the fact that the terms of the [Balfour] Declaration referred to do not contemplate that Palestine as a whole should be converted into a Jewish National Home, but that such a Home should be founded *in Palestine*.

But this statement has not removed doubts, and His Majesty's Government therefore now declare unequivocally that it is not part of their policy that Palestine should become a Jewish State. They would indeed regard it as contrary to their obligations to the Arabs under the Mandate, as well as to the assurances which have been given to the Arab people in the past, that the Arab population of Palestine should be made the subjects of a Jewish State against their will. . . .

> . . . When it is asked what is meant by the development of the Jewish National Home in Palestine, it may be answered that it is not the imposition of a Jewish nationality upon the inhabitants of Palestine as a whole, but the further development of the existing Jewish community, with the assistance of Jews in other parts of the world, in order that it may become a centre in which the Jewish people as a whole may take, on grounds of religion and race, an interest and a pride. But . . . this community . . . should know that it is in Palestine as of right and not on sufferance. That is the reason why it is necessary that the existence of a Jewish National Home in Palestine should be internationally guaranteed, and that it should be formally recognised to rest upon ancient historic connection. . . .

8. His Majesty's Government are charged as the Mandatory authority "to secure the development of self-governing institutions" in Palestine. . . . His

Majesty's Government are unable at present to foresee the exact constitutional forms which government in Palestine will eventually take, but their objective is self-government, and they desire to see established ultimately an independent Palestine State. It should be a State in which the two peoples in Palestine, Arabs and Jews, share authority in government in such a way that the essential interests of each are secured. . . .

9. . . . (1) The objective of His Majesty's Government is the establishment within ten years of an independent Palestine State in such treaty relations with the United Kingdom as will provide satisfactorily for the commercial and strategic requirements of both countries in the future. This proposal for the establishment of the independent State would involve consultation with the Council of the League of Nations with a view to the termination of the Mandate. . . .

II. — Immigration

12. Under Article 6 of the Mandate, the Administration of Palestine, "while ensuring that the rights and position of other sections of the population are not prejudiced," is required to "facilitate Jewish immigration under suitable conditions." Beyond this, the extent to which Jewish immigration into Palestine is to be permitted is nowhere defined in the Mandate. But in the Command Paper of 1922 it was laid down that for the fulfilment of the policy of establishing a Jewish National Home it is necessary that the Jewish community in Palestine should be able to increase its numbers by immigration. This immigration cannot be so great in volume as to exceed whatever may be the economic capacity of the country at the time to absorb new arrivals. It is essential to ensure that the immigrants should not be a burden upon the people of Palestine as a whole, and that they should not deprive any section of the present population of their employment. . . .

13. . . . It has been the hope of British Governments ever since the Balfour Declaration was issued that in time the Arab population, recognising the advantages to be derived from Jewish settlement and development in Palestine, would become reconciled to the further growth of the Jewish National Home. This hope has not been fulfilled. The alternatives before His Majesty's Government are either (i) to seek to expand the Jewish National Home indefinitely by immigration, against the strongly expressed will of the Arab people of the country; or (ii) to permit further expansion of the Jewish National Home by immigration only if the Arabs are prepared to acquiesce in it. The former policy means rule by force. Apart from other considerations, such a policy seems to His Majesty's Government to be contrary to the whole spirit of Article 22 of the Covenant of the League of Nations, as well as to their specific obligations to the Arabs in the Palestine Mandate. Moreover, the relations between the Arabs and the Jews in Palestine must be based sooner or later on mutual tolerance and goodwill; the peace, security and progress of the Jewish National Home itself require this. Therefore His Majesty's Government, after earnest consideration, and taking into account the extent to which the growth of the Jewish National Home has

been facilitated over the last twenty years, have decided that the time has come to adopt in principle the second of the alternatives referred to above. . . .

14. . . . His Majesty's Government are conscious of the present unhappy plight of large numbers of Jews who seek a refuge from certain European countries, and they believe that Palestine can and should make a further contribution to the solution of this pressing world problem. In all these circumstances, they believe that they will be acting consistently with their Mandatory obligations to both Arabs and Jews . . . by adopting the following proposals regarding immigration: — (1) Jewish immigration during the next five years will be at a rate which, if economic absorptive capacity permits, will bring the Jewish population up to approximately one-third of the total population of the country. Taking into account the expected natural increase of the Arab and Jewish populations, and the number of illegal Jewish immigrants now in the country, this would allow of the admission, as from the beginning of April this year, of some 75,000 immigrants over the next five years. . . .

(3) After the period of five years no further Jewish immigration will be permitted unless the Arabs of Palestine are prepared to acquiesce in it. . . .

III. — Land

16. The Administration of Palestine is required, under Article 6 of the Mandate, "while ensuring that the rights and position of other sections of the population are not prejudiced," to encourage "close settlement by Jews on the land," and no restriction has been imposed hitherto on the transfer of land from Arabs to Jews. The Reports of several expert Commissions have indicated that, owing to the natural growth of the Arab population and the steady sale in recent years of Arab land to Jews, there is now in certain areas no room for further transfers of Arab land, whilst in some other areas such transfers of land must be restricted if Arab cultivators are to maintain their existing standard of life and a considerable landless Arab population is not soon to be created. In these circumstances, the High Commissioner will be given general powers to prohibit and regulate transfers of land. These powers will date from the publication of this statement of policy and the High Commissioner will retain them throughout the transitional period.

4

WORLD WAR II AND THE CREATION OF THE STATE OF ISRAEL

1939–1949

THE IMPACT of World War II on Palestine and the future of Zionism went far beyond the military campaigns themselves. In 1941, Adolf Hitler initiated his plan to eradicate people designated as inferior according to Nazi ideology and its cult of Aryan supremacy. Although the retarded, the insane, and homosexuals were included in this category, Hitler's intent was, first, to exterminate European Jews and, second, European gypsies. It was for them that the crematoria and gas chambers were built in the concentration camps that had originally held German political prisoners. Special attention was paid to the collection of Jews (see Document 4.1). By war's end, approximately 6 million, two-thirds of European Jewry, had been slaughtered, along with between 200,000 and 250,000 gypsies. In addition, millions of Slav prisoners, rated just above Jews and gypsies, were exploited as forced labor until they either died or were deliberately killed; 3.5 million out of 5.5 million Russian prisoners of war died in German hands. In all, German troops and police murdered approximately 10 million people, either exploited at forced labor until death or, particularly in the case of Jews, rounded up purposefully and with great effort for extermination.[1]

To Jews in Palestine and elsewhere, especially the United States, knowledge of the Holocaust, available from late 1942 onward, meant that the Allies should exert all possible efforts to take in refugees. Equally important was their demand that Palestine now be recognized as a Jewish state to house those who survived. To Britain and the United States, these questions were less important than victory over Germany and Japan, especially because the Zionists often tied the refugee topic to Palestine, creating a political issue that the British in particular sought to evade. By war's end, Zionism and the fate of the remnants of European Jewry had become intertwined in the United States, setting the American government in opposition to postwar British policy. For the British, already confronted with Zionist terror in Palestine aimed at driving them out, the burden became too much. The Labour government handed over the issue to the United Nations, setting the stage for war between Jews and Arabs in Palestine and the declaration of the Israeli state on May 14, 1948.

PALESTINE, ZIONISM, AND THE WAR EFFORT, 1939–1945

As we have noted, the 1939 White Paper appeared on May 17, 1939, following the German invasion of Czechoslovakia on March 15 and Italy's conquest of Albania in April. During the summer Europe moved ever closer to war. On August 23 the Nazi-Soviet Non-Aggression Pact was signed, prompting Great Britain to enter an alliance with Poland that promised aid if it were invaded. German forces entered Poland on September 1, leading Britain and France to declare war on Germany on September 3. Russia then invaded Poland on September 17 and Polish resistance ended on September 27 when the country was partitioned between Germany and Russia.

The next stage of Germany's offensive began in April 1940, when it absorbed Norway and Denmark. The British failure to block Germany's occupation of Norway led to Neville Chamberlain's resignation as prime minister; Winston Churchill succeeded him on May 10. Germany then invaded the Low Countries and France, overwhelming the combined British-French forces. France sued for peace and signed an armistice on June 22. Hitler reigned supreme in Western Europe, now joined by Mussolini, who entered the war on his side on June 10. Great Britain faced a Nazi-held Europe alone. In the Battle of Britain, fought in August and September 1940, the Royal Air Force beat back the Luftwaffe (German air force), but England remained under intensive German air raids well into 1942. In 1940–1941, approximately 43,000 civilians were killed in these attacks.[2] Pressure was relieved somewhat when Hitler ordered the invasion of Russia, which began on June 22, 1941 and established a second front, but the Axis powers, including Japan, continued to score significant victories.

World War II and the Middle East

The spring of 1942 was especially critical. German forces advanced swiftly through western Russia and, in North Africa, drove British forces back to El-Alamein in Egypt, fifty miles from Alexandria; in the Far East the Japanese took Singapore, the largest British naval base in the Eastern Hemisphere. Only in November 1942, with the decisive British victory at El-Alamein, did the German threat to Egypt, the Suez Canal, and Palestine recede. That, coupled with the successful Russian defense of Stalingrad in the winter of 1942–1943 and the American naval victories against the Japanese in the Pacific, established a firmer basis for conducting the war.

In the Middle East, the British had come under intense military pressure once Italy declared war on June 10, 1940. The Italian position in Libya posed a direct threat to British security in Egypt and Palestine. Additionally, the Italian fleet and air force, supplemented by German air assaults, attacked British convoys crossing the Mediterranean. The Red Sea port of Suez thus became the major supply depot for goods reaching British forces in Egypt. Palestine throughout the period served as a training area for troops. Haifa, once its oil refinery was completed in June 1940, became the major source of fuel for the British fleet, refining oil sent by pipeline from Iraq. This supply, along with oil shipped from the Abadan refinery in Iran and stored at Haifa, enabled operations in the Mediterranean and North Africa to continue. For the British, the Suez Zone–Persian Gulf connection across Palestine, Transjordan, and Iraq was crucial to its immediate war effort.[3]

British military fortunes were at a particularly low ebb in the spring of 1941, once the Germans, under Erwin Rommel, took command of the desert war and drove British forces back into Egypt. The British were further threatened when, in April, the Iraqi prime minister, Rashid Ali al-Gaylani, ordered his troops to encircle the small British contingents that remained and called for German military aid. Steadfast British action undermined al-Gaylani's resolve and ultimately forced him and his pro-German retinue, including the mufti Hajj Amin al-Husayni, to flee. Because the Vichy French in Syria had granted landing rights to German planes sent to aid al-Gaylani's revolt, British forces, aided by Jewish units, invaded Syria and occupied it and Lebanon in a campaign lasting from May into July.

The need for British troops to deal with security in Arab states while confronting the Germans along the Egyptian border again raised the question of Arab loyalty. This led the foreign secretary, Anthony Eden, to issue a declaration just before the attack on Vichy French forces in Syria that offered British support for any Arab attempts to achieve unity. This appeal, which included acceptance of Syrian postwar independence—to the fury of the Free French forces under Charles de Gaulle—clearly indicated British wishes to harness Arab nationalism to their own goals after the war, recalling their support for Faysal against the French in 1918–1919. Eden's announcement also alarmed Zionist leaders, who saw it as further evidence of British wishes to restrict the scope of the Jewish National Home and ultimate statehood. But until early 1943, when the danger of a German assault through Egypt into Palestine receded, Zionist officials cooperated militarily with Great Britain while striving to undermine the White Paper and ultimately the British position in Palestine. British officials were aware of this situation, perhaps best expressed by Ben-Gurion when he told the Zionist Congress in August 1939 that "for us the White Paper neither exists nor can exist. We must behave as if we were the State in Palestine until we actually become the State in Palestine."[4]

Palestine: Jewish Immigration and the British Response

Yishuv leaders had decided in 1938, before the 1939 White Paper, to step up the illegal immigration of Jews into Palestine; the unauthorized immigrants in 1939 totaled 11,156 out of the 27,561 who arrived.[5] With the outbreak of war in September, plans to arrange the transfer of more refugees intensified: thousands were trying to flee Europe, often with Gestapo encouragement. These efforts brought Zionists and British officials into immediate conflict in London as well as Palestine. The British placed illegal immigrants in internment camps in Palestine, which led the Zionists to try to flood the country with immigrants to negate the effectiveness of such tactics. The British then decided to send the refugees who reached Palestine on to the island of Mauritius in the Indian Ocean. At the same time the Foreign Office attempted to stem the flow of refugees from Europe by encouraging countries such as Turkey to deny them transit. An impossible situation arose after September 1939 that created "almost ... a war within a war."[6] Jews became increasingly bitter at what they saw as British inhumanity. The British felt the same toward the Zionist leadership, whom they saw as demanding special attention and a diversion of war materials at a time when the major theaters of war required all available aid.

Catastrophes occurred as a result. In November 1940, over 1,700 refugees from two ships intercepted by British naval patrols were transferred to the SS *Patria* in the port of Haifa for scheduled deportation to Mauritius. The Hagana, under Jewish Agency direction, placed a bomb near the hull to disable the ship, intending to force British authorities to permit the Jews to stay. The plan miscarried, and the ship sank with over 200 casualties. In response to Zionist outrage and propaganda blaming the British for the incident, the British cabinet permitted the survivors of the *Patria* to remain in Palestine. One final disaster occurred when the *Struma*, a rickety vessel with 769 Romanian Jews aboard, docked off Istanbul in December 1941 for engine repairs while the British tried to persuade the Turks to forbid its passage into the Mediterranean toward Palestine. Negotiations and debate went on for over two months. A British concession that children between the ages of eleven and sixteen should be permitted to proceed overland to Palestine was blocked by the Turks, who would permit sea travel only. In the end, the Turks sent the ship back into the Black Sea, where it sank on February 25, 1942; there was one survivor.[7]

To the Zionists, the *Struma*'s sinking proved British perfidy and those seen as most responsible for the loss of life—Harold MacMichael, high commissioner, and Lord Moyne, colonial secretary—were later targeted for assassination attempts; that on Moyne in November 1944 was successful. For British officials, the *Struma* affair, though tragic, was just one incident in the midst of a continuing series of crises threatening the survival of the empire and its ability to wage war. Egyptian demonstrations in January 1942 calling for a German victory had forced a showdown in Cairo; on February 4, the British ambassador compelled King Faruq to accept the nationalist leader, al-Nahhas, as prime minister, under threat of forced abdication. The Zionist conception of Palestine as a haven for European Jewry conflicted with a British concern about the continuing stability of a region they deemed crucial to the conduct of the war.

The Jewish Division and the Question of Jewish Military Capabilities

Another issue of contention was Chaim Weizmann's proposal to form a Jewish division that would fight as a distinct unit under the Zionist flag alongside British troops against the Nazis. British officials had encouraged both Palestinian Arab and Jewish enlistments, intending to use these troops in British units or as auxiliaries in reserve in Palestine. Jewish enlistments far outnumbered Arab, and Hagana representatives cooperated with British special forces in training Jewish soldiers for secret missions in both the Middle East and Europe. However, the idea of a separate Jewish division aroused some controversy. The British cabinet approved Weizmann's proposals in principle but resisted his demand that the Jewish Agency be identified with the mobilization of the troops. This was seen correctly as a political move designed, with the creation of a separate Jewish fighting force, to enhance Zionist claims to Palestine at the peace conference after the war.[8] Prime Minister Winston Churchill, long sympathetic to Zionism, supported the idea of a Jewish division, but opposition at the highest civil and military levels delayed approval until late 1944, when a Jewish brigade was formed that fought as a separate unit in Europe. In addition, many Jewish soldiers fought as part of British companies.

The dispute over the Jewish brigade and its implications illustrated the complexity of the relationship between the Zionists and the British and the motives behind each side's actions and proposals. The Zionists "still hoped for a peaceful post-war change of British policy which would allow for the creation of a Jewish State. . . . On the other hand, they wished to insure against the possibility of British post-war persistence in the White Paper policy."[9] When Jewish Agency officials argued for Jewish mobilization, they did so knowing that the Hagana could exploit the opportunity to gain greater military experience and, equally important, to have greater access to British arms. In the Hagana's view, Jews "took upon themselves the twofold mission of fighting in the ranks of the British army . . . and at the same time doing whatever they could to ensure the arming of the Yishuv. It was their firm conviction that the one mission did not conflict with the other but that . . . they complemented each other."[10] As a result, Hagana agents carried out numerous raids to steal arms from storage depots in Palestine and the western desert with the cooperation of Jewish soldiers or Jewish guards, not to mention the bedouin. And Jewish units in Europe maintained contact with their Hagana leaders in Palestine and established networks for both the transfer of refugees to Palestine and the theft of arms that could then be shipped there to build up Hagana strength for war. Estimates of Jewish weapons vary, but the Hagana in 1942–1943 had approximately 12,000 pistols, 18,000 rifles, 450 submachine guns and automatic rifles, and 162 machine guns, most in excellent condition and carefully stored. In addition, the Hagana had begun some arms manufacturing and was producing mortars.[11]

The British knew of these activities and their motives. Foreign Office and Colonial Office officials agreed in 1942 that "there seems little doubt that . . . the Jews intend to resort to direct action if they fail to secure a postwar settlement compatible with their present aspirations."[12] But during the early years of the war, they could do little about such arms acquisitions, as they needed Hagana cooperation in case of a German breakthrough in Egypt. Once the possibility of a German onslaught into Egypt and Palestine faded, British officials in Palestine initiated extensive arms searches—seldom successful—and brought to trial those Jews and British soldiers whom they discovered smuggling arms to the Hagana. Raids on suspected arms caches brought open Jewish resistance and public threats of retaliation by Yishuv leaders. Aware that the British could not cope with such a possibility, the high commissioner advised the military to desist, but he believed that by 1944 the Zionist leadership in Palestine was, in effect, claiming the right to arm itself in the face of British authority in order to oppose it (see Figure 4.1).

Figure 4.1 ■ The Jewish Agency Executive Building, May 1942

This impressive complex on St. George Street attests to the organizational powers held by the Labor Zionist movement, essentially a separate government under the auspices of the British mandate.

The Biltmore Conference and Its Consequences

British fears of a confrontation with Zionism after the war owed much to the growing strength of militant American Zionism and its support of Ben-Gurion's activism against Weizmann's gradualism. This alliance had resulted from developments in the early stages of the war, especially the conference held at the Biltmore Hotel in New York City in May 1942.

The conference had been organized by Weizmann's associates who hoped to unite American Jewish organizations behind a program designed to undertake fund-raising and political activity on behalf of Zionism. They assumed that thousands, if not millions, of Jewish refugees would seek to go to Palestine after the war. The resolutions passed by the conference called for the opening of Palestine to immigration and Jewish Agency control of that immigration and the authority required to develop Palestine; after the war Palestine should "be established as a Jewish Commonwealth integrated in the structure of the new democratic world."[13] Intended to mobilize American Jews, the Biltmore declarations were extraordinarily successful, especially once news of the Holocaust began to spread in the latter half of 1942. Membership in Zionist organizations and publicity for the Zionist cause increased substantially, along with books that were published and distributed with Jewish financial aid.[14] In addition, millions of leaflets were sent to members of Congress and to their constituents to send to their representatives. And Zionists established two Christian organizations to back the call for a Jewish state in Palestine, the American Palestine Committee and the Christian Council on Palestine. Both received Zionist subsidies and proved to be extremely effective in mobilizing support that included demanding that United States oppose the 1939 White Paper. As a result of these efforts, both the Republican and Democratic platforms of 1944 endorsed the creation of a Jewish commonwealth as designated in the Biltmore resolutions.

Jewish groups were less successful in their attempts to galvanize the U.S. government to support operations designed to aid refugees fleeing Nazi-held Europe. Official American refusal to accept Jewish refugees or to exert efforts to find havens elsewhere lasted into mid-1944. Various studies of the question have either charged responsible officials with blatant anti-Semitism or have stressed the general fear that diversion of materials to an issue not contributing to military victory would have undermined the war effort.[15] It seems clear that administration officials wished to evade the refugee question in general, and the Jewish issue in particular, until after the war. Indeed, growing public support for a postwar Jewish Palestine did not translate into intensive pressure on the American government by non-Jews to strive either to rescue Jews or to even make public statements condemning the atrocities that were occurring. Only in 1944, with President Franklin D. Roosevelt's backing, was a War Relief Board created to facilitate the flight of several thousand refugees.

What is difficult to ascertain is how many Jews, if any, could have been saved if the British and American governments had opened their doors to them from

1942 onward. The official U.S. response to Jewish calls for action was hindered by divisions within the ranks of American Jewry. Here politics and the question of Palestine intervened. Many American Jews supported the principle of establishing havens for refugees anywhere, even the idea of "free ports" in Palestine where Jews would be permitted to remain throughout the war. They accepted the argument that the temporary presence of these refugees in Palestine did not constitute recognition of their right to stay afterwards as part of the Jewish population. This proposal, intended to avoid the political ramifications of immigration for the war's duration, met with strong Zionist opposition. Zionists stipulated that any proposed refugee scheme should designate Palestine as the only haven, serving their goal of effectively rescinding the 1939 White Paper and furthering the prospect of a Jewish state. The Zionist stance led to charges that they appeared to be "more interested in having the White Paper revoked than in circumventing its effects by means of temporary havens" and that Zionist politics blocked efforts that might have saved many Jews.[16] The Zionists' linkage of any proposed rescue of refugees to the right to enter Palestine immediately, thus circumventing the White Paper, has remained a sensitive issue among American Jews.[17]

Despite the impetus the Biltmore Conference gave to American Zionism, it also reopened the Weizmann–Ben-Gurion rivalry over Zionist policy. Ben-Gurion became infuriated at what he considered to be Weizmann's obsessive reliance on British policymaking and on diplomacy as the primary tool to achieve Zionist goals. He was determined to have the Zionist leadership in Palestine, namely, himself, direct the movement toward statehood, which he considered achievable as much by direct action against Great Britain as by cooperation and negotiation with it. The split widened when Ben-Gurion, as head of the Jewish Agency Executive, challenged Weizmann's right, as leader of the World Zionist Organization, to suggest any policy without his approval. Weizmann responded by accusing Ben-Gurion of "political assassination." The aftermath of the quarrel, fueled by fundamental differences in objectives, saw their increasing estrangement.[18] Weizmann hoped to persuade the British to revive the 1937 partition plan proposed by the Peel Commission. In contrast, Ben-Gurion wanted to establish a Jewish state in all of western Palestine, a goal he considered more attainable by direct Jewish action there and lobbying in the United States than through negotiations with London. By the end of 1942, however, the British cabinet was itself reviewing its postwar options for Palestine. This process, with Churchill's encouragement, led to a reassessment of the White Paper and a revival of partition as the only feasible option.

The White Paper, Partition, and Britain's Place in the Middle East, 1942–1945

In December 1942, the war cabinet commissioned a study of Britain's postwar position in the Middle East. The committee report envisioned the end of the mandates as nations achieved independence and stressed that Great Britain should retain ties with these newly independent regimes through treaty relationships in order to preserve its paramount strategic position in the region. Palestine, in this view, remained vital to British interests. If the mandate were altered, Britain should retain access to the port of Haifa and be able to secure the Haifa-Baghdad road and the Haifa-Kirkuk oil pipeline; military installations to protect these interests would be necessary.[19] In short, the value of Palestine for British imperial planners, including the chiefs of staff, remained essentially what had been outlined in the de Bunsen report of 1915 before the Balfour Declaration. British officials anticipated success in achieving these goals within the framework of the settling of the question of Palestine, which called for imposing the clauses of the 1939 White Paper, a matter of increasing importance as the war progressed. The period defined for Jewish immigration of up to 75,000 ended in April 1944 (it was extended). But the military and the Foreign Office were increasingly concerned at the apparent success of Zionist propaganda in the United States. They foresaw the need to counter expected American pressure on the matter of the White Paper, a source of potential rivalry, along with the broader question of conflicting oil interests once the war ended.

Nevertheless, a cabinet committee on Palestine was established in July 1943 at Churchill's instigation to examine alternatives to the White Paper. In December 1943, the committee recommended partition. Opposition to the proposal, led by foreign secretary Anthony Eden and backed by the chiefs of staff and British diplomats in the Middle East, inspired intense debate throughout the first half of 1944. Churchill and the committee held firm, although they reduced the area allotted to the Jewish state. In September, final discussions began, and by early November, the war cabinet was ready to examine and approve a partition plan that would become official British policy after the war. Weizmann was fully aware of this, as was Ben-Gurion in Jerusalem. Not only had the White Paper been suspended, though not officially, but London had also rejected an American trusteeship proposal, supported by Eden, that would have placed Palestine under the auspices of the United Nations, a plan the State Department later revived.[20]

Then, on November 6, members of the Jewish terrorist group LEHI (Fighters for the Freedom of Israel, formerly Stern Gang) assassinated Lord Moyne, deputy minister of state for Middle East Affairs in Cairo and a close friend of Churchill. Churchill reacted by shelving the partition scheme he had seen through, against stiff opposition from his ministers. The prime minister declared to the House of Commons that "if our dreams for Zionism are to end in the smoke of assassins' pistols and our labours for its future to produce only a new set of gangsters worthy of Nazi Germany, many like myself will have to reconsider the position we have maintained so consistently in the past."[21] Partition was not discussed again during Churchill's term as prime minister, leaving it to the Labour government that took over in July 1945. In the meantime, Churchill's warning to the Zionist leadership produced action: they stopped underground activities that seemed to threaten the likelihood of any cooperation with a British government after the war.

Jewish Terrorism, the Hagana, and the British, 1940–1945

The British declaration of the 1939 White Paper had led the Revisionist terrorist group, the Irgun, to shift its focus from the Arabs to the British. It had begun to attack British administrative buildings and police personnel and to bomb gathering places. Once the war began, Jabotinsky called for the Revisionists to support the British effort against the Nazis. While most of the Irgun in Palestine accepted this directive, a small faction, led by Abraham Stern, refused to cease operations. Thus the Stern Gang emerged in 1940, willing to rob Jewish concerns, such as a Histadrut bank, with Jewish loss of life as well as assault British officials. At the same time, Stern decided that he should establish contact with German and Italian representatives to offer his services to their cause for the duration of the war. The fact that they all were anti-British was sufficient, despite the anti-Semitic basis of the Nazi regime. As a result, the Stern group was condemned by both the Hagana and the Irgun, who gave British police information leading to its temporary destruction; Stern was killed in a British police raid in February 1942.[22]

With the leaders of the Stern Gang dead or in prison, there was little underground activity from early 1942 to the beginning of 1944. Jabotinsky's death in 1940 had deprived the Irgun of strong leadership until Menachem Begin's arrival in Palestine in April 1942. A former member of Betar in Poland and a future prime minister of Israel, Begin saw himself as the heir to Jabotinsky's Revisionist ideals. By the end of 1943, members of both groups were again preparing for anti-British action, inspired by both the receding German threat in the Middle East and the ongoing tensions in Zionist-British relations, exacerbated particularly by the legacy of the refugee ships and the growing awareness of the Holocaust. This led to an accommodation between Begin and members of the Stern Gang who had escaped from prison and who now renewed their actions against the British under the name of LEHI (Fighters for the Freedom of Israel). Among them was Nathan Yellin-Mor, who had been close to Begin as a member of Betar in Poland, and Yitzhak Shamir, who in 1980 became foreign minister in the government led by Begin and prime minister in 1986.

Both groups demanded a Jewish state that included all of original Palestine, Transjordan restored, and parts of southern Lebanon and Syria, though they disagreed on tactics until the end of the war. LEHI resumed its assassinations of British officials, civilian and military. Begin directed the Irgun to bomb only civilian installations linked to the mandatory authority, not military sites. That, he reasoned, would show that the Irgun was not seeking to impede the war effort, even though Irgun operations did kill British personnel. Throughout much of 1944, the Hagana objected more strenuously to LEHI than to the Irgun, considering it a "'classic' terrorist group," whereas the Irgun was principally a political threat to the program pursued by the Yishuv leadership.[23]

Matters came to a head with the LEHI-sponsored assassination of Lord Moyne in November 1944. In response to British police requests for aid, the

Hagana intensified its efforts against both the Irgun and LEHI, rounding up operatives, mostly Irgun, interrogating and occasionally beating them, and handing over some Irgun members to the British police; LEHI leaders agreed to suspend operations after negotiations with Hagana envoys. This operation, called "The Season," lasted from November 1944 into the spring of 1945. Hagana focus on the Irgun, despite LEHI's more active assassination policies, indicated Jewish Agency concern for the greater appeal that the Irgun might have among the population. But Begin's refusal to retaliate against the Hagana, and the Hagana's inability to destroy the Irgun, strengthened the Irgun and gave it credibility among the populace as loyal to Zionist goals, whatever the extremes of its actions.[24] With the end of the European war on May 8, 1945, terror resumed as part of a new era in British-Jewish relations in Palestine.

Palestinian Arab Leadership and the Question of Arab Unity, 1939–1945

The Arab Higher Committee had collapsed at the conclusion of the Arab Revolt in early 1939. Many of its leaders were in exile, having fled Palestine to avoid capture by the British.[25] The mufti had been officially banned from the country following his escape in October 1937. With the outbreak of war, British officials in Palestine made overtures to the mufti, by now in Baghdad, to seek his support for the White Paper and implementation of its immigration restrictions. They did so out of fear of his ability to arouse general Arab hostility toward the British position in the Middle East at that time. Al-Husayni rejected these requests and the White Paper itself. Instead, he aligned himself with the Iraqi rebellion against Great Britain in April 1941, and once it failed he made his way, via Iran, to Italy and Germany. There he spent the war supporting the German war effort and German barbarity against the Jews (see Figure 4.2).

Arab Society. Other members of the Higher Committee accepted British offers of safe return to Palestine in return for promises not to engage in overt political activity. Between February 1940 and November 1942, a number of high officials of the Istiqlal and the Palestine Arab Party that represented the Husaynis, along with Husayn al-Khalidi of the Reform Party, reestablished themselves in the country. In general they indicated their cautious acceptance of the 1939 White Paper and distanced themselves from the mufti, whom they depicted as only one member of the Arab Higher Committee. Despite the intense Axis propaganda beamed to Palestine during 1941 and 1942, which included the mufti's exhortations to rebel, Arab Palestine remained calm. Though due in part to the presence of large numbers of Allied military personnel, other factors contributed to the apparent tranquility of Arab society. Among them was the fact that Palestine, following years of economic deprivation for its Arab population, now entered a period of prosperity that included the Arabs, the result of

Figure 4.2 ■ Hajj Amin al-Husayni and Adolf Hitler Meeting in Germany, circa November 1941

The mufti fled to Axis Europe from Iraq via Iran, arriving in Italy in October 1941. Though he initially sought German/Italian backing to oust the British, as did some other Arab nationalists, he subsequently adopted language in his pronouncements, including references to Jews, that indicated Nazi influence. These statements would later serve to tarnish the Palestinian cause generally with the label of anti-Semitism once the Holocaust became widely known.

the great expansion of demand for all goods and services owing to the presence of British military forces. The peasants in particular benefited from the captive market for their crops and the expansion of the labor force, which they entered.

With the mufti in Germany and his cousin, Jamal al-Husayni, interned in Southern Rhodesia for the duration of the war, the field was open for rivals to seek to dominate Arab politics. Those in the forefront were the members of the Istiqlal who sought to use the economic boom in Palestine as a means of boosting Arab resistance to Zionism, in particular Ahmad Hilmi, Awni Abd al-Hadi, and Rashid Ibrahim. They had acquired control of the Arab National Bank and through it appealed to a newly emerging Arab bourgeoisie. They also took over the Arab National Fund, which they used as a vehicle to acquire land that might otherwise be bought by Zionists. The fund attracted widespread support. Branches were opened throughout Palestine, with many contributions by peasants who suddenly had spare cash as a result of the new prosperity. In a very real way the fund captured the attention and imagination of the Arab population, but this in itself was seen by the al-Husayni faction as a threat to its anticipated resurgence. In addition, the Istiqlal enjoyed a broad base of support, often commercially oriented and not tied to traditional local power affiliations. As a result, the Istiqlal found itself opposed by all the major clans in Jerusalem that might contend with one another; the al-Nashashibis as well as the al-Husaynis had rejected the Istiqlal in the late 1930s. Its main opposition was still the al-Husayni power base, local leaders and village headmen loyal to their traditional source of authority in Jerusalem. The Palestine Arab Party of the mufti reappeared in April 1944, its real leader being a Greek Orthodox named Emile al-Ghuri while Jamal al-Husayni remained in exile.

By the end of the European war in May 1945, the Palestine Arab Party was once again the most powerful political voice in the Arab community, although the Istiqlal also commanded widespread respect; it had been active in combating Zionism during the war, in contrast to the more propagandistic nature of the al-Husayni appeal. The differences between the two groups were significant, though neither espoused views acceptable to the Zionists. The Istiqlal called for strict implementation of the White Paper, which by 1944 the British were avoiding. This stance, though untenable in Zionist eyes, did from the Istiqlal's perspective recognize the existence of a Jewish National Home composed of those Jews then in Palestine. The Zionists wanted unlimited immigration and a Jewish state in which they were a majority. The Palestine Arab Party, on the other hand, called for the dissolution of the Jewish National Home and the creation of an Arab government in charge of the entire country. This maximalist position—rejection of any Jewish presence in Palestine beyond that traceable to before 1917—was analogous to the Irgun and LEHI calls for a Jewish state on both sides of the Jordan. The difference was that these Jewish groups were minorities within the Jewish community, whereas the Palestine Arab Party seemed to reflect the position of a majority of Palestinian Arabs, at least those in positions of local leadership.

Discussion of these factions leaves open the question of Palestinian public opinion which, though opposed to a Jewish state, might have varied on the nature of the society envisioned after the war. It is clear that major structural changes occurred in Arab Palestine between 1939 and 1945, and especially from 1943 onward, following the creation of the Arab National Fund. Muslims began to enroll in the government educational system in growing numbers, a reflection of the increased interest of peasant village communities. "Between 1943–45 Arab peasants voluntarily contributed [the equivalent of] more than $1.5 million for educational purposes, as compared to $187,200 for the years 1941–42."[26] New professional groups emerged, a Palestine Arab Medical Association was created, and Palestinian Arab women began to achieve professional status in the medical and legal professions, establishing the nucleus for what later became the Palestinian professional class in the greater Arab world following the Arab exodus and the creation of Israel.

The ongoing disputes among the Palestinian political elite meant that real leadership and representation of the Palestinian cause devolved once more to heads of neighboring Arab regimes, a process that continued through 1948. Among these Arabs, there was greater consensus on Palestine than on most other issues confronting them. Some had themselves sought to encourage a unified Palestinian front to strengthen the Palestinian Arab stance, but to no avail. Whether such a stance would have benefited the Palestinians is open to question given Zionist determination to prevail with the Palestinians at best in a subordinate status, but it would have created the impression of a Palestinian Arab polity with its own leadership instead of a cause advocated by surrogates from neighboring countries.[27]

Arab Nationalism and Regional Rivalries.   Their concern for Palestine notwithstanding, the attention of most Arab heads of state throughout the war had been directed principally to the question of regional unity, long an Arab ideal, which had been encouraged by Anthony Eden in May 1941. Whatever the expediency of his declaration, made in concert with British preparations for an invasion of Vichy-held Syria and for recognition of an independent Syrian state after the war, it gained the attention of both Nuri al-Said of Iraq and, once he took office in February 1942, Mustafa al-Nahhas, the Egyptian prime minister and leader of the most popular nationalist party, the Wafd. Al-Nahhas, recognizing the spirit of Arab nationalism, was determined to include Egypt in any forthcoming discussions to bring Arab states closer together, hoping that Egypt might dominate such a group. On the other hand, plans already existed for Arab unity in the Levant that specifically excluded Egypt. These were the Fertile Crescent schemes, so named because they applied to Transjordan, Palestine, Lebanon, Syria, and Iraq. But such proposals sparked rivalries. Both the Iraqi and Transjordanian governments, related by Hashemite blood, vied for control over any such Arab government. In turn, Syrian nationalists, as heirs to Faysal's Arab kingdom of 1919–1920, considered themselves the logical leaders of an Arab state. The Saudis and the Egyptians continued to encourage the Syrians to resist Iraqi or Transjordanian overtures. The Saud dynasty's anti-Hashemite stance harked back to World War I rivalries while Egyptian politicians feared being excluded from a large Arab state that would challenge its assumed right to influence Arab politics. These disputes and intrigues dominated Arab politics well into the 1960s and beyond.

Arab heads of state met in Alexandria, Egypt, in October 1944. The Alexandria Protocol issued by that conference called for the formation of a league of Arab states that could further coordinate their political and commercial activities. Palestine was singled out for consideration in a resolution declaring that:

> Palestine constitutes an important part of the Arab world and that the rights of the Arabs [Palestinian] cannot be touched without prejudice to peace and stability in the Arab world. . . .
>
> The Committee also declares that it is second to none in regretting the woes that have been inflicted upon the Jews of Europe by European

dictatorial states. But the question of these Jews should not be confused with Zionism, for there can be no greater injustice and aggression than solving the problem of the Jews of Europe by another injustice, that is, by inflicting injustice on the Palestine Arabs of various religions and denominations.[28]

Therein lay the heart of the Arab argument, whether Palestinian or otherwise, against Zionism, one that has lasted to the present day. With the war's end it confronted a Zionist call for unlimited immigration into Palestine to resolve precisely the injustice that Nazi Germany had imposed on European Jews.

In the meantime, a League of Arab states was formed in March 1945, pursuant to the recommendations of the Alexandria Protocol. The league's charter relaxed the stress on potential Arab unity found in the earlier document. On the other hand, it established more specific provisos for the defense of Palestinian Arabs and created a seat for a Palestinian Arab representative despite Palestine's lack of independence. With this machinery in place, the league also undertook to represent the Palestinian Arab case before the Western world and to persuade the powers to deny the achievement of Zionist goals. Certain leaders, such as King Ibn Saud, had already engaged in such efforts; when he met President Franklin D. Roosevelt in early 1945, Saud gained his promise that no steps would be taken concerning Palestine without consultation with Arab leaders. This informal statement seemed to contradict American policy as declared in party platforms, but it reflected American concern for the stability of the Arab world and its oil, considered vital to the soundness of the Western economies.

In the end, such promises meant little. Roosevelt died in April 1945 and was succeeded by his vice president, Harry Truman, whom Roosevelt had left generally uninformed as to American foreign policy. Truman had his own ideas about resolving the question of Palestine. In England, elections in July led to Churchill's stunning defeat and the rise to power of a Labour government headed by Prime Minister Clement Attlee. In 1944, the Labour Party platform had called not only for a Jewish state in Palestine but also for the transference of the Arab population to Transjordan. Now its leaders confronted a situation in which Zionist anticipation of Labour's fulfillment of its promises conflicted with the staggering problems of attempting to maintain Britain's imperial position in the world.

THE END OF THE MANDATE AND THE CREATION OF ISRAEL, 1945–1949

The European war ended on May 8, 1945; the war against Japan on August 14. Prospects for peace soon seemed a mirage, however, especially for Great Britain, which faced nationalist demands for independence in the Middle East and Asia while confronting an economic crisis that lasted for years and seriously weakened its capacity to sustain its envisaged imperial role. The United States underwent massive demobilization after the war but soon found itself aligned with the British in a "cold war" with the Soviet Union, which, by the end of 1948, had taken most of Central and Eastern Europe under its wing. The only exception was Yugoslavia, which had declared its independence as a socialist-communist state in June of that year.

The Middle East and Postwar Tensions: Origins of the Cold War

Soviet expansion in Eastern Europe was accompanied by severe pressure on Turkey and Iran, where the Soviet Union sought to acquire territory and influence in a manner reminiscent of tsarist imperial objectives. Turkey had blocked the Bosporus Strait in 1941, fearing German reprisals if it allowed supplies through to Russia. At the war's end, Soviet Premier Josef Stalin demanded that Turkey permit the Russians to establish military bases in the perimeter around the straits whose governance should become the joint responsibility of the Black Sea powers, not simply Turkey's. Such an arrangement would have placed the Bosporus and Dardanelles under predominantly Soviet authority, thus achieving a strategic objective that had eluded the Russians throughout the entire history of the Eastern Question. The Turks resisted, with American and British backing, but Russian diplomatic pressures continued throughout 1946, as did Western fears of Soviet military actions in the area.

The situation in Iran seemed equally threatening. The Soviets occupied northern Iran at the end of the war and encouraged the creation of the autonomous Republic of Azerbaijan in December 1945 under the protection of the Soviet army; in early 1946 an adjacent Kurdish Soviet Republic was created. These developments, coupled with Soviet ultimatums to Turkey, prompted President Truman to declare in April 1946 that the Near and Middle East might become an area of international rivalry that could erupt into war. International criticism and Iran's ostensible capitulation to Soviet demands for oil concessions persuaded the Soviets to withdraw from Azerbaijan, but the experience, along with the eruption of an apparently communist-sponsored civil war in Greece, caused Western diplomats deep concern for the fate of the northern rim of the Mediterranean and the Persian Gulf.

These regions had traditionally fallen within the sphere of British imperial concerns. By early 1947, however, Britain's continuing domestic economic crisis, coupled with challenges to its imperial obligations, forced the Labour government to acknowledge that it could no longer sustain major geopolitical commitments that included the Mediterranean. In February, coincident with the British decision to withdraw from India and to hand Palestine over to the United Nations (discussed later in this chapter), the British ambassador to Washington told American officials that by early 1948 London would be withdrawing its financial and military assistance to Greece and Turkey. He expressed his government's hope that the United States would step into the role the British were abdicating out of financial necessity. The American response was the Truman Doctrine, declared on March 12, 1947, in reply to an official Greek request for aid. It signified a U.S. decision to seek to contain Soviet expansion and the threat of communism. This policy of containment led to a concerted effort by the United States to establish military alliances with the countries on the southern rim of the Soviet Union and to bolster their economies as well as their weaponry to counter communist inroads.

American leaders were equally concerned about the weakened condition of the Western European economies, including those of Germany and Italy, since their continuing poverty offered a greater likelihood of communist electoral success. This led to the Marshall Plan, first broached in late spring 1947 but not approved by Congress until nearly a year later; it committed the United States to the reconstruction of Western Europe while also supplying Greece and Turkey with military aid. Fear of communism and communist infiltration, believed to be fostered by domestic instability, governed the outlook of the State Department and many other officials in Washington.[29]

Anglo-American Perspectives on Palestine

British and American perceptions of the communist threat and the means to counter it generally coincided in 1946, but their relative capacities to respond differed greatly. Great Britain was becoming financially dependent on American aid at a time when it still sought to maintain a reduced imperial posture. Here, a rift developed between London and Washington with respect to Palestine and Zionist claims to statehood.

British Foreign Secretary Ernest Bevin's cardinal concern from 1945 to 1948 was the security of British strategic interests in the Middle East and Asia. Although the Labour government was committed to granting independence to India, the route through Suez remained vital because of British oil holdings in the Persian Gulf and its military bases in Aden and southern Asia. Bevin strove to retain a military presence in the Middle East and hoped that Arab leaders might accept a continued British imperial role in return for recognition of their calls for total independence. The question was where British troops could be stationed, especially during 1946 when a tentative agreement with Egypt, never ratified, foresaw the withdrawal of all British troops from that country by 1949. For Bevin in 1946, the logical place for those forces was Palestine. This in turn spurred Bevin to assure Arab nationalist opinion that Zionism would not achieve an independent Jewish state in Palestine. From the Zionist perspective, the British desire to remain in the country signified their opposition to a separate Jewish entity at a time when the Zionist leadership focused its attention on the plight of Jewish refugees in Europe and the need to bring them to Palestine. Although the Labour government continued the 1939 White Paper immigration quotas of 1,500 a month, it ordered British ships to block Zionist efforts to land Jews seeking asylum in Palestine, repeating the situation of 1939–1941.

Immigration became the nexus of British-American-Zionist interactions. A key tenet of Zionist ideology during and after the war was that European Jews should be sent only to Palestine; thus Truman was advised by an aide sympathetic to Zionism not to offer haven to Jewish displaced persons in the United States because that would dilute the argument that an independent Jewish state was required to absorb them.[30] Truman was deeply affected by the plight of European Jews, but his support of Zionism was not simply altruistic. He knew the political implications of his actions and was constantly advised by aides, such as David Niles and Clark Clifford, of the domestic political impact that his pronouncements on Palestine might have on Jewish voters. At the same time, State Department officials cautioned him to coordinate his policy with the British in order to counter Soviet moves and the likelihood of growing instability in the Middle East.[31]

Beset by conflicting advice, Truman identified with the underdog. To him, and to many other Americans, the Jews were the downtrodden who needed refuge. In this he was probably not so much influenced by public opinion as he was a part of it. Though deeply resentful of organized Jewish pressure on him, Truman was moved by emotional appeals from persons such as Chaim Weizmann to make decisions with far-reaching implications without consulting those in the State Department responsible for foreign policy. As a rule, Truman issued statements contrary to British designs but refused to commit himself to their implications—namely, support for a Jewish state. Bevin, on the other hand, attempted to create a rationale for the continuing British retention of Palestine while simultaneously consolidating a British-American alliance, crucial to Britain's economic survival, which seemed menaced at times by his Palestine policy.

Great Britain, the United States, and Zionism, July 1945–February 1947

At the end of August 1945 President Truman wrote Prime Minister Clement Attlee and requested that Great Britain sponsor the immediate admission of 100,000 Jewish refugees into Palestine. The request, based on a previous Zionist appeal to the Labour government, signaled the beginning of direct American involvement in the British handling of the question of Palestine. When Truman's letter was leaked to the press, Truman issued a public statement, calculated in part to help the Democratic Party in the forthcoming mayoral elections in New York.[32] Bevin and Attlee, increasingly concerned over the political ramifications of American statements on Palestine and their potential impact on British-American relations, then proposed a joint Anglo-American committee to examine the refugee problem in Europe and to suggest a means to disperse the refugees to new homes, preferably not in Palestine.

Bevin hoped to make the United States jointly responsible for Palestinian policy but his strategy backfired. The British draft of the committee's responsibilities made no reference to Palestine, only "to the possibility of relieving the position [of Jews] in Europe by immigration to other countries outside of

Europe." American pressure brought a redrafting that read "to make estimates of those who wish or will be impelled by their conditions to migrate to Palestine or other countries outside of Europe."[33] Having reluctantly accepted this revision, Bevin emphasized that Palestine should not be seen as the solution to the Jewish refugee problem in Europe and that it was not the committee's responsibility to view the situation in that light. Indeed, Bevin declared that he envisaged a Palestinian state, not a Jewish one, arising under a United Nations trusteeship awarded to Britain.

British Aims and Zionist Resistance.   Bevin's announcement, coupled with British continuance of the immigration quotas of 1,500 monthly, infuriated the Zionists; his use of the term "Palestinian state" clearly meant one with an Arab majority. The Palestinian Arabs also objected to Bevin's policies. They saw British willingness to extend the White Paper immigration quotas beyond the five-year transition period as violating promises made to them.

Both the Jews and the Arabs thus considered Bevin's actions to be a betrayal of Britain's perceived obligations to their respective sides, but their responses were quite different. Arab leadership continued to be divided. Though the Arab Higher Committee had been reconstituted, the hoped-for coalition between the Husayni-led Palestine Arab Party and the Istiqlal did not last. The Palestine Arab Party thus dominated the Higher Committee, led from February 1946 by Jamal al-Husayni, who was permitted to return to Palestine. In May the mufti established himself in Egypt and took over effective, if absentee, control of the committee; the British would not permit him to reenter Palestine. Squabbling within the leadership took a new turn as tensions emerged between the mufti and his cousin, Jamal, who sought compromise with the new urban elites.

The mufti's absence from Palestine had enshrined him in the memory of the peasants as the leader of resistance to Zionism and the British. Untainted by the widespread peasant hostility to other landowners and notables that was a major legacy of the Arab Revolt of 1936–1939, the mufti also was seen as symbolizing Arab nationalist goals generally, a status of which Arab heads of state were well aware. The Palestinian question, as a crucial issue in fulfillment of Arab nationalist aspirations against imperialist designs, left little room for the mufti and his backers to compromise. To that extent, in the words of one scholar, "The confrontation with Zionism became a test of [the] Arabism" of these Arab heads of state, whatever their inclinations to seek an accommodation of competing interests.[34]

Whereas Arab differences led to political immobilization and the rejection of any option other than an Arab Palestine, Zionist disputes altered but did not impede formulation of policy. Indeed, ideological disputes and disagreements over how to counter British actions often enabled the Jewish Agency, led by Ben-Gurion, to appear moderate and interested in diplomacy while benefiting from the impact of Zionist underground and terrorist activities. The Hagana now joined the Irgun and LEHI in their ventures. The only major distinction was that the Hagana did not deliberately assault British servicemen, though their deaths in raids were considered acceptable. The Irgun and LEHI had no such compunctions regarding assassinations.[35]

Ben-Gurion accepted the idea that military operations would be necessary to force the British from Palestine. He had already contacted Jewish millionaires in the United States during the summer of 1945 to arrange for the buying and storing of weapons to be shipped to the Zionists in Palestine. His willingness to encourage armed resistance was intensified by his knowledge that some members of the Hagana had rejected any policy of restraint and had joined the Irgun and LEHI. Striving to control the situation, Ben-Gurion encouraged Hagana's efforts to be consulted about Irgun-LEHI operations and to approve them beforehand, though this was not always possible.

Clashes with British forces began in October 1945, and by year's end London had sent 80,000 troops to Palestine to quell opposition to Labour policies. Their desire to strike back forcibly began to grow, especially after attacks by the Irgun or LEHI killed ten British soldiers and policemen and wounded eleven more at the end of December. Ben-Gurion and the Agency Executive now trod a fine line, seeking to benefit from military resistance against the British but wishing to keep the lines of communication open for potentially rewarding negotiations with the Labour Party. British casualties from November 1, 1945, to June 30, 1946, amounted to eighteen officers and soldiers of the army killed and 101 wounded, with British police casualties about the same. Damage from sabotage amounted to over four million British pounds, nearly one-fourth of that caused by an Irgun raid on a British airfield and more attributed to railway bombings and derailments. Extensive British searches of settlements for arms were occasionally successful, as when a cache of six hundred weapons, half a million rounds of ammunition, and a quarter-ton of explosives was discovered spread among thirty-three hiding places around one Jewish village.[36]

The Anglo-American Committee of Inquiry.   These activities provided the backdrop against which the Anglo-American Committee of Inquiry began its hearings in Washington and then moved to Europe to interview displaced persons in refugee camps. By now they numbered well over 100,000. In response to committee questions, more than 90 percent stated their wish to go to Palestine, the result of lobbying by the Jewish Agency; many had hoped, in vain, to enter the United States.[37] Americans were concerned about the plight of Jewish refugees, but not to the extent that they would support alterations in immigration laws to permit them entry to the United States. Instead, they agreed with the Zionists that Palestine should be the haven for Jews who had survived the horrors of war and the camps.

The fact that the Arab population in Palestine was still double that of the Jews meant little to anyone except the British and the U.S. State Department, who foresaw instability and upheaval in the Arab world with concomitant anti-Western hostility. Arab representatives before the Anglo-American Committee in Cairo and Jerusalem stated that the ongoing Jewish immigration would create even more Arab resistance. Albert Hourani, a young representative of the Arab Agency and later a distinguished historian at Oxford, impressed many committee members when he declared that "no room can be made in Palestine for a second nation except by dislodging or exterminating the first."[38] Weizmann, to the consternation of Ben-Gurion and the Jewish Agency Executive, agreed, though he drew different conclusions. As one committee member wrote, "He is the first witness who has frankly and openly admitted that the issue is not between right and wrong but between the greater and the lesser injustice. Injustice is unavoidable and we have to decide whether it is better to be unjust to the Arabs of Palestine or the Jews."[39] Arabs argued for a Palestinian state, based on existing population ratios, in which the Arab majority would acknowledge and ensure Jewish rights; they rejected all other solutions. Bevin hoped for a binational state, presumably under British tutelage. Zionist leaders seemed willing to accept partition in lieu of maximalist demands for a Jewish state in all of Palestine, but Arab leaders opposed that option. To give up any part of Arab Palestine would be wrong, they believed, constituting recognition of the Jewish right to have it as Ben-Gurion and others argued.

Beset by the conflicting testimonies, the report of the Anglo-American Committee of Inquiry struck a compromise between the sentiments of its British and American members. It called for the immediate entry of 100,000 Jewish refugees into Palestine and recommended the removal of the land sale restrictions in the 1939 White Paper. But as for the future of Palestine, the report remained intentionally vague: "any attempt to establish either an independent Palestinian state or independent Palestinian states would result in civil strife such as might threaten the peace of the world."[40] Consequently, Palestine should remain under the British mandate "pending the execution of a Trusteeship agreement under the United Nations." The committee seemed to envisage a binational state in which neither Arab nor Jew could dominate the other, but beyond support for admission of 100,000, it made no recommendations for future immigration, thus leaving that matter in British hands. No one was pleased, especially Bevin, who had conceived the committee as a means to draw the Americans into the problem and to compel them to share responsibility for any future actions regarding Palestine. On the day the findings of the Anglo-American Committee were announced, April 30, 1946, Truman, without consultation, declared his support of the recommendation for 100,000 immigration certificates and the relaxation of land sale restrictions but offered no assistance and did not refer to the other portions of the document.

The Morrison-Grady Committee.   Truman's selective and spontaneous comments outraged Bevin, but he needed U.S. financial assistance. Truman, though eager to retain British friendship and cooperation, also kept an eye on congressional elections scheduled for November 1946. Thus he proposed a new, cabinet-level committee to discuss the implications of the report of the Anglo-American Committee of Inquiry, to be known, after its two chairpersons, as the

Morrison-Grady Committee. In giving his instructions, Truman emphasized that the United States would make no military commitment to maintain order in Palestine, nor would it accept joint responsibility for overseeing a trusteeship administration. But he was prepared to try to gain approval to admit 50,000 refugees into the country.

The Morrison-Grady Committee's negotiations in July 1946 reached an unexpectedly quick agreement that negated major sections of the Anglo-American Committee of Inquiry Report. The American delegation accepted a British proposal for provincial autonomy in Palestine, demarcating Arab and Jewish areas with the Negev and Jerusalem under the trustee, namely, Great Britain, for an undefined period. The scheme, very close to that proposed in the 1944 British partition plan, was designed so that partition remained possible in the long term. In British eyes, the proposal permitted them to retain control of Palestine for the moment without reference to the United Nations. As the governing authority, they would regulate all important administrative matters and would oversee Palestine's foreign relations for an undefined period. The right of 100,000 Jewish refugees to enter Palestine would be conditional on acceptance of the entire plan by both Arabs and Jews. That stipulation in particular negated the Committee of Inquiry's call for the immediate admission of the 100,000, which Truman had supported. Truman's apparent inclination to back the Morrison-Grady plan as offering stability for the region under British tutelage produced intense domestic political pressure on the president. He soon retreated, leaving the British to continue to back it while he moved closer to open support of partition.[41]

Zionist Terrorism, British Crackdown, and American Politics.   The Labour government's dependence on American financial aid emphasized to Bevin and Attlee the precariousness of their Palestine initiatives, especially when one American Zionist, Rabbi Hillel Silver, linked them to congressional approval or disapproval of their loan request. In addition, Jewish resistance intensified following the British refusal to admit the 100,000 refugees, as advocated by the Committee of Inquiry's report in April. Before the report became public, a LEHI attack on a parking lot in April had killed many British soldiers. Once Bevin rejected the 100,000, the Hagana, the Irgun, and LEHI collaborated in mid-June to undertake raids on railway installations. During the third night of these attacks, June 18, Irgun forces captured three British officers and threatened to kill them if two Irgun members were hanged in accordance with their sentences. The threat succeeded; the British commuted the sentences to life imprisonment and the Irgun released their British hostages. Attlee and Bevin then decided to try to crush the Zionist resistance by raiding the headquarters of the Jewish Agency. This operation, carried out on June 29, was designed to seize agency files, arrest the Hagana leadership, and disrupt what they correctly believed to be Hagana-coordinated resistance to the British presence. Although 2,700 people were arrested and massive documentation was taken, little of significance was learned, in part because the Zionists had been forewarned.[42]

The Irgun, under Menachem Begin, reacted by proposing to blow up the King David Hotel in Jerusalem; it housed the British administrative offices and was a prime symbol of the British presence in Palestine. The Hagana assented initially, but they later withdrew support following an appeal by Weizmann to suspend resistance temporarily. Begin then carried out the operation on his own and scheduled it for the middle of the working day. The resulting explosion, on July 22, killed ninety-one British, Jewish, and Arab personnel and wounded dozens more, leading Churchill to declare in the House of Commons that Palestine was relatively unimportant to British interests; horrified at this loss of life, he questioned the need for future casualties.[43] But many in Britain wanted revenge, especially the military and the Labour Party, who were determined not to appear weak in the face of violence. Nevertheless, the logic of Zionist terrorism was bearing fruit, bringing home to the British public at large the cost of maintaining a hold on Palestine (see Figure 4.3).

Figure 4.3 ■ The Irgun Bombing of the King David Hotel, June 1946

This photo demonstrates the power of the bombs that sheared off an entire six-story segment of the British administrative offices housed in the hotel. Ninety-one people died, and many remained buried under the rubble for several days.

Determined to adhere to the idea of provincial autonomy as outlined in the Morrison-Grady proposals, Bevin called a conference of Arab and Jewish leaders to meet in London in September 1946. Palestinian Arab and Jewish Agency representatives refused to attend, leaving British officials to conduct a fruitless dialogue with delegates from Arab states; they, like the Zionists, found the Morrison-Grady clauses unacceptable. They insisted on an Arab state throughout all of Palestine, with Jews considered a religious minority, a position that reinforced the differences among the parties; Zionists insisted on partition as the minimum solution acceptable. Bevin then decided to suspend consultations in mid-September, planning to renew the London conference in early 1947 when he hoped Truman would be more amenable to British proposals.

On Yom Kippur, the Jewish Day of Atonement, which fell on October 4, Truman issued a statement that seemed to offer definitive support for the Jewish Agency's partition plan, describing it as likely to create "a viable Jewish State in control of its own immigration and economic policies in an adequate area of Palestine instead of in the whole of Palestine." Truman also reiterated his support of "the immediate issuance of certificates for 100,000 Jewish immigrants" and concluded that "a solution along these lines would command the support of public opinion in the United States."[44] Truman's timing was primarily political. He had been advised that a statement helping Democratic chances in the upcoming congressional elections in November was crucial to capturing the Jewish vote. Indeed, soon after his statement, Republican Governor Thomas Dewey of New York issued a call for permitting "several hundred thousand" Jews to enter Palestine. As a political gesture, Truman's statement proved totally inadequate. The Republicans scored a resounding triumph in November, a significant omen to American Zionist militants who had campaigned on their behalf. They had succeeded in creating "a Jewish issue in the elections" by threatening to use a "so-called Jewish bloc vote . . . for punitive means." In this manner it could serve as a warning for future campaigns, indicating that Truman would have to be much more explicit in his advocacy of a Jewish state, rather than simply calling for the admission of 100,000 refugees.[45]

Throughout the remainder of 1946, British forces in Palestine encountered harassment and attacks, including in December a car bomb attack by Jews that left several dead and numerous wounded. The Arabs later adopted such tactics. In the same month, the World Zionist Congress met in Basel, Switzerland. The congress voted to boycott the upcoming London conference, scheduled to reconvene in February 1947. Activists led by Ben-Gurion engineered the defeat of Weizmann and his call for negotiation; they also won a vote leaving the post of president of the Zionist organization unfilled. Weizmann was thus repudiated, a man with no position, isolated because he still sought a negotiated agreement with Britain at a time when violence seemed the sole means by which a Jewish state could be achieved.

Britain Abdicates: The London Conference, February 1947.   British cabinet discussions over future policy were inconclusive prior to resumption of talks. The chiefs of staff still favored retention of Palestine, assuming until early January 1947 that the military would be withdrawn from Egypt. Others argued for partition as the only possible solution; a unitary state would only lead to strife. But sentiment was also voiced for submitting the problem to the United Nations, an option that Bevin seemed increasingly to favor. The United Nations had assumed supervision of the mandate, and the British would have to report to it sooner or later. To do so and gain U.N. support for a continued British role over a state with an Arab majority would secure British ties with Arab leaders and an ongoing British role in Palestine, the option still preferred by strategic planners. At this point, in February, the British decision to leave India became an additional factor, as its loss meant the need to retain bases elsewhere. Palestine, in the face of all odds, seemed a suitable replacement because of its location flanking Egypt, which now reemerged as the real bastion in the area once Anglo-Egyptian negotiations collapsed. Finally, U.N. approval would legitimize British activities and, it was hoped, nullify U.S. objections. That seemed preferable to abdication, a choice that would not only threaten Britain's strategic stance in the Middle East but also "harm her prestige throughout the world," a criterion that found favor in the United States when dealing with Vietnam more than twenty years later. With these considerations in mind, Bevin opened the second stage of the London Conference in February; he did not expect success and was prepared to resort to the United Nations as the next phase of his efforts to retain British power and prestige in the Middle East.

Bevin and his colleagues hosted an Arab delegation that included Jamal al-Husayni as head of the Palestinian Arab Higher Executive, but he also met informally with Ben-Gurion and other agency officials. He proposed on February 6 a five-year trusteeship under British auspices that would lead to an independent Palestinian state with a Jewish minority. Immigration would be set at 4,000 monthly for two years, thus permitting 96,000 to enter by the end of that period. After that, immigration would be allowed only in accordance with the country's economic absorptive capacity. The Zionists would be given immigration, though not nearly as much as they desired. The Arabs would be given a state with more Jews than they wanted.

After much debate, Ben-Gurion offered a compromise. Fearing that the British would resort to the United Nations, he proposed a return to the situation that existed before 1939, unlimited immigration, which to Bevin meant the ultimate achievement of Jewish statehood.[46] The Arabs denounced the proposals, insisting on a declaration of an independent Palestine and an immediate end to immigration. Confronted by this chasm and facing a terrible winter that exacerbated Britain's economic crisis, with the costs of maintaining the military in Palestine amounting to nearly £40 million annually, Bevin on February 25, 1947, "hurled Palestine into the arena of the United Nations." In a speech filled with sarcasm for American support of Zionism, he openly denounced the Jewish call for statehood.[47] Bevin and the Foreign Office seem to have hoped that the United Nations would support an independent binational state under U.N. trusteeship, with Britain the responsible party. But Bevin also noted the possibility that the United Nations might reach a decision unacceptable to Britain, in which case it would hand over Palestine to the United Nations for final resolution.[48]

UNSCOP and United Nations' Ratification of Partition, February–November 1947

As the Palestinian problem came before the United Nations, Arab leadership was once more firmly in al-Husayni hands, indicating the restoration of control to the traditional authority of the notables centered in Jerusalem. Neither the peasantry nor members of the emergent urban bourgeoisie had any real representation; indeed, peasants generally identified with the idea of uncompromising nationalist resistance to Zionism that the mufti embodied.[49] On the Zionist side, the activists led by Ben-Gurion dominated the movement and, at times, had trouble restraining those wishing to focus entirely on violence as the sole means to oust the British. But the Zionists could still rely on allies abroad to apply strong pressures to influence decisions in their favor, something denied Arabs of any political affiliation. This was of immense importance to Zionist success because in Palestine itself the Jews were still a significant minority.

At the end of 1946, there were an estimated 1.269 million Arabs in Palestine and 608,000 Jews, a two-to-one ratio. Jews owned approximately 1.6 million dunams, about 20 percent of the cultivable land and slightly over 6 percent of the total land area (see Map 4.1).[50] Whatever the rigidity of the mufti, given such numbers, few Palestinians were probably willing to agree to partition. They occupied most of the area and were still a sizable majority in their homeland. For the Jews, their minority status in no way mitigated their assumption of their right to a state in all of Palestine, although Ben-Gurion had reduced Zionist demands by accepting partition. The Zionists believed more firmly than ever that a state in Palestine was their due, not only on the basis of past heritage, but even more so in light of the Holocaust. Here the need for immigrants became

Map 4.1 ▨ The 1947 United Nations' Partition Plan as a Reflection of Patterns   ▶
of Land Ownership in Palestine by Subdistrict, 1944

This map illustrates how patterns of land ownership in Palestine influenced the configurations of the proposed Arab and Jewish states in the 1947 U.N. partition plan. Seeing that Arab land ownership predominated in all areas, UNSCOP recommended partition in accordance with those sectors where the percentage of Jewish holdings was highest relative to that of the Arabs. Although an exception to this rule, UNSCOP also allotted the Negev desert to the future Jewish state, an area where Jewish land ownership was minimal but which Zionists considered crucial if they were to have a port outlet to the Red Sea.

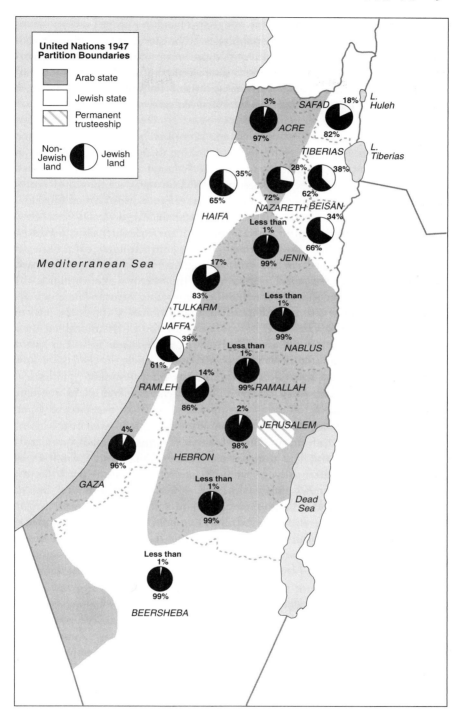

paramount, both as a solution to the refugee problem in Europe and as a means of increasing the minority Jewish population to bolster Zionist arguments that a Jewish state would be viable. Although most Western leaders, including Truman, were not convinced that a Jewish state would advance the region's stability, they were moving toward the conclusion that there was no alternative, if only because the existing situation promised even more violence.

The UNSCOP Committee Hearings and Recommendations.   The United Nations formed a special committee on Palestine to investigate conditions in the country and recommend action to the General Assembly. The United Nations Special Committee on Palestine (UNSCOP) was composed of representatives of eleven countries — Sweden, the Netherlands, Czechoslovakia, Yugoslavia, Australia, Canada, India, Iran, Guatemala, Mexico, and Peru. They undertook their assignment in an atmosphere of increasing tension and disorder in Palestine. The British had stepped up their efforts to intercept the stream of by now well-organized refugee ship contingents that approached the coast. Once the British boarded these ships, often in the face of fierce resistance, the passengers were transshipped to detention camps in Cyprus.[51] These actions spurred Hagana efforts to destroy the British patrol boats and free the Jews in temporary holding camps in Palestine. The Irgun and LEHI intensified their attacks on British military personnel and on judges considered hostile to Jews.

The committee stayed in Palestine for five weeks, leaving at the end of July. They were feted by the Zionists and boycotted by the Palestinian Arab leadership, whose bitterness and defiance could only be characterized as "exceedingly inept diplomacy" guaranteed to arouse more sympathy for the Zionists' open presentation of their case.[52] Committee members were also swayed by the intensity of British-Jewish animosity. On July 12, two British sergeants were kidnapped by the Irgun and held hostage against the death sentence given to three Irgunists. When the latter were executed on July 29, the Irgun hanged the two sergeants and booby-trapped their bodies. In addition, three committee members witnessed the British handling of a refugee ship, the *President Warfield*, renamed the *Exodus* by the Zionists (see Figure 4.4). Crammed with nearly 4,500 refugees, the ship was brought into Haifa harbor by the Royal Navy on July 18, a week after the sergeants had been kidnapped. The next day the passengers were shipped back to southern France, not Cyprus, as a lesson, one that backfired completely. From Marseilles, the ship proceeded to Germany, where the refugees from the concentration camps and the war were detained in a former camp. The resultant publicity seriously undermined the British position in world eyes at a time when the murders and bombings continued apace in Palestine, including British reprisals against Jews for the hanging of the sergeants.

The UNSCOP report, submitted to the United Nations at the end of August, was unanimous in calling for the end of the British mandate and the creation of procedures leading to the independence of Palestine (see Document 4.2). But the

Figure 4.4 ■ The Refugee Ship *Exodus*, July 1947

Carrying 4,500 refugees, the *Exodus* became a symbol of the Zionist cause when British officials sent it back to France instead of to Cyprus as was normally done; the passengers were later placed in a German camp. Arriving during UNSCOP's visit to Palestine, the *Exodus* and its fate dramatized the plight of European Jewish refugees and the Zionists' call for their settlement in Palestine.

committee split, eight to three, over what type of state should emerge. The majority called for partition into a Jewish and an Arab state and the internationalization of Jerusalem and its environs. The minority (India, Iran, and Yugoslavia) advocated "an independent federal state" after a three-year preparatory stage under U.N. trusteeship. That state would in fact comprise two separate entities with local administrative powers, but united central authority would be divided among Arabs and Jews: the minority report allotted more of Palestine to the Arabs than did the majority report.[53] The General Assembly immediately set up an ad hoc Committee on Palestine to hear both Palestinian Arab and Zionist views on the UNSCOP proposals (see Documents 4.3 and 4.4).

Britain did not wait for the debate in the General Assembly that was scheduled for November. On September 26 it declared that the British would withdraw from Palestine by mid-May, ending the mandate unilaterally and handing the matter over to the United Nations. The decision was based on many factors, all of which called attention to Britain's increased inability to meet its obligations abroad.[54]

Palestine Partitioned: The U.N. Debate.   At the United Nations, many expected that the General Assembly would deny partition; the non-European
countries would sympathize with the Arabs, and the Soviets and their allies
would presumably oppose the United States, which would lead to communist
rejection of an independent Jewish state. For the Zionists, even United States'
backing was not considered sure, but Truman aide David Niles arranged to have
Truman appoint a pro-Zionist, General John Hilldring, to the American U.N.
delegation to offset the views of the appointees from the State Department.
Through Hilldring, a direct liaison between the United Nations and Truman
was established; indeed, U.S. positions were occasionally relayed directly from
the White House without consulting the State Department. Thus, for example,
after a private conversation with Weizmann, Truman phoned the U.N. delegation and told them to reverse American backing for the Arab claim that the
Negev (southern Palestine) should be part of an Arab state; the United States
would support its inclusion in the Jewish state as recommended in UNSCOP's
majority proposal.[55]

As debate over the UNSCOP recommendations continued through November, it seemed clear to Zionists in the United States that certain delegates would
require extensive lobbying. Truman remained on the sidelines until the eve of
the vote but declared in his memoirs that he had never "had as much pressure
and propaganda aimed at the White House as I had in this instance."[56] Congressmen and senators along with Supreme Court justices were drafted to send
telegrams to heads of states and their representatives either cajoling them or,
in some cases, threatening suspension of U.S. aid. On the day the vote was
scheduled, November 27, the partition resolution appeared to be short of the
needed two-thirds majority. Filibustering gained a postponement, and Truman
approved further pressure on the delegates. Under threat of a Jewish boycott of
Firestone rubber and tire products, Harvey Firestone warned Liberia that he
would suspend plans for the expansion of plant operations there if Liberia
voted against partition.[57] Truman's approval of increased lobbying efforts may
have saved the day. Until then he and the State Department had seemed in
accord: the United States would vote for partition but not threaten or lobby
other members, leading the Arab officials to assume that they had won. On
November 29, the General Assembly voted thirty-three to thirteen, with ten
abstentions, to approve partition; the Soviets surprised many by backing the
Zionist cause. The right of the Jews to an independent state in part of Palestine
had been recognized by the international community, giving legitimacy to Jewish claims for self-rule. Whatever the nature of the Zionist accomplishment in
Palestine, the victory at the United Nations was essentially won in the United
States where

> the success of the Zionist effort in 1947 represented nearly five years of
> work, organization, publicity, education, and the careful cultivation of key
> people in different fields, . . . thus securing the help of influential men

and women in the press, the church, the arts, and above all, the government. In the process, the plight of the displaced persons in Europe played an ever-present role.[58]

Amidst the wild celebrations in New York, Tel Aviv, and the Jewish sectors of Jerusalem, both Arabs and Jews prepared for war.

The Battle for Palestine/Israel, December 1947–May 1948

Although significant, the U.N. vote in favor of partition did not guarantee the creation of a Jewish state. During the six-month period leading up to Ben-Gurion's declaration of statehood on May 14, the international community was in disarray. United States policymakers were uncertain about the wisdom of their vote and whether partition should be replaced by a U.N. trusteeship. Truman seems to have fluctuated according to the intensity of the advice given him and the direction from which it came. Much depended on the ability of the Jewish community in Palestine to achieve its goals for itself in the face of Arab resistance and a British policy of "masterly inactivity" designed primarily to lessen the number of its own casualties.

Arab-Zionist Strife Erupts.   On the Arab side, various plans for mobilization had been prepared if the United Nations approved partition. The mufti, still in Egypt, was determined to control the Palestinian Arab resistance and any aid offered by the Arab states. His forces were led by Abd al-Qadir al-Husayni, the son of Musa Kazim, the former mayor of Jerusalem.[59] In addition, there were Arab volunteers, mostly non-Palestinians, led by Fawzi al-Qawuqji and funded by the Arab League. Both al-Husayni and al-Qawuqji were veterans of the Arab Revolt of 1936–1939, but they were rivals backed by groups deeply suspicious of one another. The mufti demanded control over all funds to ensure that the fate of Palestine remain in Palestinian, most specifically his, hands. The Arab League's refusal to provide him with loans to finance resistance or to agree to create a Palestinian government-in-exile confirmed his suspicion that Arab leaders wished to decide the fate of Palestine. Egypt alone came to the mufti's aid, not so much out of loyalty to Hajj Amin as out of suspicion of Abdullah of Jordan's plan to absorb Jerusalem and central Palestine. Indeed, research on the subject supports the view that Abdullah had reached agreement with the Zionists on a division of Palestine with a view to blocking the possibility of a Palestinian entity. Britain, though hesitant, finally agreed with this objective in order to preserve influence in the area and to undermine pan-Arab aspirations.[60]

The Palestinian resistance and the Arab League's support of it were thus part of a web of rivalries and intrigue that discouraged any chance of coordinated assaults, let alone agreement on objectives. Within Palestine, rival al-Husayni–al-Nashashibi factions, the latter identified with Abdullah, engaged in intercommunal clashes. This, coupled with the lack of preparation for resistance or training in modern military techniques, severely limited the scope of Arab tactics, although their numbers and the strategic locations of their villages gave them excellent opportunities for harassing Jewish communications and attacking Jewish settlements.

Compared to the Palestinians, the Zionists had much superior leadership and organization as well as many soldiers who had benefited from the training and experience they received during World War II. Although the Irgun and LEHI were not absorbed into the Hagana, they coordinated activities with it on many occasions, especially in the spring of 1948. In general they specialized in bombing crowded Arab areas and employed other tactics designed to terrorize the Arab community. The Jewish community had a slight manpower advantage over Palestinians with more males in the twenty to forty-four age group.[61] The Zionists' major problem was one of military communications—maintaining links to isolated settlements and protecting those close to the larger urban areas. Although they lacked armaments sufficient for their people under arms, their supplies matched those of the Palestinians and were usually later models of heavier caliber. The question for the Zionist command, and many outside observers, was how they could acquire the territory allotted them by the partition scheme that lay outside the central and coastal plains in which much of the Jewish population lived. A particular and ongoing challenge was the retention of Jerusalem, reached only by narrow roads through hilly terrain ideal for interdicting communications and supplies.

The hostilities between the Arabs and Jews went through several stages. At first Arab irregulars took the initiative, attacking Jewish settlements and convoys. Hagana tactics remained essentially defensive, protecting settlements and maintaining lines of communication. In this they were mostly successful, except for the Jerusalem road, which was often cut off. From April onward, the Hagana took the offensive, establishing control over the area granted to the Jewish state and showing that the Arab force's lack of coordination severely impeded their ability to mount a sustained resistance.

Within the major cities, Tel Aviv, Haifa, and Jerusalem, a war of terror reigned that spilled over into the countryside and involved the Hagana as well as the Irgun and LEHI, who specialized in bomb and car-bomb assaults on heavily congregated Arab areas. The Arabs began to use similar tactics. A cycle of attack and retaliation ensued, each side claiming to be responding to the other's outrage. One series of incidents began with either Irgun or LEHI gunmen throwing bombs at a group of Arab workers gathered at the gates of an oil refinery in Haifa where Jews and Arabs worked together; six Arabs were killed and forty-two wounded. The Arabs, the great majority inside the plant, erupted, killing forty-one Jews and wounding forty-eight before British troops intervened. Two days later the Hagana undertook what it called a retaliatory attack to avenge the Arab murder of the Jewish refinery workers. Dressed as Arabs, they entered a village adjacent to Haifa and killed approximately sixty persons, including many women and children. For one British military observer, "No better example could be found of the type of incident which from this stage onwards happened commonly in all parts of the country where Jews and Arabs shared the same locality."[62] Terror and atrocities were committed by both sides, with little regard for noncombatants or women and children. These developments and the city bombings caused approximately 15,000 Arabs to flee during this period, most of them from the major cities, despite the mufti's call for them to stay and his request that Arab states refuse them entry.[63] The British were accused by each side of favoring the other. They were attacked by both, and their forces intervened on occasion to relieve sieges against either Arab or Jewish communities. But the British also continued to try to intercept ships carrying immigrants who, upon landing, were often prepared immediately for combat.

American Policy in Disarray.   In the midst of this conflict, American policy in Washington and New York underwent shifts in emphasis that alarmed the Zionist leadership and may have influenced their conduct of military operations in Palestine. As 1948 began, the State Department and Truman seemed to agree that the partition approved by the General Assembly would be impossible to impose except by military force, creating a situation that the Soviets could exploit. Yet the United States would not and could not commit its own troops to Palestine, nor would the British do anything but continue with their plans for withdrawal. The only recourse seemed to be a U.N. Security Council authorization for implementing the partition vote. Washington's fear of Soviet involvement in any international police force led the State Department, with Truman's blessing, to authorize Warren Austin, the U.S. delegate to the United Nations, to inform the Security Council on February 24 that the United States questioned the council's police powers. The Security Council had the right to restore peace in Palestine but not to impose partition on the unwilling inhabitants of the area, that is, the Arabs. Left unspoken but assumed by observers was the corollary to that argument: another solution should be found. For American officials, that meant a U.N. trusteeship to oversee Palestine and to prepare the respective communities for a possibly different political future to be decided by the United Nations. But such intentions were left unsaid because Truman's domestic political standing in a presidential election year prohibited him from openly endorsing such a stance.[64]

Fear of Soviet penetration of the Middle East and its intentions elsewhere were hardly a mirage at the time these decisions were made. On February 25, a Soviet-sponsored coup overthrew the legitimate Czechoslovakian government and installed a communist regime. Tension in Berlin led the governor of the U.S. military zone to warn Truman on March 5 that war could erupt at any moment. The Russians began to block Allied convoys to West Berlin at the beginning of April, leading eventually to the Berlin Airlift that began in June. Thus, Truman went further than approving a redefinition of the Security Council's role in Palestine. He accepted a declaration that rejected partition and supported creation of "a temporary trusteeship for Palestine" under U.N. auspices, a decision duly announced to that body by the American ambassador on March 19. Nevertheless, Truman immediately repudiated that statement, though not publicly, because on March 18 in a private meeting with Weizmann, he had reiterated his support of partition. He now exploded at the State Department and accused it of betraying him.

The real reason for Truman's anger lay in the timing of the U.N. announcement, not its contents, but his embarrassment was largely due to his own brand of policymaking. His private meeting with Weizmann occurred unbeknownst to the State Department and foreign policy specialists, and he did not inform Weizmann of his doubts about partition. The ensuing furor led Truman to back partition even more firmly, influenced both by domestic pressures and by advice from private aides that support of a Jewish state would not threaten peace or American interests in the Middle East: the Arabs were anticommunist and had nowhere to go but to the West, regardless of American support of partition. The pressure from the oil-producing states was minimal. Arab oil was not vital to the American market, though it was crucial to the recovery of Western Europe.[65] Truman's vacillation did not inspire confidence in Zionist circles, let alone elsewhere, especially because official American policy still seemed to back a trusteeship proposal. Truman continued to favor partition and in April assured Weizmann privately that he would recognize a Jewish state. The State Department, unaware of such promises, persisted in its efforts to arrange a U.N. peacekeeping force under the guise of a trusteeship before May 15, when Britain would hand over all power in Palestine.

Dayr Yasin and the Palestinian Refugees.   The Zionist leadership in Palestine realized that what happened there was crucial to what might be recognized internationally and that they should not rely on the United Nations to enforce partition. They agreed that by May 15 the Hagana should have established control of the zone granted to the Jews and, if possible, should have expanded the area to include those Jewish settlements outside the partition lines.[66] The Hagana thus went on the offensive at the beginning of April. By May 15, they controlled the area granted them, a Jewish state had been proclaimed, and hundreds of thousands of Palestinians had fled or been forcibly expelled in accordance with Hagana Plan Dalet.

It was during these six weeks that the fiercest fighting occurred. Although al-Qawuqji's forces now had some tanks and artillery, the Hagana began to receive major shipments from Czechoslovakia, with Soviet approval; the first consignments arrived on April 1. The Hagana offensive achieved its goals with relative ease except along the Jerusalem corridor and in the Old City, where Jewish forces encountered fierce resistance. Throughout the battle for Jerusalem and later struggles for Haifa and Jaffa, LEHI and the Irgun participated under loose Hagana auspices. In early April Abd al-Qadir al-Husayni was killed, depriving the Palestinian Arab contingents of their most respected leader. Then on April 9 there was a massacre at the Arab village of Dayr Yasin that had a major impact on the fate of the majority of the Arab population in western Palestine.

Dayr Yasin overlooked the Jerusalem road, but it had apparently entered a nonaggression pact with the Hagana. Nevertheless, a joint Irgun-LEHI force attacked the village, took it after quelling resistance, and slaughtered about 115 men, women, and children whose mutilated bodies were stuffed down wells. The Arabs retaliated on April 13 by killing seventy Jewish doctors and nurses in a medical convoy near Jerusalem. The significance of Dayr Yasin went far beyond its immediate fate. The killings and disposal of the bodies became a staple of Irgun and Hagana propaganda proclaimed from mobile loudspeaker units that beamed their messages into the Arab areas of major cities such as Haifa and Jaffa; Arab radio also publicized the incident. These broadcasts had a major impact on the Arab will to resist, especially when the population found itself betrayed by its leaders. In Haifa, the Arab military command and city officials left on April 21–22 in the face of Irgun assaults coupled with a precipitate British withdrawal of their troops and open Irgun threats of another Dayr Yasin if the Arabs remained. Fifty thousand fled in three days. In short, Zionist psychological warfare and terror tactics, which included the destruction of villages and the ousting of their populations, combined to produce a state of panic that resulted in the flight of over 300,000 Arabs by May 15.[67]

The matter of the Arab refugees has been in dispute ever since. Israeli officials claimed that the Arabs were encouraged to leave by Arab propagandists, who promised them an easy return once the Arab armies defeated the Zionists. Thus, these Arabs should not be considered refugees with the right to return after the cessation of hostilities, and Israel was justified in permitting Jewish immigrants to take over their lands and homes. This was an ex post facto Israeli stance, taken to sustain an existing situation. Recent scholarship, notably that of Benny Morris, confirms that Zionist forces acted in accordance with Plan Dalet from early April onward. The goal was to secure areas assigned to Israel by the partition plan and to expel Palestinians who did not flee, precise means for executing the plans left to local Hagana leaders. These actions, coupled with the psychological warfare and threats of future Dayr Yasins broadcast into Arab towns, meant more to the Arab civilians than did the pleas of some Jews, such as the mayor of Haifa, for the Haifa Arabs to remain. That a Zionist policy existed became apparent when some Arabs from Haifa requested permission to return ten days later, with the backing of heads of Arab states; the Hagana denied those petitions and another made in mid-May shortly after independence had been declared. Incoming Jews could be moved into the vacant homes in towns and villages, and where the villages were considered primitive, they were razed so that there would be nothing to return to; new Israeli villages were built over or adjacent to them. In this manner, a much more cohesive Jewish state with a much smaller Arab population could be achieved.[68]

Figure 4.5 ▪ **David Ben-Gurion, Israel's First Prime Minister, Reads the Israeli Declaration of Independence, May 14, 1948**

With the photograph of Theodor Herzl overseeing the event and Arab armies preparing to invade, Ben-Gurion declares the independence of the state of Israel. Second to his left is Moshe Shertok (later Sharett), Israel's foreign minister, whom Ben-Gurion would later dismiss from office because of his perceived moderation in handling Arab-Israeli tensions.

Ben-Gurion Proclaims the State of Israel.   All this took place in the midst of ongoing conflict, crisis, and, for the Jews, jubilation. On May 14, 1948, David Ben-Gurion proclaimed the state of Israel to exist within the borders awarded it by the UNSCOP partition plan, minus the Negev, where Israeli control was precarious (see Figure 4.5 and Document 4.5). On May 15 President Truman personally instructed a member of the American United Nations delegation to announce the United States' de facto recognition of Israel, the first country to do so, though the Soviet Union immediately followed suit with de jure recognition. Truman's orders came as a complete surprise to the American U.N. delegation, still trying to arrange for a trusteeship. On the same day, armies from Arab states invaded Arab Palestine and the new Israeli state, sparking a new round of warfare.[69]

The Arab-Israeli Wars and the Armistices, 1948–1949

Plans for a coordinated Arab attack had been made in April under Arab League auspices. The fighting forces included units from Iraq, Syria, Lebanon, Egypt, and Jordan with a token contingent from Saudi Arabia. Nevertheless, the Israelis held a manpower advantage over the Arab armies backed by superior military training and commitment; the only comparable units were those of Jordan's Arab Legion. In addition, there was no coordination of Arab military movements because the participants were mutually suspicious of one another's territorial ambitions. All rightly suspected Jordan's Abdullah of seeking to acquire control of the area allotted to the Palestinian Arabs under the partition plan in order to incorporate it into his kingdom, thereby enlarging his country and defeating the mufti in the process. The Israelis were well aware of Abdullah's aspirations. Zionist representatives had been in contact with him in 1947 and again in 1948, when in May he assured them of his acceptance of partition (see Document 4.6). Abdullah felt constrained to attack Israeli forces after independence when they took over areas within the Arab partition zone, but his Arab Legion, the best of the Arab forces, did not undertake sustained offensives, preferring to establish defensive perimeters around the areas Jordan coveted. Israeli and Jordanian aims generally coincided with the exception of Jerusalem, where Jordan, after fierce fighting, was able to retain control of the old, eastern sector, leaving the Israelis the newer, western section.

There were two wars (see Map 4.2). The first, from mid-May to June 11, saw the Israelis stop the Arab invasions after Arab forces penetrated Israeli territory. United Nations peacekeeping efforts then brought about a truce, which both sides were glad to accept. In theory an arms blockade was in force, imposed by the British, the Americans, and the French, but its major effect was to block shipment of Western arms to the Arabs. The Israelis stepped up their purchases from Czechoslovakia, eager for Western currency, and began to implement their long-established plans to ship arms stockpiled in Europe and the United States. When the truce ended on July 6, the Israelis were in a much better military position than the Arabs in terms of weaponry and their unitary command structure. Arab in-fighting had been such that Iraq's contingents made only a show of force while its Hashemite king accused Egypt's King Faruq of insulting him because Egypt's flag was larger than Iraq's.[70]

The truce ended because Syria and Egypt were unwilling to extend it. Beset by internal unrest caused by inflated expectations of victory, they opted for war. This second war lasted from July 6 to 19 and led to a crushing Arab defeat on all fronts. During this phase, the Israelis took over much of western Galilee, which had been included in the Arab partition zone. By the time the second truce was imposed by the United Nations, the Israelis had greatly expanded the area under their control. The only region left outside it was the Negev, allotted to Israel in the partition plan but partially occupied by Egyptian forces. In October the Israelis invaded the Negev and incorporated it into Israel. By the end of 1948, they had driven to the eastern shore of the Gulf of Aqaba, ousting the token Jordanian forces and gaining an outlet to the Red Sea.

Throughout this period, tensions were high. Israel's leaders were determined to gain as much territory as possible, taking advantage of the Arabs' disarray. The U.N. mediator, Count Folke Bernadotte of Sweden, challenged their

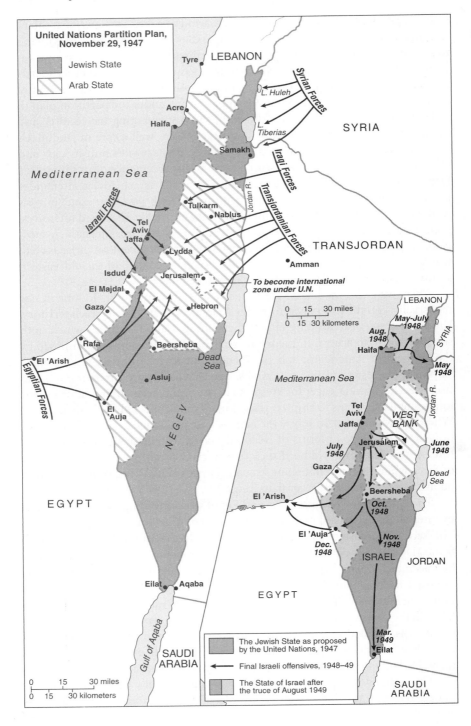

United Nations Partition Plan, November 29, 1947

Jewish State

Arab State

The Jewish State as proposed by the United Nations, 1947

Final Israeli offensives, 1948–49

The State of Israel after the truce of August 1949

assumptions. Bernadotte wanted a quick settlement in order to end the hostilities, but he believed that any agreement between the Arabs and the Israelis should achieve a balance in territorial gains to lessen irredentist emotions. With the Israelis already occupying western Galilee, he opposed their desire to have the Negev as well. They could have either one or the other but not both. But the Israelis were not about to cede the Galilee, with its rich soil, or to acquiesce in the Arab possession of the Negev, which they viewed in biblical terms as part of ancient Israel and in practical perspective as a potentially fertile area offering access to the Red Sea. The Israelis objected strongly to Bernadotte's formulations, which were accepted by both the British and the Americans. Unacceptable also was his idea that Jerusalem be internationalized, a concept equally unsatisfactory to Abdullah of Jordan. On September 18, in the midst of a vitriolic Israeli press campaign against him, Bernadotte was assassinated by members of LEHI. His successor, Ralph Bunche of the United States, conducted the armistice negotiations held between Israel and various Arab states on the island of Rhodes from January to July 1949. The agreed-upon armistice lines (see Map 4.3) defined Israel's boundaries until the 1967 war, but in principle a state of war still existed; only a cessation of hostilities had been achieved.

CONCLUSION

For the Palestinian Arabs the wars of 1948, both before and after independence, had been devastating. During the war with the Arab states, the Israelis ousted many more Arabs from the lands they captured and forced them across the lines into Arab-held territory; between 400,000 and 450,000 were expelled or fled. Of the approximately 860,000 Arabs who had lived in the area of Palestine now called Israel, 133,000 remained. Of the rest, 470,000 entered camps in Arab Palestine, controlled by Jordan, and in the Gaza Strip, held by Egypt (see Figure 4.6). The remainder were dispersed into Lebanon, Syria, and Jordan proper, with Egypt and Iraq taking lesser numbers.[71] With their dispersion, the Palestinian question became one of the refugees, to be handled by the Arab states, until the 1960s when a Palestinian national movement began to emerge, itself often the pawn of Arab state rivalries. The mufti's efforts to form an Arab government

◀ Map 4.2 ■ The 1948 War and Israeli Expansion beyond the Partition Lines to 1949

These maps show the pattern of Arab attacks and of Israeli resistance and ultimate expansion into areas not awarded by the partition plan. The uncoordinated nature of the Arab invasion enabled Israel to halt and ultimately to drive back the Arab forces other than Jordan's Arab Legion; the Arab Legion withdrew from the Lydda area in the war's second stage to consolidate its position around Jerusalem. Jordan would retain control of the Old City and a reduced area of Palestinian lands under the 1947 partition plan, known as the West Bank, until the 1967 war. (From *The Middle East: A History*, fourth edition, edited by Sydney Nettleton Fisher and William Ochsenwald, p. 642. Copyright © 1990 The McGraw-Hill Companies. Reprinted by permission of the publisher.)

LEBANON

Area under Egyptian occupation

Area under Jordanian control

Demilitarized zone

International boundary

SYRIA

Acre

Mediterranean Sea

Haifa

L. Tiberias

GOLAN HEIGHTS

Jenin

Tulkarm

Nablus

Jordan R.

Tel Aviv-Jaffa

WEST BANK

Ramleh

Ramallah

Jericho

Amman

Jerusalem

Hebron

Dead Sea

Gaza

GAZA STRIP

Beersheba

El 'Arish

ISRAEL

El 'Auja

N E G E V

JORDAN

EGYPT

Gulf of Aqaba

Eilat

Aqaba

SAUDI ARABIA

0   15   30 miles

0   15   30 kilometers

Figure 4.6 ■ **Palestinian Peasants Fleeing an Unidentified Village, October 1948**

The hostilities following the U.N. partition decision and subsequent Israeli independence shattered the Palestinian community. Hundreds of thousands of Palestinians either fled or were driven out of what had been Palestine to become refugees in neighboring Arab countries. Those pictured here were possibly fleeing the Beersheba area, which Israel attacked in October while taking the Negev (see Map 4.2).

of all of Palestine, situated in Gaza, were rejected by Abdullah, who saw it as a means of denying him authority over eastern Palestine. In December 1948, he proclaimed the unity of Arab Palestine and Jordan and appointed the mufti's old rival, Raghib al-Nashashibi, as his first military governor of Palestine, now the West Bank of Jordan.

In Israel, Ben-Gurion and his dominant Mapai Party moved to consolidate the fruits of victory. He had triumphed in a major confrontation with Begin and the Irgun in June, during the first truce, when he challenged Begin's right to

◄ **Map 4.3** ■ **The State of Israel, 1949–1967**

This map clarifies the resolution of the conflict illustrated in Map 4.2. It suggests the fragility of the borders between the West Bank and the new Israeli state. It also notes the Egyptian occupation of the Gaza Strip, until 1967, and the demilitarized zones along the Israeli-Egyptian and Israeli-Syrian borders. The Israeli-Syrian demilitarized zones would be the scenes of severe clashes because they either touched on water resources north of Lake Tiberias or lay beneath the Golan Heights overlooking the lake.

control a shipment of arms that had arrived at Tel Aviv on the SS *Altalena*. From Ben-Gurion's viewpoint, those weapons now belonged to the Israeli government and its armed forces, not to a separate unit that he feared might use them to challenge legitimate state authority. After a firefight between Hagana and Irgun forces that resulted in casualties and the beaching of the *Altalena*, the Irgun capitulated and the principal internal threat to the government was removed. With the elections of early 1949, Begin entered the Israeli parliament (Knesset) along with the leaders of LEHI and three Arabs.

By the end of 1949, the Israeli population had jumped to one million as a flood of immigrants entered the new state. Approximately half of the newcomers were Jews from Arab lands whose position had become nearly untenable, especially in Iraq, as a result of the creation of Israel. By 1952, 325,000 Jews from the Arab Middle East had migrated to Israel, ending centuries of existence as minorities under Muslim rule.[72] Only a tentative peace existed between the Arabs and the Israelis, one based on military necessity. The Arabs rejected the legitimacy of the Jewish state, whereas the Israelis were determined to convince the Arabs that they could not threaten their existence. A new phase of the conflict now began that focused on Arab-Israeli state and military interactions, influenced to a much greater degree than previously by great-power rivalries and the continuing confrontation between the Soviet bloc and the Western powers.

QUESTIONS FOR CONSIDERATION

1. What was the significance of the 1942 Biltmore Conference for U.S. policy and world Zionism?
2. What role, if any, did the Holocaust play in British and American approaches to the Palestine issue after World War II until 1948?
3. Explain the importance of the United Nations Special Committee on Palestine (UNSCOP).
4. What were the major factors creating the Palestinian refugee problem?

CHRONOLOGY

1940	Stern Gang (later LEHI) formed.
	November. Hagana blows up SS *Patria* in Haifa harbor.
1941	**June.** Germany invades Soviet Union.
	December 7. Japan attacks Pearl Harbor.
1942	**May.** Biltmore Conference takes place in New York City.
	November. British victory at El-Alamein.
1944	**November.** LEHI assassinates Lord Moyne in Cairo.
1945	**March.** League of Arab States created.
	April. U.S. President Franklin D. Roosevelt dies; succeeded by Harry S. Truman.
	May 8. War ends in Europe.
	August 14. Japan surrenders, bringing World War II to an end.
1946	**April.** Anglo-American Committee of Inquiry report. President Truman calls for admission of 100,000 Jewish refugees to Palestine.
	June. British raid Jewish Agency in Palestine.
	July. Morrison-Grady Committee Report. Irgun blows up King David Hotel.
1947	**February.** Britain submits Palestine question to United Nations.
	March. Truman Doctrine announced.
	June–July. UNSCOP visits Palestine, recommends partition.
	November 29. U.N. General Assembly approves partition of Palestine.
December 1947– May 1948	Arab-Jewish war in Palestine.
1948	**April.** Dayr Yasin massacre; Arabs take revenge on Jewish medical convoy.
	May 14. Israeli independence; David Ben-Gurion becomes first prime minister.
	May 15–June 11, July 6–19. Israel at war with Arab states.
	December. Kingdom of Jordan created.
1949	**January–July.** Armistice talks between Israel and Arab states involved in 1948 war.

Notes

1. Yehuda Bauer, *A History of the Holocaust* (New York, 1982), 200–205, 335.

2. Nicholas Bethell, *The Palestine Triangle: The Struggle for the Holy Land, 1935–1948* (New York, 1979), 95.

3. I. S. O. Playfair, *The Mediterranean and the Middle East, vol. 1, The Early Success against Italy (to May 1941)*, in *The History of the Second World War*, ed. J. R. M. Butler, United Kingdom Military Series (London, 1954), 75–79.

4. Quoted in Nevill Barbour, *Nisi Dominus* (London, 1946), 206.

5. Bernard Wasserstein, *Britain and the Jews of Europe, 1939–1945* (Oxford, 1979), 26.

6. Ibid.

7. Ibid., 71ff; and J. C. Hurewitz, *The Struggle for Palestine* (New York, 1976), 140.

8. Michael Cohen, *Palestine, Retreat from the Mandate: The Making of British Policy, 1936–1945* (London, 1978), 108ff.

9. John Marlowe, *The Seat of Pilate: An Account of the Palestine Mandate* (London, 1959), 173.

10. Munya M. Mardor, *Haganah* (New York, 1964), 163.

11. Ronald Zweig, "The Political Uses of Military Intelligence: Evaluating the Threat of a Jewish Revolt against Britain during the Second World War," in *Diplomacy and Intelligence during the Second World War: Essays in Honor of F. H. Hinsley*, ed. Richard Langhorne (Cambridge, U.K., 1985), 290. The source is an OSS report. Estimates of the quantity of arms varied, but all accounts agree on the superior quality of the Hagana's weaponry. See also Bethell, *Palestine Triangle*, 140–41.

12. Zweig, "Political Uses," 119.

13. Cohen, *Retreat*, 130ff; Yehuda Bauer, *From Diplomacy to Resistance: A History of Jewish Palestine, 1939–1945* (Philadelphia, 1970), 224–50; and Melvin I. Urofsky, *We Are One! American Jewry and Israel* (New York, 1978), 10–12.

14. Urofsky, *We Are One!* 33. Urofsky notes that "pro-Zionist books, often written by non-Jews, such as Sumner Welles's *Palestine's Rightful Destiny* and Norman MacLean's *His Terrible Swift Sword*, received Zionist subsidies, . . . [and] a number of academic studies were commissioned, all designed to refute the British contention that Palestine could not be further developed to absorb additional immigrants. One of these, Walter Clay Lowdermilk's *Palestine, Land of Promise*, published in 1944, won great popularity as a bestseller."

15. Standard works, some more sensationalist than others, are Arthur Morse, *While Six Million Died: A Chronicle of American Apathy* (New York, 1967); Henry L. Feingold, *The Politics of Rescue: The Roosevelt Administration and the Holocaust, 1938–1945* (New Brunswick, N.J., 1970); Saul S. Friedman, *No Haven for the Oppressed: United States Policy towards Jewish Refugees, 1938–1945* (Detroit, 1973); and two studies by David Wyman, *Paper Walls: America and the Refugee Crisis, 1938–1941* (Amherst, Mass., 1968); and *The Abandonment of the Jews, 1941–1945* (New York, 1984).

16. Feingold, *Politics of Rescue*, 265.

17. A commission of American Jews was formed in 1981 to conduct "an objective inquiry into the actions and attitudes of American Jewish leaders and organizations" about the Holocaust and efforts to save European Jews. Some members later resigned from the commission, which produced a truncated report that noted divisiveness over the question. See Seymour M. Finger, ed., *American Jewry during the Holocaust: A Report by the Research Director, His Staff, and Independent Research Scholars Retained by the Director for the American Jewish Commission on the Holocaust* (New York, 1984). The above quotation is from p. i.

18. Cohen, *Retreat*, 131–36.

19. Ibid., 157.

20. Ibid., 174.

21. Quoted in William R. Polk, David M. Stamler, and Edmund Asfour, *Backdrop to Tragedy: The Struggle for Palestine* (Boston, 1957), 108.

22. Bauer, *Diplomacy*, 129–39, 311–33; and J. Bowyer Bell, *Terror out of Zion: Irgun Zvai Leumi, LEHI, and the Palestine Underground, 1929–1949* (New York, 1977), 62–73.

23. Bauer, *Diplomacy*, 320–21.

24. Bell, *Terror*, 121–36. Many of the Hagana opposed these steps and refrained from participating in the campaign.

25. I am relying here principally on Hurewitz, *Struggle*, 146–55, 182–94; and the more recent study by Issa Khalaf, which is essential for the 1940s, *Politics in Palestine: Arab Factionalism and Social Disintegration, 1939–1948* (Albany, N.Y., 1991).

26. Hurewitz, *Struggle*, 190.

27. Khalaf, *Politics in Palestine*, 90–114.

28. Hurewitz, *Struggle*, 192.

29. A standard account of this period, with a good bibliography, is Bruce R. Kuniholm, *The Origins of the Cold War in the Near East: Great Power Conflict and Diplomacy in Iran, Turkey, and Greece* (Princeton, N.J., 1980). See also Melvyn P. Leffler, *A Preponderance of Power: National Security, the Truman Administration, and the Cold War* (Stanford, Calif., 1991).

30. Evan M. Wilson, *Decision on Palestine: How the U.S. Came to Recognize Israel* (Stanford, Calif., 1979), 190, n. 15.

31. Michael Cohen, *Palestine and the Great Powers, 1945–1948* (Princeton, N.J., 1982), 45. In addition to Cohen, another fine study of the question examining British and American positions is W. Roger Louis, *The British Empire in the Middle East, 1945–1951: Arab Nationalism, the United States and Postwar Imperialism* (Oxford, 1984). For Truman and the Palestine issue, see John Snetsinger, *Truman, the Jewish Vote, and the Creation of Israel* (Stanford, Calif., 1974); Zvi Ganin, *Truman, American Jewry, and Israel, 1945–1948* (New York, 1979); Kenneth Ray Bain, *The March to Zion: United States Policy and the Founding of Israel* (College Station, Tex., 1979). Wilson, *Decision on Palestine*, listed in the preceding footnote, focuses more on the diplomatic aspects of the problem from the perspective of the State Department than do the other sources mentioned. Finally, a study of American decision making regarding the Middle East since 1948 is Steven L. Spiegel, *The Other Arab-Israeli Conflict: Making America's Middle East Policy from Truman to Reagan* (Chicago, 1985).

32. Cohen, *Palestine*, 58–59.

33. Ibid., 62–64.

34. Michael N. Barnett, *Dialogues in Arab Politics: Negotiations in Regional Order* (New York, 1998), 87. See Khalaf, *Politics in Palestine*, 129–36, for discussion of these issues.

35. See Bell, *Terror*, 104ff; Bauer, *Diplomacy*, 265–345; and Eli Tavin and Yonah Alexander, eds., *Psychological Warfare and Propaganda: Irgun Documentation* (New York, 1982), especially 15–23, which note Irgun anger at the ex post facto Hagana condemnation of operations that the Irgun claimed to have been agreed on beforehand.

36. Major R. D. Wilson, *Cordon and Search: With the 6th Airborne Division in Palestine* (Aldershot, U.K., 1949), 40–61.

37. Yehuda Bauer, *Flight and Rescue: BRICHAH* (New York, 1970), 202–3, cites opinions that about 60 percent of the Jewish refugees interviewed were actually eager to go to Palestine.

38. Louis, *British Empire*, 414.

39. Richard Crossman, quoted in ibid., 412. Despite Crossman's philosophizing, he also produced wartime photos of Hajj Amin al-Husayni saluting Hitler during the testimony of Arab witnesses before the committee, an obvious attempt to taint the Arab case with the stain of Nazism.

40. Cohen, *Palestine*, 105.

41. Ibid., 116–34; Louis, *British Empire*, 434–38; and Hurewitz, *Struggle*, 249–67.

42. Bethell, *Palestine Triangle*, 242–51, states that the British had to rely on the Jews they employed to evaluate the material because so few of them knew Hebrew. But because these Jews were Hagana agents, they destroyed much incriminating evidence.

43. Ibid., 264–65; and Bell, *Terror*, 168–75.

44. Cohen, *Palestine*, 163.

45. Ganin, in *American Jewry*, 108, observes that "toward the end of 1946, . . . the Jewish Agency's efforts had secured the Yom Kippur statement, while the political action activities of the AZEC (American Zionist Emergency Council) seemed to have taught Truman and the Democrats the lesson that Jewish allegiance could not be taken for granted."

46. To return to the situation in the late 1930s would mean permitting the Jewish Agency to control immigration and have freedom to purchase land: see Cohen, *Palestine*, 220.

47. Louis, *British Empire*, 463.

48. Ibid., 445–67.

49. Pamela Ann Smith, *Palestine and the Palestinians, 1876–1983* (London, 1984), 82–84; and Khalaf, *Politics in Palestine*, 145ff.

50. *Survey of Palestine, Notes Compiled for the Information of the United Nations Special Committee on Palestine*, June 1947, vol. 1 (Jerusalem, 1947), 244; and the *Supplement to Survey of Palestine*, 10–11.

51. *Supplement to Survey of Palestine*, 15–16; and R. D. Wilson, *Cordon*, 260–63.

52. Louis, *British Empire*, 470, quoting Harold Beely of the British Foreign Office.

53. Cohen, *Palestine*, 267; and Hurewitz, *Struggle*, 294–98.

54. Cohen, *Palestine*, 269, notes that the Labour government had to impose severe austerity measures on the British public during the summer of 1947, including prohibiting the private use of gasoline.

55. Ganin, *American Jewry*, 139–41.

56. Quoted in Louis, *British Empire*, 485. Good summaries of Truman's response to these pressures are Robert J. Donovan, *Conflict and Crisis: The Presidency of Harry S. Truman, 1945–1948* (New York, 1977), 312–31, 369–87; and Spiegel, *Other Arab-Israeli Conflict*, Chapter 2.

57. Robert John and Sami Hadawi, *The Palestine Diary, vol. 2, 1945–1948* (New York, 1971), 260–64; Urofsky, *We Are One!* 143–45; Louis, *British Empire*, 484–86; and Cohen, *Palestine*, 295–300. Ganin, *American Jewry*, 144–45, discounts political factors.

58. Urofsky, *We Are One!* 147.

59. I rely here on Smith, *Palestinians*, 84–86; Cohen, *Palestine*, 305ff; and Khalaf, *Politics in Palestine*, 178–228.

60. The basic study is Avi Shlaim, *Collusion across the Jordan: King Abdullah, the Zionist Movement, and the Partition of Palestine* (New York, 1988). Khalaf, *Politics in Palestine*, 169–78, agrees in general with Shlaim but has a more nuanced view of British decision making and its inspiration. The most aggressive opponent of the work of Shlaim, Benny Morris (see n. 68), and other historians and sociologists is Efraim Karsh in his *Fabricating Israeli History: The "New Historians"* (London, 1997). For a good summary of the opposing positions, see the review of *Fabricating Israeli History* by Joel Beinin, in *The Middle East Journal* 52, 3 (Summer 1998): 448–50 and Karsh's bellicose reply to Beinin, ibid., 53, 1 (Winter 1999): 166–69. Further exchanges and discussion can be found in the Fall 1996 issue of *Israel Studies* and the special issue of *History and Memory* 7, no. 1 (1995).

61. Cohen, *Palestine*, 307.

62. R. D. Wilson, *Cordon*, 157. His casualty estimates are lower than Cohen's (*Palestine*, 308), but Cohen's account omits the initial Jewish bomb attack on the Arabs.

63. Cohen, *Palestine*, 306.

64. E. Wilson, *Decision on Palestine*, 128–37. Compare Cohen, *Palestine*, 347–54, and Louis, *British Empire*, 495–505.

65. For the oil issue, see Aaron David Miller, *Search for Security: Saudi Arabian Oil and American Foreign Policy, 1939–1949* (Chapel Hill, N.C., 1980).

66. Netaniel Lorch, *Israel's War of Independence, 1947–1949* (Hartford, Conn., 1968), 94.

67. Cohen, *Palestine*, 337, notes the nonaggression pact between the Hagana and the inhabitants of Dayr Yasin; this was confirmed indirectly by Christina Jones, *The Untempered Wind: Forty Years in Palestine* (London, 1975), 89, 130–31, who also refers to the Zionists' use of loudspeakers to terrify Arabs, as do Bell, *Terror*, 295–99, and Arthur Koestler, *Promise and Fulfillment, Palestine, 1917–1949* (New York, 1949), 160–61, 206–7. Begin's account of the propaganda value of Dayr Yasin is in his *The Revolt* (Los Angeles, 1972), 162–65, 363, in which he claims that the Hagana approved the mission.

68. The key studies of this issue are by Benny Morris, notably his *The Birth of the Palestinian Refugee Problem Revisited, 1947–1949* (Cambridge, U.K., 2004) and his *1948: A History of the First Arab-Israeli War* (New Haven, Conn., 2008). Morris demonstrates how Zionist forces undertook "cleansing" operations throughout April to mid-May and independence, essentially confirming the charges made by Ilan Pappé in his more provocative *The Ethnic Cleansing of Palestine* (Oxford, 2007).

69. See the bitter account in E. Wilson, *Decision on Palestine*, 137–49.

70. In addition to Shlaim, *Collusion across the Jordan*, see Mary C. Wilson, *King Abdullah, Britain, and the Making of Jordan* (New York, 1987); she notes Abdullah's contacts with Zionists throughout the mandate. Excellent discussion of the actions of all participants in the Arab-Israeli war can be found in Eugene Rogan and Avi Shlaim, eds., *The War for Palestine: Rewriting the History of 1948*, Second Edition (Cambridge, U.K., 2007). For Iraqi actions, see Charles Tripp, "Iraq and the 1948 War: Mirror of Iraq's Disorder," 125–49.

71. Morris, *1948*, has the most extensive coverage of these events, noted also by Yitzhak Rabin, *The Rabin Memoirs*, second, expanded, English edition (Berkeley, Calif., 1996). See also Nazzal, *Palestinian Exodus*, 64–110.

72. Lucas, *Modern History*, 272–73. There was an assault on the Jewish quarter of Baghdad in the spring of 1941, under the short-lived al-Gaylani regime, indicating anti-British as well as anti-Jewish sentiment. Such attacks did not begin to occur with any frequency until after 1945 and the growing awareness of Zionist success in Palestine and in the West. Although governments would sometimes intervene quickly, as in Egypt and Lebanon, to protect resident Jews, there was a significant loss of life and extensive damage to Jewish quarters, especially synagogues. In his *The Jews of Islam*, Bernard Lewis attributes Arab anti-Jewish sentiment to their attraction to Nazi ideology, with only passing reference to the impact of the Palestinian question on Arab attitudes toward Jews. He thus discards the concern for historical context and scholarship that pervades his discussion of the subject down to the twentieth century. In contrast, Y. Harkabi, *Arab Attitudes to Israel* (New York, 1971), depicts Arab anti-Semitic utterances as "political antisemitism," whose "rise is connected with the tension created as a result of Zionist activity, and especially the traumatic experience of defeat, the establishment of independent Israel and the struggle against her" (298).

THE "FINAL SOLUTION": NAZI EXTERMINATION OF EUROPEAN JEWRY

*This document illustrates the Nazis' comprehensive, well thought out plan to elim-
inate European Jews and shows their own estimates of the numbers killed. In this
excerpt, SS Sturmbannführer Dr. Wilhelm Hoettl recounts a conversation with
Adolf Eichmann about the numbers exterminated.*

At the end of August 1944 I was talking to SS-Obersturmbannführer Adolf Eichmann, whom I had known since 1938. The conversation took place in my home
in Budapest.

   He expressed his conviction that Germany had now lost the war and that
he, personally, had no further chance. He knew that he would be considered one
of the main war criminals by the United Nations since he had millions of Jewish
lives on his conscience. I asked him how many that was, to which he answered
that although the number was a great Reich secret, he would tell me since I, as a
historian, would be interested and that he would probably not return anyhow
from his command in Rumania. He had, shortly before that, made a report to
Himmler, as the latter wanted to know the exact number of Jews who had been
killed. On the basis of his information he had obtained the following result:

   Approximately four million Jews had been killed in the various extermination camps while an additional two million met death in other ways, the major
part of which were shot by operational squads of the Security Police during the
campaign against Russia.

Nazi Conspiracy and Aggression,
vol. V, document 2738 — PS

Source: T. G. Fraser, *The Middle East, 1914–1979* (London, 1980), 24–26.

UNSCOP'S PLAN OF PARTITION WITH ECONOMIC UNION

*This plan became the basis of the United Nations General Assembly partition pro-
posal approved on November 29, 1947. The plan recognized the inherent hostility
between the two populations and the economic imbalance favoring the proposed
Jewish state, while at the same time assuming that an economic union between
them was possible.*

Source: T. G. Fraser, *The Middle East, 1914–1979* (London, 1980), 45–47.

1. The basic premise underlying the partition proposal is that the claims to Palestine of the Arabs and Jews, both possessing validity, are irreconcilable, and that . . . partition . . . is the most likely [arrangement] to afford a workable basis for meeting in part the claims and national aspirations of both parties.

2. It is a fact that both of these peoples have their historic roots in Palestine, and that both make vital contributions to the economic and cultural life of the country. The partition solution takes these considerations fully into account.

3. The basic conflict in Palestine is a clash of two intense nationalisms. Regardless of the historical origins of the conflict, the rights and wrongs of the promises and counter-promises, and the international intervention incident to the Mandate, there are now in Palestine some 650,000 Jews and 1,200,000 Arabs who are dissimilar in their ways of living and, for the time being, separated by political interests which render difficult full and effective political cooperation.

4. Only by means of partition can these conflicting national aspirations find substantial expression and qualify both peoples to take their places as independent nations in the international community and in the United Nations. . . .

9. It is recognized that partition has been strongly opposed by Arabs, but it is felt that opposition would be lessened by a solution which definitively fixes the extent of territory to be allotted to the Jews with its implicit limitation on immigration. The fact that the solution carries the sanction of the United Nations involves a finality which should allay Arab fears of further expansion of the Jewish State.

10. In view of the limited area and resources of Palestine, it is essential that, to the extent feasible, and consistent with the creation of two independent States, the economic unity of the country should be preserved. . . .

11. Such economic unity requires the creation of an economic association by means of a treaty between the two States. . . . [creating] a common customs system, a common currency and the maintenance of a country-wide system of transport and communications.

12. The maintenance of existing standards of social services in all parts of Palestine depends partly upon the preservation of economic unity, and this is a main consideration underlying the provisions for an economic union as part of the partition scheme. . . . [although] during the early years of its existence, a partitioned Arab State in Palestine would have some difficulty in raising sufficient revenue to keep up its present standards of public services. One of the aims of the economic union, therefore, is to distribute surplus revenue to support such standards. It is recommended that the division of the surplus revenue, after certain charges and percentage of surplus to be paid to the City of Jerusalem are met, should be in equal proportion to the two States. . . .

13. This division of customs revenue is justified on three grounds: (1) The Jews will have the more economically developed part of the country embracing practically the whole of the citrus-producing area which includes a large number of Arab producers; (2) the Jewish State would, through the customs union, be guaranteed a larger free-trade area for the sale of the products of its industry;

(3) it would be to the disadvantage of the Jewish State if the Arab State should be in a financially precarious and poor economic condition.

14. As the Arab State will not be in a position to undertake considerable development expenditure, sympathetic consideration should be given to its claims for assistance from international institutions in the way of loans for expansion of education, public health and other vital social services of a nonself-supporting nature.

15. International financial assistance would also be required for any comprehensive immigration schemes in the interest of both States, and it is to be hoped that constructive work by the Joint Economic Board will be made possible by means of international loans on favourable terms.

Recommendations

A Partition and Independence

1. Palestine within its present borders, following a transitional period of two years from 1 September 1947, shall be constituted into an independent Arab State, an independent Jewish State, and the City of Jerusalem, the boundaries of which are respectively described in Parts II and III below.

> UNSCOP *Report*, vol. 1, chapter VI, part I
> Plan of partition with economic union

DOCUMENT 4.3

JAMAL AL-HUSAYNI

TESTIMONY ON PALESTINIAN ARAB REACTION TO THE UNSCOP PROPOSALS

September 29, 1947

Speaking before the U.N. Ad Hoc Committee on the Palestinian Question, Arab Higher Committee leader Jamal al-Husayni conveyed Palestinian Arab views of the UNSCOP proposals. Al-Husayni's arguments reflect the Palestinian Arabs' rejection of the decision that their fate should be subject to external forces. They also indicate an unrealistic hope for recourse to the United Nations in view of the fact that UNSCOP's actions were taken on behalf of that international body.

The case of the Arabs of Palestine was based on the principles of international justice; it was that of a people which desired to live in undisturbed possession of the country where Providence and history had placed it. The Arabs of Palestine

---

Source: T. G. Fraser, *The Middle East, 1914–1979* (London, 1980), 49–51.

could not understand why their right to live in freedom and peace, and to develop their country in accordance with their traditions, should be questioned and constantly submitted to investigation.

One thing was clear: it was the sacred duty of the Arabs of Palestine to defend their country against all aggression. The Zionists were conducting an aggressive campaign with the object of securing by force a country which was not theirs by birthright. Thus there was self-defence on one side and, on the other, aggression. The *raison d'être* of the United Nations was to assist self-defence against aggression.

The rights and patrimony of the Arabs in Palestine had been the subject of no less than eighteen investigations within twenty-five years, and all to no purpose. Such commissions of inquiry had made recommendations that had either reduced the national and legal rights of the Palestine Arabs or glossed them over. The few recommendations favourable to the Arabs had been ignored by the Mandatory Power. It was hardly strange, therefore, that they should have been unwilling to take part in a nineteenth investigation. . . .

The struggle of the Arabs in Palestine had nothing in common with anti-Semitism. The Arab world had been one of the rare havens of refuge for the Jews until the atmosphere of neighbourliness had been poisoned by the Balfour Declaration and the aggressive spirit the latter had engendered in the Jewish community. . . .

Mr. Husseini disputed three claims of world Jewry. The claim to Palestine based on historical association was a movement on the part of the Ashkenazim, whose forefathers had no connexion with Palestine. The Sephardim, the main descendants of Israel, had mostly denounced Zionism. Secondly, the religious connexion of the Zionists with Palestine, which he noted was shared by Moslems and Christians, gave them no secular claim to the country. Freedom of access to the Holy Places was universally accepted. Thirdly, the Zionists claimed the establishment of a Jewish National Home by virtue of the Balfour Declaration. But the British Government had had no right to dispose of Palestine which it had occupied in the name of the Allies as a liberator and not as a conqueror. The Balfour Declaration was in contradiction with the Covenant of the League of Nations and was an immoral, unjust and illegal promise.

The solution lay in the Charter of the United Nations, in accordance with which the Arabs of Palestine, who constituted the majority, were entitled to a free and independent State. . . .

Once Palestine was found to be entitled to independence, the United Nations was not legally competent to decide or to impose the constitutional organization of Palestine, since such action would amount to interference with an internal matter of an independent nation. . . .

In conclusion, Mr. Husseini said that he had not commented on the Special Committee's report because the Arab Higher Committee considered that it could not be a basis for discussion. Both schemes proposed in the report were inconsistent with the United Nations Charter and with the Covenant [*sic*]

League of Nations. The Arabs of Palestine were solidly determined to oppose with all the means at their command any scheme which provided for the dissection, segregation or partition of their country or which gave to a minority special and preferential rights or status. Although they fully realised that big Powers could crush such opposition by brute force, the Arabs nevertheless would not be deterred, but would lawfully defend with their life-blood every inch of the soil of their beloved country.

UNO Ad Hoc Committee on the
Palestinian Question, third meeting

DOCUMENT 4.4

RABBI HILLEL SILVER

TESTIMONY ON ZIONIST REACTION TO THE UNSCOP PROPOSALS

October 2, 1947

Commenting before the U.N. Ad Hoc Committee on the Palestinian Question, Rabbi Hillel Silver of the Jewish Agency for Palestine began by addressing al-Husayni's testimony (see Document 4.3). His response reflects Zionist assumptions of their right to Palestine on historical grounds inapplicable to the Arabs. And although apparently accepting the idea of economic union, his statement suggests that the agency reserved wide latitude for independent Jewish action.

History was not a story out of the *Arabian Nights* and the Arab Higher Committee was indulging in wishful thinking. . . .

He recalled that at the time when the Allies had liberated Palestine, the country had formed part of a province of the Ottoman Empire and there had been no politically distinct Arab nation. . . . By 636 A.D. [when the Arabs took Palestine] the Jewish people had already had 2,000 years of history behind it, and Jewish civilization, besides giving rise both to Judaism and Christianity, had also brought forth spiritual leaders venerated also by Islam. In contrast to that, Dr. Silver quoted the report of the Royal Commission of 1937, which stated that in the twelve centuries and more that had passed since the Arab conquest, Palestine had virtually dropped out of history, and that in the realm of thought, of science or of letters, it had made no contribution to modern civilization.

Palestine owed its very identity to the Jews, losing it with the Jewish dispersion and resuming its role in history only at the time of the Mandate, which had given it a distinct place alongside the Arab world.

Source: T. G. Fraser, *The Middle East, 1914–1979* (London, 1980), 51–53.

Seventeen million Arabs occupied an area of 1,290,000 square miles of great wealth, including all the principal Arab and Moslem centres, while Palestine, after the loss of Transjordan was only 10,000 square miles. The majority plan, set out in chapter VII of the Special Committee's report, proposed that that area should be reduced by one half. The plan, unlike that of the Royal Commission, eliminated western Galilee from the proposed Jewish State: that was an injustice and grievous handicap to the development of the Jewish State.

The majority plan proposed that the City of Jerusalem should be established as a separate unit. But modern Jerusalem contained a compact Jewish community of 90,000 inhabitants, and included the central national, religious and educational institutions of the Jewish people of Palestine. Moreover, Jerusalem held a unique place in Jewish life and religious traditions. It was the ancient capital of the Jewish nation and its symbol throughout the ages. "If I forget thee, O Jerusalem, let my right hand forget her cunning": that was the vow of the Psalmist, and of an exiled people throughout the ages.

Dr. Silver strongly urged that the Jewish section of modern Jerusalem, outside the walls, should be included in the Jewish State. He also reserved the right to deal later with other territorial modifications.

If that heavy sacrifice was the inescapable condition of a final solution, . . . then the Jewish Agency was prepared to recommend the acceptance of the partition solution to the supreme organs of the movement, subject to further discussion of constitutional and territorial provisions. That sacrifice would be the Jewish contribution to the solution of a painful problem and would bear witness to the Jewish people's spirit of international cooperation and its desire for peace.

The Jewish Agency accepted the proposal for economic union [but]. . . .

The limit to the sacrifices to which the Jewish Agency could consent was clear: a Jewish State must have in its own hands those instruments of financing and economic control necessary to carry out large-scale Jewish immigration and the related economic development, and it must have independent access to those world sources of capital and raw materials indispensable for the accomplishment of those purposes.

The Jews of Palestine wanted to be good neighbours in their relations not only with the Arab State of Palestine but with the other Arab States. They intended to respect the equal rights of the Arab population in the free and democratic Jewish State. What the Jews had already achieved in Palestine augured well for the future. Nevertheless, if that offer of peace and friendship were not welcomed in the same spirit, the Jews would defend their rights to the end. In Palestine there had been built a nation which demanded its independence, and would not allow itself to be dislodged or deprived of its national status. It could not go, and it would not go, beyond the enormous sacrifice which had been asked of it.

UNO Ad Hoc Committee on the
Palestinian Question, fourth meeting

DECLARATION OF THE ESTABLISHMENT OF THE STATE OF ISRAEL

May 14, 1948

This historic document subsumes within it historical links with ancient Israel, the trauma of the Holocaust, and the promise of a liberal democratic state in the future. Its call to its Arab inhabitants was mitigated, however, by Israel's expulsion of many of them to gain control of their crops and lands during the subsequent Arab-Israeli wars.

Eretz-Israel* was the birthplace of the Jewish people. Here their spiritual, religious and political identity was shaped. Here they first attained to statehood, created cultural values of national and universal significance and gave to the world the eternal Book of Books.

After being forcibly exiled from their land, the people kept faith with it throughout their dispersion and never ceased to pray and hope for their return to it and for the restoration in it of their political freedom.

Impelled by this historic and traditional attachment, Jews strove in every successive generation to re-establish themselves in their ancient homeland. In recent decades they returned in their masses. Pioneers, Ma'apilim† and defenders, they made deserts bloom, revived the Hebrew language, built villages and towns, and created a thriving community, controlling its own economy and culture, loving peace but knowing how to defend itself, bringing the blessings of progress to all the country's inhabitants, and aspiring towards independent nationhood.

In the year 5657 (1897), at the summons of the spiritual father of the Jewish state, Theodor Herzl, the first Zionist Congress convened and proclaimed the right of the Jewish people to national rebirth in their own country.

This right was recognized in the Balfour Declaration of 2 November 1917, and reaffirmed in the Mandate of the League of Nations which, in particular, gave international sanction to the historic connection between the Jewish people and Eretz-Israel and to the right of the Jewish people to rebuild its national home.

The catastrophe which recently befell the Jewish people—the massacre of millions of Jews in Europe—was another clear demonstration of the urgency

---

*Eretz-Israel: The ancient land of Israel, Palestine.—Ed.
†Ma'apilim: Immigrants who had come in defiance of British policy.—Ed.

Source: T. G. Fraser, *The Middle East, 1914–1979* (London, 1980), 66–67.

of solving the problem of its homelessness by re-establishing in Eretz-Israel the Jewish state, which would open the gates of the homeland wide to every Jew and confer upon the Jewish people the status of a fully privileged member of the comity of nations.

Survivors of the Nazi holocaust in Europe, as well as Jews from other parts of the world, continued to migrate to Eretz-Israel, undaunted by the difficulties, restrictions and dangers, and never ceased to assert their right to a life of dignity, freedom and honest toil in their national homeland.

In the second world war, the Jewish community of this country contributed its full share to the struggle of the freedom — and peace-loving nations against the forces of Nazi wickedness and, by the blood of its soldiers and its war effort, gained the right to be reckoned among the peoples who founded the United Nations.

On 29 November 1947, the United Nations General Assembly passed a resolution calling for the establishment of a Jewish state in Eretz-Israel; the General Assembly required the inhabitants of Eretz-Israel to take such steps as were necessary on their part for the implementation of that resolution. This recognition by the United Nations of the right of the Jewish people to establish their state is irrevocable.

This right is the natural right of the Jewish people to be masters of their own fate, like all other nations, in their own sovereign state.

Accordingly we, members of the People's Council, representatives of the Jewish community of Eretz-Israel and of the Zionist movement, are here assembled on the day of the termination of the British Mandate over Eretz-Israel and, by virtue of our natural and historic right and on the strength of the resolution of the United Nations General Assembly, hereby declare the establishment of a Jewish state in Eretz-Israel, to be known as the State of Israel.

We declare that, with effect from the moment of the termination of the Mandate, being tonight, the eve of Sabbath, the 6th Iyar, 5708 (15 May 1948), until the establishment of the elected, regular authorities of the state in accordance with the constitution which shall be adopted by the elected Constituent Assembly not later than 1 October 1948, the People's Council shall act as a provisional Council of State, and its executive organ, the People's Administration, shall be the Provisional Government of the Jewish state, to be called "Israel."

The State of Israel will be open for Jewish immigration and for the ingathering of the exiles; it will foster the development of the country for the benefit of all its inhabitants; it will be based on freedom, justice and peace as envisaged by the Prophets of Israel; it will ensure complete equality of social and political rights to all its inhabitants irrespective of religion, race or sex; it will guarantee freedom of religion, conscience, language, education and culture; it will safeguard the Holy Places of all religions; and it will be faithful to the principles of the Charter of the United Nations.

The State of Israel is prepared to cooperate with the agencies and representatives of the United Nations in implementing the resolution of the General

Assembly of 29 November 1947, and will take steps to bring about the economic union of the whole of Eretz-Israel.

We appeal to the United Nations to assist the Jewish people in the building up of its state and to receive the State of Israel into the comity of nations.

We appeal—in the very midst of the onslaught launched against us now for months—to the Arab inhabitants of the State of Israel to preserve peace and participate in the upbuilding of the state on the basis of full and equal citizenship and due representation in all its provisional and permanent institutions.

We extend our hand to all neighbouring states and their peoples in an offer of peace and good neighbourliness, and appeal to them to establish bonds of cooperation and mutual help with the sovereign Jewish people settled in its own land. The State of Israel is prepared to do its share in a common effort for the advancement of the entire Middle East.

We appeal to the Jewish people throughout the diaspora* to rally round the Jews of Eretz-Israel in the tasks of immigration and upbuilding and to stand by them in the great struggle for the realization of the age-old dream—the redemption of Israel.

Placing our trust in the Almighty, we affix our signatures to this proclamation at this session of the Provisional Council of State, on the soil of the homeland, in the city of Tel Aviv, on this Sabbath eve, the 5th day of Iyar 5708 (14 May 1948).

Israel Information Service

* **diaspora**: The Jewish community dispersed worldwide.—Ed.

DOCUMENT 4.6

KING ABDULLAH'S OFFER TO THE ZIONISTS
May 1948

This opening portion of a memo outlining Truman's options toward the creation of a Jewish state reports King Abdullah's offer to avoid confronting Jewish forces as long as he could absorb that area of Palestine allotted to the Palestinian state. The news was given to U.S. Secretary of State George Marshall by Zionist Foreign Affairs Secretary Moshe Shertok (later Sharett) during a meeting in Marshall's office. In light of Marshall's known opposition to American support for the creation of Israel, the statement attributed to him by Shertok's representative must be taken with caution, but the encounter does indicate close official Zionist contacts with the Truman administration prior to Israeli independence. The memo carried a note

Source: Harry S. Truman Presidential Library: http:// www.trumanlibrary.org/whistlestop/study _collections/Israel.

from Max Lowenthal, a Truman administration intermediary to the Zionists, to Clark Clifford, Truman's domestic political adviser, stating: "Clark, Please do not let anyone else read this dynamite."

Subject: Palestine

May 11, 1948

What Are the Alternatives before the President at This Moment?

    1. Secretary Marshall's Attitude

Last Saturday, May 8, at a conference in his office with Mr. Shertok, the Secretary was given a cable by Mr. Shertok from Palestine, reporting an offer from an Arab Legion colonel representing King Abdullah; the offer was for an agreement between Abdullah and the Jewish State, to enable Abdullah, without Jewish interference, to take over the Arab portion of Palestine, while leaving the Jewish area to the Jews. Mr. Shertok's Washington representative privately reports that Secretary Marshall twice said: there is nothing I would like more than such an agreement between Abdullah and the Jews. . . .

5

THE BEGINNING OF THE ARAB-ISRAELI CONFLICT
The Search for Security
1949–1957

THE CONCLUSION of the armistice agreements between Israel and the Arab states introduced an era of no war–no peace; technically, a state of belligerency still existed. Israel's successful defense of its borders had not brought official recognition of the status quo either by Arab states or by much of the international community. A major stumbling block was the question of the Palestinian Arab refugees (see Document 5.1). Western powers called on Israel to permit at least a portion to return to their homes, but the Israelis resisted this pressure or tied its acceptance to the conclusion of peace agreements with Arab governments. The latter insisted on the right of all refugees to return, at least in principle, as a preliminary step signifying Israeli good faith before they would consider peace talks. Some Arab leaders called also for a return to the 1947 partition plan, the borders of which they had previously rejected. Israel, which had benefited from that stance by expanding its sovereignty into areas allotted to the Arabs, naturally opposed these claims as being invalid, given the changing circumstances that had resulted from the wars of 1948.

In general, Israel found itself in an almost totally hostile environment. Arab leaders considered it the creation of Western imperialism, peopled by Europeans brought in with European and American encouragement at a time when other Arab countries were struggling to gain complete independence from European domination. Furthermore, the armistice lines encouraged border clashes and incidents. Drawn arbitrarily, they frequently cut off Arab villagers from their lands, which were then taken over by Jewish settlers. Palestinian Arab infiltration and Israeli retaliation, especially along the Jordanian line, became a staple of Arab-Israeli tensions. Israel's feeling of encirclement was compounded by Egypt's refusal to permit its ships through the Suez Canal, though Egypt did allow transit to ships of other flags destined for Israel. And from the early 1950s, Egypt frequently blocked traffic bound for the Israeli port of Eilat through the

Straits of Tiran into the Gulf of Aqaba, thereby barring Eilat's access to the Red Sea and Indian Ocean trade. On the other hand, interactions along Egypt's borders were relatively mild until 1955, compared with the situation existing between Israel and Jordan.

From the Israeli perspective, these Arab attitudes were unwarranted. In their view, Arab governments should recognize Israel and absorb the Palestinian Arabs into their own societies. Furthermore, Arab infiltrators should be controlled and the governments be held responsible for any damages. Given this hostility, the issue of security was paramount; it demanded military readiness and immigration to bolster the country's strength and effectively undermine the possibility that many Palestinian Arabs might be permitted to return. But Prime Minister David Ben-Gurion's conception of security was not merely defensive. He and his chief military advisers undertook a policy of retaliation against the countries from which the infiltrators came to prove to the Arab leaders that Israel could not be defeated and that peace was the only recourse. This activist policy was opposed by Foreign Minister Moshe Sharett. It resulted in serious cleavages within the Israeli cabinet in the early 1950s and led to increased hostilities with the Arab governments rather than encouraging a receptivity to negotiations.

Arab-Israeli clashes necessarily involved the Western powers, who were eager to draw Arab countries into security pacts in order to ensure opposition to Soviet overtures in the Middle East. Such efforts, fostered by Great Britain and occasionally encouraged by the United States, seemed to Israel to threaten its security further by aligning the powers with governments hostile to it. The Israelis sought, unsuccessfully, to become the basis of a Western military alliance in the Middle East that would have isolated the Arabs until they sued for peace with Israel. Though Israel's ambitions did not suit Western strategic interests, neither did the rise to power in Egypt of Gamal Abd al-Nasser, a young colonel who strove both to reform the Egyptian economy and to oust the British from the Suez Canal zone. Nasser's diplomatic successes and the prestige he gained from them in the Arab world established him in Israeli eyes as a potential threat to be nullified, a view that gained increasing acceptance in French and eventually in British eyes as well. The result was the Suez invasion of October–November 1956, a coordinated attack by Israel, France, and Great Britain that sought to break Nasser's control of the Suez Canal and overthrow his regime.

ISRAEL, THE ARAB STATES, AND THE PALESTINIAN/ISRAELI ARABS, 1949–1954

If the new state of Israel confronted rejection, now transferred from the Palestinians to the broader Arab world, it also incorporated within its own governmental system antagonisms and attitudes found in the pre-1948 Zionist community. Mapai, the dominant party during the mandate, kept its name until 1968, at which point through coalition it became the Israeli Labor Party; it retained its prominence in Israeli politics until 1977. With statehood in 1948, David Ben-Gurion, former head of the Jewish Agency, became prime minister while Chaim Weizmann was awarded the ceremonial post of president. Though other parties might be represented in succeeding cabinets, Mapai, epitomizing preindependence labor Zionism, usually controlled the key posts of prime minister, foreign minister, minister of defense, and minister of finance.

Israel: Government, Citizenship, and the Law

Israel's system of government emerged out of the institutions forged to achieve statehood and oversee military actions before and in the immediate aftermath of independence. It embodied a strong cabinet ideally reflecting a majority in the Israeli parliament, the Knesset, which was created by a Constituent Assembly in 1949; in fact, coalition governments were the norm, though usually dominated by Mapai. Like Britain, Israel never developed a constitution, opting instead for the Knesset's passage over time of certain Basic Laws. The decision not to create a constitution, which was called for in the Declaration of Independence, appears to have been Ben-Gurion's and to have stemmed from several concerns: a constitution might upset the status quo and affront Orthodox Jews; it would define and limit governmental powers and Ben-Gurion's freedom of action; and it would identify boundaries of the state, when Israel had not stipulated its boundaries in its declaration of independence.[1]

Instead, some mandate regulations remained in force. For example, religious communities (Muslim, Christian, Jewish) retained, as in the Ottoman system, their own courts for matters of personal status; Orthodox Judaism represented the Jewish community, religious or secular. Politically, Ben-Gurion preferred bargaining among parties as had occurred during the mandate; the election system was based on party lists submitted to voters nationwide. With respect to boundaries, the Declaration of Independence referred to "Eretz Israel," the land of Israel in its biblical sense, not clearly defined in the term "State of Israel." Even though Israel had signed armistices and accepted partition, it was not committed to those agreements because not all the land of Palestine had been conquered.[2]

Finally, as a Jewish state, Israel in principle offered citizenship to Jews everywhere. They had priority over non-Jewish residents, such as Arabs, who were technically citizens. Of supreme importance was establishing the authority of the state, linked closely to the military as the arm of that state and preferably of Mapai. Thus Ben-Gurion not only forced dissolution of the Irgun, the arm of Revisionist Zionism, in June 1948, but he also disbanded the Palmach, the elite unit of the Hagana, because its members were derived mostly from parties to the left of Mapai. This mistrust of Zionist rivals to the right and left of Mapai, all of whom wanted a constitution, led Ben-Gurion to form his governmental coalitions with the Orthodox, who had no position on secular affairs at that time.[3] Mapam, far more leftist than Mapai, advocated close ties with the Soviet Union; Herut, the party formed by Menachem Begin to represent Irgun ideals, supported free market policies and advocated the immediate conquest of Jordan as well as the West Bank to embrace all of ancient Israel. As a result, Israel would develop as a nonliberal democracy lacking the civil liberties embodied in a Bill of Rights. This situation permitted the state to interpret its own activities subject to subsequent Knesset or court challenge, a more desirable option in a time of crisis and transition.

As the true home of all Jews, not simply those within its borders, Israel called upon those in the Diaspora to return. This doctrine, formally decreed in the Law of Return of 1950, permitted any Jew of good character to enter Israel and receive citizenship. Between 1949 and 1952, Israel's Jewish population more than doubled as some 666,500 newcomers entered, nearly equally divided between those of European and non-European origin. Among the latter, the largest contingents were from Iraq and Yemen—nearly 125,000 Iraqi Jews and 45,000 Yemenites. Iran, Algeria, Tunisia, Morocco, and Libya also saw relatively large numbers of Jews leave, many under duress. As for Iraqi Jews, accounts of popular and government harassment must be balanced with evidence of Zionist activities in Iraq before and after Israeli independence intended to convince Iraq's Jews it would be unsafe to stay in Iraq.[4] Whether from Europe or elsewhere, nearly all of the immigrants were poor and needed state assistance. These conditions created massive pressures on the newly established Israeli state and economy, and emphasized the need for aid from abroad. In the early years of Israel's existence, this aid came from private and public contributions funneled through Zionist agencies in the United States, including the sale of Israeli bonds, which began in late 1951. During 1951 and 1952, United Jewish Appeal pledges amounted to approximately $150 million and bond sales to $99 million.[5] Nevertheless, Israel faced severe economic problems then, as later, in seeking to absorb new citizens. After 1952, as shortages mounted and immigration lessened, the Law of Return was modified in practice to exclude aged and ailing individuals who had no means of support and who, in practical terms, could not contribute either militarily or financially to the security of the state.[6]

Israeli Arabs: Dispossession and Isolation

In such circumstances, the fate of the remaining Arab population in Israel, which amounted to about 170,000 by 1950, was subject to Israel's perceived security requirements and the needs of its incoming settlers. Most of these Arabs were considered potential subversives despite being classified as citizens of Israel. Most lived in areas close to the armistice lines, which had been designated military zones, outside the control of civil law and subject to the arbitrary imposition of military edicts. Lawful residents could be banished, properties confiscated, and entire villages moved by military decision.[7] In the military's view, backed by Ben-Gurion though protested by some members of the Knesset, the granting of full civil liberties to Israeli Arabs would endanger the national defense because of the continuing tensions along the armistice lines, where frequent incursions by Palestinians occurred.

Equally important in judging the status of Israeli Arabs was the designation of much of their property as "absentee," even if they still lived in Israel. The question of property was crucial to Israel's ability to house its new immigrants. In December 1948, a custodian of absentee property was appointed who had nearly absolute powers over the disposal of lands left vacant as a result of the wars of 1948. The custodian's powers were such that he

> could take over Arab property in Israel on the strength of his own judgment by certifying in writing that any persons or body of persons, and that any property, were "absentee." The burden of proof that any property was not absentee fell upon its owner, but the Custodian could not be questioned concerning the source of information on the grounds of which he had declared a person or property. . . . He could [also] take over all property which might be obtained in the future by an individual whom he certified to be absentee.[8]

The custodian's judgment was wide-ranging and applied to many Palestinian Arabs who had not left the region taken over by Israel. Any Palestinian Arab could be declared absentee if he had left his usual place of residence on or after November 29, 1947, the date of the United Nations partition resolution. This applied whether the individual had returned to that place of residence on the following day or had fled scenes of combat during the war but had not left what became Israeli territory. Tens of thousands of Israeli Arabs were so classified; only about 1 percent were able to regain some of their property. Later protests led to a decision by the Israeli government to pay compensation to some claimants and to permit Arabs to lease lands from the custodian.

The nature of the process whereby these decisions were made reflected the conditions in Israel following independence. Massive Jewish immigration led to the ad hoc occupation of deserted Arab housing in major cities and villages. Where Arab villages had been destroyed, new Jewish villages were constructed or the land was absorbed by adjacent Jewish collective settlements. Because the Jewish Agency then took over occupied property for the use of these new settlers, the property, in the custodian's view, became inalienably Jewish and could not be returned to the Arabs who had left it, even if they remained in what had become Israel. The definition of "absentee property" served to justify the taking of Arab lands and buildings for the sake of consolidating Israel's hold on the bulk of the land area. Israel's definition of its own needs also served to isolate the Arab population from consideration for development opportunities or allocation of public services considered normal for the Jewish sector, a practice that continues today.[9]

The Palestinian Refugees

Palestinian Arabs living outside their former homeland, now refugees, encountered official sympathy and unofficial suspicion that led to their isolation in most of the countries where they settled. The bulk of the Palestinian Arabs in exile, over half a million in 1956, resided in Jordan, where they then comprised one-third of the population. The only Arab state to do so, Jordan granted the Palestinians Jordanian citizenship, a move signaling Abdullah's intent to absorb the West Bank permanently and, he hoped, erase Palestinian identity among his new citizens. Even there, many Palestinians remained in refugee camps financed by the United Nations through the United Nations Relief and Works Agency (UNRWA), created in 1950 when it became clear that swift resolution of the refugee question was unlikely. Nearly 200,000 were crammed into the Gaza Strip, under Egyptian rule, where their movement was restricted. The nearly 100,000 refugees in Lebanon in 1956 had not been granted citizenship because the Maronite Christian ruling elite feared the addition of so many Muslims to the population. Of all the states bordering Israel, only Syria at that time had sufficient land for the settlement of refugees, though certainly not all of them. In May 1949 the Syrian ruler, Colonel Husni Zaim, offered to meet with Ben-Gurion to discuss arrangements whereby hundreds of thousands of Palestinians might be resettled in Syria. Despite the favorable response of Moshe Sharett, Ben-Gurion flatly rejected the offer.[10] Ben-Gurion's reaction reflected an insistence on Arab leaders' meeting certain Israeli conditions that precluded preliminary talks that might have resolved outstanding issues.

The refugees remained in camps in most countries, many of them rejecting offers of resettlement (see Figure 5.1). Arab leaders demanded their return to former Palestine. The government of Israel, from 1950 onward, insisted on their resettlement in Arab lands as part of an equal exchange of populations that, by 1952, included the influx into Israel of over 300,000 Jews from Arab countries. Disorganized and subject to the whims of their hosts, the Palestinians remained an important factor in Arab-Israeli tensions down to 1956 but were then effectively controlled until the emergence of the Palestinian Liberation Organization in 1964, itself created to serve the interests of the Arab states.

The Western Allies, Israel, and the Arab-Israeli Conflict

From the viewpoint of the Western powers—the United States, France, and Great Britain—the Middle East was a source of tension whose causes should be resolved as quickly as possible. Ongoing Arab-Israeli border clashes became the responsibility of the Mixed Armistice Commission (MAC) formed by the United Nations General Assembly to resolve disputes. There were separate committees for Israel and each of its Arab neighbors, including representatives from both sides and U.N. officials. The commission had no independent authority. It

Figure 5.1 ■ Palestinian Refugee Camp at Nahr al-Barid in Northern Lebanon, Winter 1948–1949

Initially conceived as temporary havens, the camps, with tents provided by the United Nations, could remain the home of refugees for years if host countries were reluctant to absorb them and offer employment, as was the case in Lebanon.

could investigate complaints brought by one side or the other, assess responsibility, and report its findings to U.N. headquarters in New York. Its ability to arbitrate depended on both sides permitting the MAC to proceed.

At the same time, the West sought to neutralize the military capabilities of the antagonists and align the participants, especially the Arab states, against any possible Soviet incursion. A French-British-American Tripartite Declaration of May 25, 1950, pledged to maintain the existing armistice lines, to limit arms supplies to those required for local security needs, and to refrain from major weapons deals that might alter the balance of power and initiate an arms race. Israel was considered well equipped for its security requirements and superior in its military training and combat readiness to its Arab neighbors. Israel, however, sought more specific guarantees of support from the West. The Ben-Gurion government opposed the Tripartite Declaration and sought Israel's inclusion in a regional defense system envisaged for the area, an extension of the NATO (North Atlantic Treaty Organization) concept of regional military alliances designed to contain the Russians. But Allied plans did not include Israel at this time. The containment principle seemed more suitable for Arab participation than Israeli, given the size of the Arab population and its potential for social unrest. Social tensions could be addressed by the economic aid that would be part of the assistance granted to any member of such a defense system.

Israeli Views of Arabs and the World

Israeli leaders resented Western interest in Arab participation in regional alliances. They wanted to be part of a Western alliance that would exclude the Arab states. Membership would bring with it arms supplies and much-needed economic assistance to help provide for the great infusion of immigrants. The arms supplies, although supposedly preparing Israel to defend itself against the Russians, would ensure its military superiority over the Arab states. Conversely, Arab membership in such a system would bolster Arab military stockpiles, which Israel considered to be aimed at it. But if Ben-Gurion eagerly pursued such an alliance, especially with the United States, he rejected any condition that might restrict his freedom of movement. Thus he refused an American suggestion of a security pact while seeking an arms deal only. The latter would permit him to direct Israeli actions unhindered, a vital factor in Israel's policy toward its Arab neighbors.[11]

Israel's attitude toward the Arabs and its relations with the outside world were predicated on the Jewish experience in Europe, the Holocaust, and the Arab hostility it encountered in the Middle East. Whereas Jews had previously been subject to the will of non-Jews, Israel, as the Jewish state, would never submit to constraints imposed by others. In Ben-Gurion's view, Israel alone was responsible for its existence; though it might rely on outside economic or military assistance, that would not signify its willingness to limit its independence in any way. For Ben-Gurion and his political allies, the opinions of the outside world meant little, regardless of the aid other countries might give. He made a nearly absolute distinction between Israel and world Jewry on the one hand, and the goyim, or non-Jews, on the other. If the latter did not fulfill their perceived obligations to Israel, they would at best be ignored, and at worst fought.

Ben-Gurionist Activism.   This attitude, called "Ben-Gurionism" or "activism," emerged initially in Zionist perceptions of the British.[12] For Zionists the British had an obligation to fulfill regarding the creation of the Jewish state. When they drew back, they had to be confronted, militarily and diplomatically, so that Jewish rights could be achieved. As for the Palestinian Arabs, Ben-Gurion assumed they would understand only armed might. Once they learned that opposition to Zionism was futile, they would ultimately accept it and submit to Jewish rule. Thus Ben-Gurion testified before UNSCOP in July 1947 that he would approach the Palestinian Arabs and "tell them, here is a decision in our favour. We are right. We want to sit down with you and settle the question amicably. If your answer is no, then we will use force against you."[13] After independence, Ben-Gurion extended his perception of Arab hostility and how to confront it to Arab states. Because the Arabs denied Israel's right to exist, they had to be shown the power of Israel time and again until they were compelled to concede its military superiority and sue for peace.

For the activists, who included Moshe Dayan, appointed chief of staff in 1953, evidence of Arab hostility should be challenged immediately to remind the particular state that Israel would not tolerate any act that seemed to violate its sovereignty and well-being. This policy of retaliation was implemented with particular harshness on the Israeli-Jordanian frontier, the scene of numerous border transgressions. Many involved the theft of crops but, in the early 1950s, increasingly included personal assaults. Most of these forays came from Palestinian Arab villages in the West Bank area, which were separated from Israel and often their former farmlands by just a few hundred yards. From 1952 onward, the Israeli military ordered retaliatory assaults on Arab villages that might have housed individuals responsible for attacks on Israelis or Israeli property. In 1953 Unit 101, a special force led by Colonel Ariel Sharon, was formed to undertake punitive raids. In October 1953, following the killing of an Israeli mother and two children, this force attacked the Palestinian village of Qibya, dynamiting houses, killing over fifty inhabitants, and wounding fifteen others.[14] The intention was to impose a price on the Arab community disproportionate to the crime committed against Israel in order to encourage deterrence by the host government.

The practice achieved deterrence for a while on the Jordanian frontier, though it brought neither side closer to peace, the presumed objective of such retaliatory actions. So far as Dayan and his aides were concerned, any infringement should be punished, even if no threat to life resulted. Thus, when some prize sheep were stolen from an Israeli kibbutz, Dayan recommended a retaliatory attack against an Arab border village. He was rebuffed by Moshe Sharett, then prime minister, who deplored the activist policy that the majority of Israeli officials supported. The sheep were later returned through U.N. intercession.[15]

Ben-Gurionist activism combined a sense of being threatened with a belief in Israel's military superiority. In this context Israeli military actions were often intentionally aggressive. Israeli forces frequently engaged in maneuvers close to the borders of Jordan and later Egypt, actions that sparked clashes and that were seen by U.N. officials as deliberately provocative.[16] Although Israeli reprisals were designed initially to force Arab governments to restrain infiltrators into Israel, their success on the Jordanian frontier did not inhibit Israeli military units from undertaking unilateral actions. These tactics were important in Dayan's view, not only to make Arab governments control their borders, but primarily to "make it possible for us to maintain a high level of tension among our population and in the army. Without these actions (assaults) we would have ceased to be a combative people and without the discipline of a combative people we are lost."[17] On occasion, that might require provoking an incident designed to justify a reprisal. It might also signify cross-border raids by Israeli troops, which became "routine." Though they were violations of the armistice, they were not limited to reprisals because they were considered useful military training exercises.[18]

Moshe Sharett and the Activists.   In such an atmosphere, advocates of a more conciliatory approach to the Arabs and the world at large were relatively few, though they predominated in the Foreign Ministry. Moshe Sharett's conception of Israel's relations with outsiders has been characterized as "Weizmannist," part of the moderate school that opposed Ben-Gurionist activism.[19] That is, he was more disposed to rely on outside aid to resolve disputes and to acknowledge it rather than stressing absolute Jewish self-reliance. Although he recognized Arab hostility, he was willing to seek a reconciliation of differences through negotiation and compromise, if that were possible. Sharett did not rule out force as an option, but it remained one choice among several rather than the primary response to problems that arose with Arab neighbors. To react immediately in a military manner prevented any possibility of searching for grounds for discussions with Arab leaders, if only secret or indirect, that might create a more rational atmosphere even if a full peace accord was not achieved.

Sharett decried the militarism that he believed to permeate the Ben-Gurionist camp. To him it meant that Israel

> must . . . invent dangers, and to do this it must adopt the method of provocation-and-revenge. . . . And above all—let us hope for a new war with the Arab countries, so that we may finally get rid of our troubles and acquire our space. (Such a slip of the tongue: Ben-Gurion himself said that it would be worthwhile to pay an Arab a million pounds to start a war.)[20]

For their part, Dayan and his contemporaries viewed Sharett with contempt as a weak man whose views would enfeeble the country. Ben-Gurion agreed, once declaring that "Sharett is cultivating a generation of cowards."[21] During Ben-Gurion's temporary retirement in 1953–1954, Dayan and Minister of Defense Pinhas Lavon routinely ordered exercises without consulting Sharett and were not averse to falsifying reports afterwards. Much of this activity fell more broadly into the framework of preparing for the next war, when the activists hoped to extend Israel's borders to the Jordan River; there was little thought of using military action to foster peace talks. But the actions of the activists indicated also that the militarists, with Ben-Gurion's tacit blessing, were beyond the control of the political leadership centered in Sharett.[22]

Israel did make official peace proposals from time to time, based on Arab recognition of the existing borders with minor modifications and compensation for Arab refugees. But these offers did not meet Arab demands for major border revisions and the refugees' right to return. Often fearing domestic opposition in the midst of increasing social turmoil, no Arab state was able to discuss openly the prospect of peace with Israel. Conversely, the Israeli offers were made more with an eye to public consumption abroad than out of any expectation of positive response: "the main impetus for these announcements was pressure from the Western powers for a more conciliatory attitude."[23] And these offers, whatever their motives, drew criticism from sectors of the Israeli public.

Some argued that any Israeli overture would only be interpreted by the Arabs as a sign of weakness and might encourage a greater steadfastness in their plans to destroy Israel; military preparedness and continual demonstrations of Israel's power were the only means to bring the Arabs to the peace table. Territorialists, such as Menachem Begin, denounced the idea of talks because Ben-Gurion seemed willing to accept the existing armistice lines as future boundaries. Begin and his Herut party still advocated an immediate Israeli conquest of the West Bank and the forcible expulsion of its Arab population to pave the way for Jewish settlement of land linked biblically to ancient Israel. Ben-Gurion shared Begin's aspirations for territorial expansion but regarded him as impetuous. He preferred to await a propitious moment when Western backing might be possible, as demonstrated in his proposals during planning for the Suez attack in the autumn of 1956.

Suez gave Ben-Gurion the opportunity to implement his plans for an attack on Egypt, with possible territorial gain in the Sinai, an area he thought might pose a threat to Israel's security. With Gamal Abd al-Nasser's assumption of power in mid-1954, these expectations took on the guise of a self-fulfilling prophecy, buttressed by Ben-Gurion's preference for direct military action. In the words of one Israeli analyst:

> The Israeli approach (which granted priority to the attainment of short-range goals even at the expense of the long-range goal) stemmed from the assumption that existence *per se* takes precedence over peaceful existence. . . . From this stemmed the Israeli tendency to give priority to short- and middle-range security considerations over long-range political considerations. . . .[24]

As a result, Sharett's interest in compromise led Ben-Gurion in 1956 to decide that "Sharett was a serious liability in the preservation of Israel's vital interests."[25] He arranged Sharett's ouster as foreign minister, thus ensuring that he could plan an invasion of Egypt without strong opposition within the cabinet.

The Arab States: Domestic Turmoil and Regional Rivalries

Most Arabs considered the military defeat at the hands of the Israelis a disaster, a shock that seriously undermined the credibility of the regimes that had committed their forces to battle. Many, especially of the younger generation, saw Israel's existence as symbolic of Arab humiliation at the hands of a superior power relying on the Western technology that they were denied. Here there existed a desire for revenge coupled with the fear of Israeli military might and possible future expansion.

On the other hand, plans for retaliation played little, if any, role in Arab politics, despite the resentment felt at Israel's creation. Arab attention focused on domestic issues and problems of development; the Israeli victory seemed to many a symbol rather than a cause of the corruption and inefficiency they associated with their existing political systems. The Arab states did not develop a policy toward Israel individually or collectively, in contrast with the opposing activist and moderate policies that influenced Israel's actions toward its Arab opponents. The only course on which Arab leaders agreed was to refuse recognition to the new state. The exception to this rule was King Abdullah of Jordan, who in private negotiations sought to reach a peace agreement with Israel that would ratify the boundaries created in the 1948 war. Success would have meant recognition of his control over the West Bank, thus denying any possibility of a Palestinian state, an interest shared by the Israelis as well. The negotiations failed when news of their existence led to severe criticism of Abdullah by other Arab states. His assassination in Jerusalem in 1951 by a Palestinian was a consequence of his efforts to reach that agreement.

Arab Rivalries and the Struggle for Syria.   Arab rivalries at this time focused primarily on efforts to unite the Fertile Crescent, principally Iraq, Jordan, and Syria, but possibly including Lebanon as well; before World War II, these plans had included Palestine. Its major sponsors were Iraq and Jordan, the two Hashemite kingdoms that derived from the descendants of Sharif Husayn. The chief prize was Syria, considered the heartland of Arab nationalism. Both countries, especially Iraq, intervened in Syrian politics to encourage the rise to power of a ruler favorable to such a union. Egypt and Saudi Arabia, eager to block any merger that excluded them, strove to foster Syrian protégés who would oppose these schemes. Differing domestic priorities and relations with Western powers also played a part in these disputes. Though nominally independent, both Iraq and Jordan were closely allied to Great Britain and permitted it to use military facilities in their countries, whereas Egypt tried to oust the British.

Syria experienced serious upheavals following its defeat in the war against Israel. There were three coups in 1949, all bringing colonels to power. Although these changes of government reflected tensions in the military stemming from the war with Israel, they also indicated shifting alliances relating to Fertile Crescent matters. The first of the three colonels, Husni Zaim, was anti-Hashemite; the second, Sami Hinnawi, was pro-Iraqi and approached Baghdad with the idea of uniting the two countries; the third, Adib Shishakli, steered a middle course between the Hashemite and pro-Egyptian factions, ruling Syria with an iron hand until he was overthrown in February 1954. Although domestic resentment played an important role in Shishakli's demise, equally significant was the Iraqi financing of the coup in the hope of installing a pro-Hashemite regime, apparently with British support. This, in turn, prompted the French to support Shishakli as a means of fostering the restoration of French influence in Syria.[26]

The returns from the free elections held in October 1954 stressed the role of independents in Syrian politics, but the socialist party, the Baath, scored significant gains. Its advocacy of Arab unity and neutrality in great-power affairs aroused Western concern, intensified by Syria's hostility toward countries such as Iraq that seemed willing to consider alliances with the West. Throughout this period, tensions flared periodically along the Israeli-Syrian frontier, often sparked by disputes over the fate of the demilitarized zones established by the armistice agreements at points along Lake Tiberias at the base of the Golan Heights. The agreements guaranteed the right of these areas' inhabitants to stay, but the issue of sovereignty remained unresolved. Syria argued that the question could be decided only in a final peace accord; Israel claimed sovereignty over the zones and the right to act freely in them.

Nasser and the 1952 Egyptian Revolution.   Egypt, with King Faruq still in power until July 1952, experienced great domestic unrest during the late 1940s. Nationalists demanded complete independence from Great Britain and the removal of British personnel from their bases in the Suez Canal zone. The Muslim Brotherhood called also for drastic socioeconomic reforms based on Islamic principles to redress the inequities that plagued Egyptian society. In the turmoil following Egypt's defeat in Palestine, members of the Muslim Brothers assassinated the prime minister in December 1948; the Egyptian police retaliated by killing the leader of the Brothers, Hassan al-Banna, two months later. Resultant tensions over the canal zone erupted on January 26, 1952, with the burning of much of westernized Cairo. That led to the July 23 bloodless coup in which a group of young military officers, headed by Gamal Abd al-Nasser, ousted Faruq and took power. Although Egyptian propaganda was often violent in its condemnation of Israel during Nasser's first two years in office, the Egyptian-Israeli frontier was relatively quiet as he concentrated on domestic reform and securing his own position within the new regime. A major accomplishment was Nasser's success in reaching an agreement with the British in July 1954 whereby British forces would be withdrawn from their bases in the canal area by June 1956.

For a younger generation of Arabs, Nasser's success in gaining British agreement to withdraw its forces, initialed in July and signed officially in October 1954, aroused a general desire to break military ties with Western countries. This occurred at a time when both the British and the United States sought to reinforce such links, although their motives differed. The British, with Churchill back in office as prime minister and Anthony Eden as foreign minister, viewed Nasser with disdain and sought to reinforce their bonds with Jordan and especially with Iraq. The United States, with Dwight Eisenhower as president and John Foster Dulles as secretary of state after January 1953, shared the British desire for military alliances designed to block communist expansion but, until 1956, viewed Nasser more favorably. They believed that British efforts to retain bases in Egypt aroused nationalist opposition and created conditions more conducive to neutrality and a possible turning to the Soviets. In American eyes, if any Arab leader was to be wooed, it was Nasser and Washington hoped to persuade him to join a military pact.[27]

Nasser did not consolidate his position as ruler of Egypt until 1954. Although he had led the young officers who overthrew Faruq in July 1952, they had chosen a better known figure as leader, General Muhammad Naguib, with

Nasser the dominant policymaker behind the scenes. But Naguib acquired increasing power because of his popularity, and by early 1954 he seemed to favor the restoration of democracy, which had been suspended following the revolution. A struggle for power in the spring ended with Nasser the victor. He now emerged as the real leader of Egypt but faced challenges, especially from the Muslim Brothers, who were embittered by their continued exclusion from the government. When a member of the Brotherhood attempted to assassinate Nasser in October, Nasser used the incident to crack down on its leadership. They were arrested and brought to trial, and six members identified with efforts to instigate violence were executed.

It was precisely at this time, the beginning of 1955, that new crises erupted that affected Egypt's relations with the West and its stance toward Israel: the first was the Baghdad Pact, a military alliance between Iraq and Turkey, signed on February 24, which the British joined a month later; the second resulted from an Israeli attack on an Egyptian post in the Gaza Strip that left heavy Egyptian casualties.

THE COLD WAR AND THE MIDDLE EAST: LOOKING FOR ALLIES, 1953–1955

The Baghdad Pact was the outgrowth of an Anglo-American search for allies in a Middle Eastern defense system aimed at limiting Soviet advances. Both countries saw merit in the northern tier concept, whereby the countries along Russia's southern border—Turkey, Iran, and Pakistan—would join alignments backed by the West. Where they diverged was in their prognosis for Arab involvement in such a pact, coupled with British resentment at what they perceived as American attempts to usurp traditional British spheres of influence.

Containment and the Northern Tier Concept

Eisenhower's secretary of state, John Foster Dulles, was a determined backer of containment and an inveterate seeker of regional alliances designed to bolster countries and areas considered strategically important to the West. But following a tour of the Middle East in mid-1953, Dulles recognized that the Egyptians would not enter any pact that required Western military bases on Egyptian soil. At most, they might agree to an Arab collective security alliance buttressed by Western arms. That too awaited success in Nasser's negotiations with Eden over British withdrawal from the canal zone. Dulles, convinced that no Arab security arrangement would succeed without Egypt's participation, sought to encourage Nasser by promising American assistance once an accord was reached. In the meantime he placed his hopes on the non-Arab northern tier countries, which seemed more willing to accept direct Western ties.

Here Dulles had success. Turkey had become a NATO member in February 1952. During 1953, the United States established closer ties with Pakistan and arranged the coup that restored the Shah of Iran to his throne. With American prodding, Turkey and Pakistan reached a military accord in April 1954, followed by an announcement of U.S. military aid to Pakistan. This agreement linked the Pakistanis to two regional defense systems, one based on its treaty with Turkey and the other through its membership in SEATO (Southeast Asia Treaty Organization), created to bar Chinese as well as Russian inroads into that region. Dulles and Eisenhower seemed in 1954 to have preferred a northern tier arrangement that excluded all Arab states so as not to draw the ire of nationalists who favored neutrality. Though they appreciated the loyalty of Iraq's Nuri al-Said, they considered him less likely than Nasser to foster Arab acceptance of any collective security pact.[28]

Eden resented the American inroads into Pakistan and Iran, where British interests had once been paramount, and was particularly upset by what he perceived as American pressure to reach an agreement with Nasser in order to supplant the British in Egypt. Determined to reassert British prestige in the Arab world, Eden considered Nasser an upstart whose nationalism should be checked, best done, he believed, through open military alliances with Arab allies. Iraq was the most likely candidate, given the pro-Western sympathies of Nuri al-Said and Nuri's fear of the younger generation represented by Nasser and the anti-Hashemites in Damascus. Furthermore, Nuri was eager to promote an alliance of Arab states linked to Turkey, Iran, and Pakistan with Western military backing, a framework that presumably would have stiffened the more conservative regimes and furthered Hashemite ambitions.

The Baghdad Pact

In January 1955, Nuri announced Iraq's intention to enter a military pact with Turkey, signed on February 24. Britain, the sponsor, joined a month later and Iran and Pakistan followed, creating a union officially known as the Central Treaty Organization, more commonly designated the Baghdad Pact. The pact was Eden's answer to Dulles and he declared in the House of Commons after British entry into the group that "I think . . . we have strengthened our influence and our voice throughout the Middle East."[29] Dulles thought otherwise and refused to commit the United States to full membership, opting for observer status. He believed that open British membership weakened the Western position in the region, especially because the pact's headquarters were in Baghdad. If Iraqi membership were desirable, then the Western powers should have financed the pact behind the scenes rather than being identified openly with one regime in the Arab world.

Nasser vilified Nuri's stance as a betrayal of Arab nationalist interests, which called for neutrality; he identified instead with India's Jawaharlal Nehru, who had criticized Pakistan's membership, in part because such arrangements brought great infusions of arms, which its regional rivals would have to offset. (Israel objected to the Baghdad Pact for the same reason.) Nasser also believed that the pact violated his informal understanding with the United States about the creation of an independent Arab military alliance. Nevertheless, he still looked to the West, especially the United States, for military assistance, assuming it to be part of the aid Dulles promised in 1953; an economic accord had been reached with Washington in November 1954. Nasser's search for arms intensified following an Israeli attack on Gaza on February 28, 1955, four days after the Baghdad Pact was announced. The raid highlighted Egyptian military weaknesses and was a catalyst in the increase of Egyptian-Israeli border tensions. Its motives stemmed primarily from Israeli domestic considerations. It reflected the split between Sharett and Ben-Gurion and can be considered a turning point in the modern history of the region.

Israel, the Lavon Affair, and the Gaza Raid

Moshe Sharett had become acting prime minister in July 1953 when Ben-Gurion decided to enter semiretirement at his desert kibbutz, but the latter did not officially resign his post until December. During the interim, Moshe Dayan, who remained chief of staff, and other colleagues continued to consult Ben-Gurion without always deferring to Sharett, their nominal superior. Similarly, the new defense minister (Ben-Gurion had occupied both posts), Pinhas Lavon, regarded Sharett with scorn and sided generally with the school advocating military reprisals. Thus the retaliatory raid against Qibya in October, proposed by Dayan and assigned to Ariel Sharon, was approved by Lavon and tacitly sanctioned by Ben-Gurion, but Sharett was informed only in an offhand way, and his objections were ignored; as noted previously, the military was operating without reference to the political leadership in office.[30] Once Sharett became prime minister in December, retaining his post as foreign minister, he tried to contain military ventures and established a private dialogue with Nasser that lasted at least until the Gaza raid.[31]

Lavon, however, sought to assert himself as defense minister, and ultimately incurred the wrath of Dayan and the military because of what they considered his meddling in their affairs. In the summer of 1954, his plotting led to a scheme designed to abort the Anglo-Egyptian agreement for withdrawal of troops from the bases in the canal zone. In alliance with the head of Israeli military intelligence, Lavon decided that the removal of the British troops would open the way for Egyptian military penetration of the Sinai Peninsula, thus creating a potential threat to Israel's existence.[32] He arranged for an Israeli spy ring in Cairo, composed mainly of Egyptian Jews, to plant bombs at the American and British embassy complexes and at buildings frequented by Westerners. The explosions would be attributed to the Muslim Brotherhood and were intended to create an atmosphere of distrust and doubt about Nasser's ability to protect foreigners. As a result, the British would presumably keep their troops in Egypt to protect their citizens. The plan quickly collapsed. The conspirators were caught in late July and brought to trial in December. Two members of the spy ring were condemned to death, others to jail sentences; one committed suicide in his cell. Those given the death sentence were hanged on January 31, 1955, despite pleas from abroad and a personal request from Sharett. Nasser had just executed the leaders of the Muslim Brotherhood for conspiracy, and he could not appear to bow to Israeli requests for leniency in such circumstances.

What became known as the Lavon Affair had an immense impact on Israeli opinion, especially because the Israeli public was not informed of the actual chain of circumstances until 1960; they believed until then that Nasser had trumped up the charges in order to persecute Jews. Israel imposed complete censorship at the time because Sharett, the prime minister, had not known of the planned operation. Once informed, he decided, with the agreement of all concerned, to keep it hidden from the public for fear that Israeli confidence in their leadership might be shaken too severely. An investigation resulted in Lavon's resignation after a commission failed to establish guilt or responsibility; there was evidence that the head of military intelligence and others had falsified documents. With the government in disarray and public emotions approaching hysteria, overtures to Ben-Gurion to return to government intensified. On February 17 he was installed as defense minister, the acknowledged leader of Israel and the symbol of the Israeli will to fight. Eleven days later came the Gaza raid, resulting in over forty Egyptian soldiers dead and scores wounded.

The Gaza Raid and the Czech Arms Deal

It is generally agreed that the Gaza raid was a turning point for Nasser. It radically changed his stance toward Israel and inspired a determined effort to acquire arms, given the potent reminder provided by the Israelis of how inadequate his forces were.[33] Although some incidents, including the killing of an Israeli, had occurred in the two months preceding the attack, there had been no major activity, as suggested by Israel, to justify its assault. Indeed, as Egyptian and Israeli documents indicate, "it is difficult to connect the Israeli raid with the activity of infiltration, because the Israeli action came precisely during a period of relative calm in that area and in the wake of major efforts on the part of the Egyptian regime to stop infiltrations in the Gaza Strip."[34] The real reasons seem to have been domestic, the need to reassure Israelis that a firm hand was once more guiding the state. But the raid also reflected the activist mentality, aiming to impress upon Nasser the risks of confronting Israel in the future. The attack became a self-fulfilling prophecy: Nasser's actions following the Gaza incident became much more specifically hostile to Israel. He approved the organization of Palestinian infiltration into Israel and attacks on the population beginning in the late spring. In addition, he undertook a search for arms that ultimately transformed him into the threat that Ben-Gurion envisioned.

Nasser first turned to the United States. Washington would supply arms only if American military advisers oversaw their preparation and use, a condition Nasser refused. He then turned to the Soviets, who in early May assured Nasser that they would grant him "any quantity of arms, including tanks and planes of the latest design, against deferred payment in Egyptian cotton and rice," conditions that seemed advantageous set against the payment schedules established by the West.[35] With U.S. officials in Egypt apparently aware of the Soviet offer but Washington unwilling to counter it, Nasser proclaimed the arms deal on September 27, identifying the Czechs as the partner, a transparent subterfuge given the Russian role.

The Egyptian arms agreement with the communist bloc undercut Dulles's attempts to isolate the Arab world from Soviet influence. Indeed, British backing for the Baghdad Pact, tacitly but not openly supported by the United States, contributed to this development, along with the Israeli attack in Gaza. The Gaza raid jolted Egypt into a search for arms. The Baghdad Pact inspired Nasser to intensify his opposition to Iraq and to proclaim his own leadership of an Arab world united in its determination to oust all colonial influence. This vague conception of Arab unity, undefined with respect to specific political arrangements but clearly linked to Third World neutrality, seemed in Western eyes to encourage Soviet influence and undermine theirs. This was especially the case when calls for unity were buttressed by increasingly strident Egyptian propaganda during 1955 against Arab countries having military alliances with the West. Nevertheless, Dulles and Eisenhower remained far more reserved in their questioning of Nasser than did the French and British. The latter, for different reasons, came to agree with Ben-Gurion that the Egyptian leader should be attacked and possibly overthrown.

Israel and France Draw Closer

France and Israel had had discussions regarding arms going back to 1953, well before major problems with Egypt arose. Ben-Gurion was determined to maintain Israel's military supremacy by circumventing the Tripartite Declaration of 1950. The United States and Britain generally adhered to that statement, though they had supplied limited quantities of arms to Jordan and Iraq. Israel turned secretly to France, which from 1954 onward proved a willing accomplice, especially members of the French Defense Ministry, who feared continued deterioration of France's colonial strength. Indochina was slipping away, symbolized by the North Vietnamese victory at Dien Bien Phu. Then the Algerian revolution began in October, striking at what many French people believed to be French national territory, not simply an imperial possession.[36] To the French military, the Algerian resistance was sparked by Arab nationalism, epitomized by Nasser's call for liberation from foreign bonds. Worse, they became convinced that Nasser was giving the Algerian rebels crucial military and financial assistance, without which the rebellion would collapse. Israel thus became an anti-Arab ally to be bolstered, a perception encouraged by Shimon Peres, Ben-Gurion's envoy from the Israeli Defense Ministry.[37] One arms agreement, reached in August 1954, provided jets, tanks, and radar equipment, shipped under great secrecy, although the Egyptians apparently became aware of these developments. French opposition to the Baghdad Pact cemented the Israeli-French bond. France saw the pact through World War I lenses as a move designed to expand British influence against the French in Syria. The French military approved a major arms transaction early in 1955, but final agreement was delayed until after Nasser's announcement of the Czech arms deal because of French Foreign Office objections, backed by American pressure; Dulles later withdrew his opposition. The November 1955 arms pact included the latest Mystère 4 jets and tanks. They did not approach the quantity of weapons the Russians had begun to supply to the Egyptians, but Dayan was confident that the Israelis could absorb their deliveries into the military far more quickly than could the Egyptians.

Border Clashes and Blockade of the Straits of Tiran

Not the least of the ironies of the Suez crisis was that France and Israel ultimately joined with Great Britain, the author of the Baghdad Pact whose creation had consolidated their own relationship. These developments took place amidst increasing tensions along the Egyptian-Israeli frontier, most specifically the area defined by the Gaza Strip. Raids organized by Palestinians (*fedayeen*) under Egyptian sponsorship became more numerous and destructive from August 1955 onward. Israeli retaliatory assaults against Egyptian installations and Palestinian civilian areas resulted. Additional acrimony erupted over strategic demilitarized zones where, contrary to armistice agreements, Israel established a military settlement disguised as a civilian kibbutz. Egyptian countermoves led to frequent exchanges of fire and more casualties. Israel was provocative—not simply responding to border incursions—in part, to show Egypt its weakness in circumstances that seemed increasingly intolerable to the Ben-Gurion government. Since that September the Egyptians had fully blockaded the Straits of Tiran, forcing ships going to Israel to request permission in advance and prohibiting transit of the airspace above the area.

This full blockade and the accompanying hostilities prompted Dayan to propose an attack on Egypt to Ben-Gurion, who became prime minister once more in November; he retained the defense ministry while Sharett remained foreign minister. Ben-Gurion backed the idea, but it was defeated by the cabinet in early December. Nevertheless, the option of a military initiative remained open. The Israeli military wanted it not simply to remove the blockade but also to destroy the Egyptians' military arsenal before they had fully absorbed their new Russian equipment. Egypt had sought these armaments to defend itself against future Israeli attacks; Israel now intended to wreck the Egyptian supplies, which it saw as an offensive threat.

Israel embarked on a campaign to seek more weapons, emphasizing publicly its feeling of military weakness, although Dayan felt his troops could defeat the Egyptians with little difficulty. What Ben-Gurion really wanted was an alliance, preferably with the United States, to offset the Egyptian-Russian alignment. Yet, here too, Ben-Gurionism neutralized the search for American arms. While Sharett was in Washington in December seeking an agreement, Ben-Gurion ordered an Israeli assault on Syrian positions that inflicted heavy casualties. Though his justification was a supposed Syrian provocation, the planning of the operation suggested otherwise. It was one more lesson to be delivered to the Egyptians as well as the Syrians, intended to show them that they were no match for Israel; the two countries had formed a military alliance in October.

Here too the interaction of factors and their interpretation reflected different preoccupations. The Egyptian-Syrian defense pact was designed essentially to enhance Nasser's position as an Arab leader by blocking Hashemite plans to undermine the Syrian regime. Though lip service was paid to the protection of the Arabs against Israel, Nasser did not pursue implementation of the agreement's military provisions. But the pact was viewed by Ben-Gurion as designed to encircle Israel, and an editorial in the *Jerusalem Post* expressed the hope that "the Israeli raid has convinced many Syrians that the military pact with Egypt has increased the dangers to Syria instead of guaranteeing Syria's defense."[38] The opposite occurred. Like the Gaza raid, the Israeli action encouraged further militarization. Syria intensified its purchases of Soviet arms and moved closer to Egypt. In addition, the attack undercut any chance that Sharett had of convincing the United States that Israel was in serious danger and needed not only more arms but possibly even a military alliance. Dulles and Eisenhower believed that Israel was at least as aggressive as the Arabs and militarily superior to them, not the weak, beleaguered nation portrayed to outsiders.

Israel wanted the United States and, if possible, all the Western powers to "go on with Israel alone. If the Arabs have no alternatives and enough pressure is put on them . . . they may acquiesce and make peace as they did once before when they signed the armistice agreements."[39] Washington officials considered the Israeli arguments logical but narrow and shortsighted. Dulles disliked Nasser's neutralism and viewed Egyptian propaganda as potentially destabilizing, but to reject Nasser would be to ensure Soviet paramountcy, since no alternative would be left. This prospect was much worse than neutrality. But the risk of confrontation was not unthinkable to Ben-Gurion or, increasingly, to the French as their difficulties in Algeria mounted in early 1956. And although Great Britain retained ties to Egypt, Anthony Eden, prime minister since April 1955, was growing more eager to blunt Nasser's appeal. The catalyst for an alliance among the three was Nasser's nationalization of the Suez Canal following the Western withdrawal of an offer to build the Aswan Dam.

COUNTDOWN TO SUEZ: FAILED DIPLOMACY AND DREAMS OF EMPIRE, JANUARY–NOVEMBER 1956

The Aswan Dam symbolized to Nasser and many Egyptians the key to their progress and agricultural and industrial stability. The regime had considered the idea since late 1952 and their eagerness to build it was well known, but serious discussions did not arise until the fall of 1955, and then with the United

States and Great Britain. American willingness to entertain the financing of the project was related to political considerations. The Eisenhower administration was alarmed at the ramifications of the Soviet arms deal and hoped that the project would establish bonds to Egypt that would reinforce its ties to the West.

Carrots and Sticks: Projects and Peace Proposals

Dulles and Eisenhower hoped that a U.S. offer to back the venture could be linked to efforts to achieve peace between Egypt and Israel, indirect leverage to pressure Nasser to enter negotiations. This peace effort, designated Project Alpha, was initially conceived in late 1954 but had made little progress. Now, in December 1955, an agreement was reached in principle, whereby the United States, Great Britain, and the International Bank for Reconstruction and Development (IBRD) would commit themselves to funding a large portion of the expenses, with a major share coming from the Egyptians.[40] The stage was set for negotiations to arrange the nature of the payments and Egypt's obligations to its Western creditors. At the same time, Robert Anderson, later secretary of the treasury, was entrusted with a highly secret mission to see whether Nasser and Ben-Gurion would consent to negotiate based on Project Alpha, by then a year old.

Project Alpha and the Anderson Mission.   Conceived in October 1954, Project Alpha emerged as an ambitious effort to reach an Arab-Israeli peace predicated on an initial Egyptian-Israeli rapprochement. It envisaged a settlement of the Palestinian refugee problem to be financed by the United States, with some refugees returning to Israel but most resettled in Arab countries. It also foresaw a land link between Egypt and Jordan through the Negev Desert, while still leaving the Negev in Israel's hands, and removal of Egyptian restrictions on Israeli shipping through the Suez Canal. Peace agreements between Israel, Syria, and Jordan would be encouraged by an economic development plan for the Jordan River valley.

Although some proposals may have reflected exchanges between Nasser and Sharett, neither Egypt nor Israel was fully committed to the scheme, whose fortunes were buffeted by events. Anthony Eden first broached the idea to Nasser in February 1955, but the latter's attention was diverted by the announcement of the Baghdad Pact and the Israeli raid on Gaza that occurred the following week. As 1955 progressed, Nasser came to resent Washington's apparent linkage of promised aid to Egypt's positive response to Project Alpha. On the Israeli side, Ben-Gurion opposed ceding any territory in the Negev or absorbing refugees, ideas that Sharett had been willing to discuss. The announcement of Egypt's Czech arms deal in September further antagonized Israel, but paradoxically encouraged Dulles's advocacy of the Aswan Dam, with the idea of linking U.S. aid to the Alpha peace plan.

Anderson's talks with Nasser and Ben-Gurion were intended to push Alpha while intimating to Nasser that acceptance of its terms was necessary to ensure Aswan Dam funding. The talks lasted from January to March 1956 in a hardly propitious atmosphere; Ben-Gurion and Dayan had sought cabinet approval for an invasion of the Sinai the previous December. Nasser professed interest in continuing secret discussions to consider the creation of a route through the Negev linking Egypt to Jordan and the right of Palestinian refugees to return to live in their former homeland, with compensation if they desired. Ben-Gurion rejected these issues out of hand and stressed that there should be direct public negotiations between him and Nasser if peace were to be discussed. Nasser refused. He would not agree to direct talks, especially because Ben-Gurion insisted on recognition of Israel's existing frontiers and acceptance of compensation for refugees.[41] The Anglo-American effort to create a basis for talks collapsed, encouraging further questioning of the Western commitment to the Aswan Dam enterprise.

Aswan Dam Project in Trouble.   From February 1956 onward, difficulties multiplied between the Egyptians and their Western partners. The IBRD had approved its share of the funding, but Nasser still had to reach an accord with Dulles and Eden, who had pledged $70 million to initiate the scheme. Nasser wanted a commitment for the full amount to avoid having to seek annual approval for renewed funding. The latter process in his view would open the possibility of political pressures being imposed, something he had recognized in the timing of the Anderson visit. But in London and Washington the sense that Nasser was a threat to Western interests was intensifying. On March 1, King Husayn of Jordan had dismissed General John Glubb, head of the Arab Legion for twenty-five years. This came at a time when Nasser had led a campaign to replace the ongoing British financial subsidy to Jordan with an Arab grant and after a propaganda campaign aimed at Husayn's defensive alliance with the British. Husayn's step was interpreted in the West as a great victory for Nasser and a deliberate insult to Britain. Eden now believed that "Nasser was the incarnation of all the evils of Arabia who would destroy every British interest in the Middle East unless he himself were speedily destroyed."[42] Eden was moving closer to the perception of Nasser held by Guy Mollet, French premier since January, who believed that Nasser was another Hitler aiming to disrupt world peace.

Dulles did not share these views, but he too was increasingly distrustful of Nasser; the United States had approved French arms shipments to Israel in late 1955. The promise to assist the Aswan Dam project was becoming a political liability in an election year, with various factions opposing the grant. Southern senators lobbied heavily against it. They feared increased competition from Egyptian cotton if the dam were built and more land was placed under cultivation. Pro-Israeli supporters, encouraged by the Israeli embassy, lobbied members of Congress, arguing that Nasser posed the only threat to peace. Cold war activists opposed to aiding those with ties to the Russians were equally outraged. The lineup was impressive but not crucial. What mattered was the commitment of the administration, and to them Nasser's actions were offensive. His objections to having conditions attached to the loan annoyed Dulles. Far worse, Dulles suspected Nasser of seeking better terms from the Russians, a possibility that led him to consider withdrawing U.S. aid, if only to punish the Egyptians. The catalyst seems to have been Nasser's recognition of Communist China in May, a step Dulles considered an insult that had to be repaid.

Nasser Nationalizes the Canal

A cardinal point of Dulles's foreign policy was not simply the containment but also the denial of the existence of Communist China, a point the United States made annually by mobilizing support to block it from membership in the United Nations. Hence Dulles's conviction that Nasser's disloyalty should not be rewarded by American assistance. He was encouraged in this view by the China lobby, which threatened to block the entire foreign aid bill in Congress. The question was how to evade the U.S. promise to support the dam venture.

Dulles appears to have hoped that Nasser's bargaining over terms would prolong the issue so that it might ultimately die of its own accord; Eden agreed, out of both his own dislike of Nasser and his increasing concern over Britain's financial stability. But the Egyptians decided instead to accept the American conditions. Their ambassador returned from Cairo to declare, on July 18, that "all decisions now are up to Washington and London."[43] Dulles's hand had been called, but in his meeting with the ambassador the following day he told him that the United States was withdrawing its commitment to fund the dam. He implied that the Egyptians were seeking to blackmail the Americans by threatening to go to the Russians; if they wished to do so, they should. Dulles believed that he was teaching Nasser a lesson, as he doubted the Soviets would fund the dam, thus leaving Nasser adrift. The secretary of state's actions "mystified" many Western diplomats who believed that he had rebuffed Nasser just when the latter was moving closer to the United States. It infuriated the American head of the IBRD, Eugene Black, who later stated that "it was the greatest disappointment of my professional life. . . . It was a classic case where long-term policy was sacrificed because of short-term problems and irritations. And war came shortly after."[44] Dulles, acting almost entirely alone, had decided to show Nasser that neutralists should not dally with the United States. He chose to punish him publicly, knowing that Eden agreed and apparently convinced that the Russians would not step in.[45]

Nasser had told his ambassador to accept the American offer but to expect rejection. What he did not anticipate was Dulles's pique and apparent intent to humiliate him. Confirmed in his suspicion of U.S. and British hostility, he then decided to teach Dulles and Eden a lesson while asserting Egyptian independence. On July 26, he nationalized the Suez Canal, to great popular acclaim (see Document 5.2 and Figure 5.2).

Figure 5.2 ■ **Gamal Abd al-Nasser after Nationalizing the Suez Canal, September 1956**

Here Nasser speaks to military cadets just after foreign pilots who guided ships through the canal quit their jobs. He accused Britain and France of encouraging the walkout to cripple the canal's operations. Soviet replacements along with Egyptian pilots took over, permitting the canal to remain open. Nasser defended his nationalization of the canal as legal under international law and promised to resist Western attempts to force his capitulation. Seated just behind his left shoulder, legs crossed, is Abd al-Hakim Amr who, as chief of staff of the Egyptian army, would later be held responsible for the debacle in the 1967 war.

Invasion Plans Take Shape

Nasser's nationalization of the Suez Canal set in motion a series of events lead-ing to a joint Israeli-French-British attack on Egypt. His action was not so much the cause of their aggression as the excuse for it. All had expressed before nationalization, separately or jointly, the desire to invade Egypt and destroy Nasser. In June, the French and the Israelis had reached agreement on a massive arms sale, including 200 tanks and 72 Mystère 4 jets; they began arriving secretly in late July. Ben-Gurion was by now determined to attack Egypt, preferably in alliance with France but alone if necessary. He had forced Sharett's resignation as foreign minister in June to ensure that the latter would not lead opposition to his plans in future cabinet meetings. Ben-Gurion replaced Sharett with Golda Meir, who could be counted on to follow his lead.

Nevertheless, Israel was left out of discussions in the immediate aftermath of the nationalization because of British objections to their inclusion; the French kept the Israelis informed nonetheless. Eden and Mollet led Anglo-French talks aimed at coordinating an attack, only to be checked by Dulles. A muted confrontation between Dulles and Eden arose. Eden agreed with the French that the Suez crisis should be exploited to achieve political goals in the Middle East, which they believed to be best served by either humiliating Nasser or creating "a pretext for the use of force to unseat him."[46] Dulles, on the other hand, hoped to resolve the dispute peacefully by gaining Nasser's acceptance of arrangements backed by the international community, designed to guarantee the canal's secure operation. In this he was aided somewhat by Egypt's assurance of compensation to shareholders of the canal company, a gesture that exasperated Eden, Mollet, and Ben-Gurion. For them, Egypt's promise to live up to all international obligations pertaining to the canal's operation was an obstacle rather than a sign of conciliation.

Eden continued to seek American backing for more forceful action while the French began consultations with the Israelis in early September regarding a joint attack, keeping them informed of their separate discussions with the British. It was only in late September that the British entered the French-Israeli scheme for an assault. By then Eden was convinced that Dulles had betrayed him by seeming privately to approve a forceful response but publicly undercutting him. American officials believed that Eden deluded himself. Beset by ill health and increasingly obsessed by Nasser, he viewed the crisis as the replication of the Nazi assault on international order in the later 1930s.[47] In this, his view of Nasser coincided with Mollet's mistaken belief that the Algerian rebellion would collapse without Nasser, enabling the French to retain a vital colonial possession.

There was general agreement that any operation should be undertaken by the end of October to take advantage of still-favorable weather conditions and, equally important, to invade toward the end of the U.S. election campaign. The participants assumed that Eisenhower would not oppose Israel and risk the Jewish vote so near to election day. Representatives of Israel, France, and Great Britain met secretly in France on October 21. At the initial meeting, Ben-Gurion proposed settling all outstanding issues. First priority went to "the elimination of Nasser," but beyond that he called for

> the partition of Jordan, with the West Bank going to Israel and the East Bank to Iraq. Lebanon's boundaries would also be moved, with part going to Syria, and another part, up to the Litani River, to Israel; the remaining territory would become a Christian state. In newly expanded Syria, the regime would be stabilized by being under a pro-Western ruler. Finally, the Suez Canal would enjoy international status and the Straits of Tiran would be under Israeli control.[48]

Ben-Gurion's scheme required American as well as Anglo-French approval, highly unlikely under the circumstances. He also envisaged that Israel would take over much if not all of the Sinai Peninsula, which he refused to believe was part of Egypt. His plans indicated an Israeli hope of fulfilling the initial Zionist conception of Israel's borders (minus eastern Palestine) presented in 1919.[49] The French expressed interest but stressed the need to concentrate on Nasser. Final agreement was achieved on October 23; Israel would invade the Sinai on October 29. With their forces already sailing for Egypt from Malta, the British and French governments would call for a truce on October 31, demanding that both sides withdraw to ten miles from the banks of the canal. In effect, this would give the Israelis the right to continue their attack until they reached that boundary, while the Egyptians should withdraw all their forces from the Sinai. Because Nasser would presumably not agree to this, Eden and Mollet could blame him for continuing hostilities and thus justify their scheduled attack.

The Attacks and Their Aftermath

Israeli forces entered the Sinai and the Gaza Strip as scheduled (see Map 5.1). Once Nasser refused the October 31 Anglo-French ultimatum, British planes from Cyprus attacked Egyptian airfields. That caused Nasser to withdraw his forces from the Sinai, precipitating a rout by the Israelis after some initial stiff defense by some Egyptian units. As the crisis deepened, British radio called for the Egyptian people to arise and overthrow their leader. Still, no Anglo-French assault occurred until November 5, and no landings were made until the following day. Although successful in military terms, the operation was by now thoroughly compromised: the fiction of Anglo-French neutrality and goodwill had been exposed. Eisenhower and Dulles were infuriated at what they considered to be Allied deception and stupidity. They disliked Nasser, but they did not believe that armed force would resolve the matter. In this they were correct. Dulles had resisted Eden and Mollet primarily to ensure that the canal remain open; after the attack, the Egyptians scuttled ships in the channel, blocking passage for months. To his chagrin, Dulles found himself leading the opposition to the Suez attack at the United Nations in unwitting tandem with the Russians. It was particularly galling because the Hungarian rebellion had occurred at the same time as the Suez crisis. After some hesitation, the Soviets had invaded and crushed the uprising, but the Allied action against Egypt prevented Dulles from using the Hungarian crisis to prove the immorality of communism and the need for all nations to rely on the West.

Eisenhower and Dulles now pressured Eden to agree to end the operation. They refused to relieve financial pressure on the beleaguered pound or release oil supplies until he acquiesced. Under great strain Eden capitulated after being deserted by colleagues such as Harold Macmillan, who would succeed him as prime minister and who had strongly advocated the Suez venture. The United States voted with a large majority in the United Nations to censure the aggressors. British and French forces withdrew from Port Said by December 23. Eden resigned on January 9 after stating to the House of Commons in late December that Great Britain had not conspired with Israel in the attack, a denial that further damaged his reputation.

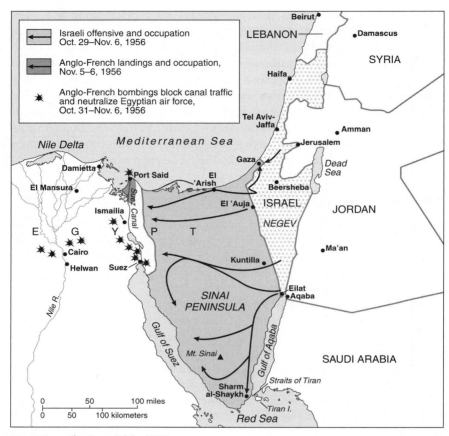

Map 5.1 ▪ The Suez Crisis, 1956

This map indicates the trajectory of the Israeli assaults and the focus of the Anglo-French landings in the Port Said zone at the head of the Suez Canal. Sharm al-Shaykh is at the point of the southernmost arrow indicating the Israeli attack toward the area overlooking the Straits of Tiran. (From *The Middle East: A History*, fourth edition, edited by Sidney Nettleton Fisher and William Ochsenwald, p. 702. Copyright © 1990 The McGraw-Hill Companies. Reprinted by permission of the publisher.)

There remained Israel to deal with. Ben-Gurion was determined to remain in the Gaza Strip and at Sharm al-Shaykh; the latter was the point of land in the southern Sinai that dominated access to the Straits of Tiran. Extensive discussions and pressure from the United States finally led to his agreement to withdraw in March 1957, but only on the condition that the United Nations Emergency Forces assigned to the area occupy Sharm al-Shaykh and patrol the Gaza Strip to prevent fedayeen infiltrations. If Egyptian forces once again occupied Sharm al-Shaykh and blockaded the entrance to the Gulf of Aqaba, Israel would consider this a *casus belli* (an act justifying war), a condition it imposed in June 1967 (see Document 5.3).

CONCLUSION

The Suez invasion and its failure signaled the end of Britain's tenure as the dominant imperial nation in the Middle East; it also scuttled Anthony Eden's career. An obituary in the *London Times* in 1977 declared that "he was the last prime minister to believe Britain was a great power and the first to confront a crisis that proved she was not."[50] Britain's collapse weakened its allies in the area, Iraq and Jordan, and left them more vulnerable to Nasser's propaganda, especially because Britain had conspired with Israel. For the French, the invasion was a fiasco for which they blamed Eden's caution, not the goals themselves. The Israelis considered Suez a major success. They had achieved a significant military victory with relatively few casualties. They had opened the Straits of Tiran, freeing Israeli shipping from the Gulf of Aqaba to the east. Finally, they had secured a de facto, if not an official, peace along the Israeli-Egyptian frontier, which remained quiet for the next ten years, patrolled by U.N. forces. Ben-Gurionism had not brought Nasser to the peace table, but it seemed to have brought security.

An added benefit for Israel was greater sympathy in the U.S. government, facilitated by effective lobbying by Jewish groups in early 1957, when Ben-Gurion sought to retain control of Sharm al-Shaykh. Many congressmen and the American public began to look at the Middle East in terms of a Soviet threat where Israel appeared to be a potential bulwark against Russian influence because it had attacked Nasser. This view was reinforced when the Soviets escaped their repression of the Hungarian revolt relatively unscathed, whereas Israel was being pushed to withdraw from a portion of the Sinai.[51]

Nasser emerged a victor despite Egypt's military defeat. The Israeli-French-British attack provided many Arabs with clear evidence of continuing Western imperial collusion with Israel to seek to impose outside control on developments within the Arab world. It seemed to prove Nasser's contention that nonalignment and rejection of Western arms agreements were the best means to retain Arab freedom. The Suez crisis and Nasser's defiance greatly enhanced his status as an Arab hero and weakened those who argued for continued reliance on Western pacts. Ironically, Egyptians looked to Washington more hopefully after Suez, believing that American opposition to the attack and pressure on Israel to withdraw from Sharm al-Shaykh would lead to improved relations. In this they were disappointed. Throughout 1957 Washington froze Egyptian funds under its custody and halted food and grain shipments under programs that had previously provided such assistance. Nasser thus turned to Moscow, which supplied the needed food and other goods blocked by Washington, giving further proof to Nasser's critics in Washington that he favored Soviet over U.S. aid.

Determined to back the more moderate, pro-Western Arab states against Nasser, Eisenhower and Dulles now undertook to strengthen regimes such as Iraq against the spread of Egyptian influence. Because the regional pact idea had proved futile, they decided to establish conditions whereby the United States could intervene openly to combat communist infiltration or aggression.

Eisenhower developed the strategy in what became known as the Eisenhower Doctrine, first proposed by him in early January 1957 but not approved by Congress until March. The doctrine provided for military and economic assistance to be granted "to any nation or group of nations which desires such aid." In addition, Eisenhower was authorized to commit American military forces "to secure and protect the territorial integrity and political independence of such nations, requesting such aid, against overt armed aggression from any nation controlled by International Communism."[52] That such an overture was aimed against Nasser was clear from the promise of economic aid given in the declaration following Washington's refusal of Nasser's request for assistance.

Eisenhower's rationale for the doctrine was that "the existing vacuum in the Middle East must be filled by the United States before it was filled by the Russians."[53] The "vacuum" was the loss of British and French prestige after Suez, which prevented them from intervening openly to back allies. Having castigated its European partners for colluding with Israel in the bid to overthrow Nasser, the United States now encouraged friendly Arab states, "with all the subtlety of temperance crusaders in a distillery," to invite its own intervention; it also sought to overthrow regimes considered hostile to American interests, resulting in even closer relations between these governments and the Russians.[54] Cold war containment triumphed over concern for regional rivalries and rapidly changing sociopolitical conditions in the Arab Middle East. No member of the State Department concerned with the region was consulted before Eisenhower proposed his plan.[55] The United States now embarked on a period of active intervention in Arab regional politics that in the long run led it closer to Israel.

QUESTIONS FOR CONSIDERATION

1. In their own views, what were the basic differences in David Ben-Gurion's and Moshe Sharett's approaches to Israeli relations with Arab states?

2. How did cold war considerations influence American and British policies toward the Middle East in the 1950s? How did American and British officials view Gamal Abd al-Nasser?

3. How did the Aswan Dam question contribute to the 1956 Suez crisis?

4. Discuss the ways in which British, French, and Israeli motives for attacking Egypt were similar or different.

CHRONOLOGY

1949	**January.** First elections held for Israeli Knesset. Chaim Weizmann elected president; David Ben-Gurion, prime minister.
1951	**July 20.** King Abdullah assassinated in East Jerusalem by a Palestinian.
1952	**July 23.** Gamal Abd al-Nasser leads coup of Egyptian officers, ousts King Faruq.
1953	**October.** Israel launches retaliatory attack on Qibya.
1954	**January.** Moshe Sharett becomes prime minister, Pinhas Lavon defense minister.
	Spring. Nasser gains control of Egyptian government.
	July–October. British agree to withdraw from Suez Canal zone. Lavon authorizes Israeli spy ring in Cairo.
1955	**January 31.** Two Israeli agents executed in Cairo.
	February 17. Ben-Gurion returns as defense minister.
	February 24. Iraq and Turkey sign Baghdad Pact (Britain joins a month later).
	February 28. Israel launches raid on Gaza.
	September. Czech-Egyptian arms deal announced.
	November. Ben-Gurion becomes prime minister.
	December. United States, Britain, and International Bank for Reconstruction and Development (IBRD) reach tentative agreement for financing Aswan Dam.
1956	**May.** Egypt recognizes Communist China.
	July 19. United States withdraws offer to fund Aswan Dam.
	July 26. Nasser nationalizes Suez Canal Company.
	October 29. Israel invades Sinai Peninsula.
	November 5. British and French troops invade Egypt.
	December 23. Britain and France withdraw from Egypt.
1957	**March.** Israel withdraws from Sinai. Eisenhower Doctrine approved.

Notes

1. This discussion is drawn from Philippa Strum, "The Road Not Taken: Constitutional Non-Decision Making in 1948–1950 and Its Impact on Civil Liberties in the Israeli Political Culture," in *Israel: The First Decade of Independence*, ed. S. Ilan Troen and Noah Lucas (Albany, N.Y., 1995), 83–104; and Ilan Peleg, "Israel's Constitutional Order and the *Kulturkampf*: The Role of Ben-Gurion," in *Israel Studies* 3 (Spring 1998): 230–50. A good overview that considers Israeli political rivalries is Peter Y. Medding, *The Founding of Israeli Democracy, 1948–1967* (New York, 1990).

2. Don Peretz and Gideon Doron, *The Government and Politics of Israel*, 3rd ed. (Boulder, Colo., 1997), 43–44.

3. Strum, "The Road Not Taken," 89.

4. For Jewish immigration, see the statistical tables in Bernard Reich, *Israel, Land of Tradition and Change* (Boulder, Colo., 1985), 15. For the story of Iraq's Jews, see Abbas Shiblak, *Iraqi Jews: A History of Mass Exodus* (London, 2005), and Nadje Sadig Ali, *Iraqi Women: Untold Stories from 1948 to the Present* (New York, 2007), especially 24–27.

5. Melvin I. Urofsky, *We Are One! American Jewry and Israel* (New York, 1978), 203.

6. Ernest Stock, *Israel on the Road to Sinai, 1949–1956* (Ithaca, N.Y., 1967), 11.

7. Don Peretz, *Israel and the Palestine Arabs* (Washington, D.C., 1958), 94ff; see also Ian Lustick, *Arabs in the Jewish State: Israel's Control of a National Minority* (Austin, Tex., 1980).

8. Peretz, *Israel*, 151.

9. For Israeli Arabs, see Lustick, *Arabs in the Jewish State*, especially Chapter 4; and Fouzi el-Asmar, *To Be an Arab in Israel* (London, 1975).

10. See Yoram Nimrod's review of Yehoshua Freundlich, ed., *Documents on the Foreign Policy of Israel*, vol. 3 (Jerusalem, 1983), in *Studies in Zionism* 5 (1984): 154–56; and Benny Morris, *Border Wars, 1949–1956* (New York, 1993), 17–20.

11. Livia Rokach, *Israel's Sacred Terrorism: A Study Based on Moshe Sharett's Personal Diary and Other Documents* (Belmont, Mass., 1980), 44, quoting Sharett's account of a meeting with Dayan and Ben-Gurion. Sharett also favored an alliance with the United States, but a defensive one designed to prevent hostilities. See also the diary entry quoted in Itamar Rabinovich and Jehuda Reinharz, eds., *Israel in the Middle East: Documents and Readings on Society, Politics and Foreign Relations, 1948–Present* (New York, 1984), 95–96. The major study of Sharett is Gabriel Sheffer, *Moshe Sharett: Biography of a Political Moderate* (New York, 1996).

12. Michael Brecher, *The Foreign Policy System of Israel* (New Haven, Conn., 1972), 282–90, 378–91, notes the differences between Ben-Gurion and Sharett, as do Morris, *Border Wars*, especially 226–36, and Sheffer, *Sharett*, which has extensive treatment of the subject.

13. United Nations Special Committee on Palestine, *Report to the General Assembly*, vol. 3, annex A (Official Records of the 2nd session of the General Assembly, supplement 2, 1947), 56; quoted in George Kirk, *The Middle East in the War, Survey of International Affairs, 1939–1946* (London, 1953), 243.

14. Brecher, *System*, 390–91; Elmo Hutchison, *Violent Truce* (New York, 1956), 43–45; and Morris, *Border Wars*, 227–63, deal with Qibya.

15. E. L. M. Burns, *Between Arab and Israeli* (New York, 1962), 41–44; Brecher, *System*, 261.

16. Burns, *Arab and Israeli*, 66–67.

17. Quoted in Sharett's diary, Rokach, *Sacred Terrorism*, 44.

18. Morris, *Border Wars*, 182 and 240, n. 55.

19. Brecher, *System*, 282–90, 378–91, Morris, *Border Wars*, and Sheffer, *Sharett*, cover these questions in great depth.

20. Rokach, *Sacred Terrorism*, 44.

21. Michael Bar-Zohar, *Ben-Gurion* (London, 1978), 217–18. Sharett did see the value of some reprisals, as noted in Rokach, *Sacred Terrorism*, 95–97, and Sheffer, *Sharett*, Chapters 21–23.

22. Morris, *Border Wars*, 182–83, 245–46, 255, n. 130, and 410–11; Sheffer, *Sharett*, especially 693, 712–39, and 770ff; and Medding, *Israeli Democracy*, 127.

23. Stock, *Road to Sinai*, 104.

24. Dan Horowitz, quoted in Baruch Kimmerling, *Zionism and Territory: The Socio-Territorial Dimensions of Zionist Politics* (Berkeley and Los Angeles, 1983), 153.

25. Ibid., 390.

26. Patrick Seale, *The Struggle for Syria: A Study of Post-War Arab Politics, 1945–1958* (Oxford, 1966), 132–47.

27. For the British perspective, see Anthony Nutting, *Nasser* (New York, 1972); Anthony Nutting, *No End of a Lesson: The Story of the Suez Crisis* (London, 1967); and the critical study of Eden by David Carlton, *Anthony Eden: A Biography* (London, 1981). The American viewpoint is well summarized in Townsend Hoopes, *The Devil and John Foster Dulles* (Boston, 1973); Stephen Ambrose, *Eisenhower, vol. 2, The President* (New York, 1984); Wilbur Crane Eveland, *Ropes of Sand: America's Failure in the Middle East* (London, 1980); and Miles Copeland, *The Game of Nations: The Amorality of Power Politics* (New York, 1969). Both Eveland and Copeland served in the Central Intelligence Agency, occasionally as rivals, according to Eveland.

28. Seale, *Syria*, 200–201, and sources in n. 27.

29. Quoted in Keith Wheelock, *Nasser's New Egypt: A Critical Analysis* (New York, 1960), 221.

30. Brecher, *System*, 390–91; and Bar-Zohar, *Ben-Gurion*, 202–6. It is noteworthy that these sources, from the 1970s, contained the relevant information now discussed in more detail in Sheffer, *Sharett*, and Morris, *Border Wars*, as listed in nn. 19 and 22.

31. Nutting, *Nasser*, 92–96. Sharett also tried to initiate substantive peace talks with Nasser through American auspices in late 1955, even though strongly opposed by Ben-Gurion; see Eveland, *Ropes of Sand*, 155–57.

32. Bar-Zohar, *Ben-Gurion*, 209–16. Sheffer, *Sharett*, 750–82, deals with the Lavon Affair, which he depicts as "The Mishap" and portrays subsequent Sharett–Ben-Gurion interactions as "A State of Law and Order or of Robbery?"—a not inaccurate description of cabinet and defense ministry relations.

33. For example, Burns, *Arab and Israeli*, 17–21, 75ff; Nutting, *Nasser*, 92–96; Seale, *Syria*, 235–36.

34. Ehud Yaari, *Egypt and the Fedayeen, 1953–1956* (in Hebrew) (Givat Havivah, Israel, 1955), 18–23, quoted in Rabinovich and Reinharz, eds., *Israel in the Middle East*, 78; a statement backed by Wheelock, *New Egypt*, 222; Burns, *Arab and Israeli*, 21; and now confirmed by Morris from the Israeli archives, *Border Wars*, 322–23, n. 184.

35. Seale, *Syria*, 235, quoting a confidant of Nasser.

36. Algeria was considered a part of metropolitan France rather than a colonial possession. A superb study of the Algerian revolution and the French response is Alistair Horne, *A Savage War of Peace: Algeria, 1954–1962* (New York, 1978).

37. The most detailed account of Israeli-French contacts is that of the major Israeli emissary, Shimon Peres, *David's Sling* (New York, 1970), 47–65. See also Anthony Moncrieff, ed., *Suez, Ten Years After* (New York, 1967), 38–39, 61–66.

38. Quoted in Seale, *Syria*, 254, where he discusses the pact and its terms.

39. Stock, *Road to Sinai*, 144. See also Eveland, *Ropes of Sand*, 150–51; and Chester L. Cooper, *The Lion's Last Roar: Suez, 1956* (New York, 1978), 91–92.

40. Robert Bowie, *International Crises and the Role of Law: Suez 1956* (New York, 1974), 11.

41. Donald Neff, *Warriors at Suez: Eisenhower Takes America into the Middle East* (New York, 1981), 130–31ff; Michael Brecher, *Decisions in Israel's Foreign Policy* (New Haven, Conn., 1975),

259ff; and Kennett Love, *Suez, the Twice-Fought War* (New York, 1969), differ over whose hard-line policies undermined the possibility of further talks. For coverage of Project Alpha from the American and British sides, see William J. Burns, *Economic Aid and American Policy toward Egypt, 1955–1981* (Albany, N.Y., 1985), 62–63; Peter L. Hahn, *The United States, Great Britain, and Egypt, 1945–1956: Strategy and Diplomacy in the Early Cold War* (Chapel Hill, N.C., 1991), 188ff; and Evelyn Shuckburgh, *Descent to Suez: Diaries, 1951–56*, ed. John Charmley (London, 1986). Shuckburgh was Eden's private secretary from 1951 to 1954 and then undersecretary in charge of Middle East affairs at the Foreign Office from May 1954 to June 1956.

42. Quoted in Nutting, *Nasser*, 122–23. Eden's mercurial personality and emotionalism are well depicted in Shuckburgh, *Descent to Suez*.

43. Quoted in Cooper, *Lion's Last Roar*, 97.

44. Quoted in Love, *Twice-Fought War*, 297. Love has an extensive discussion of this matter, 297–327.

45. Cooper, *Lion's Last Roar*, 98–99; Hoopes, *Devil*, 338–40.

46. Bowie, *Suez*, 15. The major study of this crisis, especially that of British politics, Anglo-French collaboration, and Anglo-American discord, is Keith Kyle, *Suez* (New York, 1991). Ben-Gurion's diary for the period notes French information as early as August 1. See Selwyn Ilan Troen and Moshe Shemesh, eds., *The Suez-Sinai Crisis, 1956: Retrospective and Reappraisal* (New York, 1990), p. 292.

47. Carlton, *Eden*, 298–309, 327–30, 428ff; and Shuckburgh, *Descent to Suez*, 327, 341, 344, where Nasser is Mussolini reincarnated.

48. Bar-Zohar, *Ben-Gurion*, 236. Ben-Gurion had recorded his goals in his diary; see the relevant entries in Troen and Shemesh, *Suez-Sinai Crisis*, 306–7.

49. See ibid., 242, and Morris, *Border Wars*, 428, for discussion of Ben-Gurion's "expansionist war." Ben-Gurion's denial that he hoped to annex the Sinai, in Moncrieff, ed., *Suez, Ten Years After*, 71, is contradicted by his diary entries for the crisis: presented in Troen and Shemesh, *Suez-Sinai Crisis*, 313, 318ff. For Lebanon, see Rokach, *Sacred Terrorism*, 24–25.

50. Quoted in Neff, *Warriors at Suez*, 437.

51. Stephen L. Spiegel, *The Other Arab-Israeli Conflict: Making America's Middle East Policy from Truman to Reagan* (Chicago, 1985), 77–81, and Isaac Alteras, *Eisenhower and Israel: U.S.-Israeli Relations, 1953–1960* (Gainesville, Fla., 1993).

52. Ambrose, *Eisenhower*, 382; see also Spiegel, *Other Arab-Israeli Conflict*, 83–86.

53. Quoted in Hoopes, *Devil*, 406.

54. Quoted in William Burns, *Economic Aid*, 110. See Burns's general discussion of American aid policy and anticommunism in the aftermath of Suez, 105–12.

55. Copeland, *Game of Nations*, 216.

LETTER ON THE POSITION OF THE PALESTINIAN REFUGEES

November 17, 1949

This letter from the chairman of the United Nations Conciliation Commission for Palestine to the secretary general describes the stark conditions of the refugees in the wake of the 1948–1949 war. It inspired the formation of the United Nations Relief and Works Agency (UNRWA) for Palestine Refugees in the Near East.

The Problem

The Arab refugees — nearly three-quarters of a million men, women and children — are the symbol of the paramount political issue in the Near East. Their plight is the aftermath of an armed struggle between Arabs and Israelis, a struggle marked by a truce that was broken and an armistice from which a peace settlement has not emerged.

Before the hostilities in Palestine these families lived in that section of Palestine on the Israeli side of the present armistice lines. Abandoning their homes and villages, their fields and orange groves, their shops and benches, they fled to nearby Arab lands. Tens of thousands are in temporary camps; some are in caves; the majority have found shelter in Arab towns and villages, in mosques, churches, monasteries, schools and abandoned buildings. Some seventeen thousand Jewish refugees, too, fled from their homes in and around Jerusalem and territories on the Arab side of the armistice lines. They entered into Israel where most of them have now been absorbed. . . .

On 11 December 1948 the General Assembly adopted a resolution stating: ". . . that the refugees wishing to return to their homes and live at peace with their neighbours should be permitted to do so at the earliest possible date, and that compensation should be paid for the property of those choosing not to return. . . ."

The same resolution established a Conciliation Commission for Palestine to negotiate a settlement of outstanding differences between Israel and the Arab States of Egypt, Iraq, Jordan, Lebanon, Saudi Arabia, Syria and the Yemen.

No settlement has been reached.

The Arab refugees have not been able to return to their homes because Israel will not admit them. Israel has to date offered to repatriate only 100,000, and only as a part of a general peace settlement of all other issues.

The Arab refugees have not been able to gain a livelihood in the Arab lands where they are because there is insufficient opportunity for them to do so.

Source: T. G. Fraser, *The Middle East, 1914–1979* (London, 1980), 78–79.

The Arab refugees have not yet received compensation for the property they abandoned, nor have the Jewish refugees in their turn.

The refugees are still on relief.

United Nations funds so far subscribed for the feeding of refugees will not last through the winter.

Recommendations

In the light of these findings, the Economic Survey Mission* makes the following recommendations, which are explained later in the report. . . .

3. An agency should be established to organize and, on or after 1 April 1950, direct, the programmes of relief and public works herein recommended.†

*The UN Economic Survey Mission was deputed by the Conciliation Commission for Palestine to examine economic conditions in the Middle East.—Ed.
†This became the United Nations Relief and Works Agency for Palestine Refugees in the Near East (UNRWA).—Ed.

DOCUMENT 5.2

GAMAL ABD AL-NASSER

SPEECH JUSTIFYING NATIONALIZATION OF THE SUEZ CANAL COMPANY

July 28, 1956

This speech, a good example of Nasser's style, blends anti-imperialist rhetoric with anticipation of forthcoming criticism. A major point of Anglo-French arguments for retaking the canal would be that Egyptians were incapable of managing it.

The uproar which we anticipated has been taking place in London and Paris. This tremendous uproar is not supported by reason or logic. It is backed only by imperialist methods, by the habits of blood-sucking and of usurping rights, and by interference in the affairs of other countries. An unjustified uproar arose in London, and yesterday Britain submitted a protest to Egypt. I wonder what was the basis of this protest by Britain to Egypt? The Suez Canal Company is an Egyptian company, subject to Egyptian sovereignty. When we nationalized the Suez Canal Company, we only nationalized an Egyptian limited company, and by doing so we exercised a right which stems from the very core of Egyptian sovereignty. What right has Britain to interfere in our internal affairs? What right has Britain to interfere in our affairs and our questions? When we nationalized the Suez Canal Company, we only performed an act stemming from the

Source: T. G. Fraser, *The Middle East, 1914–1979* (London, 1980), 88–89.

very heart of our sovereignty. The Suez Canal Company is a limited company, awarded a concession by the Egyptian Government in 1865 to carry out its tasks. Today we withdraw the concession in order to do the job ourselves.

Although we have withdrawn this concession, we shall compensate shareholders of the company, despite the fact that they usurped our rights. Britain usurped 44 per cent of the shares free of charge. Today we shall pay her for her 44 per cent of the shares. We do not treat her as she treated us. . . .

The Suez Canal would have been restored to us in 12 years. . . . What difference is it if the canal is restored to us now or in 12 years' time? Why should Britain say this will affect shipping in the canal? Would it have affected shipping 12 years hence? . . .

We have not interfered with shipping, and we are facilitating shipping matters. However, I emphatically warn the imperialist countries that their tricks, provocations and interference will be the reason for any hindrance to shipping. I place full responsibility on Britain and France for any curtailment of shipping in the Suez Canal when I state that Egypt will maintain freedom of shipping in the Suez Canal, and that since Egypt nationalized the Suez Canal Company shipping has been normal. . . .

Compatriots, we shall maintain our independence and sovereignty. The Suez Canal Company has become our property, and the Egyptian flag flies over it. We shall hold it with our blood and strength, and we shall meet aggression with aggression and evil with evil. We shall proceed towards achieving dignity and prestige for Egypt and building a sound national economy and true freedom. Peace be with you.

SWB, Part IV, Daily Series
no. 6, 30 July 1956

DOCUMENT 5.3

GOLDA MEIR

SPEECH TO THE UNITED NATIONS GENERAL ASSEMBLY

March 1, 1957

This statement by Foreign Minister Golda Meir reiterated Israel's contention that the Gulf of Aqaba and Straits of Tiran were international waterways and could not be interdicted by any nation. Meir's warning in paragraph 13 would be significant in light of Egyptian actions in May 1967 that reimposed a blockade over these waterways.

Source: T. G. Fraser, *The Middle East, 1914–1979* (London, 1980), 95–96.

The Government of Israel is now in a position to announce its plan for full and prompt withdrawal from the Sharm-el-Sheikh area and the Gaza strip, in compliance with General Assembly resolution 1124(XI) of 2 February 1957. . . .

2. We have repeatedly stated that Israel has no interest in the strip of land overlooking the western coast of the Gulf of Aqaba. Our sole purpose has been to ensure that, on the withdrawal of Israeli forces, continued freedom of navigation will exist for Israel and international shipping in the Gulf of Aqaba and the Straits of Tiran. Such freedom of navigation is a vital national interest for Israel, but it is also of importance and legitimate concern to the maritime Powers and to many States whose economies depend upon trade and navigation between the Red Sea and the Mediterranean. . . .

11. The Government of Israel believes that the Gulf of Aqaba comprehends international waters and that no nation has the right to prevent free and innocent passage in the Gulf and through the Straits giving access thereto, in accordance with the generally accepted definition of those terms in the law of the sea. . . .

13. Interference, by armed force, with ships of Israel flag exercising free and innocent passage in the Gulf of Aqaba and through the Straits of Tiran, will be regarded by Israel as an attack entitling it to exercise its inherent right of self-defence under Article 51 of the United Nations Charter and to take all such measures as are necessary to ensure the free and innocent passages of its ships in the Gulf and in the Straits.

UNO GAOR, Eleventh Session
666th Plenary Meeting

6

FROM SUEZ TO THE SIX-DAY WAR

1957–1967

THE DECADE between 1957 and 1967 was, in the final analysis, dominated by inter-Arab rivalries that centered on the personality and prestige of Gamal Abd al-Nasser. Though not always in control of events, he was usually in their forefront, seeking to maintain his stature as leader of an increasingly hostile Arab world in which rivals began to challenge his dominance of Arab politics. From 1964 onward, those ruling in Damascus were his principal antagonists, seeking to exploit Palestinian grievances against Israel to establish themselves as the true representatives of the Arab nationalist cause. Arab-Israeli hostilities, dormant during much of the period, once again intensified. In May 1967 Nasser attempted to use anti-Israeli sentiment to reassert his prominence in Arab circles by reoccupying the Sinai Peninsula and evicting the United Nations Emergency Forces (UNEF) contingents. His brinkmanship failed. The Israelis seized the opportunity to destroy the Egyptian forces then massed in the Sinai. Whereas the Suez affair had greatly enhanced Nasser's prestige, the 1967 war nearly toppled him. It introduced a new era in which the Palestinians emerged as an independent force in Arab politics.

THE STRUGGLE FOR SYRIA AND THE CREATION OF THE UNITED ARAB REPUBLIC, 1957–1958

Syria had long been the focus of attention among Arab states trying to dominate Arab politics, especially Iraq and Egypt. As early as June 1956, the socialist Baath Party in the Syrian government called for union with Egypt as the first step toward the goal of one Arab nation. This, combined with increasing Soviet aid to Damascus, inspired an Iraqi plot, backed by Great Britain, to overthrow the Baath and install a pro-Western government that might join Nuri al-Said's Fertile Crescent scheme.

The United States, Syria, and the Cold War

During that summer, the Central Intelligence Agency (CIA) also became involved in planning a coup, but its efforts were not necessarily coordinated with the British; they may even have been rivals, played off against each other by Syrian politicians.[1] The revolt never occurred because the timing of the Suez invasion compromised Iraqi participation. In the words of an American agent, "it was a totally unprofessional CIA operation,"[2] one whose traces had already been recognized by Syrian intelligence. On November 23, Damascus announced its discovery of plans to overthrow the government. Amidst the publicity, "the failure of the conspiracy powerfully reinforced the radical pro-Egyptian factions in Syria by eliminating from the scene their most dangerous opponents."[3] The Syrian government, reshuffled to include more Baathists, joined Cairo in attacking Nuri al-Said's government in Baghdad, accusing him of treachery and of sacrificing Iraq's independence to Western interests.

This was the regional context in which the Eisenhower Doctrine was proclaimed in January 1957 and in which the United States openly joined the Baghdad Pact in March. The Lebanese government of Camille Chamoun accepted the doctrine. Nuri al-Said and King Husayn of Jordan indicated their approval, though they declined to embrace it officially. These developments led to more intense propaganda attacks from Radio Cairo and Radio Damascus calling for the overthrow of their regimes; they in turn further convinced officials in Washington that Damascus was the principal conduit for Soviet propaganda designed to undermine Western influence in the Arab world.

In the aftermath of a new Syrian-Russian economic and military aid agreement announced in June 1957, the CIA financed another coup attempt, but Syrian officials discovered its traces and expelled three members of the American embassy linked to the plot. The United States reacted by announcing that Syria was about to become communist and mobilized pro-Western forces in the region. U.S. officials openly discussed plans to airlift arms to Iraq, Jordan, and Lebanon and arranged for Turkish army units to undertake maneuvers along the Syrian border, accompanied by threats of an invasion and calls for a popular uprising against the government. These developments did not encourage Syrian rulers to become more pro-Western. Realizing the folly of the American approach, the Saudis attempted to mediate the crisis, distancing themselves from the United States but also trying to isolate Nasser from their resolution of the problem. He in turn sent troops to Syria on October 13, declaring that they were prepared to defend the country. Though essentially a publicity move, it served to link Syria's security to Egypt's and furthered Baathist ambitions for union, precisely what Washington had hoped to avoid.

The United Arab Republic: Context and Significance

Baathist calls for Arab unity were both ideological and practical in motivation. Michel Aflaq, the leading theoretician of the Baath, believed unity to be the destiny of the Arab people, with Syria acting as the catalyst because, in his eyes, it was the heartland of Arab nationalism. But Aflaq also realized that Egypt's exclusion—given Nasser's prestige—could guarantee its failure. The Baath seemed to dominate the governments of 1956–1957, but its leaders feared that the continuing crises and attempted coups could only strengthen the hand of the Syrian communists, however few they were, at Baathist expense. Nasser initially resisted Baath overtures; whatever mileage he gained from calling for Arab unity, "he had sought to control Syria's foreign policy . . . not to assume responsibility for her government."4 Syria's continuing internal disarray and repeated Baath overtures finally convinced him to accept the invitation, if only to forestall any further increase in the popularity of Syria's communists. To a degree Nasser was a victim of his own image-making as the leader of the Arab cause. To reject unification would mean rejecting unity, the presumed goal of Arab nationalism, whose ideals he claimed to embody. He decided to control Syrian politics while trumpeting the union as representative of the aspirations of Arabs generally.5 The United Arab Republic (UAR) was proclaimed on February 1, 1958.

The Syrian-Egyptian merger lasted three and a half years, ending with Syria's abrupt secession in September 1961. By then most Syrians had had enough of Egyptian protection. Nasser had refused to share power with the Baath, allotting key positions to Egyptians, who dominated the Syrian administration. The final straw came in the summer of 1961 when Nasser imposed nationalization decrees on the Syrian economy following those he had declared for Egypt. Despite the apparent strength of Baathist socialism, the Syrian economy had remained essentially private. Most Syrians backed their country's withdrawal from the United Arab Republic and the formation of a new government from which the Baath was excluded.

The Syrian-Egyptian rift left a legacy of distrust and resentment that would contribute to the outbreak of the 1967 war. Equally important, however, were events elsewhere in the Arab world that had been affected by the formation of the UAR, in particular its impact on Lebanon and Iraq. Subsequent developments led the United States to invoke the Eisenhower Doctrine and land forces in Lebanon in July 1958.

LEBANON: POLITICAL STRIFE, CIVIL WAR, AND REGIONAL CRISIS, 1957–1958

The underlying causes of the Lebanese Civil War of 1957–1958 lay in the political structure created to balance competing religious and communal interests. Lebanese politics had been characterized by the principle of confessionalism in which political representation was based on religious affiliation and the size of one's religious community. This system had been first applied in 1861 to Mount Lebanon as a separate administrative unit governed by an Ottoman Christian from outside the area following the Druze-Maronite clashes of 1860. Nevertheless, France never lost sight of Mount Lebanon and its environs as the basis of its influence in the Middle East. In their turn, most Maronite Catholics still looked to France as the European power willing to guarantee their continued separation from the predominantly Arab Muslim world of the interior.

Maronite Catholics and Lebanese Political Alignments

French acquisition of Lebanon and Syria after World War I was a mixed blessing for the Maronites. Though eager to guarantee Maronite ascendancy in the new Lebanon, France also strove to ensure its own imperial presence in the region. French officials therefore created the country to be known as Lebanon by taking land from Syria and adding it to Mount Lebanon; the additions included the interior Biqa' Valley and a second range of mountains known as the anti-Lebanon, along with the coastal plain. They did this because "Lebanon" would be under their direct control, serving as their imperial base, and "Syria" under their indirect rule according to the clauses of the Sykes-Picot accord. This extension of French rule more than doubled the territory and greatly altered the population ratios according to religious affiliation.[6] The Sunni Muslim population leaped nearly eightfold, the Shi'i Muslims almost fourfold, and the Maronites by about a third.

The French creation of Greater Lebanon reduced the Christian majority to slightly over 50 percent of the population. Within this segment, Maronite Catholics clearly predominated; the next largest group was the Greek Orthodox, with smaller numbers belonging to various Catholic and Orthodox denominations (Syrian Orthodox and Catholic, Armenian Orthodox and Catholic). On the Muslim side, Sunnis held a slight but definite majority over the Shi'is, with the Druze about one-third of the Shi'i population.[7] The French sought to establish political institutions that would formalize these ratios and ensure Christian rule, particularly that of the Maronites, with whom they were most closely allied. The constitution drawn up in 1926 established that the president would always be a Christian; practice made him a Maronite. Likewise, the prime minister was a Sunni Muslim. The principle became rooted that other offices and parliamentary representation would reflect the size of one's religious community, with percentages based on the 1932 census; it established that Christians outnumbered Muslims by a six-to-five ratio.

The same procedure was followed for administrative posts once Lebanon attained independence in 1943. The president was a Maronite, the prime minister a Sunni Muslim, the speaker of the chamber of deputies a Shi'i, and the deputy prime minister and deputy speaker Greek Orthodox. Similarly, the foreign minister was generally a Maronite, the interior minister a Sunni, and the defense minister a Druze.[8] Nevertheless, the ratification of these arrangements in 1943 was ambiguous, part of an unwritten "National Pact" that sought to guarantee the status of Lebanon as a separate nation and to calm the fears of the major religious communities. The pact enshrined the principle that Lebanese Christians would not seek foreign protection, alluding to the wish of many

Maronites to retain a French mandate, even if under a different guise. On the other hand, Muslims agreed to support Lebanese independence, meaning they would forgo union with Syria or any other Arab state.

Despite the "national" aura surrounding the National Pact, its success depended on preserving the status quo, guaranteeing rights held by the major communities usually identified with specific regions of the country. Political power often belonged to local lords, who held nearly feudal authority over the surrounding villages. As a result, Sunni leaders aligned themselves with Maronites because as the two largest sects they divided many perquisites of influence. In general, the arrangement preserved in enlarged form the system founded under the Ottomans, to the extent that the highest religious officials of various sects, such as the Maronite patriarch, retained great prestige and did not hesitate to challenge political officials from their own community. Indeed, lines of allegiance did not always follow religious identities. Serious clan cleavages frequently undermined Maronite unity. Other Christian sects, particularly the Greek Orthodox, often sympathized with Muslim suspicion of the Francophile outlook many Maronites retained.

These factors and their potential for divisiveness became increasingly significant during the 1950s. There were sectors within both the Maronite and the Muslim communities that still longed for more specific ties to either Europe and the West or the Arab world; tensions mounted as Arab nationalism came to the fore under the banner of the Baath or Nasser. At the same time, many groups in Lebanon felt increasingly resentful of the continuing power of the Maronites; their role and general Christian dominance rested on the 1932 census, which the Maronite president and Christian-controlled chamber of deputies refused to update. The president could veto any legislation approved by the chamber and could be overridden only by a majority of that body, a virtual impossibility.[9] As a result, the president could block any initiative to revise the proportional system based on the 1932 census, which most observers agreed was out of date: by the late 1950s, the Muslims were believed to be a majority of the population.

Most Arab states viewed Lebanon as a useful anomaly in the Arab world. Its links to the West served various interests and opened the way for profits that might not be realized elsewhere. It served as a port of entry for goods going on to Syria, Iraq, Jordan, and the Persian Gulf principalities. Of vital importance were Lebanon's lack of foreign exchange controls and the creation of the Beirut port as a free-trade zone, which established the city as a freewheeling center for world commerce and finance. Conditions were so favorable for banking and exchange that in the early 1960s there were twenty-one branches of foreign banks in Lebanon and thirty-six local banks. These institutions serviced the funds generated by the oil boom in the Persian Gulf, Saudi Arabia, and Iran. Despite the fragility of its political framework, Lebanon appeared to be an island of stability in a sea of political coups and revolutions, from which it profited. The country became a haven for people fleeing failed plots, bringing with them money put to good use.[10] These circumstances also attracted foreign intelligence services, who could finance payments to agents and conspirators without fear of accountability.

Lebanon's Civil War and the Iraqi Revolution

Most Arab leaders accepted Lebanon's independence, but the composition of its government became subject to greater regional as well as domestic scrutiny in the latter half of the 1950s. The president at that time was Camille Chamoun, a Maronite whose support rested more on the burgeoning middle class than on traditional clan patronage. His foreign minister, Charles Malik, was a distinguished scholar of Greek Orthodox persuasion totally committed to close ties to the West, especially the United States. These views aroused controversy during and after the Suez affair, when Chamoun and Malik refused to sever diplomatic relations with England and France and openly accepted the Eisenhower Doctrine. In response, Egypt and Syria launched propaganda campaigns against the Chamoun-Malik tandem. Within Lebanon, various groups accused the government of subverting Lebanon's traditional neutrality by seeking to bind itself to the West. A significant critic was the Maronite patriarch.

These disputes became intertwined with Chamoun's political ambitions. Presidents could not govern in consecutive terms, but Chamoun hoped to amend the constitution and run for reelection when his term of office expired in September 1958. Though he did not openly declare his intent to do so, his supporters did, and Chamoun himself intimated that he was awaiting the right moment to take that step.[11] There is little doubt that the 1957 elections were engineered to bring in Chamoun supporters who might vote for such a constitutional amendment, even at the expense of alienating other Maronite families and the Maronite patriarch, who joined the opposition.[12]

By then external forces were involved. The Egyptians funded the opposition, and the United States openly backed Chamoun.[13] The results of the 1957 elections stacked the chamber of deputies with Chamoun adherents and inaugurated a fierce round of fighting in the mountains above Beirut that continued sporadically for nearly a year. The formation of the UAR in February 1958 exacerbated tensions. Muslim delegations went to Damascus to greet Nasser, as did representatives of the Maronite patriarch. In the meantime, the opposition front, largely composed of Druze and Muslim leaders but including Maronites and other Christians opposed to Chamoun, received arms smuggled across the Syrian border. Open civil war erupted in May following the assassination of a Maronite journalist critical of Chamoun's policies. Beirut became an armed camp, split by barricades erected by Chamounist and opposition factions.

The Lebanese Civil War of 1958 reflected various strands of allegiance beyond religious loyalties.[14] Some Sunni dignitaries sided with Chamoun, whereas several prominent Maronites backed the United Front opposing him. Chamoun defined the struggle in terms of a Muslim assault on Christian

Lebanese in order to appeal to public opinion abroad. At the same time, he found he could not rely on the Lebanese army, whose Maronite commander, Fuad Shihab, refused to commit his forces to resolve an internal dispute. Chamoun asked the United States for support, hoping to invoke the Eisenhower Doctrine and use the appearance of U.S. troops to bolster his position. Eisenhower hesitated, though he later claimed that he and his advisers shared a "deep-seated conviction that the Communists were principally responsible for the trouble and that President Chamoun was motivated only by a strong feeling of patriotism."[15]

The crisis might have ended quietly once Chamoun made it known in early July that he would step down in September. But then, on July 14, the Iraqi revolution occurred, a brutal uprising in which the Hashemite monarchy and the government of Nuri al-Said were overthrown and most of their members killed. Chamoun immediately demanded American military intervention, claiming that he was threatened by the Iraqi coup. Though not necessarily agreeing with the logic behind his request, Eisenhower acceded to it. American Marines landed on the beaches of Beirut on July 15, to be met by bikini-clad bathers and ice-cream vendors who recognized an opportunity for increased sales. But the troops were also confronted by the small Lebanese army led by General Shihab, now arrayed to confront the invading force. Swift intervention by the American ambassador resolved a potentially dangerous situation. It was agreed that General Shihab would succeed Chamoun in September, an orderly transition effected under the protective guise of the American military, which left the country by October 25.

The Arab World in American Perspective: The Cold War Context

The final resolution of the Lebanese crisis adhered closely to Nasser's proposals to the United States made in June—that Shihab replace Chamoun.[16] But from Washington's perspective, the United States had sent troops to Lebanon to stabilize a country friendly to the West, a step signaling a defeat for Nasser and the Soviets. Eisenhower and Dulles believed that the USSR had been "stirring up trouble" in various parts of the world where the "United States had for one reason or another often been unable to lend a hand."[17] By requesting aid, Lebanon offered the United States the opportunity to show the Soviets that it could and would act. From that perspective, the operation was a success. Not only had "the Communists come to be aware of our attitude," but "the peoples of the Middle East, inscrutable as always to the West, have nevertheless remained outside the Communist orbit."[18] Indeed, the new Iraqi regime of Colonel Abd al-Karim Qasim, whose nationalism and apparent pro-Nasserite sympathies had provoked the American action, soon seemed to be independent of the Egyptian leader. When U.S. special envoy Robert Murphy finished his mediation efforts in Beirut, he flew to Baghdad to meet Qasim. The United States recognized his government on August 2.

In October, the Russians and Egyptians reached an agreement for the construction of the Aswan Dam. Surprisingly, this did not worsen American-Egyptian relations, which took a turn for the better. Economic aid resumed in 1959 shortly after a series of American actions directed against Nasser and Nasserism, whereas Dulles had refused to grant such assistance after the Suez crisis. The change may have been due to Dulles's fatal illness, which forced his retirement. Equally important was the perception that "Eisenhower was comforted by having finally acted decisively towards the Egyptian leader." Lebanon was a "catharsis" whose resolution — relieving frustrations stemming from the fear that America had not responded to apparently communist-provoked agitation — permitted the president to focus his attention elsewhere.[19]

The Lebanese crisis is an instructive example of how a local problem, fanned by regional rivalries, can be evaluated by a great power in light of the message it can send to its principal adversary. Nevertheless, "the 1957–1958 tensions between the Chamoun regime and the Syro-Egyptian partnership, though eased after Shihab's advent, was more than just an episode. It was a dramatic symptom of Lebanon's endemic schizophrenia in the presence of pan-Arab nationalism."[20] These tensions exploded into a much more brutal civil war in the 1970s.

INTER-ARAB AND ARAB-ISRAELI TENSIONS, 1958–1964

The events of July 1958 and their resolution seemed to portend even greater scope for Gamal Abd al-Nasser's influence within the Arab world. His union with Syria had been expanded to include Yemen; the conclusion of the Lebanese crisis had installed a government less closely identified with the West; and the Iraqi revolution of July 14 had overthrown his chief rival, Nuri al-Said. But this vision soon proved ephemeral. The new Iraqi leader, Abd al-Karim Qasim, reasserted Iraqi's independence of regional alignments while attacking and even mocking both Nasser and the Baath. Iraq remained the strongest opponent of Egypt's Arab aspirations, all the more upsetting because it too espoused a neutralist, independent policy. Having called Nuri al-Said a lackey of Western imperialism, Nasser now accused Qasim of being "a stooge of international Communism" who compromised the goal of true Arab nationalism, separation from all power blocs.[21]

Nasser Strives to Dominate Arab Politics

Egyptian-Iraqi relations remained strained until Qasim's overthrow and death in February 1963 at the hands of Iraqi Baathist officers, who seemed eager to establish closer ties with Nasser. A month later, a similar coup in Damascus ousted those who had led the secession from the UAR. The Syrian Baath returned to office. They and their Iraqi counterparts immediately called for talks designed to create a new union, but negotiations with Nasser during

March and April proved fruitless.[22] None of the participants would subordinate his country's sovereignty to that of another, whatever their rhetoric about one Arab nation. Nasser used the talks to humiliate his visitors, proposing terms he knew were unacceptable to them.

Hostile propaganda resumed. As Egyptian-Syrian invective escalated, Syria drew closer to Iraq, but no union resulted. By the end of 1963, General Abd al-Salam Arif, an admirer of Nasser, had removed the Baath from office in Baghdad and Egyptian-Iraqi relations were once again amicable while Syrian-Iraqi contacts degenerated into open hostility. Nasser appeared to hold the high ground amidst the coups and countercoups that roiled Syrian and Iraqi politics. He presented himself as in the vanguard of progressive Arab nationalism, superior to his Syrian Baathist rivals and in confrontation with the "feudalistic reactionary" monarchies of Saudi Arabia and Jordan, which were allied with the West, especially with the United States. He believed he had reinforced that image through his support of the Yemen revolution, which had erupted in September 1962, pitting "progressive" young colonels against the Islamic rule of the Zaydi Imamate. Saudi Arabia backed the forces of the imam; they managed to hold the countryside and mountain ranges while the colonels retained the cities and adjacent areas. Nasser saw Yemen as a suitable arena for a productive clash with Riyadh and Amman that would enhance his stature in the Arab world to the detriment of aspiring leftist challengers in Damascus and Baghdad. But in the long run, Nasser found himself in a quagmire, committing 40,000 troops to bolster the new military regime.

Immersed in these Arab rivalries, Nasser strove to avoid direct confrontation with Israel. He thus found himself in early 1964 seeking to moderate a new flare-up of Syrian-Israeli friction in order to guarantee that he would not be drawn into clashes for which he and his military were unprepared. This led him to seek a rapprochement with other Arab leaders, including King Husayn of Jordan and King Faysal of Saudi Arabia, in response to Syria's demands for military action against Israel because of the latter's plans to divert water from the Jordan River.

Water Wars: Israeli-Syrian Clashes and the Arab Response

Arab-Israeli animosity over exploitation of the Jordan River's waters had existed since 1950. The river was crucial to the agricultural plans of Jordan and Israel. Its headwaters originated in Lebanon, Syria, and Israel, whence it dropped down into Lake Tiberias (Sea of Galilee) and flowed southward to end in the Dead Sea; more water entered it from the Yarmuk River originating in Jordan, south of Lake Tiberias. Israel had previously tried to divert water unilaterally from the Jordan at a point within the Syrian-Israeli demilitarized zone, to which it claimed sovereignty. Armed clashes led to U.N. condemnation of Israeli plans but also resulted from 1953 to 1955 in American-sponsored efforts to reach a water-sharing agreement among the riparian states. When negotiations failed, the United States in 1958 backed separate Israeli and Jordanian projects aimed at diverting water for irrigation purposes. Jordan initiated a project using water from the Yarmuk River, while Israel undertook to channel water out of Lake Tiberias where it lay within Israel's boundaries, thereby avoiding further confrontation with Syria in the demilitarized zone (see Map 6.1).[23]

Nonetheless, Israel's actions had political as well as economic implications. Taking water from Lake Tiberias for use throughout the country, and especially to irrigate the Negev Desert in the south, would significantly reduce the Jordan River water available to Jordan south of the lake. Construction of the water carrier took place in an atmosphere of frequent confrontations with Syria over border disputes and Israeli forays into demilitarized zones. United Nations observers believed that Israeli actions frequently violated U.N. agreements and were intended to provoke retaliation and justify Israeli accusations of Arab hostility.[24]

Israel's pending completion of this diversion in late 1963 aroused renewed Arab, particularly Syrian, concern. Nasser called for a meeting of Arab heads of state under Arab League auspices to determine an appropriate but muted Arab response. Collaboration denied the Syrian Baath the opportunity to accuse him of evading his responsibilities as the dominant Arab figure. The January 1964 summit in Cairo approved the diversion of those tributaries of the Jordan River lying in Arab territories north of Lake Tiberias. That project, if implemented, would have endangered Israeli water resources by drastically reducing the amount available for diversion from the lake for their own national water scheme. Syrian work on the project led to Israeli attacks on Syrian construction

Map 6.1 ■ Israeli-Syrian Demilitarized Zones and Water Issues   ▶

These zones, scenes of much tension, led to major clashes between the two countries in the 1950s and 1960s. The northernmost zone sat adjacent to the Banias River and its springs, in Syrian territory in the Golan Heights. The Banias and the Dan River, west of the Banias, flow south into Israel and feed the Jordan River. The Jordan itself ran through the demilitarized zones north of Lake Tiberias, into the lake, and then out of it southward where it constituted the pre-1967 border between Israel and Jordan until reaching the West Bank area. The southernmost zone lay directly beneath that portion of the Golan overlooking Lake Tiberias. Supposedly to be left for negotiations, this area saw much violence as Israel asserted its right to farm and evicted Syrian farmers and drew Syrian fire.

The map shows how Israel's national water carrier drew directly out of Lake Tiberias at its northern end and ran the length of the country. This arrangement alarmed Jordan because its Jordan River waters, from the south of the lake, were much reduced. With Israel's tolerance, Jordan then established its own carrier from the Yarmuk River before it entered the Jordan River — the East Ghor Canal. Syria attempted to create a major diversion scheme, never completed, in the north from the Banias headwaters south to the Yarmuk. It was this action that precipitated major clashes with Israel; such a diversion would have deprived Israel of major components of Jordan River water.

The fact that the northern Golan contains the headwaters of the Banias and Dan rivers, the major sources of the Jordan and hence Lake Tiberias, has major implications for any Syrian-Israeli peace treaty. Israel will demand assurance of continued access to these water supplies or guarantees that their flow into Israel remains unimpeded.

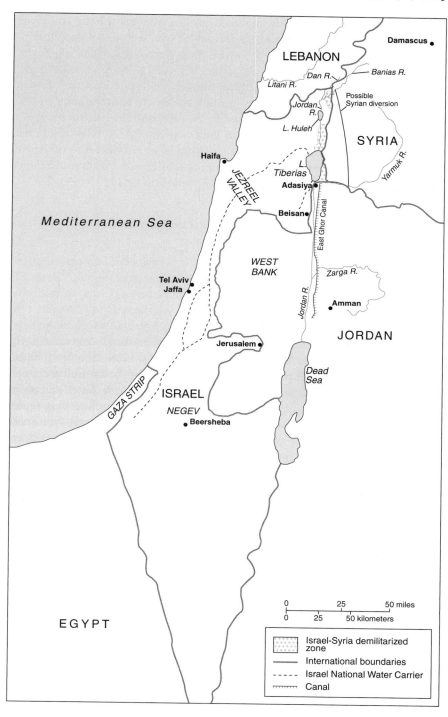

Damascus

LEBANON

Dan R.

Banias R.

Litani R.

Possible
Syrian diversion

Jordan
R.

L. Huleh

SYRIA

Haifa

L.
Tiberias

Yarmuk R.

JEZREEL
VALLEY

Adasiya

Mediterranean Sea

Beisan

East Ghor Canal

WEST
BANK

Zarga R.

Tel Aviv
Jaffa

Jordan R.

Amman

JORDAN

Jerusalem

Dead
Sea

GAZA STRIP

ISRAEL

NEGEV

Beersheba

EGYPT

| 0 | 25 | 50 miles |
| 0 | 25 | 50 kilometers |

Israel-Syria demilitarized
zone

International boundaries

Israel National Water Carrier

Canal

sites in 1965 and 1966 and greatly increased tensions between the two countries. But for the moment, the Arab summit decision of 1964 served to postpone consideration of a military response, for which most Arab states, including Egypt, were unprepared.

In keeping with this spirit of compromise, Nasser restored ties with Jordan and Saudi Arabia, hoping particularly to reach agreement with the latter so that the Yemen conflict could be settled and he could withdraw his troops. For a time, a mood of conciliation seemed to dominate inter-Arab relations, but it was soon broken, in part out of Syrian obduracy, in part because of Israeli domestic tensions, and in part because of another decision taken at the Cairo summit: to create the Palestine Liberation Organization (PLO).

The Palestine Question in Arab Politics: The Palestine Liberation Organization and al-Fatah

The decision of the Arab League to sponsor the formation of an organization that would represent Palestinians and strive toward "the liberation of Palestine," in the words of the Cairo summit, presumably indicated a new Arab commitment to the Palestinian cause. In fact, Arab leaders interpreted the significance of the PLO very differently. Nasser backed the idea in order to integrate the new group within the league under his control. This would prevent Palestinians from undertaking actions against Israel that might draw Egypt into a confrontation. His purpose was consistent with his motives in calling for the summit meeting: to defuse Syrian demands for a military challenge to Israel's water diversion plans. Such tactics also placed him once more in the forefront of the Arab cause as one deeply concerned about the Palestinian issue. Syrian-Egyptian tensions stemming from the breakup of the UAR had led to Syrian charges that Nasser hoped to shelve the Palestinian issue, accusations that Cairo denied vehemently.[25]

PLO Initiatives and Arab Government Reactions.   Arab leaders chose as head of the PLO Ahmad al-Shuqayri, an aging Palestinian lawyer who had served for years as Saudi Arabia's representative to the United Nations. Known principally for his bombast, he was considered Nasser's man. Similarly, the Palestinian Liberation Army was placed under the Arab unified command headed by an Egyptian. Once the PLO held its inaugural conference in May 1964, Shuqayri began to tour Arab capitals and Palestinian refugee camps to rouse both support and recruits. It soon became clear, however, that Shuqayri's efforts were designed to create an activist facade behind which nothing would occur; he specifically foreswore organizing raids against Israel. Nevertheless, the formation of the PLO aroused consternation in the almost forgotten offices of the Arab Higher Committee of Hajj Amin al-Husayni, which still existed in Beirut; he denounced the PLO as "a colonialist, Zionist conspiracy aiming at the liquidation of the Palestinian cause."[26] At the other extreme was King Husayn of Jordan, who viewed Shuqayri and the idea of the PLO with mounting alarm.

Husayn ruled over a population that was nearly 60 percent Palestinian. He also controlled the West Bank, deemed essential to the Jordanian economy. Two months after the PLO's founding, Shuqayri declared, in Amman, that all of Jordan, east and west banks, was part of Palestine, as was Israel, and should be recovered for Palestinians. An infuriated Husayn then barred the organization from all activities, including recruitment, in his country. But if Shuqayri's efforts appeared ominous to Husayn, they seemed far too tame to the Syrians, who realized that Nasser had outmaneuvered them at the Cairo summit of January 1964, sidestepping their demands for militant action. They began during 1965 to try to co-opt Shuqayri for their own purposes, to acquire credit for support of the Palestinians at Nasser's expense. More significantly, they turned to a smaller Palestinian organization, al-Fatah, which was prepared to undertake operations into Israel (see Document 6.1). The Syrian backing of Fatah molded the pattern of Arab-Israeli and inter-Arab interaction essential to the outbreak of the 1967 war.

Fatah: Background and Policies.   Formed in 1958, Fatah's core group was composed of young Palestinians who had fled to Gaza when Israel was created.[27] Several had dominated the Palestinian Students League while attending classes at Cairo University in the mid-1950s. Among them were Salah Khalaf, Khalil al-Wazir, and Yasir Arafat, who was related on his mother's side to Hajj Amin al-Husayni. They left Cairo following the Suez war, in part because of Egypt's close surveillance of Palestinians and in part to search for better-paying jobs, and settled in Kuwait, as many Palestinians had done previously. There they began to publish a journal called *Our Palestine*, which was issued from time to time in Beirut. Several factions emerged that later evolved into small but significant entities, most identified with the current trends of Arabism and Arab unity under the rubric of the Arab National Movement (ANM) led by George Habash. Within this framework the liberation of Palestine could occur only after Arab unity had been achieved, a process that delayed encouragement of military activities. For the leaders of Fatah, however, the proper procedure was precisely the opposite. The liberation of Palestine had to precede Arab unity, meaning also that militancy and military action were the preludes to politics. These sentiments reflected the recent success of the Algerian revolt against the French and the belief propounded by Franz Fanon, deeply influenced by the Algerian experience, that violence was the only way to purge oneself of the stigma of defeat and dependence.

Subsequent manifestos by Fatah's leadership suggest that the group's philosophy of action changed according to its circumstances, but by mid-1965, when Fatah had begun to attack Israeli installations and to develop plans for terrorizing the population, its pamphlets argued that these activities would help establish a desirable state of tension between Israel and its Arab neighbors. Israeli military threats would necessarily bring about Arab unity to confront them, resulting ultimately in an Arab victory and the liberation of Palestine from Israeli control. This view assumed Arab military superiority over Israel in conventional weapons. War seemed desirable sooner, not later, because Israel was rumored to have developed a nuclear capability. This might be the last opportunity to engage Israel in conventional warfare in which Arab numbers should prevail.[28]

The Syrian-Fatah Alliance.   Although these arguments seemed to be in accord with Fatah's precepts, they also indicated that Syrian sponsorship of Fatah aimed at reestablishing its primacy in the Arab revolutionary struggle, stymied since 1964. That Fatah's raids would eclipse Shuqayri and the PLO was in the interest of both the Baathists and Fatah, and it also attracted the ANM, which began to compete with Fatah.[29] The Baathist leadership in Damascus did not necessarily envisage open war with Israel, which was precisely what Fatah hoped to provoke. The military factions dominating the regime were seen to be using the Israeli factor, legitimated in part by Israeli provocations, to enhance their stature in Syria as well as the broader Arab world. Nonetheless, Syria hoped to prevent Israel from using its water diversion projects and to avenge the latter's raids on its own. Accordingly, the first Fatah raid was aimed at Israeli water installations.

By the end of 1965, at least thirty-nine operations had been carried out. Most were harassments consisting of random bombings that inflicted relatively few casualties but aroused intense Israeli concern about this new threat to its security. Less clear initially was which state was backing the raids, since they were undertaken from Jordan rather than Syria. This naturally aroused Jordanian fears of Israeli retaliation, despite their lack of involvement in the operations, which later proved justified: Fatah's first casualty was due to Jordanian efforts to stop its infiltrations. Equally prescient in light of later developments was Egypt's negative reaction to the news of these early raids. Both Husayn and Nasser feared an outbreak of hostilities, but their caution served Syrian interests, which were to paint each with the brush of being soft on Israel. At a meeting of the Palestinian National Conference in Cairo in May 1965, Syrian Baathists had accused Nasser of hiding behind the United Nations Emergency Forces (UNEF) stationed in Sinai since 1957, but Nasser held his ground. He declared openly in September that "he had no plan to liberate Palestine," to Shuqayri's discomfort.[30] At this point, Nasser chose to scorn Syrian criticism and seek to retain good ties with both Jordan and Saudi Arabia because he still hoped to gain an agreement that would enable him to withdraw his troops from the Yemen. Nonetheless, his stance encouraged accusations from his rivals that he lacked commitment to the Palestinian cause.

Two events in February 1966 undermined Nasser's overtures to Husayn and Faysal. One was the breakdown in Egyptian-Saudi efforts to mediate between opposing Yemeni factions; the other was Britain's declaration in the same month that it planned to withdraw in two years from the Aden Protectorate, contiguous to Yemen's southern border. These developments led Nasser to keep his forces in Yemen, but not only to assist the revolutionaries. He also hoped to influence events in Aden and establish his ascendancy there through nationalist protégés once the British left. This decision would return to haunt him during the June 1967 crisis because it required the retention of 40,000 troops in Yemen when war erupted. Equally important was the coup that took place in Damascus in February 1966. It installed a more radical Baathist regime under the guidance of the chief of staff, Salah Jadid, who took over as head of the Syrian Baath party.

Jordan between Arab Radicalism and Israeli Retaliation.　Nasser's eagerness to reassert his Arab nationalist credentials led him closer to Syria as the revolutionary-conservative split once more emerged in Arab politics. The rift was now exacerbated by the Syrian backing of Fatah; the new Baathist regime sought to arouse Palestinian opposition to King Husayn with the aim of toppling him. This goal was abetted by the intensification of Israeli retaliation raids aimed primarily at Palestinian towns on the West Bank, raids that aroused Husayn's fears of Israeli territorial designs even as he was aware of his own isolation in Arab political circles. At the same time, clashes erupted between Israeli and Syrian forces on Israel's frontier, more intense than at any time since 1955–1956. They were accompanied by mutual accusations of amassing troops on the other's borders, a foretaste of the situation that would erupt a year later.

To a great degree, the crisis was being managed by the Syrian Baathist regime, which hoped to radicalize Arab society under its leadership and bring Nasser within its orbit in the process. Israeli reprisals, aimed principally against Jordan, helped the Syrian cause; they proved Husayn's weakness and the futility of his reliance on the United States, which also armed Israel. The fact that Husayn had barred the PLO and Fatah from Jordan and forbidden them to recruit in the refugee camps there bolstered Syrian propaganda attacks against him. In Israel, however, Husayn's inability to block all access to its borders made little impression. A policy of retaliation against Jordan, a fellow ally of the West, was more convenient and would draw a less drastic response than would one against a more hostile and unpredictable government such as the Syrian Baath.

Husayn became increasingly isolated in his alliance with Saudi Arabia as Nasser moved toward the radical camp in the summer of 1966. Israel bombed the Syrian water diversion project in mid-July. At the end of the month, Nasser declared that he now rejected collaboration with the "reactionary forces" and would seek to "liberate Palestine in a revolutionary manner and not in a traditional way."[31] Such rhetoric sought to enhance his reputation among radicals while being vague enough to enable him to control events and to avoid a major confrontation with Israel. On November 7, 1966, he signed a mutual defense treaty with Damascus, and diplomatic relations were restored after a prolonged rupture. The joint military command purported to give Egypt a deciding voice in any future confrontation. Nearly a week later, on November 13, Israeli forces undertook a major retaliatory raid against the town of Samua on the West Bank, evicting the population and blowing up 125 homes. The responding Jordanian forces were ambushed and suffered extensive casualties. Husayn was caught between the Syrians and the Israelis, unable to stop all raids by Fatah, counter Israeli attacks, or maintain his credibility among his Palestinian subjects. Massive Palestinian demonstrations followed the Samua raid, protesting their exposure to Israeli attacks and the lack of adequate Jordanian protection. Husayn's only recourse was to meet Syrian and Egyptian propaganda charges with his own. If, as Radio Cairo charged, he was now the "harlot of Amman," Nasser was to Radio Amman the coward who hid behind UNEF forces in the Sinai and refused to protect fellow Arabs from Israeli assaults, the same charge leveled against him for years by the Syrians.

As 1966 ended, the world of Arab politics remained as fragmented as before. Nasser now faced the challenge of restraining Damascus while simultaneously indicating that he was the true leader of the Arab front against Israel, all the while avoiding conflict with that country. Most Arab leaders feared a major confrontation and were concerned, Jordan's King Husayn especially in light of the Samua assault, that Israel sought the opportunity to reassert its power over its antagonists.[32] Reminiscent of its retaliatory tactics in the mid-1950s, Israel's behavior also reflected strains within its political structure.

ISRAELI POLITICS TO 1967

Israel's political alignments had experienced severe tremors in the decade since 1957, resulting in the decline of Ben-Gurion's prestige and his resignation in 1965 from the Mapai Party he had led for many years. Ben-Gurion left the Mapai when a long-standing confrontation between different branches of government spilled over into a generational conflict. It was complicated by the role played by Pinhas Lavon, the former defense minister and the apparent architect of the abortive espionage operation of 1954, the Lavon affair.

At the heart of the problem were the question of military involvement in politics and the role of the defense ministry in matters considered by diplomats subject to their own expertise. Ben-Gurion had long nurtured young men, such as Moshe Dayan and Shimon Peres, who shared his concern for Israel's military preparedness and who were personally loyal to him. Loyalty rather than merit had often motivated his selection of high military personnel, notably his choice of Dayan over Yigael Allon as chief of staff, and key positions related to military matters were generally unavailable to those outside the Mapai Party.[33]

In 1960, Lavon, now head of the Histadrut and still prominent in Labor Zionist circles, asked Ben-Gurion, as prime minister, to clear him of responsibility for the events of 1954. Ben-Gurion refused, angering Lavon, who then brought the question into the open, the first time the public knew of the Lavon affair. Lavon's accusations impugned the integrity of Shimon Peres and Moshe Dayan by suggesting that they had been involved. Infuriated by this challenge to the reputation of his aides and of the military in general, Ben-Gurion decided to pursue a judicial investigation to clear the military, against the wishes of many Mapai officials who had hoped to resolve the matter quickly to save the party from further embarrassment. With Ben-Gurion absent, the cabinet, led by Finance Minister Levi Eshkol, formed a committee that exonerated Lavon. The Lavon crisis of 1960 thus symbolized the rift within the Mapai. Eshkol, Golda Meir, and others sought to spare the party, whereas Ben-Gurion strove to vindicate the military, especially Peres and Dayan, regardless of the harm done to the party. Meir's role symbolized Mapai tensions. Seen as a Ben-Gurion loyalist who had replaced Moshe Sharett as foreign minister in June 1956, she too resented the continued interference of the defense ministry, personified in Peres and Dayan, in foreign policy matters, leading her to side with Eshkol.[34]

Ultimately, the conflict over Lavon caused Ben-Gurion to leave Mapai. He had resigned as prime minister in 1963, to be succeeded by Eshkol. In 1965 the new Mapai leadership began considering a coalition with their main rival for labor support, the Ahdut Ha'Avodah. Ben-Gurion objected and challenged Eshkol in a bitter public debate that focused more on their handling of Lavon than on the question of coalition. The new leadership, centered in Eshkol and Meir, defeated Ben-Gurion, who resigned and, with Peres and Dayan, established the Rafi (Israeli workers) Party. The Rafi failed to prevent the Mapai from returning to office after the 1965 elections, but the heroes of the 1950s were now in the Rafi, their public image that of the victors at Suez. This would lead in 1967 to public suspicion that the new Mapai leaders were not equal to the task of defending Israel, with Eshkol in particular subjected to severe criticism from Ben-Gurion and his allies. Yet, following the war, when the Mapai and the Ahdut Ha'Avodah decided to expand their alignment into a full merger, they included the Rafi, whose justification for existence had been its opposition to such a union. The amalgamation of these three groups in 1968 became the Israeli Labor Party.[35]

On the right, another symbol of Zionist militancy began to gain greater credibility during the 1960s. Menachem Begin's Herut Party insisted on its vision of an Israel that controlled all territory considered Palestine in World War I: namely, Jordan east and west of the Jordan River. Herut had become the second-largest party in Israel as of the 1955 elections, but Begin remained discredited in Ben-Gurion's eyes; he even refused to use Begin's name when addressing him in the Knesset.[36] The Eshkol government initiated a public rehabilitation of the Irgun, bringing the remains of Vladimir Jabotinsky back to Israel and adding to the image of national legitimacy to be granted to Begin and the Irgun as well.

In 1965, Herut merged with the Liberal Party to become the Gahal Party. The merger did not help the party in new elections, but it furthered the process of acceptance. Also useful was the growing outspokenness of members of a younger generation, who agreed with Begin's call for Israeli expansion. Among them was Ezer Weizmann, nephew of Chaim Weizmann and chief of operations for the Israeli Defense Forces. He and others in command positions were eager to acquire more of what had been ancient Eretz Israel.[37]

In sum, Israeli politics had undergone a shift in focus with serious implications for future stability. The new Mapai leadership had abandoned Ben-Gurion's militancy and close adherence to military interests, alienating Dayan and Peres, who followed Ben-Gurion out of the party. Eshkol's focus on social and economic issues carried with it a willingness to exercise more restraint toward Arab incitements and to seek cooperation with the United Nations to reduce tensions, the opposite of Ben-Gurion's activist approach. As a result, Eshkol occasionally found himself under siege, openly berated by Ben-Gurion, Peres, and Dayan for his supposed weakness toward the Arabs. Yet at the same time, Eshkol, in the spirit of accommodation, opened doors to Revisionist respectability, a step that further infuriated Ben-Gurion. It also gave more voice to Menachem Begin's call to acquire the territories not taken in the 1948 wars.

The situation resembled the Ben-Gurion–Sharett disputes of the mid-1950s, but with a difference; Ben-Gurion was now isolated from power, whereas previously he had always influenced if not controlled developments, especially with respect to the military and often against Sharett's wishes. Some Israeli observers believed that Eshkol ordered the massive raid on Samua in November 1966 in part to divert attention from domestic issues, such as an economic recession, but also to rehabilitate himself in the public eye as a defender of Israel. Although it was aimed at a domestic audience, the intensity and size of the raid had regional repercussions and encouraged King Husayn, suspicious that Israel sought an excuse for seizing the West Bank, to be more receptive to the idea of alliances with Arab rivals.[38]

GREAT POWER RIVALRIES IN THE MIDDLE EAST TO 1967

Domestic political turmoil in Israel did not undermine a growing closeness between Israel and the United States during the 1960s, especially once Eshkol replaced Ben-Gurion and once Lyndon Johnson became president following John F. Kennedy's assassination in November 1963. President Kennedy had balanced different strands of policy during his brief tenure as president. He owed much to Jewish backing, apparently based on his proclamations of American support for Israel, for his extremely narrow margin of victory in 1960.[39] In the Middle East he pursued a two-pronged approach, seeking closer ties with Israel while establishing better relations with the Arab neutralist camp, led by Nasser. Economic aid agreements with Egypt were increased, especially regarding grain shipments, but at the same time greater economic assistance was also given to Israel. And in a major move, the Kennedy administration decided to enter the Middle East arms race by providing military aid to Israel; in this case, Hawk antiaircraft missiles, which were deemed necessary to balance Soviet military shipments to Iraq and Egypt.

The United States between Israel and the Arabs

The United States thus began a process of ever-deeper involvement in supplying its allies in the Middle East, often with apparently contradictory purposes in mind. As radical-conservative Arab rivalries intensified from 1963 onward, the United States sent assistance to regimes, such as Jordan and Saudi Arabia, to bolster them against threats from their Arab enemies, who included Nasser. This in turn made it impossible to refuse the demands of Israel's supporters that it needed more arms to counter shipments to conservative Arab states, which could be used against Israel. The apparent fragility of the conservative Arab governments led many Washington officials to see a strong Israel as all the more important to American hopes of combating Soviet influence in the region, a view encouraged by the Israelis, who profited from the continuance of American-Soviet rivalries. Israeli views were well known in Washington because of the close links established between Israeli intelligence (Mossad) and the CIA; during 1966 the CIA received from Mossad increasingly alarmist reports about Soviet intentions. Such assessments, accepted more readily in the Pentagon and the CIA than at the State Department, bolstered Israel's image as an ally against the Soviets and their clients, all the more important as America became increasingly involved militarily in Southeast Asia.

At the time of Kennedy's death in November 1963, certain issues between Israel and the United States had remained unresolved. One was Kennedy's effort to address the question of the Palestinian refugees, an inquiry that failed owing to uncertainty on both sides as to the number of refugees they would have to accept. Another was Israel's development of a nuclear reactor, initially denied by Ben-Gurion following its chance discovery by American intelligence in 1960. The American agreement to sell Hawk missiles to Israel was conditioned on the latter's willingness to permit on-site inspection of the reactor by the United States.⁴⁰ These matters faded in importance once Lyndon Johnson assumed office at a time when Syrian-Israeli tensions were mounting. Although Nasser initiated his summit policy at the beginning of 1964, failure to resolve his dispute with Saudi Arabia over Yemen led the Johnson administration to support an Islamic alliance of the Saudis and Jordanians against Nasser's apparent control of the radical Arab states and his backing of Yemeni colonels. In addition, clashes over U.S. policy in Africa seriously strained American-Egyptian relations at the end of 1964, leading Egyptian officials to suspect CIA efforts to undermine Egyptian prestige and possibly the regime. American aid to Egypt declined and was finally suspended in early 1967. The State Department played an increasingly minor role in decision making during this period and "during late 1966 and early 1967 the State Department Policy Planning Council did not have a member assigned to the Middle East."⁴¹

Lyndon Johnson and Israel

Mutual antipathy between Nasser and Johnson, encouraged by Johnson's sympathy for Israel and by Nasser's increasing assertiveness against his Arab rivals, fueled the deterioration of U.S.-Egyptian relations. For Johnson, emotions and worldviews blended easily. Johnson's perceptions of Nasser harked back to those of Dulles but in cruder fashion, given his lack of experience in foreign affairs. His judgments, often visceral, were based on his sense of loyalties and his and his aides' increasing obsession with Vietnam, where they saw themselves confronted by world communism. Nasser's permission for the Vietnamese Liberation Front to open an office in Cairo in the spring of 1966 hardly helped matters. It recalled his recognition of Communist China in the months before the Suez crisis that had so infuriated Dulles.[42]

Johnson personally felt great affinity with Israel and Israelis, based in part on his religious upbringing and reading of the Old Testament and in part on his identification with the Israelis as a frontier people—"a modern-day version of the Texans fighting the Mexicans."[43] Americans and Israelis were alike in his eyes, a feeling shared and encouraged by most of his domestic advisers, who were themselves strong supporters of Israel. These associations became particularly important following the intensification of Syrian-Jordanian hostility in 1965. Though backing military assistance to King Husayn, the Johnson administration also decided to grant Israel's request for tanks, a major step, since these were the first truly offensive weapons the United States had authorized for that country. Johnson's willingness to accelerate a U.S. commitment to arm Israel would prove important when France, Israel's traditional arms supplier, refused to continue in that role on the eve of the 1967 war.[44]

The Soviet Union and the Arab World

From the Soviet perspective, continuing military and economic assistance to Egypt, Syria, and Iraq provided a wedge for gaining access to the Arab world. Growing American identification with Israel in the 1960s offered more opportunities for Soviet inroads into the region. Ideology played a minor role. The Soviets willingly tolerated the suppression of local communist parties for the sake of geopolitical strategy during the Khrushchev era (1955–1964); mere support of neutralism worked to the Russians' advantage, given its condemnation by the Eisenhower administration. From the Soviet perspective, Egypt became all the more important as the 1960s progressed. Once the United States began bombing North Vietnam in 1965, Soviet aid to that country increased drastically. The Suez Canal and its security were crucial to the swift transit of Soviet arms and oil to its ally, achieving an importance analogous to what it had once held for the British.[45]

The Soviet Union's close ties to Egypt and other Arab states were also spurred by competition from its main communist rival, China, which sought to extend its influence in "progressive" Third World countries at Russia's expense. The Soviets now found themselves forced to defend their credibility against a communist challenger while striving to unite the radical Arab states—Syria, Iraq, and Egypt—in order to form an "anti-imperialist camp" that would counter American interests in the region. They seemed to have tried to gain a more forceful image as a defender of Syria in particular. Israeli complaints against Syrian sponsorship of guerrilla attacks were blocked by Soviet vetoes in the U.N. Security Council. On several occasions during 1966, Soviet diplomats accused Israel of fomenting disturbances and massing troops on its Syrian frontier. At the same time, the Brezhnev government paid little attention to the rise of Fatah and condemned the PLO, reiterating its concern for the legal status of Palestinian refugees in terms close to those used by the United States.[46] Throughout the period, U.S. emphasis on combating communism, buttressed by its perceptions of the struggle it had now intensified in Vietnam, led it to increase military aid to Saudi Arabia as well as Israel. This in turn reinforced Egyptian suspicion of U.S. motives in aiding its rivals and seems to have encouraged the Soviets to back their clients more emphatically. Soviet supplies to Egypt, Syria, and Iraq clearly outweighed Israel's in quantity and probably contributed to Nasser's confidence during the initial stages of the 1967 crisis. Qualitatively, however, the Israelis had a clear edge.

Each Soviet weapons system had been balanced by a Western one, and the offensive capability of the Israelis' weapons, especially aircraft, far outdistanced that of the Arabs. It seems likely, given the increasing potential for American-Soviet involvement in the region, that once the United States became an arms supplier to Israel, the Soviets wished to avoid a direct confrontation. Moscow provided weapons designed for defensive or limited offensive purposes, but not sufficient "to allow contemplation of successful first strike or total victory."[47] In contrast, the Israeli arsenal possessed significant offensive capabilities, including long-range attack bombers. Its personnel were capable of handling advanced weapons technology, training that the Arab military, especially the air force, lacked in abundance. Once the possibility of war developed in May 1967, the Israeli military leadership had little doubt they could demolish the Egyptians in the Sinai. The question was whether the Eshkol government would permit them to do so.

THE CRISIS ESCALATES: MILITARY CLASHES, MISLEADING ASSURANCES, AND FAILED DIPLOMACY

As the year began, Fatah increased its infiltrations into Israel and left explosives designed to kill civilians and create an atmosphere of terror. This presumably would instigate the hoped-for crisis that would unite the Arab governments against Israel and lead to war. The Syrian military was now much more openly involved.

Syrian-Israeli Tensions and Threats

Border clashes along the Golan Heights escalated quickly in January to include tank and artillery exchanges, creating an atmosphere of tension that lasted throughout the spring. The Syrian president, Nureddin al-Attassi, declared his country's support for a Palestinian war of liberation modeled after that of Algeria's against the French and of the Vietnamese against the United States. In response, Prime Minister Eshkol warned of Israeli retaliation amid increasing pressure from his military commanders to undertake major reprisals against Syria. Jordan remained under intense criticism from Cairo and Damascus, now for refusing to accept Egyptian, Syrian, and Iraqi forces as part of an Arab defense system against future Israeli attacks. The Arab propaganda war continued, with Amman mocking Nasser for hiding behind the UNEF in Sinai.

Then, on April 7, Syrian-Israeli exchanges of fire again erupted over the demilitarized zone beneath the Golan Heights, long a bone of contention. Syrian air support provoked an Israeli reply in which six Syrian fighters were shot down and the Israeli planes mockingly buzzed Damascus. Although President al-Attassi referred to that clash as "very useful to us" in furthering the liberation cause, Cairo was clearly alarmed and high Egyptian officials went to Damascus for consultations. Syrian spokesmen became more vocal about a joint CIA-Israeli scheme to threaten them, whereas in Israel, experiencing more attacks by Fatah, tensions mounted.

During the weekend of May 12–13, a prelude to Israeli independence day ceremonies, reports of speeches made by various officials indicated plans for a major retaliatory raid against Syria if attacks from there continued. According to one press release, "a highly placed Israeli source said here today (12 May) that if Syria continued the campaign of sabotage in Israel, it would immediately provoke military action aimed at overthrowing the Syrian regime."[48] This news aroused concern in the United Nations and elsewhere. On May 13, a secret Soviet message to Nasser falsely informed him that Israel had massed forces on the Syrian frontier. Nasser apparently accepted the information at face value, although he was later told it was inaccurate. Subsequent testimony suggests that Moscow never authorized such a statement.[49]

The Egyptian Blockade of the Tiran Straits

Nasser mobilized his army and ordered Egyptian troops into the Sinai on May 14. On May 16, he had emissaries in the Sinai request that the UNEF withdraw, thus removing the international buffer between him and Israel. Controversy still exists as to whether Nasser intended only a partial ouster of UNEF forces that would leave Sharm al-Shaykh in U.N. hands. What is clear is that U Thant, secretary general of the United Nations, believed that a partial withdrawal was impossible: it had to be full or not at all, and he accepted Egypt's right to make such a request. Egypt formally demanded a full withdrawal on May 18, and its troops began occupying U.N. posts along the frontier. U Thant then asked Israel to accept U.N. forces to act as a buffer, but Israel refused. Yet as tensions mounted, Nasser still refused to occupy Sharm al-Shaykh overlooking the Straits of Tiran while taunted by the Saudis and Jordanians that he was afraid to do so. He finally took that step on May 21 and on the next day closed the Straits of Tiran to all shipping destined for Israel. This action re-created the casus belli, the circumstances Israel had stipulated as justifying war in 1957.[50]

Despite taking these actions, Nasser did not think they would necessarily lead to war. If Israel did attack, he believed his forces could hold their ground based on assurances from his chief of staff, Abd al-Ḥakim Amr. Unknown at the time was the likelihood that Nasser did not control his army, whose leaders were more eager for war than he. Nasser's real goal was to achieve a clear political victory in the cause of Arabism that would deflate Syrian pretensions and send news of his own militancy "to the chanceries and streets of the Arab world."[51] He occupied Sharm al-Shaykh to blunt Arab criticism, not as a prelude to an offensive. He stressed defensive preparations and insisted that Egyptian forces in the Sinai adopt a defensive posture, albeit in forward, offensive positions.[52] The confusion probably reflected his military chiefs' desire for war. His war minister, Shams al-Din Badran, returned from Moscow on May 25 and lied to Nasser, telling him he had Soviet backing for war when in fact Moscow was desperately urging restraint.

Nevertheless, at times Nasser lent his voice to the war hysteria. Although he insisted that Egypt would not attack and that any conflict would be initiated by Israel, he also stated that such an act would result in the restoration of the situation that had existed in 1948, presumably referring to the abolition of Israel. But this rhetoric also included references to avenging the Suez conflict of 1956 and to the liberation of Aden from British control, language clearly invested with the aura of Arab nationalism confronting imperialism (see Document 6.2). Others were not so circumspect. Ahmad al-Shuqayri was quoted as stating that Israel was about to be destroyed and few if any Jews would survive.[53] Ironically, Shuqayri's speech was delivered in Amman. On May 30, King Husayn had signed a joint defense pact with Nasser, placing his forces under the command of an Egyptian general. Husayn had just previously broken off relations with Syria after a car filled with explosives blew up at a Jordanian border post. Egypt now had defense pacts with two nations who were sworn enemies of each other. Militant rhetoric notwithstanding, the Arab military was hardly united.

Israeli Debates: Eshkol and the Generals

Yet if Nasser seemed to be moving from expectation of Israeli attack to cautious optimism that he would achieve a diplomatic triumph, Israel was progressing in the opposite direction, from considering his actions a bluff to believing that war was necessary and probably imminent, if only to achieve Israel's own objectives. The Eshkol cabinet had countered Egypt's placement of troops in the Sinai by mobilizing its own forces; all reserves had been called up following the closure of the Straits of Tiran. For most of the Israeli public, the strident Arab propaganda established an atmosphere of encirclement that became increasingly oppressive as the crisis wore on. Eshkol hesitated, apparently fearing that Israel might be forced to attack but seeking guarantees of U.S. support. Officials in the Johnson administration strove during the last days of May to avoid war, assuring Israeli emissaries, including foreign minister Abba Eban, that they would do

everything possible to open the Straits of Tiran (see Figure 6.1). With that backing, but denied the public American commitment to support Israel that Eban
had sought, the Eshkol cabinet voted on the evening of May 27–28 not to go to
war but to accede to Johnson's request to delay such a decision for two weeks
while his administration attempted to mobilize international support to open
the straits.

Now, more than ever, Eshkol faced the wrath of his generals. In the words of
one analyst, "the legitimacy of Eshkol's cabinet in the security sphere disintegrated" during these weeks of hesitation in May. The military leadership, backed
by reserve officers prominent under Ben-Gurion, "saw his efforts to solve the
crisis by diplomatic means as hesitancy, vacillation and lack of authority; . . .
they wanted a minister who would unleash a war" they were convinced they
would win and which for some would signal the hoped-for expansion of Israel's
borders to include Jerusalem and the West Bank.[54] Recognizing Eshkol's weakness, the military now demanded that he include the Rafi and Gahal parties, the
latter led by Begin, in a national cabinet in order to add to the cabinet's militancy. On June 1, Eshkol succumbed to the pressures; he appointed Moshe

Figure 6.1 ■ Israeli Foreign Minister Abba Eban Calls on U.S. President Lyndon B. Johnson,
May 26, 1967

During this visit Eban sought to ascertain American willingness to intervene to resolve the ten-
sions resulting from Egypt's closure of the Straits of Tiran. To Eban's right is Secretary of Defense
Robert McNamara, who would indicate on June 1 to Meir Amit, head of Mossad, that the United
States would not object to an Israeli attack. To McNamara's right, his back to the camera, is Assis-
tant Secretary of State Joseph Sisco. Israeli ambassador Avraham Harman is to Johnson's left.
Behind him is Israeli Minister Counsellor Ephraim Evron.

Dayan, symbol of the Suez campaign, as minister of defense and installed Menachem Begin as minister without portfolio.[55] These additions, along with Husayn's joining a defense pact with Nasser, suggested to many that war was inevitable. The question was when.

Israel Attacks: U.S. Assurances and the Pending Egyptian Peace Initiative

Immediate attack seemed advisable for several reasons: the element of surprise, the ongoing mobilization of troops that might create economic problems, and the increasing unease among the public amid the barrage of Arab propaganda threatening to destroy Israel. A decisive factor was the news on June 2 that in response to American requests, Nasser had agreed to send his vice president, Zakariya Mohieddine, to Washington on June 7 to discuss measures to defuse the potential for confrontation over the Tiran blockade. This was totally unacceptable, even to Eban, who had resisted the military option until June 1: "It was probable that this initiative would aim at a face-saving compromise—and that the face to be saved would be Nasser's, not Israel's. For us the importance of denying Nasser political and psychological victory had become no less important than the concrete interest involved in the issue of navigation."[56] Egyptian occupation of Sharm al-Shaykh and the blockade might be the casus belli justifying attack, but Israel was also determined to deny Nasser his political triumph in the Arab world.

In this context, the Eshkol government had received reports that Washington would condone such a move. Meir Amit, the head of Mossad, whose reports to the CIA about Soviet penetration of the Middle East helped align Israel and Washington, flew to the United States incognito to ascertain American opinion regarding a possible Israeli strike. He consulted only with CIA and Pentagon officials. He informed them on June 1 and 2 of Israel's intent to attack in order to gauge their response; he received encouragement, particularly from Secretary of Defense Robert McNamara. Amit did not consult with State Department officials, whose diplomatic efforts were aimed in the opposite direction. Assurances of support were also transmitted by private channels to Israeli officials from the White House.[57] With increased confidence in American acquiescence, determined to punish Nasser and thwart the intent of Mohieddine's forthcoming visit to Washington, the Israeli cabinet on June 4 approved Dayan's plan to attack Egypt the next morning.

THE SIX-DAY WAR: ISRAEL'S CONQUESTS AND AMERICAN EXPECTATIONS

Within three hours of the initial Israeli air strikes on airfields in the Sinai, the Egyptian air force was nearly obliterated, its planes destroyed on the ground. Although Israeli forces did not achieve all their objectives—occupying Sharm ar Shaykh and reaching the Suez Canal—until June 9, the Sinai war had, for all practical purposes, been decided. Egyptian troops had no air cover in the desert to shield them from Israeli air and ground attacks. The Eshkol cabinet appealed to Husayn to stay out of the fighting, but once it became clear that Jordanian shelling would continue, the cabinet decided to fulfill the "historic opportunity" afforded them, namely, the taking of the old city of Jerusalem. In keeping with Dayan's plans, Israeli forces also moved into the West Bank toward the Jordan River. Fierce fighting ensued, especially in and around East Jerusalem. As the conflict continued, Israeli diplomats in Washington and New York tried to gain U.S. support to delay pressing for a cease-fire until "the opportunity for a permanent settlement was created. Israel needed time to finish the job."[58] The United Nations Security Council had called for an immediate cease-fire, but Israel was able to delay acceptance because the Arab states refused. Nevertheless, Israel, fearing implementation of the Security Council resolution, hastened to take old Jerusalem beforehand, securing the area by midday on June 7. Israel then pressed on toward the Jordan River, declaring its support for a cease-fire but moving swiftly before Husayn announced his acceptance, as he did later in the day. On June 8 Egypt accepted the cease-fire. Shortly after midnight on June 9, Syria, which had contributed so much to the crisis, also did so. But this was unacceptable to Dayan. There had not yet been a major confrontation between Israel and Syria, whose involvement had been restricted mainly to sustained artillery barrages against Israeli villages. He now ordered an all-out assault on the Golan Heights without informing either Prime Minister Eshkol or Chief of Staff Yitzhak Rabin of his decision; it was an act reminiscent of Ben-Gurion's style as minister of defense, anticipating civilian objections.[59]

But Eshkol, though angered at Dayan's modus operandi, pushed for deeper advances into the Golan than Dayan had envisaged. If possible, he wanted to gain control of the headwaters of the Jordan River. Israel finally stopped after occupying the key town of Qunaitra on June 10, abandoned by the retreating Syrians. The Six-Day War had ended.

American intelligence had predicted a clear-cut Israeli victory whether against Egypt alone or on all three fronts. Yet despite apparent Pentagon and CIA support for an Israeli attack, especially into the Sinai, Israeli planes and torpedo boats staged an apparently deliberate assault on an American intelligence-gathering ship, the U.S.S. *Liberty*, on June 8, killing thirty-four and wounding more than seventy.[60] The ship was stationed off the Sinai near Israel to monitor radio signals from all sources. The Israelis probably acted to forestall American awareness of their plans to move against Syria. Johnson and his aides accepted Israeli apologies for the "accident," relieved that the attackers had not been the Russians.

Yet there may well have been conflicting motives behind the U.S. search for a diplomatic resolution to the crisis. Whereas the State Department pursued a resolution with hope of success, predicated on the forthcoming Mohieddine visit, Johnson encouraged one out of fear that the United States might be forced to intercede on behalf of Israel if war erupted; this in turn fed on apprehension that the Russians would intervene on behalf of the Arabs, inducing a great-power conflict while the bulk of U.S. forces were committed to Vietnam. Once it became clear that the Soviets were sincere in seeking to blunt the crisis, the Johnson administration felt able to back Israel while relieved that it had not openly associated the United States with its effort. Vietnam was a major distraction for the White House at the time, a period during which Congress began to question the president's increasing commitment of troops to the war. Comparatively little attention could be paid to the Middle East, especially if one's ally seemed able to protect itself.

For its part, the Israeli government had been told unofficially and, at first, ambiguously, from May 25 on that the United States would not object to its attack against Egypt. They were assured of this more explicitly from May 30 onward, notably by Supreme Court Justice Abe Fortas and U.N. Ambassador Arthur Goldberg, acting on Johnson's behalf. In general, Israeli officials had great access to all levels of the administration in ascertaining its position. In contrast, Egyptian officials had no access, in part because of Egyptian suspicion of American motives, and also because the United States had no ambassador in Cairo during the crisis. Egyptians would later make the point that Washington advised them to hold back until a diplomatic resolution was reached while encouraging Israel to attack.[61]

None of these factors explains Nasser's behavior in closing the Straits of Tiran, which afforded Israel a legal justification to attack. Moreover, White House support for Israel reflected the assumption, encouraged by Israel, that as a result of the attack, there was now an opportunity for peace. Johnson accepted the arguments Israel presented when it sought American support for war and for the conditions it set for returning the territories it would occupy. Israel would withdraw only in return for peace agreements with Arab states, thus ending the state of belligerency that had existed since 1949. Here, Johnson and his advisers believed they had Israeli assurances, given on June 5, that Israel did not intend to expand its borders as a result of the conflict. Even before the war's end, a special committee in the White House began investigating proposals for possible peace settlements, but State Department officials were not informed of this stance, which overturned long-standing U.S. policy.[62]

Nevertheless, it is unlikely that anyone, including the Israelis themselves, anticipated the scope of their victory, including Jerusalem, the West Bank, and the Golan Heights in addition to the Sinai. Certain areas, especially East Jerusalem, were incorporated into Israel, regardless of past promises (see Map 6.2). As soon as the area was secured, Israeli officials ordered the demolition of the Maghrebi Quarter opposite the Western Wall and the eviction of over 600 Muslim residents so that Jews coming to worship at the holiest site in Judaism on the next Sabbath would be secure and have ample room to pray. This was done swiftly to create new realities and preempt any U.N. resolution regarding Israel's administration of East Jerusalem (see Figure 6.2).

Territory occupied by Israel, June 1967

0   50   100 miles

0   50   100 kilometers

Mediterranean Sea

Beirut

Sidon •Damascus

LEBANON

Qunaitra
GOLAN
HEIGHTS

Haifa SYRIA

Nazareth

Tel Aviv Nablus   Jordan River
Jaffa WEST •Amman
BANK
Jerusalem Jericho
Bethlehem
Gaza Hebron Dead
Sea
Beersheba

ISRAEL JORDAN

NEGEV

EGYPT

•Ma'an

Port Sa'id

Suez Canal

Cairo

Nile River

Suez

SINAI Eilat
Taba Aqaba

Gulf of Suez

Gulf of Aqaba

SAUDI ARABIA

Straits of Tiran

Sharm
al-Shaykh

Red Sea

Figure 6.2 ■ Israeli Bulldozers Destroy the Maghrebi Quarter Facing the Western Wall in East Jerusalem, June 1967

On capturing the old city of Jerusalem, Israel declared its annexation to Israel. The Eshkol government then ordered the destruction of the Maghrebi Quarter to create a large plaza for Jewish worshippers. In the background can be seen the Dome of the Rock. For the former view of the Western Wall, see Figure 1.4, which shows the wall and narrow passageway around 1900.

In the meantime, over 100,000 new Palestinian refugees from within Israel as well as the West Bank crossed into East Bank Jordan, many forcibly evicted from their homes; their villages were bulldozed to ensure that they would not return. Eshkol declared in a report to the Israeli people that "there should be no illusion that Israel is prepared to return to the conditions that existed a week ago. . . . We have fought alone for our existence and our security, and are therefore justified in deciding for ourselves what are the genuine and indispensable interests of our state and how to guarantee our future. We shall never return to the conditions prevailing before."[63] With this and other statements (see Document 6.3), Israel's prewar assurances that it would not expand its borders became moot, overrun by euphoria and a sense of having broken the noose of encirclement that seemed to threaten it, but also by the opportunities created for those who had hoped to expand Israel's borders. Here Arab propaganda,

◀ **Map 6.2 ■ Territory Acquired by Israel in the 1967 War**

Israel occupied the Sinai Peninsula, the West Bank, and the Golan Heights as a result of the 1967 war. It would return the Sinai to Egypt following their 1979 peace treaty, but Israel still retains most of the West Bank and all of the Golan (see Map 10.1).

n itself and aimed at self-inflation, provided to many in the West more
quate justification for the Israeli attack.

, this left the United States in the position of publicly backing an Israeli
promise to return conquered lands, some of which, unofficially, Israel intended
to keep. Johnson seemed unconcerned with the new Israeli position as stated
by Eshkol, or in Abba Eban's reply to Secretary of State Dean Rusk: "We had
changed our minds." His domestic advisers had already suggested that he not
insist on the restoration of the territorial status quo. Such circumspection
"could lead to a great domestic bonus—and not only from the Jews. Generally
speaking it would seem that the Mid-East crisis can turn around a lot of anti-
Vietnam, anti-Johnson feeling, particularly if you use it as an opportunity to
your advantage."[64]

Yet the Vietnam preoccupation notwithstanding, the question remained as
to how all parties would deal with a radically new situation. The United States
assured both sides of its good offices while not appearing to place excessive
pressure on Israel because of domestic political considerations. For its part,
Israel was determined to establish itself in a new territorial framework whose
boundaries, still undefined, would be quite different from those existing previously. The Arab governments would strive to restore the pre-1967 borders. As
for Fatah, its leaders, with their initial hypothesis of an Arab victory demolished, viewed the debacle as a justification for their increased independence
from Arab state constraints in confronting Israel. Despite the magnitude of the
Israeli victory, the Palestinian factor in the Arab-Israeli equation would assume
far greater importance in the years ahead.

CONCLUSION

The significance of the 1967 war cannot be overstated in terms of both its creation of new territorial frameworks still subject to negotiation and of the manner of its evolution into conflict. The prelude to the war illustrates how crises can
erupt and decisions be made based on misperceptions of their potential impact,
or for domestic or regional political reasons having little to do with the object of
the immediate actions. The long-term ramifications of such steps remained
unconsidered, as true of the United States as of the Arab-Israeli combatants.

To be sure, there were concrete issues, particularly the long-standing tensions over the demilitarized zones between Syria and Israel, which the latter had
exploited for its own use. The completion of the Israeli water diversion project
revived the question, and Syria's own diversionary plans initiated renewed
Israeli-Syrian clashes. Added to this volatile mix was the element of Palestine
and the Palestinians, salient but exploited by rival Arab regimes more as a
rhetorical marker of their comparative militancy against Israel than as an indi-
cator of intended actions with envisioned consequences. To enhance the image
of a new, radical government, Syrian militarism encouraged Egyptian actions
over which Nasser may not have had full control. Nasser's recklessness, aimed at

an Arab audience, encouraged the Israeli military command to intimidate its civil superiors into preparing for an offensive that some hoped would lead to acquisition of Arab lands; the expansionists had ramifications in mind. Jordanian involvement reflected fears of Israeli desire for expansion, born out of previous Israeli retaliatory raids, especially Samua. From an Israeli perspective, that raid had been inspired more by the domestic political weakness of Prime Minister Eshkol than by any intent to expand Israel's borders; he sought to demonstrate his concern for Israel's security. The Israeli wish to attack and their assurances regarding the future peace process were approved directly and indirectly by an American president through personal intermediaries and counsellors who were themselves sympathetic to Israel, not via official channels or after discussion with his specialists on the region. No serious consideration of the policy implications of the move, or of the idea of Israeli retention of territories, took place. Attempts to resolve the consequences of these events continue today.

QUESTIONS FOR CONSIDERATION

1. Why did the Eisenhower administration respond to the Lebanese crisis of summer 1958 by landing troops?
2. What was the United Arab Republic? What impact did its breakup have on Arab politics during the 1960s?
3. Why was the PLO created? Would you consider it an ally or rival of al-Fatah leading up to the 1967 war?
4. What do you see as the key factors leading to the outbreak of the 1967 war?

CHRONOLOGY

1958	Fatah established.
	February 1. Egypt and Syria form United Arab Republic.
	July 14. Iraqi revolution; Hashemite dynasty overthrown.
	July 15. United States lands troops in Lebanon.
1961	**September.** Syria secedes from United Arab Republic.
1962	**September.** Yemeni revolution breaks out.
1963	Levi Eshkol succeeds David Ben-Gurion as Israeli prime minister.
	November 22. President John F. Kennedy assassinated; Lyndon B. Johnson succeeds him.
1964	**January.** Palestine Liberation Organization (PLO) created.
	Summer. Israel inaugurates national water carrier system.
	November. Israel attacks Syrian water diversion efforts.
1965	Ben-Gurion forms Rafi Party; Menachem Begin's Herut Party joins with Liberal Party to form Gahal Party.
	January. Fatah initiates raids against Israel.
1966	**July.** Israel bombs Syrian water diversion project.
	November 7. Egyptian-Syrian mutual defense treaty signed.
	November 13. Israeli raid on Samua in West Bank Jordan.
1967	**January–May.** Syria and Israel clash along Golan Heights.
	May 12. Israel warns of military action against Syria.
	May 14. Nasser orders Egyptian forces into Sinai.
	May 21. Egyptian forces occupy Sharm al-Shaykh.
	May 23. Nasser closes Straits of Tiran to Israeli shipping.
	May 30. Jordan enters mutual defense pact with Egypt.
	June 1. Moshe Dayan and Menachem Begin join Israeli cabinet.
	June 2. The United States informs Israel that Egyptian vice president Zakariya Mohieddine will arrive in Washington on June 7.
	June 5. Israel attacks Egypt, inaugurating Six-Day War, which ends June 10.

Notes

1. Patrick Seale, *The Struggle for Syria: A Study of Post-War Arab Politics, 1945–1958* (London, 1966), 270–82, and Wilbur Crane Eveland, *Ropes of Sand: America's Failure in the Middle East* (New York, 1980), 158–230, discuss these events extensively. David Lesch, *Syria and the United States: Eisenhower's Cold War in the Middle East* (Boulder, Colo., 1992), closely analyzes the Eisenhower years and especially U.S. policy, 1955–1957. Eveland was active as a CIA representative in the area during the period.

2. Eveland, *Ropes of Sand*, 220.

3. Seale, *Struggle for Syria*, 281.

4. Ibid., 321.

5. Michael N. Barnett, *Dialogues in Arab Politics: Negotiations in Regional Order* (New York, 1998), 130; see also Malik Mufti, *Sovereign Creations: Pan-Arabism and Political Order in Syria and Iraq* (Ithaca, N.Y., 1996).

6. Fahim I. Qubain, *Crisis in Lebanon* (Washington, D.C., 1961), 16ff.

7. Albert Hourani, *Syria and Lebanon: A Political Essay* (London, 1954), 121, relying on 1938 French estimates.

8. Michael C. Hudson, *The Precarious Republic: Political Modernization in Lebanon* (New York, 1968), 23.

9. Qubain, *Crisis*, 19.

10. Charles Issawi, "Economic Development and Political Liberalism in Lebanon," in *Politics in Lebanon*, ed. Leonard Binder (New York, 1966), 74–78.

11. See the speeches quoted in Hudson, *Precarious Republic*, 108.

12. Qubain, *Crisis*, 56–57.

13. Eveland, *Ropes of Sand*, 246–55.

14. See Hudson's detailed analysis, *Precarious Republic*, 109–17.

15. Dwight D. Eisenhower, *The White House Years: Waging Peace, 1956–1961* (New York, 1965), 266. Eisenhower's account is a bit muddled in that he admits that Chamoun was wrong to try to amend the constitution.

16. Ibid., 268.

17. Ibid., 266.

18. Ibid., 289, 291.

19. Steven L. Spiegel, *The Other Arab-Israeli Conflict: Making America's Middle East Policy, from Truman to Reagan* (Chicago, 1985), 89.

20. Malcolm H. Kerr, "Political Decision Making in a Confessional Democracy," in Binder, ed., *Politics in Lebanon*, 209.

21. Malcolm H. Kerr, *The Arab Cold War: Gamal 'Abd al-Nasir and His Rivals, 1958–1970*, 3rd ed. (London, 1971), 17. Kerr's study remains the best discussion of this subject, but see also the broader treatment by Fawaz Gerges, *The Superpowers and the Middle East: Regional and International Politics, 1955–1967* (Boulder, Colo., 1994).

22. See the excellent survey of these talks in Kerr, *Arab Cold War*, 44–78.

23. Fred J. Khouri, *The Arab-Israeli Dilemma*, 3rd ed. (Syracuse, N.Y., 1985), 225–29.

24. Don Peretz, "River Schemes and Their Effect on Economic Development in Jordan, Syria, and Lebanon," *The Middle East Journal* 18, 3 (Summer 1964): 297; Lesch, *Syria*, 36. For the view of the U.N. observers, see Carl von Horn, *Soldiering for Peace* (New York, 1966), 76–77ff, and especially 127–40.

25. Kerr, *Arab Cold War*, 39.

26. Quoted in Helena Cobban, *The Palestinian Liberation Organization: People, Power, and Politics* (Cambridge, U.K., 1984), 31.

27. Yezid Sayigh, *Armed Struggle and the Search for State: The Palestinian National Movement, 1949–1993* (Washington, D.C., 1997), 80–87. Sayigh's book has the most extensive coverage of Palestinian movements, policies, and rivalries.

28. Fuad Jabber, "The Palestinian Resistance and Inter-Arab Politics," in *The Politics of Palestinian Nationalism*, ed. William Quandt (Berkeley and Los Angeles, 1973), 160.

29. Sayigh, *Armed Struggle*, 119–42, has extensive discussion of the interactions and differences among Fatah, the PLO, and the ANM.

30. Ibid., 132; see also Ehud Yaari, *Strike Terror: The Story of Fatah* (New York, 1970), 61–62.

31. Robert Stephens, *Nasser: A Political Biography*, Penguin Series, Political Leaders of the Twentieth Century (London, 1973), 461.

32. An article published at the time suggesting that this state of tension could lead to war is Fred J. Khouri, "The Policy of Retaliation in Arab-Israeli Relations," *The Middle East Journal* 20, 4 (Autumn 1966): 435–55.

33. Yoram Peri, *Between Battles and Ballots: Israeli Military in Politics* (Cambridge, U.K., 1983), 51–69; and Tom Segev, *1949: The First Israelis* (New York, 1986), 11.

34. I rely here on Peri, *Between Battles and Ballots*, 70–80; Noah Lucas, *The Modern History of Israel* (New York, 1975), 391–407; and Michael Bar-Zohar, *Ben-Gurion* (London, 1978), 282–97.

35. The reappearance of the Ahdut Ha'Avodah requires explanation. Led by Ben-Gurion, the party had merged with the Hapoel Hatzair in 1930 to become the Mapai. As Ben-Gurion concentrated on leadership of the Jewish community and called for Jewish statehood, leftist members of the Mapai objected, calling for achievement of socialism in Palestine before statehood. They took the name Ahdut Ha'Avodah when they split with Ben-Gurion and the Mapai in the mid-1940s over the issue of the Biltmore Declaration, and later merged with the Hashomer Hatzair to form the Mapam in 1948. They subsequently seceded from that party and then reunited with the Mapai and the Rafi to become the Labor Party in 1968. See Lucas, *Modern History*, 128–30, 190–92, 282, 311–12, 399–406.

36. Rael Jean Isaac, *Party and Politics in Israel: Three Visions of a Jewish State* (New York, 1981), 139, 149.

37. Donald Neff, *Warriors for Jerusalem: The Six Days That Changed the Middle East* (New York, 1984), 46–47. For Begin, see Eric Silver, *Begin: A Biography* (London, 1984), 124–29; and Isaac, *Party and Politics*, 135–51.

38. For the Jordanian response to Samua, see Richard B. Parker, ed., *The Six-Day War: A Retrospective* (Gainesville, Fla., 1996), 100–102, 169, 176, 181. For the overall context and Eshkol's motivations, see Yair Evron, *The Middle East: Nations, Superpowers, and Wars* (New York, 1973), 66–75; and Anthony Carhew, "After the Raid on Es-Samua," *New York Times Magazine*, December 18, 1966, quoted in Khouri, *Arab-Israeli Dilemma*, 237.

39. Spiegel, *Other Arab-Israeli Conflict*, 97.

40. Ibid., 113; and Stephen Green, *Taking Sides: America's Secret Relations with a Militant Israel* (New York, 1984), 148–79, where he discusses the probability that Israeli agents arranged to steal uranium from a nuclear plant built in Pennsylvania for that purpose, with the acquiescence if not the collusion of some American officials.

41. Spiegel, *Other Arab-Israeli Conflict*, 119–20. For the question of American aid to Egypt, its underlying political rationale, and rising Egyptian-American tensions, see William J. Burns, *Economic Aid and American Policy towards Egypt, 1955–1981* (Albany, N.Y., 1985), 149–73; and Evron, *The Middle East*, 58–63.

42. Burns, *Economic Aid*, 167.

43. Spiegel, *Other Arab-Israeli Conflict*, 123.

44. French-Israeli relations soured following revelations that Meir Amit, Mossad director, had collaborated in a rogue operation with French and Moroccan security forces in kidnapping a Moroccan opposition figure, Mehdi Ben Barka, in Paris and transporting him to Morocco,

where he was murdered. The French officers involved acted on their own, as did Amit, without Eshkol's authorization. See Peri, *Between Battles and Ballots*, 240–44.

45. Karen Dawisha, *Soviet Foreign Policy towards Egypt* (New York, 1979), 27ff; and Galia Golan, *Yom Kippur and After: The Soviet Union and the Middle East Crisis* (Cambridge, U.K., 1977), 1–18.

46. Galia Golan, *The Soviet Union and the Palestine Liberation Organization: An Uneasy Alliance* (New York, 1980), 7; and Theodore Draper, *Israel and World Politics: Roots of the Arab-Israeli War* (New York, 1968), 34–39.

47. Jon D. Glassman, *Arms for the Arabs: The Soviet Union and War in the Middle East* (Baltimore, 1975), 36.

48. Quoted in Walter Laqueur, *The Road to War: The Origin and the Aftermath of the Arab-Israeli Conflict 1967–8* (Baltimore, 1968), 89. See discussion in Parker, *Six-Day War*, 68–69.

49. Parker, *Six-Day War*, 35–73, has an extensive discussion of this question.

50. The most detailed accounts are those of the commander of the UNEF in the Sinai, Indar Jit Rikhye, *Sinai Blunder* (London, 1980); and the texts and commentary in Rosalyn Higgins, *United Nations Peacekeeping, 1946–1967: Documents and Commentary*, 4 vols. (New York, 1969), vol. 1, *The Middle East*, 271, 326, 338–39, and especially 345–49, where the official and oral Egyptian requests are given verbatim. Higgins argues that U Thant could have stalled and did not have to accede to the Egyptian demand. For a different view, see Brian Urquhart's comments and general discussion in Parker, *Six-Day War*, 74–118.

51. Kerr, *Arab Cold War*, 127.

52. See Rikhye, *Sinai Blunder*, 96–97; he inspected the positions.

53. Stephens, *Nasser*, 480.

54. The quotations are from Peri, *Between Battles and Ballots*, 79 and 250, respectively. See also Michael Brecher, with Benjamin Geist, *Decisions in Crisis: Israel, 1967 and 1973* (Berkeley, 1980), 99–100.

55. Peri, *Between Battles and Ballots*, 244–51; Brecher, *Decisions*, 150; and Parker, *Six-Day War*, 126–32, 141.

56. Quoted in Neff, *Warriors*, 181.

57. Amit confirms his conversation with McNamara in Parker, *Six-Day War*, 136–41, 144–51.

58. Brecher, *Decisions*, 273.

59. Peri, *Between Battles and Ballots*, 80; Brecher, *Decisions*, 278–80. The Israelis benefited from the enormous confusion caused by Egyptian leadership of the joint command that was overseeing Jordanian operations, as detailed by Samir A. Mutawi, *Jordan in the 1967 War* (Cambridge, U.K., 1987). For the Syrian role in the war, see Nadav Safran, *From War to War: The Arab-Israeli Confrontation, 1948–1967* (New York, 1969), 370–82.

60. Controversy remains over the nature of the attack on the U.S.S. *Liberty*. Green, *Taking Sides*, 212–42; Neff, *Warriors*, 246–66; and James M. Ennes, Jr., *Assault on the Liberty: The True Story of the Israeli Attack on an American Intelligence Ship* (New York, 1979) all assert that the attack was deliberate. Ennes was an officer on the ship at the time. Official U.S. inquiries have backed Israeli claims that the attack was a mistake, but prominent American military officers have argued that the investigations were shams and that the evidence backing claims of a deliberate assault was suppressed; these include officers who conducted an official inquiry, such as Rear Admiral Isaac Kidd and Captain Ward Boston, along with former Chief of Naval Operations and head of the Joint Chiefs of Staff, Admiral Thomas Moorer and former CIA director Richard Helms. James Bamford, *Body of Secrets: Anatomy of the Ultra-Secret National Security Agency* (New York, 2002) discusses the *Liberty* attack, pp. 185–239, and sides with the above-mentioned individuals. Jay Cristol, *The Liberty Incident: The 1967 Attack on a U.S. Navy Spy Ship* (Washington, D.C., 2002), defends the Israelis and attempts unsuccessfully to demolish Bamford's case. What appears certain is that Israeli military officials made no attempt to identify the

ship, contradicting Cristol. For a summary of the issues, see David C. Walsh, "Friendless Fire?" *U.S. Naval Institute Proceedings* 129, 6 (June 2003): 58–64.

61. William B. Quandt, "Lyndon Johnson and the June 1967 War: What Color Was the Light?" *The Middle East Journal* 46, 2 (Spring 1992): 198–228; this article contains the most detailed discussion of these matters. See also the comments by observers, including Quandt in Parker, *Six-Day War*; for example, 121, 204, 209–10, 259, 272–73, 303.

62. Parker, *Six-Day War*, 317–18 and footnote 1, also indicating direct Israeli access to the White House. The most thorough source, with official U.S. documents, for the crisis is now Harriet Dashiel Schwar, editor, *Foreign Relations of the United States, 1964–1968*, Volume XIX, *Arab-Israeli Crisis and War, 1967* (Washington, D.C., 2004); it can also be accessed online at http://www.state.gov/r/pa/ho/frus/johnsonlb/xix.

63. Quoted in Neff, *Warriors*, 299.

64. Green, *Taking Sides*, 219–20, quoting from a memo to Johnson from Ben Wattenberg and Larry Levinson, drafted after a visit to them the same day by David Brody, head of the Jewish Anti-Defamation League. For Eban's remark to Rusk, see Parker, *Six-Day War*, 243, taken from Rusk's memoirs.

COMMUNIQUÉ NO. 1 FROM HEADQUARTERS OF ASIFA FORCES (FATAH)

January 6, 1965

This communiqué marked the appearance of Fatah and the launching of its raids into Israel. The title al-Asifa (The Storm) was used initially to avoid Arab government wrath in case of Israeli retaliation. The attacks were aimed at water diversion projects, a source of great tension between Israel and Syria, mentioned in the communiqué. Note also the specific reference to Palestine but in the context of an appeal to the "single Arab nation," which reflects the pan-Arab currents of the time.

From among our steadfast people, waiting at the borders, our revolutionary vanguard has issued forth, in the belief that armed revolution is our only path to Palestine and freedom. Let the imperialists and Zionists know that the people of Palestine are still in the field of battle and shall never be swept away.

Our enemies have forgotten our strength and our history of revolutions. We are determined to resort to armed conflict whatever the obstacles, until all conspiracies are foiled. The Zionists have planned to stay long in our country by executing diversion and reconstruction projects aimed at increasing their potential for aggression and forcing the Arab world to accept the fait accompli.

Because of all these threats and since time is running out, our revolutionary vanguard had to move fast in order to paralyze the enemy's plans and projects. In this task, we rely upon our own strength and on the capabilities of the people of Palestine.

We hereby declare to the whole world that we are bound indissolubly to the soil of our homeland. Our moving force is our own faith that this is the only means which can reactivate our problem which has been dormant for so long. But we must also inform the world that we are bound, by our destiny and struggle, to the Arab nation which will help us, both materially and morally.

We appeal to the Arabs of Palestine, to our single Arab nation and to lovers of freedom everywhere to aid the fighting men of the Asifa in their heroic struggle. We pledge ourselves to fight until Palestine is liberated and resumes its place in the very heart of the Arab world. Long live the Arab nation. Long live our Arab Palestine.

Source: Documents on the Middle East, Ralph H. Magnus, ed. (Washington, D.C., 1969), 192.

DOCUMENT 6.2

GAMAL ABD AL-NASSER

SPEECH TO MEMBERS OF THE EGYPTIAN NATIONAL ASSEMBLY

May 29, 1967

These excerpts indicate Nasser's rhetorical perspective as the 1967 crisis escalated. Egypt confronts not only Israel but the Western powers. He links the 1956 Suez crisis to the creation of Israel in 1948 and recalls the plight of the Palestinians, whose situation will be "restored." But he also calls attention to his stance as the true Arab nationalist leader, addressing the people of Aden, whose political future he hoped to control. Finally, his references to the Soviet messages relayed by War Minister Shams Badran indicate the possibility of Badran's duplicity. The Soviets have always claimed that they encouraged caution, not confrontation.

The circumstances through which we are now passing are in fact difficult ones because we are not only confronting Israel but also those who created Israel and who are behind Israel. We are confronting Israel and the West as well—the West, which created Israel and which despised us Arabs and which ignored us before and since 1948. They had no regard whatsoever for our feelings, our hopes in life, or our rights. The West completely ignored us, and the Arab nation was unable to check the West's course.

Then came the events of 1956—the Suez battle. We all know what happened in 1956. When we rose to demand our rights, Britain, France and Israel opposed us, and we were faced with the tripartite aggression. We resisted, however, and proclaimed that we would fight to the last drop of our blood. God gave us success and God's victory was great.

Subsequently we were able to rise and to build. Now, 11 years after 1956, we are restoring things to what they were in 1956. This is from the material aspect. In my opinion this material aspect is only a small part, whereas the spiritual aspect is the great side of the issue. The spiritual aspect involves the renaissance of the Arab nation, the revival of the Palestine question, and the restoration of confidence to every Arab and to every Palestinian. This is on the basis that if we are able to restore conditions to what they were before 1956 God will surely help and urge us to restore the situation to what it was in 1948 [prolonged applause].

Brothers, the revolt, upheaval and commotion which we now see taking place in every Arab country are not only because we have returned to the Gulf of Aqabah or rid ourselves of the UNEF, but because we have restored Arab honour and renewed Arab hopes.

Source: The Israel-Arab Reader: A Documentary History of the Middle East Conflict, rev. ed., Walter Laqueur and Barry Rubin, eds. (New York, 1984), 185–89.

Israel used to boast a great deal, and the Western powers, headed by the United States and Britain, used to ignore and even despise us and consider us of no value. But now that the time has come — and I have already said in the past that we will decide the time and place and not allow them to decide — we must be ready for triumph and not for a recurrence of the 1948 comedies. We shall triumph, God willing.

Preparations have already been made. We are now ready to confront Israel. They have claimed many things about the 1956 Suez war, but no one believed them after the secrets of the 1956 collusion were uncovered — that mean collusion in which Israel took part. Now we are ready for the confrontation. We are now ready to deal with the entire Palestine question.

The issue now at hand is not the Gulf of Aqabah, the Straits of Tiran, or the withdrawal of the UNEF, but the rights of the Palestine people. It is the aggression which took place in Palestine in 1948 with the collaboration of Britain and the United States. It is the expulsion of the Arabs from Palestine, the usurpation of their rights, and the plunder of their property. It is the disavowal of all the UN resolutions in favour of the Palestinian people. . . .

If the United States and Britain are partial to Israel, we must say that our enemy is not only Israel but also the United States and Britain and treat them as such. If the Western Powers disavow our rights and ridicule and despise us, we Arabs must teach them to respect us and take us seriously. Otherwise all our talk about Palestine, the Palestine people, and Palestinian rights will be null and void and of no consequence. We must treat enemies as enemies and friends as friends. . . .

After my statements yesterday I met the War Minister Shams Badran and learned from him what took place in Moscow. I wish to tell you today that the Soviet Union is a friendly Power and stands by us as a friend. In all our dealings with the Soviet Union — and I have been dealing with the USSR since 1955 — it has not made a single request of us. The USSR has never interfered in our policy or internal affairs. . . . When I met Shams Badran yesterday he handed me a message from the Soviet Premier Kosygin saying that the USSR supported us in this battle and would not allow any Power to intervene until matters were restored to what they were in 1956. . . .

Brothers, we will work for world peace with all the power at our disposal, but we will also hold tenaciously to our rights with all the power at our disposal.

This is our course. On this occasion, I address myself to our brothers in Aden and say: Although occupied with this battle, we have not forgotten you.

We are with you. We have not forgotten the struggle of Aden and the occupied South for liberation. Aden and the occupied South must be liberated and colonialism must end. We are with them; present matters have not taken our minds from Aden.

I thank you for taking the trouble to pay this visit. Moreover, your presence is an honour to the Qubbah Palace, and I am pleased to have met you.

Peace be with you.

DOCUMENT 6.3

ABBA EBAN

SPEECH TO THE U.N. SECURITY COUNCIL ON ISRAEL'S REASONS FOR GOING TO WAR
June 6, 1967

Delivered the day after Israel attacked Egypt, Israeli Foreign Minister Abba Eban's account illustrates the official Israeli rhetorical perspective, but likewise reflects the impact of Arab rhetoric and threats of Israel's destruction. According to Eban, Egypt intended to attack, as did other Arab forces. Israel stood alone but determined to act against a dictator, Nasser, whose actions are compared to Adolf Hitler and his extermination of the Jews during the Holocaust.

I thank you, Mr President, for giving me this opportunity to address the Council. I have just come from Jerusalem to tell the Security Council that Israel, by its independent action and sacrifice, has passed from serious danger to successful resistance. . . .

Let me try to evoke the point at which our fortunes stood.

An army, greater than any force ever assembled in history in Sinai, had massed against Israel's southern frontier. Egypt had dismissed the United Nations forces which symbolized the international interest in the maintenance of peace in our region. Nasser had provocatively brought five infantry divisions and two armoured divisions up to our very gates; 80,000 men and 900 tanks were poised to move.

A special striking force, comprising an armoured division with at least 200 tanks, was concentrated against Elath at the Negev's southern tip. Here was a clear design to cut the southern Negev off from the main body of our State. For Egypt had openly proclaimed that Elath did not form part of Israel and had predicted that Israel itself would soon expire. The proclamation was empty; the prediction now lies in ruins. . . .

Jordan had been intimidated, against its better interest, into joining a defence pact. It is not a defence pact at all: it is an aggressive pact, of which I saw the consequences with my own eyes yesterday in the shells falling upon institutions of health and culture in the City of Jerusalem. Every house and street in Jerusalem now came into the range of fire as a result of Jordan's adherence to this pact; so also did the crowded, and pathetically narrow coastal strip in which so much of Israel's life and population is concentrated.

Iraqi troops reinforced Jordanian units in areas immediately facing vital and vulnerable Israeli communication centres. Expeditionary forces from Alge-

Source: T. G. Fraser, *The Middle East, 1914–1979* (London, 1980), 107–9.

ria and Kuwait had reached Egyptian territory. Nearly all the Egyptian forces which had been attempting the conquest of the Yemen had been transferred to the coming assault upon Israel. Syrian units, including artillery, overlooked Israeli villages in the Jordan Valley. Terrorist groups came regularly into our territory to kill, plunder and set off explosives, the most recent occasion was five days ago.

In short, there was peril for Israel wherever it looked. Its manpower had been hastily mobilized. Its economy and commerce were beating with feeble pulses. Its streets were dark and empty. There was an apocalyptic air of approaching peril. And Israel faced this danger alone.

We were buoyed up by an unforgettable surge of public sympathy across the world. The friendly Governments expressed the rather ominous hope that Israel would manage to live, but the dominant theme of our condition was danger and solitude.

Now there could be no doubt what was intended for us. I heard President Nasser's speech on 26 May. He said: "We intend to open a general assault against Israel. This will be total war. Our basic aim is the destruction of Israel." On 2 June, the Egyptian Commander-in-Chief in Sinai, General Murtagi, published his order of the day, calling on his troops to wage a war of destruction against Israel. Here, then, was a systematic, overt, proclaimed design at politicide, the murder of a State.

The policy, the arms, the men had all been brought together, and the State thus threatened with collective assault was itself the last sanctuary of a people which had seen six million of its sons exterminated by a more powerful dictator two decades before.

7

WAR AND THE SEARCH FOR PEACE IN THE MIDDLE EAST

1967–1976

OR ITS CITIZENS and Jews everywhere, Israel's victory in the Six-Day War was an unprecedented triumph, interpreted by many as an almost mystical deliverance from the Arab foe. The victory gave the Jewish state a new set of frontiers that promised greater security by distancing Arab armies from the nation's heartland. Israel now considered the borders established by the 1949 armistice agreements to be invalid. Its leaders declared that they would not withdraw from any territory except in return for full peace agreements negotiated directly with Arab states.

For the Arabs the 1967 war was a shocking debacle. Nasser resigned from office, only to be swept back in by a massive public outcry of support. But his policies and those of his allies were in disarray. At the Khartoum Conference in August 1967 the Arab states appeared open to diplomacy but also called for immediate restoration of the captured territories without specifying any concessions such as peace agreements on their part.

Officially, the United States backed Israel's position of no withdrawal without peace agreements. However, the Johnson administration and later the Nixon administration expected that Israel would ultimately withdraw from nearly all the lands it occupied in 1967 and that any border changes would be minor. The United States supported the United Nations resolution condemning Israel for unilaterally annexing East Jerusalem. Nevertheless, Johnson and his aides treaded cautiously out of sympathy and because of the tremendous outburst of American public support. American Jews were mobilized as never before, both monetarily and politically. Consequently, the United States expressed in public full support for Israel but sought in private to moderate its position. Israeli governments tried to "forge a de facto if not formal alliance" with the United States to ensure that the United States did not try to balance Israeli and Arab interests. Israel hoped to force the Arabs to meet its terms, which were not Washington's.[1]

Diplomatic initiatives between 1967 and 1975 were seriously affected by governmental and organizational factionalism. Israeli cabinets were often paralyzed by differences over what territories should be retained and what should be offered in return for peace. Nasser attempted to balance his hope for negotiations with the desires of his military command for renewed hostilities, all the while facing increasing domestic unrest. Soviet policy was divided. Diplomats and Communist Party heads apparently backed the negotiations, whereas military officials opposed them out of fear that they would lose access to the Egyptian bases they had recently acquired.

The Nixon administration's approaches to the Arab-Israeli conflict were severely hampered by the rivalry between National Security Adviser Henry Kissinger and Secretary of State William Rogers. Rogers and the State Department viewed the issue principally as a regional problem that should be resolved through negotiations, in concert with the Soviet Union if necessary. Kissinger, a globalist, wanted to oust the Soviets from the region before undertaking such talks in order to establish total American dominance of the negotiating process. The State Department thus backed joint Soviet-American efforts to bring Israel and Egypt together while Kissinger worked to frustrate them.

This stalemate lasted until the Egyptians and the Syrians attacked Israel in October 1973, hoping to compel American diplomatic involvement that might promote peace talks. Kissinger exploited the new circumstances to force discussions between Egypt and Israel. These exchanges and later negotiations with Syria led to agreements in 1974–1975 to disengage forces on the Golan Heights and in the Sinai that resulted, on the Egyptian side, in the Camp David Accords of 1978.

THE SEARCH FOR NEGOTIATING LEVERAGE, 1967–1971

Officially, Israel called for direct negotiations without preconditions, presenting a public image of conciliation that enabled Israel, with Arab rejection of these terms, to avoid defining what it might seek to absorb. This was the only way the Eshkol cabinet could survive, but it indicated a "paralysis in decision making" that served the interests of those advocating settlements in all the lands, not simply the West Bank.[2] With respect to that area, Menachem Begin, minister without portfolio, seemed to support de facto annexation. He demanded full government approval of Jewish settlements there, a position espoused also by a new movement, the Greater Land of Israel, that arose immediately following the war. The Greater Land of Israel movement included many who belonged to the Labor camp, indicating a spectrum of support beyond that of Begin's Herut ideology. Moshe Dayan juggled competing political platforms. He appeared to favor West Bank settlements, but he did not rule out autonomy for the Arab population or a possible restoration of Jordanian sovereignty over the Arab residents while the region remained part of Israel. On the other hand, he admitted that encouraging settlements in the West Bank would guarantee Jordanian rejection of that option, leaving the area open to full Israeli control. The labor minister, Yigael Allon, drafted a plan in July 1967 that would provide for an

Israeli security belt along the Jordan River valley, strategically situated to block any Arab invasion route. Otherwise, he seemed more amenable to recognizing Jordanian sovereignty over the Arab inhabitants of the West Bank and most of the land. He focused on settling and keeping the Golan Heights.[3]

This debate occurred as citizens began to establish settlements in the conquered territories during the summer of 1967, seeking, as they had during the mandate, to "create facts" to establish a Jewish presence on land that would become inalienable, thereby negating future calls for compromise. They thus preempted government policymaking, at times with the collusion of cabinet members, despite official government assurances that most occupied lands, excluding the West Bank, would be returned in exchange for peace agreements.

Some of these settlements were in the West Bank, but two others were in the Golan Heights and the Sinai, areas the government had told the United States were likely to be returned to Syria and Egypt. Indeed, the Golan settlement began in mid-July, supported by the military commanders in the region. Labor Minister Allon then unilaterally allotted unemployment funds to the settlers to finance their efforts and lobbied successfully to gain ex post facto cabinet approval; in late September the new kibbutz was awarded 6,000 dunams (1,500 acres) in the Qunaitra region. This action set a precedent that would be repeated, despite the opinion of the Foreign Ministry's legal counsel that civilian settlements in the territories violated international law.[4]

By mid-November, the U.S. State Department considered that Abba Eban's promise of June 9 that "Israel was [not] seeking territorial aggrandizement and had no 'colonial' aspirations" no longer carried weight. Instead, Israel's increased demands for direct talks with Arab leaders to the exclusion of other options now represented a tactic signaling "the prospect of permanent Israeli occupation of the territories now held."[5] By mid-1968 Israel's initial proposals to the United States were quietly dropped as a consensus to keep the Golan Heights emerged, but no Israeli government stated this openly until the elections of 1969 when the Labor Party was forced to present its platform for the lands taken in 1967.

Arab reactions to the defeat in the June war reflected the stances that various leaders had assumed before the conflict and offered Israeli expansionists ammunition for their arguments. Husayn of Jordan sought the United States' assurances that it would seek to restore the West Bank to him and would help rebuild his armed forces. Syria, backed by Iraq and Algeria, refused to consider a diplomatic resolution to the crisis. Nasser combined military threats of retaliation with diplomatic overtures. Seeking greater Soviet assistance to rebuild his forces, he granted them additional military facilities, especially in the port of Alexandria, where a Soviet naval presence might offset the power of the American Sixth Fleet. Countering Israeli troops on the east bank of the Suez Canal, which remained closed until 1975, was a major priority.

On the other hand, Nasser drew closer to Husayn and King Faysal of Saudi Arabia, hoping to use them to create contacts with the United States, with whom he had broken diplomatic relations in June. Despite his defiant rhetoric, Nasser's interests lay principally with the Arab moderates. Both he and Husayn hoped to receive subsidies from the oil states of Saudi Arabia, Kuwait, and Libya to replace the revenues lost through the war. He also wished to resolve the Yemen imbroglio, cutting costs and again improving relations with the Saudis. But he preferred to accomplish these tasks within the framework of a unified Arab position, which meant that no public response to Israeli or Western overtures was possible until an Arab summit was held.[6]

The Khartoum Conference

The Khartoum Conference took place in Khartoum, Sudan, at the end of August 1967. Most heads of state attended, although the Syrians boycotted the sessions. Nasser and King Faysal resolved their differences over Yemen, and subsidies to Egypt and Jordan were approved. The key resolution stated that

> the Arab heads of state have agreed to unite their political efforts at the international and diplomatic level to eliminate the effects of the aggression and to ensure the withdrawal of the aggressive Israeli forces from the Arab lands which have been occupied since the aggression of 5 June. This will be done within the framework of the main principles by which the Arab states abide, namely, no peace with Israel, no recognition of Israel, no negotiations with it, and insistence on the rights of the Palestinian people in their own country.[7]

The text was a compromise. The first sentence, backed by Nasser and Husayn, stressed political resolution of the problem. The second sentence appeared to negate the first by rejecting negotiations. Nasser and Husayn, however, believed that they had gained agreement for pursuing diplomatic options with a nod to the intransigence demanded by the Syrian regime and the Palestinians, a stance recognized by the U.S. State Department and confirmed by recent scholarship. They recognized the need to give Israel de facto, though not de jure, recognition through negotiations conducted by third parties, specifically the United Nations, if Israel would return to its prewar frontiers. They could discard the Palestinians at the proper moment.

Israel and the Arab states interpreted the stalemate in ways that vindicated their stances. The Israelis refused intermediaries, fearing outside attempts to compromise their position: withdrawal only in return for full peace agreements signed through direct negotiations with individual Arab states. Determined to keep some territory and to have Arab states acknowledge its right to do so, Israel would benefit from a continuing status quo; it gave them military advantages, which they would not cede in exchange for promises that might re-create the conditions that led to the 1967 war.

But this position, reinforced in the Israeli perspective by Syrian and Palestinian calls for armed struggle to regain the territories, justified to many Arabs their rejection of Israeli terms. They stressed Israel's withdrawal from the territories as a precondition for the tacit recognition of Israel's right to exist, whereas Israel demanded explicit recognition in return for partial withdrawal from the lands they had acquired. They viewed Israel's call for direct negotiations as an attempt to humiliate them and as a pretext for progressive annexation, regardless of Israeli statements that no conditions existed. For them, proof existed in Israel's immediate incorporation of East Jerusalem and its declaration that its status was nonnegotiable, as well as in the various statements by its ministers indicating that regions such as the West Bank should not be returned.

Deliberate Ambiguity: Security Council Resolution 242

Despite their cold war rivalry and the chasm between the Arab and Israeli negotiating platforms, the Soviet Union and the United States attempted to reach an agreement on a suitable framework within which peace talks might be held. The Soviet Union was willing to rearm Egypt but encouraged Nasser to be open to diplomatic overtures. Similarly, the United States, while committed to ensuring Israel's military parity with, if not superiority over, its Arab opponents, also favored discussions. And if, in the words of Moshe Dayan and Golda Meir, Israel sat by the phone waiting for the Arabs to call, the Americans occasionally tried to lend the Arabs a phone booth and an area code that might satisfy some of their demands as well.

In July 1967 the United States and the Soviet Union negotiated a draft agreement they were prepared to present to the U.N. General Assembly as a basis for resolving the questions raised by the Israeli occupation of Arab lands. This preliminary effort, once modified, led to the passage of Security Council Resolution 242 on November 22, 1967 (see Document 7.1). It has remained the official basis of negotiating efforts to the present.

Lord Caradon, British representative to the council, drafted the final version. As he saw it,

> the Arab countries insist that we must direct our special attention to the recovery of their territories. The Israelis tell us that withdrawal must never be to the old precarious peace but to secure boundaries. Both are right. The aims of the two sides do not conflict. To imagine that one can be secured without the other is a delusion. They are of equal validity and equal necessity.[8]

The resolution stressed the "inadmissibility of the acquisition of territory by war and the need to work for a just and lasting peace in which every state in the area can live in security." It called for "withdrawal of Israel from territories occupied in the recent conflict" and for "termination of all claims or states of belligerency and respect for and acknowledgment of the sovereignty, territorial integrity, and political independence of every state in the area and their right to live in peace within secure and recognized boundaries free from threats and acts of force." Another clause referred to "a just settlement of the [Palestinian] refugee problem." The resolution concluded by requesting the appointment of a special U.N. representative to initiate negotiations based on the principles espoused in the document.[9]

Resolution 242 incorporated language from the Soviet-American draft of July, specifically the reference to the inadmissibility of acquiring territory by war. But whereas that draft called for Israel's withdrawal from "the territories" occupied, Resolution 242 deliberately omitted the word "the" from the clause because Israel refused to agree to withdraw from all the territories it had taken. Nevertheless, the Arab states were assured that the omission was insignificant and that only minor border changes were envisaged; the operative statement was the initial reference to "the inadmissibility of the acquisition of territory by war." Jordan agreed to sign the document only after being told by the United States' U.N. delegate, Arthur Goldberg, that his country would strive to return the West Bank to Jordan.

The United States continued to tell Israel in private that it expected a "virtually complete withdrawal."[10] Nevertheless, Israel immediately offered a different interpretation, namely, that secure boundaries were the key to any peace and that this would require significant rather than minor revisions of the 1949 armistice lines. This position was later supported by Goldberg, who argued that "the resolution does not insist on only 'minor border rectifications,'" a statement that was legally correct but that differed from the American position he defended at the time and that was held also by Great Britain, France, and the Soviet Union.[11] Finally, Eshkol issued a statement shortly after the approval of Resolution 242 insisting on direct negotiations, a stance that rejected the negotiating framework established by the document. From his point of view, the role of the U.N. negotiator, Gunnar Jarring of Sweden, was to be confined to attaining the Arabs' agreement to such talks.

The negotiating climate was hardly propitious. Egypt reacted to Eshkol's statement by arguing that Jarring should focus solely on Israeli withdrawal. Syria refused to sign the resolution and called for renewed raids by Palestinians against Israel. The Palestinians were themselves determined to thwart Jarring's efforts. The reference in Resolution 242 to "a just settlement of the refugee problem" threatened to establish the Palestinian question as a nonpolitical issue, which would deny the PLO the sovereignty it claimed over its former homeland. These Arab positions in turn reinforced the arguments of those Israelis who called for the retention of the territory as security buffers because the Arabs would never agree to peace.

With the stage set for further confrontation, the United States began to withdraw from active involvement in the region. The Tet offensive in Vietnam in February 1968 led to Lyndon Johnson's decision in March not to run for reelection. He had already promised Prime Minister Eshkol in January that the

United States would furnish Israel with Phantom jets along with the grant of Skyhawk aircraft promised in October 1967, thus giving Israel clear air superiority in the area. The presidential election campaign, in which both candidates declared full support for Israel, precluded any likelihood of diplomacy in the Middle East.[12] American initiatives now awaited the installation of the new president, Richard Nixon, in January 1969.

PALESTINIAN AGENDAS AND THEIR REGIONAL REPERCUSSIONS

In the midst of Arab and Israeli efforts to define their terms of diplomatic engagement, Palestinian groups reevaluated the means by which they could overcome Israel and regain control of Palestine. Yasir Arafat, the Fatah leader, advocated a war of liberation from within the newly occupied West Bank; he assumed that Fatah could mobilize great support among the million Palestinians now suddenly brought under Israeli rule. He entered the West Bank in July 1967 to direct the effort, but it failed due to effective Israeli retaliation and intelligence efforts and the unwillingness of most Palestinians there to participate.[13]

Jordan and the Palestinians

Fatah's failure in the West Bank led to a marriage of convenience between Arafat and Jordan's King Husayn. Husayn, unable to submit to Israel's terms for direct negotiations because of existing political tensions, sought indirect talks with Israel mediated by the United States. He decided to tolerate Fatah's assaults on Israeli posts in the West Bank, hoping to discourage Israeli settlement efforts and possibly encourage American diplomatic intervention. Husayn assumed he could discard Arafat and Fatah if the prospect of talks arose. Conversely, Arafat hoped to use Jordan as a springboard for escalating the violence of the confrontation with Israel. Once begun, Husayn found it increasingly difficult to restrict Fatah's raids or those of other Palestinian groups that began to emerge.

Israeli reprisals into the Jordanian East Bank began in February 1968, intended, as in the 1950s, to force Husayn to quell the resistance. But now the situation was different in that there were organized groups to rally the Palestinians from the camps to their cause. A massive Israeli response against the Jordanian town of al-Karamah in February met with stiff Palestinian opposition, staffed mainly by Fatah and aided by Jordanian artillery. Though technically a defeat for the Palestinians, they stood their ground and inflicted numerous casualties on the Israelis. Karamah became a great propaganda victory for Fatah. Recruits flocked to join, just as they did following further Israeli raids on the towns of Irbid and Salt. As time went on, Fatah and rival groups began to take control of the refugee camps in Jordan and removed them from Husayn's authority.

Palestinian Factions and the PLO

Fatah's larger size seldom enabled it to direct the Palestinian resistance, as the movement became increasingly fragmented. A major rival had emerged in December 1967 with the creation of the Popular Front for the Liberation of Palestine (PFLP) under Dr. George Habash.[14] Sympathetic to the pan-Arab nationalism of the 1950s, Habash had directed the Palestinian-dominated group called the Arab National Movement (ANM) during much of the 1960s. He now formed the PFLP with Ahmad Jibril who, unlike Habash, had good relations with the Syrian Baathist leadership. Habash was imprisoned by the Syrians for much of 1968 while seeking Damascus's approval for raids from Syrian territory. During the year, three factions split from the PFLP. Jibril formed his own group, backed by Syria, and another faction received Egyptian assistance. Finally, many of the younger members of the PFLP broke with Habash in early 1969 to follow Nayif Hawatmah in creating the Popular Democratic Front for the Liberation of Palestine (PDFLP).

The differences among these groups were both ideological and tactical. Fatah, led by Arafat, was composed primarily of Sunni Muslims who focused their attention on the recovery of Palestine. Arafat stressed that the Palestinians should not become involved in Arab state rivalries. Habash and Hawatmah were Christians. Habash sought to form a broad Arab revolutionary front that would radicalize the regimes of the Arab world as the first step toward the liberation of Palestine. Hawatmah agreed but saw himself as more truly imbued with Marxist-Leninist principles than Habash was. Factionalism became endemic in the Palestinian movement. Because the Syrians backed Hawatmah as well as Jibril, and Nasser helped another faction, Habash turned to Iraq for financial assistance. Fatah sought to maintain contacts with all regimes.

These disputes became implanted in the structure of the Palestine Liberation Organization itself. Ahmad al-Shuqayri had been forced to resign as its head at the end of 1967. After a year of interim leadership, the PLO decided to absorb the commando groups, giving them membership on the Palestine national council. Fatah gained the most seats, and at the national congress held in February 1969, Arafat was elected head of the PLO. Fatah held 33 of the 57 seats allotted to the commandos out of a total of 105. This distribution suggested that Arafat could not easily lead the PLO or coordinate its activities despite the call in the revised charter, issued in 1968, for different groups to submerge their identities to unite in a common struggle to liberate Palestine (see Document 7.2). What often mattered most was the nature of Palestinian militancy, stressed in the 1968 charter. It declared that "armed struggle was the only means to liberate Palestine," to be accomplished through commando actions, often undertaken by factions competing for prestige and recruits.

Armed struggle was a long-term strategy, not a tactic to be discarded if diplomacy seemed preferable. In addition, the title of the 1968 charter changed from that of 1964, from *Mithaq al-Qawmi* to *Mithaq al-Watani*. This change signaled a major revision of the significance of the word "national," from one linked to pan-Arabism and Arab unity to one that stressed a distinct Palestinian nationalism and political identity, a victory for Arafat over the broader Arab concerns of Habash.[15]

A particular problem was the hostility of Habash's PFLP to Arafat and Fatah. The former was determined to pursue his course of overthrowing conservative Arab monarchs, regardless of the opposition of the majority of the PLO. In the view of a colleague of Arafat's,

> it wasn't that we didn't want to [get rid of the PFLP]. But it was practically impossible to unify the commando organizations when each one of them was supported and subsidized by one or another Arab country whose causes and quarrels they espoused. That is why the Central Committee of the Palestinian Resistance, instead of being a coordinating and decision-making body, turned out to be a sort of parliament where all the conflicts and intrigues of the Arab world were reflected. Yasir Arafat, speaking for more than half the Fidayin members, had to deal as an equal with the delegate of a tiny group just because the latter was the protégé of one of the richest Arab states [Iraq]. That's how difficult, if not impossible, it was to enforce even a minimum of discipline at the very heart of the movement.[16]

This uncoordinated militancy by groups vying with one another for prestige left little room for a firm policy to be established with respect to goals or activities. It also placed greater pressure on Israel to respond not only against Jordan but also against Lebanon, where Palestinian groups were seeking to expand their activities.

Lebanon, the Palestinians, and Israel

The Lebanese had long avoided involvement in the Arab-Israeli conflict, but from 1968 onward, various groups inside and outside the PLO tried to establish a new front in southern Lebanon for attacks on Israel. At the same time, rival factions within the PFLP began to use Lebanon as a base for hijacking operations. Jibril oversaw the hijacking of an El Al (Israeli) plane to Algiers in July, perhaps seeking to acquire prestige against both Arafat and his supposed ally, Habash, who was still in prison. In December, Habash ordered an attack on an El Al plane in Athens in which two were killed, an action displaying militancy but also competition with a rival for recruits. In response, Israeli forces landed at the Beirut airport the same month and destroyed thirteen planes belonging to Arab airlines. Israel announced that it held the Lebanese government responsible for tolerating PFLP activities.[17] Israel's action, a classic Ben-Gurionist response of massive if selective retaliation designed to teach the Lebanese a lesson, again had the opposite effect. It aroused an uproar that forced the collapse of the government and led to civil strife as Lebanese groups either backed or opposed support for the Palestinians. From this point onward, the question of the Palestinians became part of the question of Lebanese society with all its confessional splits and rivalries.

Palestinian refugees, who numbered 14 percent of the Lebanese population in 1968, had never been permitted to integrate into Lebanese society. The Maronite Catholic community feared that the infusion of more Muslim citizens would renew calls for a new census, and viewed PLO activities as an additional provocation. Most Lebanese Muslims sympathized with the Palestinians and their cause, based in part on their general feeling that they too were deprived of rights due them by their numbers but continually unrecognized by the Maronite hierarchy, which was determined to preserve its long-standing dominance. Throughout much of 1969, Lebanese military and security forces confronted Palestinian groups and sought to restrict their actions in the midst of growing domestic tensions that remained unresolved until they exploded into true civil war in 1975.

The immediate crisis was overcome only after the signing of the "Cairo Agreement" of 1969 between Arafat and the Lebanese government that granted significant concessions to the PLO. In return for Arafat's acceptance of Lebanese sovereignty and promise to respect it, the government granted the PLO autonomy in controlling the refugee camps that had previously been supervised by Lebanese security forces. Lebanon also gave the PLO specific routes of access to the Israeli frontier and permitted Syrian supply lines to the groups in southern Lebanon. In return for a modus vivendi, Lebanon had decided to look the other way, but the result was intensified Maronite opposition accompanied by the expansion of Christian paramilitary groups outside government control that prepared to confront the Palestinians.[18]

By the end of 1969, Israel faced greatly increased PLO activity on both the Jordanian and Lebanese borders. At the same time, a new Israeli cabinet, headed by Golda Meir following the death of Levi Eshkol, decided to try to destroy Nasser. This decision, taken amidst American and U.N. peace overtures, resulted in a massive infusion of Soviet personnel into Egypt that served to neutralize the Egyptian-Israeli frontier along the Suez Canal.

WARS OF ATTRITION AND COLD WAR DIPLOMACY: THE ROGERS PLAN

Although the term "war of attrition" has usually been applied to Egyptian-Israeli clashes between March 1969 and August 1970, when a cease-fire was achieved, intermittent strife had begun much earlier. In September 1968, in a failed attempt to arouse renewed diplomatic interest at the United Nations, the Egyptians initiated a new round of artillery duels with Israeli forces across the Suez Canal. Israel reacted by raiding deeper into Egypt and by accelerating the construction of a massive fortification along its side of the canal, the Bar-Lev line. The Egyptians then undertook a more extended war of attrition in March 1969, intended to weaken the Israeli defenses through intensive artillery barrages, and to create conditions conducive to an attack across the canal that would establish a limited bridgehead. The war and Egyptian gains would then compel the great powers to intercede to stop the fighting, thus opening the way for diplomacy to deal with the newly created circumstances—precisely what would happen in 1973.

These duels across the Suez Canal were accompanied by Egyptian and Israeli demands for the latest weapons technology from their respective sponsors, the Soviets and the Americans. Nasser, under Soviet pressure, had agreed to Security Council Resolution (SCR) 242. In return, the Soviets shipped aid to the point that by October 1968, Egyptian military supplies were superior in quality and quantity to those available at the outbreak of the 1967 war. It was this infusion of weaponry that inspired him to initiate combat with the Israelis that September.[19]

Israeli officials were determined to maintain their vaunted military superiority throughout the region, not simply over Egypt, especially regarding offensive weapons; this would permit them to refuse negotiations that failed to meet their terms. American officials tried to restrict arms sales, hoping to pressure Israel to be more flexible in its negotiating stance. Israel reversed the nature of the exchange, demanding guarantees of arms deliveries before agreeing to discuss diplomatic initiatives. A fundamental contradiction thus emerged in the American-Israeli relationship as the Nixon administration took office in January 1969. Israel sought arms to secure the territorial status quo until the Arab states submitted to its conditions, which entailed direct talks and substantial border revisions. The United States, in contrast, hoped to use promises of arms to gain Israeli concessions that far exceeded what Israel was willing to consider. Israel's ability to use its supporters in Congress and pressure groups to modify or preempt administration policies often proved successful.

Egypt's escalation of March 1969 also failed. By July, Israeli retaliatory raids had wiped out Egypt's protective air defense missile systems as well as its heavy weapons. Israel then moved at will from July to December with full air superiority, apparently placing Egypt at its mercy. By January 1970, Israeli jets were flying over the pyramids outside Cairo, tactics that were intended to humiliate the Egyptian populace as well as the military; the Meir cabinet hoped to encourage Nasser's removal from office.

But the Israeli raids backfired. In desperation Nasser went to Moscow, asking not only for more weapons but also for Soviet combat personnel and technicians. The Soviets complied. By mid-March 1970, new and extensive emplacements of advanced SAM (surface-to-air) missiles were operational, and Soviet pilots were flying missions. Israeli forces were once more restricted to the canal zone area, where their air force suffered significant losses during the summer. This military stalemate led to the August 1970 cease-fire, but only after intense debates and rivalries within the Nixon administration, triggered in part by the developments along the Suez Canal.[20]

Competing Agendas: Nixon Administration Rivalries and Middle East Policy

Throughout 1969, Egyptian-Israeli hostilities had been accompanied by ongoing talks between the Soviet Union and the United States intended to establish conditions for a cease-fire and subsequent negotiations toward a full peace accord. As a result of these efforts, Secretary of State William Rogers proposed the "Rogers Plan," announced on December 9. Rogers's terms reflected assumptions found in the majority interpretation of Resolution 242: nearly full Israeli withdrawal in return for an indirectly negotiated mutual recognition of sovereignty via United Nations auspices.

Rogers's initiative infuriated the Israelis. Golda Meir's cabinet immediately authorized bombing raids into Egypt far beyond the limits previously imposed. As noted, it was this January 1970 escalation that induced Nasser to seek Soviet intervention. Ironically, Israel chose this course of action on the advice of its ambassador in Washington, Yitzhak Rabin, Israeli chief of staff during the 1967 war. He reported American encouragement of Israeli efforts to destroy Egypt's military and indirectly humiliate the Soviets.[21] Here, the cold war faction in the Nixon administration, centered around Henry Kissinger and Nixon, encouraged Israel to undermine U.S. State Department diplomatic overtures.

The Soviet military presence in Egypt sparked new diplomatic initiatives by Secretary of State Rogers, who suggested a cease-fire that included a memorandum of understanding. It stated that both parties accepted Security Council Resolution 242 as the basis of negotiations, with a specific reference to "Israeli withdrawal from territories occupied in the 1967 conflict." Egypt and Jordan welcomed Rogers's proposals but the Israeli government accepted them under duress and only after Nixon had assured Prime Minister Golda Meir that American military support would continue and that the United States would not back calls for Israel's withdrawal to the prewar lines of June 4, 1967; left unresolved was the wide gap between American and Israeli conceptions of what Israel's future frontiers might be. Even then, Israel's acceptance was costly. Members of the Gahal Party, led by Menachem Begin, resigned from the Meir cabinet to protest Israeli acknowledgment of the principle of its withdrawal from territory before peace terms had been established with the Arab states. Israeli acceptance of the cease-fire, which went into effect in August 1970, marked the first time the government had publicly declared its willingness to withdraw from any territory taken in 1967.[22]

The August 1970 cease-fire granted Nasser a respite that enabled him to consolidate new missile defense systems. But he concluded, wrongly, that Rogers's intervention opened lines of communication with the United States that might free him from total reliance on Soviet diplomatic efforts. Most Nixon administration officials still viewed the Middle East conflict more in terms of an American-Soviet rivalry than as a series of disputes stemming from regional antagonisms. Indeed, Rogers's attempts to spark negotiations had been conducted in an atmosphere of rivalry within the Nixon administration where the president quietly undermined proposals he had supposedly approved.

Globalism vs. Regionalism under Nixon: Analysis

This dysfunctional approach derived from the Nixon-Kissinger focus on the global, cold war rivalry with the Soviets set against Rogers's Middle East efforts. Although immersed in Vietnam, Nixon and Kissinger, then national security adviser, decided to challenge Moscow by balancing tactics of détente and confrontation, using the latter to encourage the former with respect to trade and diplomacy.[23] As for the Middle East, Kissinger believed that diplomacy should await the moment when the United States could dominate the negotiating process and exclude the Soviets. He saw a willingness to work with the Soviets as undermining American power, whereas Rogers and the State Department argued that cooperation with the Soviets had merit if each power could bring its satellite to the bargaining table. Also fueling this tension was Kissinger's ego. He strove to control all foreign policy and automatically denigrated ideas he had not proposed.[24]

Israeli officials recognized the Rogers-Kissinger impasse and cultivated Kissinger. During Israel's election campaign in the fall of 1969, the Labor Party had committed itself to retaining the Golan Heights, Sharm al-Shaykh, and Gaza along with unspecified areas of the West Bank; Jerusalem was declared nonnegotiable. These terms clearly contradicted implementation of Resolution 242 as envisaged by Rogers. Israel's belief that it could discount Rogers was reinforced when Nixon established "a special channel between Kissinger and [Ambassador] Rabin to sidestep the State Department" in September.[25]

Then, in December 1969, Rogers announced his diplomatic initiative, unaware that Nixon had already assured Rabin he would not press for its acceptance. These assurances led Rabin to urge Golda Meir to order more extensive raids into Egypt in January 1970 that instead of forcing Nasser's removal resulted in the arrival of 15,000 Soviet military personnel. In short, the Nixon/Kissinger gambit to discredit Rogers resulted in a cold war crisis, a fiasco resolved only when the United States pushed for the August 1970 cease-fire, achieved thanks to Rogers's diplomacy.

Nonetheless, Kissinger's cold war globalist vision trumped Rogers's diplomatic initiatives, with Kissinger becoming secretary of state as well as national security adviser in 1973. He was willing to seek Israeli concessions but only after Arab leaders with ties to the Soviets abandoned them and turned to the United States: "Arab leaders would, I thought, have to come to us in the end."[26] In fact, an Arab dialogue with the United States would occur only after the 1973 war that was inspired by Arab frustration at the Nixon administration's disinterest in diplomacy. In the interim, Israel's hopes of blocking great-power pressures were aided by renewed Palestinian-Jordanian tensions that had far-reaching implications.

Jordan and the Palestinians, August–September 1970

If the Israeli government was upset at the August 1970 cease-fire established by the United States, the groups that comprised the PLO were horrified that Nasser and Husayn had signed such an agreement. Here there arose a symbiotic relationship between Israel and the Palestinians. Each dreaded peace plans that might undermine its position, but from differing vantage points. Israel feared outside intervention that might force it to give up territory it felt essential either for security reasons or, for many, because the West Bank was part of ancient Israel, the provinces of Judea and Samaria. The Palestinians watched their Arab sponsors for signs of willingness to reach a peace agreement that would include SCR 242's reference to the Palestinian refugee problem and ignore Palestinian rights of self-determination. From this perspective, Husayn and even Nasser were caught, at times, between the Israeli hammer and the Palestinian anvil, apparently willing to abandon the latter but offering conditions unacceptable to the former. For many Palestinians, however, the message was clear. The cease-fire should be destroyed if possible, and the means to do so existed in Jordan. Habash and Hawatmah now decided to overthrow King Husayn.

Palestinian-Jordanian relations had long been strained. PLO forays into the Israeli-held West Bank had accomplished little and had resulted in Israeli retaliations that caused many civilian casualties and damaged Jordan's economic infrastructure. What Arafat ultimately hoped for, the destruction of Israel, was to Husayn a fantasy; what Arafat might conceivably settle for, the West Bank, was unacceptable to the king. Husayn wanted the West Bank for himself and at most would permit Palestinian autonomy under the cloak of Jordanian sovereignty. Furthermore, the PLO sought a secure base of operations in Jordan, "a place where the revolutionaries [had] complete control and authority," which naturally meant a corresponding decrease of government legitimacy.[27] Palestinian militias began flouting Jordanian laws and intimidating the citizenry. Clashes erupted, most notably in June 1970 when animosity between Palestinian groups and Husayn's Arab Legion led to the PFLP's taking as hostages many Westerners staying in tourist hotels that the group commandeered. They were released only after Husayn agreed to realign his cabinet in accordance with Habash's demands, a humiliation not likely to be forgotten.

With the cease-fire declared in August, Arafat and a majority of the PLO hesitated, unwilling to confront Husayn directly but equally unwilling to challenge the PFLP and the PDFLP, who called for Husayn's overthrow. Matters came to a head when the PFLP hijacked four airliners between September 6 and 9, forcing three of them to land at an airfield twenty miles from Husayn's palace. Husayn once more capitulated to ensure the safety of the hostages, but when they were released and the planes were blown up, he turned against the Palestinians. The civil war began on September 16. Pitched battles erupted between Jordanian forces and most Palestinian groups, and Jordanian artillery shelled the refugee camps where the various organizations had their offices.

Over three thousand were killed and over eleven thousand wounded, the majority Palestinians and many of them civilians, before the conflict finally ended on September 25.

Husayn's triumph had not come easily. He had faced a Syrian tank invasion in support of the Palestinians that had early successes before his forces repulsed it. He had borne the censure of other Arab leaders, who strove to preserve the Palestinian resistance without causing Husayn's overthrow in the bargain. Intense negotiations brokered by Nasser finally contained the struggle, but only after Husayn agreed in principle to PLO leadership of the Palestinians in Jordan, an arrangement he subsequently ignored. In the process, exhausted by the strain of negotiations, Gamal Abd al-Nasser collapsed and died on September 28, 1970.

The Jordanian crisis prompted American considerations of great-power competition that redounded to Israel's benefit. Once the fighting erupted, Nixon declared that American intervention might be required and called for a show of force by the Sixth Fleet in the Eastern Mediterranean. But the Syrian tank strike called Nixon's hand with troubling implications: "U.S. military maneuvers were designed primarily to convey signals to the USSR . . . not to intervene directly in the fighting." American face was saved by Israeli promises of intervention on Husayn's behalf. The king committed his air force to attacks against the Syrian tank column only after assurances of supporting Israeli air strikes if requested. Israeli compliance "helped protect the United States from having its bluff exposed as a rather empty one."[28] In the end a regional confrontation had been resolved satisfactorily for Husayn, Israel, and the United States, whose leaders were pleased at what they believed to be the defeat of Soviet-sponsored unrest. Nixon and Kissinger had interpreted events in the global, cold war context where their allies had prevailed. Israel's offer of cooperation enhanced its image as an anticommunist ally, pushing into the background its obstructionist reputation regarding regional peace proposals. Nixon and Kissinger now advocated arms shipments to Israel that could be used to counter envisioned Soviet-encouraged machinations while the United States committed most of its resources to Vietnam.

The Jordanian Crisis: Regional and International Repercussions

The Jordanian civil war had numerous and far-reaching ramifications. The PLO had suffered a major setback that finally forced all Palestinian organizations to withdraw from Jordan after a renewed flare-up of fighting in July 1971. They moved to Lebanon, where their appearance in force further destabilized that country's domestic politics while embroiling it ever more directly in the conflict. Fatah-PFLP antagonisms over tactics continued, but even elements of Fatah now embarked on terrorist missions against Israelis abroad.

The most famous was undertaken by the Black September group, named after the September 1970 Jordanian affair, when it took eleven Israeli athletes and coaches hostage at the 1972 Olympic Games in Munich. All, along with five of their Palestinian captors, were killed, most during an abortive attempt by German forces to kill the Palestinians and rescue the Israelis. But Black September operations during the Olympics were only the most visible signs of a continuing war in which Palestinian groups sought to assassinate Israelis abroad, and Israeli agents and commandos retaliated in kind.

Here Lebanon again became the focal point of Israeli punitive raids. Air strikes and armed incursions into southern Lebanon against PLO positions resulted in many civilian as well as guerrilla dead and wounded. During 1973, Israeli squads landed near Beirut and assassinated three Fatah officials in their apartments. Other PLO officials were killed and wounded by car and letter bombs, indicating that Israeli agents could operate in Beirut with relative impunity. At the same time, PLO rocket attacks into northern Israel from Lebanon continued, with occasional casualties among the population of the northern settlements.

Not the least among the ironies related to the concentration of the PLO in Lebanon was the appearance in November 1970 of a new head of state in Syria, Hafiz al-Assad. Assad had sponsored the Syrian backing of Fatah and Arafat in 1965, but as president he sought to control Arafat. He used the Syrian-supported Palestinian militia, al-Saiqa, against Fatah and other groups when necessary and refused to allow PLO operations from Syria against Israel. Assad's fear that the Palestinians might draw the Syrians into an unplanned conflict with Israel greatly exacerbated Syrian-Palestinian tensions. Conversely, eschewing the confrontational style of his predecessor, Salah Jadid, Assad tried to restore relations between Syria and its former rivals, Egypt, Jordan, and Saudi Arabia.[29]

For Egypt, Nasser's sudden death inaugurated a series of changes that gradually led his successor, Anwar al-Sadat, to seek an accommodation with the United States regarding Israel. Much of Sadat's motivation was economic. Nasser's state capitalism had become mired in inefficiency in the mid-1960s. The 1967 conflict and the subsequent war of attrition undermined Egypt's economic health still further.[30] Sadat hoped to break both the diplomatic deadlock and Egypt's economic stagnation by appearing more forthcoming in negotiations and seeking American financial assistance in the process.

Most American policymakers considered Sadat a neophyte whose tenure as head of Egypt might be short. Rogers and the State Department continued to prod U.N. Ambassador Gunnar Jarring's attempt to implement Resolution 242 through mid-1971, at which point Jarring abandoned his efforts. Kissinger continued to criticize Rogers and Jarring to Nixon and to the Israelis through Ambassador Rabin. American initiatives were often uncoordinated; the State Department and Kissinger were undertaking inquiries without informing the other.[31]

Jarring withdrew from the negotiating process following his failure to get Israel to agree with Egypt to "parallel and simultaneous commitments" that might settle their differences. He asked Israel in February 1971 to withdraw to the pre-1967 borders in return for security arrangements that included extensive demilitarization of the Sinai and U.N. forces at Sharm al-Shaykh; Israel would also receive freedom of navigation through the Suez Canal. He asked Egypt to enter a peace agreement with Israel that included an end of belligerency and respect for Israel's independence and right to exist in secure boundaries. Sadat agreed to all terms and added others, which included settlement of the refugee problem in accordance with U.N. resolutions. Sadat's stance on refugees indicated that he had broken with the positions taken by the PLO and at the Khartoum Conference. Refusing to withdraw to prewar lines and insisting on direct negotiations without prior conditions, Israel rejected Sadat's offers; the Meir cabinet was determined to retain at least Sharm al-Shaykh and a strip of land connecting it to Israel.[32]

At year's end, American-Israeli relations were closer than ever. Kissinger had gradually taken over control of Middle East policy, at Nixon's behest, to create a positive climate conducive to Nixon's 1972 reelection campaign. Part of Nixon's campaign strategy was to divert Jewish votes from the Democrats by appearing supportive of Israel. Kissinger "assured Rabin that plane deliveries would continue and that State Department pressure would stop."[33] Rabin, in turn, openly backed Nixon's candidacy. At the same time the Nixon administration took advantage of Israel's popularity in Congress to place funding requests for recipients such as South Korea, Taiwan, and Cambodia on Israeli assistance bills.[34] The White House had no intention of openly concerning itself with the Middle East until after the 1972 elections.

THE 1973 WAR AND ITS CONSEQUENCES

Once Kissinger assumed control of Middle East policy in early 1972, he incorporated it within his concept of linkage. He investigated the possibility of Soviet agreement on principles for future approaches to the region while forgoing specific overtures until after Nixon's reelection in November. He and the Soviets reached a consensus on principles in the spring of 1972 that closely resembled the Jarring package that Sadat had accepted and the Israelis, with Kissinger's encouragement, had rebuffed in February 1971 — namely, support for peaceful coexistence and Resolution 242. However, the U.S.-Soviet joint communiqué to that effect had unintended consequences.

The Arabs: Seeking Responses to Signals

Though it was ostensibly threatening to Israel, it was Egypt that reacted angrily to the Soviet-American statement. Unaware of the Soviet talks with Kissinger and already frustrated with delays of arms supplies from Moscow, Sadat and his advisers believed the Soviets were allying themselves with the United States to maintain the status quo in the region. Given ongoing American aid to Israel, this would place Egypt at a disadvantage. It was particularly embarrassing to Sadat, who had been proclaiming since 1971 that the "year of decision" was at hand, threatening a new war in order to compel new diplomatic efforts that would end the diplomatic impasse. Sadat's military command resented Soviet control over many Egyptian military installations, and Sadat knew from various American channels that the United States demanded the expulsion of the Soviets before moving to attain peace in the Middle East.

On July 8, Sadat ordered that Russian advisers and military personnel leave Egypt within one week, a move that caught Washington as well as Moscow by surprise. Sadat acted for domestic as well as diplomatic reasons. He could mollify his military while still sending a message to Washington that its terms had been met. The timing, in the midst of an American election campaign, meant that Egypt did not expect an immediate response but that Cairo anticipated an American initiative once the elections were over. Sadat received assurances of this from Kissinger through private channels and Kissinger met privately twice in early 1973 with Sadat's security adviser, Hafiz Ismail. But no such undertaking occurred. By this time, Kissinger was on the verge of running the entire government, not simply its foreign policy. The scandal of the Watergate break-in was beginning to isolate Nixon from other matters, leaving in limbo most diplomacy other than that for Vietnam.

Kissinger assumed that the Middle East stalemate would last. His complacency solidified Egypt's determination to force the issue and finally convinced the Soviets that the United States would not undertake any corrective diplomacy following the elections. From February 1973 onward, the Soviets began supplying Egypt with offensive weaponry and the means of countering Israeli air strikes that they had withheld previously out of fear of encouraging an Egyptian attack.[35]

Kissinger also misjudged the circumstances in which other Arab leaders, not only Sadat, found themselves regarding the impasse in the region. Of particular importance was the role of Saudi Arabia, long close to the United States and seeking its protection against any threat of communist subversion. The Saudis agreed with Kissinger that the Soviets should be excluded from the region, but they challenged his argument that American support of Israel contributed to the success of that policy. Here also Saudi leaders became increasingly agitated about the continuing Israeli dominance of Jerusalem, a holy city to Islam and one that the Saudis, as the declared true practitioners of the faith, were determined to have returned to Muslim control. Once it became clear during 1973 that the United States might not act to break the Arab-Israeli deadlock, representatives of King Faysal began to warn American officials, as did Sadat, that war might erupt. The Saudis were also willing to consider the threat of a cutback in oil production that could seriously affect America's energy supplies.

American policymakers, recalling the Saudi-Egyptian hostility of the Nasser era, dismissed the idea that Egypt and the Saudis could achieve a rapprochement and considered an energy pinch improbable. But here a conjunction of factors created an unforeseen crisis. The Organization of Petroleum Exporting Countries (OPEC) had been formed in 1960 to create a common front to achieve higher prices and a greater share of the profits for the oil-producing countries. OPEC had had little success until the end of the decade. Then increasing demand and radical politics led to greater assertiveness by the oil states and greater willingness by the oil companies to reach agreements more beneficial to the former. Libya's Muammar al-Qadhdhafi, who took power in a coup in 1969, led the way in demanding at least 50 percent of the profits and a rise in price per barrel. He was supported in this by his ideological opposite, the shah of Iran, who, as America's ally, needed additional funds to buy the arms America wanted to sell him. Here the Saudis found themselves in the middle, seeking to moderate oil price increases but to gain a greater share in the running of the Arabian American Oil Company (ARAMCO), the oil consortium that controlled production in Arabia.[36]

From 1970 onward, experts warned that the United States was increasingly vulnerable in that its energy consumption and demand far outstripped its domestic production.[37] Unaware of the implications of this and distracted by Nixon's problems, Kissinger viewed Sadat's threat of war and Faysal's linking of oil prices to the Arab-Israeli issue as mere rhetoric. But Sadat was now joined by Syria's Assad, who also felt that Arab willingness to negotiate had been rebuffed. He had announced his acceptance of Resolution 242 in 1972, with no response. Eager to regain control of the Golan Heights, he joined Sadat in a concerted effort to create an Arab fait accompli and force new diplomatic probes that would achieve terms more favorable to the Arabs.

Israel and the Politics of Expansion: The Galili Document

On the eve of the 1973 war, Arab frustration was matched by Israeli confidence. Minister of Defense Dayan declared repeatedly during 1972 and 1973 that he did not envisage a war for at least a decade. The influx of new American weapons to Israel ensured its qualitative advantage over its Arab neighbors, meaning that Israel could reject Arab overtures it did not consider totally acceptable. This in turn enabled the Meir cabinet to avoid having to define the concessions that Israel might make, thus averting a domestic political storm. When Meir had stated in 1971 that Israel would retain the Golan Heights, Sharm al-Shaykh and a connecting road to Israel, and parts of the West Bank with the Sinai demilitarized once it was returned to Egypt, Begin attacked her for being too lenient.[38] But as new elections approached, scheduled for November 1973, the Labor Party suddenly found itself making a major shift toward annexation of territories it had previously defined as subject to negotiation and at least partial return.

As noted earlier, Israel's continued retention of the territories captured in the 1967 war fostered calls for their absorption into Israel. At the beginning of 1973, forty-four settlements had been installed on the West Bank, the Golan, and in the northern Sinai. Fifty more were scheduled to be created by year's end, most of them intended for the Sinai and the West Bank, where paramilitary camps (Nahal) depicted as defense outposts would gradually turn into civilian sites. In this way the Allon Plan, envisioning only defense perimeters on the

West Bank, was being manipulated to further create facts on the ground for retention of the area. Their implications for responses to peace overtures had already emerged in 1972, when King Husayn proposed that the West Bank enter a federation with Jordan following Israel's withdrawal. Allon called it promising, but the Knesset (Israel's parliament) went on record that it "reaffirms and confirms the historic right of the Jewish people over the Land of Israel."[39]

As the 1973 election campaign progressed, the Meir cabinet was forced further toward Land of Israel ideology by its minister of defense, Moshe Dayan, who was in charge of the conquered territories (see Figure 7.1). Until this point, no land had been sold to private individuals. Rather, land had been appropriated by the military government of the territories, acting as it had after the 1948 war. It could declare land "abandoned" and did so in order to make it available to settlements, especially when Arab owners refused to sell desirable property even under considerable pressure. Now, however, the prospect of private investment in the West Bank arose, encouraged by Dayan to ensure a Jewish presence.[40]

Figure 7.1 ■ Moshe Dayan Confers with Golda Meir, circa 1973

Dayan was minister of defense in Prime Minister Meir's cabinet, a post he had held since entering Levi Eshkol's coalition cabinet just prior to the 1967 war. Both Dayan and Meir would resign in April 1974 in response to criticism of Israel's state of readiness when Egypt and Syria attacked in October 1973. Dayan had been targeted because he had proclaimed in mid-1973 that Israel had a ten-year threshold of military superiority over the Arabs and had called for Israel's permanent occupation of the West Bank and annexation of parts of the Sinai.

Prime Minister Meir initially rejected Dayan's proposals, bolstered by international alarm and by opposition to the plan in her own party, but Dayan was not finished. Still highly popular, he threatened to withdraw from the Labor Party in the midst of the election campaign unless its platform recognized the right of individuals to buy land for the development of industrial centers in heavily settled Arab areas of the West Bank. The plan also intended to expand Israeli settlements around Jerusalem, where a belt suitable for occupation by 100,000 Israelis had already been mapped out, and to facilitate extensive acquisition of land by the Israeli Land Authority. In the Sinai, Dayan called for the creation of a new city to be called Yamit in the northeast sector of the peninsula, significantly expanding Israeli control there. Finally, he proposed a partitioning of the Sinai from Eilat west to the Gulf of Suez, a slicing of the peninsula along the eastern coast and its southern third that would have also given Israel permanent control of the oil fields captured from Egypt in 1967.

After much cabinet debate, opposition faded owing to the "political common sense" of the moderates, who recognized that Labor might be threatened if it opposed calls for absorption of Arab lands that seemed to have great popular support. Meir's approval came in the form of the Galili Document, written by her minister without portfolio, which became the Labor Party's program for the occupied areas. Dayan and Galili envisioned these new regions to be settled primarily by incoming Russian Jewish émigrés; this in part explained Israeli eagerness to pressure the Soviet Union on this matter and to seek American political support for this cause.[41] Labor's adoption of this platform effectively nullified its previous declarations regarding Resolution 242 and the territories it would be willing to return in exchange for peace. It angered Sadat and probably encouraged him to attack when he did so as to forestall its ratification by the electorate.[42]

The 1973 War: The Chance for Diplomacy

The 1973 war can be quickly summarized. Egyptian and Syrian forces attacked Israeli units on October 6, the Jewish holy day of Yom Kippur and the Muslim anniversary of the Prophet Muhammad's first victory over his Meccan adversaries at the battle of Badr (624 CE). The war officially ended on October 22 following a second cease-fire agreed upon by all parties, but Israeli efforts to deny Egypt its territorial gains in the Sinai led to continued attacks that brought the United States and the Soviet Union to the brink of nuclear confrontation.[43]

The war moved through several stages, from initial Arab victories that shocked and in places overwhelmed Israeli defenders to what amounted to a total Israeli military victory on the Syrian front and a partial triumph along the Suez Canal. The fighting was extraordinarily fierce with Arab forces attacking and resisting Israeli troops far more effectively than in past encounters. On the Golan Heights, Syrian tanks almost broke through Israeli lines but were finally stopped; Israeli counterattacks then added more territory in the Golan to that taken in 1967. On the Egyptian front, Egyptian soldiers crossed the Suez Canal and broke through the Bar-Lev line, stunning the Israeli command. A Soviet-supplied missile umbrella protected Egyptian ground forces close to the canal against Israeli air attacks. Fear of such attacks beyond the range of this missile system probably prevented the Egyptians from gaining more territory in the first days of the war. Israeli forces then counterattacked effectively and those under Ariel Sharon's command crossed the canal and occupied much of its west bank. At war's end, Egyptian forces still held out in two major pockets along the east bank of the canal, establishing an Egyptian presence in Israeli-held territory in the Sinai. Israeli troops were engaged in bitter house-to-house fighting, trying futilely to take the city of Suez, block supply lines to the Egyptian Third Army across the canal, and force a withdrawal that would have restored the status quo.

The Nixon administration had assumed a quick Israeli victory once Israel recovered from its opening setbacks, and proposed a cease-fire on October 12 that would preserve some Egyptian gains and set the stage for talks. Israel accepted, but Sadat refused the offer, believing that Egyptian forces could gain the strategic Giddi and Mitla passes. The Nixon administration then decided to release major arms supplies to Israel that it had previously withheld. The American allocation of these supplies enabled Israel to regain the initiative, but the subsequent announcement of a $2.2 billion appropriation for Israel on October 19 led Saudi Arabia's King Faysal to invoke an oil embargo and cut back production. It also encouraged the Israelis to seek a total victory, driving Egyptian forces out of the Sinai.

Kissinger, though angered by Sadat's rejection of the first cease-fire offer, still intended to preserve at least a minor Egyptian military presence in the Sinai. He was determined to establish a framework for negotiations that took these circumstances into account. They created a new bargaining environment where Israel did not have the dominance it had maintained for over six years. His efforts led to increased American-Israeli and American-Soviet tensions. Israel resisted, trying to regain the Sinai, while the Soviets strove to block any further Egyptian losses. When the October 22 cease-fire was finally implemented, U.N. peacekeeping contingents had been established in place (see Map 7.1 and Figure 7.2).[44]

Kissinger's Shuttle Diplomacy and the Partial Withdrawal Agreements. Henry Kissinger, secretary of state since August while also remaining national security adviser, was now in full control of American foreign policy. He believed, in the aftermath of the war, that reliance on Israel's military might to maintain peace in the Middle East had been wrong and that Israeli unwillingness to make concessions had contributed to the outbreak of hostilities. Though appreciating Israel's security concerns, he thought that compromise rather than insistence on unattainable terms better served peace and American interests; prolonged stalemate could only aid the Soviets. Kissinger thus strove to establish his and the United States' dominance of the negotiations, through which he hoped to move the Arab-Israeli question toward some resolution.

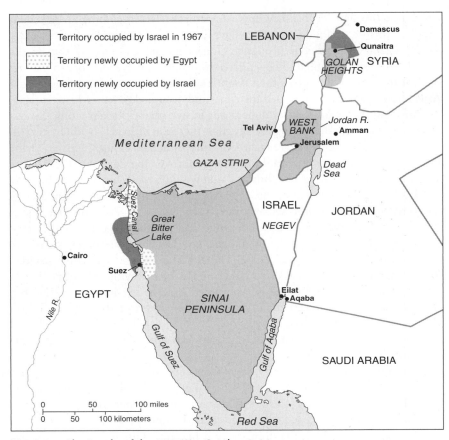

Map 7.1 ■ The Results of the 1973 War, October 6–24

Egypt and Syria undertook a joint attack to force negotiations over lands taken in 1967. In the Golan Heights, the Syrian attack nearly succeeded but Israeli forces held and ultimately captured more territory, which Israel retained. In the Sinai, Egyptian troops overwhelmed the Israeli defensive line on the Suez Canal and penetrated into the Sinai. Their advance halted initially because of logistical and operational inefficiencies and finally because of a sustained Israeli counteroffensive that crossed the canal and occupied Egyptian land on the west bank. The end of the war led to extensive negotiations, brokered by Henry Kissinger, in which Egypt retained its positions in the Sinai, setting the stage for the limited withdrawals of 1974 and 1975. (From *The Middle East: A History*, fourth edition, by Sydney Nettleton Fisher and William Ochsenwald, p. 699. Copyright © 1990 The McGraw-Hill Companies. Reprinted by permission of the publisher.)

This approach meant balancing several issues. Kissinger agreed to a Soviet request that a Geneva Conference be called, held for one day in December, to give the Soviets the impression he would pursue peace in tandem with them. He then undertook direct talks with Sadat and the Meir cabinet, newly reelected in December, to seek an interim or step-by-step accord that he preferred, without Soviet involvement. Sadat encouraged this strategy. He had decided to seek

Figure 7.2 ■ **Kilometer 101, the Cease-Fire Line**
Here Israeli and Egyptian army officers meet on November 11, 1973, separated by members of Finland's military force delegated to the United Nations; they had just signed the cease-fire agreement officially ending hostilities of the 1973 war. This accord set in motion negotiations sponsored by Henry Kissinger that ultimately led to the 1978 Camp David talks and the 1979 Egyptian-Israeli peace treaty.

American support in negotiations and to sever his ties with the Soviets if necessary. Kissinger thus began his renowned shuttle diplomacy that in the end produced two withdrawal agreements between Egypt and Israel (1974, 1975) and one between Israel and Syria (1974). His initial successes caused Faysal to end his oil embargo and also alleviated tensions between the United States and its European allies; they and Japan were nearly totally dependent on Arab oil and had been seriously affected by the oil cutbacks.

In principle Kissinger operated according to the framework established in Security Council Resolution 338, passed on October 22 (see Document 7.3). It called on all parties to begin "implementation of SC Resolution 242 in all its parts" through negotiations "under appropriate auspices aimed at establishing a just and durable peace in the Middle East." In practice Kissinger bypassed the United Nations as well as the Russians, hoping to achieve partial agreements that could establish trust between the signatories and create momentum that might lead to final peace accords. But Kissinger's methods often undermined his supposed final goal because he promised the parties different results. He told the Israelis that signing accords now would relieve international pressure for further concessions. By giving up a little, Israel might be able to retain more in the end. He told the Arabs the opposite, that moving toward partial peace agreements with Israel would create an impetus for future pacts leading to a final peace with, he intimated, nearly full Israeli withdrawal from the Sinai and the Golan Heights.[45]

After extremely hard bargaining, Kissinger gained two partial withdrawal agreements in the first six months of 1974. On January 18, Egypt and Israel signed a "Disengagement of Forces Agreement" providing for the final withdrawal of Israeli troops from the west side of the Suez Canal and delineation of the zones in which Egyptian forces could be stationed on the east bank. Syria and Israel signed a disengagement pact on May 31, 1974, whereby Israel withdrew just beyond the key town of Qunaitra in the Golan Heights, deliberately demolishing what remained of the town as they left. Assad agreed in a private memorandum to prevent Palestinian groups from undertaking attacks and terrorist activities by Syria.[46]

Israeli Politics and Regional Diplomacy.   Attainment of these pacts had been hampered in part by long-standing suspicions between enemies, but also by growing instability within the Israeli political alignments. The Labor Party, led by Golda Meir and Moshe Dayan, had won delayed elections held in December 1973 but with a reduced plurality; it acquired 39.6 percent of the vote and fifty-one seats, as opposed to 46.2 percent and fifty-six seats in the 1969 elections. Much of Labor's loss had been the gain of a new party, formed by General Ariel Sharon in September, before the war. Sharon, angered at being passed over for a command assignment, had resigned from the military. He then engineered the formation of a new coalition, combining Menachem Begin's Herut and the Liberal Party, already linked together as the Gahal, with smaller parties on the right. The result was the Likud, still led by Begin, who deeply admired Sharon. When Sharon emerged from the war as a hero following his crossing of the Suez Canal, his prestige and Begin's warnings about surrendering territory led the Likud Party to acquire 30.2 percent of the vote and a significant thirty-nine seats in the Knesset.[47] The dominance of Labor-led coalitions harking back to independence was beginning to crumble.

Worn out by the war and political infighting, Meir resigned as prime minister in April 1974, as did Dayan, who had been severely criticized by the public for the army's state of unreadiness. Meir was succeeded by Yitzhak Rabin, former chief of staff of the army and ambassador to Washington, who won the post within the Labor Party conclave by a narrow margin over Shimon Peres, formerly of the Rafi and Rabin's archrival. The Rabin-Peres antagonisms and competition for prestige within and outside Israel lasted until the early 1990s.[48] Peres became defense minister, with Yigael Allon as deputy prime minister; the three disagreed frequently, with Peres and Rabin each trying to undercut the other. Rabin did sign the second disengagement accord with Egypt in September 1975, removing Israeli forces beyond the strategic passes and giving Egypt access to some oil fields in the Gulf of Suez.

It was agreed that any future pact between Israel and Egypt would be a final peace accord. The United States also assured Israel that it would push for only minor territorial concessions in any forthcoming negotiations with Syria and would not press Israel toward any partial treaty with Jordan. Only a full peace treaty would be acceptable. Finally, Kissinger promised Israel that the United States would not talk to the PLO unless it specifically recognized the former's right to exist under Resolution 242, something he assumed unlikely if not impossible.

These latter stipulations indicated the direction Israel's policies would take in regularizing its relations with its Arab neighbors and how it hoped to retain U.S. backing in the process. Israel was determined to remain in the Golan Heights, regardless of the Syrian agreement to abide by Resolution 242. Israel also insisted on a full pact with Jordan mainly because it knew this would be unacceptable to Husayn, given Israeli terms. This enabled the cabinet to hold the West Bank and avoid an internal crisis over disposition of the territory. Israel also hoped to isolate Egypt from the rest of the Arab world, especially Syria. Success in this tack would give Israel a free hand to dispose of the territories other than the Sinai through direct dialogues or confrontation, without fear of an Egyptian military threat, a strategy Rabin admitted openly in December 1974.[49] Here Sadat's willingness to sign a second disengagement agreement with Israel in September 1975, without prior consultation with Damascus, indicated to Assad and others that Egypt could be induced to abandon a general Arab position. In their view Sadat appeared to pursue an Israeli-designed plan intended to further its own military and territorial aims. Finally, Kissinger's assurance regarding the PLO came at a time when that organization was redefining its objectives with a view to political as well as military strategies, a shift Israel was determined to block with American cooperation if at all possible.

Tactics and Ultimate Intentions: The PLO and Israel, 1973–1977

Israel's stance toward the West Bank following the 1973 war helped Arafat and the PLO, while undermining King Husayn's stature in Arab decision-making circles. Husayn had hoped for a partial pullback of Israeli forces on the West Bank, analogous to what had occurred in the Sinai and in the Golan Heights. That would have restored Jordanian sovereignty over part of the region and given Husayn greater authority to speak for the Palestinians there against the claims of the PLO. Husayn's failure correlated with a general willingness among Arab leaders to give the Palestinians a greater prominence in international gatherings, which reflected what seemed to be a move toward a negotiating posture by the Palestinian leadership.

The Rabat Declaration: The PLO Debates Its Objectives.   In October 1974 an Arab summit meeting in Rabat, Morocco, recognized "the right of the Palestinian people to establish an independent national authority under the command of the Palestinian Liberation Organization, the sole legitimate representative of the Palestinian people, in any Palestinian territory that is liberated." A month later Arafat and the PLO received international recognition when he spoke before the U.N. General Assembly (see Figure 7.3), which granted the PLO observer status[50] (see Documents 7.4 and 7.5).

The Rabat Declaration stripped Husayn of power to negotiate for the West Bank and its Arab inhabitants, a decision he accepted. Kissinger considered the declaration a disaster. He believed that Israel should have dealt with Husayn, if only to deny the PLO the appearance of legitimacy it derived at Husayn's expense. In Kissinger's view, Husayn's survival was in America's interests, but his credibility in the Arab world, based on his ties to the United States, had been weakened in part by America's chief ally, Israel. Kissinger now sought to isolate the PLO at precisely the moment when Arafat was eager to pursue further contacts based on changes in positions that were beginning to emerge within the Palestinian leadership.

The official stance of the PLO, based on its 1968 charter, called for the liberation of Palestine through "armed struggle" and the establishment of a secular democratic society in the place of Israel. No clear distinction was made between

Figure 7.3 ■ PLO Head Yasir Arafat Clasps His Hands over His Head as He Addresses the United Nations General Assembly, November 13, 1974

Arafat carried an olive branch and wore an empty holster, arguing that the choice was between further war or peace. He defended armed struggle, mentioned in the 1968 PLO Charter (Document 7.2), as legitimate resistance to occupation. He called for Palestinian self-determination and creation of a democratic secular state in what was Israel (Document 7.4).

pre- and post-1967 Israel. Moreover, as noted earlier, leftist groups such as George Habash's Popular Front for the Liberation of Palestine (PFLP) and Nayif Hawatmah's Popular Democratic Front for the Liberation of Palestine (PDFLP) had demanded revolutionary change in the wider Arab world, specifically the overthrow of King Husayn, as a precondition to undertaking a direct confrontation with Israel.

By late 1972, Hawatmah and the PDFLP had begun to modify this vision, concluding that Husayn would remain in power and alarmed by the expansion of Israeli settlements in the West Bank. They proposed the term "national authority"; intended to apply to the West Bank and Gaza, it signified a willingness to accept sovereignty over what had been part of Palestine rather than stressing conquest of what was now Israel. The PDFLP proposal sought to create conditions that might block Israeli retention of the occupied lands while establishing an alternative to Husayn's plans for them. The Soviet Union encouraged Hawatmah. Moscow armed the Palestinians but also backed Palestinian political compromise because it sought a role in any negotiations for a diplomatic solution, something Kissinger hoped to deny.

Hawatmah's proposal met strong opposition from what became known as the Rejection Front, Habash's PFLP and Ahmad Jibril's PFLP General Command. Both argued that to declare these limited objectives meant open abdication of the ultimate goal, control of all of former Palestine, while receiving no assurance of Israeli concessions. Furthermore, this tack tacitly abandoned the Arab revolutionary goal to overthrow King Husayn. The debate over the idea of Palestinian national authority in any lands taken from Israel lasted for years, but its basic terms were accepted in the Rabat Declaration of October 1974. This meant that such lands, though directly "liberated" from Israel, were also being indirectly liberated from Jordan, given Husayn's own ambitions. The question remaining was the exact position of Arafat and the PLO central leadership, an issue that remained in doubt for some time.[51]

PLO Vacillation and Israel's Reply. It seems clear that Arafat from 1973 onward was attracted to the idea of a negotiated settlement that might regain the West Bank and Gaza. But he hesitated to openly advocate this option for fear of losing control of the PLO. Despite his prominence, he still had to take into account the attitudes of various factions; to splinter the organization over such a debate could cause him and the PLO to lose credibility as representatives of the Palestinian cause. The problem became more complex after 1973 because West Bank Palestinians, eager to retain what they had, increasingly favored a limited settlement. On the other hand, the Palestinian refugees in the camps, who made up the fighting cadres, had come from what was now Israel. They resisted suggestions to abandon their hope of achieving their former homeland.[52]

Arafat's strategy was to float suggestions of negotiated settlements through aides without committing himself or the organization to them. He sought a positive response to such ideas from Arab states, the Soviet Union, and especially the United States. Explicit American interest could permit him to present the peace options more directly to the PLO National Council for approval. A crucial stumbling block for Arafat was the United States' insistence on a specific PLO overture that accepted Resolution 242 and recognized Israel as a precondition of official discussions. Arafat wanted the opposite, open American willingness to deal with the PLO to encourage Palestinian moderation. The principal obstacle was Resolution 242, which referred only to the Palestinian refugee problem. Arafat suggested in 1974 that the resolution be amended to refer to Palestinian rights of self-determination, permitting him to bring this concession to the PLO National Council.

A further problem was PLO obtuseness in defining what "national authority" really meant. Did it mean a state? If it did, this might signify open acceptance of limited goals, a Palestinian state in the West Bank and Gaza, that accepted an Israeli state. The PLO shied away from the term for several years, despite Soviet encouragement to present the idea in order to open the way for possible acceptance into the diplomatic arena. In addition, PLO references to national authority stipulated that this was only the first step toward a final goal, namely, the liberation of all of Palestine. Differing factions might disagree as to what that meant—future armed struggle or peaceful contacts leading to an integration of Palestinian and Israeli societies—but no one would speak clearly on the subject to oppose the rejectionist viewpoint.[53]

The PLO's vacillation served Israel's interests. Israeli leaders could point quite logically to these proposals as smoke screens rather than serious questions. In addition, Arafat's inability or unwillingness to control various Palestinian groups also bolstered Israel's position. In April 1974, a PFLP squad infiltrated the Israeli village of Kiryat Shimona, took hostages, and was wiped out along with several of its captives. A month later a PDFLP unit undertook a suicide attack on Maalot in northern Israel, holding Israeli schoolchildren hostage; twenty-four were killed along with the Palestinians and sixty-three wounded in the ensuing shoot-out when Israeli troops stormed the school. The fact that two ideologically opposed groups should undertake these assaults highlighted the tension among the factions and their need to prove that they had not abandoned armed struggle. In this particular context, the raids were also designed to foil Kissinger's shuttle diplomacy between Tel Aviv and Damascus, tactics recognized by the Israeli leaders and Kissinger, who continued the talks.[54] Nevertheless, the terrorist raids gave further weight to the Israeli refusal to deal with the PLO as a whole, attributing responsibility to its leader. This left the way open for Israel to increase its settlements on the West Bank without much fear of American protest.

The Labor government's support of new settlements was based on various factors. The signing of the second disengagement pact with Egypt in September 1975, coupled with the upcoming American presidential election campaign in

1976, meant there would be little official criticism of Israel. In fact, President Gerald Ford suspended American diplomatic efforts in the Middle East during the year to avoid offending American Jewish voters.[55] In addition, the Labor Party, under Prime Minister Yitzhak Rabin, was weakened by the "endemic personal rivalry between [him] and Shimon Peres, the Minister of Defense."[56] The leadership thus submitted to pressures imposed by its coalition partner, the National Religious Party, and a new organization that emerged in 1974, Gush Emunim (Bloc of the Faithful). Once opposed to annexation of the conquered territories, the National Religious Party had been taken over by a militant wing that called openly for the absorption of the West Bank, thus incorporating the ideology of the Greater Land of Israel Movement into the Labor coalition. At the same time, Gush Emunim committed itself to creating illegal settlements in the heart of Arab populations and forcing the government to accept them. Their goal was to shift the focus of Israeli settlement activity from a strategic perspective to one that insisted on the right of Jews to colonize all areas of the region as part of what had been Eretz Israel. In this, Gush Emunim had the behind-the-scenes backing of Peres and military leaders responsible for the area, leaving Rabin helpless to oppose faits accomplis that brought the Labor Party much closer to the posture of annexation called for by Begin. The founding of new settlements approved by the Labor Party rose by 45 percent between mid-1975 and 1977.[57]

CONCLUSION

Political events brought new faces to power in the United States and Israel in early 1977. Jimmy Carter became president of the United States in January, and Menachem Begin was elected prime minister of Israel in March, assuming office in June. At the same time, the PLO National Council, meeting in March, declared for the first time its willingness to seek an "independent national state" as part of the Palestinian right to self-determination. The council also called for PLO participation in a Geneva conference, the clearest expression yet of a wish to engage in international diplomacy. Yet even here, concessions to the rejectionists meant that the West Bank and Gaza were not mentioned, nor was there any offer to recognize Israel. The Carter presidency signaled major changes in the American approach to Arab-Israeli and Palestinian issues. The Nixon and Ford administrations had, with Kissinger controlling most policy decisions, interpreted regional problems within the cold war framework where Kissinger sought limited agreements between enemies. Carter would seek talks aimed at a general peace, exchanges that would include the Soviets and possibly the Palestinians. But Israeli policy was now to shift from the piecemeal expansion of settlements to full-fledged sponsorship with the Likud's Begin, now prime minister, just as opposed to dealings with the PLO as had been Yitzhak Rabin.

In these circumstances, PLO vacillation in explaining its diplomatic goals helped Israel harden its position in the face of new challenges from the United States. The collision of these approaches resulted in the Camp David Agreement of 1978. It was a major victory for the Israeli strategy of seeking to isolate Egypt, as expounded by Rabin in 1974, and seemed to Begin to assure Israel's control of the West Bank.

QUESTIONS FOR CONSIDERATION

1. How did the Israeli position on establishing settlements in the newly conquered territories develop after the 1967 war?
2. What were the major differences between the Rogers and Kissinger approaches to Arab-Israeli issues once Richard Nixon assumed office in 1969?
3. What do you see as the major factors contributing to the outbreak of the 1973 war? What changes in American policy emerged after the war?
4. Can we say that there was a PLO "policy" regarding diplomatic resolutions that developed during this period? If not, why not?

CHRONOLOGY

1967	**August.** Khartoum Conference.
	November 22. U.N. Security Council approves Resolution 242.
1968	**January.** Israeli Labor Party formed.
	March. Israeli-Palestinian battle at Karamah, Jordan.
	July. Palestinian National Charter revised.
1969	**January.** Golda Meir installed as Israeli prime minister; Richard M. Nixon becomes president of the United States.
	February. Yasir Arafat elected head of the PLO.
	March 1969–August 1970. Egyptian-Israeli war of attrition.
1970	**August.** Egyptian-Israeli cease-fire along Suez Canal.
	September 16–25. Jordanian civil war.
	September 28. Egyptian president Gamal Abd al-Nasser dies. Succeeded by Anwar al-Sadat.
	November. Hafiz al-Assad takes power in Syria.
1972	**July.** Sadat orders departure of Soviet troops, advisers.
	September. Black September group abducts eleven Israeli Olympians in Munich Olympics. All die.
	November. Nixon reelected.
1973	**September.** Israeli Likud Party formed.
	October 6–22. Yom Kippur War. Egypt and Syria attack Israel.
	October 22. Cease-fire declared. U.N. Security Council Resolution 338 passed.
	October 24. Israel agrees to cease-fire.
1974	**January 18.** First Egyptian-Israeli Disengagement of Forces Agreement.
	February. Gush Emunim (Bloc of the Faithful) formed.
	April. Meir resigns, succeeded by Yitzhak Rabin.
	May 31. Syrian-Israeli disengagement agreement.
	October 28. Rabat summit, PLO declared "the sole legitimate representative of the Palestinian people."
	November 13. PLO chairman Arafat addresses the U.N. General Assembly.
1975	**September 4.** Second Egyptian-Israeli disengagement agreement.

Notes

1. Michael Brecher, *Decisions in Israel's Foreign Policy* (New Haven, Conn., 1975), 444.

2. Ibid., 462.

3. Rael Jean Isaac, *Israel Divided: Ideological Politics in the Jewish State* (Baltimore, 1976), 115–26; and Shlomo Aronson, *Conflict and Bargaining in the Middle East: An Israeli Perspective* (Baltimore, 1978), 87ff, discuss the different approaches to the problems. For statements made in 1967, see Daniel Dishon, ed., *Middle East Record, 1967* (Jerusalem, 1971), 276–77.

4. William Wilson Harris, *Taking Root: Israeli Settlement in the West Bank, the Golan and Gaza-Sinai, 1967–1980* (New York, 1980), 34–44. Gershom Gorenberg, "Israel's Tragedy Foretold," *New York Times*, March 10, 2006.

5. Harriet Dashiell Schwar, editor, *Foreign Relations of the United States, 1964–1968*, vol. 19, *Arab-Israeli Crisis and War, 1967* (Washington, D.C., 2004). Compare Document 227, June 9, 1967, "[U.S. Ambassador to the United Nations Arthur] Goldberg Talk with [Israeli Foreign Minister Abba] Eban," pp. 386–87 with Document 530, November 17, 1967, "Information Memorandum from the Assistant Secretary of State for Near Eastern and South Asian Affairs ([Lucius] Battle) to Secretary of State (Dean) Rusk, pp. 143–45. A new comprehensive study of Israeli settlement policy is Idith Zertal and Akiva Eldar, *Lords of the Land: The War for Israel's Settlements in the Occupied Territories, 1967–2007* (New York, 2007).

6. Robert Stephens, *Nasser: A Political Biography* (Middlesex, England, 1973), 520–24; Malcolm Kerr, *The Arab Cold War: Gamal 'Abd al-Nasir and His Rivals, 1958–1970* (London, 1971), 137–40.

7. For the Khartoum Declaration and Nasser's position, see Yoram Meital, "The Khartoum Conference and the Egyptian Policy after the 1967 War," *Middle East Journal* 54, 1 (Winter 2000): 64–82. The U.S. analysis can be found in Schwar, editor, *Crisis and War, 1967*, Document 455, October 3, 1967, "Memorandum from the President's Special Assistant ([Walt] Rostow) to President Johnson," p. 867.

8. Institute for the Study of Diplomacy, Georgetown University, *U.N. Security Council Resolution 242: A Case Study in Diplomatic Ambiguity* (Washington, D.C., 1984), 5.

9. The text is in Walter Laqueur and Barry Rubin, eds., *The Israel-Arab Reader: A Documentary History of the Middle East Conflict* (New York, 1984), 365–66.

10. See Lord Caradon in *Resolution 242*, 13–15; and William B. Quandt, *Decade of Decisions: American Policy toward the Arab-Israeli Conflict, 1967–1976* (Berkeley and Los Angeles, 1977), 65.

11. Goldberg in *Resolution 242*, 23. To add to the confusion, the French and Russian translations of the document refer to "the territories," adding the article omitted in the English original.

12. Quandt, *Decade*, 66, discusses the arms deal that included tanks for Jordan. For American domestic politics and the timing of Middle East diplomacy, see William B. Quandt, *Camp David: Peacemaking and Politics* (Washington, D.C., 1986), 6–29.

13. Ehud Yaari, *Strike Terror: The Story of Fatah* (New York, 1970), 123–50.

14. Helena Cobban, *The Palestinian Liberation Organization: People, Power and Politics* (Cambridge, England, 1984), 141–47. Yezid Sayigh, *Armed Struggle and the Search for State: The Palestinian National Movement, 1949–1993* (Washington, D.C., 1997), has the most detailed discussion of issues.

15. Sayigh, *Armed Struggle*, 218–23. The remaining 48 of the 105 seats were held by representatives of student and labor groups, the Palestinian Liberation Army, and so on.

16. Eric Rouleau, "Les Palestiniens face au trône jordanien, IV: Le dilemme," *Le Monde*, 4 December 1970, quoted in Kerr, *The Arab Cold War*, 145.

17. John Cooley, *Green March, Black September: The Story of the Palestinian Arabs* (London, 1973), 146–48; Sayigh, *Armed Struggle*, 214–15.

18. Kamal S. Salibi, *Crossroads to Civil War: Lebanon, 1958–1976* (New York, 1976), 32–51; Sayigh, *Armed Struggle*, 192–94.

19. For Soviet arms shipments to Egypt and other Arab states, see Alvin Z. Rubenstein, *Red Star on the Nile: The Soviet-Egyptian Relationship since the June War* (Princeton, N.J., 1977), and Jon D. Glassman, *Arms for the Arabs: The Soviet Union and War in the Middle East* (Baltimore, 1975).

20. I rely on the following sources for the war of attrition and accompanying diplomatic efforts to resolve it: Yaacov Bar-Siman-Tov, *The Israeli-Egyptian War of Attrition, 1969–1970* (New York, 1980); Yaacov Bar-Siman-Tov, "The Myth of Strategic Bombing: Israeli Deep-Penetration Air Raids in the War of Attrition, 1969–70," *Journal of Contemporary History* 19 (1984): 549–70; Rubenstein, *Red Star*, 66–117; and Lawrence L. Whetten, *The Canal War: Four-Power Conflict in the Middle East, 1967–1974* (Cambridge, Mass., 1974), which covers a broader period, 1967 to 1974.

21. Yitzhak Rabin, *Rabin Memoirs* (New York, 1979), 157–65. See also Bar-Siman-Tov, "Myth of Strategic Bombing," 553; and Nadav Safran, *Israel, the Embattled Ally* (Cambridge, Mass., 1978), 436.

22. Brecher, *Decisions*, 488–95; and Rabin, *Memoirs*, 177.

23. I rely principally on Steven L. Spiegel, *The Other Arab-Israeli Conflict: Making America's Middle East Policy, from Truman to Reagan* (Chicago, 1985); Raymond L. Garthoff, *Détente and Confrontation: American-Soviet Relations from Nixon to Reagan* (Washington, D.C., 1985); Seymour M. Hersh, *The Price of Power: Kissinger in the Nixon White House* (New York, 1983); Tad Szulc, *The Illusion of Peace: Foreign Policy in the Nixon Years* (New York, 1978); Richard M. Nixon, *RN, The Memoirs of Richard Nixon* (New York, 1978); Henry Kissinger, *White House Years* (Boston, 1979); and Quandt, *Decade*, 72–104.

24. Kissinger, *White House Years*, 351–57. Roger Morris, *Uncertain Greatness: Henry Kissinger and American Foreign Policy* (New York, 1977), a bitter account of Kissinger's handling of policy and his staff; and Barry Rubin, *Secrets of State: The State Department and the Struggle over U.S. Foreign Policy* (Oxford, England, 1985), who notes, 146, that Kissinger would not tolerate questions from his staff regarding the substance of the policy he and Nixon had selected.

25. Quoted in Spiegel, *America's Middle East Policy*, 185. For Israeli cabinet discussions, see Brecher, *Decisions*, 454–78.

26. *White House Years*, 379. It is difficult to know how much of Kissinger's attribution of foresight to himself is the product of hindsight.

27. *Fatah*, April 17, 1970, quoted by Jabber in Quandt, Jabber, and Lesch, *Palestinian Nationalism*, 196–97. Sayigh, *Armed Struggle*, 251–81, covers the Jordanian strife and PLO factionalism through the civil war and its aftermath.

28. William B. Quandt, "Lebanon, 1958, and Jordan, 1970," in Barry M. Blechman, Stephen S. Kaplan, et al., eds., *Force without War: U.S. Armed Forces as a Political Instrument* (Washington, D.C., 1978), 278–79.

29. For rivalries within the Syrian political elite, civilian and military, see Nikolaos Van Dam, *The Struggle for Power in Syria: Sectarianism, Regionalism and Tribalism in Politics, 1961–1978* (New York, 1979), especially 83–97, which treat the Assad-Jadid feud; and Moshe Ma'oz and Avner Yaniv, "On a Short Leash: Syria and the PLO," in Moshe Ma'oz and Avner Yaniv, eds., *Syria under Assad: Domestic Constraints and Regional Risks* (London, 1986), 191–208.

30. John Waterbury, *The Egypt of Nasser and Sadat: The Political Economy of Two Regimes* (Princeton, N.J., 1983), 112ff. See also the overview by William J. Burns, *Economic Aid and American Policy towards Egypt, 1955–1981* (Albany, N.Y., 1985), 173–77.

31. As Kissinger acknowledges, *White House Years*, 1276–1300.

32. Quandt, *Decade*, 130–43; Whetten, *Canal War*, 139–95, who has a very detailed treatment of the issues; and Aronson, *Conflict and Bargaining*, 139–54.

33. Marvin Kalb and Bernard Kalb, *Kissinger* (New York, 1975), 208.

34. Spiegel, *America's Middle East Policy*, 203. During the early 1970s, Congress increased aid to Israel by nearly 9 percent over the White House's requests while reducing total foreign aid expenditures by 25 percent: Marvin C. Feurwerger, *Congress and Israel: Foreign Aid Decision-Making in the House of Representatives, 1969–1976* (Westport, Conn., 1979), 40 and passim.

35. Dina Rome Spechler, "Soviet Policy in the Middle East: The Crucial Change," in Paul Marantz and Blema S. Steinberg, eds., *Superpower Involvement in the Middle East: Dynamics of Foreign Policy* (Boulder, Colo., 1985), 133–71.

36. Anthony Sampson, *The Seven Sisters: The Great Oil Companies and the World They Shaped* (New York, 1976), especially 186–310; and Peter R. Odell, *Oil and World Power* (New York, 1979).

37. See the articles in Raymond Vernon, ed., *The Oil Crisis* (New York, 1976), especially those by Joel Darmstadter and Hans H. Landsberg, "The Economic Background," 15–38; and Edith Penrose, "The Development of the Crisis," 39–58.

38. Aronson, *Conflict and Bargaining*, 162.

39. Quoted in Isaac, *Israel Divided*, 128. See also Harris, *Taking Root*, 42–57.

40. Baruch Kimmerling, *Zionism and Territory: The Socio-Territorial Dimensions of Zionist Politics* (Berkeley and Los Angeles, 1983), 164–65. Dayan's mercurial nature is well treated in Conor Cruise O'Brien, *The Siege: The Saga of Israel and Zionism* (London, 1986), 507–8.

41. *Jerusalem Post Overseas Edition*, August 21, 1973, September 11, 1973, and October 2, 1973, covers the discussions. Aronson, *Conflict and Bargaining*, 408–9, lists the provisions of the Galili plan. For American Jewish efforts to gain greater Soviet Jewish emigration, backed by Senator Henry Jackson, who hoped to exploit the matter for a possible presidential candidacy in 1976, see Paula Stern, *Water's Edge: Domestic Politics and the Making of American Foreign Policy* (Westport, Conn., 1979), and the second volume of Kissinger's memoirs, *Years of Upheaval* (Boston, 1982), 250–56, 986–97.

42. Mohamed Haykal, *The Road to Ramadan* (London, 1971), 22, 205.

43. Capable summaries of the war can be found in Frank Aker, *October 1973: The Arab-Israeli War* (Hamden, Conn., 1985); and Trevor N. Dupuy, *Elusive Victory: The Arab-Israeli Wars, 1947–1974* (New York, 1978), 387–617.

44. Aronson, *Conflict and Bargaining*, 168–211; and Quandt, *Decade*, 165–206.

45. Quandt, *Decade*, 251; see also Edward R. F. Sheehan, *The Arabs, Israelis, and Kissinger: A Secret History of American Diplomacy in the Middle East* (New York, 1976); and Matti Golan, *The Secret Conversations of Henry Kissinger: Step-by-Step Diplomacy in the Middle East* (New York, 1976). Compare Sheehan's comments on Matti Golan, *Secret History*, 81.

46. Texts in Sheehan, *Secret History*, 238–44.

47. The statistics are in Itamar Rabinovich and Jehuda Reinharz, eds., *Israel in the Middle East: Documents and Readings on Society, Politics, and Foreign Relations, 1948–Present* (New York, 1984), appendices (unpaginated). See also Eric Silver, *Begin, a Biography* (London, 1984), 144–46.

48. In *The Rabin Memoirs*, every indexed reference to Peres is critical, sarcastic, or both. For a reaction to these memoirs, see Matti Golan, *Shimon Peres, a Biography* (New York, 1982), 232–35.

49. Golan, *Secret Conversations*, 229; and Quandt, *Decade*, 261.

50. The quote is from Cobban, *Palestine Liberation Organization*, 60

51. My discussion of PLO debates and positions relies on Alain Gresh, *The PLO, the Struggle Within: Towards an Independent Palestinian State*, trans. A. M. Berrett (London, 1985), especially 118–210, which provide a detailed treatment of the issues; Galia Golan, *The Soviet Union and the Palestine Liberation Organization: An Uneasy Alliance* (New York, 1980), 56–58; and Sayigh, *Armed Struggle*, 333–57, who dates discussions to after the 1973 war.

52. Gresh, *Struggle Within*, 133–38.

53. Cobban, *Palestine Liberation Organization*, 61–62, 154–56; Gresh, *Struggle Within*, 143–49.

54. Golan, *Secret Conversations,* 202–3. Israeli policy was not to bargain with terrorists but to attack and kill them, even if this risked the loss of hostages' lives.

55. William B. Quandt, *Camp David: Peacemaking and Politics* (Washington, D.C., 1986), 33.

56. Meron Benvenisti, *The West Bank Data Project: A Survey of Israel's Policies* (Washington, D.C., 1984), 52.

57. Ibid.; and Harris, *Taking Root,* 126ff. For Gush Emunim, see the following sources in addition to Benvenisti: David Newman, ed., *The Impact of Gush Emunim: Politics and Settlement in the West Bank* (London, 1985); David J. Schnall, *Radical Dissent in Contemporary Israeli Politics: Cracks in the Wall* (New York, 1979), 139–55; David J. Schnall, *Beyond the Green Line: Israeli Settlements West of the Jordan* (New York, 1984), which includes interviews with leaders of Gush Emunim and with West Bank Arabs; and the broader survey by Ehud Sprinzak, *The Ascendance of Israel's Radical Right* (New York, 1991).

DOCUMENT 7.1

U.N. SECURITY COUNCIL RESOLUTION 242
November 22, 1967

This resolution remains the official basis of negotiations to resolve the results of the 1967 war. Israel insisted that Principle (i) under Article 1 should not have the word "the" before "territories" to enable it to ensure "secure" boundaries as mentioned in Article 1, Principle (ii). Debate over how much land is required to ensure such secure boundaries continues to the present. Menachem Begin's attempt to remove the West Bank from the resolution's scope failed.

The Security Council,

Expressing its continued concern with the grave situation in the Middle East, *Emphasizing* the inadmissibility of the acquisition of territory by war and the need to work for a just and lasting peace in which every state in the area can live in security,

Emphasizing further that all Member States in their acceptance of the Charter of the United Nations have undertaken a commitment to act in accordance with Article 2 of the Charter,

1. *Affirms* that the fulfilment of Charter principles requires the establishment of a just and lasting peace in the Middle East which should include the application of both the following principles.

(i) Withdrawal of Israel[i] armed forces from territories occupied in the recent conflict;

(ii) Termination of all claims or states of belligerency and respect for and acknowledgement of the sovereignty, territorial integrity and political independence of every State in the area and their right to live in peace within secure and recognized boundaries free from threats or acts of force.

2. *Affirms further* the necessity

(a) For guaranteeing freedom of navigation through international waterways in the area;

(b) For achieving a just settlement of the refugee problem;

(c) For guaranteeing the territorial inviolability and political independence of every State in the area, through measures including the establishment of demilitarized zones;

3. *Requests* the Secretary-General to designate a Special Representative to proceed to the Middle East to establish and maintain contact with the States concerned in order to promote agreement and assist efforts to achieve a peaceful and accepted settlement in accordance with the provisions and principles in this resolution;

4. *Requests* the Secretary-General to report to the Security Council on the progress of the efforts of the Special Representative as soon as possible.

Source: T. G. Fraser, *The Middle East, 1914–1979* (London, 1980), 117.

THE PALESTINIAN NATIONAL CHARTER: RESOLUTIONS OF THE PALESTINE NATIONAL COUNCIL

July 1–17, 1968

PLO RESOLUTION ON SECURITY COUNCIL RESOLUTION 242

June 1974

This revised charter stresses a distinct Palestinian identity within the framework of Arab nationalism. The Palestinian nation should be reborn in what was then Israel, a goal to be achieved through armed struggle. Article 33 was invoked when the Palestine National Council voided articles calling for Israel's destruction in 1996, a move accepted by the Labor government but later challenged by Israeli Prime Minister Binyamin Netanyahu (1996–1999). Netanyahu insisted on a meeting of the Palestine National Congress, apparently hoping that gaining another two-thirds majority to amend the charter and accept Israel's existence would be impossible to achieve. This would have enabled him to refuse any further discussions under the Oslo Accord.

The 1974 resolution highlights the PLO's rejection of Resolution 242 because it treated the Palestinian question as one of resolving the refugee issue.

The Palestinian National Charter: Resolutions of the Palestine National Council (1968)

Charter

1. Palestine is the homeland of the Arab Palestinian people; it is an indivisible part of the Arab homeland, and the Palestinian people are an integral part of the Arab nation.

2. Palestine, with the boundaries it had during the British Mandate, is an indivisible territorial unit.

3. The Palestinian Arab people possess the legal right to their homeland and have the right to determine their destiny after achieving the liberation of their country in accordance with their wishes and entirely of their own accord and will.

4. The Palestinian identity is a genuine, essential, and inherent characteristic; it is transmitted from parents to children. The Zionist occupation and the dispersal of the Palestinian Arab people, through the disasters which befell

Source: The Israel-Arab Reader: A Documentary History of the Middle East Conflict, Walter Laqueur and Barry Rubin, eds. (New York, 1984), 366–71.

them, do not make them lose their Palestinian identity and their membership in the Palestinian community, nor do they negate them.

5. The Palestinians are those Arab nationals who, until 1947, normally resided in Palestine regardless of whether they were evicted from it or have stayed there. Anyone born, after that date, of a Palestinian father—whether inside Palestine or outside it—is also a Palestinian.

6. The Jews who had normally resided in Palestine until the beginning of the Zionist invasion will be considered Palestinians. . . .

8. The phase in their history, through which the Palestinian people are now living, is that of national struggle for the liberation of Palestine. . . . The Palestinian masses, . . . whether . . . residing in the national homeland or in [the] diaspora, constitute . . . one national front working for the retrieval of Palestine and its liberation through armed struggle.

9. Armed struggle is the only way to liberate Palestine. Thus it is the overall strategy, not merely a tactical phase. The Palestinian Arab people assert their absolute determination and firm resolution to continue their armed struggle and to work for an armed popular revolution for the liberation of their country and their return to it. They also assert their right to normal life in Palestine and to exercise their right to self-determination and sovereignty over it.

10. Commando action constitutes the nucleus of the Palestinian popular liberation war. This requires its escalation, comprehensiveness, and the mobilization of all the Palestinian popular and educational efforts and their organization and involvement in the armed Palestinian revolution. . . .

12. The Palestinian people believe in Arab unity. In order to contribute their share toward the attainment of that objective, however, they must, at the present stage of their struggle, safeguard their Palestinian identity and develop their consciousness of that identity, and oppose any plan that may dissolve or impair it. . . .

14. The destiny of the Arab nation, and indeed Arab existence itself, depend upon the destiny of the Palestine cause. From this interdependence spring the Arab nation's pursuit of, and striving for, the liberation of Palestine. . . .

15. The liberation of Palestine, from an Arab viewpoint, is a national duty . . . and aims at the elimination of Zionism in Palestine. Absolute responsibility for this falls upon the Arab nation . . . with the Arab people of Palestine in the vanguard. . . .

19. The partition of Palestine in 1947 and the establishment of the state of Israel are entirely illegal, regardless of the passage of time, because they were contrary to the will of the Palestinian people and to their natural right in their homeland, and inconsistent with the principles embodied in the Charter of the United Nations, particularly the right to self-determination.

20. The Balfour Declaration, the Mandate for Palestine, and everything that has been based upon them, are deemed null and void. Claims of historical or religious ties of Jews with Palestine are incompatible with the facts of history and the true conception of what constitutes statehood. Judaism, being a religion, is not an independent nationality. Nor do Jews constitute a single nation with an identity of its own; they are citizens of the states to which they belong. . . .

22. Zionism is a political movement organically associated with international imperialism and antagonistic to all action for liberation and to progressive movements in the world. It is racist and fanatic in its nature, aggressive, expansionist, and colonial in its aims, and fascist in its methods. Israel is the instrument of the Zionist movement, and a geographical base for world imperialism placed strategically in the midst of the Arab homeland to combat the hopes of the Arab nation for liberation, unity, and progress. Israel is a constant source of threat *vis-à-vis* peace in the Middle East and the whole world. Since the liberation of Palestine will destroy the Zionist and imperialist presence and will contribute to the establishment of peace in the Middle East, the Palestinian people look for the support of all the progressive and peaceful forces and urge them all, irrespective of their affiliations and beliefs, to offer the Palestinian people all aid and support in their just struggle for the liberation of their homeland. . . .

33. This Charter shall not be amended save by [vote of] a majority of two-thirds of the total membership of the National Congress of the Palestine Liberation Organization [taken] at a special session convened for that purpose.

PLO Resolution on Security Council Resolution 242 (1974)

1. The PLO reaffirms its previous attitude concerning Security Council Resolution 242 which obliterates the patriotic and national rights of our people and treats our national cause as a refugee problem. It therefore refuses categorically any negotiations on the basis of this Resolution at any level of inter-Arab or international negotiation including the Geneva Conference. . . .

DOCUMENT 7.3

U.N. SECURITY COUNCIL RESOLUTION 338

October 22, 1973

Resolution 338 sought to end hostilities in the 1973 war and to resume negotiations based on Resolution 242. Since then the two resolutions have been linked. Henry Kissinger's step-by-step diplomacy did not reject these resolutions but envisaged their gradual implementation under American rather than international auspices.

The Security Council,

1. *Calls upon* all parties to the present fighting to cease all firing and terminate all military activity immediately, not later than 12 hours after the moment of the adoption of the decision, in the positions they now occupy;

Source: T. G. Fraser, *The Middle East, 1914–1979* (London, 1980), 131.

2. *Calls upon* the parties concerned to start immediately after the cease-fire the implementation of Security Council Resolution 242 (1967) in all of its parts;

3. *Decides that,* immediately and concurrently with the cease-fire negotiations start between the parties concerned under appropriate auspices aimed at establishing a just and durable peace in the Middle East.

DOCUMENT 7.4

YASIR ARAFAT

ADDRESS TO THE U.N. GENERAL ASSEMBLY
November 13, 1974

Arafat's address to the U.N. General Assembly summarized Palestinian history within the context of Zionism as imperialism and racism. He presented Palestinian resistance as part of a non-Western struggle similar to that experienced by many members of the General Assembly, who had themselves been labeled terrorists. Although he called for peace instead of continued bloodshed, he did so in a framework within which Israel would no longer exist. Nonetheless, his appeal to Jews then in Israel to live in a secular, democratic state contradicted Article 6 of the 1968 PLO Charter (see Document 7.2), which offered residency only to those Jews who were in Palestine before the "Zionist invasion," usually dated to the Balfour Declaration of 1917. Compare his reference to the Balfour Declaration with those made by Sadat and Begin in November 1977 (see Documents 8.2 and 8.3).

Mr. President, I thank you for having invited the Palestine Liberation Organization to participate in this plenary session of the United Nations General Assembly. . . .

The roots of the Palestinian question reach back into the closing years of the nineteenth century . . . to that period which we call the era of colonialism and settlement as we know it today. This is precisely the period during which Zionism . . . was born; its aim was the conquest of Palestine by European immigrants, just as settlers colonized, and indeed raided, most of Africa. This is the period during which . . . colonialism spread into the further reaches of Africa, Asia, and Latin America, . . . cruelly exploiting, oppressing, plundering the people of those three continents. This period persists into the present. Marked evidence of its totally reprehensible presence can be readily perceived in the racism practised both in South Africa and in Palestine. . . .

Between 1882 and 1917 the Zionist Movement settled approximately 50,000 European Jews in our homeland. . . . Its success in getting Britain to issue the

---

Source: The Israel-Arab Reader: A Documentary History of the Middle East Conflict, Walter Laqueur and Barry Rubin, eds. (New York, 1984), 504–18.

Balfour Declaration once again demonstrated the alliance between Zionism and imperialism. Furthermore, by promising to the Zionist movement what was not hers to give, Britain showed how oppressive the rule of imperialism was. As it was constituted then, the League of Nations abandoned our Arab people, and Wilson's pledges and promises came to nought. In the guise of a mandate, British imperialism was cruelly and directly imposed upon us . . . [to] enable the Zionist invaders to consolidate their gains in our homeland. . . .

As a result of the collusion between the mandatory Power and the Zionist movement and with the support of some countries, this General Assembly early in its history approved a recommendation to partition our Palestinian homeland. . . . [and]

With support from imperialist and colonialist Powers, [Israel] managed to get itself accepted as a United Nations Member. It further succeeded in getting the Palestine Question deleted from the agenda of the United Nations and in deceiving world public opinion by presenting our cause as a problem of refugees in need either of charity from do-gooders, or settlement in a land not theirs. . . .

It pains our people greatly to witness the propagation of the myth that its homeland was a desert until it was made to bloom by the toil of foreign settlers, that it was a land without a people, and that the colonialist entity caused no harm to any human being. No: such lies must be exposed from this rostrum, for the world must know that Palestine was the cradle of the most ancient cultures and civilizations. Its Arab people were engaged in farming and building, spreading culture throughout the land for thousands of years, setting an example in the practice of freedom of worship, acting as faithful guardians of the holy places of all religions. . . .

Those who call us terrorists wish to prevent world public opinion from discovering the truth about us and from seeing the justice on our faces. They seek to hide the terrorism and tyranny of their acts, and our own posture of self-defense.

The difference between the revolutionary and the terrorist lies in the reason for which each fights. For whoever stands by a just cause and fights for the freedom and liberation of his land from the invaders, the settlers and the colonialists, cannot possibly be called terrorist; otherwise the American people in their struggle for liberation from the British colonialists would have been terrorists, the European resistance against the Nazis would be terrorism, the struggle of the Asian, African and Latin American peoples would also be terrorism, and many of you who are in this Assembly Hall were considered terrorists. This is actually a just and proper struggle consecrated by the United Nations Charter and by the Universal Declaration of Human Rights. As to those who fight against the just causes, those who wage war to occupy, colonize and oppress other people—those are the terrorists, those are the people whose actions should be condemned. . . .

When the majority of the Palestinian people was uprooted from its homeland in 1948, the Palestinian struggle for self-determination continued under the most difficult conditions. . . . All along the Palestinian dreamed of return. . . . Nothing could persuade him to relinquish his Palestinian identity or to forsake his homeland. . . . When our people lost faith in the international community which persisted in ignoring its rights . . . our people had no choice but to resort to armed struggle. . . . A national liberation movement . . . materialized in the Palestine Liberation Organization. . . .

The Palestine Liberation Organization has earned its legitimacy . . . by representing every faction, union or group as well as every Palestinian talent, either in the National Council or in people's institutions. This legitimacy . . . was consecrated during the last Arab Summit Conference [Rabat] which reiterated the right of the Palestine Liberation Organization, in its capacity as the sole representative of the Palestinian people, to establish an independent national State on all liberated Palestinian territory. . . .

I am a rebel and freedom is my cause. I know well that many of you present here today once stood in exactly the same resistance position as I now occupy and from which I must fight. You once had to convert dreams into reality by your struggle. Therefore you must now share my dream. . . .

In my formal capacity as Chairman of the Palestine Liberation Organization and leader of the Palestinian revolution I proclaim before you that when we speak of our common hopes for the Palestine of tomorrow we include in our perspective all Jews now living in Palestine who choose to live with us there in peace and without discrimination.

. . . I call upon Jews to turn away one by one from the illusory promises made to them by Zionist ideology and Israeli leadership. They are offering Jews perpetual bloodshed, endless war and continuous thraldom. . . .

We offer them the most generous solution, that we might live together in a framework of just peace in our democratic Palestine.

In my formal capacity as Chairman of the Palestine Liberation Organization, I announce here that we do not wish one drop of either Arab or Jewish blood to be shed; neither do we delight in the continuation of killing, . . . I appeal to you to accompany our people in its struggle to attain its right to self-determination. This right is consecrated in the United Nations Charter and has been repeatedly confirmed in resolutions adopted by this august body since the drafting of the Charter. I appeal to you, further; to aid our people's return to its homeland from an involuntary exile imposed upon it by force of arms, by tyranny, by oppression, so that we may regain our property, our land, and thereafter live in our national homeland, free and sovereign, enjoying all the privileges of nationhood. . . . Only then will our Jerusalem resume its historic role as a peaceful shrine for all religions. . . .

Today I have come bearing an olive branch and a freedom-fighter's gun. Do not let the olive branch fall from my hand. I repeat: do not let the olive branch fall from my hand.

War flares up in Palestine, and yet it is in Palestine that peace will be born.

DOCUMENT 7.5

YOSEF TEKOAH

RESPONSE TO ARAFAT'S ADDRESS

November 13, 1974

Israeli U.N. Ambassador Yosef Tekoah's references to the PLO as murderers and ter-rorists reflect the Israeli experience under PLO assaults as well as Israeli determina-tion never to deal with an organization whose claims contradicted their own asser-tions of the right to exist in their historic homeland. Tekoah's identification of Jordan as a Palestinian Arab state, even including the bedouins, is noteworthy in itself and as the position of a Labor government, then headed by Yitzhak Rabin. It would be a basic stance of Likud governments after 1978. Compare Tekoah's depic-tion of the PLO with the position of the later Rabin government, which signed the Oslo Accord of 1993 (Document 10.1).

On 14 October 1974 the General Assembly turned its back on the UN Charter, on law and humanity, and virtually capitulated to a murder organization which aims at the destruction of a State Member of the UN. On 14 October the UN hung out a sign reading "Murderers of children are welcome here." Today these murderers have come to the General Assembly, certain that it would do their bidding. Today this rostrum was defiled by their chieftain, who proclaimed that the shedding of Jewish blood would end only when the murderers' demands had been accepted and their objectives achieved. . . .

The United Nations is entrusted with the responsibility to guide man-kind away from war, away from violence and oppression, toward peace, toward international understanding and the vindication of the rights of peoples and individuals.

What remains of that responsibility now that the UN has prostrated itself before the PLO, which stands for premeditated, deliberate murder of innocent civilians, denies to the Jewish people its right to live, and seeks to destroy the Jewish State by armed force? . . .

Now, as a result of centuries of acquisition of territory by war, the Arab nation is represented in the UN by twenty sovereign States. Among them is also the Palestinian Arab State of Jordan.

Geographically and ethnically, Jordan is Palestine. Historically both the West and East Banks of the Jordan River are parts of the Land of Israel or Pales-tine. Both were parts of Palestine under the British Mandate until Jordan and then Israel became independent. The population of Jordan is composed of two

---

Source: T. G. Fraser, *The Middle East, 1914–1979* (London, 1980), 140–43.

elements—the sedentary population and nomads. Both are, of course, Palestinian. The nomad Bedouins constitute a minority of Jordan's population. Moreover, the majority of the sedentary inhabitants, even on the East Bank, are of Palestinian West Bank origin. Without the Palestinians, Jordan is a State without a people. . . .

Indeed, the vast majority of Palestinian refugees never left Palestine, but moved, as a result of the 1948 and 1967 Wars, from one part of the country to another. At the same time, an approximately equal number of Jewish refugees fled from Arab countries to Israel.

It is, therefore, false to allege that the Palestinian people has been deprived of a State of its own or that it has been uprooted from its national homeland. Most Palestinians continue to live in Palestine. Most Palestinians continue to live in a Palestinian State. The vast majority of Palestinian Arabs are citizens of that Palestinian State.

The choice before the General Assembly is clear. On the one hand, there is the Charter of the UN; on the other there is the PLO, whose sinister objectives, defined in its Covenant, and savage outrages are a desecration of the Charter.

On the one hand, there is Israel's readiness and desire to reach a peaceful settlement with the Palestinian Arab State of Jordan in which the Palestinian national identity would find full expression. On the other hand, there is the PLO's denial of Israel's right to independence and of the Jewish people's right to self-determination. . . .

The United Nations, whose duty it is to combat terrorism and barbarity, may agree to consort with them. Israel will not.

The murderers of athletes in the Olympic Games of Munich, the butchers of children in Ma'alot, the assassins of diplomats in Khartoum do not belong in the international community. They have no place in international diplomatic efforts. Israel shall see to it that they have no place in them.

Israel will pursue the PLO murderers until justice is meted out to them. It will continue to take action against their organization and against their bases until a definitive end is put to their atrocities. The blood of Jewish children will not be shed with impunity.

Israel will not permit the establishment of PLO authority in any part of Palestine. The PLO will not be forced on the Palestinian Arabs. It will not be tolerated by the Jews of Israel.

8

LEBANON, THE WEST BANK, AND THE CAMP DAVID ACCORDS

The Palestinian Equation in the Arab-Israeli Conflict

1977–1984

THE CARTER White House staff and advisers "achieved a rare degree of consensus" regarding the approach to be taken toward the Arab-Israeli conflict.[1] Unlike the Rogers-Kissinger rivalry during Nixon's first term in office, Secretary of State Cyrus Vance and National Security Adviser Zbigniew Brzezinski concurred that an international conference of all parties seeking a full peace agreement was preferable to Kissinger's step-by-step procedures. Administration officials also agreed that the Palestinian question had to be addressed and resolved. Though committed to Israel, Washington defined its security more in terms of treaties than retention of territories, believing that Israel's settlement policies were counterproductive to peace efforts.

A potential obstacle to an international conference was Egypt's Anwar al-Sadat, who hoped to reach a separate accord with Israel that would accelerate the infusion of American economic assistance to his beleaguered economy. Egypt had witnessed serious outbreaks of unrest in January 1977 after the government temporarily raised prices on staples in order to reduce its subsidies on those goods. Sadat's hesitancy was only one of several factors that thwarted Carter's plans. Israel's prime minister, Menachem Begin, was determined to retain the Golan Heights and the West Bank and would tolerate at most a separate peace with Egypt. On the Arab side, various states, especially Syria, preferred an international conference with Soviet participation and viewed Sadat's eagerness for an accord with suspicion. Syria's Assad had little interest in negotiations unless the Arabs formed a united front, although he accepted U.N. Resolution 242. The period of diplomacy that culminated in the Camp David Accord of September 1978 was marked by major developments elsewhere, on the West

Bank and in Lebanon. Under Begin, Israeli settlement projects in the West Bank increased, at times in apparent violation of commitments given to the Carter administration. In Lebanon, the aftermath of a vicious civil war saw the south caught up in a struggle among Palestinian groups, Israeli proxies, and Israel itself, which acted at times in direct alliance with Maronite politicians and paramilitary forces.

The problems deriving from the Lebanese Civil War establish the backdrop for Camp David and its impact, especially on West Bank Palestinians. That conflict erupted in the mid-1970s during the period that saw Kissinger achieve the Israeli-Egyptian and Israeli-Syrian limited withdrawal agreements. For West Bank Palestinians, the Egyptian-Israeli Camp David agreement seemed a disaster because it appeared to confirm their continued subjugation to Israeli rule. This in turn bolstered Arafat's prestige. He seemed the only leader able to achieve recognition of Palestinian rights. PLO strength in southern Lebanon and continued unrest in the West Bank, often fanned by Israeli attempts to destroy nationalist sentiments there, resulted in a long-planned Israeli invasion of Lebanon in June 1982. The attack sought to eradicate the Palestinian presence in Lebanon, in collaboration with Maronite allies, and thus to erase any hope among West Bank Arabs that they had an alternative to Israeli rule. In this manner, the fates of Lebanon and the West Bank became increasingly intertwined following the Camp David Accord.

THE LEBANESE CIVIL WAR AND ITS AFTERMATH, 1975–1978

Scholars date the period of the Lebanese Civil War from April 1975 to October 1976, when an Arab summit led to the formation of a peacekeeping force to maintain order in central Lebanon. These dates are technically correct, but tensions between the Maronites and the Palestinians on the one hand, and between the Maronites and the Lebanese Muslim and leftist forces on the other, long predated the war.

Roots of the Lebanese Conflict

Domestically, the major issue remained that of Christian, especially Maronite Catholic, control of the government and the patronage system related to it. This system was increasingly challenged by a coalition of Muslim and leftist groups headed by the Druze patriarch, Kamal Junblat, who formed the National Movement in 1969. As depicted in its program announced in 1975, the National Movement called for the "deconfessionalization" of the government, to be achieved by the taking of a new census and the subsequent allocation of governmental and electoral posts on the basis of majority rule; the proposal posed a direct threat to Maronite ascendancy.[2]

The National Movement was a radical front that included Christians along with Muslims, often opposing their own leaders who acquiesced in denial of their rights. A purely religious delineation of the conflict overlooked the complexity of allegiances. For example, the parliamentary elections of 1972 witnessed "the overwhelming victory of a young neo-Nasserist candidate against an established conservative rival in Beirut," an event that showed the "crystallizing Moslem radical mood." Both candidates were Greek Orthodox Christians, but the district was composed primarily of Sunni Muslims. And the Greek Orthodox victor, by being a "neo-Nasserist," belonged to a faction financed by Libya's Muammar al-Qadhdhafi.[3]

The Maronite leadership, as in 1958, presented the question as one of Muslim-Christian strife. Here, the matter was complicated by the growing alliances between the National Movement and elements of the PLO, especially the Marxist-oriented PFLP and PDFLP controlled by George Habash and Nayif Hawatmah. Finally, there was the matter of the PLO attacks on Israel that brought Israeli retaliation and greater sympathy for the Palestinian cause on the part of many Muslims and leftists. As a result of the Cairo Accords of 1969, the PLO controlled the refugee camps, located in the poorer suburbs of Beirut or in the south, and had gradually created a ministate within Lebanon.[4] These developments spurred the growth of private Maronite militias. Formed to confront the Palestinians, they fought each other as well, striving to dominate Maronite politics; the Phalange under the Gemayels, and the paramilitary forces linked to the families of Camille Chamoun and Sulayman Franjiyah[5] (see Figure 8.1).

Figure 8.1 ■ Maronite Militia Leaders Dany Chamoun and Bashir Gemayel, April 12, 1978, Press Conference

Ostensibly united against the PLO, Chamoun, seen here speaking, and Gemayel were bitter rivals. Both were sons of Maronite Catholic patriarchs, Camille Chamoun, former prime minister, and Pierre Gemayel. Bashir Gemayel would later cement his leadership of the Maronite militias by ordering the massacre of Dany Chamoun's family, forcing Chamoun to flee into exile.

Arab Factions and Alignments vis-à-vis Syria and Israel

A final element in the Lebanese equation was the alignment of states and factions either supporting or rejecting U.S. diplomacy and the 1974–1975 disengagement accords, especially Sadat's agreement to sign the second pact with Israel in September 1975. Within the PLO, the "Rejection Front," backed by Libya and Iraq, joined Junblat's National Movement to work to redress the political balance in Lebanon.[6] Arafat and Fatah hedged, seeking to avoid immersion in Arab communal strife. Arafat's later commitment to the radical alignment in the civil war was in part motivated by realization that the PLO would gain no benefits from great-power diplomacy. As for Syria, it joined Iraq and Libya in condemning the Sinai II Accord of September 1975, but for the most part Hafiz al-Assad attempted to balance the competing demands of international diplomacy and Syria's regional security. Assad's primary fear was that PLO actions might force Syria into a war with Israel.

Once the civil war erupted in April 1975, Syria sided cautiously with the Rejection Front, when it seemed that Palestinian-leftist forces might overrun Maronite positions and communities, Syria switched sides during 1976 and backed the Maronites, blocking the potential defeat of the major Christian groups. Assad preferred a balance of power in which the Maronites preserved their political and military role, but this meant that Assad ordered his troops to permit the ongoing Maronite blockade, aided by Israel, of a major refugee camp, Tal al-Zaatar. The camp finally succumbed in August 1976; after they surrendered, many of its inhabitants were lined up and killed outright by Maronite militiamen, adding to the atrocities committed by both sides during the conflict.

Syria's actions illustrated in microcosm how allegiances could shift as the war continued. Equally complex were the sources of armaments for the combatants, with manifest contradictions in their implications for state policies. Although the Saudi ruling house discreetly backed the Maronites in the beginning, other Saudi princes funded the Palestinians. The Maronites used money from the Saudis and conservative Arab states, such as Kuwait, to buy arms from Czechoslovakia and Bulgaria, communist regimes whose master, the Soviet Union, was arming Syria and, through it, the PLO. Once the communist supplies to the Maronites ended, the Maronites bought weapons on the open market and ultimately found their new supplier in Israel. Beginning in May 1976, Israel began shipping arms and tanks to the Maronites in the north while building up Maronite enclaves in the south. Israeli advisers were also sent to Maronite territory north of Beirut. These advisers and vehicles with Israeli markings took part in the final siege of Tal al-Zaatar.[7] Thus during the summer of 1976, both Israel and Syria were either directly or indirectly backing the Maronites against the Palestinians.

In the end, following an Arab summit in Riyadh in October, a deterrent force composed primarily of Syrians remained in central Lebanon to try to restore peace. By now, Lebanese politics had become even more splintered as many small factions, unanswerable to any recognized political authority, clashed for control of urban neighborhoods; Beirut once more became a war zone. As a final irony, the Riyadh Accords called for the PLO to transfer its forces from central Lebanon to the south, where their presence contributed to the tensions that finally caused the Israeli invasion of southern Lebanon in March 1978.

Israel had its own priorities. Strengthening the Maronite militias meant the possible destruction of the Palestinian camps and their inhabitants. Israel initiated an open fence policy along its northern border and, from 1976 onward, facilitated the transfer of Maronite militiamen through Israel into south Lebanon to bolster the Maronite position there. The Israelis linked their efforts with those of a dissident Lebanese army officer, Saad Haddad. A Greek Catholic, Haddad opted for close relations with Israel as a way to combat the Palestinians in the region and enhance his own prestige. Israel supplied Haddad's forces and helped them expand their control, especially once Menachem Begin took office. Begin likened the Maronites, and Christians in general, to Jews exterminated by the Nazis in World War II. By extension, the Arabs, and especially the Palestinians, were the incarnations of Nazis and should be given no quarter, an analogy he developed more specifically as time passed.

Haddad's expansion of his authority increased tensions with the Palestinian forces returning to the south from around Beirut. In the midst of these clashes, Israel notified Syria that its forces could not extend beyond a "red line," which remained undefined but was assumed to be the Litani River. Accepting this limit to its sphere of interest, the Syrians tried to restrict the PLO's activities and backed Lebanese government efforts to establish the principle of Lebanese authority in the region. In July 1977 Syria, the PLO (Arafat), and Lebanese President Elias Sarkis reached an agreement at Shtaura whereby the Palestinians would withdraw their forces from the border regions adjacent to Israel and permit Lebanese army units to enter. Haddad and Begin rejected this idea. They opposed restoration of any central authority that might limit their freedom of action in their own sphere of interest between the Litani River and the Israeli frontier.

U.S. Diplomacy amid Regional Strife

These activities took place during a period of intense American diplomacy (discussed in detail later) that aimed during most of 1977 to establish conditions suitable for a Geneva conference of all parties to the conflict, including, at one point, the PLO. Washington's abandonment of these goals and subsequent support for Sadat's peace overture to Israel in November 1977 inspired the PLO, including Fatah, to intensify their raids into Israel. Terrorist assaults could strengthen Begin's resolve not to capitulate to American pressures. More Israeli settlements were preferable to a conference that excluded Palestinians from talks that could decide the fate of the West Bank.

On March 11, 1978, for example, eight Palestinian commandos belonging to Fatah landed on an Israeli beach along the coastal highway between Haifa and Tel Aviv. They commandeered a passenger bus and headed for Tel Aviv. In the shoot-out that followed, six of the Palestinians and thirty-four Israelis died, with seventy-eight more wounded. Fatah timed the raid to interrupt a visit of Begin to Washington, scheduled for March 14. It was intended to enable Begin to resist American pressure to soften the Israeli position on the future of the Palestinians on the West Bank.[8] The immediate result of the raid was the Israeli invasion of south Lebanon on March 15, which led to an occupation that ended in June.

Ostensibly aimed at the PLO, the invasion by approximately 20,000 troops had long been planned, with the primary objective of ousting most Lebanese civilians, other than Maronites, from the area. This would give freer rein to military actions by Israel and Colonel Haddad. The intensive shelling caused an evacuation of over 100,000 Lebanese, many of them Shi'ites.[9] In the short run, Fatah strategy seemed to work. PLO casualties in south Lebanon were slight, and "the terrorist attack greatly strengthened Begin's position." Many in the United States shifted from criticizing his hard-line stand on West Bank settlements, which seemed to block progress in talks, to stressing the need to bolster Israel's security.[10]

President Jimmy Carter and his advisers had hoped to bring in the PLO to attain a lasting peace, but by mid-1978 they realized that their initial objectives were impossible to achieve. Their best course was to salvage an Egyptian-Israeli pact that could serve as a guide for future negotiations with other states, an upgraded version of the Kissinger model.

THE CARTER ADMINISTRATION AND CAMP DAVID, JANUARY 1977–SEPTEMBER 1978

The first efforts to define the parameters within which agreement might be reached indicated the difficulties ahead. Prime Minister Rabin, facing elections in March 1977, had told the United States that Israel could give up most of the Sinai but none of the Golan Heights; the West Bank was the most delicate, although he left room for compromise. As for the PLO, Rabin continually reminded Washington that Kissinger's 1975 promise still held; no contacts with the PLO were possible until it accepted Resolution 242, to which Israel presumably adhered. Once Begin took office in June, he insisted that SCR 242 did not apply to the West Bank. During his electoral campaign, he had promised never to give up any portion of Judea and Samaria, as he called the region (see Document 8.1). In addition, Begin emotionally declared that the PLO was a Nazi organization; even if the PLO accepted Resolution 242 and recognized Israel, he would never deal with them, a statement that had widespread approval in Israel.[11]

Begin's assertions clarified the forthcoming confrontation. Husayn of Jordan, eager to be included in any international summit meeting, supported inclusion of the PLO because he could not afford to oppose it. But he could not countenance the supposed goal of such participation, namely, the creation of an independent Palestinian state in the West Bank and Gaza; he wanted the West Bank to be returned to Jordan. He therefore proposed that Palestinians outside the PLO be permitted to attend a Geneva meeting as part of his Jordanian delegation, hoping to counter the PLO's demands for a state and gain international recognition of his own title to the land. Begin, in turn, refused to consider Jordanian recovery of the region.

The PLO's various groups debated the possibility of attending a summit in light of the Lebanese crisis they had just experienced.[12] They refused to accept Resolution 242 because it referred to Palestinians only as refugees; the matter of statehood had to be considered. It was only in March 1977 that Arafat gained PLO approval of a call for a Palestinian state to be created in "the territories from which Israel withdraws," an apparent though indirect acceptance of Israel's existence in its pre-1967 form.[13] This served as a signal of Arafat's eagerness to be included in any international conference that was convened.

Carter's Failed Attempts to Restructure Negotiating Parameters

Unlike Henry Kissinger, Jimmy Carter genuinely believed that the PLO should be involved in peace talks conditional upon the organization's acceptance of Resolution 242. He was willing to have the PLO add a reservation that disclaimed the resolution's reference to the Palestinian issue solely in terms of refugees, something Arafat had proposed. In Carter's view, this would indicate the PLO's acceptance of Israel and would enable it to be included in the Geneva conference, where a separate Palestinian entity might be accepted, although linked to Jordanian sovereignty over the West Bank. There were pitfalls. Eager to instill new life into resolving the Middle East conflict, Carter had remarked in March 1977 that the Palestinians should be given a "homeland" as part of an overall resolution of the Arab-Israeli stalemate. Though couched in terms that called for Arab acceptance of Israel, the code word "homeland" seemed to suggest a separate state, and Carter was later forced to repudiate his remarks because of their domestic political repercussions.[14]

Carter's effort failed, despite various American overtures to Arafat including a State Department announcement on September 12 that "the Palestinians must be involved in the peacemaking process. Their representatives will have to be at Geneva for the question to be solved," assuming these delegates had accepted Resolution 242.[15] Arafat could not overcome rejectionist arguments that the United States could not be relied on to force Israel to withdraw from the West Bank and Gaza.[16] Interim developments prior to the PLO meeting had seemed to prove their point. Pro-Israeli criticism of the State Department's September 12 announcement had led Carter to deny on September 16 that he had ever committed himself to the PLO or that he envisioned a separate Palestinian state; he was calling only for Palestinians to be represented at the conference.[17]

Defeat did not mean the end of American efforts, however. The Carter administration reached agreement with the Soviet Union on a joint declaration of principles that could guide the forthcoming Geneva summit, another significant departure from Kissinger's strategy. Moscow agreed to omit references to the "national rights" of the Palestinians and to Israel's withdrawal to "the" 1967 borders; the communiqué referred to Israeli withdrawal from territories and to the "legitimate rights" of the Palestinians, placing the statement more squarely within the context of Resolution 242.[18]

Sadat welcomed the news, but for Israel and its American supporters, the agreement signified a major setback that would have to be neutralized. During a tense meeting with Carter and his chief aides on October 4, Foreign Minister Moshe Dayan threatened to go to the American Jewish community to mobilize them against Carter because of his supposed rejection of commitments to Israel. He gained from Carter a declaration including the sentence "acceptance of the Joint U.S.-U.S.S.R. Statement of October 1, 1977, is not a prerequisite for the reconvening and conduct of the Geneva Conference." This meant that Israel would not be bound by the principles established for the meeting, even if all other participants accepted them. The United States was forced to back Israel's position even though it had jointly proposed those principles.[19]

Israel opposed Soviet involvement, fearing that the Russians might persuade the Syrians and the Palestinians to be more amenable to compromise. This would have placed greater international pressure on Israel to withdraw from the Golan Heights and the West Bank in return for peace; as Dayan made clear, that was unacceptable.[20] Carter's retreat from the Soviet-American declaration convinced Sadat that direct negotiations with Israel were preferable to an international forum where discussions over procedures would greatly lengthen the negotiating process. Aware of Israeli interest in a direct dialogue, Sadat announced on November 9 to a stunned Egyptian National Assembly, with Arafat in the audience, that he was willing to go to Jerusalem.[21] Exchanges with Begin led to his historic visit on November 19 (see Documents 8.2 and 8.3), setting in motion the contacts that, after several false starts, led to Camp David and the subsequent Egyptian-Israeli peace accord.

The Road to Camp David, November 1977–September 1978

Both Sadat and Begin wanted a peace agreement to justify their diametrically opposed stances on the fate of the West Bank Palestinians. Sadat demanded references in the agreement to Israeli recognition of Palestinian rights to self-rule; Begin sought clauses that would guarantee continued Israeli control of the West Bank, ensuring denial of any semblance of an independent Palestinian entity. The potential for stalemate emerged soon after Sadat's visit to Jerusalem. On January 18, 1978, he summarily recalled his negotiating team from that city.

During their exchanges, the Egyptians had been angered by Begin's continued references to Palestinians and, by inference, other Arabs, as Nazis. In addition, the Begin cabinet had approved a proposal by Agricultural Minister Ariel Sharon to create dummy settlements in the Sinai beyond those already in place west of Gaza. Sharon's aim, accepted by Begin and Dayan, was either to gain more land in the Sinai or to bargain with Sadat by openly abandoning these fake encampments in order to keep the existing Jewish communities. Begin also proposed retaining rights to the oil fields in the Sinai and the air bases built there, even if the Sinai was returned to Egypt. These latter proposals could be seen as bargaining tactics, but the new settlements appeared to be a breach of faith, arousing intense Egyptian hostility, which in turn angered the Israelis.[22]

A six-month hiatus set in. Carter's efforts, in tandem with Sadat, to pressure Begin to relax his stand regarding the West Bank, especially his refusal to apply Resolution 242 to the area, proved fruitless. As for Sadat, the president and his advisers concluded that the Egyptian leader would settle for a vague formula regarding the Palestinians. Sadat would not demand guarantees for the Palestinians, and even if he did, Begin would not provide them. Given this impasse, Carter decided in July to call a summit to resolve the discord between Begin and Sadat, conceding that his hopes for a broader peace in any form had been dashed. His only option was a separate agreement, precisely what the Israelis had been hoping for and what they believed, as Carter now did, Sadat would accept.[23]

The Camp David talks lasted from September 5 to 17, 1978. Two sets of agreements resulted. One established arrangements for determining the future of the West Bank and the Gaza Strip (see Document 8.4). The other comprised principles whereby an Egyptian-Israeli peace treaty would be formulated to ratify the conclusion of hostilities and the establishment of normal relations between the two countries (it was signed in March 1979). Success came only at the very end, with most of the participants near exhaustion and several crucial details left open to interpretation (see Figure 8.2).

Camp David Exchanges: The West Bank and the Gaza Strip

Throughout the talks, Begin refused to agree to withdraw the Sinai settlements; he finally compromised by declaring that he would accept the vote of the Knesset on the matter, meaning that he could not be accused of abandoning Jewish territory. As a result, Israel undertook a staged pullback from the Sinai that was completed in April 1982. But in return, Begin and his aides were able to delete references to Resolution 242 as applying to the West Bank. They had also deleted the reference to its clause noting the "inadmissibility of territories acquired by war," implying by omission the acceptability of retaining some territory by such means. No reference to Jerusalem appeared, which suggested Sadat's acceptance of a united Jerusalem under Israeli rule, although official positions remained to the contrary. And finally, from Begin's perspective, "the Sinai had been sacrificed, but Eretz Israel had been won," referring to the manner in which understandings pertaining to the West Bank had been deliberately left open.[24]

Figure 8.2 ■ Sadat, Carter, and Begin Clasp Hands on the North Lawn of the White House after Signing the Peace Treaty between Egypt and Israel on March 26, 1979

The apparent amity of the scene masked the mutual antipathy between Begin and Sadat. The negotiations were tense, and American diplomats served as intermediaries. Begin's aides, Moshe Dayan and Ezer Weizman, pushed him to be more forthcoming. Sadat's aides were horrified at his willingness to make concessions.

Here differences of opinion emerged that weakened American credibility in the Arab world. In seeking an accord on the fate of the West Bank and Gaza, Begin had accepted inclusion of the term "the legitimate rights of the Palestinian people," because he considered it meaningless in light of the guaranteed Israeli occupation of the region. But he later informed Carter that by "people" he meant the inhabitants of the areas, whereas Carter and Sadat had assumed this meant other Palestinians as well and thus theoretically did not rule out PLO participation. Though left unresolved, Begin's qualification was later accepted by the Reagan administration, with major implications for American policy in the region.[25]

In addition, there was the question of Israeli settlements in these areas. Carter had wanted Israel's commitment to freeze implantation of new settlements during the period required to negotiate the autonomy of the areas, which would take at least five years. Carter and other officials believed they had Begin's oral acceptance of this proposal, but Begin then informed Carter in writing that he would accept only a three-month moratorium. This suspension applied to the period envisaged as necessary to conclude the Israeli-Egyptian peace treaty, not the autonomy talks regarding the West Bank and Gaza. The gap in interpretation resulted from arguments on the final day of the talks that were left unresolved; Begin apparently agreed verbally to the longer moratorium but refused to sign anything. Carter then decided to leave the matter open in order to conclude the talks successfully. He and his aides remained convinced, however, that the context of the original discussion clearly tied Begin's oral agreement to the autonomy negotiations and that he later reneged. With no written document, however, the point remained moot.[26]

The Egyptian-Israeli Peace Treaty: The Carter Legacy

The Egyptian-Israeli peace treaty, signed in March 1979, was not linked to resolution of the autonomy scheme for the West Bank, despite Sadat's belated efforts to connect the two and defend himself against charges that he had abandoned the Palestinians. The negotiations leading to the final treaty were acrimonious and exhausting, but both sides compromised. Sadat agreed to an exchange of ambassadors and full diplomatic relations before Israel had completed its withdrawal from the Sinai; the latter reduced the period of its departure from five to three years.

Negotiations over the format of autonomy for the West Bank, begun in May 1979, dragged on for over a year with no agreement. The Begin government reasserted its claim to the West Bank. It interpreted "autonomy" as personal not political, and as not applying to land and water rights, which would belong to Israel. This assertion came during accelerated efforts to extend Jewish settlements in the area (discussed later). Sadat called for full governing autonomy for the territory, not simply for its inhabitants, within a Jordanian entity, a stance that had American backing but little will to support it forcefully.

Already looking ahead to the 1980 Democratic primary and reelection campaign, Carter found himself confronted by crises elsewhere that eroded his leadership image. The departure of the Shah from Iran in January 1979 and the arrival of the Ayatollah Khomeini in February signaled a new era for that country and sparked political turmoil that culminated in the taking of American hostages in the U.S. embassy in Teheran in November. This, coupled with the Soviet invasion of Afghanistan in December, left the president little room for maneuvering in the Arab-Israeli forum. The official American position remained as before — Israeli settlements in occupied territory were illegal and East Jerusalem was considered to be occupied territory despite its incorporation into Israel — but Carter preferred not to argue this openly in the midst of an election campaign.[27] He had achieved the Camp David Accords and the Egyptian-Israeli peace treaty, but at personal and political cost. Holding to established American positions, when declared openly, harmed his chances for a second term and helped the cause of the new president, Ronald Reagan.

THE REAGAN ADMINISTRATION AND THE ARAB-ISRAELI CONFLICT

Ronald Reagan assumed the presidency in January 1981 at a time of increased regional strife in the Middle East. In addition to the Soviet occupation of Afghanistan and a hostile regime in Iran, Iraq had attacked Iran in September 1980 to overthrow the regime of the Ayatollah Khomeini. The Ayatollah's pronouncements about the advent of a Shi'ite revolution under Iranian auspices had struck fear throughout the Persian Gulf region, where Arab oil-producing states, including Saudi Arabia, had significant Shi'i minorities.

The Reagan administration viewed these events in a global context dominated by the supposed Soviet ability to exploit them to their advantage. Reagan believed that the Soviets were an evil presence on earth whose machinations (if not their very existence) should be ended. This vision affected most of his other perceptions. His lack of knowledge about foreign affairs was equaled by his lack of interest in rectifying that situation. The new president "was well known for lack of mastery over finite material" and responded mainly to information that confirmed his preconceptions.[28] In the Middle East, Reagan saw Israel, following the Shah's departure from Iran, "as perhaps the only remaining strategic asset in the region on which the United States can truly rely. . . . Only by full appreciation of the critical role the State of Israel plays in our strategic calculus can we build the foundation for thwarting Moscow's design on territories vital to our security and our national wellbeing."[29] Reagan also identified with Israel in light of Old Testament prophecies as proclaimed by fundamentalist Christian groups, which lobbied him on behalf of Likud expansion in the territories.[30]

The Anticommunist Crusade: The Middle East in Global Perspective

Unconcerned with detail, the president left policy formulation to his advisers. They, especially Secretary of State Alexander Haig, hoped to align Israel and the conservative Arab states, in particular Egypt and Saudi Arabia, in an anti-Soviet military defense system. This search for a "strategic consensus" ignored the underlying reality of continuing Arab-Israeli hostility, which made such an initiative impossible to achieve. In addition, the Reagan administration's support for this policy aroused strong opposition in Washington when, in the spring of 1981, funding was requested for arms packages to Arab states as well as to Israel. Congress approved aid to Israel, but a furor erupted over proposed assistance to Saudi Arabia as part of the same strategic approach, especially the offer to sell five AWACS (Airborne Warning and Command Systems) planes. Though intended to buttress Saudi defense systems in the Persian Gulf against either Soviet or Iranian aggression, Israel's supporters viewed them as a threat to its security. The proposed package, with modifications, finally passed, but only after Reagan's direct intervention. The fray angered both sides, the Israelis because they had lost the battle and the Saudis because they had been forced to justify their need for such weapons in what they deemed a humiliating manner. In early June, in the midst of the controversy, Israeli planes had bombed an Iraqi nuclear reactor. The planes had crossed Saudi airspace to reach their target.

In these tense circumstances, chances for a strategic consensus on the Middle East were slight, but the Reagan administration sought to apply the concept elsewhere. In Central America, rebels called "contras" sought to overthrow the Marxist government of Nicaragua with strong administration backing. Reagan's support of the AWACS sale to Saudi Arabia was apparently tied to a private agreement that the Saudis would fund anticommunist movements. Initially conceived to back Afghan resistance against the Soviets, it later included giving $32 million to the contras. Israel also contributed to the contra effort as a result of its involvement in arms shipments to Iran in collusion with Reagan administration officials, and in violation of U.S. law. The money paid for these arms was then diverted to back the contras against the leftist government in power.[31]

This led to the following situation: Israel sold arms to Iran for use against Iraq, at times with American assistance; Washington intended to use the proceeds to fund anticommunist movements in Central America. At the same time, the Reagan administration was also backing Iraq against Iran, giving it strategic information on Iranian deployments and encouraging military and economic assistance to Baghdad via its European allies. These friendly relations with the Saddam Husayn regime would continue up to the eve of the Gulf Crisis of 1990.

The contrast with the Carter administration could not have been greater. Where once a consensus existed on Middle East policy, now there was none, with major rifts appearing within the Reagan administration. Whereas Carter had immersed himself in details, perhaps overly so, Reagan ignored both the details and the need to coordinate policy. As a result, officials fought among themselves while forced to respond to events, often instigated by the logic of Israel's policies that helped intensify hostilities in the region. The search for a strategic consensus among anticommunist Middle Eastern countries was justified only because Saudi and Israeli resources could be exploited to fund resistance to leftist regimes outside of the Middle East, not to establish a common front in the area of direct confrontation.

In the Middle East, the year 1981 was characterized by increasing violence in Lebanon. Tensions between Syria and Israel escalated, sparked by Maronite militias, PLO factions, and the units under Saad Haddad, as well as by Israel's continuing policy of preemptive air strikes on Palestinian positions. By the end of the year, Menachem Begin and Ariel Sharon, who had been appointed defense minister in August, had drafted plans for a massive invasion of Lebanon, as far as Beirut, designed to wipe out the PLO and possibly force most Palestinians from the country. An important by-product of this accomplishment would be consolidation of Israel's control over the West Bank. Destruction of the PLO would presumably demoralize Arafat's supporters in the area and compel them to accept Israeli rule.

The West Bank factor had become more significant following the assassination of Anwar al-Sadat on October 6, 1981, the eighth anniversary of the Egyptian crossing of the Suez Canal, which opened the 1973 war. Sadat had been playing for time, planning to become more forceful in his criticism of Israel's West Bank policies once he had regained the Sinai. But his tactics had opened him to severe criticism in Egypt. He had visited Israel before the June elections, a clear gesture of support for Begin designed to ensure progress toward recovery of the Sinai. Three days after his departure, Israel had bombed the Iraqi nuclear reactor, associating Sadat with the plan by default. In September he had ordered massive arrests of critics of his policies, both on the left and on the right. Egyptian disillusionment showed itself in the nearly total absence of public remorse at his death. His successor, Husni Mubarak, indicated his adherence to the Camp David Accord, but it was clear that Begin could not afford to pressure him for further concessions before proceeding with the final withdrawal from the northeast corner of the Sinai, scheduled for April 1982. The Begin government thus turned to imposing new administrative measures to consolidate its control over the West Bank, increasingly the focus of regional and international attention.

West Bank and Israeli Arabs between Jordan and Israel, 1948–1977

Since 1948 the West Bank, inhabited by Palestinian Arabs, had experienced the determined efforts of Jordan and Israel to erase its affiliation with mandatory Palestine. The term refers to the area taken by Jordan's King Abdullah in the 1948 war with Israel, which comprised most of the region in eastern Palestine allotted to the Arabs in the 1947 partition plan. Abdullah officially annexed the West Bank to his kingdom to create the Hashemite Kingdom of Jordan, and deliberately expunged the word "Palestine" from all sources that referred to it. It would be known as the West Bank to distinguish it from the East Bank, which had made up Abdullah's former principality of Transjordan. Abdullah set about cementing ties with West Bank notables who had opposed the mufti. He appointed many of them to prominent posts in government and to administrative positions dealing with West Bank affairs, among them the al-Nashashibis, Abd al-Hadis, and the Tuqans. King Husayn, who assumed the throne in 1952 at the age of sixteen, continued his grandfather's policy of maintaining ties with prominent Palestinian families from the West Bank. He also kept close surveillance over political activity among the general populace, which identified more closely with Arab nationalist currents prevalent in Cairo or Damascus.

Economically, the West Bank saw its relative prosperity decline vis-à-vis the East Bank. Agriculture remained the predominant occupation, while industrial development was concentrated in the East Bank. Those few with fairly large landholdings benefited from exporting their produce to East Jordan and to the Arab shaykhdoms of the Persian Gulf, but the bulk of the population continued to be small landholders with a sizable tenant farmer component. Circumstances in the West Bank were complicated by a greater concentration of refugees than in the East Bank—360,000 added to the 400,000 West Bank Palestinians already there in 1948. The small size of properties and the lack of opportunity for growth meant that many West Bankers emigrated, most to the East Bank initially but later into the wider Arab world and abroad. This outward flow stabilized the population at about 900,000, despite a birthrate of nearly 3 percent.[32] The aggregate of these factors suited Hashemite interests. The monarchy pursued a policy of political fragmentation, and this, along with Jordan's economic backwardness, prevented the formation of large political parties or newly wealthy groups independent of its control that might challenge Husayn's rule.

Israel's absorption of the West Bank in 1967 did not signal a change of political direction for the region. Like the Hashemites, Israel pursued the practice of political and social fragmentation by dealing with village leaders individually and seeking to prevent the growth of a collective identity as Palestinians. This reflected the Israelis' perception that they were "the only legitimate collective in the land of Israel [including the West Bank] and therefore all Palestinian claims to communal (economic and political) rights are illegitimate and, by definition, subversive."[33] Economic practices developed that were aimed at subverting West Bank Palestinian interests to those of Israel, but their impact also reflected the government's political tactics.

The West Bank Economy under Israeli Control. The material prosperity of West Bank Palestinians increased enormously under Israeli domination, particularly from 1967 to 1973 when the Israeli economy experienced a boom. Agricultural production rose, as did rural income. However, the tremendous increase in rural income per se, from a per capita revenue of $133 in 1966 to one of $930 in 1975, was principally the product of West Bank labor working in Israel, not on West Bank farms.

Many of the crops grown by West Bankers in 1967 competed with those cultivated by Israeli farmers. The Israeli government forbade the sale of some West Bank produce in Israel and placed quotas on others so that they would not compete with Israeli products. In addition, the Israelis received extensive government subsidies denied to the West Bankers; not being citizens, they were considered outside the Israeli system politically but were integrated into the economic system to benefit Israeli producers. Israeli farmers could dump excess produce into the West Bank at lower prices than those considered viable by Palestinians. The Israeli government also reserved the region as a special zone for its industrial goods, to the exclusion of those from other countries.[34] Little relief was found in Jordan. Israel permitted West Bankers to retain economic ties to the East Bank, meaning that much of the surplus agricultural crops traditionally farmed went there, but Jordanian quotas to protect East Bank agriculture left West Bank sales at the 1967 level. As a result, increased agricultural productivity did not greatly increase prosperity in the agricultural sector for those traditionally identified with landed wealth, namely, the old-time leaders that the Israelis sought to cultivate. Instead, these larger farmers lost laborers to the Israeli economy, which undermined their prestige and weakened them financially. This in turn led to the rise in status and wealth of members of the lower classes who formerly depended on the largesse of the landed class.[35]

It was here that the West Bank became integrated into the Israeli economic network. A development of great significance, the infusion of Arab labor into Israel meant the subordination of the West Bank economy and labor force to Israeli needs. Continued prosperity depended on Israel's economic fortunes. From the early 1970s, employment among the West Bank labor force averaged about 98 percent. Although the Palestinians (including the Gaza Strip workers) amounted to no more than 5 percent of the Israeli workforce, their representation in low-wage sectors and menial labor was important, "constituting almost one-third of the total labor force in the construction branch, and . . . a majority of unskilled laborers on actual construction sites."[36] These workers were the major contributors to West Bank income, particularly rural income, as they came from that sector. Their presence enabled the Israeli economy to experience a major economic boom in the mid-1970s by postponing mechanization in many areas, reducing costs, and paying wages unacceptably low to most Israeli workers but comparatively high to many Arabs. Although Arab workers were legally required to return to their homes at night, violations were often tolerated.[37]

Israeli control of the West Bank and the Gaza Strip proved economically beneficial to both parties but on different levels. Arab laborers in Israel received social security benefits, but they also paid income taxes. Customs duties were levied on non-Israeli goods entering the territories, but Israeli-owned industries in the West Bank were allowed to "export" their products to Israel duty free, in contrast to the regulations governing Arab agriculture. In many ways the regions paid for themselves until the 1987 uprising, leading one student of the process to conclude that "two-thirds of military government expenditure on the local population has been covered by revenues collected from the population. . . . There are indications that the territories place no fiscal and monetary burden . . . [and] it may well be that the territories are a net source of revenue to the Israeli Treasury."[38]

Israeli West Bank Tactics and Domestic Politics.   Beyond the perceived economic and strategic advantages to retaining the territories, especially the West Bank, there was a political factor of significance for one sector of Israeli society, the Jews from Arab lands. These oriental (Sephardic) Jews, now a majority of the Jewish population in Israel, had long considered themselves, with justification, as having been discriminated against by the dominant European Jewish (Ashkenazi) elite. The upward mobility of oriental Jews, though impressive over the years, did not erase the gap between their overall economic level and that of the Ashkenazim, leaving a legacy of bitterness.

The influx of Arab laborers from the territories after 1967 proved a boon to the oriental Jews. It helped to push them up the ladder out of jobs with which they had traditionally been associated.[39] Oriental Jews were well aware of these circumstances and the benefits they accrued from Israel's retention of the territories and the Arab labor force. Many feared that if these lands were returned for peace, they would be forced back by the Ashkenazi into the menial positions they had escaped. It was no accident that a majority of oriental Jews supported Begin and his call for holding the West Bank (Judea and Samaria) in perpetuity. They strongly identified with him as outsiders in an Israel controlled until 1977 by the Ashkenazi-dominated Labor Party. In addition, his desire to retain the West Bank for historical and religious reasons blended perfectly with their conception of their ability to preserve their economic gains. Oriental Jews backed Begin by a nearly three-to-one ratio in the 1977 elections, and he received the vote of over 50 percent of a younger generation that had grown up in an Israel that included the area.[40]

With this backing, Begin could feel that he had great popular support for his already determined plan to retain the West Bank. He facilitated the efforts of the Gush Emunim to establish settlements in heavily populated Arab sectors, tactics that the Labor Party had opposed. He identified with the Gush Emunim's combination of mystical attachment to areas of ancient Israel and practical steps to ensure a continued Jewish presence in the region. Religiosity and land went together, a connection fostered by Ariel Sharon who, as minister of agriculture, encouraged settlements to preempt any idea of concessions in the area.[41]

Israeli Arabs in the Israeli State. Israel's expansion of settlements into high-density Arab areas on the West Bank coincided with its renewed attention to the Arabs who had remained in Israel since 1948. Here, as on the West Bank, the Likud Party's policies reflected an intensification of past Labor practices rather than a radical shift of emphasis.

As noted previously, the status of Israeli Arabs had loomed as a threat to the integrity of the Jewish state of Israel immediately following independence. Although technically citizens of that state, these Arabs were seen as part of the enemy, fifth columnists whose possession of land obstructed the settlement of incoming Jews. Under the absentee laws, land had been expropriated from individual Arabs and Arab villages. When the legal clauses did not apply, forcible expulsion could be used. Initiated during the 1948 war, these practices lasted until 1953. Nearly 1 million dunams of Arab land were "redeemed" for Jewish ownership by transference to the Jewish National Fund, so that it became inalienably Jewish. In 1953 the Israeli law of compensation for lands taken or to be taken in the future based the value of a dunam on rates current in 1950, regardless of the inflation of Israeli currency or increases in land values.[42]

An additional motive for expelling entire villages arose from the fact that most Arab settlements were clustered in the upper Galilee near the Lebanese border, creating a region with very little Jewish settlement. From the early 1950s, efforts were made to "Judaize the Galilee," albeit with little success. However, when settlements such as Maalot or Kiryat Shimona were founded, they were often situated where Arab villages had once stood; the Arab inhabitants had been ousted from Israel and pushed across the Jordanian border to make room for Jewish towns that would break up the Arabness of the region. When villages were not destroyed, a frequent practice was to expropriate valuable land from them. This opened the way for Jewish settlement or development of that land and served to deny the potential for Arab expansion on lands once theirs. The frequency of these occurrences decreased dramatically after 1956, principally because government attention was focused elsewhere, but they increased again once the Likud entered office in 1977.

As a rule, Israeli policy toward Israeli Arabs sought to "reinforce the internal fragmentation of the Arab population and its isolation from the Jewish majority."[43] This could be done through land expropriation or the imposition of Jewish settlements among the Arabs, but it could be furthered only by stimulating the development of Jewish sectors at a pace unavailable to the Arab inhabitants. Technically, this did not reflect deliberate governmental decision making but, rather, the process of state development aided by the Jewish National Fund. Thus, most Arab villages did not have basic amenities because these would have to be paid for out of taxes levied on the inhabitants, mostly poor farmers. Consequently, little money was available for such services, whereas the Jewish settlements received nearly free electricity, paved roads, sewage systems, and the like.[44] These practices isolated Arab regions from the national economy and kept them agricultural and dependent on a Jewish industrial and larger agricultural base unless they could finance their own development, usually an impossibility.[45]

This approach, along with the practice of encouraging educated Israeli Arabs either to leave or not to return from education abroad for advanced degrees, served the same purpose. Arab resentment exploded at times, as happened following the demonstrations in May 1976 to protest Israeli expropriation of land. The communist-sponsored Land Day rally attracted large crowds; Israeli soldiers fired on the protesters, killing six and wounding many, thereby establishing a legacy of bitterness that remains.

Sharon's Vision: Israel, Israeli Arabs, and the West Bank, 1977–1982

On assuming power in 1977, Begin and his colleagues had called attention to the concentration of Arab settlements in northern Israel. Minister of Agriculture Ariel Sharon declared that he had undertaken an "offensive" to "stem the hold of foreigners on state lands," to be achieved in part through Judaizing the Galilee.[46] Sharon's militaristic terminology and his reference to Arab citizens of Israel as foreigners coincided with his attitude toward West Bank Arabs living in what had been Israel; he identified them all as alien to a Jewish state. His assumptions resembled those of Meir Kahane, former head of the right-wing party, Kach, who in the 1980s called for the expulsion of all Israeli Arabs in order to purify Israel by ridding it of alien blood.[47] These activities and their stated justification created a greater sense of kinship between Israeli and West Bank Arabs after 1977 than might have otherwise existed.

In the occupied territories, Ariel Sharon expanded Jewish settlements on the West Bank and in Gaza, especially the former. Sharon had close ties to the Gush Emunim and backed the group's efforts to settle in areas adjacent to large Arab centers of population, a strategy designed to ensure the enlargement of the Jewish population of the West Bank and intimidate the Arab inhabitants. Sharon was aided by the fact that the West Bank was governed by an Israeli military administration whose acquisition of private land for supposedly military purposes traditionally went unchallenged by Israeli courts; in many cases, this land was then handed over to the agriculture ministry for Jewish settlement. When unilateral acts by the Gush Emunim brought this policy into question, Sharon used his ties with and financial backing from the Jewish National Fund, part of the World Zionist Organization, to acquire sectors considered public or state land rather than privately owned land.⁴⁸

When the process proved time-consuming and indicated that too much land might be considered private property, the government decided in 1980 to declare arbitrarily as "state land" large tracts regardless of title. It stipulated that the land could be turned over to Israeli settlers in three weeks if Arab claimants could not prove ownership during that period, an unlikely prospect in the Begin government's view. Judgment over the status of ownership would be made by military tribunals within the territory with no appeal.

Done hastily, this "process of declaration and seizure [was] not the outcome of a long, multistage judicial process but was intended specifically to preempt it."⁴⁹ Authorities designated for acquisition over two million dunams (500,000 acres), or 40 percent of the total land area (see Figure 8.3). At the same time the World Zionist Organization authorized plans to purchase extensive private property where the Arabs were willing to sell. This had been the primary form of land acquisition during the mandatory period, but now the proportion of land acquired through buying and selling, as opposed to state requisition, was less, perhaps 25 percent of the total by 1983, and the cost relatively high because land values had risen enormously.⁵⁰

Begin and the West Bank after Camp David

With Begin's narrow electoral victory in June 1981 behind him and Sharon now his minister of defense, he decided to implement his own version of Palestinian autonomy while claiming that it fulfilled the intent of the Camp David Accord. On November 8, 1981, the Begin cabinet announced that it had created a separate civilian administration designed to handle all local concerns except military and security matters on the West Bank and abolished the military government established after the 1967 war. This was a subterfuge. The Israeli military remained in control of affairs on the West Bank and civilian officials remained

Figure 8.3 ■ **Ariel Sharon Shows Map of Plans for New Settlements in the West Bank to Visiting Members of the Likud Party, 1984**

Then Minister without Portfolio, Sharon displays a map that shows the careful planning undertaken by Likud to consolidate control of the West Bank as called for by the Likud Platform (Document 8.1). Once he became prime minister in 2001, Sharon continued to pursue such efforts in the face of the second Palestinian intifada and calls for a two-state solution.

subordinate to them. The only difference was that the military authority was now situated in Israel rather than centered in the West Bank. This enabled the Begin government to claim that it was fulfilling the clauses requiring that the military government and "its civilian administration" be removed "as soon as a self-governing authority had been freely elected."[51]

Having "removed" the military government by transferring its headquarters, Israeli officials set about trying to constitute a Palestinian self-governing authority staffed by individuals who would accept their directives. Here, they focused on an arrangement of local village leagues created in 1978 around Hebron and decided to use this structure as a basis for developing an areawide system run by Palestinians. These leagues would be given legislative powers, excluding elected mayors and village officials who rejected the Israeli initiative. Village league heads would control patronage, have the power to issue permits, and have the sole right to carry arms. This authority would presumably enable them to win support either through their control of purse strings or through intimidation. West Bank Palestinians mounted strong resistance to these moves, which were accompanied by an "iron fist" policy of retaliation and harassment encouraged by the chief of staff, Rafael Eitan. As a result, the West Bank became a scene of intensified repression during the first six months of 1982, with military officials tolerating, if not encouraging, settler violence toward Arab residents.[52]

LEBANON: THE STRUGGLE FOR HEGEMONY

By the end of 1980, Bashir Gemayel and his Phalange militia had established their dominance over all the Maronite military forces in Lebanon. As noted, Israel's West Bank strategy paralleled its plans to undertake a massive invasion of Lebanon designed to destroy the PLO and facilitate the re-creation of a united Lebanon under Gemayel's presidency.

The Phalange-Likud Alliance

Gemayel had long been in contact with Israeli leaders. Many of his assistants had received extensive training in Israel during and following Israeli intervention on the side of the Maronites in 1976. In Lebanon, Gemayel was backed by the Maronite religious establishment now centered in the monastic orders, which contributed fighters to paramilitary groups. Despite their minority status, they were determined to regain total Maronite control of the country, a goal supported by Begin and Sharon. It would ensure a state on their northern frontier governed by a religious minority in the Middle East, just as they were. And they, like Gemayel, intended to remove the PLO from Lebanon. Its existence threatened any chance of Maronite success and, from Israel's perspective, any assurance that their northern frontiers would be spared the possibility of raids and rocket attacks. But Gemayel went further. He and his Maronite advisers spoke openly of the removal from Lebanon of most if not all Palestinians, not just the PLO, the methods to be left to their discretion.[53]

The first half of 1981 saw the increasing coordination of Israeli-Maronite activities against Syria as well as the PLO, despite the fact that Syria also strove to restrict Palestinian freedom of action where it could. The problem lay in Syrian hopes of influencing the outcome of Lebanese presidential elections, scheduled for September 1982. It was no secret that Hafiz al-Assad hoped to install as president Sulayman Franjiyah, the one Maronite with whom he had close ties. This threatened Bashir Gemayel's presidential aspirations, which Israel encouraged. As a result, Gemayel decided to challenge Syria by gaining control of Zahle, an important city adjacent to the Beirut-Damascus highway in central Lebanon, whose population was primarily Greek Orthodox and Greek Catholic. With Syria's forces situated just east of the city, the Maronite action could incite hostilities that would draw Israel in on Gemayel's side and enable him to claim he had defended Christians other than Maronites. Begin had promised him in 1978 that if Syrian planes attacked Christian forces, Israeli planes would intervene on their behalf.[54]

At the beginning of April 1981, clashes between Phalangist and Syrian forces erupted in and around Zahle. Gemayel called for Israeli aid and Israeli planes responded by downing two Syrian helicopters.[55] Assad replied by installing ground-to-air missiles in the hills overlooking Zahle, a significant escalation; these weapons covered airspace heretofore open only to Israeli reconnaissance and to their attacks on Palestinian positions. A "missile crisis" ensued, with the

United States sending veteran diplomat Philip Habib to restrain both sides, a task he concluded successfully in May.

American Diplomacy and Its Impact

Despite its accomplishments, the Habib mission illustrated the disarray in America's Middle East policy. Secretary of State Alexander Haig had visited the Middle East in late March and early April. He had pointedly omitted Syria from his itinerary and, during his stay in Israel, had referred to Assad's regime as Soviet-dominated and a threat to peace. On the other hand, Habib found it necessary to work with Assad. He seems to have encouraged him to believe that further progress on an overall peace agreement might develop with American approval and, Habib hoped, with Saudi backing in the near future.

The disparity between the Haig and the Habib visits, one a junket and the other a specific effort to dampen hostilities, highlighted the contradictions in Reagan administration policy. Washington's search for a strategic consensus against the Soviets encouraged confrontation with Soviet "clients," whereas efforts to resolve regional disputes necessarily included clients such as Syria, whose truculence was inspired in part by its determination not to be omitted from any peacekeeping efforts. This disparity in interpretations would recur, with bloody ramifications for U.S. troops, after the 1982 Israeli invasion of Lebanon.

In the spring of 1981, the PLO found itself caught between the Maronite militias to the north and a possible Israeli invasion from the south (see Map 8.1). In addition, those factions supporting Arafat found that they faced increasing Syrian hostility. Damascus feared he might seek an accord in tandem with Jordan that would further isolate Syria in a direct confrontation with Israel while its forces were divided between the Golan region and Lebanon. There was some basis for Syrian alarm. Although Arafat's approaches to Washington had failed, his diplomatic overtures had scored impressive gains. In June 1980 the nine-member European Economic Community issued the Venice Declaration, which called for recognition of the Palestinians' right to self-determination and the PLO's right to be linked with any peace initiative.

This statement and subsequent pronouncements indicated the Europeans' unease with the Camp David process and their belief that the American initiative

Map 8.1 ■ Lebanon: Regional Topography Indicating Population Distribution   ▷
by Religious Affiliation and Refugee Camps, 1985

As this map indicates, Lebanon's mosaic of religious communities established sectors of regional power for certain groups at the expense of others. Assuring sufficient representation for all affiliations in the face of Maronite efforts to retain dominance was further complicated by the influx of Palestinians after 1970–1971. Although the PLO had mostly withdrawn by 1985, the bulk of the Palestinian refugee population remained in Lebanon. This map also identifies the locations of major refugee camps that had been the scenes of conflict in 1975 and 1982 or, as in the south, were the targets of Israeli reprisal raids.

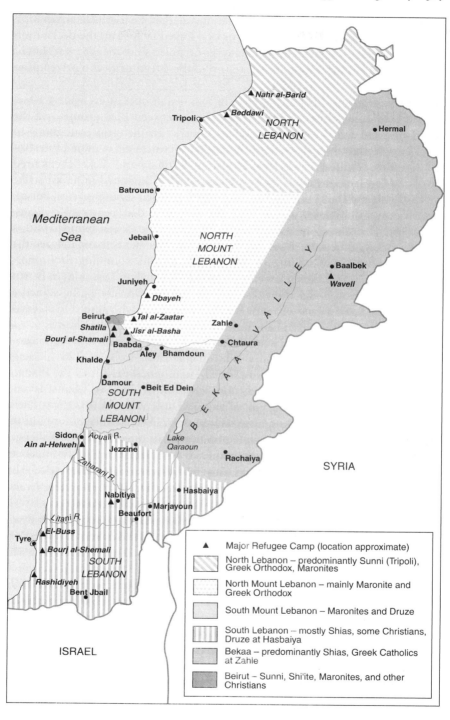

Mediterranean
Sea

**NORTH
LEBANON**

▲ *Nahr al-Barid*

Tripoli

▲ *Beddawi*

● Hermal

Batroune ●

Jebail ●

**NORTH
MOUNT
LEBANON**

● Baalbek

▲ *Wavell*

Juniyeh ●

▲ *Dbayeh*

Beirut ●

▲ *Tal al-Zaatar*

Shatila ▲

Bourj al-Shamali

▲ *Jisr al-Basha*

Zahle ●

Baabda ●

Aley ● Bhamdoun ●

● *Chtaura*

Khalde ●

Damour ●

● Beit Ed Dein

**SOUTH
MOUNT
LEBANON**

B E K A A   V A L L E Y

Sidon ● *Aouali R.*

Ain al-Helweh ▲

Jezzine ●

Lake
Qaraoun

● Rachaiya

SYRIA

Zaharani R.

● Hasbaiya

Nabitiya ▲

● *Marjayoun*

Beaufort ●

Litani R.

Tyre ● ▲ *El-Buss*

▲ *Bourj al-Shemali*

**SOUTH
LEBANON**

Rashidiyeh ▲

Bent Jbail ●

ISRAEL

▲	Major Refugee Camp (location approximate)
	North Lebanon – predominantly Sunni (Tripoli), Greek Orthodox, Maronites
	North Mount Lebanon – mainly Maronite and Greek Orthodox
	South Mount Lebanon – Maronites and Druze
	South Lebanon – mostly Shias, some Christians, Druze at Hasbaiya
	Bekaa – predominantly Shias, Greek Catholics at Zahle
	Beirut – Sunni, Shi'ite, Maronites, and other Christians

was doomed to fail. Though not stipulating whether such self-determination should result in an independent state or one linked to Jordan, the declaration specified that Israeli settlements in territories occupied since the 1967 war should be dismantled in preparation for the return of these territories as a prerequisite for peace.[56]

As Arafat pushed his peace option in 1981, Fatah operations against Israel seemed to decline, although numerous clashes between PLO groups and the Israeli-supplied militia of Saad Haddad occurred in the strip contiguous to Israel's northern border. Then, in early July, Israeli forces again raided Palestinian positions, resulting in a war of escalation. Artillery and rocket shells fired into Israel led Israel to intensify its attacks, which culminated in an air strike against Fatah and the PDFLP headquarters in a crowded suburb of West Beirut. Casualties were estimated at 200 dead and 600 wounded, nearly all civilians, with about 30 assumed to be members of the PLO. The PLO responded with a massive rocket bombardment of northern Israeli settlements that paralyzed the region for several days, killing six Israeli civilians and wounding fifty-nine.[57] The intensity of these exchanges and the numerous civilian casualties in Beirut brought U.S. envoy Philip Habib back to the region. On July 24, he gained a cease-fire, mediated separately with the PLO and Israel, who agreed to a cessation of hostilities in southern Lebanon and along Israel's Lebanese border.

In the eyes of many Israeli analysts, the PLO-Israeli cease-fire, though negotiated indirectly through Habib, posed a major threat to Israel. First, it suggested Israel's implicit recognition of the PLO. Second, it permitted the PLO to resume its buildup of forces in Lebanon, which might be used against Israel. Third, the willingness of the United States to deal with the PLO was itself alarming, even though Washington's position on PLO acceptance of Resolution 242 remained unchanged. Once again, the Palestinians posed a greater challenge to Israel as a peacemaking organization than as a military one; the continuance of the cease-fire was more unsettling than its collapse. This was particularly galling because Arafat was unwilling to denounce PLO incursions into Israel from Jordan; he held that the cease-fire applied only to Lebanon, whereas Israel argued that it was all-embracing. Following the cease-fire, Begin became even more convinced that the PLO should be destroyed rather than permitted to exist behind a truce.

The Israeli Invasion of Lebanon, August 1981–September 1982

The inauguration of the second Begin-led cabinet in Israel in August 1981 coincided with more insistent demands from various Arab states that Washington undertake peace initiatives. While in the American capital from August 4 to 8, Sadat had proposed using the PLO-Israeli cease-fire as a stepping-stone to "mutual and simultaneous recognition" of each other that could form the basis of lasting peace. Then, on August 7, during Sadat's stay in Washington, Crown Prince Fahd of Saudi Arabia called for the scrapping of the Camp David agreements, Israeli withdrawal from all territories occupied in 1967, and the creation of a Palestinian state with its capital in East Jerusalem. He dealt with Israel by declaring that "all states in the region should be able to live in peace."[58] Some saw this pronouncement as a major step forward, implying Arab recognition of Israel, but the only state mentioned specifically was that proposed for the Palestinians. Israel denounced the plan.

Washington treated it more cautiously, fearful of alienating the Saudis but aware that Fahd's proposals repudiated the Camp David process to which the United States remained committed. Sadat dismissed Fahd's remarks, which were obviously designed to upstage his visit. He would regain all of the Sinai in April 1982 only as part of the Camp David Accords. Nevertheless, Fahd's overtures seemed to indicate movement in the Arab camp toward a negotiating forum, something that itself could challenge Begin's desire to consolidate his control over the West Bank. Consequently, in September 1981, he and Ariel Sharon, his defense minister, began to plan Israel's invasion of Lebanon.

Sharon's Plan for Lebanon and the PLO.   Ariel Sharon intended to destroy the PLO military infrastructure and, if possible, the PLO leadership itself; this would mean attacking West Beirut, where the PLO headquarters and command bunkers were located. In addition, Sharon envisaged a major confrontation with the Syrians, driving them out of Lebanon. This would ensure the presidency of Bashir Gemayel, to be elected under Israeli auspices. As payment for Israeli assistance, Sharon expected Gemayel, once installed as president, to sign a peace treaty with Israel, presumably stabilizing forever Israel's northern border. Sharon visited Maronite headquarters north of Beirut several times during 1981–1982, as did the Israeli staff assigned to coordinate arrangements for the attack.

The idea in its totality seems to have been Sharon's, though he had the support of Begin, Foreign Minister Yitzhak Shamir, and Chief of Staff Rafael Eitan. But many high-ranking officers objected to part or all of the plan, preferring a sweep of the southern region akin to the invasion of 1978. The Israeli cabinet remained uninformed until December 1981, when the scheme was placed before it for approval. Cabinet criticism forced Begin to table the idea.[59]

What remains uncertain from this time onward is whether Begin remained committed to the full invasion plan or whether he decided to opt for a limited strike that would satisfy his cabinet. What is clear is that Sharon and Eitan continued to prepare for the larger-scale invasion, whereas Begin presented the cabinet with proposals for a limited attack in order to gain its assent. Indeed, Begin and Sharon dispatched the chief of military intelligence, Yehoshua Seguy, to Washington in February 1982 to consult on the expanding PLO military infrastructure in southern Lebanon and apparently to seek approval for a strike against the PLO under appropriate circumstances. Secretary of State Haig, evidently under the impression that such an operation would be restricted to the south, stressed that there could be no assault without a major provocation from Lebanon.

On various occasions during the spring of 1982, the Israeli military command sought approval for strikes that might provoke PLO retaliation forceful enough to justify to the world Israel's right to attack. By this time, news reports had appeared in both Israel and the United States from March onward noting the likelihood of an Israeli assault. In late May, Sharon met Haig and his staff in Washington. He showed them maps and detailed plans for two different invasions, one restricted to south Lebanon and the other going north to Beirut. Haig again informed Sharon that such an undertaking required a major provocation, but in a subsequent private meeting with Sharon, Haig may well have been more encouraging than he was in front of his aides.[60]

The catalyst for the Israeli invasion of Lebanon came with the attempted assassination of the Israeli ambassador in London on June 3. British intelligence sources identified the act as that of the Abu Nidal group, now probably sponsored by Iraq. Israeli intelligence evaluations agreed, but Begin, Sharon, and Eitan had their excuse and ordered Israeli jets to attack West Beirut, strikes that resulted in over one hundred casualties. These air attacks were intended to cause PLO gunners to shell northern Israel, thus providing the justification to invade. They succeeded.

With the PLO rocket and artillery barrage, the Israeli cabinet met to approve the invasion. What they were told and what was planned were two different things. Sharon informed them of a plan for an invasion of twenty-five miles to wipe out PLO positions in southern Lebanon, whereas he and Eitan had actually ordered the armed forces to proceed directly toward Beirut, which they did once the invasion began on June 6. From then on, the cabinet was briefed in piecemeal fashion as Sharon carried out his plan. Warned not to clash with the Syrians, he apparently ordered his troops to fire on Syrian positions to provoke a response that he could use to justify an attack. In this manner he and Eitan escalated the cabinet-approved limited strike to fit his prearranged design.[61]

By June 15 Israeli forces were on the outskirts of Beirut. Sharon had hoped to have the Maronite forces enter the Palestinian strongholds of West Beirut but his advisers, regarding Maronite military capabilities with contempt, rejected this proposal. The alternative, an Israeli assault, seemed equally unpalatable given the expected casualties. In the resulting stalemate, the United States pushed for an immediate PLO withdrawal of all forces from Lebanon. Sharon ordered air strikes and indiscriminate bombardment of West Beirut and adjacent areas, with heavy loss of civilian life, not always Palestinian. Negotiations over terms for withdrawal dragged on as Arafat sought guarantees for the Palestinian civilians left behind and to salvage some political gain from the crisis.[62]

U.S. Intervention and the Reagan Plan.   The White House had approved Israel's objective—the removal of the PLO from any role in future peace talks—but U.S. officials were appalled at Israeli tactics and disregard for civilian lives. Haig, who admired Sharon, was asked to resign and Washington once again dispatched Philip Habib, now to try to reach agreement on the terms of withdrawal.

He succeeded on August 12, but only after a Sharon-ordered day-long bombard-ment of West Beirut that many observers interpreted as a last-ditch attempt to undermine the cease-fire. With the truce, a multinational peacekeeping force arrived, including U.S. troops, whose mission was to oversee the departure of the PLO and to guarantee the safety of civilians in the refugee camps. By Sep-tember 1, Palestinian forces had left Beirut for other Arab countries, and Ameri-can forces were withdrawn.

On the same day, September 1, President Reagan proposed a new initiative designed to reinvigorate the Camp David Accords. The Reagan Plan called for a freeze on Israeli settlements on the West Bank and denied Israeli claims of sovereignty over either that area or Gaza. At the same time Reagan rejected the idea of an independent Palestinian state. Instead, he called for "full Palestinian autonomy," to be realized through confederation with Jordan in such a manner that "the legitimate rights of the Palestinians" would be realized without com-promising the "legitimate security concerns of Israel." Reagan repudiated the basic PLO and Israeli positions. He pointedly remarked that in America's view, "the withdrawal provision of Resolution 242 applies to all fronts, including the West Bank and Gaza," thereby denying Begin's claim that these areas were ex-cluded. At the same time Reagan implicitly and the new secretary of state, George Shultz, explicitly dismissed the right of Palestinians to "self-determination," since to them it meant an independent state.[63]

What then was the purpose of Reagan's initiative in itself or as clarified by Shultz, who had declared that "the legitimate needs and problems of the Pales-tinian people must be addressed and resolved—urgently and in all their dimen-sions"?[64] The Reagan Plan was intended to influence discussions at an upcoming Arab summit scheduled to be held in Fez, Morocco, on September 9. It failed because it never mentioned, nor was it meant to include, the PLO. Both Reagan, and Shultz in later remarks, stressed that the PLO had left Beirut, opening the way for consideration of the needs of the "Palestinian inhabitants of the West Bank and Gaza." Having informed Arab leaders that the United States would address the Palestinian problem in its entirety, Reagan had presented a plan, sup-posed to aid Arab moderates, that removed the PLO from the peace equation, ignoring the Rabat Declaration of 1974; the inhabitants of the territories were the only Palestinians to be considered under the agreement.[65] Such an approach— meeting Begin's terms—following on the Israeli invasion of Lebanon, appeared ludicrous. On the other hand, Begin was horrified by American references to Palestinian rights to full autonomy, presumably in a relationship with Jordan, which clashed with Israeli designs to deny them any political rights. Thus both sides opposed the plan, and the Arab summit reaffirmed the Rabat Declaration of 1974 that the PLO was the sole representative of the Palestinian people.

Reagan's pronouncement, the basis of future American policy, publicly dis-approved of Israeli intentions for the West Bank yet defined terms in ways that backed Israel's positions. In such circumstances the United States did not appear as the honest broker it claimed to be. Sharon had already declared that the removal of the PLO from Beirut created the possibility for agreement between Israel and "moderate" Palestinians, a clear reference to the West Bank aspect of the invasion of Lebanon.[66]

Gemayel's Assassination and the Sabra-Shatila Massacres.   In Lebanon, however, Israel encountered unexpected obstacles, notably the assassination of Bashir Gemayel on September 14. Gemayel's relations with Begin and Sharon had been strained. He had resisted their demands for an immediate peace treaty between Lebanon and Israel and opposed their plan for Saad Haddad and his forces in south Lebanon to remain under Israel's military authority once Lebanon's national unity was reestablished. But they had reached agreement on September 12 that Phalangist forces would enter the Palestinian camps outside Beirut, supposedly to clear out some 2,000 PLO fighters reputed to be there.[67] Gemayel's death set in motion a series of events that led to the massacres in the Sabra and Shatila refugee camps.

After paying their condolences to the Gemayel clan and consulting with their staff and Phalangist leaders, Sharon and Eitan—without informing the Israeli cabinet—ordered Israeli troops into West Beirut in violation of the truce negotiated by Philip Habib. The Israeli military command then arranged for Phalangist militias, numbering about 200, to be transported to the area surrounding the camps, which they entered at 6 PM on September 16. Though the ostensible purpose was to wipe out an estimated 2,000 PLO fighters, the small number of Maronite forces suggests differently. Aided by Israeli flares to assist them at night, the Phalangists undertook a massacre of Palestinians that continued until the morning of September 19. High-level officers ignored word of the atrocities, which emerged on September 17, as apparently did Chief of Staff Eitan when told of the events in Beirut on the afternoon of September 18. He and his staff approved a Phalange request to remain in the camps until the next morning.

The Maronites exited on September 19, leaving behind at least 800 dead, none apparently members of any PLO unit and a majority of them women and children. A subsequent Israeli commission of inquiry rejected the military's initial claims that the Phalange entered the camps without the assistance or even the knowledge of the Israeli command. The Kahan Commission found Israeli officials, especially Sharon and Eitan, indirectly responsible for the massacre, in that they should have known what would occur: the Phalange had repeatedly declared what they intended to do with Palestinians they found, and some Israeli leaders had stated candidly that they hoped to "purify" Lebanon of Palestinians.[68]

America's Lebanon Policy, September 1982–February 1984

In the massacre's aftermath, the United States reintroduced its troops as part of the multinational force, aware that its original mission had been intended to protect Palestinian civilians. Secretary of State George Shultz declared that the

Palestinians were fully justified in seeking "a place with which they can identify" and that Israel would have to cede territory to gain peace in accordance with Resolution 242. During the fall the Reagan administration tried to bring King Husayn into the negotiations. The United States offered enticements, asking Congress not to increase aid to Israel in light of recent events and to approve shipment of sophisticated jet fighters to Amman. Congress rejected the latter and upped Israeli assistance, moves that reflected "the continued political advantages of supporting Israel." Congress also demanded that Husayn negotiate directly with Israel without the PLO, a stipulation that mirrored Israel's conditions.[69] Seeing no hope, Husayn broke off talks and refused to negotiate directly with Israel.

Angered by the collapse of the American overture to Husayn when the Soviets were rearming Damascus, Shultz, after much wrangling over terms, engineered a Lebanese-Israeli security agreement, signed on May 17, 1983, that provided for Israel's withdrawal from Lebanon. This was conditional on a similar commitment from Damascus, highly unlikely because Shultz had excluded Syria from the talks. The agreement in effect ratified continued Israeli control of southern Lebanon through proxies. Haddad's forces would be integrated with other troops from the southern region into the reconstituted Lebanese army that would oversee the area; no troops from central and northern Lebanon could enter the south. If implemented, the treaty would have forced Syria to concede the loss of any influence in Lebanon but allowed Israel to retain a major foothold through Haddad.

Not the least of the pact's ironies was that this arrangement violated the provisions Bashir Gemayel had insisted on before his assassination, namely, that Haddad, whom he despised, be subordinated to his authority as president of Lebanon. Israel had rejected his request.[70] Bashir's successor, his older brother Amin, lacked his charisma and accepted the agreement as a means of gaining American backing against both Israel and Syria as he attempted to weave his way through the literal and metaphorical minefields of Lebanese politics.

The signing of the treaty followed, by a month, a bomb attack on the U.S. embassy in Beirut that had caused extensive casualties and killed the CIA's leading Arab affairs analyst (see Figure 8.4). Possibly Syrian sponsored, it indicated both Assad's and Lebanese Muslim anger at the changing American role in the country. Supposedly neutral, American representatives now seemed intent on securing Maronite paramountcy. The security agreement appeared to give Israel what it had not gained by its invasion. Non-Christian groups in Lebanon began to snipe at American military positions. U.S. marines became more vulnerable in September when the government of Yitzhak Shamir, who had replaced Begin as prime minister, pulled Israeli forces out of the Shouf Mountains overlooking Beirut, over Washington's strong objections. The withdrawal exposed American forces to increased harassment as the Druze regained control of their traditional stronghold. The White House, over the objections of the marine commander in

Figure 8.4 ■ **The U.S. Embassy in Beirut after the Terrorist Attack on April 18, 1983**

This massive explosion destroyed entire wings of the embassy building and killed sixty-three persons, including seventeen Americans; among the latter was the chief CIA officer overseeing Middle East affairs. An attack in October destroyed the marine barracks, killing 241 marines and forcing the Reagan administration to withdraw its forces from Lebanon.

Beirut, then ordered naval bombardments of Druze positions, which resulted in numerous casualties, mostly noncombatant.[71] The reply to the American bombardments came in the form of the suicide bombing of the marine-naval barracks outside Beirut in October 1983, which caused 241 deaths.

The demolition of the barracks and its aftermath reflected the disparity between Arab and Reagan administration perceptions of its causes. Druze leader Walid Junblat warned of further incidents if the United States pursued "its hostile policy towards the Arab and Islamic world." Reagan argued that keeping the marines in Lebanon was "central to U.S. credibility on a global scale" and to stopping the Middle East as a whole from being "incorporated into the Soviet bloc."[72] In the renewed clash between regional tensions and global anti-Soviet perceptions of their significance in Washington, the latter again emerged victorious, to Israel's benefit. Shultz and Reagan, over Defense Department objections, decided to offer Israel a strategic agreement aimed at increasing "military and political cooperation" to counter "the threat to our mutual interests posed by increased Soviet involvement in the Middle East." The agreement also offered advanced military technology and favorable aid terms.[73] No conditions applied, and Israel did not restrict its settlement activities on the West Bank, which the United States opposed.

In Lebanon itself, the United States escalated its attacks on Syrian positions, which culminated in air strikes and bombardments by the U.S.S. *New Jersey* at the turn of the year. With his aides divided on the merits of further confrontation, Reagan played both sides of the issue. Having accused his critics of seeking to surrender American interests, he decided to remove the troops from Lebanon and to deploy them on ships offshore. He then ordered renewed shelling of Druze and Shi'i positions, creating a facade of militancy behind which the American navy sailed away in February 1984, leaving Lebanon an open battleground for regional competitors.[74] With Syria the apparent victor, Amin Gemayel now declared the security agreement with Israel to be dead. Assad would be the new broker of a Lebanese political pact if any could be achieved.

As American forces departed from Lebanon's shores in early 1984, the U.S. policy lay in ruins, the victim of the perceptions of its policymakers as well as the entangled web of regional and communal hatreds. The Reagan administration had assumed contradictory postures. Despite Syria's importance to any agreement, Washington did not address Syrian concerns; it excluded Syria from its strategic alliance aimed at expelling Soviet influence from the region. Though opposed in principle to Israeli actions, the administration either willingly or unwittingly became captive to Israel's strategic designs encompassed within the framework of the 1982 war. Frustrated by Israeli excesses and those of its clients, the Reagan government then tried to restore the internal balance in Lebanon by gaining the withdrawal of both Syria and Israel, but it did so without Syria's agreement and in terms clearly supportive of Israel's objectives. America's inability to impose its will on Syria aroused Washington's wrath, resulting in bombardments that indicated petulance rather than strategy. The retaliatory bombing of the marines' barracks signaled the bankruptcy of the United States' attempt to force the issue. What remained was a return to a total global perspective, dominated by the polarization of American and Soviet interests and clients, in which Israel played a willing and prominent role.

LEBANON POSTSCRIPT, 1984–2006

Lebanese politics remained in chaos following the departure of American troops in early 1984. Rival gangs fought for control of neighborhoods or strongholds; car bombings became more frequent, often timed to foil upcoming peace negotiations. Syria pushed its plan, first proposed in 1976, for a revision of the political system. The Maronites would retain the presidency but would preside over a parliament divided equally between Christians and Muslims, thereby erasing the long-standing six-to-five ratio. The plan also overturned presidential powers by stipulating that the president could not dismiss his cabinet without parliamentary approval. Druze, Shi'ite Amal, and some Christian notables, including Maronites linked to the Phalange (indicating the existence of rifts within the Phalange hierarchy), accepted the 1976 plan in an accord signed at the end of 1985. Elie Hobeika, an intelligence chief under Bashir Gemayel who was linked to the Israelis and to the direction of the Sabra-Shatila massacres, went over to the Syrian side and backed political reform in September 1986.[75]

Diehard Maronite paramilitary groups, led by General Michel Aoun, commander of the Lebanese army, blocked the plan's acceptance. Determined to oust the Syrians from Lebanon, Aoun found an unexpected ally in Iraq's Saddam Husayn, who offered military aid to counter his rival, Syria's Hafiz al-Assad.

Seeking to resolve the turmoil, Arab heads of state met at Taif, Saudi Arabia, in 1989 and drafted a peace plan modeled on the 1976 principles. The Lebanese Parliament accepted the Taif Accord in October, but General Aoun did not. He repudiated the new Maronite president, elected by parliament, who was assassinated by a bomb on November 22, an event that triggered fratricidal warfare, this time between rival Maronite factions.

The bloody stalemate was not resolved until October 1990 during the American mobilization of forces in Saudi Arabia against Iraq, a coalition that Syria had agreed to join. With attention focused on the Gulf, President Ilyas Hrawi, a moderate, invited Syria to oust his fellow Maronite, General Aoun, from the presidential palace he had occupied since 1988. The move succeeded and Aoun took refuge in France. Though officially denied, it seemed that the Syrian action had been cleared with Washington, one of the many payoffs to result from American efforts to form an alliance against Saddam Husayn.

The national unity government in office, based on the Taif Accord, began to assert Lebanese national authority, which had been nonexistent for over fifteen years. As of May 1991, Syria, which was initially granted authority over internal affairs—and later security and foreign policy—by the Lebanese government, became de facto ruler of Lebanon. The government's attention then shifted to southern Lebanon where Shi'ites continued their assaults on the Israeli-controlled enclave, another legacy of Israel's 1982 invasion.

Shi'ites had initially welcomed Israel's assault as a means of ousting the PLO. But they and most southern Lebanese soon turned against Israel, angered by its exploitation of the region including blockading access to northern markets and dumping Israeli goods on the domestic economy to deliberately undercut local merchants. These steps, coupled with roundups and abductions of suspected "terrorists," ignited attacks and suicide bombings, both locally inspired and directed from Damascus. In retaliation, Israeli terror squads invaded villages and assassinated those who they claimed were involved in the assaults.

Here, Israel faced a new and formidable adversary, the Iranian-backed Shi'ite force Hizbollah (Party of God), which replaced Amal as the major military wing of the Shi'ite community in Lebanon. Hizbollah's militancy challenged Israel as well as its client Lebanese forces in the southern zone, and triggered Israeli air strikes and the kidnapping of Hizbollah leaders.[76] These confrontations reached such intensity, with increasingly high Israeli casualties, that in 2000 Israeli Prime Minister Ehud Barak ordered Israel's unilateral withdrawal from the enclave, accompanied by many Lebanese refugees who had sided with Israel since the 1980s.

Lebanon once more asserted authority over the region, except for a disputed area in the southeast retained by Israel, Shaba Farms, but its domestic political structure remained fragile. The American attack on Iraq in March 2003 (discussed in Chapter 11) brought renewed pressure on Syria to relinquish its control of Lebanese politics, which the administration of George H. W. Bush had sanctioned in 1991. Resulting turmoil and the assassination of opposition politician and former prime minister, Rafik Hariri, in February 2005, exacerbated tensions and led to Syria's apparent withdrawal of most of its forces. But Syria retains a role in Lebanese affairs, and international investigations of Syria's suspected complicity in the Hariri murder have proved inconclusive.

CONCLUSION

By 2006 Lebanese political life, even with the 2005 Hariri assassination, appeared relatively stable, but matters remained unsettled, notably the place of Hizbollah in Lebanese politics. Although part of the government, Hizbollah retained control of its own weaponry, a fact that alarmed some but was accepted by others. The conservative Maronite, Michel Aoun, long in exile, returned and allied himself with Hizbollah on occasion.

Then in July 2006, Hizbollah attacked an Israeli patrol, killing several soldiers and kidnapping two (see Chapter 11). Israel responded with a classic Ben-Gurionist assault on Lebanon's infrastructure, not just on Hizbollah positions and Shi'i districts of Beirut. The Bush administration delayed United Nations efforts to achieve a cease-fire in order to assist Israeli military objectives.

From a military standpoint, the conflict ended inconclusively and an international force was assembled to control Lebanon's borders with Israel and Syria. Within Lebanon, criticism of Hizbollah's kidnapping of the Israeli soldiers was balanced by fury at the magnitude of Israel's reply, leaving much of the last decade's redevelopment efforts in ruins. The precise course of Lebanon's governmental and economic restructuring remains unclear, but American ability to influence Lebanese politics seems to have been weakened by the Bush administration's blocking of an immediate cease-fire that led to much damage and more civilian casualties.

QUESTIONS FOR CONSIDERATION

1. How did the Carter administration's first approach to resolving Arab-Israeli issues differ from that of Henry Kissinger's during the Nixon and Ford administrations?
2. Why were Anwar al-Sadat and Menachem Begin willing to consider a peace treaty between Egypt and Israel? Were their motives similar or different?
3. How did the Camp David Accord address the Palestinian problem?
4. Why did Israel invade Lebanon in 1982? Did the assault achieve the goals sought by Ariel Sharon?

CHRONOLOGY

April 1975– October 1976	Lebanese Civil War.
1977	**January.** Jimmy Carter becomes president of United States.
	June. Menachem Begin sworn in as prime minister of Israel.
	November 9. Anwar al-Sadat declares his willingness to go to Jerusalem.
	November 20. Sadat addresses Israeli Knesset.
1978	**January 18.** Egyptian-Israeli talks suspended, renewed in August.
	March 11. Fatah terrorist attack into Israel.
	March 15. Israelis invade south Lebanon; withdraw in June.
	September 5–17. Camp David talks end in peace accord.
	December. Sadat and Begin awarded Nobel Peace Prize.
1979	**January–February.** Iranian revolution. Ayatollah Khomeini assumes power.
	March 26. Egyptian-Israeli peace treaty.
	November. Iranians seize U.S. embassy personnel as hostages.
	December. Soviet invasion/occupation of Afghanistan.
1980	**September.** Iraq invades Iran, starting eight-year Iraq-Iran War.
1981	**January.** Ronald Reagan becomes president of United States.
	June. Israeli air raid destroys Iraqi nuclear reactor. Begin reelected prime minister of Israel.
	October 6. Sadat assassinated. Husni Mubarak becomes president of Egypt.
	December. Israel annexes Golan Heights.
1982	**June 6.** Israeli invasion of Lebanon.
	August 12. Cease-fire in Lebanon.
	September 14. Bashir Gemayel assassinated.
	September 16–19. Maronite massacre of Palestinians at Sabra and Shatila.
1983	**August.** Begin resigns as prime minister, succeeded by Yitzhak Shamir of Likud.
	October 23. Suicide bomber kills 241 U.S. marines in Beirut.
1984	**February.** American forces withdraw from Lebanon.
1989	**August.** Taif Accord revises Lebanese political system.
	October. Lebanese Parliament ratifies Taif proposals, rejected by Maronite separatists led by General Michel Aoun.
1990	**October.** Syria ousts Aoun and takes full control of Lebanon.

Notes

1. William B. Quandt, *Camp David: Peacemaking and Politics* (Washington, D.C., 1986), 37.

2. Walid Khalidi, *Conflict and Violence in Lebanon: Confrontation in the Middle East* (Cambridge, Mass., 1979), 42ff.

3. Ibid., 42, and 164, note 42.

4. Rashid Khalidi, *Under Siege: PLO Decision Making during the 1982 War* (New York, 1986), 10.

5. Walid Khalidi, *Conflict and Violence*, 68–72. A good general account dealing with various factions is John Bulloch, *Death of a Country: The Civil War in Lebanon* (London, 1977).

6. Helena Cobban, *The Palestinian Liberation Organization: People, Power, and Politics* (Cambridge, England, 1984), 149.

7. This discussion relies on Walid Khalidi, *Conflict and Violence*, 84–85; and the collection of essays in P. Edward Haley and Lewis Snider, eds., *Lebanon in Crisis: Participants and Issues* (Syracuse, N.Y., 1979), along with Anthony Sampson, *The Arms Bazaar: From Lebanon to Lockheed* (New York, 1977), 5–15. For estimates of Israeli military aid to the Maronites ranging from $100 million to $150 million, see Lawrence L. Whetten, "The Military Dimension," 290, note 46 in Haley and Snider, *Lebanon in Crisis*; and Ze'ev Schiff and Ehud Ya'ari, *Israel's Lebanon War* (New York, 1984), 18.

8. The preliminary talks between American and Israeli officials are discussed in Cyrus Vance, *Hard Choices: Critical Years in America's Foreign Policy* (New York, 1983), 207ff. Vance was secretary of state under President Carter.

9. For Amal and the Shi'ite population of south Lebanon, see Augustus Richard Norton, *Amal and the Shi'a: Struggle for the Soul of Lebanon* (Austin, Tex., 1987). A broader discussion of the Lebanese Shi'a is Fouad Ajami, *The Vanished Imam: Musa al-Sadr and the Shi'a of Lebanon* (Ithaca, N.Y., 1986). For Israeli efforts to terrorize civilians into flight, see Lewis P. Snider et al., "Israel," in Haley and Snider, eds., *Lebanon in Crisis*, 95–103; and Frederic C. Hof, *Galilee Divided: The Israel-Lebanon Frontier, 1916–1984* (Boulder, Colo., 1985), 87–93.

10. Vance, *Hard Choices*, 209. The United States also sharply criticized Israel for its use of cluster bombs against civilian targets.

11. *Los Angeles Times*, August 10, 1977. Begin repeated these references to the Palestinians in his banquet toasts to the Egyptian delegation in January 1978.

12. Itamar Rabinovich, *The War for Lebanon, 1970–1985* (Ithaca, N.Y., 1985), 48–49 and appendix.

13. Cobban, *Palestine Liberation Organization*, 84, quoting Farouq al-Qaddumi, who was responsible for foreign affairs in the PLO.

14. I rely for my discussion of Camp David primarily on Quandt, *Camp David*; Vance, *Hard Choices*; Ezer Weizman, *The Battle for Peace* (New York, 1981); Zbigniew Brzezinski, *Power and Principle: Memoirs of the National Security Adviser, 1977–1981* (New York, 1983); Moshe Dayan, *Breakthrough: A Personal Account of the Egypt-Israel Peace Negotiations* (New York, 1981); and Steven L. Spiegel, *The Other Arab-Israeli Conflict: Making America's Middle East Policy, from Truman to Reagan* (Chicago, 1985). Spiegel is much more critical of Carter than of previous presidents and depicts Brzezinski as "arrogant," using personal criteria he has not heretofore employed.

15. For a good discussion of Arab rivalries and Saudi attempts to mediate, see Nadav Safran, *Saudi Arabia: The Ceaseless Quest for Security* (Cambridge, Mass., 1985), 253–55.

16. Quandt, *Camp David*, 48–103, for a detailed treatment of these matters.

17. Quandt, *Camp David*, 111.

18. Galia Golan, *The Soviet Union and the Palestine Liberation Organization: An Uneasy Alliance* (New York, 1980), 113–42.

19. Quandt, *Camp David*, 132. The conversations had been tense. Brzezinski, *Power and Principle*, 108, uses the term "blackmail" to describe Dayan's tactics, but his overall account is less

detailed than is Quandt's, 126–31. Dayan, *Breakthrough*, 65–71, stresses Carter's threat of confrontation rather than his own.

20. Dayan, *Breakthrough*, 68–70.

21. Ibid., 38–54, discusses his meeting with Hassan Tuheimi, the deputy prime minister of Egypt.

22. Weizman, *Battle for Peace*, 142–47, criticizes the Begin cabinet for acting like stereotypical Jews and then attacks the Egyptian newspapers that depicted them in that way, thereby intensifying the growing mutual animosity.

23. Quandt, *Camp David*, 168–205. Spiegel, *Other Arab-Israeli Conflict*, 346–49, discusses the arms sales furor.

24. The quotation is from Quandt, *Camp David*, 256.

25. For Begin's interpretation of the word "people" as inhabitants of the West Bank and Gaza, see Yehoshafat Harkabi, *The Bar Kokhba Syndrome: Risk and Realism in International Politics*, trans. Max D. Ticktin and ed. David Altshuler (Chappaqua, N.Y., 1983), 171. The Carter government included Palestinians from the territories in the term "people": see Quandt, *Camp David*, Appendix H, 388.

26. Compare Quandt, *Camp David*, 247–51, and Spiegel, *Other Arab-Israeli Conflict*, 362, on the dispute over the proposed freeze on settlements. Spiegel argues the Israeli position, relying on the notes of an Israeli adviser, Aharon Barak. Quandt contradicts Spiegel, saying that Barak's notes prove just the opposite.

27. Compare Spiegel, *Other Arab-Israeli Conflict*, 375–79, where he states that Vance's position on the settlements angered Carter, and Vance, who makes no mention of the settlement flap in his memoirs. Another furor had arisen over unauthorized contacts with PLO representatives made by the U.S. ambassador to the United Nations, Andrew Young, which were discovered by Israeli espionage and leaked to the press. Young initially denied the contacts but was subsequently asked to resign.

28. Ibid., 401–2.

29. *Washington Post*, August 15, 1979, 25; quoted in Spiegel, 406.

30. For a look at Christian fundamentalist support of Israel and Reagan's ties to Jerry Falwell and Pat Robertson, see Grace Halsell, *Prophecy and Politics: Militant Evangelists on the Road to Nuclear War* (Westport, Conn., 1986), 171–73, 191. Paul Findley, *They Dare to Speak Out: People and Institutions Confront Israel's Lobby* (Westport, Conn., 1985), 238–64; and Nimrod Novik, *The United States and Israel: Domestic Determinants of a Changing U.S. Commitment* (Boulder, Colo., 1986), 86–93. Novik's depiction of how Menachem Begin used his ties to Falwell to lobby Reagan foreshadows Binyamin Netanyahu's use of Falwell to lobby Congress against Bill Clinton after 1996.

31. Joel Brinkley, "Iran Sales Linked to Wide Program of Covert Policies," *New York Times*, February 15, 1987; and Doyle McManus, "Private Contra Funding of $32 Million Disclosed," *Los Angeles Times*, March 6, 1987. See also Lawrence E. Walsh, *IRAN-CONTRA, The Final Report* (New York, 1994), for example, 88–146, 211–21. For probable Israeli aid to Argentina for training the contras on behalf of the United States, see Aaron S. Kleiman, *Israel's Global Reach: Arms Sales as Diplomacy* (Washington, D.C., 1985), 96 and 156–57.

32. Joel S. Migdal, *Palestinian Society and Politics* (Princeton, 1980), 39–45. See also Don Peretz, *The West Bank: History, Politics, Society, and Economy* (Boulder, Colo., 1986), 39ff; and Pamela Ann Smith, *Palestine and the Palestinians, 1876–1983* (London, 1984), 87ff.

33. Meron Benvenisti, *The West Bank Data Project: A Survey of Israel's Policies* (Washington, D.C., 1984), 12.

34. Ibid., 10.

35. Migdal, *Palestinian Society*, 67–73.

36. Benvenisti, *Data Project*, 10.

37. See the discussion of conditions in which these workers reside overnight in Rafik Halabi, *The West Bank Story: An Israeli Arab's View of Both Sides of a Tangled Conflict* (San Diego, 1981), 275–79.

38. Benvenisti, *Data Project*, 10.

39. Sammy Smooha, *Israel: Pluralism and Conflict* (Berkeley and Los Angeles, 1978), 103; see also his discussion of Ashkenazi attitudes toward oriental Jews and Arab-Jewish relations, 86–95, 135–207, also treated by Tom Segev in his analysis of the attitudes of Israel's founders, *1949: The First Israelis* (New York, 1986). An excellent study of Israel and Israeli Arabs is Ian Lustick, *Arabs in the Jewish State: Israel's Control of a National Minority* (Austin, Tex., 1980).

40. Asher Arian, *Politics in Israel: The Second Generation* (Chatham, N.J., 1985), 136–44. Efraim Torgovnik, "Likud 1977–81: The Consolidation of Power," in *Israel in the Begin Era*, Robert O. Freedman, ed. (New York, 1982), 7–27, has a good overview of the first Begin government.

41. Lilly Weisbrod, "Gush Emunim Ideology—From Religious Doctrine to Political Action," *Middle Eastern Studies* 18 (1982): 265.

42. Lustick, *Arabs in the Jewish State*, 130, 167; and Sabri Jiryis, *The Arabs in Israel* (New York, 1976), 80ff, 127, and tables in the appendix. See also Elia T. Zureik, *The Palestinians in Israel: A Study in Internal Colonialism* (London, 1979), for a broader overview of issues pertaining to this discussion.

43. Lustick, *Arabs in the Jewish State*, 129.

44. Ibid., 168.

45. Ibid., discussion on 186 and the map on 187, outlining plans for state-funded development of industrial zones that included the new Jewish town of Nazareth but excluded the adjacent old Arab city of the same name.

46. Ibid., 258.

47. Meir Kahane, *They Must Go* (New York, 1981). Two unsympathetic but accurate portrayals of Kahane and his views are Yair Kotler, *Heil Kahane*, trans. Edward Levin (New York, 1986); and Robert Friedman, *The False Prophet: Rabbi Meir Kahane: From FBI Informant to Knesset Member* (New York, 1990). Kahane was assassinated in New York City in November 1990.

48. This discussion relies on Ian Lustick, "Israel and the West Bank after Elon Moreh: The Mechanics of De Facto Annexation," *Middle East Journal* 35 (Autumn 1981): 562ff; and Peter Demant, "Israeli Settlement Policy Today," in *Occupation: Israel over Palestine*, ed. Naseer H. Aruri (Belmont, Mass., 1983), 143–64.

49. Benvenisti, *Data Project*, 34.

50. Ibid., 34–35. The World Zionist Organization allocated $30 million for purchases for the period 1983–1986.

51. Ibid., 43–45.

52. Ibid., 46–47; and *The Karp Report: An Israeli Government Inquiry into Settler Violence against Palestinians on the West Bank* (Washington, D.C., 1984).

53. For the events leading up to the Israeli invasion of Lebanon in 1982, consult Schiff and Ya'ari, *Israel's Lebanon War*; Shai Feldman and Heda Rechnitz-Kijner, *Deception, Consensus and War: Israel in Lebanon*, Jaffee Center for Strategic Studies, Tel Aviv University, Paper no. 27 (October 1984); Jonathan C. Randal, *Going All the Way: Christian Warlords, Israeli Adventurers, and the War in Lebanon* (New York, 1983); Itamar Rabinovich, *War for Lebanon*; *The Beirut Massacre: The Complete Kahan Commission Report* (Princeton, N.J., 1983).

54. Itamar Rabinovich, "The Lebanese Crisis," in *Middle East Contemporary Survey* (hereafter abbreviated MECS) 5 (1980–1981): 171. Rabinovich is less explicit about the nature of this commitment in his *War for Lebanon*, saying only that Israel had promised to "not allow the Syrian air force to operate against it [the Maronite position]" (117).

55. Schiff and Ya'ari, *Israel's Lebanon War*, 31–34, treat this as a threat of military escalation that the Begin government had not clearly thought through. Rabinovich, *War for Lebanon*, 117–18, suggests that the Israeli air strike was actually "a message that Israel was willing to accept Syrian hegemony in Zahle," an odd way of doing so.

56. See Saadallah A. S. Hallaba, *Euro-Arab Dialogue* (Brattleboro, Vt., 1984), and D. Allen and A. Pijpers, eds., *European Foreign Policy-Making and the Arab-Israeli Conflict* (The Hague, 1984).

57. Moshe Gammer, "Armed Operations," in *MECS* 5 (1980–1981): 214–20.

58. Moshe Gammer, "The Middle East Peace Process," in *MECS* 5 (1980–1981): 159–64, covers the Sadat and Fahd proposals, including the text of Fahd's interview.

59. Schiff and Ya'ari, *Israel's Lebanon War*, 38–51, discuss the December 1981 meeting, and Feldman and Rechnitz-Kijner, *Deception, Consensus and War*, 54–55, note Eitan's differences with Sharon.

60. Feldman and Rechnitz-Kijner, *Deception, Consensus and War*, 22–23; and Rabinovich, *War for Lebanon*, 134, note Israeli, Arab, and American news comments on Israeli plans up to three months before the invasion. For differing views of Haig's conversations with Sharon, compare Schiff and Ya'ari, *Israel's Lebanon War*, 67–77, who believe Haig approved an attack, with Haig, who presents himself in his memoirs as forcefully opposed to Sharon's designs when they met; Haig, *Caveat, Realism, Reagan, and Foreign Policy* (New York, 1984), 334–35. Doubts about Haig's continued opposition to Sharon's plans were shared by his own staff, including his chief negotiator, Philip Habib, who in an interview with Rashid Khalidi accused both Sharon and Haig of collusion and of lying regarding the process of negotiations for the PLO withdrawal from Beirut in the summer of 1982. See Rashid Khalidi, *Under Siege*, 172, and especially n. 10, 212.

61. Schiff and Ya'ari, *Israel's Lebanon War*, 111–15, 163–66.

62. Rashid Khalidi, *Under Siege*, 135, and n. 8, 209, where he observes that the editors of the *New York Times* censored the word "indiscriminate" from an article by Thomas Friedman describing the bombardments of August 4. See also John Bulloch, *Final Conflict: The War in Lebanon* (London, 1983), especially 86–89, 119–36; and Randal, *Going All the Way*, 219ff.

63. U.S. Department of State, *The Quest for Peace: Principal United States Public Statements and Related Documents on the Arab-Israeli Peace Process* (Washington, D.C., 1984), 108–29. Shultz refers to self-determination on 118.

64. Quoted in Spiegel, *Other Arab-Israeli Conflict*, 419.

65. Ibid., 412, and n. 46.

66. As reported in the *Washington Post*, August 30, 1982; and noted in the "Chronology" of the *Middle East Journal* 37 (1983): 70, listing for August 29.

67. Schiff and Ya'ari, *Israel's Lebanon War*, 230–46.

68. For the chronology of events, see *Kahan Commission Report*, 6–50, which also refers to Israeli awareness of Phalangist attitudes toward the Palestinians. For a critical evaluation of the *Kahan Report*, see Ammon Kapeliouk, *Sabra and Shatila: Inquiry into a Massacre* (Belmont, Mass., 1984). Kapeliouk refutes the commission argument that Israeli observers could not see into the camp from their post high above it, a point also made by journalists who were there at the time: Loren Jenkins in the *Washington Post*, September 20, 1982; and Thomas Friedman in the *New York Times*, September 26, 1982. For references to "purifying" and "purging" the camps of Palestinians, see Kapeliouk, *Sabra and Shatila*, 34 and 83, and the transcript of an Israel Defense Forces Radio Announcement broadcast on September 16, 1982, found in *The Beirut Massacre, Press Profile*, Claremont Research and Publications (New York, 1984).

69. Both quotes from Spiegel, *Other Arab-Israeli Conflict*, 422–23.

70. Hof, *Galilee Divided*, 105–11, analyzes the agreement; Schiff and Ya'ari, *Israel's Lebanon War*, 131, 231–34, treat Gemayel's dislike of Haddad.

71. Spiegel, *Other Arab-Israeli Conflict*, 426.

72. Junblat is quoted in the *New York Times*, October 25, 1983. Reagan's remarks were reported in the *Washington Post* on October 25 and 28, 1983. See "Chronology," *Middle East Journal* 38 (1984): 286.

73. Fred J. Khouri, *The Arab-Israeli Dilemma*, 3rd ed. (Syracuse, N.Y., 1985), 450. For U.S. defense contractors and their relations with the Israeli military and defense establishment, see Sheila Ryan, "U.S. Military Contractors in Israel," *Middle East Report (MERIP)* 17 (January–February 1987): 17–22. See also the breakdown of military aid to Middle Eastern countries generally, 23–26.

74. See Spiegel, *Other Arab-Israeli Conflict*, 428, for an account of Reagan's intervention to settle a major dispute among his advisers as to what course they should follow.

75. For discussion of attempts at political reform in Lebanon, see the *New York Times*, December 29, 1985; and the *London Observer*, March 17, 1985. For Elie Hobeika's break with the Phalange, see the *New York Times* and the *Los Angeles Times*, September 28, 1986.

76. Augustus R. Norton, *Hezbollah: A Short History* (Princeton, N.J., 2007).

PLATFORM OF THE LIKUD COALITION
March 1977

These excerpts from Prime Minister Menachem Begin's election platform illustrate Revisionist Zionist beliefs. Although claims to Jordan had been dropped, the right to the West Bank (Judea and Samaria) was absolute. Equally concrete was the Likud objection to a Palestinian state and to the PLO. Likud responses to peace initiatives, including Sadat's overture of November 1977 (see Document 8.2) must be read in light of these ideals. Likud was supposedly open to "direct negotiations . . . without pre-conditions," but its own set of conditions was well established.

The Right of the Jewish People to the Land of Israel (Eretz Israel)

a. The right of the Jewish people to the Land of Israel is eternal and indisputable and is linked with the right to security and peace; therefore, Judaea and Samaria will not be handed to any foreign administration; between the sea and Jordan there will only be Israeli sovereignty.

b. A plan which relinquishes parts of western Eretz Israel undermines our right to the country, unavoidably leads to the establishment of a "Palestinian State," jeopardizes the security of the Jewish population, endangers the existence of the State of Israel, and frustrates any prospect of peace.

Genuine Peace — Our Central Objective

a. The Likud government will place its aspirations for peace at the top of its priorities and will spare no effort to promote peace. The Likud will act as a genuine partner at peace treaty negotiations with our neighbors, as is customary among the nations. The Likud government will attend the Geneva Conference. . . .

d. The Likud government's peace initiative will be positive. Directly or through a friendly state, Israel will invite her neighbors to hold direct negotiations, in order to sign peace agreements without pre-conditions on either side and without any solution formula invented by outsiders ("invented outside"). At the negotiations each party will be free to make any proposals it deems fit.

Settlement

Settlement, both urban and rural, in all parts of the Land of Israel is the focal point of the Zionist effort to redeem the country, to maintain vital security

---

Source: *The Israel-Arab Reader: A Documentary History of the Middle East Conflict,* Walter Laqueur and Barry Rubin, eds. (New York, 1984), 591–92.

areas and serves as a reservoir of strength and inspiration for the renewal of the pioneering spirit. The Likud government will call the younger generation in Israel and the dispersions to settle and help every group and individual in the task of inhabiting and cultivating the wasteland, while taking care not to dispossess anyone.

Arab Terror Organizations

The PLO is no national liberation organization but an organization of assassins, which the Arab countries use as a political and military tool, while also serving the interests of Soviet imperialism, to stir up the area. Its aim is to liquidate the State of Israel, set up an Arab country instead and make the Land of Israel part of the Arab world. The Likud government will strive to eliminate these murderous organizations in order to prevent them from carrying out their bloody deeds.

DOCUMENT 8.2

ANWAR AL-SADAT

SPEECH TO THE ISRAELI KNESSET

November 20, 1977

Egyptian president Sadat's epoch-making visit to Jerusalem would eventually lead to what appeared to be a separate peace, his statement of intention to the contrary. Still, his remarks about occupation of land, the Palestinian issue, and security through peace agreements as superior to security through land acquisition remain basic questions to resolve. Compare his remarks about the Balfour Declaration and his references to Israeli use of force to impose peace to Begin's remarks in his reply (see Document 8.3).

In the Name of God, Mr. Speaker of the Knesset, ladies and gentlemen. . . .

God's peace and mercy be with you. God willing, peace for us all . . . in the Arab land and in Israel and in every part . . . of this wide world. . . . All of us in this land, the land of God, Moslems, Christians and Jews, worship God and no other god. God's decrees and commandments are: love, honesty, chastity and peace. . . .

Ladies and gentlemen: There are moments in the life of nations and peoples when those who are known for their wisdom and foresight are required to look beyond the past, with all its complications and remnants. . . . We must rise above all forms of fanaticism and self-deception and obsolete theories of superiority. It is important that we should never forget that virtue is God's alone. If I

Source: T. G. Fraser, *The Middle East, 1914–1979* (London, 1980), 151–63.

say that I want to protect the Arab people from the terrors of new, terrifying wars, I declare before you with all sincerity that I have the same feelings and I carry the same responsibility for every human being in the world and, most certainly, for the Israeli people. . . . Destiny has decreed that my visit to you, my visit of peace, should come on the day of the great Islamic feast, the blessed Id al-Adha, the feast of sacrifice and redemption when Ibrahim [Abraham], may peace be upon him, the forefather of both the Arabs and the Jews, our father Ibrahim submitted to God and dedicated himself completely to Him, not through weakness but through colossal spiritual power and through his free choice to sacrifice his son, which arose from his firm, unshakable belief in the sublime ideals which gave a deep meaning to life.

Ladies and gentlemen, let us be frank with each other. . . . How can we achieve a just and lasting peace? . . .

Firstly, I did not come to you with a view to concluding a separate agreement between Egypt and Israel, this is not provided for in Egypt's policy. The problem does not lie just between Egypt and Israel; . . . Even if a peace agreement was achieved between all the confrontation states and Israel, without a just solution to the Palestinian problem it would never ensure the establishment of the durable, lasting peace the entire world is now trying to achieve. . . . I have come to you so that together we can build a lasting and just peace, so that not one more drop of the blood of either side may be shed. . . .

We used to reject you, and we had our reasons and grievances. Yes, we used to reject meeting you anywhere. Yes, we used to describe you as "so-called Israel." . . . But I say to you today and I say to the whole world that we accept that we should live with you in a lasting and just peace. . . . There existed between you and us a huge high wall. You tried to build it over a quarter of a century, but it was demolished in 1973. In its ferocity the wall continued the war psychologically. Your wall was a threat with a force capable of destroying the Arab nation from end to end. . . . Indeed some of you said that even after another fifty years the Arabs would never achieve a position of any strength. . . . We must admit together that this wall has fallen, it collapsed in 1973. But there is still another wall, this second wall forms a complex psychological barrier between us and you. It is a barrier of doubt, a barrier of hatred, a barrier of fear of deception, a barrier of illusions about behaviour, actions or decisions, a barrier of cautious and mistaken interpretation of every event or statement. . . .

Ladies and gentlemen, the truth is . . . that there can be no peace in the true sense of the word, unless this peace is based on justice and not on the occupation of the territory of others. It is not right that you seek for yourselves what you deny to others. In . . . the spirit which prompted me to come to you, I say to you: you have finally to abandon . . . the belief that force is the best means of dealing with the Arabs. You have to absorb very well the lessons of confrontation between ourselves and you; expansion will be of no avail to you. . . . To put it clearly, our territory is not a subject of bargaining; it is not a topic for wrangling. . . .

What is peace to Israel? To live in the region, together with her Arab neighbours, in security and safety.... For Israel to live within her borders secure from any aggression — this is a logic to which I say: "Yes." For Israel to get all kinds of assurances that ensure for her these two facts — this is a demand to which I say: "Yes."... But how can this be achieved?... There are facts that must be confronted with all courage and clarity. There is Arab land which Israel has occupied and still occupies by armed force. And we insist that complete withdrawal from this land be undertaken and this includes Arab Jerusalem, Jerusalem to which I have come, as it is considered the city of peace and which has been and will always be the living embodiment of coexistence between believers of the three religions. It is inadmissible for anyone to think of Jerusalem's special position within the context of annexation and expansion. It must be made a free city, open to all the faithful. What is more important is that the city must not be closed to those who have chosen it as a place of residence for several centuries....

Let me tell you without hesitation that I have not come to you, under this dome, to beg you to withdraw your forces from the occupied territory. This is because complete withdrawal from the Arab territories occupied after 1967 is a matter that goes without saying.... There can never be peace established or built with the occupation of others' land....

As regards the Palestine question, nobody denies that it is the essence of the entire problem. Nobody throughout the entire world accepts today slogans raised here in Israel which disregard the existence of the people of Palestine and even ask where the people of Palestine are. The problem of the Palestinian people, and the legitimate rights of the Palestinian people ... are facts that meet with the support and recognition of the international community.... Even the USA — your first ally, which is the most committed to the protection of the existence and security of Israel ... has opted ... to recognize that the Palestinian people have legitimate rights, and that the Palestine question is the crux and essence of the conflict.... In all sincerity, I tell you that peace cannot be achieved without the Palestinians, and that it would be a great mistake, the effect of which no one knows, to turn a blind eye to this question or to set it aside.

I shall not recall events of the past, since the issue of the Balfour Declaration sixty years ago. You know the facts quite well. And if you have found it legally and morally justified to set up a national homeland on a land that was not totally yours, you are well placed to show understanding to the insistence of the Palestinian people to set up their own state anew, on their homeland.... You must face the reality courageously, as I have faced it.... There can never be peace through an attempt to impose imaginary situations on which the entire world has turned its back.... There is no use in creating obstacles, for either they will delay the march of peace or peace itself will be killed....

When the bells of peace ring, there will be no hand to beat the drums of war; should such a hand exist, it will not be heard. Imagine with me the peace agreement in Geneva, the good news of which we herald to a world thirsty for peace: (Firstly) a peace agreement based on ending the Israeli occupation of the Arab territory occupied in 1967; (secondly) the realization of basic rights of the Palestinian people and this people's right to self-determination, including their right to setting up their own state; thirdly, the right of all the countries of the region to live in peace within their secure and guaranteed borders, through agreed measures for the appropriate security of international borders, in addition to the appropriate international guarantees; fourthly, all the States in the region will undertake to administer relations among themselves in accordance with the principles and aims of the UN Charter, in particular eschewing the use of force and settling differences among them by peaceful means; and fifthly, ending the state of war that exists in the region. . . .

The experiences of past and contemporary history teach us all that missiles, warships and nuclear weapons, perhaps, cannot establish security. On the contrary, they destroy all that was built by security. For the sake of our peoples, for the sake of a civilization made by man, we must protect man in every place from the rule of the force of arms. We must raise high the rule of humanity with the full force of principles and values which hold man high. . . .

DOCUMENT 8.3

MENACHEM BEGIN

REPLY TO PRESIDENT SADAT

November 20, 1977

Israeli Prime Minister Menachem Begin stresses Israel's continuing desire for peace set against Arab threats and aggression. He rejects Sadat's interpretation of the Balfour Declaration and, implicitly, any Palestinian rights to what was then Palestine. He also links the departure of Jews from Palestine/Israel, their homeland, at the turn of the Christian era with World War II and the Holocaust, creating a historical foundation for Israeli security policy extending beyond the immediate present and its concerns.

Mr. Speaker, Mr. President of the State of Israel, Mr. President of the Arab Republic of Egypt, Ladies and Gentlemen, members of the Knesset, we send our greetings to the President, to all the people of the Islamic religion in our country, and wherever they may be, on this the occasion of the Feast, the Festival of the Sacrifice, Id al-Adha. This feast reminds us of the binding of Isaac. This was the way in which the Creator of the World tested our forefather, Abraham—our common forefather—to test his faith, and Abraham passed this test. . . . Thus

Source: T. G. Fraser, *The Middle East, 1914–1979* (London, 1980), 163–69.

we contributed, the people of Israel and the Arab people, to the progress of mankind, and thus we are continuing to contribute to human culture to this day.

I greet and welcome the President of Egypt for coming to our country and on his participating in the Knesset session. The flight time between Cairo and Jerusalem is short, but the distance between Cairo and Jerusalem was until last night almost endless. President Sadat crossed this distance courageously. We, the Jews, know how to appreciate such courage, and we know how to appreciate it in our guest, because it is with courage that we are here and this is how we continue to exist, and we shall continue to exist.

Mr. Speaker, this small nation, the remaining refuge of the Jewish people which returned to its historic homeland—has always wanted peace and, . . . in the Declaration of Independence in the founding scroll of our national freedom, David Ben-Gurion said: We extend a hand of peace and goodneighbourliness to all the neighbouring countries and their peoples. We call upon them to cooperate, to help each other, with the Hebrew people independent in its own country. . . .

But it is my bounden duty, Mr. Speaker, and not only my right, not to pass over the truth, that our hand outstretched for peace was not grasped and, one day after we had renewed our independence—as was our right, our eternal right, which cannot be disputed—we were attacked on three fronts and we stood almost without arms, the few against many, the weak against the strong, while an attempt was made, one day after the Declaration of Independence, to strangle it at birth, to put an end to the last hope of the Jewish people, the yearning renewed after the years of destruction and holocaust.

No, . . . we have never based our attitude to the Arab people on might; quite the contrary, force was used against us. Over all the years of this generation we have never stopped being attacked by might, the might of the strong arm stretched out to exterminate our people, to destroy our independence, to deny our rights. . . . With the help of Almighty God, we overcame the forces of aggression, and we have guaranteed the existence of our nation. . . . We believe . . . only in right and therefore . . . we want full, real peace, with complete reconciliation between the Jewish and the Arab peoples. . . .

I do not wish to dwell on memories of the past, although they are bitter memories. . . . For it is true indeed that we shall have to live in this area. . . . Therefore we must determine what peace means. . . . The first clause of a peace treaty is cessation of the state of war, for ever. We want to establish normal relations between us, as they exist between all nations, even after wars. . . . Let us sign a peace treaty and let us establish this situation forever, both in Jerusalem and in Cairo, and I hope the day will come when the Egyptian children wave the Israeli flag and the Egyptian flag just as the children of Israel waved both these flags in Jerusalem. And you, Mr. President, will have a loyal ambassador in Jerusalem and we shall have an ambassador in Cairo. And even if differences of opinion arise between us, we shall clarify them, like civilized peoples, through our authorized envoys.

We are proposing economic cooperation for the development of our countries. There are wonderful countries in the Middle East, the Lord created it thus: oases in the desert, but we can make the deserts flourish as well. Let us cooperate in this field, let us develop our countries, let us eliminate poverty, hunger, homelessness. . . .

As I pointed out, . . . I am renewing my invitation to the President of Syria to follow in your footsteps, Mr. President, and come to us to open negotiations . . . so that we may sign a peace treaty between us. . . . I invite King Husayn to come to us to discuss all the problems which need to be discussed between us. And genuine representatives of the Arabs of Eretz Yisra'el, I invite them to come and hold clarification talks with us about our common future, about guaranteeing the freedom of man, social justice, peace, mutual respect. And if they invite us to come to their capitals, we shall [go to] Damascus, . . . Amman or . . . Beirut, . . . in order to hold negotiations with them there. . . .

Mr. Speaker, it is my duty today to tell our guest and the peoples watching us . . . about the link between our people and this land. The President [of Egypt] recalled the Balfour Declaration. No, sir, we did not take over any strange land; we returned to our homeland. The link between our people and this land is eternal. . . . We had our prophets here and their sacred words stand to this day. . . . This is where we became a people, here we established our Kingdom. And when we were expelled from our land, . . . we never forgot it for even one day. We prayed for it, we longed for it, we believed in our return to it from the day these words were spoken: When the Lord restores the fortunes of Zion, we shall be like dreamers. Our mouths will be filled with laughter, and our tongues will speak with shouts of joy. These verses apply to all our exiles and all our sufferings, giving us the consolation that the return to Zion would come. This, our right, was recognised. The Balfour Declaration was included in the mandate laid down by the nations of the world, including the United States of America, and the preface to this recognised international document says: Whereas recognition has the bible given to the historical connection of the Jewish people with Palestine and to the grounds for reconstituting their national home in that country . . . , that is, in Eretz Yisra'el.

In 1919 we also won recognition of this right by the spokesman of the Arab people and the agreement of 3 January 1919, which was signed by Prince Faysal and Chaim Weizmann.* It reads: Mindful of the racial kinship and ancient bonds existing between the Arabs and the Jewish people and realising that the surest means of working out the consummation of the national aspirations is the closest possible collaboration in the development of the Arab State and of Palestine. . . . That is our right. The existence—truthful existence.

. . . I accompanied you this morning, Mr. President, to Yad Vashem.† With your own eyes you saw the fate of our people when this homeland was taken from it. It cannot be told. Both of us agreed, Mr. President, that anyone who has

*See Document 2.3 on page 98.—Ed.
†**Yad Vashem:** Memorial in Jerusalem to the Jews murdered by the Nazis.—Ed.

not seen with his own eyes everything there is in Yad Vashem cannot understand what happened to this people when it was without a homeland, when its own homeland was taken from it. And both of us read a document dated 30 January 1939, where the word "vernichtung"—annihilation—appears. . . . And during those six years, too, when millions of our people, among them one and a half million of the little children of Israel who were burnt on all the strange beds, nobody came to save them, not from the East and not from the West. And because of this, we took a solemn oath, this entire generation—the generation of extermination and revival—that we would never again put our people in danger. . . . It is our duty for generations to come to remember that certain things said about our people must be taken with complete seriousness. . . .

President Sadat knows and he knew from us before he came to Jerusalem that we have a different position from his with regard to the permanent borders between us and our neighbours. However, I say to the President of Egypt and to all our neighbours: Do not say there is not, there will not be negotiations about any particular issue. I propose, with the agreement of the decisive majority of this parliament, that everything be open to negotiation. . . . No side will . . . present prior conditions. We shall conduct the negotiations honourably. If there are differences of opinion between us, this is not unusual. Anyone who has studied the history of wars and the signing of peace treaties knows that all negotiations over a peace treaty began with differences of opinion between the sides. And in the course of the negotiations they came to an agreement which permitted the signing of peace treaties and agreements. And this is the road we propose to take.

DOCUMENT 8.4

A FRAMEWORK FOR PEACE IN THE MIDDLE EAST AGREED AT CAMP DAVID
September 17, 1978

These excerpts from agreements reached at the Camp David talks note the reliance on Resolutions 242 and 338. They also stress, for the West Bank and Gaza, the procedures intended to lead to "full autonomy" for the Palestinian inhabitants, with Jordanian involvement, and refer to the "elected representatives" of these areas deciding how they should be governed. The Likud Party rejected this interpretation. The Egyptian-Israeli peace treaty of March 1979 would refer to negotiations intended to implement these terms, but they were never concluded satisfactorily. The stipulations for a five-year transitional period, with final status talks beginning no later than the third year of that period, show how this framework became the model for future negotiations, including those of the 1993 and 1995 Oslo Accords (see Chapter 10).

Source: T. G. Fraser, *The Middle East, 1914–1979* (London, 1980), 171–76.

Muhammad Anwar al-Sadat, President of the Arab Republic of Egypt, and Menachem Begin, Prime Minister of Israel, met with Jimmy Carter, President of the United States of America, at Camp David from 5 September to 17 September 1978, and have agreed on the following framework for peace in the Middle East. They invite other parties to the Arab-Israeli conflict to adhere to it. . . .

- To achieve a relationship of peace, in the spirit of Article 2 of the United Nations Charter, future negotiations between Israel and any neighbor prepared to negotiate peace and security with it, are necessary for the purpose of carrying out all the provisions and principles of Resolutions 242 and 338.
- Peace requires respect for the sovereignty, territorial integrity and political independence of every state in the area and their right to live in peace within secure and recognized boundaries free from threats or acts of force. Progress toward that goal can accelerate movement toward a new era of reconciliation in the Middle East. . . .

Framework

Taking these factors into account, the parties . . . agree that this framework as appropriate is intended by them to constitute a basis for peace not only between Egypt and Israel, but also between Israel and each of its other neighbors which is prepared to negotiate peace with Israel on this basis. With that objective in mind, they have agreed to proceed as follows:

West Bank and Gaza

1. Egypt, Israel, Jordan and the representatives of the Palestinian people should participate in negotiations on the resolution of the Palestinian problem in all its aspects. To achieve that objective, negotiations relating to the West Bank and Gaza should proceed in three stages:

(a) Egypt and Israel agree that, in order to ensure a peaceful and orderly transfer of authority, and taking into account the security concerns of all the parties, there should be transitional arrangements for the West Bank and Gaza for a period not exceeding five years. In order to provide full autonomy to the inhabitants, under these arrangements the Israeli military government and its civilian administration will be withdrawn as soon as a self-governing authority has been freely elected by the inhabitants of these areas to replace the existing military government. To negotiate the details of a transitional arrangement, the Government of Jordan will be invited to join the negotiations on the basis of this framework. . . .

(b) Egypt, Israel, and Jordan will agree on the modalities for establishing the elected self-governing authorities in the West Bank and Gaza. The delegations of Egypt and Jordan may include Palestinians from the West Bank and Gaza or other Palestinians as mutually agreed. The parties will negotiate an agreement which will define the powers and responsibilities of the self-governing authority to be exercised in the West Bank and Gaza. A withdrawal of Israeli armed forces will take place and there will be a redeployment of the remaining Israeli forces into specified security locations. . . .

(c) When the self-governing authority (administrative council) in the West Bank and Gaza is established and inaugurated, the transitional period of five years will begin. As soon as possible, but not later than the third year after the beginning of the transitional period, negotiations will take place to determine the final status of the West Bank and Gaza and its relationship with its neighbors, and to conclude a peace treaty between Israel and Jordan by the end of the transitional period. These negotiations will be conducted among Egypt, Israel, Jordan, and the elected representatives of the inhabitants of the West Bank and Gaza. . . . The negotiations will be based on all the provisions and principles of UN Security Council Resolution 242. The negotiations will resolve, among other matters, the location of the boundaries and the nature of the security arrangements. The solution from the negotiations must also recognize the legitimate rights of the Palestinian people and their just requirements.

In this way, the Palestinians will participate in the determination of their own future through: (1) The negotiations among Egypt, Israel, Jordan and the representatives of the inhabitants of the West Bank and Gaza to agree on the final status of the West Bank and Gaza and other outstanding issues by the end of the transitional period.

(2) Submitting their agreement to a vote by the elected representatives of the inhabitants of the West Bank and Gaza.

(3) Providing for the elected representatives of the inhabitants of the West Bank and Gaza to decide how they shall govern themselves consistent with the provisions of their agreement.

(4) Participating as stated above in the work of the committee negotiating the peace treaty between Israel and Jordan.

2. All necessary measures will be taken and provisions made to assure the security of Israel and its neighbors during the transitional period and beyond. To assist providing such security, a strong local police force will be constituted by the self-governing authority. It will be composed of inhabitants of the West Bank and Gaza. The police will maintain continuing liaison on internal security matters with the designated Israeli, Jordanian, and Egyptian officers. . . .

9

FROM PARIAH TO PARTNER
The PLO and the Quest for Peace in Global and Regional Contexts

1984–1993

THE YEARS 1984–1993 witnessed major transformations in the world order as well as within the Middle East. In Europe, the Soviet Union officially dissolved in December 1991, the Communist Party was banned, and Moscow became the capital of the new Russian republic. Former Eastern European satellites regained their independence and numerous independent states emerged along the southern rim of the former Soviet empire, many with Muslim majorities. West and East Germany reunified in December 1990. The cold war was over.

In the Middle East, a revolution began and the Iraq-Iran War ended. The consequences of these developments led initially to further conflict, but ultimately to peace efforts that resulted in the Israeli-Palestinian accord of September 1993.

The revolution was the Palestinian intifada (literally, a "shaking off" of a condition), which erupted in Gaza in December 1987. It galvanized a moribund PLO and encouraged its historic declaration of an independent state of Palestine and its recognition of the existence of Israel in November–December 1988. In response, the United States opened a dialogue with the PLO through its embassy in Tunis, where Yasir Arafat had established himself after leaving Lebanon.

In June 1990 the United States, under President George H. W. Bush (who succeeded Ronald Reagan in January 1989), suspended the United States–PLO talks following an abortive Palestinian raid on Israel. They would not be renewed until the Oslo Accords of September 1993. These events coincided with a major repercussion of Soviet liberalization, namely, Moscow's willingness to permit massive Soviet Jewish emigration. An average of 10,000 Jews a month went to Israel, where they immediately became a significant factor in the struggle for control of the territories. The Likud Party and its backers proclaimed the salvation of the Golan Heights and the West Bank for Israel because room would be needed to house these new immigrants.

In the midst of this discord, a regional crisis erupted that ultimately affected Palestinian-Israeli relations. In July 1988, Iraq emerged victorious from its eight-year war with Iran, albeit with few tangible gains. The Iraqi ruler, Saddam Husayn, found himself beset with debts owed to those who had financed his war effort, especially the oil-rich shaykhdoms of the Persian Gulf; Kuwait began to request repayment of its loans. Unable to finance the rebuilding of his military and economy because of lowered oil prices, Saddam Husayn sent troops to the Kuwait border in July 1990, seeking agreement for a rise in oil prices as well as boundary modifications. When Kuwait scorned further negotiations, Iraq invaded on August 2 and announced that Kuwait had become a province of Iraq. In reply, the United States formed a military coalition, including Egyptian and Syrian troops, that attacked Iraqi forces in January 1991 and liberated Kuwait—a conflict now known as the first Gulf War. Further assaults on Iraq were suspended. Kurdish and Shi'ite insurgencies against Saddam's regime in northern and southern Iraq, respectively, encouraged by the United States, were crushed by Saddam, although a Kurdish zone protected by international forces was created in the north.

This first Gulf War had several ramifications that impinged upon the Arab-Israeli peace process. The United States had prevailed upon Israel not to involve itself in the war, even if attacked by Iraq. At the same time the Bush administration had promised Arab coalition partners that the United States would pursue peace efforts with Israel once hostilities had ended that would include the Palestinians. After several tours of the Middle East, Secretary of State James Baker succeeded in convening a peace conference on October 30, 1991, in Madrid, Spain, cosponsored with the then still existing Soviet Union. The PLO permitted itself to be represented by Palestinians from the territories as part of a Palestinian-Jordanian delegation.

The Madrid talks lasted nearly two years with little progress, unaffected by the Israeli elections in June 1992 that saw the ouster of the Likud and the return of the Labor Party, headed by Yitzhak Rabin. But private Israeli-Palestinian negotiations, removed from the Madrid talks, had been initiated in Oslo, Norway. These led to the first Oslo Accord where Israel and the PLO exchanged statements of mutual recognition and, on September 13, 1993, signed a Declaration of Principles on Interim Self-Rule for the Palestinians in a ceremony at the White House.

PEACE GAMBITS, TERRORISM, AND POLITICAL STRIFE, 1984–1987

With the PLO established in Tunis after its departure from Beirut in 1982, Yasir Arafat attempted to salvage something from the Lebanon disaster. Beset by opposition in his own ranks, Arafat found little encouragement outside. Official Israeli policy remained that espoused by Menachem Begin and reiterated by Yitzhak Rabin: the PLO should be denied a role in negotiations "even if it accepts all the conditions of negotiations on the basis of the Camp David agreements (in addition to Resolutions 242 and 338) because the essence of the willingness to speak with the PLO is the willingness to speak about a Palestinian state, which must be opposed."[1]

Competing Agendas and Coalition Politics: Israel and the Jordanian Option

The United States seemed to agree with this position. It would talk to the PLO and consider a role for it in negotiations only when it "publicly and unequivocally" accepted Resolution 242. When Arafat sought American recognition of the Palestinian right to "self-determination," even if in the context of a confederation with Jordan, the Reagan administration objected; self-determination meant a Palestinian state, which the United States refused to consider. The United States appeared to reject Arafat's diplomatic overtures unless he met conditions that would deny statehood, a stance nearly identical to Israel's.

Apparent U.S. backing for Israel did not mean complete agreement, however. The Reagan administration wanted a Jordanian solution to the West Bank situation, one that envisaged Israel giving up more territory than any Israeli politician seemed likely to do. It would also accept as negotiators Palestinians from the West Bank and Gaza who were linked to the PLO, provided they were acceptable to Israel. The administration seemed to be pressuring Israel to be forthcoming while permitting it to veto U.S. proposals.

The results of Israeli elections in July 1984 further confused matters. The Labor Party, led by Shimon Peres, won a slight plurality, but Peres failed to form a coalition government out of the fifteen minority parties that had won seats in the Knesset. Reluctantly, he accepted a coalition with Likud in which power would be shared and posts distributed equally. The Labor Party would govern for the first eighteen months, with Peres as prime minister and Yitzhak Shamir of Likud as foreign minister; Yitzhak Rabin, Peres's rival in the Labor Party, was defense minister, and Ariel Sharon reemerged on the Likud side as minister of commerce and industry. (Shamir would become prime minister in October 1986.)

Peres hoped to achieve a settlement with King Husayn of Jordan that excluded the PLO. Success might enable him to call for new elections before he had to hand the prime ministership over to Shamir, but he had to tread cautiously or risk being accused by the Likud of caving in to the PLO. For their part, hoping to annex the West Bank to Israel, Shamir and Sharon opposed any negotiations with Jordan. They encouraged further settlement activity that Peres tried to restrain in order to bring Husayn to the peace table.

Temporary Allies: The Husayn-Arafat Accord

Diplomatic bargaining intensified in 1985, as did the equally determined efforts to derail that process. In February, King Husayn and Yasir Arafat issued a joint call for a Palestinian state on the West Bank that would include East Jerusalem, but this "state" would exist in confederation with Jordan, whose ruler would have final authority over it. Israel would withdraw completely from the occupied territories in return for peace. Jordanian officials said that by accepting inclusion in a confederation with Jordan, Arafat was implicitly abandoning the 1968 PLO Charter that called for Palestinian statehood in what was now Israel. This meant acceptance of Israel's existence, to be acknowledged openly if a settlement were reached.

Husayn would have preferred to regain the West Bank without Arafat, but he needed an alliance with the PLO to legitimize his aspirations in the eyes of the Arab world as well as in those of West Bank Arabs. For his part, Arafat had no love for Husayn but saw him as a vehicle through which to gain U.S. support for PLO involvement in the negotiating process. Both viewed American approval of their overtures as a way to stop further Israeli settlements in the territories, but Arafat's gambit was restricted by obligations to his constituency. He would not recognize Israel before being accepted into the international diplomatic arena, since to do so would prejudice his position within PLO councils. Thus, he could not take the one initiative that would have forced the American hand, namely, open acceptance of Resolution 242.[2]

Given these obstacles, little progress was made. Many blamed the stalemate on the United States. Among those disenchanted with Washington was the government of Margaret Thatcher of Great Britain, normally Ronald Reagan's staunchest defender. Seeking to break the deadlock, she invited two Fatah members of the Palestine National Council (PNC) to meet with her in October 1985. This decision, announced in mid-September, was a "calculated gesture designed to distance Britain from both the U.S. and Israel. It is the clearest possible hint to the Americans, who have so far refused to talk to the PLO, that they should stop making difficulties and start making peace in the Middle East."[3]

The upcoming meeting between Thatcher and Fatah representatives posed a serious threat to those who opposed Arafat's participation in the peace process. They included not only Palestinian factions such as the Popular Front for the Liberation of Palestine (PFLP) and the Popular Democratic Front for the Liberation of Palestine (PDFLP), but also Israel, because such overtures might place pressure on the United States to modify its hostility to the PLO. A series of events took place in which radical Arab and Israeli governmental interests coincided.

On September 25, 1985, a Palestinian assassination squad (including one British citizen) killed three Israelis in Cyprus. When captured, the group claimed to belong to Force 17, an elite PLO group linked to Fatah and Arafat, although he and other PLO spokesmen denounced the killings. The incident gave the Peres government the opportunity to retaliate. On October 1, hoping to kill Arafat, Israeli planes bombed the PLO headquarters outside Tunis; more than fifty were killed and wounded, including some Tunisians. Ostensibly a mission to avenge the deaths of the Israelis in Cyprus, the raid was designed to derail Arafat's peace offensive. Whereas European and Arab leaders depicted the Israeli strike as an attempt to destroy the peace process, President Reagan called it a "legitimate response," which was later toned down to "understandable but unfortunate."[4]

The American reaction angered the Tunisians. Washington's tolerance of Israeli violations of Tunisian airspace contrasted with its condemnation, a week earlier, of Libyan overflights. The American stance was particularly galling because, in 1982, Tunis had agreed to house the PLO at Washington's request. On the other hand, the raid buttressed Shimon Peres's image in Israel as he tried to entice King Husayn into direct talks, which his Likud partners continued to oppose. One Israeli analyst declared on October 3 that "nobody will accuse Labor of being soft on the PLO or soft on terrorism now."[5]

The disintegration of the peace initiative continued. On October 8, PLO members commandeered a cruise ship, the *Achille Lauro*, in the Mediterranean, apparently intending to disembark in Israel and avenge the Tunis bombings. Arafat condemned the undertaking and asked the hijackers to surrender, but they did so only after murdering a disabled American Jew in his wheelchair and dumping his body overboard. At worst, especially in American eyes, Arafat had proven his terrorist tendencies. At best, he had been shown to lack control over units supposedly under his command: the head of the *Achille Lauro* operation was based in Tunis.

This sequence of events undermined the meeting with Thatcher and led to its cancellation. The culmination of this episode was Shimon Peres's address to the United Nations on October 21, in which he called for peace talks with Jordan. The United States approved the Peres overture, a stance suggesting implicit acceptance of the Israeli assault on the PLO headquarters.[6] In Israel, on the other hand, Peres's speech was immediately vilified by the Israeli right, which had no intention of ceding any territory.

The United States and Israel: Cold War Calculations

The Reagan administration had viewed Israel as a strong component of its anti-communist crusade from the time the president took office. In 1984 with U.S. troops withdrawn from Lebanon, Secretary of State George Shultz initiated a closer strategic alliance with Israel that included technological exchanges related to the Strategic Defense Initiative (the SDI, or Star Wars, project). Shultz declared in late 1986 that the goal of American-Israeli strategic cooperation was "to build institutional arrangements so that eight years from now, if there is a secretary of state who is not positive about Israel, he will not be able to overcome the bureaucratic relationship between Israel and the United States that we have established." This cooperation could have domestic benefits as well. The administration encouraged Israel's involvement in the Star Wars project in part to overcome opposition to it from liberal congressmen, who usually backed Israel.[7]

These goals promised close ties to Israel regardless of the nature of Likud actions toward the Palestinians or the potential clash of Israeli and American interests elsewhere. In the administration's view, the PLO remained isolated from major bases of support, leaving Arafat with one choice, an alliance with Jordan. Beyond this, "the PLO [had] no military option and [lacked] an effective political strategy beyond perpetuating its own survival."[8] Jordan's overture in 1985 that the PLO was weak and open to concessions had met with the response that "if the PLO was weak it should be excluded entirely from the diplomatic process."[9] In 1993, however, it was precisely this weakness that made Arafat and the PLO an attractive partner for peace in Israeli eyes.

But circumstances were about to change. The Palestinian rebellion against Israeli rule would create a new set of circumstances challenging the foundations of American policy based on the Jordanian option. These foundations would then be shattered by the Iraqi invasion of Kuwait and the U.S. decision to oppose Iraq militarily in the hope of reasserting American power not only in the Middle East but globally.

THE INTIFADA

On December 8, 1987, an Israeli tank-transport truck crashed into several Arab cars in Gaza, killing four Palestinians and injuring others. Demonstrations erupted during the funerals of the victims, initiating an upheaval that spread rapidly to the West Bank. These developments inaugurated a new phase in Palestinian Arab resistance to an Israeli rule designed to deprive them of their land and, in Likud's eyes, to oust them from the territories.

Roots of the Intifada

The intifada was a spontaneous eruption of hatred and frustration, directed mostly at Israel but to some extent also at the external Palestinian leadership.[10] Much of the fury resulted from personal factors not directly related to politics or economics—the daily harassments, arrests, and beatings that ordinary Palestinians had faced for years.

As noted in previous chapters, Arabs derived significant benefits from employment in Israel after 1967 that produced a boom in living standards for Palestinians, especially in the West Bank, for most of the 1970s. Wages were better than under Jordanian rule and were often supplemented by funds repatriated from Palestinians working in the Gulf, where a thriving economy existed. In addition, Israeli occupation, until 1977, did not seem particularly onerous to most Arabs in the territories. Jewish settlements were relatively isolated from Arab communities and their rate of growth was slight, especially compared with what occurred once Menachem Begin took office in 1978. Whereas an annual average of 770 Israelis settled in the territories from 1967 to 1977, that average increased under Likud to 5,960 annually from 1978 to 1987.[11] The location of settlements also changed: now they were often deliberately planned to abut Arab communities and to take over their lands, visible threats designed from Ariel Sharon's point of view to intimidate Arabs and encourage them to leave (see Map 9.1).

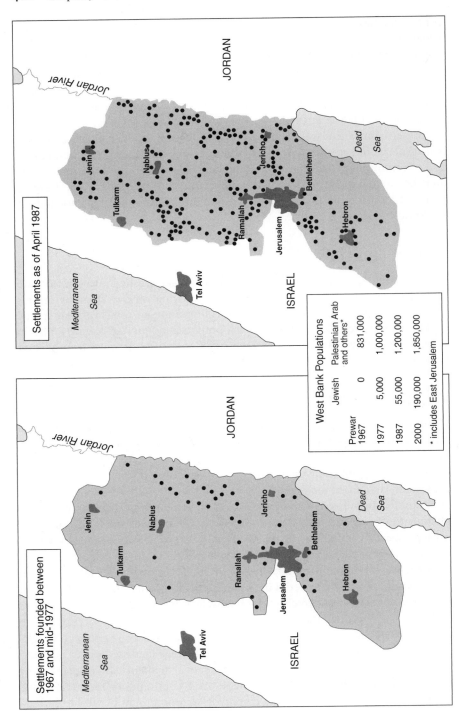

Settlements as of April 1987

Settlements founded between 1967 and mid-1977

West Bank Populations		
	Jewish	Palestinian Arab and others*
Prewar 1967	0	831,000
1977	5,000	1,000,000
1987	55,000	1,200,000
2000	190,000	1,850,000
* includes East Jerusalem		

The 1980s witnessed the intensification of this strategy. The village leagues created at the end of 1981 were accompanied by the reappearance of the "iron fist" policy, proclaimed by Sharon and Chief of Staff Rafael Eitan as the best means of crushing Palestinian Arab resistance. Arab demonstrations in the spring of 1982 met with arrests and beatings, though they did not approach the scale that would emerge later. The period immediately following the Israeli invasion of Lebanon until 1985 was relatively quiescent; then aggressive land requisitions recurred. It was not unusual for the military authorities simply to fence off Arab land and declare it to be Jewish property, leaving the owners with no legal recourse. The military administration was the law in the territories, as it had been in administering the absentee property law in Arab sectors of Israel immediately after independence. The Israeli military, now under Defense Minister Yitzhak Rabin, responded to Arab protests in August 1985 with a new "iron fist" campaign that intensified hatred on both sides.

For the Arabs, Israeli expansionist goals seemed on the verge of fulfillment in the vista of new bedroom communities for Jews being built on the West Bank. At the same time, a new generation of Arabs was emerging in the territories. Born under Israeli rule, they questioned their parents' submission to the daily humiliations they witnessed. For the younger generation, this submission meant capitulation to Israel where their elders had always viewed it as fortitude or endurance, *sumud*. Where the parents still placed their hopes in the PLO leadership, the youth saw that hope fade with the decline of the PLO in the mid-1980s. In addition, recession and inflation in Israel during that period caused economic decline for all sectors. As the Palestinian economy was tied to the shekel, its revenues and the purchasing power of individuals also suffered. Concomitantly, the steady decline in oil prices and slowing of economic growth in the Gulf, affected to some degree by spillover from the Iran-Iraq War, meant that jobs in Gulf states and funds sent back to the territories diminished.[12]

In such circumstances, sumud suggested acceptance of conditions that endangered one's future. Demonstrations increased from 1985 onward. So did random violence and assaults by Arabs and more controlled reprisals by Israelis, whether settlers on a raid or military patrols. Arrests of Arabs spiraled and a punishment used initially by the British in the 1930s, demolition of the

◁ **Map 9.1** ▪ **The West Bank: Israeli Settlements, 1967–1987**

These maps distinguish between settlement policies under Labor governments and those that began with Likud's assumption of power in 1977. Other than the expansion of Jerusalem, the focus of efforts under Labor was establishing a defensive perimeter along the Jordan River.

Few settlements were created near major Arab towns, the exception being Hebron where an illegal settlement, Qiryat Arba, was founded by Gush Emunim and allowed to stay. Under Likud we see a much more forceful settlement effort. East Jerusalem expands farther east, many more settlements arise near the 1967 borders, and there is a determined concentration of settlements adjacent to Arab towns and villages with the intent to take over land and possibly encourage Arabs to leave. The population statistics for 2000 are included to highlight issues pertaining to final status talks treated in Chapter 10.

homes of suspected rioters, was reinstituted. Rabin escalated the practice of administrative detention, which meant that Palestinians could be held for six months without trial. Whereas only 62 Palestinians had been held without trial during the period 1980–1985, 131 were detained in the last five months of 1985. Many more were arrested and later released, but only after brutal treatment. According to an Israeli lawyer who sought to defend Palestinians: "If you are arrested, the general rule is: after you confess you can see a lawyer. Everyone is beaten when they are arrested or to get a confession out of them. You must be very tough not to break in these circumstances."[13] Some did break and became informers against fellow Palestinians. But many others did not and used the prison experience, as had their predecessors in the 1970s, to formulate ties and strategies for the future. For them, "Prison was like an education."[14]

In retrospect, this experience was a turning point for many younger Palestinians in the territories. In the past they had frequently been victims of Jewish terrorism, itself a response to Arab terrorism initiated from outside. In the early 1980s a particular flash point had been Hebron, site of the massacre of many Jews in 1929 and a focal point of Israeli settler attention from the mid-1970s, when a Jewish (Gush Emunim) community reestablished itself there under military protection. An attack on settlers in May 1980 by Palestinians from outside the territories, killing six and wounding sixteen, led to a Jewish response—the car bombings of several Arab mayors. The stabbing death of a yeshiva student in Hebron in 1983 prompted random booby-trapping of Arab schools by a Jewish terrorist ring. Before the group was caught, it had planned to blow up the Dome of the Rock/Haram al-Sharif areas on the Temple Mount. Prison sentences for Jewish terrorists were often commuted after intense pressure from settler groups and right-wing politicians.[15]

Starting in 1985, Arab violence in the territories was more likely to be inspired from within rather than by groups or individuals sent from outside the area. Also different was the Israeli reaction, which included more frequent military retaliation to crush disturbances. Arabs in the territories, whether they were involved in riots or not, came into daily confrontations with Israeli troops. Nowhere was tension more rife than in Gaza.

The Gaza Strip

Conditions in the Gaza Strip have always been harsh owing to the extraordinary population density of the area, perhaps second only to Bangladesh. Refugees from 1948 and 1967 made up about 70 percent of the population in an area one-fifteenth the size of the West Bank. The Palestinian population had been further squeezed by the Israeli expropriation of 42 percent of Arab land after 1967 (see Map 9.2). As Sara Roy notes, "One [refugee] camp, Jabalya, is home to sixty thousand people living on one-half square mile of land, giving the camp a population density . . . double the density of Manhattan. The Strip's population is very young, with nearly 50 percent comprised of children 14 years of age and younger" (see Figure 9.1). With such a dependent population, the Strip became the major source of cheap labor in Israel: before the intifada, approximately 70,000 Gazans worked in Israel. On the other hand, sixteen Jewish settlements created out of land taken from Arabs housed approximately 2,500 Israeli settlers, compared to a Palestinian population of 750,000. Water-use restrictions imposed on Arabs to benefit Israeli settler agriculture resulted in a severe decline in the productivity of the Gaza citrus industry. When population imbalances are set against resource allocations, "individual Israelis consume[d] seven times the amount of water consumed by individual Gazans."[16]

Gaza had a long tradition of opposing Israeli rule. The Israeli occupation in 1967, followed by the announcement that Israel would retain control of the area in any subsequent peace agreements, had led to armed resistance, which intensified in 1971 following Israeli deportation of Arab families. One successful Israeli retaliation, directed by Ariel Sharon, saw sections of camps bulldozed to open roads for military access. Hostilities erupted again at the end of 1981, and in early 1982 a number of Gazans were killed by Israeli soldiers stationed outside mosques during Friday prayers.[17]

The place of Islam has always been more significant politically in the Gaza Strip than in the West Bank, derived primarily from the influence of the Gaza branch of the Muslim Brotherhood based in Cairo. The Brothers addressed the harsh socioeconomic environment of Gaza and sought to provide social and

Figure 9.1 ■ Jabalya Palestinian Refugee Camp, Gaza

This rooftop view of the Jabalya refugee camp offers a perspective on Palestinian living conditions. Refugees from the 1948 and 1967 wars, along with their descendants, make up about 70 percent of Gaza's inhabitants.

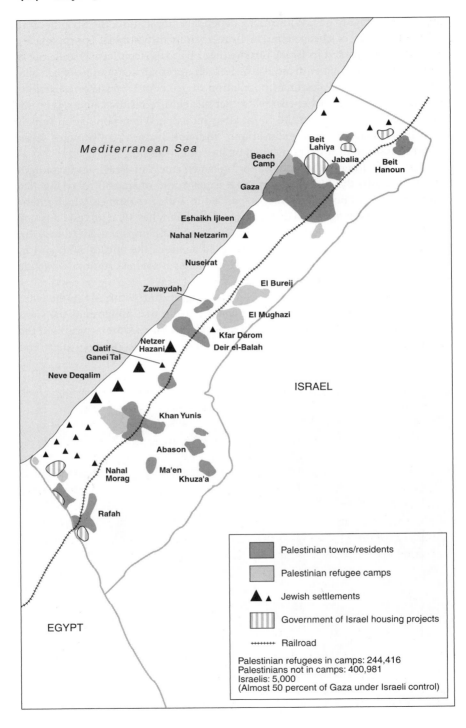

Mediterranean Sea

Beit Lahiya

Beach Camp

Jabalia

Beit Hanoun

Gaza

Eshaikh Ijleen

Nahal Netzarim

Nuseirat

El Bureij

Zawaydah

El Mughazi

Kfar Darom

Netzer Hazani

Deir el-Balah

Qatif

Ganei Tal

Neve Deqalim

ISRAEL

Khan Yunis

Abason

Ma'en

Khuza'a

Nahal Morag

Rafah

EGYPT

Palestinian towns/residents

Palestinian refugee camps

Jewish settlements

Government of Israel housing projects

Railroad

Palestinian refugees in camps: 244,416
Palestinians not in camps: 400,981
Israelis: 5,000
(Almost 50 percent of Gaza under Israeli control)

moral alternatives to the alienation imposed by those circumstances. Various offshoots of the Brothers appeared, some more militant against Israel than others. Most called for personal reform (*jihad*) as the dominant moral imperative and did not present themselves to the populace as an alternative to the PLO, whose goal of a Palestinian state they approved. The Brothers helped found the Islamic University of Gaza and two universities, al-Najah and Hebron, located in the West Bank.

Aggressive militancy emerged with the formation of Islamic Jihad in the mid-1980s, another offshoot of the Muslim Brotherhood. It argued that armed resistance against Israel was the only path to liberation. Its appearance indicated frustration at the doctrine of self-development and moral reform fostered by the Brotherhood during a period of increasing socioeconomic repression under Israeli rule, but it also showed that Israeli policy toward the religious groups had turned against itself. Israeli occupation and intelligence officials had encouraged the growth of the Muslim Brothers in Gaza from the later 1970s, through funding and by imposing fewer restrictions on their movements than they did on known PLO sympathizers. They assumed that increased adherence to Islam would undercut loyalty to the PLO and its secular political goals. These officials permitted militant students to travel from Gaza to Bir Zeit University in Ramallah, outside Jerusalem, to rough up PLO supporters, and the Israeli governor of Gaza told a journalist that "The Israeli Government gave me a budget and the military government gives to the mosques."[18]

Though successful to a small degree, these Israeli tactics were compromised by the general tenor of Israel's approach to the territories and its confiscation of land. As a result, no serious rift occurred at that time between members of Islamic groups and PLO sympathizers, who found common accord in their analysis of conditions within the territories.[19] Nevertheless, the decline of PLO prestige during the mid-1980s enabled local militants to assume more authority and initiative. The cycle of protest and repression intensified during 1987. On December 7 of that year, an Israeli was stabbed to death by a Gazan. When the tank-transport truck crashed into several Arab cars the next day, rumors spread immediately that the Israeli driver was a relative of the deceased and had been seeking revenge. The funerals of the Arab victims of the crash launched the massive demonstrations that inflamed the West Bank as well. The uprising had begun.

◀ Map 9.2 ■ The Gaza Strip, 1988

The Gaza Strip was created as a result of the 1949 armistices following the 1948 Arab-Israeli wars. Approximately 26 miles long and 5 miles wide, it contains one of the highest population densities in the world for its Arab population, whether in refugee camps or large towns (see also Figure 9.1). This map shows the Arab areas of concentration as well as the Jewish settlements situated either close to Israel's border in northern Gaza or along the coast; the different sizes of the settlement icons indicate their relative populations. Heavily fortified and isolated from nearby Arab population centers, the settlers moved under military escort when leaving their compounds. Israel withdrew from Gaza in 2005 (see Chapter 10).

Intifada: The First Two Years, December 1987–December 1989

A spontaneous uprising undirected by any higher committee or organization, the intifada spread rapidly from Gaza to the West Bank. It sustained itself through an extensive network of local committees formed over the previous decade and of neighborhoods that organized for mutual assistance. At its heart, the intifada was a rebellion of the poor and the young, the less-advantaged sectors of the population, who organized popular committees that PLO representatives then sought to co-opt under their own direction.[20]

Various decisions were made on the spot. One restricted the protests to demonstrations and stone-throwing; knives and guns were banned. Those directing the protest realized that the image of the Palestinian populace confronting with stones armed Israeli troops who shot to kill was one that would affect world opinion. Violence, controlled and restricted in its weapons, was for many Palestinians an important means of asserting open opposition to Israeli hegemony. But a political agenda quickly appeared. In January 1988, the leadership in the territories called for an independent Palestinian state, led by the PLO, that would coexist with Israel. Resolution of issues should await an international conference sponsored by the U.N. Security Council, a proposal that had been suggested by the PLO in April 1987. Within the territories, special taxes imposed on Arabs should be rescinded.

These principles, called the Fourteen Points, were initially announced by individuals not connected to the intifada, men more widely known to the outside world as "moderates," such as Sari Nuseibeh and Faysal al-Husayni, who had their own ties to the PLO in Tunis. As members of a social elite they were viewed with suspicion by both the popular leadership and PLO committee heads when these points were first declared. Subsequently, with direction from Tunis, the Fourteen Points became the official agenda of the intifada.[21] The integration of the various groups was never fully achieved, but they collaborated successfully. The local committee heads formed the unified command (Unified National Leadership, UNL), which in general agreed on tactics and issued joint directives that were then taken up at the street level (see Documents 9.1 and 9.2); coordination among factions in the territories often surpassed the inclination of their leaders to agree when meeting in Tunis. The Islamic Jihad (discussed later in this chapter), organized on the basis of cells, initially followed the UNL lead, mainly through its ties to Fatah.

The intifada radically affected the relationship of Arabs in the territories with PLO headquarters in Tunis and with the Israelis. The PLO had always tried to repress local leadership independent of its control, even if such individuals identified themselves with PLO goals. Now, necessity demanded not only cooperation but reliance on information and advice from the territories. This interactive balance would prove crucial in encouraging the leadership to consider diplomatic compromise once the resistance in the territories demanded it. On the other hand, Arafat's assumption of power in Gaza and Jericho following the

1993 accord with Israel gradually turned Arabs in the territories against him because they viewed him as imposing the authority of overseas Palestinians and ignoring local leaders.

The Israeli Perspective.   Israelis, and the government leadership in particular, interpreted the intifada in light of their preconceptions of Arab protests. For some, it was unacceptable behavior; for others, such as Defense Minister Yitzhak Rabin, it was "terrorism" and should be dealt with accordingly. He believed that Arabs understood force, nothing else. Military repression, including shooting at demonstrators, was acceptable; the beating of prisoners to "teach them a lesson" was encouraged. Many soldiers who had grown up with Arabs in subordinate positions to them reacted with fury to Arabs who defied them. Mass beatings occurred during patrols, and tear gas was used frequently in closed as well as open settings (a violation of the Geneva Convention). Houses adjacent to the site of stone-throwing were routinely vandalized and teargassed without evidence of the complicity of the occupants or regard for the frequent presence of pregnant women and children.

What Rabin explained as a policy designed to break Arab will—"beatings never killed anybody"—at times turned into soldier-inspired riots against the population of entire areas. Those arrested could expect serious beatings; those stopped, even aged adults or children under five years of age, might experience the same. As one Israeli journalist explained it:

> There is democracy in Israel but none in the territories. A whole generation of Israelis grew up with a nondemocratic system next to them, as nondemocratic rulers. There is a difference between the arrest of Arabs and Jews. When you [a Jew] get arrested, the police or secret service people will say, "We will give you Jewish treatment." You will be slapped around perhaps but not tortured. Arabs who are arrested are beaten and tortured. It is difficult to convince Israelis that this undemocratic way of ruling and treating Arabs is wrong or evil. Israelis see it as a normal practice [toward Arabs, not themselves].[22]

Eventually the excesses would stir public criticism within Israel, and in some cases lead to legal actions against soldiers charged with exceeding their orders. Their defense, that they were following orders issued by superiors (including Rabin), was denied, causing officers as well as soldiers to hurl accusations of lying at the military leadership and Rabin.[23]

The violence of the Israeli response aroused international criticism: in the first five weeks of the intifada, 33 Palestinians had been killed, more than 250 had been wounded, and nearly 2,000 had been imprisoned. Israel had suffered no fatalities, although 60 soldiers and 40 civilians had been wounded, the latter mostly settlers who joined the fray. The threat to Israel was twofold. First, Israel had to suppress the uprising in order to control the territories that its rightist government hoped to keep. Second, the government had to stem any hope of a political resolution to the uprising. In April 1988 the coalition cabinet approved the assassination of Khalil al-Wazir (Abu Jihad) at his home in Tunis. Wazir had directed the intifada and had counseled refusal to use arms. The cabinet's decision to kill him, fully supported by Likud members and by Defense Minister Rabin of the Labor Party, reflected the hope of quelling the uprising but also sought to stymie peace efforts. The timing of the assassination served to undercut calls for an international conference that had the approval of Rabin's rival, Shimon Peres.[24]

The Palestinian Response.   From the Palestinian perspective, the intifada had two sides: a popular resistance to Israeli oppression and an offer of coexistence once a Palestinian state was created. Both tracks had the same goal, getting rid of Israeli domination, but the second was just as threatening to most Israeli politicians as the first. For Israeli leaders, the Israeli-Arab relationship could not be one of equality. Arabs who espoused compromise were often incarcerated. For example, two Arab lawyers from Gaza were invited to speak on the goals of the intifada at a gathering at Tel Aviv University in the spring of 1988. They did so, advocating peaceful coexistence in separate states. Within two weeks each had been arrested and sentenced to six months detention without legal recourse in Ansar 3, a new prison built in the Negev to house such individuals. The Israeli organizers of the conference had no doubt about the reasons for such detention: advocacy of peace was again more threatening than pursuit of violence.[25]

Rather than crush the uprising, Israeli repression unified it, solidifying ties that had been tenuous. Originally an uprising of the young and the poor centered in Gaza, the intifada appealed mainly to the youth from the refugee camps when it spread to the West Bank; many members of the middle class at first questioned their motives. What finally united the middle class with the younger generation was the indiscriminate nature of Israeli retaliation—you were beaten because you were a Palestinian, regardless of your status or what you happened to be doing at the time a demonstration began. General though not universal cooperation developed regarding acts of civil disobedience. Palestinians boycotted Israeli goods and refused to pay Israeli taxes designed to finance the occupation. The UNL-sponsored strikes and shutdowns of businesses survived Israeli attempts to break them. Israeli countertactics, principally the denial of food supplies to villages, full quarantines, and the like, were countered by the spread of family gardens that became a symbol of resistance. Israeli authorities at times arrested Arabs for growing their own food (as happened in the Christian village of Bayt Sahur) (see Figure 9.2).

Labor groups and women's committees joined the resistance. The Palestinian labor movement had existed for years and was somewhat factionalized. A more recent women's movement, which had fewer ideological splits, expanded its activities during the intifada. Many women who had previously remained at home took jobs to support families or became political activists, joining in strikes and demonstrations. Once Islamist organizations became more involved

Figure 9.2 ■ **Palestinian Christian Women Support the Intifada, 1988**

This march, with the outlawed Palestinian flag, took place in the Christian West Bank village of Bayt Sahur, where Israeli troops later destroyed gardens to undermine Palestinian refusal to buy Israeli goods. Note the stone in the woman's right hand. Compare the dress of these women to that of the Hamas supporters in Figure 9.3. Since the al-Qaida attacks on the United States of September 11, 2001, stereotypes of Palestinian opposition to Israeli occupation label it as Muslim in inspiration and participation, but Palestinian Christians have been strong supporters of the resistance and part of the movement; the most recent Palestinian ambassador to the United States, who ended his tour in 2006, was Greek Orthodox.

in the intifada, they began to criticize the open involvement of women in the resistance because their public actions challenged traditional conceptions of women's social behavior.[26]

The first two years of the intifada, from 1987 to the end of 1989, can be characterized as a period of intensifying violence on both sides. Israeli rules for military response were stretched to permit snipers in civilian clothes to be stationed where they could assassinate stone-throwers. Computerized tax lists led to confiscation of property, often automobiles, and village raids frequently resulted in the destruction of gardens and orchards to force Palestinians into economic dependence on Israel.

By the end of 1989, an estimated 626 Palestinians and 43 Israelis had been killed, 37,439 Arabs wounded, and between 35,000 and 40,000 arrested.[27] Increased pressures on Arab society had prompted individual acts of violence, beyond those sanctioned by the leadership. These incidents encouraged assaults on Arabs by individual Israelis. In addition, Palestinians turned against fellow Arabs they suspected of collaborating with Israeli intelligence. Individual Palestinian militancy was buttressed by the growing prominence of Islamic resistance organizations, which began to supplant PLO authority as the intifada continued.

The Intifada and Islamic Resistance

As noted earlier, Islamic resistance to Israeli control of the territories had intensified in the early 1980s with the creation of Islamic Jihad. Its leaders had been inspired by the activities of Egyptian Islamic organizations opposed to the policies of Anwar al-Sadat that emerged in the 1970s and were linked to his assassination in 1981. Influenced by the Egyptian thinker Sayyid Qutb (d. 1966), these groups had called for jihad as holy war to end the reign of alien Western secular ideologies and to restore Islam as the basis of life in the Islamic world. Another key influence was the Iranian Revolution of 1979, which signified to these militants that success was possible.

The Islamic Jihad group in Gaza had broken off from the Muslim Brotherhood, which espoused educational and social reforms as a means of spreading Islam. Jihad leaders also recalled the example of the Palestinian cleric Izz al-Din al-Qassam, who died in 1935 while organizing armed resistance to Zionism. Although Islamic Jihad at first cooperated with Arafat and Fatah, they parted company once Arafat's two-state policy became known. The group advocated the recovery of all of former Palestine by armed struggle and the creation of a new Islamic state, the antithesis of the democratic secular state that was the PLO's goal. Islamic Jihad activists had undertaken armed assaults on Israelis even before the intifada began. The outbreak of the intifada reinforced their belief that resistance was mandatory and finally brought the more quietist Muslim Brotherhood into the arena; it created an armed wing called Hamas that would gain prominence as Israeli crackdowns weakened Islamic Jihad efforts.

The formation of Hamas (Harakat al-Muqawama al-Islamiyya—the Islamic Resistance Movement) in February 1988 was a direct outgrowth of the intifada.

Its founders were Muslim Brothers, such as Shaykh Ahmad Yasin, who decided to extend the brotherhood's ideology into politics.[28] Hamas, like Islamic Jihad, posed an alternative to PLO political guidelines. It too called for the creation of a Palestinian state, founded on religious principles, in all of former Palestine. For the time being, however, Hamas and Palestinians tied to secular groups overlooked their differences in order to combine their efforts against Israel. Hamas affiliation varied, being 20 percent in Gaza and much less initially in the West Bank. A particular Hamas West Bank stronghold was Nablus, a nearly totally Muslim town where the incidence of Arab-Israeli attacks was higher than elsewhere. Gaza's militancy was not simply Islamic, however. Khalil al-Wazir had been raised there, and his assassination by Israel provided new impetus for opposition in the camps.

The advent of 1990 saw the PLO, especially Fatah, lose influence in the territories as hope of a diplomatic settlement turned to despair. The intifada continued, but Palestinian militancy now frequently took the form of armed attacks more often identified with Islamic activists. Hamas established a military wing, called the Izz al-Din al-Qassam brigade, which committed itself to the assassination of Israelis and the revenge killing of Palestinians suspected of collaborating with Israel. As PLO prestige, especially Fatah's, seemed to wane as a result of its failed diplomacy, the appeal of Islamic groups increased. They alone appeared determined to achieve the goal of Palestinian independence, albeit to create a religious instead of a secular state.

The Intifada and International Politics, 1988–1991

The intifada sparked major changes in international politics relating to the Middle East and to the Palestinian future. The PLO, moribund on the eve of the uprising, took on new life. Arafat, through his deputy Bassam al-Sharif, presented a position paper at the Arab League Emergency Summit, which met in Algiers in June 1988 where he called for mutual recognition of the right of Palestinians as well as Israelis to peace and security.[29] The paper generated a muted response. Although the league called for an international conference to reach a settlement, league members refused to contribute to a fund to support the intifada and to sustain workers who had lost jobs.

The Declaration of Palestinian Independence.   Heads of state with close ties to the United States worked to encourage a dialogue between Arafat and Washington. In November, a meeting of the PNC in Algiers proclaimed the existence of "the state of Palestine . . . with its capital in the holy Jerusalem." In addition, the PNC announced its readiness to negotiate with Israel on the basis of Resolutions 242 and 338 under the aegis of an international peace conference, with the condition that mutual recognition occur and that Israel also recognize Palestinian rights. This stance met sharp criticism from Islamic groups because it indicated a willingness to settle for only part of Palestine and because of the PNC's stress on a confederation between a future Palestinian state and Jordan. Indeed,

Arafat now hoped to satisfy U.S. hopes for a Jordanian solution despite the fact that four months earlier, in July, King Husayn had openly renounced any claims to Palestine and rescinded the subsidies Jordan had paid into the West Bank. He had reacted with anger to the Fourteen Points issued by the UNL leadership that ignored Jordan.[30]

Arafat's efforts to gain international recognition for his peace proposal found success in December 1988, when Washington agreed that, by renouncing terrorism and accepting Resolution 242, he had met its conditions. He had done so by responding to a draft of a PLO declaration, written by U.S. Secretary of State George Shultz, which referred to "the democratic Palestinian state which [the PLO] seeks to establish in the West Bank and the Gaza Strip."[31] The PNC November Declaration of Palestinian Independence had been recognized by many Arab and Muslim states and by the Soviet Union. In the same month, a group of American Jews had met PLO officials, including Arafat, in Stockholm to encourage the American-PLO rapprochement. In early December, they issued a joint declaration arguing that the PNC had renounced terrorism in all forms and recognized Israel's existence. Under domestic pressure, Shultz initially rebuffed the Stockholm Declaration and the State Department denied Arafat a visa to address the United Nations in New York, forcing the transfer of the meeting to Geneva. There the PLO head again appealed for peace in terms finally acceptable to Washington. An American-PLO dialogue was established through the U.S. ambassador in Tunis, where PLO headquarters remained. Despite Israeli and PLO Rejection Front opposition to these developments, the stage had been set for a new entry into the peace process.

Shamir Strives to Derail Peace Efforts.   The United States had agreed to talk to the PLO at a time when a new administration, headed by George H. W. Bush, was about to take office. While pressure on Israeli Likud Prime Minister Yitzhak Shamir could be expected, he had been strengthened by Knesset elections in early November 1988. Although Likud barely beat Labor in the polls, the strength of religious parties helped Shamir to form a new National Unity Government in which Likud controlled the most important cabinet posts, including the foreign ministry, though Rabin of the Labor Party remained as defense minister, responsible for quelling the intifada.[32] Faced with Washington's requests for proposals to talk to the PLO, backed by calls for progress from the American Jewish community, Shamir proposed an election plan for the territories. It was designed to stall the negotiating process, not to promote it, and to enable further consolidation of Israeli power in these areas. The stalemate would last until June 1990.

Shamir's plan called for "free and democratic elections" among Palestinian Arabs in the territories in May 1989; they would supposedly lead to autonomy that would grant them authority over their [unspecified] "affairs of daily life." Israel would retain control of security, foreign affairs, and all aspects of policy pertaining to the settlers in the territories. Shamir revealed his real intent when he responded to rightist critics, such as Ariel Sharon, who charged that any promise of autonomy would lead to Palestinian independence: "We shall not give the Arabs one inch of our land, even if we have to negotiate for ten years. We won't give them a thing. . . . We have the veto in our hands. . . . The status quo of the interim arrangement will continue until all parties reach agreement on the permanent arrangement," which would ratify acceptance of the territories as part of Israel. No restrictions on further settlements would be imposed.[33] A codicil to the government proposals affirmed Shamir's intention that Israel would never talk to the PLO, let alone permit a Palestinian state in the territories.

Palestinians in the territories rejected the plan, as did the PLO in Tunis. Both groups called for coexistence with Israel, which required a state. The United States, however, welcomed Shamir's initiative as a working document; it established linkage between elections in the territories and resolution of the final status of the occupied regions in subsequent negotiations. The Bush administration foresaw the end of Israeli occupation of the territories, something Israel would not accept, but decided to give Shamir a year to find Palestinian leaders in the West Bank or Gaza who would discuss his ideas; the PLO was excluded. As expected, no Palestinians offered to participate. This gave Israel another year to suppress the intifada and add more settlements while fending off American efforts to broaden the scope of Shamir's offer.

These developments further undermined Arafat's credibility among Palestinians. He had conceded PLO exclusion from any talks in return for U.S. efforts to expand the scope of Palestinian representation, only to see Shamir reject American attempts to reach that objective; Israeli politicians acknowledged that they were trying to drive a wedge between Palestinians in the territories and the PLO leadership. The only concessions were those made by Arafat at a time when Israel's harsher repression of the intifada during the summer of 1989 took a greater toll of Palestinian lives.

Frustrated by Shamir's intransigence, President Bush declared on March 3, 1990, that the United States opposed further Israeli settlements in East Jerusalem, the West Bank, and Gaza. Shamir immediately replied that Israel intended to settle as many Soviet Jews in East Jerusalem as it could. When the Labor Party, with American encouragement, threatened to dissolve the coalition unless Washington's points of negotiation, including the participation of East Jerusalem Arabs, were accepted, Shamir, as prime minister, then fired Peres, his finance minister: the Labor Party left the coalition on March 15.

Peres was given the first chance to form a new cabinet, but he failed, leaving the field open to Shamir. By mid-June, Shamir had put together a Likud cabinet without Labor. On June 28, Shamir officially rejected the plan for negotiations he had proposed in May 1989.

Washington Discards Arafat.   With Labor out of the coalition, Yitzhak Shamir used its absence to press Likud's policy of settlements in the territories and in East Jerusalem. At the same time, Yasir Arafat, sensitive to criticism of his policy of rapprochement, began strengthening his ties with Iraq's Saddam Husayn. He hoped to compel negotiations based on threat of force rather than on the conciliation advocated by Egypt's Husni Mubarak. Saddam Husayn himself, in early April and at an Arab summit in Baghdad May 28–30, would call for a more militant posture toward American tolerance of Israeli actions, especially in light of the massive Soviet Jewish immigration into Israel.

Negotiations at the United Nations in early May indicated American sympathy but no support for an Arab-sponsored resolution criticizing Israeli settlement policies, especially that of placing Soviet Jewish immigrants in the territories. Then, on May 20, an Israeli killed seven Gazans waiting for rides to work in Israel. During the ensuing demonstrations and military reprisals, at least seventeen more Arabs were killed, and an estimated 600 to 700 were wounded. The PLO immediately requested that Arafat address the U.N. Security Council on conditions in the territories. When the U.S. government refused to allow him entry into the country, the meeting was held instead in Geneva on May 25. There, Arafat asked that the Security Council order an international team to investigate Palestinian complaints and conditions, a request that received backing from fourteen of the fifteen members; the United States alone opposed it because Israel would not accept it.[34]

In the midst of these tensions, Saddam Husayn hosted the May 28–30 Arab summit in Baghdad. Those attending, including Egypt's Mubarak, approved a harsh statement criticizing American support for Israel. On May 30, the Israelis intercepted a Palestinian attack from the Mediterranean backed by Abu al-Abbas, author of the 1985 hijacking of the *Achille Lauro* and now based in Baghdad. On May 31, using that attack as justification, the United States vetoed the Security Council Resolution supported by all other members calling for an investigation of conditions in the territories.

The European Community (EC) now broke ranks with the United States. On June 2, the EC backed an investigation and also voiced its support for an international conference with the PLO in attendance as representative of the Palestinian people, a stance opposed by the United States. On June 13, Secretary of State Baker strongly criticized Shamir for rejecting U.S. peace proposals, but then condemned Arafat because his criticism of those who had ordered the May 30 raid was considered too mild. Finally, on June 20, the Bush administration suspended its dialogue with the PLO until U.S. terms were met. In doing so, President Bush acknowledged that his "strongest allies" in Europe and the "most reasonable and moderate" Arab states disagreed with the U.S. course.[35]

In June Shamir emerged from the transition period as head of a new cabinet that either supported his policies or tried to push him further to the right. Arafat, on the other hand, had been considerably weakened. In April 1990, reports appeared that Hamas and the PFLP were forming an alternative leadership to the Unified Command in the territories, and in June Hamas delegates won a majority of seats on a United Nations Relief and Works Administration (UNRWA) staff council in Gaza.[36] Control of the intifada seemed to be slipping away, along with any hope of progress in talks brokered by Egypt and the United States. These factors, coupled with the Arab condemnation of Washington at the Baghdad summit in May, further encouraged Arafat to edge closer to Iraq. American tolerance of Israeli intransigence suggested that only Baghdad could pose the credible military threat necessary to force Israeli concessions. This position challenged Washington's long-standing goal of controlling talks, since it might force an international conference at which U.S. policies would be criticized by its allies as well as its foes.

In this context Iraq's invasion of Kuwait on August 2 was both a threat and an opportunity to the Bush administration. It endangered Kuwait's oil reserves and potentially those of Saudi Arabia, major components of Western and Japanese economic stability, but it also provided the United States with the opportunity to defend its Arab allies. In doing so, Washington could destroy the challenge that Saddam Husayn posed, not only to the Gulf region but to American influence in the area.

THE FIRST GULF CRISIS

The diplomacy and subsequent political and military alignments that followed the Iraqi invasion of Kuwait on August 2, 1990, were enormously complex.[37] Coalition forces led by the United States recaptured Kuwait and destroyed much of Iraq's military and civilian infrastructure in a campaign that began on January 16, 1991. A cease-fire was imposed on February 28. The scale of the military triumph was unquestioned; less clear was the anticipated political resolution of the conflict with respect to both the Persian Gulf and Arab-Israeli issues.

The United States: Motives and Opportunities

The Iraqi invasion of Kuwait was preceded by a diplomatic confrontation in mid-July in which Iraq threatened Kuwait unless the latter agreed to raise oil prices. Kuwait and the United Arab Emirates (UAE) were known to be exceeding quotas, and their overproduction deprived Iraq of badly needed revenues in the aftermath of the Iraq-Iran War. Kuwait acceded to Iraqi demands. Following this crisis, the U.S. Central Command, which oversaw U.S. interests in the Persian Gulf, mounted a staff war-game exercise that "postulated a major threat to U.S. interests in the Middle East requiring a swift and massive military commitment"; this exercise ended on July 29. At the same time, Washington instructed its ambassador in Baghdad to tell Saddam Husayn, in a July 26 meeting, that the United States had "no opinion" about his quarrels and relations with neighboring states, "like your border disagreement with Kuwait," a reference to Iraqi claims to the Kuwaiti islands of Warba and Bubiyan and disputes over the neutral zone between the two countries.[38]

Once Iraq invaded Kuwait, however, the Bush administration immediately called for emergency sessions of the U.N. Security Council to condemn the aggression, and dispatched Secretary of Defense Richard Cheney to the region to gain Arab agreement to the positioning of large numbers of American troops in Saudi Arabia and Kuwait. As early as August 6, press reports noted President Bush's determination to overthrow Saddam Husayn. The administration refused to talk to the Iraqi leader and decided not to send its ambassador, then in London, back to Baghdad for discussions because "We don't have anything to say to him." It seems clear that President Bush sought to establish a climate of confrontation to discourage compromise and ensure a stalemate that would justify the military alternative.[39]

There is little doubt that oil played a role in triggering the American response. As one "key policymaker" explained, "if a country less important than Kuwait had been invaded and if the principal product of Kuwait and Saudi Arabia were artichokes instead of oil, we would not have proceeded as we did."[40] Still, the U.S. interest in a military response was rooted more in its concern about the global implications of the crisis than in worry over its regional ramifications. The Soviet withdrawal from the cold war enabled the United States to act unilaterally to enforce its will without fear of a great-power confrontation. President Bush declared that "a new world order" was in the making, which required "new thinking and new concepts and there is a feeling that it is better to talk to people who see things in global terms rather than regional specialists whose thinking has been much slower to catch up with this new kind of situation." This "new thinking" was actually based on the parameters of the old world order in which the global rather than the regional approach took priority and area specialists were once more excluded from consultations about policy.[41] What had changed was the removal of the major adversary to unfettered U.S. action, creating an opportunity for the unchallenged expansion of American power.

Arab and Israeli Reactions to the Gulf Crisis

Most Arab heads of state condemned Saddam Husayn's assault and called for Iraq's withdrawal from Kuwait. Yasir Arafat, on the other hand, defended Saddam, hoping to use his gambit to pressure the United States and its allies into concessions, a major miscalculation that severely weakened his standing in Arab capitals and elsewhere.[42] But these same Arab leaders who called for Saddam's withdrawal also criticized the United States for engaging in a self-serving power play and for what appeared to be an American double standard. The United States vetoed U.N. resolutions aimed at Israel, refusing to punish it despite its treatment of Palestinians under the intifada, but was eager to use the United Nations to back its own immediate response to an Arab transgression.

The primary exponent of this view was Jordan's King Husayn. In trying to mediate the crisis, he found himself upstaged by the American-led coalition and confronted by an embargo whose sanctions threatened Jordan's economic survival. Dependent on Iraq for oil and for revenues from its own trade, Husayn now found himself adrift. Saudi Arabia cut off monetary subsidies because of

Jordan's criticism of its actions, at a time when Jordan confronted a massive influx of refugees as hundreds of thousands of Palestinians fled Kuwait. Finally, King Husayn's criticism of the United States led to cuts in American aid. From Husayn's perspective, he had little choice. Jordan's population, over 60 percent Palestinian, supported Saddam out of anger against American allies. Israel's Ariel Sharon repeatedly referred to Jordan as the state of Palestine, strongly intimating that all Arabs from the territories should be removed to Jordan to overthrow Husayn and create the state for which they longed. In these circumstances, Husayn's defiance of his traditional great-power ally brought him more domestic approval than ever before.[43]

The motives of Washington's principal Arab partners in the coalition—Egypt, Saudi Arabia, Kuwait, and Syria—were clear-cut, if diverse in inspiration. Saudi Arabia could not tolerate a challenge to its oil fields, let alone a new contender for dominance in Gulf affairs. Egypt viewed Saddam as a rival for primacy in the Arab world, re-creating the divisive Iraqi-Egyptian axis of the 1950s. For Assad of Syria, Saddam's downfall would relieve him of pressure on his northern flank as he turned to seek a peace agreement with Israel under American auspices. In return, Washington promised major arms sales to the Saudis, later scaled down because of Israeli opposition.[44] Egypt was relieved of obligations to Washington totaling $7 billion for past economic and military assistance.

Israel, equally desirous of an American-led military assault that would destroy the Iraqi military machine, encouraged American mobilization against Saddam, but the Bush administration eyed the Israeli stance warily. Officials feared that Israel would intervene in the war, thereby undermining the Arab coalition backing the United States. This fear increased once Iraqi Scud missiles landed in the Tel Aviv–Haifa coastal strip. Visits to Israel by Undersecretary of State Lawrence Eagleburger ensured that Israel did not respond. In return, the United States promised Israel $13 billion—$3 billion for damages incurred by these attacks and $10 billion to be paid over five years to aid in the settlement of Russian Jews; the Bush administration warned Shamir that these Jews should not be settled in the disputed territories.

The Intifada, the Gulf Crisis, and the Negotiating Process

The most obvious outcome of the Persian Gulf Crisis beyond that region was a renewed American effort to resolve Arab-Israeli matters, including the future of the Palestinians. As Secretary of State James Baker discovered during visits to the Middle East in March and April 1991, the Arab states, especially Syria, wanted an international conference sponsored jointly by the United States and the Soviets to oversee direct negotiations with Israel for return of the Golan Heights. In contrast, the Likud leadership pushed for a temporary international conference setting up immediate face-to-face talks with Syria, with no further international input.

By July Baker had gained Syrian, Lebanese, and Jordanian acceptance of the negotiating framework. Syria, the key Arab player, agreed to direct talks with Israel. They would meet for one day in Madrid under the guise of an international conference sponsored by the United States and the Soviet Union. In case of an impasse, recourse to the United States and the U.S.S.R. was permitted, meeting Syrian concerns, but appeals to the United Nations could be vetoed by a participant in negotiations. This provision recognized Israeli objections to U.N. involvement. Syria's Hafiz Assad also received U.S. assurances that it considered Israel's 1981 annexation of the Golan Heights to be illegal and that Security Council Resolution 242 applied to the Golan and the West Bank, interpretations that contradicted the Israeli Likud position that Shamir advocated. In another development, Saudi Arabia, Syria, and Jordan joined Egypt in agreeing to support the end of the Arab economic boycott of Israel if Israel would stop building settlements.

These developments aroused consternation in Israeli government circles. Rightist minority parties vowed to leave the Shamir cabinet if Shamir agreed to enter talks, but the possibility of a U.S. refusal to fund housing of Soviet Jewish immigrants loomed if he rejected the U.S.-backed Arab overtures. As a sweetener, the Soviet Union restored diplomatic relations with Israel, suspended since the 1967 war. As for the Palestinians, Baker told West Bank leaders that the PLO representatives could not attend the talks, but that Palestinians linked to the PLO and from East Jerusalem might be part of a joint Jordanian-Palestinian delegation. On record as supporting American peace efforts, Arafat agreed, as he had in 1989, to remain aloof from the talks so long as Palestinians from within and outside the territories were permitted to attend. Shamir decided to participate, though he lost some militant backing by doing so.

The Palestinian delegation to the Madrid talks was led by Haydar Abd al-Shafi, a Gaza physician. He was accompanied by Faysal Husayni and Hanan al-Ashrawi, the latter a highly articulate activist from the territories who had received her doctorate in literature in the United States. They consulted frequently with the PLO in Tunis, but at times achieved a prominence beyond that accorded Arafat, who found himself and the PLO in desperate financial straits. Arab Gulf states, Kuwait and the Saudis in the forefront, canceled their contributions, which had buttressed PLO activities for years, as punishment for PLO support of Saddam. In addition, Kuwait had expelled thousands of Palestinians whom they suspected, often erroneously, of backing the Iraqi leader; this meant lost remittances from these families to the organization. PLO losses amounted to at least $100 million annually; by spring 1993, the PLO would be closing offices at its headquarters in Tunis for lack of funds.

Arafat's decline in prestige was countered by the enhanced reputations of Islamic groups. They too initially lost funding from Saudi Arabia and Kuwait for sympathizing with Saddam, but they found compensation in contributions from countries and groups identified with the Islamic resurgence, Iran most notably, but also Sudan and members of the Saudi ruling house. Indeed, Iran's new significance as a beneficiary of the Gulf crisis and Saddam's defeat led Hamas to establish a permanent mission in Teheran in 1991. Hamas also drew closer to rejectionist groups within the PLO, notably those that had criticized Arafat's concessions to U.S. terms in 1988; Hamas, Habash's PFLP, and Hawat-meh's revised DFLP issued a joint statement in October 1991 condemning Arafat's willingness to sanction Palestinian participation at Madrid.

DIPLOMACY AND CONFLICT: THE MADRID TALKS, OCTOBER 1991–SUMMER 1993

The Madrid talks would ultimately consist of nine rounds before being pre-empted by the Palestinian-Israeli Accord of September 1993. The conference split into a series of panels so that Israeli teams negotiated with their Arab counterparts from Lebanon, Syria, and a joint Jordanian-Palestinian delegation. The Jordanians provided the umbrella for Palestinian participation, but each group met separately.

The Madrid talks were historic in that the participants were engaging in official direct negotiations for the first time. The talks were based on U.N. Resolutions 242 and 338, as well as the Camp David Accords of 1978. The U.N. resolutions declared the principles of land in exchange for peace and the need for direct negotiations (see Documents 7.1 and 7.3). The operative Camp David points involved the idea of "interim" stages for ironing out differences prior to final negotiations, especially in relation to the Palestinians and the fate of the occupied territories (see Document 8.4). Beyond Madrid, great-power sponsors established multilateral talks on topics of regional significance, such as water, arms control, and trade—discussions intended to establish bases for practical cooperation in the entire Middle East.

Despite their significance, the talks produced little discernible progress, except between Israel and Jordan. The Palestinians and the Israelis remained far apart. Palestinian delegates, with PLO approval, had agreed to interim stages for deciding the fate of the territories, as stated at Camp David, but they insisted that self-determination, meaning a Palestinian state, be the final outcome. The Shamir government in Israel adhered to its position of autonomy for the Palestinian people but continued Israeli control of the land. Shamir's intent, as he admitted after leaving office in June 1992, "was to drag out talks on Palestinian self-rule for 10 years while attempting to settle hundreds of thousands of Jews in the occupied territories," giving the appearance of accommodation while working to ensure Israeli retention of the territories.[45]

The rigidity of these stances caused increasing despair among Palestinians in the territories and intensified the violence often promoted by Hamas and a revived Islamic Jihad. Shamir's bellicosity ultimately prodded America to impose sanctions in February 1992. Because of Israel's settlement activity, which amounted to a reported 18,000 new housing units since June 1990, the Bush administration withheld the $10 billion in loan guarantees promised during the Gulf War.[46] Shamir responded with even more settlements. The United States undertook successful efforts to undermine Likud credibility and to assist a Labor Party victory in elections scheduled for June 1992. Labor won the mandate, with Yitzhak Rabin as prime minister and Shimon Peres as foreign minister; the coalition included representatives of parties on the left that supported peace and territorial compromise more openly than Labor. The Bush administration now released the loan guarantees in return for Rabin's promise to halt settlement construction nonessential for security.

Rabin declared his commitment to the principle of land for peace rejected by Shamir. He curtailed financial incentives, such as low-interest mortgages, for settling in the territories and for the construction of what he called "political settlements." Still, Rabin refused to stop construction of what he called "security settlements" in the Golan Heights and around Jerusalem, the latter the most sensitive point of dispute.[47] In December 1992, he pushed through the Knesset a bill permitting official contacts with the PLO, reversing past policy and acknowledging the reality that informal Israeli-PLO links had existed for some time.

Though he was clearly more forthcoming than his predecessor, Rabin's actions seemed contradictory. He advocated more settlements in the Golan Heights while simultaneously broaching the prospect of withdrawing from them in return for a full peace with Syria. He backed the idea of land for peace but left no doubt that sizable portions of the West Bank, especially near Jerusalem, would remain Israeli. And he emphatically opposed the idea of a Palestinian state, meaning that an arrangement with Jordan over the West Bank would be mandatory. A major problem for Rabin was the strength of the conservative forces he had just defeated; they remained a powerful counterweight to any decisive peace effort.

Violence and terror accompanied the Madrid talks from 1991 to 1993 as the security of both Arabs and Israelis continued to deteriorate. In a two-month period, from December 1992 to mid-February 1993, 50 Palestinians were killed by Israeli troops, who often fired into crowds to quell demonstrations, and 10 Israelis died at Palestinian hands. During March 1993, 12 Israelis were stabbed to death. Some of the killers belonged to groups such as Islamic Jihad but others were apparently individuals acting spontaneously. Conversely, at least 23 Palestinians were killed during the same month.[48]

Israeli efforts to prevent assaults only intensified them. The early 1993 outbreak stemmed from the Israeli deportation of 416 Hamas and Islamic Jihad members on December 16, 1992, a reaction to the killing of an Israeli border policeman. Intended to reduce Islamist activities, Rabin's decision, condemned as illegal, instead publicized the plight of the deportees, whom Lebanon refused to accept. The efforts of Hamas and Islamic Jihad to expand their cause at the expense of Fatah were aided rather than undermined by the expulsion.[49]

Violence in the territories was matched by that in the Israeli security zone in southern Lebanon. Hizbollah, backed by Iran and at times by Syria (which controlled Lebanon), intensified its attacks on Israeli troops and their allies of the Southern Lebanese Army in the security zone from March onward, joined at times by PFLP detachments. In April, Israel replied with helicopter assaults on Hizbollah positions and sent troops ashore against PFLP camps in Lebanon. Tensions heightened in June and July, especially once five Israeli soldiers died from Katyusha rocket attacks in the security zone as some missiles struck Israeli territory. Israel then initiated "Operation Accountability," an air and artillery shelling of southern Lebanon villages intended, according to Rabin, "to cause a mass flight of residents" from the region and open it up to Israeli attacks against Hizbollah; the policy replicated that implemented in the Israeli invasion of southern Lebanon ordered by Menachem Begin in March 1978 to oust the PLO. Nearly 500,000 Lebanese, one-tenth of Lebanon's population, fled northward but Hizbollah attacks increased, as did Lebanese civilian casualties from Israeli shellings.[50]

In the cease-fire brokered by Secretary of State Warren Christopher, which took effect on July 31, Hizbollah agreed to attack only the security zone and not Israeli territory. Lebanon declared that it would not restrict Hizbollah activities because the Israeli presence in the zone violated Lebanese sovereignty. When nine Israeli soldiers were killed in the zone by Hizbollah on August 19, Rabin declared that this did not violate the cease-fire of July 31.[51] Rabin's equivocation suggested that other issues were at work, which included the imminent PLO-Israeli accord but also the critical role of Islamic resistance groups in justifying this development.

CONCLUSION

Throughout the period 1984–1993, the PLO found itself stranded between the competing aspirations of various factions and countries. Would it be undermined by Israeli Labor's success in promoting the Jordanian option with Washington or left to encourage local Palestinian resistance in the face of Likud's annexationist ambitions?

The intifada was as much a shock to Arafat and the PLO leadership in Tunis as it was to Israel, but it did afford the leadership the opportunity to demand recognition of Palestinian grievances. With the advent of George H. W. Bush to the American presidency in 1988, Palestinians believed initially but wrongly that greater American sympathy might be immediately forthcoming in light of Israeli Likud recalcitrance. This did not happen and the sudden eruption of the first Gulf Crisis, with Arafat's desperate backing of Iraq's invasion of Kuwait, made him a pariah with Arab heads of state, leaving the field open to Hamas to argue that it alone could resist ongoing Israeli settlement expansion.

By the summer of 1993, the PLO appeared on the verge of political and financial bankruptcy. The Madrid talks were stalled and tensions had increased between Arafat and his Palestinian negotiators from the territories. At the same time, the prestige of the PLO's Islamic opponents had risen sharply. In the eyes

of many Palestinians, they were confronting Israel on the ground while the PLO had agreed to nonparticipation in unproductive talks. For their part, Israeli leaders, like Arafat, viewed the Islamist surge with alarm. The increasingly Islamic nature of Palestinian assaults on Israelis indicated that Israel's encouragement of Muslim groups in the 1980s had backfired. Though the Islamists' rise in popularity had weakened Arafat, as intended, their own strength now seemed ominous (see Figure 9.3). Also threatening was Palestinian anger at a stalemate that tolerated Israeli consolidation of their occupation. This anger intensified with the news, in October 1992, that Jordan and Israel had drafted a formal peace treaty, to be ratified if a comprehensive peace were achieved. The announcement signaled Jordan's eagerness to conclude such a peace, but for Palestinians it seemed to symbolize PLO inability to fulfill Palestinian aspirations for self-determination.

At the same time, however, secret negotiations were under way in Oslo, Norway, setting the stage for an agreement in which Israel and the PLO would recognize each other. The PLO and the Rabin cabinet had found the prospect of an agreement mutually beneficial. Rabin was eager to rid Israel of Gaza, the source of most of the violence. And he preferred a weakened Arafat to the Islamic alternative. For their part, the PLO leadership welcomed the chance to gain Israeli recognition of their status, restoring badly needed prestige. But Arafat wanted territory on the West Bank, not just Gaza, to affirm the Palestinian claim there as well. He proposed Jericho as the place to implant an official Palestinian presence as a prelude to assumed extension of Palestinian sovereignty. Where Arafat grasped the opportunity for an agreement to revive his failing fortunes, Israel seized upon Arafat's damaged status to achieve concessions (even if unwritten) that he might not have offered otherwise. If a weakened PLO in the 1980s had

Figure 9.3 ■ Palestinian Muslim Women Attend a Hamas Rally at Bir Zeit University, ▶
West Bank, circa 1992

Palestinian women, religious and secular (see Figure 9.2), played an important role in supporting the intifada. These modestly dressed Hamas backers sit before a poster of an armed figure breaking through the Star of David, the emblem of Israel. The figure's *kaffiyeh* (headdress) is one worn by men, but the garment and the gloves are feminine, suggesting the unity of the sexes in the sacred cause to liberate Palestine for Islam. The banner in the figure's right hand displays the emblem, "There is no God but God," the Islamic profession of faith. The statement on the left is from the Quran (Sura: "The Night Journey") and refers to God's punishment of the Jews for disobeying His commands.

The literal translation, "We sent against you men loyal to us who possessed great bravery," can be interpreted to mean armies (Assyrians) that wreaked havoc and destruction, invading and destroying the houses of the Jews and the Temple, just as Hamas serves as God's avengers in the present.

The slogan on the lower right is from a Hamas prison song. The literal translation, "I shall return soon from my captivity and illuminate the land with my faith," can be interpreted to mean that these Hamas prisoners will redeem the Islamic land of Palestine by taking it from their captors who have defiled it, the Israelis. Compare these images and statements to those displayed by Israeli settlers against Prime Minister Yitzhak Rabin in 1995 (see Figure 10.2).

justified to Americans and Israelis its continued isolation, a wounded Arafat now encouraged recognition when the alternatives were considered.

Historic in its conception, the hopes embodied in the 1993 Oslo Accord masked both the difficulties of its implementation and the fury it aroused among its opponents. That fury would lead to the November 1995 assassination

of the Israeli signatory, Yitzhak Rabin, in order to block further progress requiring Israeli territorial compromise. The specter of a Palestinian state, however distant and restricted its achievement might be, challenged long-standing Israeli and American rejection of this prospect and would mobilize strong resistance in both countries to undermine its realization.

QUESTIONS FOR CONSIDERATION

1. What was the "Jordanian option" that the Reagan administration favored for Palestinians?
2. What inspired the Palestinian intifada? How did Israel respond to it?
3. What do you see as the major reasons for the emergence of Hamas in Gaza?
4. What was the Madrid Conference, and why was it held? Did it produce any agreements between Israel and any Arab state?

CHRONOLOGY

1984	**February.** American forces withdraw from Lebanon.
1985	**September 15.** PLO Force 17 assassinates three Israelis in Cyprus.
	October 1. Israel bombs PLO headquarters.
1986	**October.** Likud's Yitzhak Shamir succeeds Shimon Peres as Israeli prime minister.
1987	**December 9.** Intifada begins.
1988	**January.** Intifada/PLO announce the Fourteen Points.
	February. Hamas founded.
	June. PLO calls for mutual Israeli-Palestinian recognition.
	July. King Husayn officially renounces claims to Palestine.
	November. Palestine National Council declares creation of a Palestinian state with Jerusalem its capital, asserts readiness to negotiate with Israel on basis of Resolutions 242 and 338.
	December. United States acknowledges contacts with PLO in Tunis.
1989	**May.** Prime Minister Shamir gains Knesset approval for election. Arab League readmits Egypt to membership.
	October. Lebanese Parliament endorses Taif Accord.
1990	**May 20.** Israeli kills 7 Palestinians. Ensuing riots leave 17 Palestinians dead, over 600 wounded.
	May 28–30. Arab summit meeting in Baghdad attacks American policy on Israel and the occupied territories.
	May 30. Palestinian terrorist raid initiated from Baghdad intercepted by Israel.
	June 20. Bush administration suspends dialogue with PLO.
	August 2. Iraq invades and occupies Kuwait.
1991	**January–February.** U.S.-led assault on Iraq; Kuwait liberated.
	February 28. Cease-fire in war against Iraq.
	October. Arab-Israeli talks begin in Madrid.
	December. Dissolution of Soviet Union, creation of independent republics.
1992	**July.** Labor Party wins Israeli elections, Yitzhak Rabin elected prime minister.
	December. Israeli Knesset approves official contacts with PLO.

Notes

1. Quoted in Noam Chomsky, *The Fateful Triangle: The United States, Israel, and the Palestinians* (Boston, 1983), 112.

2. Thomas L. Friedman, "Seeking Peace in the Middle East," *New York Times*, March 17, 1985; and "Chronology," *Middle East Journal* 39 (Autumn 1985): 800; along with Dan Fisher, "Israeli Right Assails Peres' Peace Bid to Jordan," *Los Angeles Times*, October 23, 1985.

3. Nigel Hawkes, "Thatcher Takes a Big Risk over PLO Talks," *London Observer*, September 22, 1985.

4. The sequence of events can be followed in the "Chronology," *Middle East Journal* 40 (Winter 1986): 115–17.

5. Quoted in *Facts on File*, October 4, 1985. For details on the *Achille Lauro* hijacking, see the articles in the *New York Times*, October 10, 1985.

6. "U.S. Acting as Go-Between in Jordan Talks, Peres Says," *Los Angeles Times*, October 8, 1986; and Dan Fisher, "Israel, Jordan Stepping Up Cooperation on West Bank," ibid., October 2, 1986. For a more detailed analysis of American policy, see William B. Quandt, *Peace Process: American Diplomacy and the Arab-Israeli Conflict since 1967* (Berkeley, 1993), 352ff.

7. The quotation is from *The Link* 19 (October–November 1986). Wolf Blitzer, "Why the U.S. Wants Israel in the Star Wars Project," *Jerusalem Post International Edition*, February 2, 1986.

8. Aaron David Miller, "The PLO in Retrospect: The Arab and Israeli Dimensions," in *The Arab-Israeli Conflict: Two Decades of Change*, ed. Yehuda Lukacs and Abdalla M. Battah (Boulder, Colo., 1988), 130.

9. Quandt, *Peace Process*, 355.

10. Robert Hunter's *The Palestinian Uprising: A War by Other Means* (Berkeley and Los Angeles, 1991) is the best sustained analysis of the intifada, Israeli efforts to suppress it, and Palestinian strategies to maintain it. Two volumes containing excellent essays are Zachary Lockman and Joel Beinin, eds., *Intifada: The Palestinian Uprising against Israeli Occupation* (Washington, D.C., 1989) and Jamal R. Nassar and Roger Heacock, eds., *Intifada: Palestine at the Crossroads* (New York, 1990). Good background treatment appears in Ann Mosely Lesch and Mark Tessler, *Israel, Egypt, and the Palestinians from Camp David to Intifada* (Bloomington, Ind., 1989). Most studies rely heavily on the volumes produced if not written by Meron Benvenisti under the rubric of *The West Bank Data Project* and *The Gaza Data Project*. See in particular Benvenisti, *The West Bank Handbook: A Political Lexicon* (Jerusalem, 1986) and his 1987 *Report: Demographic, Economic, Legal, Social, and Political Developments in the West Bank* (Jerusalem, 1987); Benvenisti and Shlomo Khayat, *The West Bank and Gaza Atlas* (Jerusalem, 1988); and Sara Roy, *The Gaza Strip* (Jerusalem, 1986).

11. Hunter, *Palestinian Uprising*, 48.

12. See the articles in George T. Abed, ed., *The Palestinian Economy: Studies in Development under Prolonged Occupation* (London, 1988).

13. Hunter, *Palestinian Uprising*, 55.

14. Ibid., 27.

15. The best single treatment of this subject is still David Shipler, *Arab and Jew: Wounded Spirits in the Promised Land* (New York, 1986, second edition 2002), which deals with both Arab and Israeli self-images set against images of "the other."

16. Both quotes come from Sara Roy, "From Hardship to Hunger: The Economic Impact of the Intifada on the Gaza Strip," *American-Arab Affairs* (Fall 1990): 109–10. I rely mainly on Roy for my discussion here, but see also Ziad Abu-Amr, "The Gaza Economy: 1948–1984," in Abed, ed., *Palestinian Economy*, 101–20, and two articles by Ann Lesch, "Gaza: History and Politics" and "Gaza: Life under Occupation," in Lesch and Tessler, *Israel, Egypt, and the Palestinians*, 223–54.

17. Lesch, "Gaza: History and Politics," 235.

18. Shipler, *Arab and Jew*, second edition, 156.

19. Hunter, *Palestinian Uprising*, 34–35. For Palestinian institutions and political developments in the West Bank, see Emile Sahliyeh, *In Search of Leadership: West Bank Politics since 1967* (Washington, D.C., 1988).

20. For Palestinian communal organizations in the context of the intifada, see Yazid Sayigh, *Armed Struggle and the Search for State: The Palestinian National Movement, 1949–1993* (New York, 1997), 607–37; and Joost R. Hilterman, *Behind the Intifada: Labor and Women's Movements in the Occupied Territories* (Princeton, N.J., 1991).

21. The points or demands also called for Israeli adherence to the Geneva Conventions covering treatment of civilians, release of Palestinians in Israeli prisons, and trials of Israeli soldiers for crimes against Arabs. See the text of the Fourteen Points in the *Journal of Palestine Studies* (Spring 1988): 63–65, and reprinted in Don Peretz, *Intifada: The Palestinian Uprising* (Boulder, Colo., 1990), Appendix 3.

22. Hunter, *Palestinian Uprising*, 107. An Israeli account of routine Israeli torture of Palestinians in prisons is Ari Shavit, "On Gaza Beach," *The New York Review of Books*, July 18, 1991, 3–6.

23. "Officer Claims General Mitzna Lied," *Jerusalem Post International Edition*, November 10, 1990, discusses orders given to deliberately break bones when beating Arabs.

24. Hunter, *Palestinian Uprising*, 81, and Peretz, *Intifada*, 60–62.

25. Private communication with members of the peace group "Ad Kan."

26. Hilterman, *Behind the Intifada*, 56–172, has extensive treatment of the labor and women's movements. See also Julie Peteet, *Gender and Crisis: Women and the Palestinian Resistance Movement* (New York, 1991).

27. Hunter, *Palestinian Uprising*, 215.

28. The word *hamas* means "zeal." For detailed analysis of the origins and thought of Hamas and Islamic Jihad, see Azzam Tamimi, *Hamas: A History from Within* (Northampton, Mass., 2007), and Khaled Hroub, *Hamas: Political Thought and Practice* (Washington, D.C., 2002).

29. Peretz, *Intifada*, 208–10.

30. Ibid., 109–10, 184–87.

31. The text and explanatory material are in Quandt, *Peace Process*, 373ff.

32. Two articles on this election and the role of religious parties are Don Peretz and Sammy Smooha, "Israel's Twelfth Knesset Election: An All-Loser Game," and Robert O. Freedman, "Religion, Politics, and the Israeli Elections of 1988," *Middle East Journal* 43, 3 (Summer 1989): 388–405 and 406–22, respectively.

33. Peretz, *Intifada*, 154. See also Hunter, *Palestinian Uprising*, 178–79.

34. See "Chronology," *Middle East Journal* 44, 4 (Autumn 1990): 674. The Israeli was sentenced to life imprisonment in March 1991.

35. Excerpts from news conference held at Huntsville, Alabama, June 20, 1990, *Journal of Palestine Studies* 20, 1 (Autumn 1990): 187.

36. "Chronology," *Middle East Journal* 44, 4 (Autumn 1990): 676.

37. My sources are mostly journalistic. I have relied mainly on articles from the *New York Times* and the *Washington Post*, and broadcasts on National Public Radio, and have found Elizabeth Drew's "Letter from Washington" in *The New Yorker* to be particularly insightful. A competent summary of events, from a great-power perspective, is Lawrence Freedman and Efraim Karsh, *The Gulf Conflict, 1990–1991: Diplomacy and War in the New World Order* (Princeton, N.J., 1993).

38. The staff war exercise is discussed in Bob Woodward and Rick Atkinson, "Mideast Decision: Uncertainty over a Daunting Move," *Washington Post*, August 26, 1990. Elizabeth Drew, "Letter from Washington," *The New Yorker*, September 24, 1990, 104–5, notes how the administration used April Glaspie as a scapegoat. The islands of Warba and Bubiyan lay offshore from

the mouth of an Iraqi canal built to give Iraq direct access to the Persian Gulf from the Shatt al-Arab, rather than traversing that route, which had been blocked by Iran during the war.

39. The quote is in "U.N. Votes Embargo on Iraq," *Washington Post*, August 7, 1990. See also "Bush Orders Effort Aimed at Destabilizing, Toppling Iraqi Leader," ibid., August 6, 1990, and David Hoffman, "White House Counts on Military Buildup to Force Saddam's Hand," *Washington Post*, August 15, 1990, who notes White House interest in provoking a confrontation rather than letting the embargo drag on. See the interview with General Norman Schwarzkopf in the *New York Times*, November 2, 1990, in which he expresses his distaste for the military alternative.

40. Elizabeth Drew, "Letter from Washington," *The New Yorker*, September 24, 1990, 106. The Kuwaiti portfolio is discussed in Clyde H. Farnsworth, "Bush, in Freezing Assets, Bars $30 Billion to Hussein," *New York Times*, August 3, 1990; and Steven Mufson, "Kuwaiti Assets Form Vast Frozen Empire," *Washington Post*, August 6, 1990.

41. John Goshko, "Bush Seen Seeking Little Advice from U.S. Experts on Arab World," *Washington Post*, November 25, 1990. Similar behavior characterized formulation of the Eisenhower Doctrine and U.S. responses to the 1958 Lebanese crisis and the 1970 Jordanian civil war.

42. For a Palestinian Arab analysis of the crisis that is highly critical of Saddam, see Walid Khalidi, "The Gulf Crisis: Origins and Consequences," *Journal of Palestine Studies* 20, 2 (Winter 1991): 5–28.

43. Ann Devroy, "Bush, in Saudi Arabia, Says U.N. Will Meet on Kuwait," *Washington Post*, November 22, 1990; and Valarie Yorke, "Hussein Fights to Save Country and Throne," *Middle East International*, November 23, 1990. Secretary of State Baker deliberately omitted Jordan from the itinerary of his postwar tour of the region in mid-March "in protest over King Husayn's support of Iraq during the Gulf War."

44. Ann Mosely Lesch, "Contrasting Reactions to the Persian Gulf Crisis: Egypt, Syria, Jordan, and the Palestinians," *Middle East Journal* 45, 1 (Winter 1991): 30–50; "Chronology," *Journal of Palestine Studies* 20, 2 (Winter 1991), covers these issues.

45. David Hoffman, "Shamir Plan Was to Stall Autonomy: Rabin Says He'll Cut Subsidies to Settlers," *Washington Post*, June 27, 1992.

46. Jackson Diehl, "Israel Said to Speed Settlement Construction," *Washington Post*, January 9, 1992.

47. Hoffman, "Shamir Plan."

48. See "Chronology," *Journal of Palestine Studies* 22, 4 (Summer 1993): 162–72; Avi Shlaim, "Prelude to the Accord: Likud, Labor, and the Palestinians," ibid., 23, 2 (Winter 1994): 16; and Clyde Haberman, "As Attacks on Israelis Mount, Leaders Debate Self-Defense," *New York Times*, March 29, 1993.

49. For example, David Hoffman, "Rejectionist Palestinians Flex Muscle in West Bank Campus Vote," *Washington Post*, November 12, 1992; and Hoffman, "Rabin Tried to Keep Expulsions Secret to Avoid Court Test," ibid., December 22, 1992.

50. See David Hoffman, "Israeli Offensive Draws Criticism," *Washington Post*, July 29, 1993; Nora Bustany, "A Summer's Journey from Hope to Despair," ibid., July 30, 1993; and "Chronology," *Journal of Palestine Studies* 23, 1 (Autumn 1993): 173.

51. "Chronology," *Journal of Palestine Studies* 23, 2 (Winter 1994): 160–61.

COMMUNIQUÉ NO. 1 OF THE INTIFADA ISSUED BY THE UNIFIED NATIONAL LEADERSHIP

January 8, 1988

The Unified National Leadership (UNL) declaration acknowledges the PLO and advises the Arab inhabitants of the territories on how to conduct themselves. It identifies specific occupations and professions and their responsibilities. Compare the tone and content of this message with that of the first leaflet issued by Hamas the same month (Document 9.2). Subsequent UNL communiqués would contain the directives found here but would also celebrate the "throwers of stones and Molotov cocktails" and invoke the name of Shaykh Izz al-Din al-Qassam, perhaps to match the tone and allusions invoked by Hamas, which created a Qassam brigade.

27. *Communiqué of the Intifada No. 1, January 8, 1988*

In the name of God, the merciful, the compassionate. Our people's glorious uprising continues. We affirm the need to express solidarity with our people wherever they are. We continue to be loyal to the pure blood of our martyrs and to our detained brothers. We also reiterate our rejection of the occupation and its policy of repression, represented in the policy of deportation, mass arrests, curfews, and the demolition of houses. We reaffirm the need to achieve further cohesion with our revolution and our heroic masses. We also stress our abidance by the call of the PLO, the Palestinian people's legitimate and sole representative, and the need to pursue the bountiful offerings and the heroic uprising. For all these reasons, we address the following call:

All sectors of our heroic people in every location should abide by the call for a general and comprehensive strike until Wednesday evening, 13 January 1988. The strike covers all public and private trade utilities, the Palestinian workers and public transportation. Abidance by the comprehensive strike must be complete. The slogan of the strike will be: Down with occupation; long live Palestine as a free and Arab country.

Brother workers, your abidance by the strike by not going to work and to plants is real support for the glorious uprising, a sanctioning of the pure blood of our martyrs, a support for the call to liberate our prisoners, and an act that will help keep our brother deportees in their homeland. Brother businessmen and grocers, you must fully abide by the call for a comprehensive strike during the period of the strike. Your abidance by previous strikes is one of the most splendid images of solidarity and sacrifice for the sake of rendering our heroic people's stand a success.

Source: *The Israeli-Palestinian Conflict: A Documentary Record*, Yehuda Lukacs, ed. (New York, 1992), 390.

We will do our best to protect the interests of our honest businessmen against measures the Zionist occupation force may resort to against you. We warn against the consequences of becoming involved with some of the occupation authorities' henchmen who will seek to make you open your businesses.

We promise you that we will punish such traitor businessmen in the not too distant future. Let us proceed united to forge victory.

Brother owners of taxi companies, we will not forget your honorable and splendid stand of supporting and implementing the comprehensive strike on the day of Palestinian steadfastness. We pin our hopes on you to support and make the comprehensive strike a success. We warn some bus companies against the consequences of not abiding by the call for the strike, as this will make them liable to revolutionary punishment.

Brother doctors and pharmacists, you must be on emergency status to offer assistance to those of our kinfolk who are ill. The brother pharmacists must carry out their duties normally. The brother doctors must place the doctor badge in a way that can be clearly identified. General warning: We would like to warn people that walking in the streets will not be safe in view of the measures that will be taken to make the comprehensive strike a success. We warn that viscous material will be poured on main and secondary streets and everywhere, in addition to the roadblocks and the strike groups that will be deployed throughout the occupied homeland. Circular: The struggler and brother members of the popular committees and the men of the uprising who are deployed in all the working locations should work to support and assist our people within the available means, particularly the needy families of our people. The strike groups and the popular uprising groups must completely abide by the working program, which is in their possession. Let us proceed united and loudly chant: Down with occupation; long live Palestine as a free and Arab country.

DOCUMENT 9.2

LEAFLET NO. 1 OF THE ISLAMIC RESISTANCE MOVEMENT (HAMAS)

January 1988

During the intifada, Hamas would come to epitomize Islamic resistance to Israel and Jewish occupation of Muslim land. This leaflet invokes Quranic sanction for resistance. It insults the Egyptians as cowards because of Camp David while recalling past Islamic leaders of Egypt who had resisted foreign invaders. The threat of roadside bombings would soon be carried out.

Source: Shaul Mishal and Reuben Aharoni, *Speaking Stones: Communiqués from the Intifada Underground* (Syracuse, N.Y., 1991), 201–3.

In the Name of Allah the Merciful and Compassionate

The infidels *"will not cease from fighting against you till they have made you rene-gades from religion, if they can. And whoso becometh a renegade and dieth in his disbelief such are they whose works have fallen both in the world and in the Here-after. Such are rightful owners of the fire: they will abide therein."**

O *murabitun*[†] on the soil of immaculate and beloved Palestine: O all our peo-ple, men and women. O our children: the Jews — brothers of the apes, assassins of the prophets, bloodsuckers, warmongers — are murdering you, depriving you of life after having plundered your homeland and your homes. Only Islam can break the Jews and destroy their dream. Therefore, proclaim to them: Allah is great, Allah is greater than their army, Allah is greater than their airplanes and their weapons. When you struggle with them, take into account to request one of two bounties: martyrdom, or victory over them and their defeat.[‡]

In these days, when the problem is growing more acute and the uprising is escalating, it is our duty to address a word to the Arab rulers, and particularly to the rulers of Egypt, the Egyptian army, and the Egyptian people, as follows: What has happened to you, O rulers of Egypt? Were you asleep in the period of the treaty of shame and surrender, the Camp David treaty? Has your national zealousness died and your pride run out while the Jews daily perpetrate grave and base crimes against the people and the children?

And you, O army of Egypt, O descendants of Salah al-Din al-Ayyubi,[§] Qutuz[||] and al-Zahir Baybars,[#] what has happened? Have the rulers paralyzed your movement and stripped you of your power, making you so impotent that even the usurpers are no longer frightened of you?[**] And you, O defeated Egyptian people, which is incapable of doing anything, God will help you and us. We greet you through the pioneer Muslims who have come out of al-Azhar and all the universities in order to express their solidarity with their brethren in Palestine, strengthen their hands, and cry out to the usurpers that their end shall come in the morning — is the morning far off — is it not near? [Know] that God does not abandon but gives respite.

Let the whole world hear that the Muslim Palestinian people rejects the sur-render solutions, rejects an international conference, for these will not restore

---

* Surah of The Cow (2), 217. The translations from the Quran are taken from Mohammed Mar-maduke Pickthall, *The Meaning of the Glorious Koran* (New York, 1953).

† Muslims who settled in outlying areas during the initial period of the Muslim conquests in order to defend the borders.

‡ In Islamic tradition, one of two bounties is requested from Allah: victory or martyrdom in battle.

§ The victorious commander over the Crusaders in the Battle of Hittin (1187).

|| Mamluk Sultan of Egypt (1259–1260), who defeated the Mongols in the Battle of 'Ayn Jalut, near Nablus, in 1259.

Mamluk Sultan of Egypt (1260–1277), who fought in the Battle of 'Ayn Jalut.

** Salah al-Din, Qutuz, and Baybars vanquished the empires of the time. By implication, Israel, another empire, can also be defeated.

our people's rights in its homeland and on its soil. The Palestinian people accuses all who seek this [solution] of weaving a plot against its rights and its sacred national cause. Liberation will not be completed without sacrifice, blood and jihad that continues until victory.

Today, as the Muslim Palestinian people persists in rejecting the Jews' policy, a policy of deporting Palestinians from their homeland and leaving behind their families and children—the people stresses to the Jews that the struggle will continue and escalate, its methods and instruments will be improved, until the Jews shall drink what they have given our unarmed people to drink.

The blood of our martyrs shall not be forgotten. Every drop of blood shall become a Molotov cocktail, a time bomb, and a roadside charge that will rip out the intestines of the Jews. [Only] then will their sense return. You who give the Jews lists containing the names of youngsters and spy against their families, return to the fold, repent at once. Those who deal in betrayal have only themselves to blame. All of you are exposed and known. To you our Muslim Palestinian people, Allah's blessing and protection! May Allah strengthen you and give you victory. Continue with your rejection and your struggle against the occupation methods, the dispossession, deportations, prisons, tortures, travel restrictions, the dissemination of filth and pornography, the corruption and bribery, the improper and humiliating behavior, the heavy taxes, a life of suffering and of degradation to honor and to the houses of worship.

Forward our people in your resistance until the defeat of your enemy and liquidation of the occupation. Then the mark of Cain shall be erased. O our people of clean conscience! Spare no efforts [to fan] the fire of the uprising until God gives the sign to be extricated from the distress. Invoke God's name plentifully, for "lo! with hardship goeth ease, / Lo! with hardship goeth ease."*

The Islamic Resistance Movement
January 1988

---

* Surah of Solace (94), 5–6.

10

ISRAELI-PALESTINIAN/ARAB NEGOTIATIONS AND AGREEMENTS

1993-1999

THE ISRAELI-PALESTINIAN pact of 1993 was fraught with obstacles. Each side held radically different conceptions of what its terms signified, especially regarding the status of Jerusalem, Israeli settlements, and Palestinian sovereignty. Many of the accord's provisos were never implemented, requiring a second agreement, Oslo 2, or "The Interim Agreement," of September 1995. The additional handovers of land outlined in Oslo 2 led to the assassination of Prime Minister Yitzhak Rabin in November 1995, a traumatic event with lasting implications for the peace process. The specter of future assassination or of civil war in Israel if many settlements were removed appears to have encouraged Israeli prime ministers such as Ehud Barak to back settlement expansion while declaring their eagerness for peace with the Palestinians. It also led U.S. negotiators to tolerate such developments for the sake of Israel's domestic political stability while aware of their negative impact on the peace process itself.

Rabin was ultimately succeeded by a Likud prime minister, Binyamin Netanyahu. Netanyahu, who had encouraged the opposition to Oslo 2 and vilified Rabin, strove to evade implementation of the Oslo and subsequent agreements in an atmosphere of bitterness and violence on all sides. His maneuvers eventually split the Likud Party and resulted in the election of Ehud Barak as prime minister of Israel in May 1999. Barak promised to achieve full peace accords with the Palestinians.

THE 1993 OSLO ACCORD

The 1993 Israeli-Palestinian accord was produced independently of the Madrid talks and without American involvement. The catalysts were Yossi Beilin, deputy foreign minister in the Rabin cabinet after June 1992 and a close ally of Shimon Peres, and Terje Rod Larsen, a Norwegian researcher studying Israeli rule in the occupied territories; as a Knesset member, Beilin had long advocated direct talks with the PLO. Beilin delegated two Israeli history professors, Ron Pundak and Yair Hirschfeld, to pursue initiatives with a PLO representative, Ahmad Quarai, who happened to be the PLO treasurer. With nongovernmental negotiators, Israel could always deny the substance of talks if they seemed unproductive.

The negotiations lasted from December 1992 to August 1993, nearly all conducted in locales in and around Oslo, with more official Israeli representatives joining the talks as they progressed.[1] The newly elected Clinton administration knew of the meetings but not of their content or progress. The United States still refused to talk to the PLO as a result of the events of May–June 1990. Clinton's Middle East representatives remained wedded to the Madrid formula and the president appeared more sympathetic to rightist Israeli opinions than had the Bush administration of the 1990s.

The Terms

There were two aspects to what can be termed the Israeli-Palestinian Accord: the Declaration of Principles (DOP) and the letters of mutual recognition. The DOP was initialed in Oslo on August 20, 1993, but the official signing occurred at the White House on September 13 (see Document 10.1). The DOP was conditional on the exchange of letters of recognition by Yasir Arafat, as chairman of the PLO, and Yitzhak Rabin, as prime minister of Israel (see Figure 10.1).

Although depicted as "mutual," the types of recognition given were unequal because of the disparity in status of the signatories—one a state, the other an organization. The PLO recognized "the right of the State of Israel to exist in peace and security" and accepted U.N. Resolutions 242 and 338. In his September 9 letter, Arafat declared that the PLO renounced terrorism and would strive to control elements that might engage in it. He also asserted that those clauses in the 1968 PLO Charter that denied Israel's existence and called for her overthrow by "armed struggle" were "now inoperative and no longer valid" and that he would propose their removal from the charter to the Palestinian National Council. In return, Rabin wrote to Arafat on the same day that "the Government of Israel has decided to recognize the P.L.O. as the representative of the Palestinian people and commence negotiations with the P.L.O. within the Middle East peace process."

Israeli negotiators in Oslo refused to permit any reference to a Palestinian state in the agreement. Israel accepted the PLO as the organization with whom it would negotiate, but the status of that organization was left undefined, as was the goal of the negotiations. From a Palestinian rejectionist viewpoint, Arafat had done what they had always feared; he recognized Israel's existence without gaining mutual acknowledgment of a Palestinian right to self-determination. Conversely, from an Israeli rejectionist standpoint, the very fact that the existence of a Palestinian people, let alone the PLO, had been acknowledged was

Figure 10.1 ■ The Handshake: Yitzhak Rabin and Yasir Arafat Shake Hands with President Bill Clinton as Onlooker Following the Signing of the Declaration of Principles, September 13, 1993

A historic moment symbolizing the end of one stage of the Palestinian-Israeli conflict. Rabin had been reluctant to shake hands with Arafat, who to him embodied Palestinian terrorism. Arafat, on the other hand, saw this ceremony as signifying full international recognition, including Israeli, of the Palestinians' ultimate right to self-determination.

anathema and the prelude to a Palestinian state in areas they were determined to retain for Israel.[2]

The intent of the declaration was to create a Palestinian Interim Self-Government Authority (PISGA—the future Palestinian Authority, or PA) comprised of an elected council that would govern the Palestinians in Gaza and the West Bank for "a transitional period not exceeding five years." Elections for this council were scheduled for nine months after the Declaration of Principles went into force—July 13, 1994. However, these elections were dependent on the conclusion of the Interim Agreement (Article VII) that would define the structure and authority of the council. Negotiations for this interim agreement were distinct from those required before the projected Israeli military withdrawal from Gaza and Jericho began in December 1993.

The transitional, or "interim," period of five years would date from the election of this council, supposedly from July 1994, with "permanent status" negotiations commencing no later than the third year of the interim period—July 1997. These permanent status negotiations would cover issues deliberately excluded from the jurisdiction of the elected council and therefore from any

points of discussion during the interim period, as they were still subject to unilateral Israeli control; they included "Jerusalem, refugees, settlements, security
arrangements, border relations and cooperation with other neighbors, and
other issues of common interest." Once the Palestinian Council had been
installed, the Israeli Civil Administration would be "dissolved and the Israeli
Military Government . . . withdrawn."

Nonetheless, the Israeli withdrawal and creation of Palestinian civil authority, including local police, did not signify Israeli recognition of Palestinian control over these areas: ". . . subsequent to the Israeli withdrawal Israel [would]
continue to be responsible for external security, and for internal security and
public order of settlements and Israelis. Israeli military forces and civilians may
continue to use roads freely within the Gaza Strip and the Jericho area." In
short, Israel's military authority would override Palestinian civil authority and
"the withdrawal of the military government [would] not prevent Israel from
exercising the powers and responsibilities not transferred to the council." Israel,
therefore, could decide which powers it wished to award to the council and
which it wished to retain.[3] Nothing denoting Palestinian sovereignty or unilateral authority, independent of Israeli supervision, had been ceded by Israel;
most matters were still subject to negotiations where there was wide latitude for
disagreement.

Negotiators immediately deadlocked on the size of the council and differed
on the size of the "Jericho area" from which Israel would withdraw; was it 15
square miles as the Israelis proposed or 150 square miles as the PLO suggested?
Another dispute centered on whether "withdrawal" meant total withdrawal or
merely "redeployment," which connoted a repositioning of troops, possibly still
within the area allocated to the Palestinians.[4]

The deadlines were never kept. Palestinian self-rule in Gaza and Jericho,
with Israeli troop withdrawals, did not begin until mid-May 1994; six months
later, in November, agreement was finally reached on the extent of limited
Palestinian authority to be exercised at border crossings with Jordan and Egypt,
supposedly part of the self-rule accord of May.[5] Still left in abeyance was negotiation of the Interim Agreement. Initially envisaged for July 1994, the Interim
Agreement (Oslo 2) was not concluded until September 1995 with the council,
to be known as the Palestinian Authority, elected in January 1996 following the
Rabin assassination.

Analysis of the Accord

In the spring of 1993, the Israeli leadership had begun to debate how Israel
might reach agreement with Palestinians and on what grounds. Should there be
an interim period of transition where Palestinians established a bureaucratic
structure preparatory to ultimate self-rule and proved themselves capable of
governing, or should Israel negotiate final status issues immediately?[6] Shimon
Peres favored immediate final status negotiations. Rabin differed; he feared that

settler opposition might help Likud in an immediate debate and apparently looked to the interim stage as a period during which general confidence in Palestinian self-governing abilities would grow.

Four other factors loomed large when contrasted to Palestinian expectations. Both Rabin and Peres, from different vantage points, still favored a Palestinian confederation with Jordan based on "a common interest with Amman in restraining the territorial ambitions of the Palestinians," the basis of Labor proposals in the 1980s.[7] Second, they considered land for peace to mean Israeli retention, by unilateral annexation if necessary, of at least 20 percent of the West Bank, presumably with Jordan's agreement. The bulk of it would be the greater Jerusalem area and the corridor to adjacent settlements, encompassing two-thirds of the settlers and, from a domestic political perspective, isolating the most militant. From this standpoint, Palestinian self-rule in an interim stage had to be severely restricted in order to prevent "a precedent that would make annexation of the 20 percent much harder five years from now."[8] Third, the time was propitious. The Gulf War and the end of the cold war had brought about American global primacy and discredited the Arab radical camp—a combination that offered Israel greater leverage to impose its terms. Finally, Arafat's financial and political weakness provided an opportunity to force concessions, particularly because the Palestinians negotiating with their Israeli counterparts in Washington under the Madrid umbrella (Haydar Abd al-Shafi and Hanan Ashrawi) were demanding recognition of a Palestinian state and that the issues of settlements and Jerusalem be addressed. Arafat would accept much less to reappear as the leader of the Palestinians.

East Jerusalem and the Settlements

From the Israeli perspective at Oslo, avoidance of reference to East Jerusalem was essential. Israel claimed all of Jerusalem as its capital, forever united after the 1967 war. Palestinians viewed East Jerusalem as the capital of a future Palestinian state. A key issue was and still is: What is meant by "East Jerusalem"? It originally signified the Old City of Jerusalem, within the walls, including the Temple Mount and Dome of the Rock, annexed by Israel as a result of the 1967 war. Sacred to Jews as the site of the ancient temple of worship, the Temple Mount is revered by Muslims as *Haram al-Sharif* ("the noble sanctuary"), a term indicating its status as a holy city in Islam superseded only by the two sacred sanctuaries, Mecca and Medina.

Once Israel annexed the Old City in 1967, the Eshkol government had immediately constructed apartments on the hills overlooking it, in the West Bank, and subsequently expanded the concept of "East Jerusalem" to encompass 105 kilometers north and south of Jerusalem proper; this territory extends northward to just below the Arab town of Ramallah and south toward Bethlehem. Israel annexed this additional territory as "East Jerusalem" in 1980 and has declared it to be part of Jerusalem proper and therefore nonnegotiable, creating the impression it was part of the original city. At the same time, Israel undertook to strengthen the Jewish position in the Old City, and in Arab East Jerusalem generally, while permitting Arab sectors to deteriorate in the hope of encouraging emigration where dispossession was impossible.

Whereas former U.S. administrations had characterized "East Jerusalem" as part of the occupied territories, meaning that it was considered West Bank land subject to negotiation, even before the 1993 accord Clinton started to call it "disputed territory," the status of which would be resolved in final talks. Administration spokespersons argued that extension of Israeli settlements around Jerusalem, which now included significant portions of the West Bank, did not violate American criteria for loans. Neither did the United States want to discuss whether Israeli expansion of settlements around Jerusalem after the accord was "an obstacle to peace," as noted by previous administrations (see Map 10.1). Instead the administration declared itself unwilling to take a position on the legality of the settlements or on other issues because Jerusalem's status had been deferred to permanent status talks.[9]

Once the accord had been signed, Rabin admitted his doubts that the Palestinians would ever have agreed to a "united Jerusalem . . . under Israeli control and outside the jurisdiction of the Palestinians for the whole interim period"; or to continuation of settlements; or to "keeping all options open for the negotiations on a permanent solution." The Palestinians could "stick to their goals," but for Rabin: ". . . Jerusalem must remain united under Israeli sovereignty and be our capital forever. . . . I don't believe there is room for an additional state between Israel and Jordan."[10] For Rabin, this interim stage afforded Israel the opportunity to consolidate control of territory it wished to retain permanently because Arafat had left Jerusalem under Israeli auspices until final status talks began. At that point, there might be nothing to negotiate because an Israeli fait accompli would have occurred. Rabin seemed to intend for Jerusalem what Shamir had sought for all the territories—protracted negotiations that enabled consolidation of Israel's fundamental objectives.

For Arafat and his chief negotiator, Nabil Shaath, Oslo 1 was the first step toward the ultimate creation of a Palestinian state with East Jerusalem as its

---

Map 10.1 ■ **Israel and the Territories Subject to Negotiation, 1993–2000**   ▶

This map highlights those lands occupied by Israel down to the Camp David talks, July 2000 (discussed in Chapter 11), where resolution of final status by withdrawal or negotiation remains unresolved. It reflects changes made by the 1993 Oslo Accord, which awarded self-government to Jericho in the West Bank and most of the Gaza Strip; Israeli settlements in the Gaza Strip remained under full Israeli control. The West Bank other than Jericho was redefined as a result of the 1995 Oslo 2 Accord and is the subject of Map 10.2. Note also the nature of Jerusalem, especially East Jerusalem, in the inset, where the Old City, former East Jerusalem, has been expanded and unilaterally annexed by Israel in an attempt to make the area nonnegotiable. Israel voluntarily withdrew from the security zone in south Lebanon in May 2000, restoring it to Lebanese sovereignty, except for the far southeast corner, which it retains, a status disputed by Lebanon and especially by Hizbollah.

Territory still subject to negotiation

Palestinian self-governing areas, 1994

Israeli security zone, 1994
(Israeli troop withdrawal, 2000)

0   15   30 miles

0   15   30 kilometers

LEBANON

Israeli security zone

GOLAN HEIGHTS

SYRIA

Acre

Haifa

L. Tiberias

Mediterranean Sea

Jenin

Tulkarm

Nablus

Jordan R.

Tel Aviv

WEST BANK

Ramallah

Jericho

Amman

Jerusalem

Hebron

Dead Sea

Gaza

GAZA STRIP

ISRAEL

JORDAN

EGYPT

Gulf of Aqaba   Eilat   Aqaba

East Jerusalem (annexed by Israel in 1980)

Old City (annexed by Israel in 1967)

Jerusalem

capital. For Haydar Abd al-Shafi, the Palestinian negotiator at the Madrid talks, the accord was a flawed document "phrased in generalities that leave room for wide interpretations. . . . We are trying to read into it what is not there." As he saw it, Israel had "no intention of ever allowing a state," as they admitted openly, and the agreement contained nothing about stopping settlements in the territories, especially around Jerusalem. Given the "terrible asymmetry in . . . power and force" between Israel and the Palestinians, the negotiators could not rely on United Nations Resolutions 242 and 338 because they could not be imposed from without. He envisioned popular disillusionment, as did many Palestinians who had "already concluded [before the signings] that the peace plan will not be able to develop as Mr. Arafat expects it to."[11]

Why, then, sign the accord? For Nabil Shaath, the Palestinians were addressed inclusively "as a people," not simply as the residents of the territories. The accord stressed that Resolution 242, land in exchange for peace, would be the basis of negotiations. Equally important from Shaath's perspective, yet diametrically opposed to Rabin's assumptions, were the issues of settlements and Jerusalem:

> Our agreement to temporarily relegate these issues to the permanent settlement [permanent status talks] constituted a very important breakthrough from the Israeli point of view [see Rabin's previous comments]. What made it possible for us to agree was, first, the fact that these issues were placed on the agenda not just as issues to be raised but as matters to be settled, and, second, that the permanent status talks were given a specific time frame—either as soon as possible or a maximum of two years. In the case of Jerusalem, our acceptance was made a little easier by the fact that Jerusalemites can vote and be nominated in elections, and that the Palestinian institutions in East Jerusalem would be run by the Palestinian authority. . . .[12]

But Shaath admitted that Israel was "not willing to commit [itself] in writing to any specific issue relating to settlements in the interim period and that remains a major problem," as was the lack of commitment in writing to "freeze settlements in the West Bank and Jerusalem." Rabin had stressed the same issue to indicate that Israel retained all options.

Shaath's reference points were the (1978) Camp David declarations, which "had the Palestinians tucked under a Jordanian umbrella, and this has clearly ended." He admitted that "all the modalities . . . are to be discussed," but apparently assumed that the identification of the topics to be negotiated took precedence over the specific procedural issues whereby disputes over these topics would be resolved.

Rabin assumed the opposite; negotiations over procedures were crucial. Defining the modalities included discussion of sovereignty or nonsovereignty, how or when authority might be handed over, and the like. Their delay in resolution afforded Israel opportunities to consolidate its position in areas such as Jerusalem, thereby preempting issues to be discussed in permanent status talks.

These talks, originally scheduled for the third year of the interim period (not the second as Shaath stated), no sooner than July 1997 according to Oslo 1, did not begin until July 2000.

Equally crucial to Rabin was the question of Palestinian ability to control the areas allotted to them. Could Arafat govern capably and control dissidents who might threaten the accords and Israeli citizens, essentially taking over Israel's security duties? If he could not, Rabin reserved the right for Israel to withdraw from talks and, in principle, return to the status quo ante. He seemed to make no connection between Israel's actions to consolidate its goals during this period, such as expansion of settlements, and the impact of such actions on Arafat's capacity to control dissidents.

THE POLITICS AND ECONOMICS OF VIOLENCE

In the immediate aftermath of the accord's signing, its Arab and Israeli opponents proclaimed their determination to derail its implementation. Particular flashpoints for both groups were Gaza, where Hamas had installed itself, and Hebron on the West Bank, where Gush Emunim militants had established settlements within the city and outside. But Hamas became active on the West Bank as well, where deaths of settlers were soon reported and one of the founders of Gush Emunim was wounded. Simultaneously, the intifada erupted once more, especially in Gaza, where protest demonstrations led to Israeli military reprisals.[13]

Economic and Diplomatic Inequalities

Gaza's fury was fueled by economic despair. Their nearly total dependence on employment in Israel had already been compromised; Rabin had imposed a full curfew in June 1993 that had not been lifted by January 1994, four months after the accord. Early warnings by Israeli and other experts that "Palestinian anger is stoked by poverty" were ignored, as were arguments by Israeli economists that "For growth the Palestinians must have open borders with Israel . . . [because] if you separate them [the two economies], one of them will die and it is obvious that that one will be the Palestinian economy."[14]

Intensified violence in 1994 led to larger shutdowns of Gaza, and Israel increased its importation of Asian and East European manual laborers. The sealing off of the territories could be justified for security reasons, especially after suicide bombings took numerous Israeli lives during 1994, but the policy intensified the rage already inspiring such acts. Whereas 70 percent of Gaza's labor force had worked in Israel before the intifada, 23 percent did so in June 1993 and only 11 percent by January 1994.

Palestinian frustration was fed by signs of Israeli progress on other fronts that resulted from the Oslo Accord. The Vatican established diplomatic relations with Israel in June and would later establish "official" relations with the

PLO. Jordan and Israel signed an agreement ending their state of war in late July, and an official peace accord was ratified on October 26, 1994. In one of the clauses, Israel granted Jordan a "special role" in administering Muslim shrines in and around East Jerusalem as well as "high priority" in negotiation of the city's permanent status. This clause appeared to subvert terms of the 1993 Oslo agreement by leaving Jerusalem open to Israeli-Jordanian negotiations.[15] These developments, coupled with Israel's opening of a liaison office in Tunisia in early October and its participation in an American-sponsored economic conference held in Casablanca, Morocco, in early November, suggested progressive Arab state acceptance of Israel following the 1993 accord, a stance that stood in sharp contrast to developments affecting the Palestinians themselves.[16]

Added to these issues was the question of Arafat's leadership abilities. Local Palestinian leaders resented Arafat's habit of appointing close allies from his Tunis network to key posts and ignoring Fatah and other officials from the territories, who were familiar with local conditions. But if Arafat's personal style of rule seemed to ignore the need to create a political and economic infrastructure in the territories taken over, he was hardly helped by the nature of the structure given him. Israeli transition officials often sought to hinder Palestinian assumptions of authority, whether they removed light switches from offices in Jericho or, more seriously, refused to hand over population registers or tax records. Indeed, "the Israelis dismantled their whole taxation system in Gaza and Jericho without coordinating with him [Arafat] or fully transferring taxes to his government."[17]

In the midst of these conflicts, another clash resulted from Arab attacks on Israelis: Israel demanded that Arafat show that he could establish security in the regions given to him, a key issue for Rabin. A combination of factors, primarily the interaction of Arab and Israeli violence, made this task nearly impossible to accomplish.

Prelude to Oslo 2

On February 24, 1994, Baruch Goldstein, an immigrant from Brooklyn and a follower of Meir Kahane, killed twenty-nine Arabs as they worshipped in the Mosque of Abraham situated in a cave in Hebron, also sacred to Jews as the Tomb of the Patriarchs; Arab onlookers then killed him. Goldstein had resided at Qiryat Arba, the militant settler community adjacent to Hebron. In the Arab protest riots that followed, at least twenty-five more Palestinians were killed by Israeli troops. In the end, the Israeli government banned two political parties as terrorist, Kahane's old Kach Party and "Kahane Lives," but did not restrict settler movement in and around Hebron, where a shrine was erected to commemorate Goldstein's act; Palestinian freedom of movement was sharply curtailed.[18]

Hamas seemed the only Palestinian group able to seize the initiative. It chose terror in the aftermath of the Hebron massacre; April saw two suicide car bombings with serious casualties. Then in early October Hamas kidnapped an Israeli soldier and demanded the release of 200 Arab prisoners for his return. Israel suspended peace talks and both Rabin and President Clinton, insisting that the Hamas kidnappers were in Gaza under Arafat's authority, held Arafat responsible for finding them. Then Israeli troops stormed a Hamas hideout on the West Bank, where the soldier had been held outside of Arafat's sphere of control. The captive and one of his rescuers were killed in the shoot-out along with three members of Hamas. Three days later, on October 18, a suicide bomber destroyed a bus in Tel Aviv, killing at least 22 and wounding nearly 50. Pressured to show he would crack down on Hamas as demanded by Rabin and Clinton, Arafat's police opened fire on a Palestinian protest demonstration held on November 19, killing 12 and wounding over 200. For many Arabs, the PLO appeared to have replaced the Israeli military as oppressors. On January 22, 1995, the confrontation intensified as two suicide bombers set off explosions at a military transit point in Israel, killing at least 19 soldiers and wounding scores more. The Islamic Jihad took responsibility. The toll since April 1994 rose to at least 65 Israelis killed and over 200 wounded. Many more Palestinians had been killed by Israeli troops during demonstrations.

Following these events, Israel suspended public negotiations. But behind the scenes, secret talks were under way with Arafat's aides to prepare the Interim Agreement that was called for in the 1993 Declaration of Principles but never negotiated. News of these talks appeared during the summer of 1995, a time when polls indicated a preference for the new Likud leader, Binyamin Netanyahu, who repudiated the Oslo peace process. With Israeli elections scheduled for November 1996 at the latest, Likud's Netanyahu denounced any idea of withdrawal from occupied lands and handed to the Knesset a copy of a government position paper on the Golan Heights, possibly trying to sabotage the talks.[19] When Rabin presented preliminary proposals on Israeli withdrawals from the West Bank to the Knesset in June, Netanyahu accused him of planning a full withdrawal from the territories and abandoning Israeli citizens to Palestinian terrorist attacks.

More ominously, ultra-Orthodox rabbis in Israel and in Brooklyn began to accuse Rabin and Peres of being "traitors" and "criminals," provoking charges that they were justifying a religiously sanctioned (*halachic*) sentence of death for the Israeli leaders. A similar halachic ruling forbade removing army bases from the West Bank, claiming that the Torah could not sanction "transferring the sites to the gentiles, since this contravenes a positive Torah commandment and also endangers the life and the existence of the state."[20]

Tensions soared as finalization of the Interim Agreement approached. Hamas undertook two suicide bombings during August that killed at least ten Israelis and wounded over one hundred. Settlers accused Rabin of endangering Jewish lives by pursuit of his peace plans. Police officials warned of Jewish extremist plots and settler spokespersons declared that if ministers were attacked, they would bear responsibility because of their policies. These events, and Rabin's declaration that the new accord, nicknamed Oslo 2, "was a mighty blow to the delusion of a Greater Israel" intensified emotions that would be exploited once Oslo 2 had been signed.[21]

OSLO 2 AND THE RABIN ASSASSINATION

The Oslo 2 Accord (see Document 10.2) was initialed by Prime Minister Yitzhak Rabin and Palestinian Authority Chairman Yasir Arafat on September 24, 1995. A more ceremonial signing took place at the White House on September 28. Oslo 2 was that "Interim Agreement" first mentioned in the 1993 Declaration of Principles (DOP) but never negotiated. Conclusion of this agreement had been a necessary precondition to the election of the Palestinian Interim Self-Government Authority (PISGA). Oslo 2 specified that the election of this author-ity, or "Council," would occur no later than January 1996, eighteen months after its original deadline. Once formed, the council would oversee the removal of the offending clauses from the Palestine National Charter that called for Israel's destruction, another matter suspended by the previous strife. The five-year transitional, or "interim," period now dated from May 1994, the date of Israel's withdrawal from Gaza and Jericho. Permanent status negotiations would com-mence on May 4, 1996, with the deadline for a final agreement of May 4, 1999.

Terms of the Agreement

The Interim Agreement specified the types of powers and responsibilities the Palestinian Authority (PA) would and would not have. It could sign economic, cultural, scientific, and educational pacts with foreign countries, but it could not enter into diplomatic agreements. Several hundred Palestinians in Israeli prisons would be released in stages, although major disputes would later erupt over the types of crimes that might prevent release. The agreement provided for the creation of a safe passage route between Gaza and the West Bank to enable Palestinian travel between the territories, and for a Gaza seaport, projects implemented only after Netanyahu's electoral defeat in 1999.

The agreement's 23 pages of articles were buttressed by 284 pages of annexes and appendices. The latter specified matters such as how many Palestinian police officers, vehicles, rifles, and pistols would be in each self-governing municipality and that the color of gas cylinders used by Palestinians in the territories would differ from that used in Israel or by Israelis in the territories.[22] But there were also areas that seemed deliberately ambiguous, especially on matters that were key to Palestinian optimism about the agreement.

Oslo 2 called for the West Bank to be divided into three areas labeled "A," "B," and "C." Israeli forces would withdraw from specified areas in Areas A and B prior to the election of the PA in late January 1996. Area A identified six population centers in the West Bank—Jenin, Nablus, Tulkarm, Qalqilya, Ramallah, and Bethlehem. In addition, special arrangements were made for an Israeli redeployment in Hebron, creating a Palestinian self-governing area but preserving a Jewish sector; the Hebron redeployment would not occur until January 1997. Area B comprised about 450 smaller towns and rural hamlets, often but not always adjacent to the larger towns in Area A. It was anticipated that regions within Area B could be shifted to Area A in the future just as lands from Area C would come under Area B. As for Area C, Israeli withdrawal would supposedly occur in three stages within eighteen months of the election of the council, but in contrast to Areas A and B, the areas and timing were deliberately left vague.

The Palestinian Council's authority differed according to the area. In Area A, the Palestinians would have full responsibility for overall security as well as internal affairs. In Area B, the rural areas, the Palestinian Authority, through its elected council, would oversee public order and internal security in matters involving Palestinians; however, unlike in Area A, in Area B Israel would be responsible for external security and have final authority for security matters generally. But it was Area C, and its link to issues to be decided only in the permanent status talks, that suggested how misleading certain clauses of the accord could be. Arafat claimed that Oslo 2 guaranteed the return of 80 percent of the West Bank to the Arabs while Rabin assured the Knesset that the pact left 70 percent of the same land, or all of Area C, in Israel's hands.

These differences stemmed from the linkage of promised Israeli withdrawals to exceptions "for issues [to be] negotiated in the permanent status negotiations." These issues included Jerusalem, settlements, borders, refugees, security arrangements, and the like; Jerusalem, all Israeli settlements, military installations, and border areas were in Area C. Several clauses explicitly mentioned that lands in Area C would come under the jurisdiction of the Palestinian Council in three phased withdrawals to last no more than eighteen months, yet all contained the qualifier referring to exceptions retained for permanent status negotiations.[23]

The Palestinians expected Israel to gradually withdraw from Area C except for the land actually occupied by settlements and military installations. Although Israel would later relent, it argued initially that because Area C included these settlements, military installations, and border areas, there could be no withdrawal at all until the permanent status talks. Moreover, this interpretation enabled Israel "not to freeze building and natural growth" in the settlements, meaning existing settlements could be expanded to absorb more land.[24]

Rabin and Peres had negotiated these terms to preserve as extensive an Israeli occupation as possible prior to permanent status talks. With this end in mind, Oslo 2 provided for the expansion of the network of bypass roads from Israel proper to all settlements, linking them to each other and to pre-1967 Israel. These roads were intended, in Rabin's words, to "[enable] Israelis to move without crossing the Palestinian population areas that will become the

Palestinian Authority's responsibility." Rabin did not note that the roads would also cut off Palestinian areas from each other, denying contiguity and blocking an effective imposition of any central Palestinian authority independent of Israeli security. Finally, Israel interpreted the agreement to permit it to decide unilaterally which if any parts of Area C would be ceded should that become necessary; the United States would agree with that interpretation in 1997.

Why did the Palestinians accept such terms? The negotiating team opposed them, wanting more specific guarantees for Israeli deployment from the areas that became Area C; Israel refused. In times of impasse, Israeli negotiators had Shimon Peres talk directly to Arafat, bypassing his delegation. Arafat, to his delegation's horror, accepted the clauses referring to transfer of further security powers to the Palestinian Authority "without defining the amount of territory [Area C] involved." He wanted more Palestinian authority in Areas A and B. Immediate accomplishments meant more to him than insisting on guarantees about the future. Although Arafat's decision gave the appearance of progress toward Palestinian self-rule, from the Israeli perspective it was a "real coup." Israel was not forced to identify specific sites within Area C to be placed under Palestinian control then or later, only to stipulate the land in Areas A and B that Israel was giving to the Palestinians.[25]

Palestinian public reception of the accord was cautious because Israel appeared to control more, not fewer, aspects of Palestinian life in areas granted self-rule. Once Jericho had been awarded to the Palestinians under the 1993 Declaration of Principles, they could enter or leave it only after passing through several Israeli checkpoints, inspections, and roadblocks established after it had gained autonomy. In times of unrest, Israel frequently sealed off the area. Arafat required official Israeli approval before exiting Jericho in his helicopter because the West Bank was within Israeli airspace. Whereas Palestinian merchants had traded freely from town to town when Israel controlled all the West Bank, such trade with Jericho now became nearly impossible. Autonomy had brought Jericho more restrictions and less mobility, a fate Palestinians feared could also be theirs.[26] And the Israeli bypass roads to the settlements that Arafat accepted as part of Oslo 2 required confiscation of Arab land, homes, and farms to pave the way for linking the Jewish population.

What mattered most to Arafat and to the United States, which claimed credit for the achievement, was the renewal of the peace process and the appearance of progress, not the specifics of implementation and their implications. What mattered most to the Rabin government was the granting of Palestinian authority over nearly 90 percent of the West Bank's Arab population while ceding only 30 percent of the land. This enabled the consolidation of Jewish control of areas that might be retained in the permanent settlement. Here the government focused on major settlement blocs around Jerusalem with the intention that some, such as Ma'ale Adumim and Giva'at Ze'ev, be incorporated into a greater Jerusalem. Since Jerusalem was reserved for discussion during permanent status talks, and Israel was determined to retain it as the united capital of Israel, unilaterally incorporating West Bank settlements into Jerusalem established more West Bank land that was nonnegotiable. Such actions had major implications because Ma'ale Adumim has a land area larger than Tel Aviv (see Map 10.2).[27]

Israel's ability to dictate the terms of the negotiation process shaped implementation of the Interim Agreement and the Arab reaction. Several clauses in the agreement declared that "the integrity and status [of the territories] will be preserved during the interim period" and that "neither side shall initiate or take any steps that will change the status of the West Bank and Gaza Strip pending the outcome of permanent status negotiations." Palestinian and most other observers interpreted this to mean that expansion of settlements violated the accord.[28] Israel argued that the terms referred to political status only, a reservation not mentioned in the documents. In Israel's view, Arafat could not declare a state because that would alter the political status of the territories, but as Rabin noted to the Knesset, Israel reserved "total freedom of action in order to fulfill those security and political aims that touch on the permanent solution." These aims included consolidating the settlement blocs so as to argue that uprooting them would be too disruptive, and because, as Peres had noted, "to force [settlers] to leave . . . [would] risk a civil war."[29] In the long run, this meant that to evade a civil war within Israel, Palestinian expectations regarding the Oslo process would be denied, with the apparent compliance of American negotiators, while the Palestinians would be blamed for any rupture in that process.

The Rabin Assassination

Why then was Rabin vilified by the ultra-Orthodox and extremist settlers, with Likud politicians joining in the condemnation? To them, abandoning any land they considered Jewish was heresy. Settler networks linked to radical rabbis and leaders in Hebron and Qiryat Arba, but also with ties to Netanyahu, initiated demonstrations in the summer of 1995 that condemned Rabin. A new organization, Zoe Artzenu (This Is Our Land), associated with Meir Kahane's outlawed Kach Party and centered in and around Hebron, arranged massive sit-ins at key road junctions to try to cripple the government.[30] These organizations harassed Rabin and his ministers constantly, at times with overt threats of physical harm. At demonstrations in Hebron, Moshe Levinger, founder of Gush Emunim, accused Rabin and his government of treason, murder, and "crimes against the Jewish people." Ariel Sharon, though not uttering such words, participated in the rally, as did Netanyahu. All pledged their loyalty to "the land of Israel" and Netanyahu declared that "no Jew hitherto ever longed to give up slices of the homeland."[31]

Following Rabin's assassination on November 4, 1995, his widow, Leah, accused Netanyahu of helping to foment the atmosphere that had led to her

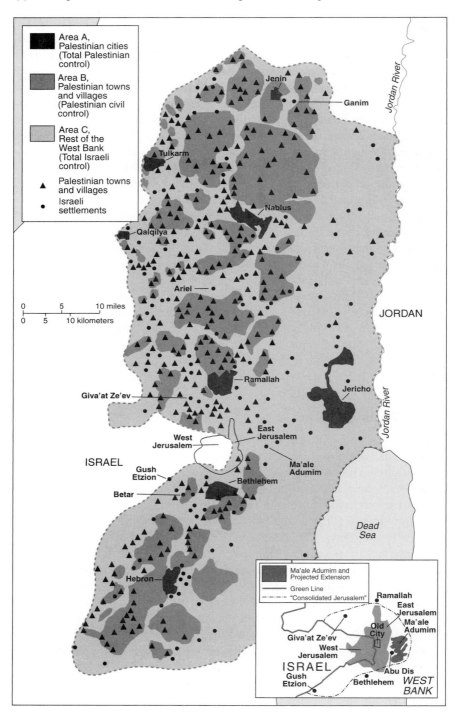

husband's death, a charge he angrily denied. Accounts indicate that at times he cautioned antigovernment demonstrations to avoid using terms such as "traitor," but Netanyahu also lent himself to the rhetoric of the religious right. During the highly charged Knesset debate where Oslo 2 was approved by a narrow 61–59 margin, he declared that Rabin and his government were "removed from Jewish tradition . . . and Jewish values" and were threatening the Jewish homeland, accusations that led Rabin to call Netanyahu a liar. Netanyahu addressed massive demonstrations that displayed posters denigrating Rabin. One depicted him in a Nazi SS uniform and another had the epithet "traitor" emblazoned beneath Rabin's picture with a sniper's sight targeting his head.[32]

Rabin accused Likud of inciting the rightist violence, inspiring similar accusations from Netanyahu and his colleagues (see Figure 10.2). From Netanyahu's perspective, Labor had never condemned those who called Menachem Begin and Ariel Sharon "murderers" in the wake of the 1982 Israeli invasion of Lebanon; therefore, "let those self-righteous, sanctimonious hypocrites not lecture and preach to us now."[33] But whereas Labor charges had been linked to Israeli killing of Arabs, Likud charges of "murderer" implied that Jewish lives were being endangered by a fellow Jew. This was the logic that justified to Yigal Amir his right to kill Rabin.

A devout student of the Torah and rabbinical writings, Amir had served in the army, where he distinguished himself by his militancy. He came to believe that Rabin was a *din rodef*, in Judaic law a Jewish "pursuer" who threatened Jewish lives. A Jew could presumably kill another Jew whose actions placed Jewish lives in danger. This concept, never prominent in Jewish legal tradition, had been revived by extremist Orthodox rabbis, most in the settlements or in Brooklyn, as part of halachic or religiously sanctioned rulings that legitimized action. The fact that other rabbis challenged this interpretation did not lessen its impact among the militants who believed that Rabin had to be stopped. The Hamas bomb attacks in the summer had confirmed to the rightists that Rabin's policies threatened Jewish lives, and they were a foretaste of what could occur if more land were given up.[34]

◀ Map 10.2 ■ The West Bank and Jerusalem in Light of the Oslo 2 Accord, Showing Areas A, B, C, and Likely Areas of Israeli Retention According to Settlement Patterns around Jerusalem (inset map). Compare this to Map 11.1, which illustrates Ehud Barak's offer at Camp David for the West Bank, and Map 11.3, which outlines the path of the Israeli barrier between Israel and the West Bank Palestinians.

This map illustrates the nature of Israeli settlement patterns and the area Israel retained in Area C after the Oslo 2 Accord. The inset map, indicating settlement patterns in the north-south arc around Jerusalem, from Giva'at Ze'ev around Ma'ale Adumim south to Gush Etzion, suggested intentions expanded upon at Camp David by Barak, who sought Israeli control from Jerusalem east to the Jordan River, barring contiguity of any Palestinian state and totally isolating Bethlehem and Ramallah from each other. Although further compromises were offered at Camp David and later (Map 11.2), current projects fostered by the Sharon government suggest that Likud in 2004 envisages a Palestinian state more along the lines of Areas A and B, as shown in this map.

The political repercussions of the Rabin assassination last to this day. While many in Labor, along with the Rabin family, still view Likud and other rightist politicians as bearing responsibility, the latter suggest a state conspiracy to stage a fake murder attempt and to taint Likud with responsibility, undermining opposition to Oslo 2. They point to the revelation that Avishai Raviv, the founder of a radical settler group called Eyal, who had launched a number of extremist ventures against Arabs and Rabin, was actually an informer for the Shin Bet government security service. Raviv had been one of those who had paraded with posters of Rabin in the SS uniform. The animosity between the camps was such that on the first anniversary of Rabin's death Netanyahu, as prime minister, refused to declare it a national day of mourning; Leah Rabin then denied him permission to speak at the ceremony[35] (see Figure 10.3).

FROM RABIN TO NETANYAHU: THE PERES GOVERNMENT AND LIKUD'S VICTORY, NOVEMBER 1995–MAY 1996

Shimon Peres succeeded Rabin as prime minister. He retained the defense ministry for himself and appointed Ehud Barak as foreign minister. Barak, a former Israel Defense Force chief of staff, had publicly criticized the security aspects of the Oslo 2 agreements with the Palestinians. Reluctant to campaign in Rabin's shadow, Peres initially resisted advice to advance the November 1996 date set for new elections, but he stressed that he too could guarantee Israel's security and reassured Israelis that the settlements would remain.[36]

With respect to the Interim Agreement, Peres implemented its terms swiftly. Israeli forces withdrew from the six major population centers in Area A and from the over 400 villages of Area B by the end of 1995. Elections for the Palestinian self-government authority were held on January 20, 1996, thus completing procedures first outlined in the 1993 Declaration of Principles. Peres then

◀ Figure 10.2 ▪ A Right-Wing Israeli Demonstration against the 1995 Interim Agreement (Oslo 2), October 5, 1995

Right-wing Israelis mounted massive demonstrations against the Interim Agreement and its planned withdrawals from parts of the West Bank. This gathering in Jerusalem drew over 10,000 protesters, either calling for Rabin's dismissal, as shown, or expressing more extreme views.

The two placards in Hebrew toward the rear of the group represent the views of the Molodet (Homeland) Party, which was ideologically to the right of Likud and an offshoot of the outlawed Kach Party of the late Meir Kahane. The sign on the right portrays the Molodet symbol and the slogan "Homeland Not for Sale," meaning that they reject the slogan "land for peace" with reference to the West Bank. The placard on the left declares "Only Transfer Will Bring Peace," "transfer" meaning the removal of all Arabs from the West Bank to make it purely Jewish land. Likud leader Binyamin Netanyahu addressed this and similar rallies, and the Likud banner is displayed in Hebrew lettering at the front of the photo. Though Likud did not officially espouse the policy of transfer, Netanyahu did bring Molodet into his coalition when he became prime minister, as did Ariel Sharon when elected prime minister in 2001.

Figure 10.3 ■ Jordan's King Husayn at Yitzhak Rabin's Funeral, November 1995

Those who mourned Rabin were not only Israelis committed to the peace process and a potential two-state solution. They also included Arab heads of state who had seen in Rabin an opportunity to resolve long-standing differences. King Husayn, in particular, had had a personal rapport with Rabin that preceded the signing of the 1994 Israel-Jordan peace treaty. Queen Noor is next to Husayn. To her right is Shimon Peres, who briefly succeeded Rabin as prime minister. Former President Jimmy Carter appears behind and between Peres and Queen Noor.

announced, on February 11, that he had advanced elections to late May. The optimistic premises underlying his decision would be undermined by events related to the aftermath of the Rabin assassination.

In early January, Peres had approved the assassination of Yahya Ayyash, "The Engineer." Israeli authorities considered Ayyash the mastermind of a string of Hamas-sponsored suicide bombings including those of July and August 1995. There were several domestic political reasons for Peres's decision. First, he hoped to display his strong stance on security, emulating Rabin, who had apparently approved the assassination of Islamic Jihad head, Fathi Shiqaqi, in Malta the previous October. Also, he was using the retirement of the former director of Shin Bet, Carmi Gillon, to provide him with a memento of achievement. Killing Ayyash would bolster Shin Bet's reputation, which had been tarnished by its failure to protect Rabin.

The press releases of the time caught the conflicting atmosphere of exultation and alarm. While the government proclaimed that "the fact that [Ayyash] is no longer alive will help us to continue on the road to peace without terror," intelligence experts warned of "a dynamic of rage in the Arab street" and that the assassination would trigger more terrorism. Israeli papers carried photos of massive Hamas demonstrations where the participants chanted "prepare the coffins, we are coming."[37]

The Ayyash killing ended a period of apparent truce between Hamas and Israel. There had been no bombings after August 1995, and in the aftermath of Oslo 2, Rabin had permitted Hamas members from Gaza to visit Sudan to discuss the possibility of forming a political party within the framework of the forthcoming elections for the Palestinian Council. Hamas representatives participated in Israeli-Palestinian talks in December.[38]

Peres's authorization of Ayyash's killing proved disastrous. Despite intense security efforts, four major suicide bombings occurred within a week, from February 25 to March 4, all but one in Jerusalem or Tel Aviv; at least 59 died and 214 were wounded. These terrorist attacks, initiated two weeks after Peres's call for new elections, enabled Netanyahu, the Likud candidate for prime minister, to quickly overcome Peres's 15 percent lead in opinion polls. Then, as hostilities with Hizbollah heated up in southern Lebanon, Peres ordered an incursion into Lebanon, linked to a full-scale artillery and air assault, the latter reaching as far as Beirut.

Israeli analysts labeled Operation "Grapes of Wrath" as a "domestically oriented operation" intended to impress the Israeli electorate. It became a public relations disaster when an Israeli artillery barrage killed over one hundred Lebanese and wounded an equal number as they took shelter in a United Nations compound. In the midst of these developments, Peres effectively suspended the peace process, blaming Arafat for the February–March bomb attacks and imposing a total closure on all towns and villages in the West Bank.[39]

The May 1996 elections saw two ballots: one an American-style election for prime minister as national leader, which focused on personality and exploited television; the second, an election of party candidates for the Knesset. Netanyahu, familiar with American television from his stint as Israel's ambassador to the United Nations, used the media far more skillfully than did Peres. Still, his margin of victory was less than 1 percent of the vote, or 30,000 ballots. In forming his cabinet, Netanyahu relied on five parties in addition to Likud, four of them religious, introducing a secular-religious mix that would prove divisive. The religious party, Shas, clashed with Yisrael Ba'aliya, which represented Russian immigrants, over control of the interior ministry. More than a quarter of recent Russian immigrants were not Jewish, a practice violently opposed by Shas but backed by Yisrael Ba'aliya as a means of boosting its electoral chances.[40]

THE NETANYAHU GOVERNMENT, JUNE 1996–JULY 1999

Binyamin Netanyahu was the product of a Revisionist Zionist household. His father had worked with Vladimir Jabotinsky against Labor Zionism during the Mandate. Though born in Israel, Netanyahu spent many of his formative years in the United States, where he attended college and developed close ties with right-wing Jewish groups.

Netanyahu condemned the Oslo Accords and sought to postpone, if not avoid, Israel's implementation of previous commitments as his settler constituency demanded. He pledged that he would hand over no more land to the Arabs, a promise that would return to haunt him. Openly hostile to Arafat, he had declared during the campaign that he would never meet with him, a vow Netanyahu was able to keep for four months.

Reciprocity and Confrontation

Netanyahu adopted a policy of "reciprocity" toward the Palestinians. Israel would fulfill its obligations only when the Palestinians had fulfilled theirs as judged by the Netanyahu government, an approach that would bring him into direct confrontation with the Clinton administration. His relations with the United States had previously been tarnished when, as deputy foreign minister in Yitzhak Shamir's government in 1990, he had charged that U.S. policy "was built upon a foundation of distortion and lies." James Baker, then secretary of state, had banned him from the State Department.[41] Equally problematic was President Clinton's openly expressed preference for Peres during the campaign, creating tension between the two governments that was exacerbated by Clinton's own domestic travails in 1997 and 1998, which culminated in unsuccessful impeachment hearings in January 1999.

Perhaps emboldened by the furor over Clinton's personal behavior, Netanyahu openly asserted his opposition to American peace proposals and received acclaim in the U.S. Congress, where an alliance of pro-Israeli supporters, Jewish or conservative Christian, aligned with the Republican opposition in seeking to undermine a weakened president. Netanyahu worked closely with American fundamentalists. When a bill was presented to the Knesset to outlaw Christian missionary activity in Israel, Netanyahu opposed it, to the consternation of his Orthodox supporters. Among those who had petitioned Netanyahu to scuttle the bill was Senator Jesse Helms, chair of the Senate Foreign Relations Committee. Netanyahu's campaign manager had previously worked for Helms. Jerry Falwell's Moral Majority and Pat Robertson's Christian Coalition were also staunch supporters of Israel's retention of the territories and lobbied Congress on Netanyahu's behalf.[42] Weakened by Clinton's scandals, the administration could do little in response as the American Israel Public Affairs Committee worked with the Israeli embassy to mobilize senatorial opposition to administration efforts to restart negotiations.

Netanyahu was confrontational in his initial approaches to the Palestinians and to his Arab neighbors, Jordan and Syria. Rabin had been close to an agreement in principle with Syria on key issues, including withdrawal from the Golan Heights, the precise boundaries still to be determined. Netanyahu assumed that the Assad regime would relinquish the Golan Heights, a serious misreading of the Syrian perspective. His first statement on Syria guaranteed stalemate. After declaring that Israel would conduct negotiations with Syria "without preconditions," he then affirmed that "retaining Israeli sovereignty over the Golan will be the basis for an arrangement with Syria," establishing a precondition that challenged the essential Syrian demands.[43]

As for Jordan, Netanyahu, like Rabin and Peres, saw King Husayn's interest in East Jerusalem and the West Bank as creating a mutuality of interests with Israel. But whereas Rabin had seemed to move toward acceptance of Palestinian statehood in the West Bank, Netanyahu, like Peres, viewed Jordan as the "linch-pin" in his strategy toward the Palestinians, believing that he and King Husayn shared a "strategic convergence" against Palestinian statehood. Husayn was initially amenable. He was the only Arab leader to publicly welcome Netanyahu's election and he appeared to accept Israel's lifting of the freeze on settlement expansion with equanimity.[44]

Conversely, Netanyahu's decision to end the four-year freeze on new settlements without consulting Arafat put the Palestinians on notice that the Oslo 2 process had changed. Netanyahu's government began subjecting the Palestinian leader to petty harassments, such as forcing his helicopter to hover for forty-five minutes before being given permission to land. Arafat accused Netanyahu of having declared war on the Palestinian people.[45]

Netanyahu's unilateralism damaged his relations with Jordan. On September 24, 1996, Israel opened a second entrance to the Hasmonean Tunnel, an archaeological site previously accessible only from near the Western Wall. Previous Israeli leaders had delayed taking this step in order to assuage Palestinian sentiments because the second entrance was in the heart of East Jerusalem, close to the Dome of the Rock. Netanyahu apparently ordered its opening as an act of defiance in response to Egyptian as well as Palestinian criticism of his government's behavior. But his actions also infuriated King Husayn, who had met with Netanyahu's chief foreign policy adviser two days prior to the tunnel opening but had not been forewarned.

The Hasmonean Tunnel opening had serious consequences not only for future Israeli-Arab relations but also for government-military trust within Israel. The territories exploded in riots that equaled if not exceeded the intensity of the intifada; eighty-six Arabs and fifteen Israeli troops died. Israel sent tanks and helicopters into the West Bank for the first time since 1967, and Palestinian security forces engaged Israeli soldiers in firefights. King Husayn, reacting to the Israeli decision, in October met Arafat in Jericho, where he declared his pleasure to be in the land of Palestine on his first visit to the West Bank since 1967. Within Israel, high-ranking military officials objected to having been left out of a decision that had serious security consequences and cost the lives of Israeli troops. Netanyahu did not trust senior officers, whom he believed to have ties to Labor leaders, evidenced when troops were ordered to appear without weapons at a review by the prime minister in early October.[46] On the other hand, the fallout from the Hasmonean Tunnel debacle spurred efforts to rescue the Oslo process, culminating in a modified agreement on Hebron, signed in January 1997.

The Hebron Agreement, January 1997

Hebron is sacred to Jews and Muslims. The Jew's Tomb of the Patriarchs is the Muslim's Mosque of Abraham, a site of Muslim worship since the seventh century. Following the 1967 war, Israeli authorities converted part of the mosque into a place where Jews could worship. Jews and Muslims had prayed in the same complex, divided into separate prayer areas, until the murder of twenty-nine Arabs by Baruch Goldstein in 1994. Hebron had been the target of Gush Emunim's first efforts to establish a Jewish presence in the West Bank, in this case to restore the Jewish community evacuated in 1929 following the Western Wall riots and the killing of many Hebron Jews. A focal point of militant Zionists, 450 Jews lived in Hebron in five fortified compounds, protected by Israeli troops, and surrounded by an Arab population of nearly 200,000. Most were followers of the late Meir Kahane and were openly dedicated to the ouster of Arabs from the occupied territories. Their fate became a focal point of militant Zionism as embraced by Netanyahu.

The essence of the Hebron arrangement was the division of the city into two areas defined as H-1 and H-2. H-1, the larger area, was handed over to the Palestinians, who assumed governing responsibilities as in other Area A cities. Israeli troops withdrew from H-1 but remained in H-2, the Old City, where they oversaw security arrangements for the 450 settlers in the midst of the 20,000 Arab residents of that quarter. In H-2, the Palestinian Council technically had authority resembling that in Area B areas for the Arab residents, that is, for their domestic security needs in dealing with other Arabs. However, Israeli soldiers retained responsibility for the Jewish residents and for overall security in cases involving Arabs and Jews.[47]

Provisions for the H-2 area were designed to separate Arabs and Jews, but they created a divided city with barbed wire defining key areas. Arabs in the Palestinian-controlled area still confronted Israeli checkpoints when leaving the city. The Jewish settlers, funded by the government and private donors abroad, had their own access routes to Qiryat Arba and to Israeli bypass roads, guarded by their own security services as well as by satellite navigational systems in their cars that could be tracked by Israeli police. The highly militant settlers in H-2 felt free to roam the area and to scrawl graffiti calling for the death or expulsion of Hebron's Arabs. Riots erupted over a poster on which the prophet Muhammad was portrayed as a pig writing the Quran, a deliberate insult to Muslims. The woman responsible for the poster came from Qiryat Arba outside of Hebron.[48]

Official American optimism over the Hebron Accord masked Arab and Jewish unease at its implications. For many Arabs, the continued presence of a

Jewish community in a city supposedly ceded to the Palestinians was an ominous harbinger of the future. A small group of militant settlers could serve as a pretext for a continued Israeli military presence, which could override Palestinian authority, precisely what Ehud Barak would propose at Camp David in July 2000. In contrast, the settlers opposed giving any authority to Arabs in Hebron and Likud stalwarts, such as Yitzhak Shamir, condemned Netanyahu for abandoning land in the "Jewish heartland."[49]

Arafat, encouraged by U.S. negotiators, had conceded the fact of continued Jewish settlement in Hebron in order to encourage further momentum for the peace process. The Palestinians committed themselves to renewed efforts against terrorist groups, to strengthening security cooperation with Israeli forces, and to completing revisions of the Palestinian National Charter by removing clauses calling for Israel's destruction. In return, Israel promised to make three further redeployments by August 1998, the first in March 1997. Israel also promised to enter negotiations on other issues related to Oslo 2 — for example, safe passage for Palestinians between Gaza and the West Bank and the openings of an airport and a seaport in Gaza.

Netanyahu referred to the Hebron Agreement as a victory, asserting that the Jewish community would always exist there under Israel's authority. Equally significant was U.S. support of Israeli claims that they could decide the area and scope of further redeployments unilaterally, confirmed in a private letter to Netanyahu from outgoing Secretary of State Warren Christopher, who also declared in it that "a hallmark of U.S. policy remains a commitment to work cooperatively to seek to meet the security needs that Israel identifies." This promise seemed to support Netanyahu's argument that Israel's security needs as identified by him required no further concessions, contradicting the official American position.[50]

With these letters in hand, Netanyahu proposed in March 1997 an initial redeployment of 9 percent of the West Bank. Arafat denounced the offer as insufficient, and Netanyahu's settler backers excoriated him for agreeing to any more handovers. Coinciding with this announcement was the Israeli decision to proceed with construction in Har Homa, a Jewish name for Arab land outside East Jerusalem. Arab riots erupted in Hebron and Bethlehem, and Jordan's King Husayn accused Netanyahu of seeking to destroy the peace process.[51]

Then, on March 21, a suicide bombing in Tel Aviv killed three Israelis and wounded dozens. The first bombing in a year, it foreshadowed further violence in April when a settler killed a Palestinian in Hebron, causing protests in which three Palestinians were killed by Israeli troops and over one hundred were wounded. Netanyahu immediately blamed Arafat and the Palestinian Authority for the bombing, suspended consideration of redeployments for the foreseeable future, and pursued expansion of the Jewish presence in East Jerusalem. Two more suicide bombings, in July and September, killed 25 and wounded at least 330 Israelis.[52]

Amidst this turmoil, outgoing U.S. ambassador Martin Indyk called the peace process a "nightmare," attributing blame to Israel as well as to the Palestinians. In Israel, Likud triumphantly labeled the Oslo process "dead and buried" while Labor warned the rightists not to abandon it. Secretary of State Madeleine Albright visited Israel and challenged both sides: Arafat should do more to try to control terrorism, but Israel should halt its continuing "provocations" of settlement expansion and land confiscation, which encouraged retaliatory violence. In reply, Netanyahu openly defied Albright during her visit, announcing a new expansion of 300 buildings in settlements.[53]

Palestinian Communal Tensions and Charges of Corruption

With no redeployments imminent, Arafat seemed helpless in the face of Israeli settlement expansion. Arab rage at these developments in the summer of 1997 was fanned by the behavior of officials of the Palestinian Authority and by the manner in which its security forces treated fellow Palestinians who had been brought into custody. As noted, Arafat had surrounded himself with those who had been with him in exile, men familiar with PLO policies and activities. Many had accrued wealth through their positions and built villas in Gaza, the area where Palestinian offices were housed. Their residences towered over the hovels of most Gazans, spreading resentment and rumors of corruption. A panel appointed by the PA recommended that Arafat dismiss his entire cabinet and indict several members on charges of exploitation of their offices. Among those named were Nabil Shaath, who had negotiated the 1993 Oslo Accord; Yasir Abed Rabbo, Arafat's chief spokesperson; and Civil Affairs Minister Jamal Tarifi. Tarifi, a contractor, was accused of having a monopoly on cement imported from Jordan and was suspected of profiting from building or expanding the very Israeli settlements his leader termed illegal.[54]

Palestinians from the territories called their counterparts from outside "the Tunisians," referring to the decade in which the PLO had had its residence in Tunisia following its ouster from Lebanon. Their wealth and their lifestyles, including the way their wives dressed, were considered too European and immodest by many local Muslims and drew extensive criticism, recalling incidents during the intifada. At that time, many women who had participated in the revolt had been stoned for not wearing headdresses, especially in Gaza, the Hamas stronghold.

Also disturbing was the behavior of Arafat's security forces. Rivalries existed among factions that sought to preserve spheres of interest against one another as well as against Israel. Israeli leaders wanted strong Palestinian security and intelligence forces; not only would this contribute to Israeli security, but in Rabin's words, the Palestinians would "rule by their own methods." They could operate without the oversight to which Israeli troops might be subjected. Several Palestinians died within twenty-four hours of being taken into custody by Palestinian security forces. Riots broke out in Gaza in July 1997 when the fourteenth fatality was announced. The dead Palestinian had been arrested by a security officer because he had confronted the officer's wife, a "Tunisian," and criticized her dress as immoral, demanding that she dress more modestly.[55]

With Arafat's position so precarious and the results of the peace process so meager, he and his cohort were unlikely to tolerate criticism. Palestinian academics or lawyers who challenged the Palestinian Authority or openly criticized corruption were often jailed for months without charges and, in certain cases, assassination attempts appear to have been made. Yet many within as well as outside the Palestinian community hesitated to criticize the Palestinian leader too sharply. Arafat was the only personage able to sign agreements with Israel and to oversee the rivalries that simmered among Palestinian factions under the umbrella of the Palestinian Authority.[56]

The Mashal Affair

Ironically, it was Netanyahu, at the apparent height of his power, who helped Arafat regain stronger American and Arab backing. Hamas cells in Amman, possibly more militant than most of those in the territories, appeared to be behind many of the suicide bombings. In late September 1997, Netanyahu authorized a Mossad assassination of Khalid Mashal, a Hamas official in Amman, by injection of poison. The attempt, carried out on a city street, seriously wounded but failed to kill Mashal. Two Israeli agents were jailed in Amman and others took refuge in the Israeli embassy. Having left King Husayn uninformed of the plan, Netanyahu then sent an emissary to ask Husayn to free the captured agents, the first the king had heard of the plot.

The ensuing crisis nearly destroyed Israel's ties to Jordan. Netanyahu initially refused Husayn's request for the poison's antidote; he relented only after Husayn threatened to close the Israeli embassy. Mashal recovered, but Jordanian-Israeli relations did not. Husayn closed the Mossad office in Amman that he had tolerated, and Netanyahu was forced to release the jailed leader of Hamas, Shaykh Ahmad Yasin, who returned in triumph to Gaza, where he was embraced by Husayn as well as Arafat.

The Mashal assassination blunder humiliated King Husayn, already viewed by his subjects as far too tolerant of Israeli settlement expansion and activities in East Jerusalem at a time when there had been no economic benefits to Jordan from the Israeli-Jordanian peace pact. In Israel, cabinet members hurled recriminations at each other over who had authorized the failed plot.[57] Netanyahu now found himself beset by fissures within his own coalition as well as external criticism. The Clinton administration suddenly asserted itself, demanding Israeli proposals for the three further redeployments scheduled in the Hebron pact. The administration withstood Israeli-backed congressional pressures that included House Speaker Newt Gingrich's labeling of Madeleine Albright as "the agent of the Palestinians." Netanyahu's flirtation with the idea of further withdrawals during the first half of 1998 triggered posters sponsored by the Hebron-based

Kach group that depicted the prime minister in an Arab headdress with the word "liar" underneath, recalling the campaign that led to Rabin's assassination. By autumn 1998, tensions within Israel seemed to approach those between Palestinians and Israelis.[58]

The Wye Memorandum and the Collapse of the Netanyahu Coalition

After nine days of tense negotiations, with Netanyahu repeatedly threatening to abandon the talks, Israel and the Palestinians signed the Wye Memorandum on October 23, 1998, named after the Wye Plantation in Maryland, where the talks were held. This was a last-ditch effort to complete Oslo 2 and initiate the Israeli redeployments specified in the Hebron Protocol.

The Palestinians agreed once more to address the matter of the 1968 Palestinian Charter, which called for destruction of Israel. The Palestine National Council convened in Gaza in December 1998, with President Clinton in attendance, and voted overwhelmingly to remove the offending clause. In return, Israel promised to undertake the three deployments mentioned in the Hebron Accord of January 1997, but Netanyahu then refused to implement them. More successful was Israel's willingness to permit the Palestinians to open an airport already constructed in Gaza and to refrain from searching Arafat's private plane as an exception to their security jurisdiction. Israel considered the airport theirs whatever the facade of Palestinian authority and approved all flight patterns since the airport was in Israeli airspace. Negotiations on the safe passage route from Gaza to the West Bank as outlined in Oslo 2 were promised but remained unfulfilled, as were calls for permanent status negotiations to begin immediately. Finally, Netanyahu sought the release of the convicted American spy for Israel, Jonathan Pollard, as compensation for the three promised deployments but Clinton refused in the face of threats of resignation from his top intelligence personnel, including the head of the CIA. For the U.S. intelligence community, Pollard's spying was "a massive betrayal of national security" to an ally, Israel, which refused to return the documents, having denied for several years that any spying had occurred.[59]

Arafat, desperate for progress, unexpectedly found a new ally in the U.S. government, exasperated by Netanyahu's delaying tactics. The Wye Memorandum called for close Palestinian security liaison with the CIA. In addition to improving Palestinian security procedures, the collaboration also would "confirm the fulfillment of Palestinian responsibilities as the Palestinian Authority carried them out in accordance with the memorandum." Netanyahu could no longer charge the Palestinians with dereliction of duty as an excuse to evade Israeli obligations if the United States was saying otherwise.[60]

The Palestinians met all deadlines. Netanyahu now faced open Likud rebellion and had to rely on the Labor Party to gain Knesset approval of the Wye

Memorandum. Beset from all sides, he suspended the withdrawals scheduled in the Wye document and agreed in late December to call for new elections, scheduled for May 1999. His cabinet had collapsed and his colleagues mocked him in the Knesset.

Jewish Communal Strife: The Culture War Intensifies

In the midst of this acrimony, religious-secular differences in Israel accelerated, particularly in areas occupied by Orthodox and ultra-Orthodox Jews such as Jerusalem. It was not uncommon for Orthodox women as well as men to berate secular women for their style of dress.[61] More serious were the political ramifications stemming from Orthodox Jewish status as the sole representative of Judaism and Israel, and from the demands of religious parties once in office.

Orthodox Judaism had been recognized as the official branch of the Jewish religion when the state of Israel was founded. Orthodox rules governed all aspects of religious life and conversions were deemed valid only if performed by an Orthodox rabbi. These statutes had begun to be challenged by Conservative and Reform Jewish congregations in the United States and in Israel, but their requests for inclusion were rebuffed, often violently, by Orthodox clerics and by their followers. In a confrontation at the Western Wall in June 1997, Orthodox Jews assaulted an American Conservative Jewish delegation, in part because women prayed with the men, hurling epithets—"Nazis" and "Christians"—along with garbage and human excrement from the window of a yeshiva school. Legal challenges to Orthodox dominance began to be approved by the secular Israeli courts. By 1999, Orthodox leaders were condemning members of the Supreme Court as "Jew-haters," and death threats were issued against prominent jurists, triggering open discussion of a "culture war" in Israel. It was not uncommon for the ultra-Orthodox to refer to secular Israelis as "Nazis," and in late 1999 an Orthodox lieutenant in the army was removed from service because he accused Conservative and Reform Jews of complicity in the Holocaust.[62]

Although personally secular, Netanyahu played the Orthodox card for political reasons. The Orthodox parties held twenty-three of the sixty-six seats in the Knesset and were key elements in his cabinet. Although they differed on the fate of the territories, they all shared the goal of ultimately forcing Israel under religious law. Their electoral strength was not limited to the religiously observant; the Shas Party's appeal attracted secular Jews, though mostly of North African origin, who benefited from their social services including neighborhood schools. But these services were expensive, precisely why Shas and other religious parties would enter any coalition in order to vie for control of the education and housing ministries to finance their particular movements. When the head of Shas and former government minister, Aryeh Deri, was convicted of corruption for funneling funds to religious schools and receiving paybacks, Sephardic Jews interpreted the sentence as further secular discrimination against them; Deri accused the prosecution of "blood libel" during the proceedings. Likud electoral success still relied on Sephardic anger at Labor Zionist discrimination, leading Ehud Barak, during the 1999 electoral campaign, to publicly apologize for past injustices committed by the Ashkenazim (Jews of European origin) in hope of attracting traditional Likud votes to Labor.[63]

DOMESTIC AND REGIONAL REALIGNMENTS, DECEMBER 1998–JULY 1999

The period in question witnessed the death of Jordan's King Husayn in February 1999 and the Israeli election campaign leading to Ehud Barak's victory in May and his assumption of office in July—events that suggested significant changes in regional policies.

Husayn's death terminated a forty-six-year reign. Though mourned, he had alienated many Jordanians because of his obvious pride in his close relations with Israeli leaders and his apparent tolerance of Israel's settlement expansion. There was also the continued stagnation of the Jordanian economy; Jordanian per capita income was lower than that of West Bank Arabs. The ongoing American-backed embargo against Iraq, in its eighth year, continued to wreak havoc. Arab Gulf states still refused to renew subsidies suspended as a result of Jordanian sympathy for Iraq during the Gulf War.

Husayn was succeeded by his son Abdullah, who assumed the title King Abdullah II. Abdullah altered his father's priorities. He stressed the need for resolution of the Palestinian question on Palestinian terms in his talks with Israel, a stance favorable to many Jordanians who viewed the Israeli peace treaty as a device intended to "neutralize Jordan so that Israel [could] do what it wants with the Palestinians."[64] Regionally, Abdullah embarked on a course of reconciliation with former enemies of Jordan's peace with Israel. Kuwait and Saudi Arabia immediately reopened their embassies that had been closed since 1991 and restored oil sales and financial assistance.

Within Israel, electoral realignments suggested important changes in the political landscape. Though the Likud Party retained its name, its leading politicians other than Netanyahu left it in order to abandon him and the party. Those on the right, such as Yitzhak Shamir, joined Benny Begin, Menachem's son, in recreating the Herut Party; it entered a coalition with the Molodet Party, which advocated expulsion ("transfer") of Arabs from the territories. Likud moderates formed their own centrist parties, calling Netanyahu a danger to Israel, but they were preempted by the Labor candidate for prime minister, Ehud Barak. He distanced himself from his party by creating a new party that included Labor, "One Israel," to the consternation of old-time Labor ideologues.

Barak's move reflected electoral realities. The new two-stage elections, first used in 1996, had transformed Israeli politics. Israeli governments had always been coalitions but usually with a dominant party—Labor until 1978, the Likud or a combination of Likud and Labor afterward. The new arrangement (which would be abolished in 2001) meant that voters could select their prime minister on ideological grounds and then vote for a Knesset party that fit their specific interests; that party would not necessarily be the party of their choice for prime minister. As a result, numerous single-issue parties acquired sufficient support to gain Knesset seats. Moreover, the identities of the two major parties had altered. Labor was no longer as strongly socialistic, while many Likud members no longer demanded Israeli sovereignty over all the land of Israel. Even Sharon acknowledged the inevitability of a Palestinian state, though seeking to impose conditions that would effectively deny Palestinian sovereignty; for him and for many others, a Palestinian state did not mean Palestinian independence.[65] Despite the campaign invective, which included Barak and Netanyahu accusing each other of resembling Adolf Hitler, there were major differences between the candidates. Netanyahu presented Israel as threatened and as having to impose its will to guarantee security before peace. Barak saw Israel "as the strongest country in a thousand miles," argued that Israel had "to get rid of this ghetto mentality," and wanted to "start with peace [in order to] achieve security."[66] And, in an unusual gesture, Barak offered expressions of sympathy for the Palestinian side by expressing his concern about Palestinian economic hardships; a year earlier, he had created a furor when he said in response to a question that, if born a Palestinian instead of an Israeli, he would have probably joined a "terrorist" organization at the appropriate age.[67] On the other hand, Barak also appealed to settler sentiments; he referred to the West Bank as Judea and Samaria, and avoided the confrontational stance that Rabin had adopted in 1995 in the face of Netanyahu's provocations.

Elected in mid-May, Barak needed seven weeks to form a broad coalition that included seven parties, some at ideological odds with others. With such an unstable government, his optimism regarding his chances for a peace accord would be severely tested.

CONCLUSION

The momentum behind the Oslo peace had faltered by the end of the 1990s. Welcomed with fanfare and hope by many, it had also confronted committed efforts to undermine it by ideologues on both sides, Palestinian and Israeli. But whereas Palestinian opponents, such as Hamas and Islamic Jihad, remained outside circles of power, Israeli opposition, personified in Likud and Netanyahu, took over the reins of government in Israel following the Rabin assassination. Likud militancy in Israel was matched by its supporters in the United States where in 1996 sympathizers drafted a proposal, "Clean Break," which advised Netanyahu to withdraw Israel from the peace process (discussed in Chapter 11). Many of those who approved of "Clean Break's" theses would be appointed to prominent posts in the George W. Bush administration in 2001.

A majority of Israelis and Palestinians supported the idea of a two-state solution, but the reality of ongoing settlement growth in the occupied territories, especially the West Bank, led many Palestinians to question the goals of the peace process and the legitimacy of Yasir Arafat's leadership of the Palestinians. Palestinian distrust of the process was matched by Israeli political disarray following the Rabin killing: the implications for any Israeli leader seeking a peace agreement were clear. Ehud Barak's peace efforts would be circumscribed by his awareness of the militancy of his Israeli opponents, fully committed to retaining the West Bank. This atmosphere of distrust among both Palestinians and Israelis did not bode well for the peace efforts that culminated in the Camp David talks of July 2000.

QUESTIONS FOR CONSIDERATION

1. How did Israelis and Palestinians interpret the letters of "mutual recognition" signed by Yitzhak Rabin and Yasir Arafat?
2. How did Israelis and Palestinians interpret the Oslo 2, or Interim Agreement, signed in September 1995?
3. What was the significance of Area C in the Oslo 2 Accord?
4. How successful were the Clinton administration's attempts to fully implement steps outlined in the Oslo 2 Accord?

CHRONOLOGY

1993   **August 20.** Israel-Palestinian Declaration of Principles initialed in Oslo, Norway.

September 13. Oslo I Accord signing in Washington, D.C.

1994   **February 24.** Baruch Goldstein kills 29 Arabs at Mosque of Abraham in Hebron.

May. Palestinian self-rule begins in Gaza Strip and in Jericho.

October 26. Jordan-Israel Peace Treaty signed.

1995   **August.** Two Hamas-backed suicide bombings kill 10 Israelis, wound over 100.

September 28. Oslo 2 Accord signing in Washington, D.C.

October. Islamic Jihad head, Fathi Shiqaqi, assassinated in Malta by Israel.

November 4. Rabin assassinated by Yigal Amir; succeeded by Shimon Peres as prime minister.

December. Israeli forces withdraw from Area A and Area B as outlined in Oslo 2.

1996   **January 5.** Hamas bomb maker Yahya Ayyash assassinated by Israeli Shin Bet.

January 20. Palestinian Interim Self-Government Authority elected.

February 25–March 4. Four suicide bombings avenge killing of Yahya Ayyash, 59 Israelis killed, 200 wounded.

March–April. Operation "Grapes of Wrath" — Israeli assaults into Lebanon respond to clashes with Hizbollah in south Lebanon.

May. Binyamin Netanyahu elected Israeli prime minister by less than 1 percent of vote; assumes office in June.

1997   **January.** Hebron Redeployment Agreement signed.

1998   **October 23.** Wye Memorandum between Israel and Palestinians signed.

December. Palestine National Council officially removes clauses from 1968 Palestine National Charter calling for Israel's destruction.

1999   **February.** Jordan's King Husayn dies; succeeded by his son, who takes title Abdullah II.

May 18. Ehud Barak elected Israeli prime minister; assumes office in July.

Notes

1. I rely here on the detailed article by Clyde Haberman, "How the Oslo Connection Led to the Middle East Pact: The Secret Peace," *New York Times*, September 5, 1993; and Avi Shlaim, "The Oslo Accord," *Journal of Palestine Studies* 23, 3 (Spring 1994): 24–40.

2. *Journal of Palestine Studies* 23, 1 (Autumn 1993): 115–24, includes the text of the letters and the Declaration of Principles. Numerous memoirs and accounts of the Oslo negotiations have appeared. Among them are Mahmoud Abbas, *Through Secret Channels* (Reading, U.K., 1995), which includes the Palestinian minutes of the talks; Yossi Beilin, *Touching Peace* (London, 1999); Jane Corbin, *Gaza First: The Secret Norway Channel to Peace between Israel and the PLO* (London, 1995); and Uri Savir, *The Process* (New York, 1998). A highly critical Palestinian analysis is Amr G. E. Sabet, "The Peace Process and the Politics of Conflict Resolution," *Journal of Palestine Studies* 27, 4 (Summer 1998): 5–19.

3. *Journal of Palestine Studies* 23, 1 (Autumn 1993): 117. Article VII, and 121, "Specific Agreements and Understandings," Article VII (5), and Annex II.

4. Ibid., 118–19. The term "withdrawal" is used in Article XIV and Annex II, but the term "redeployment" (with a very different connotation) is used in Article XIII. (See Document 10.1.)

5. There were two terminals at crossings. The Israeli terminal for travelers going to Israel was completely under Israeli authority with no Palestinian participation. In the Palestinian terminal there were two wings: for travelers going to Arab areas not under Palestinian authority, an Israeli and a Palestinian officer jointly examined documents; in the other wing, for travelers going to Gaza or Jericho, under Palestinian authority, only a Palestinian customs officer was visible at the checkpoint but he or she had to hand the person's documents through a window to an Israeli officer, who was invisible behind a two-way window. Thus, Palestinian authority appeared established but Israeli authority, though invisible, was final.

6. I rely here on the article by David Makovsky, "Rabin, Peres Diverge," *Jerusalem Post International Edition*, May 15, 1993.

7. Ibid.

8. Ibid.

9. Israel's policies toward East Jerusalem are presented by Amir S. Cheshin, Bill Hutman, and Avi Melamed, *Separate and Unequal: The Inside Story of Israeli Rule in East Jerusalem* (Cambridge, Mass., 1999). For official U.S. statements, the *Journal of Palestine Studies* 23, 1 (Autumn 1993): 159–61, and ibid., 24, 1 (Autumn 1994): 149–51.

10. "Rabin: Let's Talk about Success, Not Failure," interview with David Makovsky, *Jerusalem Post International Edition*, October 16, 1993.

11. "The Oslo Agreement: An Interview with Haydar Abd al-Shafi," *Journal of Palestine Studies* 23, 1 (Autumn 1993): 14–19.

12. "The Oslo Agreement: An Interview with Nabil Shaath," ibid., 5–13; the quote is on p. 10. That the Palestinian Authority would have offices in East Jerusalem was not mentioned in the DOP but in a separate letter from Peres to Arafat.

13. "Militants Vow Holy War," an AP bulletin from Cairo in the *New York Times*, September 3, 1993; John Kifner, "Israel's Parliament Backs P.L.O. Accord, 61–50," ibid., September 24, 1993; Clyde Haberman, "The Priority in Gaza: Israelis and P.L.O. Seem Determined to Fulfill Their Pact Despite Violence," ibid., December 2, 1993.

14. Steven Greenhouse, "Mideast Pact Success May Depend on Billions in Aid to Palestinians," *New York Times*, September 9, 1993; and Clyde Haberman, with Chris Hedges, "Economic Ties Are Regarded as Key to Israeli-P.L.O. Pact," ibid., September 18, 1993. The best study of Gaza and the problems inherent in a peace agreement is Sara Roy, *The Gaza Strip: The Political Economy of Development* (Washington, D.C., 1995).

15. The text of the Israeli-Jordanian Peace Treaty can be found in the *Journal of Palestine Studies* 24, 2 (Winter 1995): 126–43. Article 9, 130, refers to the Muslim shrines in Jerusalem.

16. Clyde Haberman, "Israel and Tunisia to Begin First Official Ties," *New York Times*, October 2, 1994; and Youssef M. Ibrahim, "Israelis and Arabs Meet to Talk Business Deals," ibid., November 1, 1994.

17. The quote is from Thomas Friedman, "Who Can Save Arafat? Arafat," *New York Times*, November 27, 1994. For an overview of Palestinian efforts to create a political infrastructure, see Glenn E. Robinson, *Building a Palestinian State: The Incomplete Revolution* (Bloomington, Ind., 1997).

18. For details on the Hebron massacre and its aftermath, see the *New York Times*, from February 25, 1994, onward: for example, Youssef M. Ibrahim, "Palestinians See a People's Hatred in a Killer's Deed," *New York Times Week in Review*, March 6, 1994. For the Goldstein memorial, see Clyde Haberman, "Hundreds of Jews Gather to Honor Hebron Killer," *New York Times*, April 1, 1994.

19. Staff, "Netanyahu Leaks IDF Position Paper on Concessions to Syria," *Jerusalem Post International Edition*, July 8, 1995; Netanyahu defended himself by arguing that a "patriot" had given him the documents.

20. Gad Ben-Ari, "A Jewish Ayatollah," *Jerusalem Post International Edition*, July 8, 1995; Herb Keinon, "Rabbis: Halacha Forbids Moving Army Bases from Judea, Samaria," ibid., July 22, 1995. The Brooklyn rabbi was Abraham Hecht. For further discussion of Hecht and his rulings, see Michael Karpin and Ina Friedman, *Murder in the Name of God* (New York, 1998), especially 147–50.

21. David Makovsky and Michal Yudelman, "PM: Oslo II Is 'Blow to Greater Israel,'" *Jerusalem Post International Edition*, August 26, 1995; and Sarah Honig, "Netanyahu Asks for Tolerance toward Government," ibid., September 9, 1995.

22. Serge Schmemann, "Lives Are at Stake: So Are Postal Services and Gas Tanks," *New York Times*, September 29, 1995. For the text of the agreement with a summary of its annexes, see "The Peace Process," *Journal of Palestine Studies* 25, 2 (Winter 1996): 123–40.

23. For example, Articles XI, clauses 2 and 3, especially 2e and 3c, and XVII, clauses 1 and 2, especially 2a, ibid., 127–28, 130–31.

24. Liat Collins, "Rabin Offers Vision for Final Settlement: Oslo 2 Gains Knesset Approval 61–59," *Jerusalem Post International Edition*, October 7, 1995; and the summary of Rabin's address in *Journal of Palestine Studies* 25, 2 (Winter 1996): 137–39.

25. Uri Savir, *The Process*, 174–204; Savir was the chief Israeli negotiator.

26. Serge Schmemann, "An Anxious West Bank City Awaits the Fine Print," *New York Times*, September 27, 1995, referring to Ramallah.

27. Deborah Sontag, "New Path of Israeli Settlers: Moving toward the Mainstream," *New York Times*, July 21, 1999; Herb Keinon, "Divide and Dismantle," *Jerusalem Post International Edition*, November 12, 1999. Both articles focus on Ma'ale Adumim, referring to Ehud Barak's strategy once in office.

28. Articles XI, clause 1, and XXXI, clause 7. See *Journal of Palestine Studies* 25, 2 (Winter 1996): 127, 134; Serge Schmemann, "Telling Vote: Most Israeli Jews Are More Fearful Than Hopeful over Peace," *New York Times*, June 2, 1996, notes that Israel was "at least as culpable" as the Palestinians in failing to fulfill obligations.

29. See excerpts of Rabin's speech to the Knesset on Oslo 2, *Journal of Palestine Studies* 25, 2, 137–39; and David Makovsky interview with Rabin, "Past the Point of No Return," *Jerusalem Post International Edition*, September 30, 1995. Peres's quote comes from his *The New Middle East* (London, 1994), 19–20.

30. Karpin and Friedman, *Murder in the Name of God*, 75–76.

31. Joel Greenberg, "Settlers Angrily Denounce, Protest Accord in Hebron," *New York Times*, September 29, 1995; and Sarah Honig, "Opposition Stages Its Own Signing, Declares Loyalty to Land of Israel," *Jerusalem Post International Edition*, October 7, 1995.

32. Collins, "Rabin Offers Vision," and Herb Keinon, "Massive Oslo 2 Protests Flood Zion Square," *Jerusalem Post International Edition,* October 14, 1995. For photographs of Rabin on posters, see Karpin and Friedman, *Murder in the Name of God,* between 148–49.

33. Sarah Honig and Batsheva Tsur, "Rabin: I Am Not Afraid of Being Attacked," *Jerusalem Post International Edition,* October 21, 1995.

34. In addition to the sources in note 20, see the important articles by John Kifner, "Israelis Investigate Far Right: May Crack Down on Speech," *New York Times,* November 8, 1995; "Zeal of Rabin's Assassins Springs from Rabbis of Religious Right," ibid., November 12, 1995; and especially "With a Handshake, Rabin's Fate Was Sealed," ibid., November 19, 1995. An important source for these articles and the subject in general is Ehud Sprinzak, *Brother against Brother: Violence and Extremism in Israeli Politics from "Altalena" to the Rabin Assassination* (New York, 1999).

35. In addition to sources cited in note 38, see Liat Collins and Sarah Honig, "Likud Asks 'Slanderers' to Apologize," *Jerusalem Post International Edition,* December 2, 1995; Joel Greenberg, "Year after Rabin Fell, Israel Is No Closer to Unity," *New York Times,* October 25, 1996; and Dan Izenberg, "Rabin Family Raises Specter of Conspiracy," *Jerusalem Post International Edition,* November 12, 1999. Raviv was indicted as an accomplice in 1999.

36. Serge Schmemann, "Israel's Leader Declines to Call Early Elections," *New York Times,* November 8, 1995; and David Makovsky, "Reality and Rhetoric: An Interview with Shimon Peres," *Jerusalem Post International Edition,* August 26, 1995.

37. On the assassination and its link to Gillon's resignation, see Joel Greenberg, "Head of Israel's Shin Bet Security Service Resigns over Rabin Case," *New York Times,* January 9, 1996; and Avishai Margalit, "The Chances of Shimon Peres," *New York Review of Books,* May 9, 1996, 18–23. On the Arab reaction and Israeli expectation of reprisals, see Serge Schmemann, "Killing of Bomb Maker Unites Palestinian Factions," *New York Times,* January 10, 1996; and Staff, "Hamas Leaders Swear Revenge for Assassination," *Jerusalem Post International Edition,* January 20, 1996.

38. Steve Rodan, "The Talks Trap," ibid., May 18, 1996, notes Hamas involvement in talks; John Kifner, "Aims and Arms: Tactics in a Holy War," *New York Times,* March 15, 1996, discusses the links between the Ayyash assassination and the subsequent bombings. For the Hamas delegation to Sudan, see "Chronology," *Journal of Palestine Studies* 25, 2 (Winter 1996): 173.

39. Serge Schmemann, "2 Suicide Bombings in Israel Kill 25 and Hurt 77, Highest Such Toll," and idem, "Israel Rage Rises as Bomb Kills 19, Imperiling Peace," *New York Times,* February 26 and March 4, 1996, respectively. For the domestic implications of the campaign and the effort to avoid killing Hizbollah officials, see articles in the April 27, 1996, edition of *Jerusalem Post International Edition,* especially Steve Rodan, "Grape Juice in a Wine Glass: Israel's Attack on Hizbollah Operations in Lebanon Never Intended to Do Any Harm."

40. Asher Arian, *The Second Republic: Politics in Israel* (Chatham, N.J., 1998), for example, 104–7, 218–26, 242–52; Ira Sharkansky, *Policy Making in Israel: Routines for Simple Problems and Coping with the Complex* (Pittsburgh, 1997), 39–45; Don Peretz and Gideon Doron, "Israel's 1996 Elections: A Second Political Earthquake," *The Middle East Journal* 50, 4 (Autumn 1996): 529–46; and Joel Greenberg, "In Israeli Votes, Orthodox Rabbis Are Key Brokers," *New York Times,* May 26, 1996.

41. David Makovsky, "The Candidate Becomes the Leader," *Jerusalem Post International Edition,* June 15, 1996; and James A. Baker, *The Politics of Diplomacy: Revolution, War and Peace, 1989–1992* (New York, 1995), 129.

42. Joseph Berger, "He Had Pataki's Ear and Now He Has Netanyahu's," *New York Times,* May 26, 1996; Haim Shapiro, "Gov't Condemns Antimissionary Bill," *Jerusalem Post International Edition,* July 12, 1997; and "Chronology," *Journal of Palestine Studies* 27, 3 (Spring 1998): 182. Helms and Benjamin Gilman, head of the House Committee on International Relations, repeatedly held up funding allotments owed to the Palestinian Authority under the 1993 Oslo Accord.

43. Douglas Jehl, "Rabin Showed Willingness to Give Golan Back to Syrians," *New York Times,* August 29, 1997; and Itamar Rabinovich, *The Brink of Peace: The Israeli-Syrian Negotiations* (Princeton, N.J., 1998). For Likud guidelines for talks, David Makovsky, "We Never Gave Up

Belief: Interview with Binyamin Netanyahu," *Jerusalem Post International Edition*, May 25, 1996; and Staff, "Netanyahu Upbeat on Syria: Offers Lebanon First, Drops Rabin's Pledge to U.S. on Golan," ibid., August 17, 1996.

44. Ibid. This article on Netanyahu and Syria also quotes Husayn criticizing the negative reaction to Israel's removal of the freeze on settlements.

45. David Makovsky, "Bibi's First 100 Days," *Jerusalem Post International Edition*, October 15, 1996; and "Chronology," *Journal of Palestine Studies* 26, 2 (Winter 1997): 168–69.

46. Arieh O'Sullivan, "State of Emergency Declared in Territories: 11 Soldiers, over 30 Palestinians, Die in Gun Battles," *Jerusalem Post International Edition*, October 5, 1996. On Netanyahu's distrust of the military, see Steve Rodan, "Shaky Soloist," ibid., November 30, 1996.

47. The text of the Hebron Agreement and relevant letters can be found in the *Journal of Palestine Studies* 26, 3 (Spring 1997): 131–39. Joint patrols were stipulated for areas of H-1 overlooking the Old City.

48. Deborah Sontag, "In Hebron, Peace Accord's Bitter Fruit," *New York Times*, October 15, 1998; Serge Schmemann, "Israeli Wounds 6 Arabs in Hebron Rampage," ibid., January 2, 1997; Schmemann, "Palestinians Protest over Arafat and Security Forces," ibid., July 2, 1997; and Schmemann, "A Day in Court for Israeli Who Enraged Muslims," ibid., July 19, 1997.

49. Douglas Jehl, "After 30 Years, the Palestinians Take Over in Hebron," *New York Times*, January 18, 1997; and Sarah Honig, "Shamir Condemns Hebron Deal," *Jerusalem Post International Edition*, January 25, 1997.

50. Serge Schmemann, "Israeli Parliament Approves Hebron Withdrawal Accord," *New York Times*, January 18, 1997; and Netanyahu and Dennis Ross statements on the Hebron Protocol and Israeli obligations, *Journal of Palestine Studies* 26, 3 (Spring 1997): 141–45.

51. Serge Schmemann, "A New Struggle for Jerusalem," *New York Times*, March 2, 1997; and Schmemann, "King Hussein Rebukes Netanyahu for 'Intent to Destroy' Peace Plan," ibid., March 12, 1997.

52. Serge Schmemann, "4 Are Killed in Suicide Bombing in Tel Aviv," *New York Times*, March 22, 1997; Joel Greenberg, "3 Palestinians Killed in Clashes with Israelis in Hebron," ibid., April 9, 1997; Schmemann, "Suicide Bombers Kill 17 in a Jerusalem Market," ibid., July 31, 1997.

53. Michal Yudelman, "Indyk: 'Oslo Dream Looks Like a Nightmare,'" *Jerusalem Post International Edition*, October 4, 1997; Steven Erlanger, "A Candid Albright Challenges Israel and Palestinians," *New York Times*, September 13, 1997; and Steven Lee Myers, "In Rebuke, Albright Insists That Netanyahu Hurt Talks," ibid., September 26, 1997.

54. Serge Schmemann, "Corruption Panel Urges Arafat to Dismiss His Cabinet," ibid., July 30, 1997.

55. Serge Schmemann, "Palestinians Protest over Arafat and Gaza Security Forces," ibid., July 2, 1997. For the factionalism within Palestinian security forces, see Graham Usher, "The Politics of Internal Security: The Palestinian Authority's New Security Services," in George Giacaman and Dag Jorund Lonning, eds., *After Oslo: New Realities, Old Problems* (Chicago, 1998), 146–61.

56. Joel Greenberg, "Palestinians Free Professor Jailed over an Exam," *New York Times*, December 3, 1997; and William A. Orme, Jr., "7 Palestinians Arrested for Criticism of Arafat," ibid., November 29, 1999.

57. Serge Schmemann, "Netanyahu Defiantly Defending Botched Assassination Attempt," ibid., October 6, 1997; Alan Cowell, "The Daring Attack That Blew Up in Israel's Face," ibid., October 15, 1997; and Douglas Jehl, "Netanyahu Enmeshed in Fiasco, Panels Told," ibid., November 5, 1997.

58. For Gingrich's comments, see Schmemann, "Gingrich, Darling of Israeli Right, Tangos with Arafat," ibid., May 28, 1998; see also Staff photo, "The Liar," *Jerusalem Post International Edition*, June 13, 1998.

59. "The Wye Memorandum," *Journal of Palestine Studies* 28, 2 (Winter 1999): 135–46; James Risen and Steven Erlanger, "C.I.A. Chief Vowed to Quit If Clinton Freed Israeli Spy," *New York*

Times, November 11, 1998; and Tim Weiner, "U.S. Now Tells of Much Deeper Damage by Pollard Than Thought," ibid.

60. "The Wye Memorandum," 139–40.

61. Tracy Wilkinson, "Modesty Squad Dressing Down Secular Israelis," *Los Angeles Times*, August 9, 1999.

62. Serge Schmemann, "Orthodox Jews Assault Jews Praying at Western Wall," ibid., June 13, 1997; and Staff, " 'Culture War' Declared in Huge J'lem Demonstrations," *Jerusalem Post International Edition*, February 19, 1999. See also, Michal Yudelman, "Haredi Columnist: Secular Jews = Nazis," ibid., December 21, 1998; and Deborah Sontag, "Israeli Army Ousting Officer for Intolerance," *New York Times*, November 23, 1999.

63. Judith Miller, "Israel's Controversy over Religion Affects Donations by Jews in U.S.," *New York Times*, November 17, 1997. On Barak's approach to the Sephardic community, see Joel Greenberg, "In Spirit of Atonement, an Apology to Sephardim," ibid., September 30, 1997; and Avashai Margalit, "The Other Israel," *New York Review of Books*, May 28, 1998.

64. For Abdullah, see William A. Orme Jr., "Jordan's New King Assuming Key Role in Mideast Talks," *New York Times*, October 7, 1999. On Husayn's ties with Israeli leaders, see his interview with Avi Shlaim, "His Royal Shyness: King Hussein and Israel," *New York Review of Books*, July 15, 1999. On Jordan's economic fears, see William A. Orme Jr., "Jordanians Grieve over the Passing of a King and Worry about the Future," *New York Times*, February 9, 1999.

65. Herb Keinon, "Gather the Clowns and Call It a Party," *Jerusalem Post International Edition*, January 22, 1999; and Danna Harmon, "Sharon Foresees Palestinian State," ibid. Sharon assumed an Israeli right to control the Palestinian economy and to ratify Palestinian economic relations with other states.

66. Deborah Sontag, "2 Who Share a Past Are Rivals for Israel's Future," *New York Times*, April 20, 1999; Tracy Wilkinson, "Acrimony Intensifies in Israeli Campaign," *Los Angeles Times*, February 3, 1999.

67. Herb Keinon, "Plenty of Clowns, But No Party," *Jerusalem Post International Edition*, March 21, 1998.

THE ISRAELI-PLO DECLARATION OF PRINCIPLES, WASHINGTON, D.C.

September 13, 1993

The Declaration of Principles (DOP) was signed following the exchange of letters between PLO Chairman Yasir Arafat and Israeli Prime Minister Yitzhak Rabin, as discussed in the text. The excerpts included here note the developments expected to occur, such as election of the Palestinian Interim Self-Government Authority and the Israeli withdrawal from Gaza and Jericho, as well as the nature of the powers to be delegated to the Palestinians. All matters were subject to detailed negotiations that could drag on for years. Lack of resolution left Israel in control or left certain matters, such as safe passage between Gaza and Jericho, unimplemented until late 1999.

. . . The Government of the State of Israel and the PLO team (in the Jordanian-Palestinian delegation to the Middle East Peace Conference) ("the Palestinian delegation"), representing the Palestinian people agree that it is time to put an end to decades of confrontation and conflict, recognize their mutual legitimate and political rights, and strive to live in peaceful coexistence and mutual dignity and security to achieve a just, lasting and comprehensive peace settlement and historic reconciliation through the agreed political process. Accordingly, the two sides agree to the following principles.

Article I

Aim of the Negotiations

The aim of the Israeli-Palestinian negotiations within the current Middle East peace process is, among other things, to establish a Palestinian interim Self-Governing Authority, the elected Council (the "Council"), for the Palestinian people in the West Bank and the Gaza Strip, for a transitional period not exceeding five years, leading to a permanent settlement based on Security Council Resolutions 242 and 338. It is understood that the interim arrangements are an integral part of the whole peace process. . . .

Article IV

Jurisdiction

Jurisdiction of the Council will cover West Bank and Gaza Strip territory, except for issues that will be negotiated in the permanent status negotiations. The two

Source: Journal of Palestine Studies 23, 1 (Autumn 1993): 115–21.

sides view the West Bank and Gaza Strip as a single territorial unit, whose integrity will be preserved during the interim period.

Article V

Transitional Period and Permanent Status Negotiations . . .

2. Permanent status negotiations will commence as soon as possible, but not later than the beginning of the third year of the interim period between the Government of Israel and the Palestinian people representatives.

3. It is understood that these negotiations shall cover remaining issues, including: Jerusalem, refugees, settlements, security arrangements, borders, relations and cooperation with other neighbors, and other issues of common interest.

4. The two parties agree that the outcome of the permanent status negotiations should not be prejudiced or preempted by agreements reached for the interim period.

Article VI

Preparatory Transfer of Powers and Responsibilities . . .

2. Immediately after the entry into force of this Declaration of Principles and the withdrawal from the Gaza Strip and Jericho area, with the view to promoting economic development in the West Bank and Gaza Strip, authority will be transferred to the Palestinians on the following spheres: education and culture, health, social welfare, direct taxation, and tourism. The Palestinian side will commence in building the Palestinian police force, as agreed upon. Pending the inauguration of the Council, the two parties may negotiate the transfer of additional powers and responsibilities, as agreed upon.

Article VII

Interim Agreement

. . . 2. The Interim Agreement shall specify, among other things, the structure of the Council, the number of its members, and the transfer of powers and responsibilities from the Israeli military government and its Civil Administration to the Council. The Interim Agreement shall also specify the Council's executive authority, legislative authority in accordance with Article IX below [not included here], and the independent Palestinian judicial organs. . . .

4. In order to enable the Council to promote economic growth, upon its inauguration, the Council will establish, among other things, a Palestinian Electricity Authority, a Gaza Sea Port Authority, a Palestinian Development Bank, a Palestinian Export Promotion Board, a Palestinian Environmental Authority, a Palestinian Land Authority and a Palestinian Water Administration Authority, and any other authorities agreed upon, in accordance with the Interim Agreement that will specify their powers and responsibilities.

5. After the inauguration of the Council, the Civil Administration will be dissolved, and the Israeli military government will be withdrawn.

Article VIII

Public Order and Security

In order to guarantee public order and internal security for the Palestinians of the West Bank and the Gaza Strip, the Council will establish a strong police force, while Israel will continue to carry the responsibility for defending against external threats, as well as the responsibility for overall security of Israelis for the purpose of safeguarding their internal security and public order. . . .

Article XIII

Redeployment of Israeli Forces

1. After the entry into force of this Declaration of Principles, and not later than the eve of elections for the Council, a redeployment of Israeli military forces in the West Bank and the Gaza Strip will take place, in addition to withdrawal of Israeli forces carried out in accordance with Article XIV. . . .

3. Further redeployments to specified locations will be gradually implemented commensurate with the assumption of responsibility for public order and internal security by the Palestinian police force pursuant to Article VIII above. . . .

Article XIV

Israeli Withdrawal from the Gaza Strip and Jericho Area

Israel will withdraw from the Gaza Strip and Jericho area as detailed in the protocol attached as Annex II. . . .

Annex I

Protocol on the Mode and Conditions of Elections

1. Palestinians of Jerusalem who live there will have the right to participate in the election process, according to an agreement between the two sides.

2. In addition, the election agreement should cover, among other things, the following issues: a. the system of elections; b. the mode of the agreed supervision and international observation and their personal composition; and c. rules and regulations regarding election campaign, including agreed arrangements for the organizing of mass media, and the possibility of licensing a broadcasting and TV station.

3. The future status of displaced Palestinians who were registered on 4th June 1967 will not be prejudiced because they are unable to participate in the election process due to practical reasons.

Annex II

Protocol on Withdrawal of Israeli Forces from the Gaza Strip and Jericho Area

1. The two sides will conclude and sign within two months from the date of entry into force of this Declaration of Principles, an agreement on the withdrawal of Israeli military forces from the Gaza Strip and Jericho area. This agreement will include comprehensive arrangements to apply in the Gaza Strip and the Jericho area subsequent to the Israeli withdrawal.

2. Israel will implement an accelerated and scheduled withdrawal of Israeli military forces from the Gaza Strip and Jericho area, beginning immediately with the signing of the agreement on the Gaza Strip and Jericho area and to be completed within a period not exceeding four months after the signing of this agreement.

3. The above agreement will include, among other things:

a. Arrangements for a smooth and peaceful transfer of authority from the Israeli military government and its Civil Administration to the Palestinian representatives.

b. Structure, powers and responsibilities of the Palestinian Authority in these areas, except: external security, settlements, Israelis, foreign relations, and other mutually agreed matters.

c. Arrangements for the assumption of internal security and public order by the Palestinian police force consisting of police officers recruited locally and from abroad (holding Jordanian passports and Palestinian documents issued by Egypt). Those who will participate in the Palestinian police force coming from abroad should be trained as police and police officers. . . .

g. Arrangements for a safe passage for persons and transportation between the Gaza Strip and Jericho area. . . .

Annex IV

B. Specific Understandings and Agreements

ARTICLE IV

It is understood that:

1. Jurisdiction of the Council will cover West Bank and Gaza Strip territory, except for issues that will be negotiated in the permanent status negotiations: Jerusalem, settlements, military locations, and Israelis.

2. The Council's jurisdiction will apply with regard to the agreed powers, responsibilities, spheres and authorities transferred to it. . . .

ARTICLE VII(5)

The withdrawal of the military government will not prevent Israel from exercising the powers and responsibilities not transferred to the Council. . . .

Annex II

It is understood that, subsequent to the Israeli withdrawal, Israel will continue to be responsible for external security, and for internal security and public order of settlements and Israelis. Israeli military forces and civilians may continue to use roads freely within the Gaza Strip and the Jericho area.

DOCUMENT 10.2

THE ISRAELI-PALESTINIAN INTERIM AGREEMENT (OSLO 2) ON THE WEST BANK AND THE GAZA STRIP

September 28, 1995

This agreement was 307 pages long; 284 of them consisted of annexes and appendices. It called for implementation of arrangements and Israeli withdrawals originally foreseen under the 1993 DOP. The selections here refer to the powers to be transferred to the Palestinian Council, once elected, and those to be retained by Israel. They also include references to retention of the integrity of the territories, the ambiguous nature of Area C lands, and whether deployment from them could occur. The ra'ees is Arafat (Arabic: ra'is) as president of the Palestinian Authority. Most suggestions would remain unfulfilled with the Hebron redeployment requiring a separate protocol in January 1997.

A. Israeli-Palestinian Interim Agreement on the West Bank and the Gaza Strip, Washington, September 28, 1995

. . . The Government of the State of Israel and the Palestine Liberation Organization (hereinafter "the PLO"), the representative of the Palestinian people;

Preamble . . .

REAFFIRMING their determination to put an end to decades of confrontation and to live in peaceful coexistence, mutual dignity and security, while recognizing their mutual legitimate and political rights; . . .

RECOGNIZING that the peace process and the new era that it has created, as well as the new relationship established between the two Parties as described above, are irreversible, and the determination of the two Parties to maintain, sustain and continue the peace process; . . .

Source: Journal of Palestine Studies 25, 2 (Winter 1996): 123–37.

DESIROUS of putting into effect the Declaration of Principles on Interim Self-Government Arrangements signed at Washington, DC on September 13, 1993, and the Agreed Minutes thereto (hereinafter "the DOP") and in particular Article III and Annex I concerning the holding of direct, free and general political elections for the Council and the Ra'ees of the Executive Authority in order that the Palestinian people in the West Bank, Jerusalem and the Gaza Strip may democratically elect accountable representatives; . . .

HEREBY AGREE as follows:

Chapter 1 – The Council

Article I

TRANSFER OF AUTHORITY

1. Israel shall transfer powers and responsibilities as specified in this Agreement from the Israeli military government and its Civil Administration to the Council in accordance with this Agreement. Israel shall continue to exercise powers and responsibilities not so transferred.

2. Pending the inauguration of the Council, the powers and responsibilities transferred to the Council shall be exercised by the Palestinian Authority established in accordance with the Gaza-Jericho Agreement, which shall also have all the rights, liabilities and obligations to be assumed by the Council in this regard. Accordingly, the term "Council" throughout this Agreement shall, pending the inauguration of the Council, be construed as meaning the Palestinian Authority. . . .

7. The offices of the Council, and the offices of its Ra'ees and its Executive Authority and other committees, shall be located in areas under Palestinian territorial jurisdiction in the West Bank and the Gaza Strip. . . .

Article IV

SIZE OF THE COUNCIL

The Palestinian Council shall be composed of 82 representatives and the Ra'ees of the Executive Authority, who will be directly and simultaneously elected by the Palestinian people of the West Bank, Jerusalem and the Gaza Strip.

Article XI

LAND

1. The two sides view the West Bank and the Gaza Strip as a single territorial unit, the integrity and status of which will be preserved during the interim period.

2. The two sides agree that West Bank and Gaza Strip territory, except for issues that will be negotiated in the permanent status negotiations, will come under the jurisdiction of the Palestinian Council in a phased manner, to be completed within 18 months from the date of the inauguration of the Council, as specified below:

    a. Land in populated areas (Areas A and B), including government and Al-Waqf land, will come under the jurisdiction of the Council during the first phase of redeployment.

    b. All civil powers and responsibilities, including planning and zoning, in Areas A and B, set out in Annex III, will be transferred to and assumed by the Council during the first phase of redeployment.

    c. In Area C, during the first phase of redeployment Israel will transfer to the Council civil powers and responsibilities not relating to territory, as set out in Annex III. . . .

    e. During the further redeployment phases to be completed within 18 months from the date of the inauguration of the Council, powers and responsibilities relating to territory will be transferred gradually to Palestinian jurisdiction that will cover West Bank and Gaza Strip territory, except for the issues that will be negotiated in the permanent status negotiations. . . .

3. For the purpose of this Agreement and until the completion of the first phase of the further redeployments:

    a. "Area A" means the populated areas delineated by a red line and shaded in brown on attached map No. 1;

    b. "Area B" means the populated areas delineated by a red line and shaded in yellow on attached map No. 1, and the built-up area of the hamlets listed in Appendix 6 to Annex I; and

    c. "Area C" means areas of the West Bank outside Areas A and B, which, except for the issues that will be negotiated in the permanent status negotiations, will be gradually transferred to Palestinian jurisdiction in accordance with this Agreement.

Article XII

ARRANGEMENTS FOR SECURITY AND PUBLIC ORDER

1. In order to guarantee public order and internal security for the Palestinians of the West Bank and the Gaza Strip, the Council shall establish a strong police force as set out in Article XIV [see original document]. Israel shall continue to carry the responsibility for defense against external threats, including the responsibility for overall security of Israelis and Settlements, for the purpose of safeguarding their internal security and public order, and will have all the powers to take the steps necessary to meet this responsibility. . . .

Article XIII

SECURITY . . .

(8) Further redeployment is from Area C and transfer of internal security responsibility to the Palestinian Police in Areas B and C will be carried out in three phases, each to take place after an interval of six months, to be completed 18 months after the inauguration of the Council, except for the issues of permanent status negotiations and of Israel's overall responsibility for Israelis and borders. . . .

Chapter 3 — Legal Affairs

Article XVII

JURISDICTION

1. In accordance with the DOP, the jurisdiction of the Council will cover West Bank and Gaza Strip territory as a single territorial unit except for: a. issues that will be negotiated in the permanent status negotiations: Jerusalem, settlements, specified military locations, Palestinian refugees, borders, foreign relations and Israelis; and b. powers and responsibilities not transferred to the Council.

2. Accordingly, the authority of the Council encompasses all matters that fall within its territorial, functional and personal jurisdiction, as follows:

   a. The territorial jurisdiction of the Council shall encompass Gaza Strip territory, except for the Settlements and the Military Installation Area shown on map No. 2, and West Bank territory, except for Area C which, except for the issues that will be negotiated in the permanent status negotiations, will be gradually transferred to Palestinian jurisdiction in three phases, each to take place after an interval of six months, to be completed 18 months after the inauguration of the Council. . . .
   c. The territorial and functional jurisdiction of the Council will apply to all persons, except for Israelis, unless otherwise provided in this Agreement.
   d. Notwithstanding subparagraph a. above, the Council shall have functional jurisdiction in Area C, as detailed in Article IV of Annex III.

Article XVIII

LEGISLATIVE POWERS OF THE COUNCIL . . .

3. While the primary legislative power shall lie in the hands of the Council as a whole, the Ra'ees of the Executive Authority of the Council shall have the following legislative powers:

a. the power to initiate legislation or to present proposed legislation to the Council;

b. the power to promulgate legislation adopted by the Council; and

c. the power to issue secondary legislation, including regulations, relating to any matters specified and within the scope laid down in any primary legislation adopted by the Council.

4.

a. Legislation, including legislation which amends or abrogates existing laws or military orders, which exceeds the jurisdiction of the Council or which is otherwise inconsistent with the provisions of the DOP, this Agreement, or of any other agreement that may be reached between the two sides during the interim period, shall have no effect and shall be void *ab initio*.

b. The Ra'ees of the Executive Authority of the Council shall not promulgate legislation adopted by the Council if such legislation falls under the provisions of this paragraph.

5. All legislation shall be communicated to the Israeli side of the Legal Committee. . . .

Article XXXI

FINAL CLAUSES

1. This Agreement shall enter into force on the date of its signing. . . .

3. The Council, upon its inauguration, shall replace the Palestinian Authority and shall assume all the undertakings and obligations of the Palestinian Authority under the Gaza-Jericho Agreement, the Preparatory Transfer Agreement, and the Further Transfer Protocol. . . .

7. Neither side shall initiate or take any step that will change the status of the West Bank and the Gaza Strip pending the outcome of the permanent status negotiations.

8. The two Parties view the West Bank and the Gaza Strip as a single territorial unit, the integrity and status of which will be reserved during the interim period.

9. The PLO undertakes that, within two months of the date of the inauguration of the Council, the Palestinian National Council will convene and formally approve the necessary changes in regard to the Palestinian Covenant, as undertaken in the letters signed by the Chairman of the PLO and addressed to the Prime Minister of Israel, dated September 9, 1993 and May 4, 1994.

11

IS THE TWO-STATE SOLUTION DEAD?

Camp David 2000, Palestinian Rebellion, and Israeli Unilateralism

1999-2009

THE DECADE from 1999 to 2009 ended in uncertainty for both Israel and the Palestinians with their societies and political parties more factionalized than previously. The Oslo process collapsed with the failure of the talks held at Camp David in 2000 and the eruption of a second intifada. In 2001, Americans and Israelis elected new leaders in President George W. Bush and Prime Minister Ariel Sharon. Palestinian-Israeli strife continued in the aftermath of the al-Qaida terrorist attacks on the United States in September 2001 and the subsequent American-led attack on Iraq in March 2003. Yasir Arafat died and Sharon suffered an incapacitating stroke. In August 2005, Israel withdrew unilaterally from Gaza and dismantled its settlements there. Hamas won Palestinian elections in January 2006 and Ehud Olmert was elected prime minister of Israel at the end of March. Whereas Israel had sparked the Oslo initiative in 1992–1993 to undermine Hamas and strengthen Arafat and the PLO, the process and its repercussions ended in 2006 with Hamas's triumph via free elections—elections initially backed by the Bush administration, which then condemned their results and worked with Israel to try to destroy Hamas in Gaza, most recently with Israel's December 2008 assault on that area. That attack, whose timing was dictated by Israeli and American political considerations, bolstered rather than undermined Hamas's reputation and also failed to benefit its political sponsors, the Kadima and Labor parties, on the eve of the February 2009 Israeli elections. The results were a standoff between Kadima and Likud with the latter's candidate, Binyamin Netanyahu, able to form a coalition whose views were further to the right than his and Likud's. The attack was also timed to end before George W. Bush left office, preempting anticipated opposition from the incoming administration of Barack Obama to such acts and to the ongoing expansion of Israeli settlements in the West Bank. That expansion has led many observers to declare the impossibility of ever achieving a viable two-state solution to the Palestine-Israel conflict.

PRELUDE TO CAMP DAVID, JULY 1999–JULY 2000

Ehud Barak's declared eagerness to achieve peace accords appeared promising although he had little leeway given rightist opposition to territorial concessions; threats of assassination were reported by the press.[1] Seeking to appease his opponents, Barak's government authorized new construction in existing settlements from July to December at a pace exceeding that seen under Netanyahu. Barak dismissed American and Palestinian complaints, stating that Arafat knew he would not get the whole West Bank. Barak froze the issue of construction permits in December, acknowledging that settlement growth undermined the credibility of Palestinian officials as preliminary negotiations began.[2]

Then Barak abruptly left the Palestinian track in January 2000 for talks with Syria, only to abandon these negotiations after three months, believing that he could not persuade his cabinet to approve a withdrawal from the Golan. News of these Syrian discussions had mobilized settlers who, suddenly alerted to what Barak might also have in store regarding Palestinian lands, staged massive demonstrations. These incidents highlighted the pitfalls inherent in Barak's efforts to mollify a militant opposition that included parties in his coalition. National Religious Party members left the coalition once he turned again to the Palestinians.[3]

THE CAMP DAVID TALKS: BACKGROUND AND CONTEXT

The Camp David summit was convened hastily as Barak's coalition disintegrated and Palestinian anger intensified over the progressive loss of land to settlement growth in the West Bank and in East Jerusalem, anger directed as much at Arafat and the peace process as at Israel. Palestinians had anticipated the eventual creation of a state in most if not all of the territories, while the period since 1993 had witnessed the near doubling of the settlements, the vast expansion of the bypass road network built on expropriated Arab land, and more restrictions on Arab movement.

The creation of Areas A and B in 1996 (see Map 10.2) and the handovers of full or limited authority to the Palestinian Authority amounted to approximately 42 percent of the West Bank. Israel then placed roadblocks and checkpoints around all Palestinian areas. Palestinians now experienced unaccustomed daily searches and harassment when leaving their areas of residence. Israeli troops and border police manning the checkpoints often vented their contempt for Arabs, engaging in random beatings that usually went unreported.

Observers noted that troops and border police were at fixed checkpoints "on about 80 percent of West Bank territory," where most incidents of this type occurred.

Although the Israeli public had acknowledged these beatings during the first intifada, they seemed unaware or unconcerned that they continued. Lawyers and police officials admitted that "This is unfortunately something regular" with young border policemen at tense checkpoints sometimes "influenced by sentiments of hatred."[4] For most Palestinians the daily realities created by the Oslo process contradicted the claims made for that process in the outside world. In May observers predicted more serious explosions of anger if concrete steps were not taken to resolve outstanding issues.

As the situation deteriorated, President Clinton feared Likud's resurgence unless Barak achieved a peace proposal on which a majority of Israelis could agree. Having intervened to encourage Barak's election against Netanyahu in 1999, and with his term in office soon to expire, Clinton pushed for renewed negotiations despite the fact that Israel and the Palestinians remained far apart "on every crucial issue."[5]

Equally problematic for Clinton was the 2000 presidential campaign in which Republican candidate George W. Bush voiced his admiration for Ariel Sharon. At an American-Israel Public Affairs Committee (AIPAC) conference in May 2000, Bush criticized Clinton and the Democratic presidential candidate, Vice President Al Gore, for favoring Barak over Netanyahu in 1999 and declared that "my support for Israel is not conditional on the outcome of the peace process," a stance directly at odds with his father's in 1991–1992.[6]

Bush's remarks captured the feelings of many at the AIPAC meeting who objected when former Israeli Oslo negotiator Uri Savir acknowledged that Israel as well as the Palestinians had not kept its Oslo commitments. Savir referred sympathetically to the gulf between Palestinians who saw "all Jews as potential beaters of their parents" and Israelis who saw every Arab as a "potential suicide terrorist." The crowd preferred Bush's quip regarding the West Bank—if the pre-1967 boundaries gave Israel only a nine-mile width at some points, "Why, in Texas, there are driveways that are longer than that."[7]

Clinton's eagerness to push for a settlement matched Barak's needs far more than Arafat's. Barak arrived at Camp David able to rely on only 42 votes of the 120-member Knesset. But whereas Barak was threatened because he might be too conciliatory in the eyes of right-wing Israelis, Arafat confronted Palestinian anger at his corrupt administration and ineffective leadership as evidenced in his willingness to tolerate Israeli settlement growth during the Oslo process. He also faced Clinton's claims that Barak had gone as far as he could given Israeli domestic pressures and that a peace agreement was necessary to save Barak and to block the election of a Likud candidate, possibly Ariel Sharon. The Palestinians distrusted Barak, believing he had misled them with respect to settlement expansion, ignored them for the sake of the Syrian talks, and now turned to them only to save his own political future, even if it endangered their chances for real independence.

Arafat and his advisers acknowledged that they were unprepared for the hastily called summit, but accounts of the talks indicate that the Israeli and American teams were equally disorganized and dysfunctional, mirroring an apparent consensus of second-tier members of all three delegations. Arafat, wary of the mounting pressure for a summit, had gained Clinton's promise not to blame him if the talks failed. Clinton would break his promise. Clinton refused to admit that Arafat's priorities and timetable did not match Barak's. Barak, with Clinton's approval, insisted that agreements reached at Camp David should be conclusive; no further negotiations to clarify or modify issues would be permitted.[8]

Barak's final proposals at Camp David were pathbreaking in that no Israeli leader had ever made such terms available to Palestinians, but they were unofficial rather than official offers, and doubts remained as to his commitment to them. Throughout the Camp David talks, he refused to talk to Arafat, even at social occasions. Moreover, Barak would not put anything in writing (he feared a record that his opponents at home could use against him) and he never made offers personally, using Clinton to suggest they were American ideas. Clinton, desperate for success, accepted this role, expanding on Barak's terms with Barak's verbal assurances that he might "consider" Clinton's initiatives. On occasion, Barak backed off from "offers" he had asked Clinton to present when he thought Clinton had expanded on them.

Barak's willingness to consider Clinton's ideas became translated into a public image of flexibility, which contrasted favorably with Arafat's supposed rigidity, an image referred to by one Israeli commentator as "the great charade." In fact Barak presented Arafat with an all-or-nothing set of choices, "a corridor leading either to an agreement or to confrontation" where the blame would be laid on the Palestinians and relations would be downgraded "[resulting in] a situation far grimmer than the status quo." These threats increased Palestinian distrust of Barak, not sympathy, but Arafat's tendency to stonewall under such pressure rather than present counteroffers raised Israeli doubts of his interest in the terms presented.[9]

WHAT HAPPENED AT CAMP DAVID? JULY 2000

Barak initially offered the Palestinians what had been reported in May: 66 percent of the West Bank would be handed over to the Palestinians. Israel would retain major settlement blocs that effectively cut the West Bank into three sections with full Israeli control from Jerusalem to the Jordan River. More land, amounting to 14 percent, would be retained for periods ranging from twelve to twenty years. These areas included land west of the Jordan River (Israel would keep the shoreline permanently for security purposes) and the militant settler compounds and settlements in Hebron and Qiryat Arba. Ultimately, after twenty years, the Palestinians would have 80 percent of the West Bank and Gaza (see Map 11.1).

- **Palestinian areas A and B, March 2000**
- **Palestinian sovereignty**
- **Temporary (12–20 years) Israeli security control**
- **Israeli sovereignty**
- ▲ **Israeli settlements to be annexed by Israel**
- △ **Israeli settlements within Palestinian sovereignty or temporary Israeli security control**

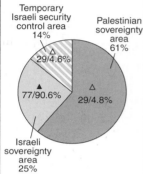

Temporary Israeli security control area 14%

Palestinian sovereignty area 61%

△ 29/4.6%

▲ 77/90.6%

△ 29/4.8%

Israeli sovereignty area 25%

West Bank sovereignty areas, including number of Israeli settlements (number at left in each section) and percentage of total number of settlers in the West Bank found in that location (percentage at right). Thus Israel would retain permanently 57.7% of the settlements, keeping 77 and returning 58, but would absorb 90.6% of the settlers who live in larger urban settings.

ISRAEL

West Bank

Gaza Strip

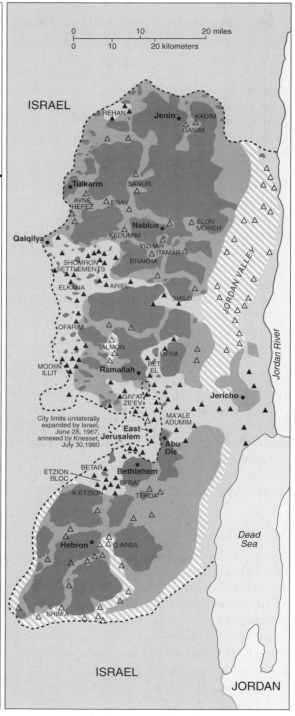

0   10   20 miles
0   10   20 kilometers

ISRAEL

REHAN
Jenin   KADIM
GANIM

Tulkarm   SANUR
AVNE   ENAV
HEFEZ

Nablus   ELON MOREH
Qalqilya   KEDUMIM
YIZHAR
ITAMAR
SHOMRON   BRAKHA
SETTLEMENTS
ELKANA   ARIEL
SHILO

OFARIM

TALMON   OFRA
MODIIN   BET
ILLIT   Ramallah   EL

GIV'AT
ZE'EV
MA'ALE   Jericho
ADUMIM

City limits unilaterally
expanded by Israel,   East
June 28, 1967,   Jerusalem
annexed by Knesset,   Abu
July 30,1980   Dis

ETZION   BETAR
BLOC   Bethlehem
EFRAT
K.ETZION   TEKOA

Hebron   Q.ARBA

SHIM'A

JORDAN VALLEY

Jordan River

Dead Sea

ISRAEL

JORDAN

Initial Negotiating Positions

With the West Bank cut into three pieces, the Palestinian "state" would lack territorial contiguity. Barak's proposal preserved 90.6 percent of the settlements in the West Bank and was intended to provide encirclement of "independent" Palestinian areas. Though they might be connected by tunnels or bridges, they would also be surrounded by barriers and checkpoints, as had occurred once areas were handed over to Palestinians after 1993 and 1996. Bypass roads would link the settlers directly to Israel.

Having rejected Barak's proposal as outlined in a map in May, the Palestinians were not about to accept it in July.[10] The Palestinians were willing to permit settlements to remain in the West Bank in return for land in Israel, but would not cede 20 percent of that region, essentially Rabin's idea before Oslo 1 in 1993. As for Jerusalem, Barak proposed creating two capitals, "Jerusalem" for Israelis and "al-Quds" for Palestinians. This was a ruse in that al-Quds, the Arabic term for Jerusalem, would be the name given to Abu Dis, the Palestinian village on the outskirts of expanded Israeli-controlled East Jerusalem that was unconnected to the Old City. Israel would retain control of all of Jerusalem, West and East. This permitted Barak to claim he preserved Israel's "unified" capital, one of his red lines, while the Palestinians had their own "Jerusalem," al-Quds. But Barak proposed that this Israeli Jerusalem be expanded to incorporate major settlement blocs such as Ma'ale Adumim, Giva'at Ze'ev, and Gush Etzion. This meant that "Jerusalem" would extend halfway to the Jordan River, with al-Quds isolated and under Israel's control.

For their part, the Palestinians demanded sovereignty over all of expanded East Jerusalem, meaning the territory annexed in 1980 and the Old City, which would be their capital, guaranteeing Palestinian control over the Haram al-Sharif. Finally, Arafat put forward the claim for the Palestinian right of return to Israel within its 1967 boundaries, a stance from which he would not budge.

◀ MAP 11.1 ■ West Bank Final Status Map Presented by Israel, May 2000

This was the map given to the Palestinians by Ehud Barak in May and again at Camp David, and rejected both times by them. The proposed Palestinian sovereignty area of 61 percent (see breakdown of percentages on left) includes Israeli settlements totaling another 4.8 percent, which explains the offer of 66 percent — those settlements would be abandoned by Israel. The horizontally striped areas would be retained by Israel for periods ranging from twelve to twenty years, and include the militant settlements in and next to Hebron.

The map indicates the careful planning of Israeli settlements along the West Bank border with Israel to link those areas to pre-1967 Israel, as well as those extended blocs around greater Jerusalem in the central region. It also makes clear that Israel intended to cut the Palestinian sectors into three separate areas with no contiguity, with the central Israeli area extending from Jerusalem to the Jordan River. Although the striped areas marked as the "Jordan Valley" would eventually be returned to the Palestinians, the banks of the Jordan River were to remain Israeli permanently, thereby encircling Palestinian sectors with Israeli checkpoints and military bases.

Note Abu Dis, carefully separated from East Jerusalem, which would be called "al-Quds" as the Palestinian capital.

Barak apparently proposed a right of return to the future Palestinian state, with a limited number allowed reentry to pre-1967 Israel.

Major differences remained. Israel's next offer of 89.5 percent was also unacceptable to the Palestinians, and Arafat's position on the right of return equally unattractive to all Israelis. Both sides were constrained by basic preconceptions unintelligible to the other. Israelis expected Palestinians to be grateful for their offer to withdraw from up to 90 percent of the West Bank. Palestinians saw this as insulting. Having lost 78 percent of former Palestine in 1948, they were determined to keep the remaining 22 percent, thereby forcing Israel's withdrawal to the 1967 lines.

Despite these obstacles, specialists made progress in "back-channel" talks, only to be undermined by Barak or Arafat. For example, Israeli negotiators had offered Palestinians 89.5 percent of the West Bank and three Arab villages in East Jerusalem. When Barak altered that to 91.5 percent and one village, Palestinians asked whom they could believe, and Clinton erupted at Barak, tired of being the go-between and not sure exactly what Barak intended. Likewise, Israeli and American negotiators were outraged when Arafat dismissed notions that the Temple Mount had once held the temple, claiming it had been situated near Nablus.

Barak's Proposal and Clinton's Role

Barak suddenly shocked his own camp and the Americans by crossing his "red lines." Israel would keep 9 percent of the West Bank, not 11+ percent, and sovereignty over 15 percent of the border with Jordan, though Israel would control the entire Jordan Valley for at least twelve years. With regard to Jerusalem,

> seven out of the nine outer neighborhoods would come under Palestinian sovereignty; in the inner neighborhoods, they would be in charge of planning and zoning; and in the Old City, the Muslim and Christian neighborhoods would come under Palestinian sovereignty. [As for] the Temple Mount/Haram [al-Sharif], the UN Security Council would pass a resolution to hand custodianship over it jointly to Palestine and Morocco [chair of the higher Islamic Commission based in Jerusalem]. . . . There would be a "satisfactory solution" to the refugee problem.[11]

These ideas went far beyond anything previously conceived, especially the partitioning of Jerusalem, including the Old City, but was the manner of their presentation to Arafat designed to gain Palestinian approval?

Barak had Clinton present his offer to Arafat as an American proposal that Clinton would try to persuade Barak to accept as the basis for concluding a deal. Clinton told Arafat that there could be no questions as to meaning, intent, or scope of the proposal; he could accept it or reject it. Clinton refused to answer or to pass on to Barak Arafat's queries as to what was meant by "custodianship" of the Temple Mount/Haram al-Sharif, what was meant by a "satisfactory solution" to the refugee question and right of return, and whether Arafat could discuss the Jerusalem idea with Arab heads of state. Clinton's stance indicated his acceptance of Barak's demand that all matters be concluded at Camp David. There would be no follow-up talks to settle issues that remained unclear.

Barak would not commit himself to any offer unless Arafat had agreed to it, and Arafat hesitated to agree to statements that could be interpreted differently, as had happened with clauses of the Oslo accords. The Palestinians correctly suspected that Clinton often acted on Barak's behalf, thus calling into question American neutrality. Finally, there was the real stumbling block of who held title, ultimately, to the Temple Mount/Haram al-Sharif. Arafat, fearing assassination, told Clinton he could not decide Jerusalem without cover from Arab states: "Do you want to come to my funeral?" Barak told his own negotiating team that "I don't have any flexibility when it comes to the Temple Mount."[12]

As for statehood, even with the Barak offer of 91 percent of the West Bank to the Palestinians, the Palestinian state would not be fully contiguous. Israel would retain a road from Jerusalem through Ma'ale Adumim to the Jordan River, under Israeli protection and over which Palestinians had no authority. Palestinians would have had actual possession of approximately 77 percent of the West Bank for up to twenty years, not 91 percent.[13]

Conflicting Interpretations

Such an offer also calls attention to the different meaning Palestinians and Israelis attached to words like "control," "sovereignty," and "authority." For the Palestinians sovereignty meant full, unimpeded authority over their areas:

> Palestinians will not tolerate Israeli Border Police or Israeli checkpoints. That is not sovereignty, that is not control. Palestinians no longer want to ask Israelis for permission to build their homes, to educate their children, to live their lives.[14]

The issue of control, or lack thereof, lay at the heart of the problem. For Palestinians, Israeli roads bisecting Palestinian lands and Israeli surveillance of Palestinian tunnels beneath those roads meant that Palestine would not be truly "independent" even if it were declared a "state." Similarly, with respect to Jerusalem, it historically had been a divided city, and East Jerusalem was split into Arab and Jewish sectors whose inhabitants wished to have no contact with one another. For Palestinians, a unified city/region was not as crucial as having control over their own lives without the interference and checkpoint harassment they had experienced previously, which had intensified under the Oslo process. For Israeli opponents of compromise, a "unified" Jerusalem meant full Israeli control of the expanded urban district with no Palestinian capital or authority in it.

Claims that the talks failed solely on the issue of Jerusalem are inaccurate but participants felt that "solving Jerusalem" would have enabled success on other matters. When Clinton refused to clarify for Arafat Barak's idea that Palestinians and Moroccans would share "custodial sovereignty" over the Haram al-Sharif, the talks collapsed. Clinton then blamed Arafat for the failure of the summit, with some sources suggesting that chief U.S. negotiator Dennis Ross encouraged him to do so at Barak's request.[15]

Barak and Arafat returned to their constituencies claiming victory. Arafat was hailed because he had not compromised Palestinian demands. Barak declared that he unmasked Arafat and the Palestinians as refusing to consider his offers and therefore fully to blame for the summit's failure, a version willingly accepted in the United States and Israel. The reality was quite different, though discovering it was more difficult in the United States than abroad. Because Israeli offers were oral and made by U.S., not Israeli, negotiators, "strictly speaking, there never was an Israeli offer" but rather American offers on Israel's behalf.[16] On the Palestinian side, Arafat's requests for clarifications of issues were falsely reported as outright rejection of offers when that had not occurred.

President Clinton and chief U.S. negotiator Dennis Ross fully backed Barak's condemnation of Arafat for American audiences. Yet, while the Palestinian version of events was not wholly accurate, it appeared on examination to be "much closer to the evidentiary record of articles, interviews, and documents produced by participants in the negotiations, journalists, and other analysts" than the official Israeli and American accounts, a judgment buttressed by later publications.[17] Indeed, what Americans heard from Dennis Ross, heaping all blame on Arafat, was not what he told a French audience:

> I think [our] biggest mistake was letting a huge gap develop between the reality on the ground and the reality around the negotiating table. The Palestinians have to stop inciting violence . . . [and] bring up [their children] differently. The Israelis have to stop . . . constructing settlements . . . stop destroying Palestinian houses and confiscating land, and [they] have to change their attitude at checkpoints. . . . [The Palestinians] got used to the idea of engaging permanent incitement and socialization of violence . . . [and the Israelis] constantly did things that created a sense of powerlessness in the Palestinians. From the very beginning we should have held both sides accountable for the commitments they made. We did not. . . . We never did anything to prepare public opinion [for peace]. Holding negotiations come what may got us nowhere. If I could do it all over again, I'd do it differently.[18]

Here, Ross held both sides accountable while admitting errors in oversight of the peace process, which had been his responsibility. In contrast, in his book, *The Missing Peace*, there is no indexed reference to settlements after the Oslo process began in 1993; his statement above refers specifically to the period 1993–2000.

Moreover, Barak's approach at Camp David had not discounted the possibility of future violence resulting from continuance of the status quo. As the press noted at the time, and as Barak claimed once the second intifada erupted, by appearing more reasonable than Arafat, he regained the strategic advantage with the United States that had been lost when the United States sided with Arafat against Netanyahu. This to Barak was a major triumph because

> the Palestinians have for a generation held international legitimacy, we succeeded in a year to turn that around, without giving up anything, not even 9 percent, or 13 percent [of the territories], we succeeded in bringing back international legitimacy to us, and in putting Arafat on the defensive. And we did that without giving up anything. . . . The world is with us and the onus is now on the other side.[19]

Indeed, official commentaries by the Clinton administration and the American media were nearly unanimous in holding Arafat responsible not only for the Camp David failure, but for the outbreak of the new intifada following Ariel Sharon's visit to the Temple Mount in September (discussed later). Sharon had already declared his rejection of "every major component of the peace deal that President Clinton put forward and [that] . . . Barak tentatively accepted . . . [acknowledging] that his only goal was [to] topple the government and force early elections."[20]

SUBSEQUENT DIPLOMACY

As the new intifada consumed attention, Palestinian-Israeli talks went largely unnoticed, with an apparent breakthrough in January 2001 obscured by the ongoing violence and the Israeli election campaign.

The Clinton Parameters

Talks resumed on September 27, 2000, but they were almost immediately derailed by Sharon's visit to the Temple Mount the next day, which incited the second intifada (discussed later). Then, in December just before Christmas, Clinton hosted Israeli and Palestinian delegations. He dictated his plan and they took notes, but no official record was to be preserved and there would be no discussion. Barak and Arafat had to accept his ideas as the basis for talks without requests for further information.

Clinton proposed that the Palestinians get 94–96 percent of the West Bank. In exchange for the remaining major Israeli settlements, Israel would allot a land swap of 1–3 percent — almost a full exchange of land for land, though the areas were not specified. As for Jerusalem, the Old City, and extended East Jerusalem, Arab and Jewish communities would be awarded to Palestine or Israel, respectively. On the right of return, only a small portion of the Palestinians in exile could return, but Israel would not "negate the aspiration of the Palestinian people to return to [former Palestine]," meaning that Israel would not openly reject the idea as a principle. The crux was the question of the Temple

Mount/Haram al-Sharif. Clinton suggested Palestinian sovereignty over the Haram. Israel would have sovereignty over the Western Wall and the land under the Haram where ancient Israeli relics existed.[21]

Barak officially "accepted" Clinton's ideas on December 28 with numerous reservations, but he withdrew that acceptance three days later. Some sources, including Dennis Ross, depict Arafat as not replying until he met Clinton on January 2, 2001. In their version, Arafat accepted the offers "with reservations," which for Clinton constituted a rejection, even though Clinton and Ross had not regarded Barak's initial reply, with twenty pages of reservations, to signal the same. In fact, Arafat had called Clinton on December 28 to accept his ideas, but requested clarifications. In his account, Ross omits news of Barak's rejection of Clinton's terms on December 31 and of Arafat's initial reply on December 28.[22]

The Taba Discussions, January 2001

Lower-level talks continued and led to the Taba negotiations, a last-ditch effort based on the Clinton parameters. Neither Barak nor Arafat participated or openly endorsed the discussions. They ended with each side acknowledging areas where no agreement had been reached, but the participants believed they had established a fruitful basis for hammering out an accord.

For once, both sides presented maps outlining their territorial demands. The Israeli offer called for retention of 5 to 6 percent of the West Bank, much reduced from Barak's Camp David proposals. In reply the Palestinians refused to accept inclusion of Ma'ale Adumim and Giv'at Zeev in Israel (see Map 11.2). Headway was made on the question of refugees' right of return, and the two sides agreed that Jerusalem would serve as the capital of both Israel and Palestine. Like the Camp David talks, there was no official record, nor was there American oversight — by this time George W. Bush was the new American president.

Map 11.2 ■ **Final Status Map Presented by Israel, Taba, January 2001**   ▶

After intensive official negotiations with President Clinton's involvement in December 2000, where progress was made but with no conclusive results, Israeli and Palestinian negotiators on their own produced this map on which all apparently agreed. But, with no official sponsorship or recognition, its findings remained moot.

Here Israel retains 5 percent of the West Bank, in significantly reduced settlement sectors compared to Barak's Camp David offer, but also proposes giving 3 percent of Israeli territory as a swap for the 5 percent kept (see vertical shaded area at bottom). The settlement blocs around Jerusalem are sharply reduced, especially to the north of the city, while the Betar and the Etzion blocs to the south are smaller, as are Ma'ale Adumim and the large settlement of Ariel in the north with links to Israel. This area includes 65 percent of all the settlers, far less than the 90.6 percent included in Barak's scheme (see Map 11.1), but still well over half of that population in light of settler concentration in these areas.

The proposed Palestinian state has full contiguity, and also has most of East Jerusalem as its capital with Abu Dis included.

Finally, note the location of Kalkilya (Qalqilya), the Palestinian town on the far western border of the West Bank. It has been fully surrounded by the portion of the security fence now completed and is isolated from other Palestinian areas.

Palestinian Areas
A and B

Palestinian sovereignty

Israeli sovereignty/
settlement built-up areas

Israeli territory offered as
part of a 3% land swap

△   Israeli settlements within
    Palestinian sovereignty

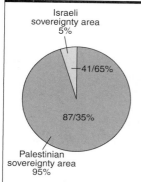

Israeli
sovereignty area
5%

—41/65%

87/35%

Palestinian
sovereignty area
95%

West Bank sovereignty areas,
including number of Israeli
settlements and percentage of
total number of settlers, excluding
East Jerusalem, which, if
included, would adjust the
percentages by at least 10%,
adding more within the Israeli
sector and reducing that in the
Arab sector.

Jewish state according to
UN Partition Plan, 1947

Palestinian state according to
UN Partition Plan, 1947

Projected Palestinian state according
to the Israeli Proposal, 2001

Proposed land-swap areas

LEBANON

SYRIA

Tel
Aviv   West
        Bank

Jerusalem
Gaza

ISRAEL

JORDAN

EGYPT

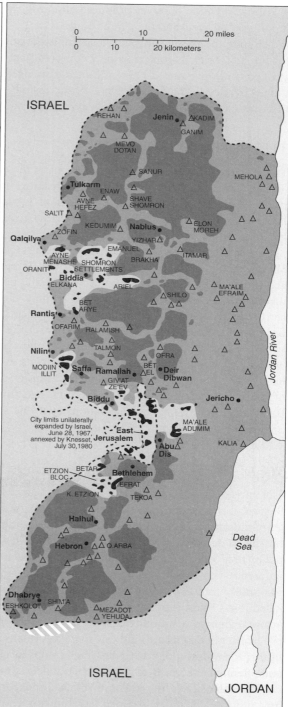

0   10   20 miles
0   10   20 kilometers

ISRAEL

REHAN   Jenin   KADIM
                        GANIM

            MEVO
            DOTAN

              SANUR   MEHOLA

Tulkarm   ENAW
          SHAVE
   AVNE   SHOMRON
   HEFEZ
SAL'IT   ELON
        KEDUMIM   Nablus   MOREH
Qalqilya   ZOFIN   YIZHAR
              EMANUEL
    AYNE   BRAKHA   ITAMAR
  MENASHE SHOMRON
ORANIT   SETTLEMENTS
     Biddia
   ELKANA   ARIEL   MA'ALE
                          SHILO   EFRAIM
            BET
Rantis   ARYE

  OFARIM   HALAMISH

Nilin   TALMON   OFRA
MODIIN   BET
ILLIT   Saffa Ramallah EL   Deir
             GIV'AT   Dibwan
             ZE'EV
        Biddu   Jericho

City limits unilaterally
expanded by Israel,   MA'ALE
  June 28, 1967,   East— ADUMIM
annexed by Knesset, Jerusalem
  July 30,1980   Abu   KALIA
                        Dis
ETZION   BETAR
BLOC   Bethlehem
          EFRAT
   K. ETZION   TEKOA

   Halhul   Dead
                                Sea
  Hebron   Q.ARBA

Dhabrye   JORDAN
  ESHKOLOT SHIM'A
            MEZADOT
            YEHUDA

Jordan River

Dead
Sea

ISRAEL

JORDAN

A European Union observer produced an unofficial text that was subsequently repudiated by Israel and the United States.[23]

Despite the participants' enthusiasm, negotiations had been overtaken by the intifada. Ariel Sharon's election victory (62.39 percent of the votes to Barak's 37.61 percent) introduced a new era already presaged by Sharon's calculated visit to the Temple Mount. Barak lobbied unsuccessfully to become Sharon's defense minister. Labor, without Barak, joined Sharon's coalition.

THE SECOND INTIFADA

The architect of settlement expansion during the 1980s (see Figure 8.3), Ariel Sharon seized the Camp David talks and rumors of territorial compromise to present himself as the prospective leader of Likud and preserver of Greater Israel in forthcoming elections. Former Prime Minister Netanyahu was ineligible to run because he was not a member of the Knesset.

On September 28, 2000, the fifth anniversary of the signing of Oslo 2, Sharon made his carefully staged visit to the Temple Mount/Haram al-Sharif, accompanied by nearly 1,000 police and media personnel, the Likud Knesset members, and Jerusalem Mayor Ehud Olmert. His visit, aimed at the Israeli electorate, was designed to discredit Barak by depicting him as willing to sacrifice a unified Jerusalem and Jewish control over the Temple Mount. Planning to seek reelection, Barak had no choice but to allow Sharon to go; the alternative was to be accused of abandoning Israel's claims to the site.[24] The ensuing violence enabled Sharon, once elected prime minister, to undertake the destruction of the Palestinian Authority as a governing structure and to reoccupy the West Bank, aided by Arafat's miscalculations as to the strategic import of Sharon's accession to office.

The Initial Stage, September 2000–March 2001

The uprising began with Palestinians throwing rocks and burning tires to protest Sharon's visit. Israeli police and soldiers met these demonstrations with live ammunition, shooting with intent to kill Israeli Arabs as well as West Bank Palestinians, as occurred at the Israeli-Arab town of Umm Fahm where troops and police fired on the crowd, killing thirteen; regular crowd-control tactics were ignored.[25] The Israeli use of massive firepower triggered a Palestinian armed response. From September 28, 2000, to year's end, at least 365 persons were killed—325 Palestinians, 36 Israelis, and 4 others. An estimated 10,600 Palestinians were injured or wounded during this period, compared to 362 Israelis. Official Israeli military records indicate that Palestinians used firearms in 27.6 percent of their demonstrations, whereas Israeli troops invariably used live ammunition and often altered crowd-control rubber bullets to make them more lethal.[26]

The intensity of the violence shocked independent observers, who noted how quickly U.S. officials joined Israel in condemning Arafat and Palestinians in general for staging the demonstrations. In contrast, they suggested that, as during the first intifada, a spontaneous outburst erupted, reflecting long existing rage (see Document 11.1). Now, however, the uprising was directed at Arafat and the Palestinian Authority as well as at Israel, in protest of a situation where "areas of Palestinian control were like disconnected islands in an Israeli-controlled sea" surrounded by checkpoints allowing no freedom of movement.

Further strife resulted from a new Israeli policy of targeted assassinations at a time when the vast majority of Palestinian protesters were unarmed. The killing of ten Palestinians appeared to occur at strategic intervals that served to arouse more Palestinian violence and stymie negotiations or undermine truces, or for domestic political reasons such as reassuring a nervous Israeli public of military efficiency. The first killing, in November, took place when Arafat was in Washington for talks with Clinton. A second, in December, killed Thabet Thabet, a Palestinian who had many Israeli friends and connections to Peace Now. Israel claimed that the Israeli Defense Forces (IDF) had "overwhelming evidence" of terrorist involvement in each case. The government offered less explanation in response to evidence that Israeli troops violated rules of engagement by killing Palestinian civilians and by denying medical units access to wounded individuals, which led to several deaths.[27]

Despite his militant rhetoric, Barak had sought to moderate the Israeli military response, but he and the political echelon had virtually no control over the military, which often ignored their orders. Led by Likud sympathizers, the army's massive retaliation helped to undermine any chance of reconciliation or achievement of a cease-fire. Highly publicized incidents of killings on both sides that inflamed public opinion in October/November 2000 (the Israeli killing of a Palestinian boy in Gaza and the Palestinian public killing of two Israeli soldiers in Ramallah) hindered Barak's willingness to publicly call for restraint, especially since his electoral rival, Sharon, called for crushing the Palestinians.[28]

The Political Context of the Intifada: Bush, Sharon, and Arafat

Ariel Sharon assumed office in March 2001, two months after George W. Bush entered the White House. Sympathetic to Sharon and lacking Clinton's knowledge of the issues, Bush declined to become involved in the intricacies of the conflict. He assured Sharon that the United States would not intervene in Israeli-Palestinian affairs and praised his "marvelous sense of history."[29]

During the next two years, Bush would meet with Sharon at the White House eight times while never inviting Arafat, whom he, like Sharon, held responsible for the violence. Arafat was further discredited in early January 2002 when Israel seized the *Karine A*, a ship carrying fifty tons of weapons and explosives that Israel claimed had been sent from Iran for Palestinian use. The White House accepted Israeli evidence of Arafat's complicity in the *Karine A* scandal, although official Israeli and American press accounts often were highly misleading.[30]

The *Karine A* incident had a major impact on U.S. policy in the aftermath of the September 11, 2001, al-Qaida attacks on the United States. It encouraged President Bush to include Iran with Iraq and North Korea in his "Axis of Evil" during his January 2002 State of the Union address. With Arafat personally implicated in the arms shipment, Bush administration officials accepted Sharon's claim that Arafat was not a partner for peace and tolerated the Israeli policy of massive reprisals. Once in office, Sharon had declared: "If they [the Palestinians] aren't badly beaten, there won't be any negotiations." Intelligence estimates that harsher military actions inspired more, not less, violence were ignored.[31]

Arafat, in the view of Palestinian analysts, completely misread the altered political environment. Although he had not initiated the intifada, Arafat believed "that continued violence would bring Sharon down by defeating his electoral pledge to provide the Israeli public with security, and that his fall would bring the Labor Party back to power." Instead, Labor joined Sharon's coalition in March 2001 and approved Israeli attacks and reprisals. Conditioned by events during the Clinton years, Arafat and his advisers made "a fundamental misreading of [the Bush] administration's worldview, and in particular of its affinity for Israel and distrust of the PA and Arafat." Arafat assumed that continued violence "would engineer a face-to-face dialogue with Bush despite evidence of Bush's clear antipathy toward him from the outset of his presidential term." By June 2002, President Bush had made Arafat's replacement as head of the Palestinian Authority a condition for American support of negotiations.[32]

Intensified Conflict and Suicide Bombings: The Israeli Barrier

Sharon had ordered the West Bank to be cut into sixty-four isolated sectors and Gaza into four using trenches, earthen ramparts, and concrete barriers, with an estimated 450 checkpoints, barriers, and roadblocks established by the end of 2002. An estimated 680 such obstacles were in place by November 2004. Despite the severe impact on the Palestinian population, armed resistance intensified[33] (see Document 11.2).

The situation would worsen during the next two years with both sides suffering great trauma. Nearly 2,000 Palestinian attacks occurred in 2001, undertaken against settlements in the territories as well as inside Israel. Palestinians killed at least 189 settlers and military personnel in the territories during 2002 in addition to the civilian casualties of suicide bombings.[34] Israel carried out at least 33 politically ordered targeted assassinations in 2001, and 37 in 2002, with 43 bystanders, including children, also killed. The Popular Front for the Liberation of Palestine (PFLP) retaliated in October 2001 for the assassination of one of its leaders by killing Rehavem Ze'evi, head of the Molodet Party and Minister of Tourism. He had called for the "transfer" of Palestinians from the occupied territories. Israeli forces often fired randomly at civilian neighborhoods and into unarmed demonstrations, killing at least 93 Palestinians and wounding more than 1,500 during 2001, as well as damaging service buildings, including hospitals.

Suicide bombings began with Sharon's election in early 2001 and his implementation of more restrictions on Palestinian movement, along with the targeted assassinations of leaders of different groups. The use of suicide bombings expanded from Islamic militias to include secular factions such as Tanzim and the al-Aqsa Martyrs Brigade, both offshoots of Fatah, as well as the PFLP. By 2002, women had become suicide bombers as well. For Hamas, the sudden participation of secular Palestinians as suicide bombers served no political purpose and contradicted the "strategic" intent of such efforts; it also removed control of such efforts from the Islamists.

Many bombings appeared to be blind acts of revenge at the circumstances in which Palestinians found themselves harassed or beaten at the numerous checkpoints or occasionally killed in "ambiguous circumstances" as they climbed over earthen barriers that blocked egress from communities. "The IDF generally did not investigate the actions of security force members who killed or injured Palestinians in such actions, leading to a climate of impunity," a situation that has continued. Israeli raids for suspected terrorists often involved occupying offices, banks, and schools as well as homes, which they frequently despoiled. Intended to humiliate Palestinians under their domination, these actions instead fueled the desire for retaliation, as did the placing of towns under curfew for months at a time. Soldiers frequently permitted settlers to pillage Palestinian lands by uprooting olive trees and either collecting the crops or blocking farmers' access to them.[35]

In similar fashion, Palestinian actions led to massive reprisals such as when a suicide bombing of a Passover seder celebration in 2002 led to the Israeli assault on Jenin in April that leveled most of the refugee camp within the town. Palestinian charges of a massacre were disproved but 4,000 Palestinians were left homeless and the army blocked access to the camp by relief and medical personnel for six days after the fighting stopped.[36]

For Israelis, beset by suicide bombings that affected most areas inside Israel, not just the occupied territories, knowledge of these corollary developments was immaterial. They accepted Sharon's methods because they valued the search for security more than the means by which it was achieved. It was clear from early 2002 that Palestinian suicide bombings inside Israel helped Sharon more than the Palestinians. The bombings permitted Sharon to argue that Israeli security justified a full military response and to blame Arafat while Sharon himself strove to undermine the results of the Oslo process. For the vast majority of Israelis, the bombings and their psychological as well as personal toll meant that there was no alternative to Sharon's promise of security through military action. The trauma of their daily lives justified for Israelis what Palestinian trauma justified for the occupants of the territories—revenge and reprisals with little concern for the targets of the actions.

Figure 11.1 ■ Israel's Security Barrier

While much of the separation barrier is an electrified fence, it becomes a wall dividing settled areas as in the West Bank town of Ram. The Palestinian side shows a town with a dirt road while the Israeli side has a well-paved highway.

Finally, during 2002 the Sharon government began constructing a barrier intended to run the length of the West Bank. Occasionally, following the 1967 border, the barrier invades the West Bank in order to incorporate Israeli settlements and to confiscate Palestinian lands for the construction route. In addition, the barrier has separated nearly 50,000 Palestinians and land amounting to 142,600 acres from the West Bank itself with restricted access. In the case of some major towns, twenty-foot walls completely enclose them with one gate for residents to use (see Figure 11.1). Ranging from eight to twenty feet high, the barrier in April 2007 was 70 percent complete; it is estimated to extend over 500 miles (see Map 11.3). Appeals to the Israeli Supreme Court and an opinion from

Map 11.3 ■ Israel's West Bank Separation Barrier, 2007 ▶

This map details the route of the barrier with changes since July 2006 that draw more of the West Bank west of the barrier while further isolating Palestinians from each other. Nearly 13 percent of West Bank land will be west of the barrier but to that must be added the 25 percent Israel plans to retain in the Jordan Valley. The Palestinian areas of 54 percent will be cantonized. See Ariel Sharon's reference to Palestinians having "transportation contiguity" in Document 11.5. Palestinians living in annexed East Jerusalem are being cut off from the West Bank and, as illustrated, the town of Qalqilya (population 40,000), in the west, is completely enclosed with one entry/exit blocked by an Israeli checkpoint.

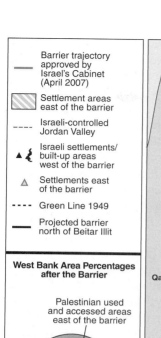

Barrier trajectory
approved by
Israel's Cabinet
(April 2007)

Settlement areas
east of the barrier

Israeli-controlled
Jordan Valley

▲ ⚶ Israeli settlements/
built-up areas
west of the barrier

△ Settlements east
of the barrier

---- Green Line 1949

Projected barrier
north of Beitar Illit

**West Bank Area Percentages
after the Barrier**

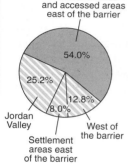

Palestinian used
and accessed areas
east of the barrier

54.0%

25.2%

12.8%

8.0%

Jordan
Valley

West of
the barrier

Settlement
areas east
of the barrier

**Principal Barrier Changes
from July 2006**

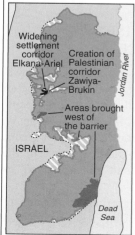

Widening
settlement
corridor
Elkana-Ariel

Creation of
Palestinian
corridor
Zawiya-
Brukin

Areas brought
west of
the barrier

ISRAEL

Jordan River

Dead
Sea

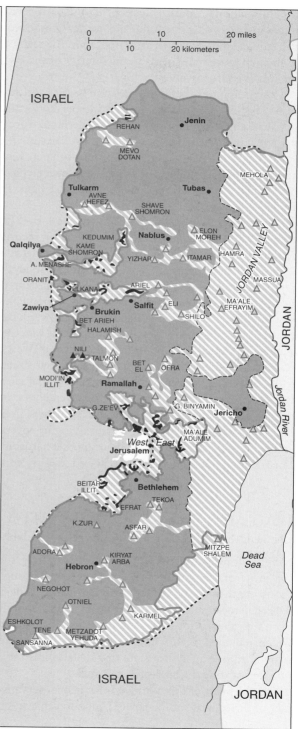

ISRAEL

0   10   20 miles
0   10   20 kilometers

REHAN

Jenin

MEVO
DOTAN

MEHOLA

Tulkarm

Tubas

AVNE
HEFEZ

SHAVE
SHOMRON

ELON
MOREH

Nablus

KEDUMIM

Qalqilya

KAME
SHOMRON

HAMRA

A. MENASHE

YIZHAR

ITAMAR

ORANIT

MASSUA

ELKANA

ARIEL

Zawiya

Brukin

Salfit

ELI

MA'ALE
EFRAYIM

BET ARIEH

HALAMISH

SHILO

NILI

TALMON

BET
EL

OFRA

MODI'IN
ILLIT

Ramallah

G.ZE'EV

G. BINYAMIN

Jericho

MA'ALE
ADUMIM

West   East

Jerusalem

BEITAR
ILLIT

Bethlehem

TEKOA

EFRAT

K.ZUR

ASFAR

ADORA

KIRYAT
ARBA

MITZPE
SHALEM

Dead
Sea

Hebron

NEGOHOT

OTNIEL

ESHKOLOT

KARMEL

TENE

METZADOT
YEHUDA

SANSANNA

ISRAEL

JORDAN VALLEY

JORDAN

Jordan River

ISRAEL

JORDAN

the International Court of Justice that the barrier violated international law in many instances suggested that the barrier's route would be altered to take less Palestinian land. However, as of mid-2007, the major changes have instead been to include more settlements in the interior of the West Bank and the east overlooking the Jordan Valley.[37]

According to Israeli estimates, the barrier and surveillance cut the number of Israelis killed by terror attacks by 60 percent, with a 30 percent reduction in total casualties. Another factor was the declared truce by Hamas, begun in January 2005, and acceptance of calm by most Palestinian groups other than Islamic Jihad. Palestinian casualties were proportionately higher due principally to the clashes in Gaza prior to the Israeli disengagement of August 2005 (discussed later). Three times as many Gazans as West Bank Palestinians were killed by Israelis during 2005.

From September 28, 2000, to early 2006, over 3,300 Palestinians and foreigners had been killed by Israeli troops or security forces; those killed by settlers were not reported. Approximately 1,030 Israelis and foreigners had been killed by Palestinians or Israeli Arabs. The injured and wounded were not reported for 2005 but, for purposes of comparison, by June 2003, the intifada, nearly three years old, saw approximately 50,000 Palestinians and 7,000 Israelis wounded. Palestinian living standards plummeted. By mid-2003, at least 40 percent of children in the West Bank and Gaza were judged to be chronically or acutely malnourished, and nearly 60 percent of West Bankers and 80 percent of Gazans were living below the poverty line; that situation has not changed. The situation in Gaza worsened following the 2005 Israeli withdrawal from all settlements (discussed later). Israel suffered severely in economic terms as a result of the intifada; it entered a recession and its citizens' lives were disrupted by fear of bombings with an increase in Israelis living in poverty.[38] However, Israelis generally did not experience the socioeconomic hardships that impacted the Palestinian population under Israel's renewed military control.

IRAQ AND THE NEOCONSERVATIVE VISION OF A U.S.-ISRAELI STRATEGIC ALLIANCE

Never before had right-wing Israeli leaders had such committed ideological support from an American administration. Throughout the 1990s, American groups with links to conservative Christian evangelical organizations openly backed Israel's retention of the West Bank, and they welcomed George W. Bush's candidacy for president. Once in office, his tolerance of developments, which included destruction of the Oslo process and transformation of the region, led one analyst to state that the administration had "subcontracted" its policy regarding the territories to Israel.[39]

At the heart of this worldview lay neoconservative eagerness to take advantage of the collapse of the Soviet Union to achieve American global dominance.

Here pro-Likud and non-Jewish neoconservative interests meshed. In June 1996, Richard Perle, a former member of the Reagan administration and long close to Likud, authored a policy paper, "Clean Break: A New Strategy for Securing the Realm," for new Israeli Prime Minister Binyamin Netanyahu. Perle and his cosigners, including Douglas Feith, also of the Reagan administration and the product of a Zionist Revisionist family like Netanyahu, advised Netanyahu to break with the comprehensive peace process embodied in the Oslo agreements. Instead, Israel, then governed by Likud, should impose its will on the Palestinian Authority and remove Arafat from power. The "land for peace" formula endangered Israel's security, a standard Likud refrain.

Regionally, Israel should focus on dismantling any threat from Syria, but the path to that objective led through Baghdad because "removing Saddam Hussein from power in Iraq—an important Israeli strategic objective in itself—would foil Syria's regional ambitions." These and other steps would help to "forge a new U.S.-Israeli relationship" based on power.

A second Likud advisory paper by David Wurmser in December 1996, "A Western and Israeli Balance of Power Strategy for the Levant," reiterated "Clean Break's" arguments. Abandoning both the Oslo process and the search for negotiated agreements with Middle East countries would open the way for a closer U.S.-Israeli "strategic alliance" that, following "regime change" in Iraq, would seek the same in Syria and "destabilize Iran."[40] In 1998, Perle, Feith, Paul Wolfowitz, and Wurmser joined other neoconservative ideologues, non-Jewish as well as Jewish Likud backers, that included Donald Rumsfeld to call for an attack on Iraq and Saddam Husayn's overthrow.[41]

Bush appointed many of these individuals to key administration posts, especially in the Department of Defense, where Rumsfeld, Wolfowitz, and Feith held the top three positions. Elliott Abrams, close to Ariel Sharon and the Christian evangelical movement, was soon placed in charge of Middle East affairs, including the Arab-Israeli peace process, at the National Security Council and David Wurmser became Middle East adviser to Vice President Richard Cheney. For one government official, it meant that "the Likudniks are really in charge now," characterized by sympathizer Rumsfeld's caustic reference to "the so-called occupied territories."[42]

In the aftermath of the al-Qaida terrorist attacks of September 11, 2001, neoconservatives immediately called for an attack on Iraq—rather than on Afghanistan, where Usama Bin Ladin was known to reside. Following the U.S. invasion of Iraq in March–April 2003, charges that intelligence justifying the attack was politically skewed focused on the Department of Defense, where undersecretary Douglas Feith, cosigner of "Clean Break," had created the Office of Special Plans, an intelligence group that sought links between Iraq and al-Qaida that had supposedly been overlooked by U.S. intelligence agencies. Reports later surfaced that Cheney and Rumsfeld had essentially "hijacked foreign policy" by taking decisions they had made to President Bush for approval without State Department knowledge of the recommendations.[43]

OFFICIAL AND UNOFFICIAL REPORTS AND PEACE EFFORTS, 2001–2005

Throughout the period of the intifada, various efforts were made to assess conditions in Israel and the occupied territories and to recommend procedures that might enable a return to negotiations. These recommendations ultimately formed the basis for President George W. Bush's approach to resolving outstanding matters, but his interpretation of the obligations of both parties reflected the ideological bent of his administration. An unofficial Israeli-Palestinian pact, the 2003 Geneva Accords, then pushed Ariel Sharon to negate its potential appeal by undertaking his own initiative, which produced the 2005 Gaza Disengagement.

The Sharm al-Sheikh Fact-Finding (Mitchell) Committee

Formed at the request of former President Clinton in November 2000 and chaired by former Senator George Mitchell, the Sharm al-Sheikh Fact-Finding Committee's mission was to investigate causes of the intifada and to recommend "a path back to the peace process."[44] The committee's mandate was to discover what had happened and how to prevent its recurrence. Its recommendations were to be nonbinding.

The committee's report confirmed Israel's use of "live ammunition and modified metal-cored rubber rounds against unarmed demonstrators throwing stones" at the outbreak of the intifada, a violation of the IDF Code of Ethics. It also backed previous reports that Palestinians did not use firearms and explosives in the vast majority of incidents during the first three months of the intifada.[45] The report called for total cessation of violence by both sides. Beyond that, the committee demanded a "maximum effort" by the Palestinians to stop terrorism and arrest terrorists, while Israel should "freeze all settlement activity, including the 'natural growth' of existing settlements." Finally, the committee recommended renewed joint security efforts to establish calm so that talks could resume, a suggestion that seemed impossible to implement given the breakdown of trust between the two sides.

Submitted to President Bush on April 30, 2001, the report was tabled even though the Palestinians had immediately accepted its recommendations. No effort was made to implement it, in part because of the mutual escalation of violence once Sharon took office and in part because Sharon rejected the idea of any halt to settlement activity. Angered that settlements were equated with terrorism as "core catalysts in eroding trust," he remained confident that his rapport with Bush would overcome calls for restrictions on Israeli actions until the uprising had been crushed.

The Rose Garden Address, June 2002

In June 2002, President Bush addressed the nation from the White House Rose Garden to demand regime change in Palestine. Influenced by Yasir Arafat's supposed involvement in the *Karine A* affair, he declared that he would not intervene in Palestinian-Israeli affairs until Arafat had been replaced as head of the Palestinian Authority.[46]

Bush's address was a landmark in U.S. policy. For the first time, an American president declared openly that the outcome of envisioned changes would be a Palestinian state, conditional on new leadership. He referred to that state as "democratic, viable, and credible"; such a "stable, peaceful state is necessary to achieve the security that Israel longs for." Siding with Sharon, Bush declared that only when greater security was achieved could he envision Israeli forces withdrawing "fully to positions they held prior to September 28, 2000," the date of Sharon's visit to the Temple Mount. In return, Palestinians could then, by 2005 at the latest, create a new democratic political structure vesting a legislative branch with authority guaranteed by a constitution. Finally, Israeli settlement activity would end, as recommended by the Mitchell Committee report.

The administration then placed further efforts on hold until coalition forces led by the United States attacked Iraq and removed Saddam Husayn in March 2003. Nonetheless, at the behest of British Prime Minister Tony Blair, Bush agreed to reassure Middle East leaders that overthrowing Saddam did not indicate unconcern for the festering Palestinian-Israeli problem. Blair's pleas led to a document, known as the "Road Map," that appeared to have international backing but that President Bush effectively undermined in June at an Israeli-Palestinian summit.

The Road Map vs. the Rose Garden Address

The Road Map stemmed from Bush's June 2002 Rose Garden call for Arafat's removal from office and the beginning of Palestinian political reform. It was composed by the "Quartet" — the United States, the European Union, Russia, and the United Nations — during summer 2002. Drafts of the document were known, but official announcement of the Road Map was withheld until April 30, 2003.[47] By then, Saddam Husayn had been removed from power and Yasir Arafat had reluctantly accepted the appointment of Mahmud Abbas (Abu Mazen) as prime minister of the Palestinian Authority. Arafat remained as the PA's chairman, but foreign emissaries could bypass him and deal with Abbas. Despite the international aura attached to the document, the United States later modified the Road Map to suit Israel without consulting other Quartet members.

The Road Map set out three development phases, although its timetable became irrelevant because the United States insisted on removing Saddam Husayn before it was issued. To undertake Phase 1, the Palestinian leadership would "issue [an] unequivocal statement reiterating Israel's right to exist." Israel, for its part, would issue a similar statement "affirming its commitment to the two-state vision of an *independent, viable, sovereign* [emphasis added] Palestinian state, as expressed by President Bush . . . ," characteristics not mentioned in Bush's Rose Garden speech.

The document was characterized as "performance-based," meaning that the Palestinians and Israelis should simultaneously take steps to seek to restore mutual confidence and to remove causes of violence and mistrust. Palestinians should immediately cease all violence and begin to build new political institutions. Israel should freeze settlement activity, as called for in the Mitchell Report, and begin immediate "dismantling of settlement outposts erected since March 2001," the date Sharon first took office.

The Quartet initially insisted that the Road Map's stipulations were not subject to modification but the Bush administration succumbed to Israeli pressure, tacitly accepting Sharon's list of fourteen demands. Then, at the Aqaba summit attended by Ariel Sharon and Mahmud Abbas, Bush contradicted the stated intent of the Road Map two months after it had been issued.

The Aqaba Summit, June 2003

Many in the Palestinian leadership had welcomed the demands for Arafat's ouster, if only to set in motion an alternative to the violence. As prime minister, Mahmud Abbas, long a confidant of Arafat, had the power to represent the Palestinians in negotiations. His presence at the Aqaba summit indicated official acceptance of his status.

Abbas, seeking to inject movement into negotiations, had accepted the Road Map as issued. Israel had immediately mobilized backers in Washington to lobby Congress and the White House against it. For Sharon, there were three major obstacles. First, the plan was performance-based, meaning mutual responsibility to act simultaneously, not "performance driven," meaning that Israel would not act until convinced Palestinians had fulfilled their obligations. Netanyahu had used the latter concept, Israel's satisfaction with Palestinian actions (reciprocity), to stall on implementing any Oslo obligations. Second, the plan envisaged immediate "dismantling of settlement outposts erected since March 2001," a stipulation Sharon rejected. Third, as noted, the Road Map specifically demanded that Israel commit itself to "the two-state vision of an independent, viable, sovereign Palestinian state."

Israel garnered support from lobbying groups including Christian evangelical organizations prior to the Aqaba summit. In May 2003, settler leaders, such as Benny Elon, appeared at rallies in the United States flanked by members of the Christian Coalition and Tom DeLay, then House majority leader. Elon's Molodet Party called for the transfer of the Palestinians from the West Bank, as did Christian evangelicals such as former Republican presidential candidate Gary Bauer. Bauer characterized the Road Map as a breach of God's covenant with Israel and reminded Bush of which votes he needed for the 2004 elections.[48]

Confronted with this lobbying, Bush reversed his stance on the Road Map, to which he had agreed for international consumption. Whereas the Road Map echoed the Mitchell Report in calling for the removal of all Israeli outposts established after March 2001, Sharon gained Bush administration acceptance—

in Bush's Aqaba speech — of a distinction between "authorized" and "unauthorized" settlements and outposts established since March 2001. Sharon thus established his own criteria for what settlements might be removed, ignoring the official texts on which U.S. policy was supposedly based and on which Palestinian actions were to be judged. Indeed, Israel had been taking steps to ensure the permanence of these outposts. An official report concluded that the Israeli government had financed paved roads and electrical connections to the main grid in an illegal process and suggested that "law violation became institutionalized."[49]

Sharon also lobbied the White House successfully, without seeking Quartet agreement, regarding the Road Map's reference to the projected Palestinian state as independent and sovereign. Instead, the state should be "stable, peaceful, viable [and] democratic," all terms Bush used in his Rose Garden address. Bush obliged. At the Aqaba summit, Bush made no mention of the Palestinian state being "independent" or "sovereign."[50] Willing to accommodate Sharon, Bush had little interest in details. On the eve of the summit, an administration official commented that the president

> often has a viscerally negative reaction when officials try to delve deeply into issues — such as final borders of Israel and a Palestinian state, or the status of Jerusalem — that are central to the conflict ... [and] does not have the knowledge or the patience to learn this issue enough to have an end destination in mind.[51]

In the aftermath of the June 2003 Aqaba conference, Mahmud Abbas sought Hamas's agreement to a truce, and an American envoy arrived in Israel on June 15 seeking to implement the Road Map. At the same time, Israel reported that it had reached an agreement with the United States, without consulting other Quartet members, on new settlement construction that "remove[d] the settlements from the framework of its road map."[52] The pattern of targeted assassination and retaliatory suicide bombings continued, the most notable victims being Shaykh Ahmad Yasin and Abd al-Aziz Rantisi of Hamas in March 2004. By then, arrangements were well under way for official Israeli abandonment of the Road Map and of any commitment to a negotiated settlement. Instead, Israel, with apparent American approval, would adopt a unilateral approach to defining its own future boundaries and the presumed boundaries of a fragmented and emasculated Palestinian state, sparked by a joint Israeli-Palestinian plan for peace.

The Geneva Initiative, October 2003

This agreement, which carried no official stamp of approval from either side, resulted from ongoing informal discussions between Israeli and Palestinian officials, many of whom had been involved in the Camp David negotiations and those that had occurred at Taba in early 2001. The chief signers were Yossi Belin and Yasser Abed Rabbo, the former a leftist Knesset member and the latter a former PLO public relations official close to Arafat. The text declared that its ɔroposals were based on Security Council resolutions 242 and 338 and fit within the framework of discussions at Camp David 2000, Taba, President Bush's June 2002 Rose Garden address, and the Road Map.[53] The signatories saw this agreement as a prelude to full Arab-Israeli peace based on the Arab League Resolution of March 2002 that offered full peace to Israel in return for its withdrawal from the West Bank and recognition of a Palestinian state; Ariel Sharon had ignored that Arab League offer.

Under the Geneva resolution, Israel would ultimately withdraw from 98 percent of the West Bank; the remaining 2 percent would be retained in exchange for 2 percent of Israeli territory. Nearly all West Bank settlements would be evacuated, and Israel would abandon its settlements in the Gaza Strip. Jerusalem would be the capital of both states, with Palestinians having sovereignty over the Haram al-Sharif/Temple Mount compound and Israel over the Wailing Wall and the Jewish quarter of East Jerusalem.

Regarding security, "Palestine would be a non-militarized state with a strong security force," meaning that it would not have a standing army, and Israel could post two early warning stations in the West Bank; the weapons permitted for the security force would be subject to inspection by a joint security commission, with additional guarantees for both sides provided by a multinational force positioned in the Palestinian state. As for Palestinian refugees, their right of return to Israel would be subject to its approval, it being expected that refugees would settle in areas evacuated by Israelis; refugees would be compensated for lost property.

Certain key issues, including that of water, were left for further discussion. Resolving that question would be difficult. Israel has relied on the Western aquifer of the West Bank for its own domestic use for decades and piped much of it back into settlements in the West Bank (see Map 11.4). Palestinians would naturally demand control of that aquifer, as it would lie in Palestine, for their own use.

The Geneva Initiative outlined an agreement that would presumably have been accepted by a majority of Israelis and West Bank and Gazan Palestinians if it had been reached by official representatives of both sides. But its major significance lay in the reaction to it by various parties. Arafat had been aware of the talks via Abed Rabbo and appeared to have approved of them. Hamas condemned the Palestinian negotiators as "traitors" who had gone beyond the "national consensus." In Israel, Ehud Barak and Shimon Peres rejected the initiative and Prime Minister Sharon called it "the most serious historic error made since Oslo"; he quickly took steps to neutralize its potential impact.[54]

Map 11.4 ▪ West Bank Aquifers   ▶

As this United Nations display indicates, the western aquifer of the West Bank flows into Israel, where it is used by Israelis. A great deal of the water is then piped back to West Bank settlements. Many West Bank Palestinians, however, must rely on wells. In any peace negotiations, Israel could claim control of this water source based on the direction of its flow, whereas Palestinians would claim the right to use based on its source, under prospective Palestinian rule.

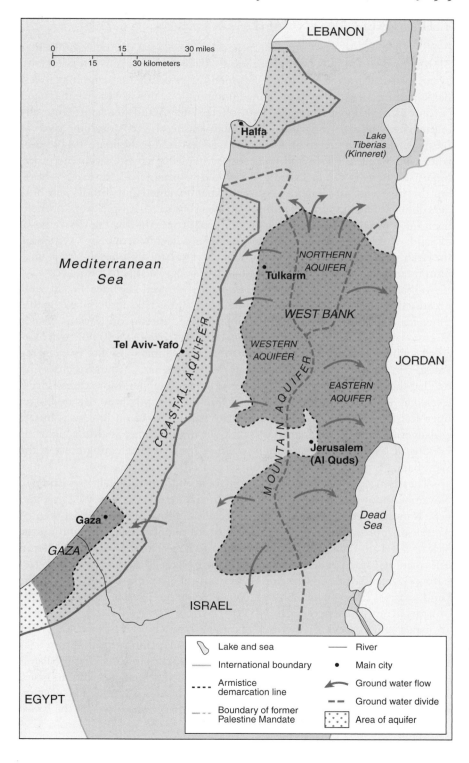

LEBANON

0   15   30 miles
0   15   30 kilometers

Halfa

Lake
Tiberias
(Kinneret)

*Mediterranean
Sea*

NORTHERN
AQUIFER

Tulkarm

WEST BANK

COASTAL AQUIFER

Tel Aviv-Yafo

WESTERN
AQUIFER

MOUNTAIN AQUIFER

EASTERN
AQUIFER

JORDAN

Jerusalem
(Al Quds)

Gaza

GAZA

Dead
Sea

ISRAEL

EGYPT

	Lake and sea	——	River
	International boundary	•	Main city
----	Armistice demarcation line	←—	Ground water flow
----	Boundary of former Palestine Mandate	--	Ground water divide
		⋮⋮⋮	Area of aquifer

THE ISRAELI DISENGAGEMENT PLAN

Public references to evacuating Gaza had first appeared in August 2002 after Bush's Rose Garden speech. The idea was that Israel would display its good faith by evacuating Gaza and granting Palestinians more contiguous land in the West Bank, joining Areas A and B as defined under Oslo 2; this would give them 49.1 percent of the region. In return, the United States would free Israel from any immediate obligation to resume peace talks, erasing the 2005 deadline given in Bush's Rose Garden speech. In the interim, Israel could consolidate its hold over land it intended to retain and then declare its willingness to negotiate peace. Negotiations, as at Camp David 2000, would be on a take-it-or-leave-it basis, but this time with Israel in possession of what it wanted and with its new borders defined. The proponents of this plan also believed that Israel would benefit from the forthcoming American attack on Iraq. The army saw the U.S. removal of Saddam as leading to a pro-Western regime in Baghdad, thereby "weakening the Arab states' and the Palestinians'" will to resist Israeli proposals "for a long-term interim agreement" that would stabilize Israel's West Bank presence.[55]

Initially disinterested, Sharon ultimately embraced the idea in fall 2003 because this unilateralism could postpone final status talks indefinitely. By that time, he had found himself under increasing criticism on various fronts. Twenty-seven pilots had signed a public letter criticizing Israel's policy of "targeted killings" and refused to participate in future missions that endangered Palestinian civilians; among the signatories was General Yiftah Spector, who had led the attack on the Iraqi nuclear reactor in June 1981. More charges were leveled at Sharon by four retired former Shin Bet directors, who declared in an open letter that Israel's focus on a security agenda based on force was in fact endangering Israel's national security. Under fire at home, Sharon sought the backing of the Bush administration to secure his goal of retaining most of the West Bank.[56]

The disengagement plan appears to have been formally hatched in Rome in November 2003 at a meeting of Sharon, his main adviser, Dov Weisglas, and U.S. National Security Middle East specialist Elliott Abrams. Israel wanted American approval before announcing the idea publicly and justified it on the lack of any Palestinian partner with whom to negotiate. In December Sharon informed the Israeli public of his goals, assuring Israelis that in return for evacuating Gaza, he would consolidate Israel's control over "those same areas of the Land of Israel [West Bank] that will constitute an inseparable part of the State of Israel in any future agreement."[57]

Israel sought specific American guarantees, namely, that Israel could annex and retain major settlement blocs in the West Bank prior to future peace talks with Palestinians. Sharon also wanted the United States to agree that the Palestinian claim to a right of return applied only to a Palestinian state, not to Israel. Determined to retain their Christian evangelical base in a presidential election year, Bush administration officials decided in January 2004 to accept the Israeli initiative after torturous negotiations in which they capitulated on nearly all Israeli demands.[58]

With the disengagement agreement and the Sharon-Bush letters (see Documents 11.3 and 11.4), prearranged and issued simultaneously on April 14, 2004, Sharon declared that Israel would withdraw fully from the Gaza Strip and from four settlements in the northern West Bank. In return, President Bush stated in his letter to Prime Minister Sharon that he welcomed the plan and that

> in light of new realities on the ground, including already existing major Israeli population centers, it is unrealistic to expect that the outcome of final status negotiations will be a full and complete return to the 1949 armistice lines and all previous efforts to negotiate a two-state solution have reached the same conclusion. It is realistic to expect that any final status agreement will only be achieved on the basis of mutually agreed changes that reflect these realities.

This statement overturned all standing American positions on the fate of the occupied territories and settlements. Although the Bush administration had refused to use the word "annex" to refer to Israelis settlements that could remain in the West Bank, Sharon and his aides interpreted Bush's statement to mean that Israel could retain many large settlements including some distant from the armistice lines, not just those adjacent to them. It clearly placed the United States as opposed to the ideas offered in the Geneva Initiative.

Other promises were open to conflicting interpretations. Bush continued in his letter to state that the security barrier was not political and was only temporary, as Sharon had assured him. He then wrote that, "as you [Sharon] know, the United States supports the establishment of a Palestinian state that is viable, contiguous, sovereign and independent." Indeed, Bush's letter was based on Sharon's professed commitment to a "mutual agreement . . . of two states for two peoples." But Sharon regarded such a Palestinian "state" as having no sovereignty or real independence. It would be separated into enclaves, with Israelis manning checkpoints and barriers at Palestinian enclave boundaries. Blocked on the west by the separation barrier, Palestinians would be blocked in the east by Israel's continued occupation of the Jordan River valley. West Bank Palestinians would have no free movement outside of their enclaves, which would remain under Israeli surveillance (see Map 11.3). Subsequent Israeli versions of the plan (May and June 2004) removed references to a Palestinian state without official consultation with Washington.[59] And although Bush referred to a Palestinian state as having contiguity, Sharon's plan referred only to "transportation contiguity" in the West Bank, meaning Palestinian tunnels under Israeli roads (see Document 11.5).

Israel's intent was to postpone if not derail a peace process based on an Israeli-Palestinian agreement, as Sharon's closest adviser, Dov Weisglas, acknowledged cynically in an interview:

The disengagement plan is . . . the bottle of formaldehyde necessary so that there will not be a political process with the Palestinians. . . . The American term is to park conveniently. The . . . plan . . . distances us as far as possible from political pressure . . . [and] legitimizes our contention that there is no negotiating with the Palestinians. . . . We received a no-one-to-talk-to certificate . . . [whereby] the geographic status quo remains intact [and] the certificate will be revoked only when this-and-that happens — when Palestine becomes Finland. . . .[60]

The Disengagement Plan and Israeli Politics

The Israelis who called for a nearly full withdrawal from all the territories saw disengagement as a ploy to retain most of the West Bank, but most ultimately backed the idea with the proviso that the Gaza disengagement was only the first of many such steps. For many in Likud, Sharon's party, and those further to the right, Sharon's plan betrayed the Likud platform that he had helped draft and that called for full absorption of Judea and Samaria into Israel (see Document 8.1).

Former Prime Minister Binyamin Netanyahu seized on the proposal to challenge Sharon for the leadership of the Likud Party once the Gaza withdrawal was carried out in mid-August 2005. When Likud split on Netanyahu's candidacy, Sharon abruptly left the party to form a new one, Kadima ("Forward"). Created on November 21, 2005, Kadima drew Labor politicians such as Shimon Peres and Haim Ramon and Likud colleagues such as deputy prime minister and former mayor of Jerusalem Ehud Olmert.

Then, with elections announced for March 28, 2006, Sharon suffered a massive stroke in January and remains in a coma as of July 2009. Olmert, Sharon's successor, pledged to fulfill Sharon's blueprint, but he altered the plan by calling for withdrawal from nearly all settlements east of the security barrier. Kadima won the elections on March 28 and Olmert formed a government by early May. His coalition, formed with the Labor Party, Shas, and a new party called the Pensioner Party, held 67 of the 120 seats in the Knesset. Likud won only 11 seats. Olmert immediately proclaimed that he would move to establish Israel's permanent borders based on the security barrier route and dismissed the likelihood of any Palestinian negotiations.[61]

In this light, Hamas's election in January 2006 appeared to be a godsend for Olmert. It enabled him to declare that Hamas was no partner for peace, thereby justifying ongoing unilateralism.

Hamas, Fatah, and the Peace Process: Conflict and Fragmentation

Having proclaimed democratic goals for the Middle East, Bush administration officials had accepted Hamas's candidacy in the Palestinian parliamentary election campaign of late 2005 while contributing $2 million to assist Fatah.[62] When Hamas won, the United States condemned the results and moved to block

Palestinian access to financial resources, hoping to engineer Hamas's downfall because of popular discontent. Israel withheld tax revenues it owed the PA and blocked all gates to Gaza. The resulting financial and political chaos severely affected Palestinians generally and resulted in fierce clashes between Hamas and Fatah groups, but analysts argued that this would strengthen Hamas in Palestinian eyes even if Hamas were forced to give up power.

Many Palestinians believed that PA officials had ignored the plight of ordinary Palestinians throughout the Oslo process because they preferred to benefit from ties to Israeli officials. Inasmuch as Abbas had no option but to appeal to Washington, he was seen by many Palestinians as bound to American-Israeli dictates, whereas Hamas, despite its American image as solely a terrorist organization, had earned Palestinian respect for both resisting Israeli occupation and providing free social and medical services under stressful conditions. In the words of one sympathetic observer, the PA, in the eyes of many Palestinians, was "at best . . . perceived as a corrupt and failing organization and at worst as a subcontractor for the bureaucracy of the occupation."[63]

Once Hamas assumed office in March 2006, the United States persuaded the European Community to cut off funding to the Palestinian Authority, still led by Mahmud Abbas in Ramallah, who presided over a Hamas-led parliament, and Prime Minister Ismail Haniya, who was based in Gaza. With access to outside funds blocked, Fatah-Hamas tensions exploded in Gaza in May when 140,000 people formerly on the PA payroll were not paid. These clashes called attention to Gaza's desperate social and economic circumstances, which had intensified once Israel evacuated its settlements there.[64]

Israel had asserted on its withdrawal from Gaza in August 2005 that it no longer had any responsibility for Palestinians living there. Gaza might not be "occupied territory," but Israel retained control of Gaza. Israeli troops supervised all entry and exit from Gaza, via gates in a wall it had built that entirely enclosed the strip by land and by naval surveillance and blockade of the coastline. President Bush had accepted this outcome in April 2004 (see Document 11.5). Subsequently, Egypt agreed to oversee the Rafah approach into the Sinai.[65]

The three gates permitting the passage of workers into Israel were to have been upgraded, which would have also facilitated shipments of Gazan agricultural products to outside markets. Instead, most produce rotted at the gates, as did Israeli goods bound for Gaza. Israel stressed fears of suicide bombers, though virtually none from Gaza had entered Israel in the prior three years. Instead, Israel's policies resulted in almost daily rocket launchings from Gaza into Israel. Though Israeli casualties were slight, Israeli retaliatory artillery fire into northern Gaza took a much greater toll. Israel stressed security concerns, but the American representative of the Quartet, James Wolfensohn, attributed much of the severe economic damages dealt Palestinians generally to "a systematic violation of commitments by Israel regarding Gaza border crossings and West Bank freedom of movement," that was backed by the Bush administration.[66] Wolfensohn had mediated the modalities of the Gaza disengagement between Israel and the

Palestinian Authority, then in power in Gaza, beginning in May 2005. In his view, he had been undermined by Elliott Abrams and the nonimplementation of the border crossings agreement, which shattered Palestinian hope of normality and encouraged the rise of Hamas at the expense of Fatah.[67]

Since June 2006, Gaza has been described as "on verge of disaster." An estimated 65 to 70 percent of Gazans are considered impoverished (compared to 30 percent in 2000) in a population estimated at 1.5 million, most of whom survive primarily on United Nations and other donor aid.[68] The situation has worsened since the December 2008 Israeli assault on Gaza (discussed below).

Israel, Gaza, and Lebanon: Rockets, Hostages, and Political Ambitions, 2006–2009

As noted, Palestinians had launched rockets into Israel once the Israeli blockade tightened around Gaza, but Hamas claimed that it continued to adhere to a truce it had declared in January 2005. Then in June 2006 Israel charged that Hamas loyalists were behind rocket firings into Israel from Gaza and intensified its shelling of that area. In response, Hamas broke its truce when an Israeli artillery round killed a Palestinian family on a beach. Then, on June 24, Israeli forces entered Gaza, the first incursion since disengagement in August 2005, and seized two Palestinians they accused of planning Hamas terrorist attacks. Hamas replied the next day by attacking an Israeli army unit outside Gaza, killing two soldiers and capturing one whom they said they would hold as hostage for exchange of Palestinian prisoners. Despite calls for negotiations backed by the captured soldier's family, Prime Minister Olmert immediately ordered a military assault that destroyed much of Gaza's civilian infrastructure including the major power plant, with significant Palestinian casualties, mostly civilian.[69]

As this crisis escalated, Hizbollah suddenly attacked an Israeli military unit in the north of Israel on July 12, kidnapping two soldiers and killing eight. This ignited a full-scale Israeli air assault on much of Lebanon's civilian infrastructure, including the Beirut airport, as well as Shi'ite regions on a scale reminiscent of Israeli punishments of governments for individual incursions begun in the 1950s; Prime Minister Olmert then ordered a ground assault into southern Lebanon to destroy Hizbollah positions. The Bush administration purposely delayed efforts to approve a cease-fire at the United Nations in order to help Israel gain a decisive victory it failed to achieve. When a cease-fire occurred, Hizbollah remained defiant and Israeli military gains were limited after four weeks of fighting. Hizbollah had launched missiles that hit major Israeli cities such as Haifa, signaling Israel's vulnerability to advanced weapons systems in the hands of nonstate actors backed by great popular support.[70]

Israel's seizure of Gazans in June that triggered hostilities was likely intended to derail the prospect of a Palestinian consensus on peace demands. Efforts to achieve a Fatah-Hamas pact were in full swing, and such an alliance would have threatened implementation of Olmert's convergence plan to withdraw from settlements east of the security barrier. In Israel, however, the clashes with Hamas and Hizbollah were interpreted as undermining Olmert's convergence plan; national security now required that Israel remain in full occupation of the West Bank rather than withdraw unilaterally behind the barrier.

At the same time, the Bush administration continued to seek the overthrow of Hamas with the collaboration of Fatah and Israel. Despite their hostility, Fatah and Hamas had agreed to a unity government in a pact brokered by Saudi Arabia in March 2007. But news reports noted that special Fatah brigades were being trained with U.S. financing and weapons in preparation for an assault into Gaza from the Sinai to oust Hamas, a plan linked to President Bush, Secretary of State Condoleezza Rice, and NSC Middle East specialist Elliott Abrams. Hamas preempted this plan in June by attacking and defeating the remaining Fatah security forces in Gaza, thereby taking full command of the area but also opening itself to accusations that it had destroyed the newly formed Palestinian coalition. This left Mahmud Abbas, president of the Palestinian Authority and head of Fatah, in the West Bank where Israeli settlement growth continued, while Hamas ruled over Gaza.[71]

THE ANNAPOLIS CONFERENCE AND ITS RAMIFICATIONS, NOVEMBER 2007–MAY 2008

It was in this context that the Bush administration arranged a major conference that took place at Annapolis, Maryland, in November 2007.[72] The declared goal was to achieve a comprehensive Palestinian-Israeli peace by the end of 2008 when Bush's term of office expired. Heads of Arab states were invited and many attended, including officials from Syria. The administration excluded Hamas, meaning that a Palestinian-Israeli peace would be negotiated between Fatah and Israel. Bush called for ongoing bilateral talks between Abbas and Ehud Olmert with only the United States overseeing implementation of the Road Map. All this was included in an Israeli-PLO Joint Understanding hammered out fifteen minutes before the conference opened, with further international input excluded, despite the fact that most of the Arab states that had signed the Arab League Peace Initiative of 2002, including Saudi Arabia, had attended the conference (see Document 11.6).

Olmert and Abbas met often in the coming year, but no progress was made, even though Olmert declared on several occasions that peace would require Israeli withdrawal from most of the West Bank and from nearly all of East Jerusalem. In the meantime, settlement building in the West Bank continued, as did the extension of Jewish neighborhoods in East Jerusalem.

In the midst of this standoff, former president Jimmy Carter visited the region in April 2008, noting Mahmud Abbas's comments that there was no hope of a peace accord by the end of the year. He decided to consult with all actors, including Hamas, and met with Hamas leaders in Cairo and Damascus; Israel denied him entry to Gaza. As he reported to the Israeli Council on Foreign Relations, Hamas officials would not renounce violence since they considered it the only way to end the occupation under the existing circumstances. But they and Carter agreed on a statement that he read to his audience.

> If President Abbas succeeds in negotiating a final status agreement with Israel, Hamas will accept the decision made by the Palestinian people . . . through a referendum monitored by international observers . . . by mechanisms agreed upon nationally, even if Hamas is opposed to the agreement. In order to ensure that the referendum can be debated and the choice of voters truly reflects the will of the Palestinian people, a national reconciliation and, in particular, between Fatah and Hamas will be necessary.

Hamas agreed to a two-state solution if the Palestinian people approved the terms achieved by Abbas and Fatah, even though Hamas had not yet acknowledged Israel's existence.[73]

Carter's report challenged the bases of Israeli-American policy. He argued that isolating Hamas produced stalemate, not progress, and, as polls showed, increased Hamas's popularity given Abbas's failure to reach an accord with Israel. This was not the first time that Hamas's calls for truces had been aired, but the declaration of acceptance of a two-state solution, sponsored by a former American president, drew international attention.[74]

President Bush reacted with fury to Carter's initiative and, in a speech to the Israeli Knesset the next month, charged that those who talked to terrorists and radicals such as Hamas and Hizbollah were analogous to those who sought to appease Hitler in 1938–1939: "We have an obligation to call this what it is—the false comfort of appeasement, which has been repeatedly discredited by history."[75] But Hamas's position, to accept a Palestinian referendum on the terms of a two-state solution, was similar to that taken by Menachem Begin on the 1979 Egyptian-Israeli peace treaty that entailed Israel's withdrawal from the Sinai. Begin refused to openly back the treaty but said that if the Knesset approved it, he would accept it.

EVENTS LEADING TO ISRAEL'S INVASION OF GAZA, DECEMBER 2008

Subsequent efforts to forge a new pact between Fatah and Hamas have failed as a result of deep mutual mistrust as well as major policy differences. Fatah's aversion to Hamas has also been fueled by American and Israeli encouragement that loyalty to their sponsorship of peace talks will produce results. But Mahmud Abbas's reliance on these powers has fostered further Palestinian disillusionment with his leadership because of daily Israeli raids into West Bank towns and ongoing settlement building. Prime Minister Olmert justified the stalemate by arguing that Abbas was too weak to reach an agreement while Hamas, as a terrorist organization, was unacceptable as a negotiating partner. But the status quo further boosted popular respect for Hamas among Palestinians, if only out of sympathy for the plight of Gaza inhabitants, as became clear when Israel again invaded Gaza in December 2008 under dubious circumstances.

Hamas and Israel had established a mutually agreed-upon truce in June 2008. The rocket attacks that occurred were accepted as those usually of Islamic Jihad until November when Israeli politicians began to suggest that Hamas's control of Gaza again had to be confronted. Their motive was linked to upcoming February 2009 Israeli elections where Netanyahu and Likud appeared to have the lead based on his charges of Kadima ineptness in dealing with the rocket problem that severely impacted the Israeli town of Sderot. With Prime Minister Olmert soon to leave office and to be indicted on corruption charges, Kadima Foreign Minister Tzipi Livni and Labor Party head Ehud Barak, defense minister in Olmert's coalition, decided to launch an assault against Hamas to bolster their candidacies against charges of being weak on the issue of Israeli national security; pollsters predicted, accurately, that the Labor Party in particular had lost popular support.[76]

On November 4, 2008, Israel broke the truce with Hamas by launching a raid into Gaza. As expected, this triggered major rocket attacks attributed to Hamas and laid the groundwork for the assault on December 27 that devastated Gaza. (See Figures 11.2 and 11.3.) It left an estimated 1,300 Palestinians dead, as opposed to 13 Israeli troops, but failed to shake Hamas's hold over Gaza or to gain the release of the Israeli hostage captured in July 2006. The timing of the

Figure 11.2 ■ Palestinian Rocket Fire from Gaza, 2008

A woman militant of Islamic Jihad holds an al-Sraya rocket during a rally in the midst of the December 2008 Israeli assault on Gaza. These rockets and the larger al-Qassams killed few Israelis but unnerved them by the very fact they were in range of these weapons.

Figure 11.3 ■ Israeli Mobile Artillery Firing into Gaza

An Israeli soldier lines up shells for an artillery unit to fire into Gaza. The type of weapons used and their firepower illustrate the disparity in military strength between Palestinians in Gaza and Israel.

mission, which ended in mid-January 2009, was designed to conclude before the inauguration of President Barack Obama, the Democratic Party victor in the American elections of November 2008. His administration was expected to take a firmer hand in criticizing Israeli settlement building and to be more actively involved in promoting peace talks.

Israel's Gaza offensive failed to influence the Israeli electorate decisively, with the Israeli press reporting that Barak, Livni, and Olmert disagreed on how or if to end the Gaza assault.[77] Livni's Kadima Party gained one more seat than Likud in the February elections; Barak's Labor Party suffered a crushing defeat. But when Livni failed to form a coalition, Netanyahu accepted the challenge and established a government that includes far right-winger Avigdor Lieberman as foreign minister but also Ehud Barak and other Laborites; determined to oppose what she saw as his determined opposition to any substantive peace talks, Livni rejected Netanyahu's offers.

Netanyahu had declared before the elections that he would not be bound by Olmert's recent statements that peace with the Palestinians would require withdrawal from many West Bank settlements and East Jerusalem. Once appointed foreign minister, Lieberman declared that Israel was no longer bound by the Annapolis Conference guidelines, but only by the Road Map as interpreted by Israel; this meant no action by Israel unless it was satisfied that Palestinians met its demands, precisely the terms of reciprocity that Netanyahu had imposed in 1997. He then challenged the new Obama administration by announcing that American policy depended on Israeli approval.[78]

CONCLUSION

Is the two-state solution dead? As of April 2009, paralysis appears likely with respect to the ability of either the Palestinian or Israeli leadership to move in the direction of peace talks. The new Netanyahu-Lieberman government has renounced even the final official effort by the Bush administration and plans settlement expansion in the West Bank. The Palestinian leadership is as divided as ever. Israel's Gaza assault, Operation Cast Lead, failed to threaten Hamas which, in a poll conducted among Palestinians, gained more popularity from it at the expense of Mahmud Abbas. This process should continue, not because a majority of Palestinians might favor Hamas under normal conditions, but because Hamas has declared an interest in a two-state solution but remains defiant. Abbas, on the other hand, has nothing to show for his acceptance of American-sponsored talks with Olmert, and he now must impotently confront Israel's declared intent to further expand West Bank settlements.[79]

At the same time, the Obama administration has reversed the Bush administration's policy of distance and will become more immediately and continually involved in Palestinian-Israeli and Arab-Israeli matters. The Bush policy of isolating Hamas may continue as Secretary of State Hillary Clinton has declared that the United States will not talk to Hamas until it recognizes Israel. On the other hand, Clinton and the newly appointed special envoy to the region, former Senator George Mitchell, have declared that the Obama administration will include the 2002 Arab League peace initiative as part of its policy toward the region. This would appear to signal a major effort at an inclusive peace between Israel and major Arab states that would necessarily include a settlement of Palestinian-Israeli issues (see Document 11.7). This is a bold effort that will clash with the declared goals of the Netanyahu-Lieberman cabinet.[80] More conflict, possibly as much within Palestinian and Israeli communities as between them, seems likely before any vision of the prospect of peace takes hold.

QUESTIONS FOR CONSIDERATION

1. What are the conflicting versions of what happened at Camp David 2000?
2. Did Ariel Sharon support or oppose the peace efforts at Camp David 2000?
3. What were the goals of Israel's Disengagement Plan?
4. How would you describe the differences between Bush administration policy toward Arab-Israeli and Palestinian-Israeli issues and the approach that the Obama administration has presented?

CHRONOLOGY

2000	**June 10.** Hafiz al-Assad dies; succeeded by his son, Bashar.
	July 11–July 25. Camp David summit.
	September 28. Ariel Sharon visits Temple Mount/Haram al-Sharif. Beginning of second intifada.
2001	**February 6.** Sharon elected prime minister of Israel. Forms coalition cabinet with Labor Party.
	April 30. Sharm el-Sheikh Fact-Finding (Mitchell) Committee submits report to President George W. Bush.
	September 11. Al-Qaida terrorist attacks on World Trade Center in New York City and Pentagon kill over 3,000.
	October. U.S. begins attacks on Afghanistan in response to 9/11 assaults.
2002	**January 18.** Israel isolates Yasir Arafat in his Ramallah compound.
	February 18. Saudi Arabia offers peace initiative; Sharon rejects it.
	June 24. President George W. Bush delivers Rose Garden address.
2003	**January 28.** Sharon reelected prime minister of Israel; forms cabinet with parties linked to settler movement.
	March. U.S. begins assault on Iraq.
	March 19. Arafat appoints Mahmud Abbas (Abu Mazen) prime minister of Palestinian Authority.
	April 30. Road Map officially issued, following Abbas's formal installation as prime minister.
	June 4. Aqaba summit.
	September. Abbas resigns as prime minister of Palestinian Authority.
2004	**March.** Israel assassinates Hamas leaders Abd al-Aziz Rantisi and Shaykh Ahmad Yasin.
	April 14. U.S. accepts Sharon's Gaza Disengagement Plan.
	November. Arafat dies in a Paris hospital.
2005	**January.** Mahmud Abbas elected president of the Palestinian Authority.
	August. Israel removes settlers, withdraws fully from Gaza Strip.
	November. Sharon resigns from the Likud Party; forms the Kadima Party.

2006	**January.** Sharon incapacitated by stroke; Ehud Olmert becomes acting prime minister of Israel. Hamas wins Palestinian parliamentary elections.
	March. Kadima Party wins Israeli elections; Olmert becomes prime minister in May.
	June 24. Israeli troops seize two Palestinians inside Gaza.
	June 25. Hamas squad enters Israel, kills two Israeli troops, takes one captive as hostage for return of Palestinian prisoners. Israel invades Gaza.
	July 12–August 14. Hizbollah-Israel war.
2007	**November.** Annapolis Conference.
2008	**June–November.** Hamas-Israel truce, broken by Israel November 4.
	December–January 2009. Israeli assault on Gaza.
2009	**January.** Barack Obama takes office as president of United States.
	February–March. Israeli elections. Kadima polls one delegate more than Likud but Binyamin Netanyahu forms coalition, becomes Israeli prime minister in March.

Notes

1. Deborah Sontag, "On Hopeful Soil, Arafat and Barak Chase an Old Dream," *New York Times*, November 2, 1999, notes Barak's concern for Jewish terrorism.

2. Deborah Sontag, "Barak Is Pledging Halt to Housing on West Bank," ibid., December 12, 1999; and Joel Greenberg, "Israel Destroys Shrine to Mosque Gunman," ibid., December 30, 1999.

3. Haim Shapiro, "NRP Rabbis Forbid Golan Pullout," *Jerusalem Post International Edition*, January 4, 2000. For the failure of the Israeli-Syrian talks, see Charles Enderlin, *Shattered Dreams: The Failure of the Peace Process in the Middle East, 1995–2002*, translated by Susan Fairfield (New York, 2003), 125–42; and Ahron Bregman, *Elusive Peace: How the Holy Land Defeated America* (New York, 2005), 23–63.

4. Lee Hockstader, "Trophy Photos Betray Israeli Police Abuse," *Washington Post*, <www.washingtonpost.com>, September 27, 2000. Israel's plans for East Jerusalem before and after Oslo are outlined in Amir S. Cheshin, Bill Hutman, and Avi Melamed, *Separate and Unequal: The Inside Story of Israeli Rule in East Jerusalem* (Cambridge, Mass., 1999), 248–49 and map on 265.

5. Deborah Sontag, "Albright in Middle East Trying to Push Israeli-Palestinian Talks," *New York Times*, June 6, 2000; Milton Viorst, "Peace in Oslo but No Peace in Jerusalem: A Pact's Built-in Edge for Israel," ibid., May 24, 2000.

6. Janine Zacharia, "Gore, Bush at AIPAC Rally Pledge Unflagging Support for Israel," *Jerusalem Post*, <www.jpost.com>, May 24, 2000.

7. Helen Freedman, "Looking at the AIPAC 2000 Conference through AFSI Eyes," <www.freeman.org/m_onlin/jun00/freedman.htm>; and Francine Kiefer, "Bush's Mideast Tête-à-tête: Cookies and Trucks," *Christian Science Monitor*, <www.csmonitor.com>, May 8, 2002, discuss the driveway remark as well as Bush's personal rapport with Sharon. AFSI (Americans for a Safe Israel) supports retention of "Judea, Samaria, Gaza and the Golan [as] Integral Parts of Israel" and essential to Israel's security; see <www.afsi.org> for additional information.

8. Robert Malley and Hussein Agha, "Camp David: The Tragedy of Errors," *New York Review of Books*, August 9, 2001, 59–65, first provided a counterargument to the official line blaming Arafat. See also Dennis Ross's reply and the Malley/Agha rejoinder, "Camp David: An Exchange," ibid., September 20, 2001. Ross's version appeared in far more detail in his memoir, *The Missing Peace: The Inside Story of the Fight for Middle East Peace* (New York, 2004), which omits information on key issues such as Israeli settlement expansion during the Oslo process. Four books countering Ross, some based on extensive interviews with members of all delegations, are Enderlin, *Shattered Dreams*, and Bregman, *Elusive Peace*, cited in note 3; and also Clayton Swisher, *The Truth about Camp David: The Untold Story about the Collapse of the Middle East Peace Process* (New York, 2004), and Yoram Meital, *Peace in Tatters: Israel, Palestine and the Middle East* (Boulder, Colo., 2006).

9. The reference to the "great charade" is in Meital, *Peace in Tatters*, 69–91. In addition to Malley and Agha, "Camp David: Tragedy of Errors," 59–60, for discussion of the specifics of the talks, see also the critique of each side's approaches by Palestinian and Israeli analysts in Tamara Cofman Wittes, ed., *How Israelis and Palestinians Negotiate: A Cross-Cultural Analysis of the Oslo Peace Process* (Washington, D.C., 2005).

10. Lamia Lahoud, "Israel Offers Palestinians 66% of WB for Initial State," *Jerusalem Post*, <www.jpost.com>, May 13, 2000.

11. Bregman, *Elusive Peace*, 107.

12. Ibid., 111–14. Bregman notes, 114, that Clinton misrepresented to Arafat at one point Barak's conditions for continuing the talks. Ross, *The Missing Peace*, 688, confirms that Barak wanted Clinton to pretend to Arafat that the ideas were Clinton's.

13. Jeremy Pressman, "Visions in Collision: What Happened at Camp David and Taba?" *International Security* 28, 2 (Fall 2003): 17–19; John Kifner, "The Holiest City, the Toughest Con-

flict," *New York Times*, July 23, 2000; Danna Harmon, "When Push Came to Shove: Ehud Barak's Assumption That He Had a Deal the Palestinians Couldn't Refuse Proved Wrong, Where Did He Fail?" *Jerusalem Post International Edition*, August 4, 2000. No minutes of the meetings and offers have been published.

14. The quote is by Khalil Shikaki in Etta Prince-Gibson, "Jerusalem: At the Conflict's Heart," *Jerusalem Post International Edition*, August 28, 2000. For Jerusalem's divisions, see the recent study by Bernard Wasserstein, *Divided Jerusalem: The Struggle for the Holy City* (New Haven, Conn., 2001) and Menachem Klein, *The Jerusalem Problem: The Struggle for Permanent Status*, trans. Haim Watzman (Gainesville, Fla., 2003).

15. Bregman, *Elusive Peace*, 120–21. Swisher, *Truth about Camp David*, 332–33, quotes an Israeli source as stating that Ross acted at Barak's request. Ross, *Missing Peace*, 708–11, skirts the issue of direct Israeli encouragement but notes that he did talk to Barak's aide Dan Meridor (709). Ross defends Clinton's praise of Barak as helping Barak domestically, but makes no mention of promises to Arafat not to blame him for the talks' failure.

16. Malley and Agha, "Camp David: The Tragedy of Errors," 62–63.

17. Pressman, "Visions in Collision," 6.

18. Enderlin, *Shattered Dreams*, 360–61. Cf. Swisher, *The Truth about Camp David*, 362, where Ross unleashes a vituperative broadside blaming Arafat for the failure of the talks. For a fuller discussion, see my review of Swisher's book in *Middle East Policy* 12, 1 (Spring 2005): 156–60. Ross, in his taped interview with Enderlin contradicts his version of Camp David as offered in his exchanges with Malley and Agha, cited in note 8.

19. Herb Keinon, "Exclusive Interview with PM Ehud Barak," *Jerusalem Post*, <www.jpost .com>, October 2, 2000.

20. Quoted in John F. Burns, "Barak Proposes Pact with Likud if Arafat Balks, but Sharon Rejects Idea," *New York Times*, August 25, 2000.

21. The text is in Enderlin, *Shattered Dreams*, 334–39.

22. Bregman, *Elusive Peace*, 141–47; Enderlin, *Shattered Dreams*, 339–41; Swisher, *Truth about Camp David*, 399–401; Pressman, "Visions in Collision," 20. Compare Ross, *Missing Peace*, 753–58.

23. Enderlin, *Shattered Dreams*, 351–57, has the text of the discussions.

24. Barak's claim of Palestinian compliance in Sharon's visit was false, as he admitted in his remarks to the Mitchell Commission, "Sharm el-Sheikh Fact-Finding Final Report," April 30, 2001, 6 <www.usinfo.state.gov/regional/mitchell.htm>; Sharon's goal of undermining potential compromises to create a shared capital is noted by Herb Keinon and Etgar Lefkovits, "Sharon Vows to Fight Division of Jerusalem," *Jerusalem Post*, <www.jpost.com>, September 29, 2000.

25. Ori Nir, "Snipers Admit They Fired Live Bullets during Nazareth Riots," *Haaretz*, <www.haaretz.com>, April 7, 2001, relates accounts of the firepower used, including rubber-coated metal bullets from fifteen yards without warning—they are lethal within thirty yards. The Or Commission, established to investigate the incidents, recommended trials but the Sharon government declined to press charges.

26. U.S. Department of State, "Israel and the Occupied Territories," *Country Reports on Human Rights Practices—2000* (February 23, 2001): 22, <www.state.gov/g/drl/rls/hrrpt/2000/ nea/794pf.htm>.

27. For Arafat and the intifada, see Larry Derfner, "The Chairman's Losing Gamble," *Jerusalem Post International Edition*, October 27, 2000; Edward Cody, "Israel's Grinding Presence Fuels a Festering Palestinian Rage," *Washington Post*, <www.washingtonpost.com>, October 27, 2000; and Amira Hass, "The Mirror Does Not Lie," *Haaretz*, <www.haaretz.com>, November 1, 2000, who commented that Israelis viewed Palestinian subordination as a natural condition that they should continue to accept. For targeted assassinations, see U.S. Department of State, "Israel and the Occupied Territories—2000," 21–23.

28. A perceptive article from the period is Amos Harel, "Wildly Throwing Punches: Key Members of the Defence Establishment Sense the IDF Has Used Excessive Force against the Palestinians," *Haaretz*, <www.haaretz.com>, December 12, 2000. Harel's sources attributed the ferocity of the military reply to Chief of Staff Shaul Mofaz and his deputy, Moshe Ya'alon, both Likud backers. Mofaz would ultimately become Sharon's minister of defense.

29. Jane Perlez, "Bush and Sharon Find Much in Common," *New York Times*, March 21, 2001, mentions Bush's appreciation for Sharon's sense of history and common ground; Glenn Kessler, "Bush Sticks to the Broad Strokes: In Mideast Peace Push, President Wary of Details and Deep Intervention," *Washington Post*, June 3, 2003.

30. For problematic official versions of the seizure of the *Karine A*, see Brian Whitaker, "The Strange Affair of the *Karine A*: Israel's Official Account of the Palestinian Authority's Connections with a Ship Found Loaded with Weapons Makes Little Sense," *Guardian*, <www.guardian .co.uk>, January 21, 2002; Zvi Bar'el, "A Perplexing Route," *Haaretz*, <www.haaretz.com>, February 16, 2002; and Sara Leibovich-Dar, "Half-Truths and Double-Talk," ibid., January 25, 2002, which ranges more widely than the *Karine A* incident.

31. Charles D. Smith, "The 'Do More' Chorus," MERIP Press Information Note 91, <www .merip.com>, April 15, 2002. Yossi Verter and Gideon Alon, "Sharon: First We'll Beat Them Badly, Then We Can Negotiate," *Haaretz*, <www.haaretz.com>, March 5, 2002; and David Kimche, "True Leaders Choose the Good," *Jerusalem Post*, <www.jpost.com>, May 14, 2001, who notes that lessons drawn from war games concluded that increasing the number of Palestinian casualties "would only intensify the hatred and desire for revenge, making the ultimate goal of reconciliation and understanding between the two peoples that much harder to achieve."

32. Yezid Sayigh, "The Palestinian Strategic Impasse," *Survival* 44, 4 (Winter 2002–2003): 8–9.

33. U.S. Department of State, *Country Reports on Human Rights Practices—2005*, "Israel and the Occupied Territories," 36, <www.state.gov/g/drl/rls/hrrpt/2005/61690.htm>.

34. I rely on the comments and statistics provided in the U.S. Department of State, *Country Reports on Human Rights Practices*, "Israel and the Occupied Territories," for 2000, 2001, and 2002 (accessed at <www.state.gov/g/drl/rls/hrrpt,2000[or2001,2002]/nea>).

35. Ibid., "Israel and the Occupied Territories—2001," 26. Harassments included forcing Palestinians to wait hours at checkpoints; in one instance, forcing schoolteachers to lie in a ditch in the rain for several hours; broadcast pornography to Palestinians, after wrecking offices they had occupied before they left: "Israel and the Occupied Territories—2002," 36. Soldiers often defecated into office equipment and soiled schools they occupied, in addition to pulling cars out into streets so that tanks could crush them; by Irene Siegel, "The Chaos of Seeing: Witnessing the Occupied Territories," *Middle East Women Studies Review* 17, 3 and 4 (Fall 2002/Winter 2003): 1–9. See also the article by Avishai Margalit, "The Suicide Bombers," *The New York Review of Books*, January 16, 2003: 36–39, and two recent studies of suicide bombers, Robert Pape, *Dying to Win: The Strategic Logic of Suicide Terrorism* (New York, 2005), and Mohammed Hafez, *Manufacturing Human Bombs: The Making of Palestinian Suicide Bombers* (Washington, D.C., 2006).

36. "Israel and the Occupied Territories—2002," 33; and ibid., 2005, 29. There is an extensive literature on Jenin: see, for example, Chris McGreal and Brian Whitaker, "Israel Accused over Jenin Assault: Red Cross and Amnesty Say Attack Violated Geneva Accords," *Guardian*, <www.guardian.co.uk>, April 23, 2002; Brian Whitaker, "Battle for Truth in Jenin," ibid.; and Suzanne Goldenberg, "Israel Blocks UN Mission to Jenin," ibid., April 24, 2002.

37. Compare "Israel and the Occupied Territories—2005," 35, with Gideon Alon and Aluf Benn, "Government Approves Changes to Fence Route near Ariel," *Haaretz*, <www.haaretz .com>, April 30, 2006, which mentions the fence being extended into the Judean desert. For the impact of the fence, including discriminatory measures, see Amira Hass, "IDF Redefines Palestinians West of the Fence," ibid., October 14, 2003.

38. "Israel and the Occupied Territories—2005," 2, 23; and Sagi Or, "This Year Has Seen the Fewest Fatalities since the Intifada Began," *Haaretz*, <www.haaretz.com>, September 28, 2005. "Israel and the Occupied Territories—2002," 35–36; and James Bennett, "In Palestinian Children, Signs of Increasing Malnutrition," *New York Times*, July 26, 2002.

39. William B. Quandt, *Peace Process: American Diplomacy and the Arab-Israeli Conflict since 1967*, 3rd ed. (Washington, D.C., 2005), 408.

40. "Clean Break: A New Strategy for Securing the Realm," <www.israeleconomy.org/strat1 .htm>, June 1996; and David Wurmser, "Coping with Crumbling States: A Western and Israeli Balance of Power Strategy for the Levant," <www.israeleconomy.org/strat2.htm>, December 1996. Both papers can also be accessed at <www.iasps.org> under "Research Papers in Strategy." IASPS (Institute for Advanced Strategic and Political Studies) is a pro-Likud think tank with offices in Jerusalem and Washington. See also Akiva Eldar, "Perles of Wisdom for the Feithful," *Haaretz*, <www.haaretz.com>, September 30, 2002. Overviews of the neoconservative movement and its views on Iraq and Israel can be found in Julie Kosterlitz, "The Neoconservative Moment," *National Journal*, May 17, 2003; Joel Beinin, "Pro-Israeli Hawks and the Second Gulf War," *Middle East Report Online*, <www.merip.org>, April 6, 2003; George Packer, *The Assassin's Gate: America in Iraq* (New York, 2005) Chs. 1–3; "Clean Break" is discussed on 30–32; and Jim Mann, *Rise of the Vulcans: The History of Bush's War Cabinet* (New York, 2004).

41. The February 1998 letter to Clinton can be found at <www.centerforsecuritypolicy.org/ index.jsp?section=papers&code=98-D_33at>; the May letter is at <www.newamericancentury .org/iraqletter1998.htm>.

42. Michael Dobbs, "Back to Political Forefront: Iran Contra Figure Plays Key Role on Mideast," *Washington Post*, <www.washingtonpost.com>, May 27, 2003; and Robert G. Kaiser, "Bush and Sharon Nearly Identical on Mideast Policy," ibid., February 9, 2003, who has the Likudnik reference.

43. Eric Schmitt, "Aide Denies Shaping Data to Justify War," *New York Times*, June 6, 2003, notes the fury of career intelligence officials who believed that Feith misrepresented what occurred. For the charge that Feith gave Likud operatives access to his office, bypassing channels and CIA-Mossad links, see Julian Borger, "The Spies Who Pushed for War," *Guardian*, <www .guardian.co.uk>, July 17, 2003. For Cheney and Rumsfeld bypassing the State Department, see Dana Milbank, "Colonel Finally Saw Whites of Their Eyes," *Washington Post*, <www.washington post.com>, August 20, 2005; and Richard Leiby, "Breaking Ranks," ibid., January 19, 2006.

44. "The Sharm-el-Sheikh Fact-Finding Committee Final Report," delivered to President Bush, April 30, 2001, <http://avalon.law.yale.edu/21st_century/mitchell_plan.asp>.

45. Ibid., 14–15, and footnote 39.

46. "President Bush Calls for New Palestinian Leadership," The Rose Garden, Washington, D.C., June 24, 2002, <www.state.gov/g/drl/rls/hrrpt/2005/61690.htm>.

47. "A Performance-Based Roadmap to a Permanent Two-State Solution to the Israeli-Palestinian Conflict," <www.state.gov/r/pa/prs/ps/2003/20062.htm>.

48. Aluf Benn, "Sharon Blasts Road Map," *Haaretz*, <www.haaretz.com>, October 23, 2002; Julia Duin, "Zionist Meeting Brands 'Road Map' as Heresy," *The Washington Times*, <www .washingtontimes.com>, May 19, 2003.

49. The quote is from the "Sasson Report," presented by Talia Sasson, "Opinion concerning Unauthorized Outposts," March 8, 2005, as excerpted in the *Journal of Palestine Studies* 34, 3 (Spring 2005), 181. For a detailed summary, go to <www.mfa.gov.il>.

50. Aluf Benn, "Israel Removes All Mention of 'Independent State' in 'Road Map,'" *Haaretz*, <www.haaretz.com>, March 16, 2003; and Chris McGreal, "No Independent Palestine, Sharon Insists," *Guardian*, <www.guardian.co.uk>, March 17, 2003.

51. Quandt, *Peace Process*, 403, quoting Glenn Kessler, "Bush Sticks to the Broad Strokes," *Washington Post*, June 3, 2003.

52. Steven R. Weisman, "Bush Rebukes Israel for Attack in Gaza," *New York Times*, June 11, 2003; and Aluf Benn, "Bush May Be 'Deeply Troubled,' But Israel Isn't," *Haaretz*, <www.haaretz .com>, June 11, 2003.

53. The text of the Geneva Initiative (or Accord) can be found at <www.haaretz.com>, October 19, 2003, and in Charles Enderlin, *The Lost Years: Radical Islam, Intifada, and Wars in the Middle East, 2001–2006*, translated by Suzanne Verderber (New York, 2007) 297–320.

54. Ibid., 212.

55. Aluf Benn, "IDF Draws Up Plan to Quit Gaza and Seven West Bank Settlements but Sharon Refuses to Discuss the Proposal," *Haaretz*, <www.haaretz.com>, August 28, 2002; and Benn, "PM: Despite Rumors, No Plans for a [Further] West Bank Pullout," ibid., September 29, 2005.

56. For the challenge to Sharon, see Gregg Myre, "4 Israeli Intelligence Experts Call for Political Solution," *New York Times*, November 14, 2003, and Myre, "4 Israeli Ex-Security Chiefs Denounce Sharon's Hard Line," ibid., November 15, 2003; and Enderlin, *Lost Years*, 207–08, 217–18.

57. Bregman, *Elusive Peace*, 281.

58. Quandt, *Peace Process*, 283–85, 405. Last-minute American efforts to modify the agreement failed. Sharon sat in his aircraft at Tel Aviv airport, refusing to take off for Washington until Condoleezza Rice backed down on the matter. Maariv Staff, "Sharon's Departure to Washington Delayed by Disagreement with US," *Maariv*, <www.maarivenglish.com>, April 12, 2004; and James Bennett, "Sharon's Tenacity Swayed Bush, Israeli Aide Says," *New York Times*, <www.nytimes.com>, April 16, 2004.

59. "Ariel Sharon's and George Bush's Letters in Full," *Haaretz*, <www.haaretz.com>, April 19, 2004. A revised Israeli version, "Appendix A," was published on May 28, 2004, in *Haaretz*, <www.haaretz.com>. A second revised version, dated June 6, 2004, can be accessed on the Israeli prime minister's Web site, <www.pmo.gov.il>; enter "disengagement plan" in the search engine, then choose option 1. For an overview, see Elisha Efrat, *The West Bank and the Gaza Strip: A Geography of Occupation and Disengagement* (New York, 2006). I rely on the version of the Disengagement Plan found in *Haaretz*, <www.haaretz.com>, April 16, 2004.

60. Ari Shavit, "The Big Freeze (Interview with Dov Weisglas)," *Haaretz*, <www.haaretz .com>, October 8, 2004.

61. "Elections 2006," *Jerusalem Post*, March 30, 2006, at <www.jpost.com/COO6/Supplements/ elections/finals.html>.

62. Shmuel Rosner and Arnon Regular, "U.S. Won't Oppose Hamas Participation in PA Elections," *Haaretz*, <www.haaretz.com>, October 21, 2005; Scott Wilson and Glenn Kessler, "U.S. Funds Enter Fray in Palestinian Elections: Bush Administration Uses USAID as Invisible Conduit," *Washington Post*, <www.washingtonpost.com>, January 22, 2006.

63. Amira Hass, "How the PA Failed," *Haaretz*, <www.haaretz.com>, November 2, 2005; Glenn Kessler, "U.S. Policy Seen as Big Loser in Palestinian Vote," *Washington Post*, <www .washingtonpost.com>, January 28, 2006.

64. Laura King, "Deadly Feud in Gaza Follows an Old Script: Battles between Security Forces Linked to Hamas and Fatah Reflect the Deliberate Dispersal of Power by the Late Palestinian Chief, Arafat," *Los Angeles Times*, <www.latimes.com>, May 28, 2006.

65. Sara Roy, "Praying with the Eyes Closed: Reflections on the Disengagement from Gaza," *Journal of Palestine Studies* 34, 4 (Summer 2005), 64–74; Arieh O'Sullivan, "Army: New Gaza Fence Is Formidable Barrier," *Jerusalem Post*, <www.jpost.com>, September 8, 2005; Danielle Haas, "Israel Plans High-Tech Barrier around Gaza," *Associated Press*, <www.washingtonpost .com>, July 28, 2005.

66. Akiva Eldar, "Quartet to Hold Key Talks on Fate of Its Mideast Peacekeeping Role," *Haaretz*, <www.haaretz.com>, May 4, 2006; Amiram Cohen, "Israeli Produce Bound for Gaza Rots at Closed Border Crossing," ibid., January 22, 2006; and Scott Wilson, "Left to Rot in Gaza: Strip's Economy Suffers as Trade Passage to Israel Remains Sealed," *Washington Post*, <www .washingtonpost.com>, March 19, 2006.

67. Shahar Smooha, "All the Dreams We Had Are Gone Now," Interview with James Wolfensohn, *Haaretz*, <www.haaretz.com>, July 19, 2007. For Wolfensohn and the abortive agreement intended to open gates, see also Amira Hass, "It's No Wonder Envoy Is Frustrated," *Haaretz*,

<www.haaretz.com>, October 26, 2005; and Akiva Eldar, "Analysis: Closure on Gaza Breaches PM's Promise to Rice," *Haaretz*, <www.haaretz.com>, December 5, 2005.

68. Akiva Eldar, "UN Aid Workers: Gaza on Verge of Disaster," *Haaretz*, <www.haaretz.com>, April 4, 2006; and Conal Urquhart, "Gaza on Brink of Implosion as Aid Cut-off Starts to Bite," *Observer*, <www.observer.guardian.co.uk>, April 16, 2006.

69. Ken Ellingwood, "2 Palestinians Held in Israel's First Arrest Raid in Gaza since Pullout," *Los Angeles Times*, <www.latimes.com>, June 25, 2006; and Josh Brannon, "IDF Arrests Hamas Members in Gaza," *Jerusalem Post*, <www.jpost.com>, June 24, 2006.

70. Augustus R. Norton, *Hezbollah: A Short History. Princeton Studies in Muslim Politics* (Princeton, N.J., 2007) considers the brief war in the broader context of Hizbollah's presence in Lebanon. Lessons of the war are assessed in Anthony H. Cordesman, with George Sullivan and William D. Sullivan, *Lessons of the 2006 Israeli-Hezbollah War* (Washington, D.C., 2007). Two studies of the conflict are Nubar Hovsepian, ed., *The War on Lebanon, a Reader* (New York, 2007) that includes accounts from Lebanon, and the analysis by Israeli journalists, Amos Harel and Avi Issacharoff, *34 Days: Israel, Hezbollah, and the War in Lebanon*, Ora Cummings and Moshe Tlamim, translators (New York, 2008).

71. The most complete account of this fiasco is David Rose, "The Gaza Bombshell," in *Vanity Fair*, <www.vanityfair.com/politics/features/2008/04/gaza200804?prin.>, April 2008.

72. Documents can be found in the *Journal of Palestine Studies* 37, 3 (Spring 2008): 74–92.

73. "Former President Jimmy Carter, Notes on Meetings with Hamas Leaders and Syrian Pres. Bashar al-Asad, and Observations Regarding the Peace Process, Atlanta, GA 22 April 2008 (Excerpts)," in *Journal of Palestine Studies* 37, 4 (Summer 2008): 182–86. The Hamas statement is on 185.

74. "Hamas Calls for End to Bloodshed," *Jerusalem Post*, <www.jpost.com>, March 26, 2006; and "Livni: Attacks on Soldiers Not Terror," ibid., April 11, 2006, where the Kadima foreign minister referred to Hamas attacks in Israel as terrorist, whereas those in the occupied territories were not. See also Amira Hass, "Haniyeh: Hamas Willing to Accept Palestinian State within 1967 Borders," *Haaretz*, <www.haaretz.com>, November 9, 2008, immediately after Israel broke the truce.

75. "Pres. George W. Bush, Address to Members of the Knesset, Jerusalem, 15 May 2008 (Excerpts)," *Journal of Palestine Studies* 37, 4 (Summer 2008): 186–88. The quote is on 186–87.

76. Richard Boudreaux, "Gaza Conflict Can Make or Break Ehud Barak's Fortunes," *Los Angeles Times*, <www.latimes.com>, January 2, 2009.

77. Aluf Benn and Amos Harel, "Barak, Livni, Olmert at Loggerheads over Exit Strategy of Gaza Operation," *Haaretz*, <www.haaretz.com>, January 8, 2009.

78. Mazal Muallem, "Netanyahu: I'm Not Bound by Olmert Pledges, Won't Evacuate Settlements," *Haaretz*, <www.haaretz.com>, January 30, 2009; Lily Galili and Barak Raviv, "Lieberman: U.S. to Accept Any Israeli Policy Decision," ibid., April 22, 2009; and Rachel Shabi, "Avigdor Lieberman Rules Out Concessions to Palestinians: Israel Never Ratified 2007 Annapolis Peace Talks, New Foreign Minister Says in Debut Speech," *Guardian*, <www.guardian.co.uk>, April 1, 2009; cf "Olmert: No Peace without Dividing Jerusalem," <www.ynetnews.com>, March 6, 2009.

79. "Poll: Hamas More Popular after Gaza Offensive," *Haaretz*, <www.haaretz.com>, March 9, 2009. For Netanyahu's plans, Sara Miller, "Peace Now: Israel Planning 73,000 New Homes in West Bank," ibid., <www.haaretz.com>, March 2, 2009, and Rory McCarthy, "Israel Annexing East Jerusalem, Says EU," *Guardian*, <www.guardian.co.uk>, March 6, 2009.

80. Barak Ravid and Yoav Stern, "U.S. Envoy: Arab Peace Initiative Will Be Part of Obama Policy," *Haaretz*, <www.haaretz.com>, April 5, 2009; and Glenn Kessler, "Clinton Pursues 'Comprehensive Peace' in Mideast," *Washington Post*, <www.washingtonpost.com>, March 2, 2009.

"YOU'LL MISS ME YET": INTERVIEW WITH MARWAN BARGHOUTI

November 9, 2001

Jailed in Israel for "terrorist activities" since 2003, Marwan Barghouti remains a prominent leader of Fatah factions in the West Bank. Though active in both intifadas, from exile in Jordan during the first, he had close ties to the Israeli peace camp and initially backed the Oslo process. His comments indicate a Palestinian view of Oslo and the Camp David talks as being undermined primarily by Israel. He, like Ami Ayalon (see Document 11.2), sees peace as being achieved only through full Israeli withdrawal from the occupied territories.

Marwan Barghouti, one of the pioneers of peace between Israel and the Palestinians, . . . is running for his life. . . . He lives underground, moves on the fringe, hides. He speaks fluent Hebrew, jokes, and remembers for a moment those good old days when he was one of the pioneers of dialogue with Israelis, when they spoke of peace, of a vision, of a dream. Today he stands at the head of the war. . . .

Q: What is your solution for ending the current situation?

A: It's simple: You must understand, once and for all, that you must . . . announce that the occupation is over and that Israel is leaving the territories. . . . Present a timetable for withdrawal from all of the territories and the dismantling of the settlements, and announce that you recognize an independent Palestinian state with its capital in East Jerusalem. Believe me, such an announcement on the part of Israel will change the situation from top to bottom. Everything will work out. . . .

Q: And the refugees? What about the refugees? You lost the support of the [Israeli] peace camp when you went back to the right of return.

A: A solution must be found for the refugee problem. I believe that such a solution will be found. The moment you announce the end of the occupation and recognize a sovereign, genuine Palestinian state, not a vassal state, at that very moment everything will change. It will be possible to solve the refugee problem as well, believe me. I mean it.

Q: . . . Your friends on the Israeli Left are asking, "what happened to Marwan?"

A: Nothing happened to me. As usual, you are asking the opposite questions and are seeing everything through your glasses. I was one of the bravest peace pioneers. I fought in the streets for Oslo. The problem is that since Rabin's assassination there hasn't been a peace process. I don't know what would have

Source: Ben Caspit, interview with Marwan Barghouti in *Ma'ariv*, November 9, 2001.

happened had Rabin not been murdered, but I know what happened after the murder. The whole of Israel society changed direction. The process stopped. You didn't leave us any choice.

Q: If Rabin had known in 1993 that you would come in 1999 and demand the right of return, he would have thrown you down the stairs.

A: You're back to that again? Put an end to this mentality of occupation mixed with panic. What are you so afraid of? Between 1967 and 1993 you built 25,000 apartments in the territories. Between 1993, after Oslo, and 2000, you built another 23,000 apartments in the territories. Had we known that this is what was going to happen, we also wouldn't have started this process.

Q: You have a degree in history. Did they teach you at Bir Zeit about the Holocaust, for example?

A: Of course. I know all of your history. But the Holocaust of the Jewish people does not justify our disaster. There is a refugee problem and it must be solved. Ways can be found. This is the most important point for Palestinians. The truth must be told. We reached a historic decision to recognize Israel, its security, its legitimacy. You still haven't reached your own decision to recognize us and our rights.

Q: You recognize Israel, but the right of return will destroy it, and it won't be a Jewish state.

A: We recognize Israel as a Jewish state. On the other hand, there is UN Resolution 194 and on the basis of that resolution it is possible to reach a solution that will satisfy everyone. . . .

Q: There was a government like that, not long ago. Barak agreed to give you the vast majority of the land and a large part of Jerusalem, and you responded with blood and fire.

A: Once again, you are both mistaken and misleading. We agreed to make do with 22 percent of historic Palestine. At Camp David you tried to take from this small portion an enclave here, a bloc there, the Jordan Valley, border crossings, Jerusalem. This is a state? This is a solution? This is justice? I'm telling you the truth. You have to count on people like me, not on the hypocrites. . . .

Q: Still, Barak's proposal could have been the basis for discussions, not for war. Oslo is based on the idea that your rifles are meant to keep order and fight terror, not shoot at us.

A: But Oslo died with Rabin. How would you feel if on every hill in territory that belongs to you a new settlement would spring up? . . . I reached a simple conclusion. You don't want to end the occupation and you don't want to stop the settlements, so the only way to convince you is by force. . . . This Intifada will lead to peace in the end. We need to escalate the conflict. It will be hard. Many of us will be killed, but there is no choice. Every one of us is willing to sacrifice himself. We have decided that Sharon will not bring you security, and we have succeeded. It's been 274 days since he was elected, and what has happened? Is there security? No. Nothing will help. Only a just agreement, the 1967 borders, a sovereign state, Jerusalem and a solution to the refugee problem. This is the formula and there is no other, and no one has the right to give up on it. . . .

DOCUMENT 11.2

"THE URGENT THING, IT IS TO UNCONDITIONALLY DISENGAGE OURSELVES FROM THE TERRITORIES": INTERVIEW WITH AMI AYALON

December 22, 2001

Appointed head of Shin Bet by Shimon Peres, Ami Ayalon resigned from his post in May 2000 on the eve of the Camp David summit. He, like Marwan Barghouti, considers a two-state solution based on Israeli withdrawal from the territories to be the only path to true peace and security and the sole means to guarantee Israeli democracy in a Jewish state. Ayalon, like Barghouti, attributes the second intifada to Palestinian anger and rejects claims of Arafat's complicity, a challenge to Barak's version. Note also his stance on the issue of the Palestinian right of return, which he rejects in principle but views as necessary to be considered as part of final negotiations, similar to Barghouti, and his comment that time favored the settlers and Hamas, not peace.

Q: How do you judge the state of the political debate in Israel?

A: Society, up to it[s] highest point, is in a state of confusion—a loss of reference points. This reality is masked by swaggering slogans: "vanquish terrorism!" At the Herziliyah colloquium [held December 16–19, 2001, and attended by the bulk of the Israeli military, security, and military industrial establishment], the army Chief of Staff declares "We are winning." He evokes the superiority of the Tsahal—the Israeli army; his "feeling [is] that the nation is gaining strength." Then he adds that "there are more Palestinian terrorists today than a year ago" and says that there will be even more tomorrow! If we are beating them, why are the terrorists gaining strength? In Israel, nobody is dealing with reality anymore. It is the consequence of a flawed perception of the peace process and of the failure of Camp David. The Israelis were provided with a one-sided version: "We were generous and they refused." This is ridiculous. And everything that follows from this misperception is flawed.

In addition, obsessed by the Palestinians, we forget to ask ourselves questions about ourselves. What do we want to be? Where are we going? No leader responds to these. . . .

Q: The great majority of the leaders, though, are convinced that time plays in the favor of Israel.

A: . . . This view obscures the consequences of our holding onto the Palestinian territories. And not only on the moral plane. Our state, in the spirit of its founders, has a reason to exist only if it furnishes a homeland for the Jewish people and if it is democratic. From these two perspectives, time is against us!

Source: Sylvain Cypel, interview with Ami Ayalon in Le Monde, December 23, 2001.

Demographically, it [time] works for the Palestinians, and politically, in favor of Hamas and the settlers.

But to fight against Hamas, it is necessary to evacuate the settlers, whose proximity with the Palestinians strengthens the hatred. Among the Palestinians, the weight of the Islamists is growing, and also that of the intellectuals who long favored the idea of two states, but now are saying "since the Israelis will never evacuate the settlements, well, eventually, there will be a binational state." But I absolutely don't want this. This would no longer be a Jewish state.

And if it remains a Jewish state, dominating an Arab population, it will no longer be democratic.

Q: Given the balance of power, do you exclude the possibility of an Israeli victory against the Palestinians?

A: The "victory"—we already had it! In 1967, we occupied all the Palestinian territories. Once "terrorism is vanquished," what will we do?

All this is absurd. The Palestinians want self-determination. Whoever imagines "vanquishing" them, then giving them bread and circuses and preventing the resumption of attacks, does not understand anything. Tsahal [the IDF] is stronger than ever, our intelligence services are excellent, so why is the problem not solved? Reoccupying the autonomous territories, killing Arafat—what would this change? Those who want "victory" want war forever.

Q: Yet, many people think that, since September 11th, Israel can change the regional situation in its favor.

A: What an illusion! September 11th changed many paradigms in the United States, but changed nothing of the basic givens in the Near East. Whatever the mistakes of Arafat, the Palestinian people will continue to exist. As long as the issue is not resolved, the region will not know stability. . . .

Q: But Israelis are traumatized by the Palestinian demand for the right of return of refugees.

A: Let's stop worrying ourselves so much with what the adversary says, or what he is made to say. What do we, ourselves, want? We reject the return of refugees. But we can only reject that if Israel recognizes unambiguously its role in the suffering imposed on the Palestinians and its obligation to participate in the solution to the problem. Israel must accept the principal of the right of return and the PLO must commit itself to not challenge the Jewish character of our state.

Q: What do you think of the strategic vision of the head of the Mossad, of Israel in the front line in the "third world war" against terrorism?

A: Whomever [sic] believes that Arafat equals Osama Bin Laden neither understands who is Arafat, nor who is Bin Laden. The latter is the guru of a very dangerous sect, marginal in Islam, that aims to create chaos and cares nothing for the international community. Arafat, for his part, dreams of being accepted by the international community. Since 1993, it is Arafat who never ceases to make reference to the international community, who demands the application of the resolutions of the United Nations, and we, the Israelis, who refuse! If we kill Bin Laden, his sect may disappear with him. If we kill Arafat, the Palestinian people will continue to want their independence.

Q: Do you fear that the Palestinian territories will become a quagmire for Tsahal [the IDF]?

A: People here say that the Palestinians behave like "madmen." It is not madness, but a bottomless despair. . . .

Yasser Arafat, contrary to what is hammered into us, neither prepared nor launched the Intifada. The explosion was spontaneous—against Israel, due to the absence of hope for the end of the occupation; and against the Palestinian Authority, its corruption, its impotence. Arafat could not repress it. . . .

Q: From Oslo to Camp David, did Israel miss a rare opportunity to make peace?

A: Yes. Everything is not the fault of the Israelis. The Palestinians, the international community, carry their part of the responsibility. But we missed an extraordinary opportunity: the situation was incredibly favorable after the end of communism, the Gulf War, the emergence of globalization—all phenomena that contributed to Israel reexamining its own assumptions. Now, we are regressing.

Q: Do you favor "unilateral separation" with the Palestinians?

A: I don't like the word separation—it reminds me of South Africa. I support an unconditional disengagement from the Palestinian territories. I would prefer that this is done in the context of an agreement. But we don't need one: withdrawing from the territories—this is the urgent thing. And a real withdrawal, that leaves the Palestinians territorial contiguity in a West Bank linked to Gaza, open to Egypt and Jordan. If they declare their state, Israel should be the first to recognize it and to propose to it state-to-state negotiations, on the basis of the last Clinton proposals, without conditions, to resolve the pending issues.

DOCUMENT 11.3

ARIEL SHARON'S LETTER TO GEORGE W. BUSH OUTLINING THE DISENGAGEMENT PLAN

April 14, 2004

As prearranged, Prime Minister Sharon presented this letter to President Bush along with his Disengagement Plan (Document 11.5). In this letter, Sharon stressed his adherence to the Road Map while acknowledging that this plan diverged from it, placing the blame on the Palestinians. He referred to a full withdrawal from Gaza, carried out in August 2005, and a withdrawal from four settlements in the northernmost West Bank. He promised that the security fence would be temporary, not permanent, and referred to a two-state solution to the Palestinian-Israeli problem.

Source: Haaretz, <www.haaretz.com/hasen/objects/pages/PrintArticleEn.jhtml?itemNo=415475>.

Dear Mr. President,

The vision that you articulated in your 24 June 2002 [Rose Garden] address constitutes one of the most significant contributions toward ensuring a bright future for the Middle East. Accordingly, the State of Israel has accepted the roadmap, as adopted by our government. For the first time, a practical and just formula was presented for the achievement of peace, opening a genuine window of opportunity for progress toward a settlement between Israel and the Palestinians, involving two states living side by side in peace and security. . . .

Having reached the conclusion that, for the time being, there exists no Palestinian partner with whom to advance peacefully toward a settlement and since the current impasse is unhelpful to the achievement of our shared goals, I have decided to initiate a process of gradual disengagement with the hope of reducing friction between the Israelis and Palestinians. The Disengagement Plan . . . will enable us to deploy our forces more effectively until such time that conditions in the Palestinian Authority allow for the full implementation of the roadmap to resume.

I attach for your review, the main principles of the Disengagement Plan. . . . According to this plan, the State of Israel intends to relocate military installations and all Israeli villages and towns in the Gaza Strip, as well as other military installations and a small number of villages in Samaria.

In this context, we also plan to accelerate construction of the Security Fence, whose completion is essential in order to ensure the security of the citizens of Israel. The fence is a security rather than political barrier, temporary rather than permanent, and therefore will not prejudice any final status issues including final borders. The route of the Fence, as approved by our Government's decisions, will take into account, consistent with security needs, its impact on Palestinians not engaged in terrorist activities. . . .

In this regard, we are fully aware of the responsibilities facing the State of Israel. These include limitations on the growth of settlements; removal of unauthorized outposts; and steps to increase, to the extent permitted by security needs, freedom of movement for Palestinians not engaged in terrorism. Under separate cover we are sending to you a full description of the steps the State of Israel is taking to meet all its responsibilities . . . [see Document 11.5].

DOCUMENT 11.4

PRESIDENT BUSH'S REPLY
TO ARIEL SHARON'S LETTER
April 14, 2004

As arranged, President Bush responded to Ariel Sharon's letter by welcoming it, though with cautionary statements regarding a "viable, contiguous, sovereign, and independent state," terms that did not appear in the June 24, 2002, speech that both he and Sharon mention. He also predetermines anticipated negotiating outcomes by his references to Israeli retention of major population centers and to denial of return of Palestinian refugees to pre-1948 Palestine.

Thank you for your letter setting out your disengagement plan.

. . . I remain committed to my June 24, 2002, vision of two states living side by side in peace and security as the key to peace, and to the road map as the route to get there. We welcome the disengagement plan you have prepared, under which Israel would withdraw certain military installations and all settlements from Gaza, and withdraw certain military installations and settlements in the West Bank. These steps described in the plan will mark real progress toward realizing my June 24, 2002, vision, and make a real contribution toward peace. . . .

The United States appreciates the risks such an undertaking represents. I therefore want to reassure you on several points. . . .

The United States reiterates its steadfast commitment to Israel's security, including secure, defensible borders, . . . as a Jewish state. It seems clear that an agreed, just, fair, and realistic framework for a solution to the Palestinian refugee issue as part of any final status agreement will need to be found through the establishment of a Palestinian state, and the settling of Palestinian refugees there, rather than in Israel.

As part of a final peace settlement, Israel must have secure and recognized borders, which should emerge from negotiations between the parties in accordance with UNSC Resolutions 242 and 338. In light of new realities on the ground, including already existing major Israeli populations centers, it is unrealistic to expect that the outcome of final status negotiations will be a full and complete return to the armistice lines of 1949, and all previous efforts to negotiate a two-state solution have reached the same conclusion.

It is realistic to expect that any final status agreement will only be achieved on the basis of mutually agreed changes that reflect these realities. I know that, as you state in your letter, you are aware that certain responsibilities face the

Source: Haaretz, <www.haaretz.com/hasen/objects/pages/PrintArticleEn.jhtml?itemNo=415475>.

State of Israel. Among these, your government has stated that the barrier being erected by Israel should be a security rather than political barrier, should be temporary rather than permanent, and therefore not prejudice any final status issues including final borders, and its route should take into account, consistent with security needs, its impact on Palestinians not engaged in terrorist activities.

As you know, the United States supports the establishment of a Palestinian state that is viable, contiguous, sovereign, and independent, so that the Palestinian people can build their own future in accordance with my vision set forth in June 2002 and with the path set forth in the road map. . . .

Mr. Prime Minister, . . . I commend your efforts and your courageous decision, which I support. As a close friend and ally, the United States intends to work closely with you to help make it a success.

DOCUMENT 11.5

ARIEL SHARON'S DISENGAGEMENT PLAN: KEY PRINCIPLES

April 2004

This text was the basis for George W. Bush's letter approving the plan where he stated that Israel could retain "major population centers" in the West Bank. It specifically mentions a Palestinian state. The "Main Points of the Plan" refer to Israel's intended actions, with the tacit admission in II.B.4 that Palestinians will not have real contiguity in the Israeli-occupied West Bank, but "transportation contiguity," meaning tunnels overseen by checkpoints. Part III, "Security Reality after the Evacuation," outlines Israel's encirclement of Gaza and retention of controls in the West Bank.

I. Overview

Israel is committed to the peace process, and aspires to reach a mutual agreement on the basis of two states for two peoples, the State of Israel as the state of the Jewish people and a Palestinian state for the Palestinian people, as part of the realization of President [George W.] Bush's vision.

Israel . . . has come to the conclusion that at present, there is no Palestinian partner with whom it is possible to make progress on a bilateral agreement. In light of this, a unilateral disengagement plan has been formulated, which is based on the following considerations:

A. . . . Israel must initiate a move that will not be contingent on Palestinian cooperation.

Source: Haaretz, <www.haaretz.com>, April 16, 2004.

B. The plan will lead to a better security reality, at least in the long term.

C. In any future final-status agreement, there will be no Israeli settlement in the Gaza Strip. However, it is clear that in Judea and Samaria, some areas will remain part of the state of Israel, among them civilian settlements, military zones and places where Israel has additional interests. . . .

F. The disengagement move will obviate the claims about Israel with regard to its responsibility for the Palestinians in the Gaza Strip.

G. The disengagement move does not detract from the existing agreements between Israel and the Palestinians. The existing arrangements will continue to prevail.

When there is evidence on the Palestinian side of the willingness, ability and actual realization of a fight against terror and of the implementation of the reforms stipulated in the road map, it will be possible to return to the track of negotiations and dialogue.

II. Main Points of the Plan

A. The Gaza Strip

1. Israel will evacuate the Gaza Strip, including all the Israeli settlements currently existing there, and will redeploy outside the territory of the Strip. . . . As a result, there will be no basis for the claim that the Gaza Strip is occupied territory.

B. Judea and Samaria

1. Israel will evacuate the area of northern Samaria . . . and will redeploy outside the evacuated area. . . .

3. The move will enable Palestinian territorial contiguity in . . . northern Samaria.

4. Israel will improve the transportation in Judea and Samaria with the aim of enabling Palestinian transportation contiguity in Judea and Samaria.

C. The Security Fence

Israel will continue to build the security fence, in accordance with the relevant government decisions. The route will take humanitarian considerations into account.

III. Security Reality after the Evacuation

A. The Gaza Strip

1. Israel will supervise and guard the external envelope on land, will maintain exclusive control in the air space of Gaza, and will continue to conduct military activities in the sea space of the Gaza Strip.

2. The Gaza Strip will be demilitarized and devoid of armaments, the presence of which is not in accordance with the existing agreements between the sides.

3. Israel reserves for itself the basic right of self-defense, including taking preventative steps as well as responding by using force against threats that will emerge from the Gaza Strip. . . .

DOCUMENT 11.6

ARAB PEACE PLAN PROPOSED BY SAUDI ARABIA AND ADOPTED AT ARAB LEAGUE SUMMIT, BEIRUT

March 27, 2002

Saudi Arabia took this step in the hope of engaging the United States in a comprehensive peace effort that settled all differences between Israel and Arab states with whom it did not have peace agreements. But this was conditioned on full Israeli withdrawal from the West Bank and Gaza and was consequently ignored by Prime Minister Ariel Sharon and by the Bush administration. That the Obama administration has embraced this idea as part of its Middle East initiative (see Document 11.7) signals its ambitious agenda for the region.

The Council of the League of Arab States at the Summit Level, at its 14th Ordinary Session,

Reaffirming the resolution taken in June 1996 at the Cairo Extra-Ordinary Arab Summit that a just and comprehensive peace in the Middle East is the strategic option of the Arab Countries, to be achieved in accordance with International Legality, and which would require a comparable commitment on the part of the Israeli Government. Having listened to the statement made by His Royal Highness Prince Abdullah bin Abdul Aziz, the Crown Prince of the Kingdom of Saudi Arabia, in which his Highness presented his Initiative calling for full Israeli withdrawal from all the Arab territories occupied since June 1967, in implementation of Security Council Resolutions 242 and 338, reaffirmed by the Madrid Conference of 1991 and the land for peace principle, and Israel's acceptance of an independent Palestinian State, with East Jerusalem as its capital, in return for the establishment of normal relations in the context of a comprehensive peace with Israel.

Emanating from the conviction of the Arab countries that a military solution to the conflict will not achieve peace or provide security for the parties, the council:

Source: Churches for Middle East Peace, <www.cmep.org/documents/Saudiproposal.htm>.

1. Requests Israel to reconsider its policies and declare that a just peace is its strategic option as well.

2. Further calls upon Israel to affirm:

    a. Full Israeli withdrawal from all the territories occupied since 1967, including the Syrian Golan Heights to the lines of June 4, 1967, as well as the remaining occupied Lebanese territories in the south of Lebanon.

    b. Achievement of a just solution to the Palestinian Refugee problem to be agreed upon in accordance with UN General Assembly Resolution 194.

    c. The acceptance of the establishment of a Sovereign Independent Palestinian State on the Palestinian territories occupied since the 4th of June 1967 in the West Bank and Gaza strip, with East Jerusalem as its capital.

3. Consequently, the Arab Countries affirm the following:

    a. Consider the Arab-Israeli conflict ended, and enter into a peace agreement with Israel, and provide security for all the states of the region.

    b. Establish normal relations with Israel in the context of this comprehensive peace.

4. Assures the rejection of all forms of Palestinian patriation which conflict with the special circumstances of the Arab host countries.

5. Calls upon the Government of Israel and all Israelis to accept this initiative in order to safeguard the prospects for peace and stop the further shedding of blood, enabling the Arab Countries and Israel to live in peace and good neighborliness and provide future generations with security, stability, and prosperity.

6. Invites the International Community and all countries and Organizations to support this initiative.

7. Requests the Chairman of the Summit to form a special committee composed of some of its concerned member states and the Secretary General of the League of Arab States to pursue the necessary contacts to gain support for this initiative at all levels, particularly from the United Nations, the Security Council, the United States of America, the Russian Federation, the Muslim States and the European Union.

REMARKS BY SECRETARY CLINTON, WASHINGTON, D.C.

February 27, 2009

In a telephone interview with David Gollust of the Voice of America, Secretary of State Hillary Clinton discusses U.S. policy toward the Middle East, including Palestinian-Israeli issues. She challenges Hamas to recognize Israel but calls for disaster aid for Gaza. And she confirms that the 2002 Arab peace initiative is part of U.S. policy for the region.

Q: . . . Madame Secretary, You are about to embark on your first trip to the Middle East, and some would argue it's coming at an inopportune time: Israel . . . is struggling to form a government; President Abbas of the Palestinian Authority—technically his term has expired; and of course you have the over-hanging split between the forces of Mr. Abbas and Hamas. Isn't this a particularly difficult time for you?

A: Well this will be my first trip to the Middle East as Secretary of State. . . . I have been there many times in the past. And as you know, George Mitchell was designated Special Envoy for Middle East Peace and is currently in the midst of his second trip to the region.

. . . At Sharm al-Sheikh I'll be joining other members of the international community to address the immediate humanitarian crisis in Gaza. We want to strengthen a Palestinian partner willing to accept the conditions outlined by the Quartet and the Arab Summit; in other words, a renunciation of violence, a recognition of Israel, and a commitment to abide by the previous agreements entered into by the Palestinian Authority.

. . . Our aid dollars will flow . . . in service of the goals that will help people feel more secure in their lives, and therefore more confident that progress toward peace would serve them better than retreating to violence and rejection-ism. . . .

So I'm looking forward to returning to Israel. . . . It's a visit with old friends. And obviously this is a sensitive time in Israeli politics . . . but I will take the opportunity to reaffirm the strength of the U.S.-Israeli relationship and talk about the best way to move peace forward. We are still committed to a two-state solution. I will also be visiting with Palestinian leaders in Ramallah to consult with them.

So I guess in summary, I will be working along with Special Envoy Mitchell to help make progress toward a negotiated agreement to end the conflict between

Source: <www.state.gov/secretary/rm/2009a/02/119886.htm>.

Israel and the Palestinians; to create an independent, viable Palestinian state in both the West Bank and Gaza; and to provide Israel with the peace and security that it has long sought and which the people deserve to have.

Q: Madame Secretary, are you in any way encouraged by the reports of progress in the Egyptian mediation efforts between the major Palestinian parties?

A: Well, I believe that it's important, if there is some reconciliation and a move toward a unified authority, that it's very clear that Hamas knows the conditions that have been set forth by the Quartet, by the Arab summit. And they must renounce violence, recognize Israel, and abide by previous commitments; otherwise, I don't think it will result in the kind of positive step forward either for the Palestinian people or as a vehicle for a reinvigorated effort to obtain peace that leads to a Palestinian state.

Q: What about the Israeli side of the equation? Benjamin Netanyahu, who is the designated—the prime minister-designate, hasn't fully embraced the two-state solution that's been a real fundamental part of U.S. policy.

A: Well, I think that our policy remains as it is the policy of the Quartet and the Arab League peace initiative to move toward a two-state solution. And there is not yet a government in Israel, so clearly, we have not had an opportunity to consult with anyone, but we will certainly convey our strong commitment to a two-state solution. . . .

EPILOGUE

JUNE 2009 marked the forty-second anniversary of the 1967 Six-Day War. Since 1967, two generations of Israelis have grown to maturity with Israel in control of Palestinians in Gaza and the West Bank, the latter through ongoing occupation, and Gaza by military surveillance and blockade after Israel's 2005 withdrawal from the Gaza Strip. Conversely, two generations of Palestinians have been raised under an occupation that has continued to expand in the West Bank, even during periods of Israeli negotiation with Palestinian officials.

This situation has now developed to the point where Jews are about to constitute a minority in the lands Israel governs or controls. As of April 2009, Israel's total population, according to Israel's Central Bureau of Statistics, was 7,411,000, with 5.6 million Jews and an Arab population of 1.5 million, the latter 20 percent of the population. Of this Jewish population, over 250,000 were West Bank settlers and approximately 200,000 lived in expanded East Jerusalem. These figures omit Palestinian Arabs. The population of the Gaza Strip approximates 1.6 million and that of the West Bank 2.5 million. This gives a total Arab population, including Gazans, West Bankers, and Israeli citizens, of 7.1 million; 5.5 million live under Israeli rule, either as Israeli citizens or as West Bank inhabitants, a figure nearly equal to that of the 5.6 million Jews.[1] With Arab birth rates being significantly higher than Israeli Jewish birth rates, an Arab majority within Israel, Gaza, and the West Bank is imminent.

In short, the moment of truth regarding Israel's choice of being a Jewish state or a bi-national one may have arrived, even as its new government appears to reject a two-state solution that would require withdrawal from most of the West Bank. That withdrawal could trigger civil war, leaving Israel with the choice of soon governing a state with an Arab majority or risking civil strife to assure its identity as a Jewish state. The dilemma facing Israeli leaders is posed more starkly when one considers the momentum of Israeli population expansion in the West Bank since 2000, the year of the Camp David talks. Whereas Israel's population has grown at an average of 2.0 percent since 2000, the West Bank settler population growth averaged 5 percent for the same period.[2]

This data highlights two movements that have gained increased momentum during this nine-year period, that of West Bank population growth and that of increasing Palestinian sympathy with Hamas at the expense of Fatah. The latter does not mean that most Palestinians would vote for Hamas in free elections with peace prospects at hand; more voted for Fatah than Hamas in the January 2006 elections under difficult conditions but Fatah's rival candidacies in many districts undermined its electoral chances. Rather, Fatah's helplessness in the face of Israeli settler expansion, which was tolerated by the Clinton and Bush administrations, has enhanced Hamas's credibility and its argument that the American-sponsored peace process has failed to fulfill its promises: West Bank Palestinians remain under occupation, Gazans remain encircled by the Israeli military.

These trends have been countered in recent decades by major changes in the perspectives of Arab and Israeli leaders. After the 1967 war, Arab heads of state originally called for full Israeli withdrawal from the conquered territories in return for an end to the belligerency. Israel, which sought to retain unspecified lands that included parts of the West Bank and Golan Heights, insisted on direct negotiations with Arab states. Here, the ambiguity of U.N. Security Council Resolution 242 proved impossible to overcome then as now. As interpreted by Israeli officials, the clause banning the retention of lands taken in war was neutralized by articles stating that all countries should live in secure and recognized boundaries, and that Israel did not have to withdraw from all the territories it acquired in the 1967 war. Israel's secure boundaries, it argued, required retention of some unspecified lands taken in the conflict.

Egypt's 1979 peace treaty with Israel met Israeli demands for direct talks and it led to Israel's withdrawal from the Sinai Peninsula. But Israeli leaders of the time saw the treaty as guaranteeing their ongoing retention of the West Bank and the Golan Heights, not as a preamble to future talks with other Arab states that would necessarily lead to similar withdrawals in return for peace. The Arab League condemned Anwar al-Sadat for signing this separate peace with Israel and expelled Egypt from the League.

More recently, in the Arab League initiative of 2002, Arab heads of state have publicly proposed a full peace with Israel based on its withdrawal to the 1967 boundary lines; thus far, Israel has failed to give an official response to these offers. And whereas Arab states and Palestinian officials linked to Fatah have continued to call for a two-state solution to the Israeli-Palestinian conflict, Israeli leaders have increasingly opted for an arrangement that would create a Palestinian state in name only, that is, fragmented areas in the West Bank without sovereignty or territorial contiguity. In fact, the new Netanyahu government appears to have rejected former Prime Minister Ehud Olmert's plan to withdraw from Israeli settlements east of the security barrier.

Into this apparent stalemate enters the Obama administration, whose policy calls for a two-state solution that incorporates the 2002 Arab League initiative. Because the Obama approach foresees an overall peace among Arab states, Palestinians, and Israel based on nearly full Israeli withdrawal from the West Bank, this stance poses a direct challenge to any Israeli prime minister. While a full return to the 1967 borders is unlikely, the exchanges of land proposed by the Geneva Initiative could resolve that issue and retain for Israel major settlement blocs north and south of Jerusalem. But the initiative excludes Ma'ale Adumim east of East Jerusalem; Netanyahu and Avigdor Lieberman will insist that it remain part of Israel even if that splits the West Bank nearly in half. Moreover, the Arab League initiative calls for the full right of Palestinian refugees to return to Israel; this is unacceptable to all Israelis. Experts believe that this demand could be negotiated, especially since the Palestinians have already accepted restrictions on that right in the Geneva Initiative.

In December 2008, on the eve of the Israeli assault on Gaza, a joint Israeli-Palestinian poll on the 2002 Arab League initiative showed 66 percent of Palestinians backing full peace with Israel based on the latter's full withdrawal from the West Bank, but 61 percent of Israelis opposed it. Forty-six percent of Israelis favored retaining 3 percent of the West Bank while giving Palestinians an equal amount of Israeli territory, but 48 percent opposed it; 54 percent of the Palestinians polled approved it with 44 percent opposed.[3]

For the moment, Netanyahu has declared that any consideration of Palestinian issues must await resolution of Iran's nuclear program. This effort to delay addressing peace talks with Palestinians may or may not succeed, but Netanyahu was not helped when Lieberman asserted that Iran was now only the third most serious threat to Israel, after Afghanistan and Pakistan. At the same time, Lieberman argued that "America accepts all our decisions," meaning the United States would do nothing without Israel's approval. That assumption of Israeli influence over America's Middle East policies will be tested in coming years. What is clear is that any strike on Iran's nuclear facilities would fail to destroy more than 15 percent of its infrastructure. But the Iranian backlash would undermine the security of American forces in Iraq and Afghanistan. The only benefit would be the domestic approval rating given to the Israeli politician who ordered the strike.[4]

Further complicating this unpromising mix are questions related to Hamas and to Iranian involvement in Palestinian-Israeli matters. Hamas's willingness to accept a two-state solution if approved by a majority of Palestinians is a far more concrete statement than that of Likud's Netanyahu, who thus far refuses to accept a Palestinian state of any kind.[5] Those opposing peace can exploit Iran's support of Hamas by citing Iranian President Ahmadinejad's denial of the Holocaust as evidence that Hamas's interest in peace is insincere. But when Saudi Arabia and Kuwait cut off their funding to the PLO and Yasir Arafat after he backed Saddam Husayn's invasion of Kuwait in 1990, Arafat opened an office in Teheran and sought Iranian assistance; that did not prevent Israel from reaching out to him to start the Oslo talks in 1992.

Iranian backing for the Palestinian cause, especially Hamas, and its links to Hizbollah, have aroused alarm among some key Arab states. It is difficult to know how much of this anxiety is based on Sunni-Shi'i tensions and how much comes from a feared loss of influence in mediating Palestinian-Israeli issues, as is the case with Egypt. It is clear that the populations of some Sunni Arab states, particularly Jordan and Egypt, are increasingly vocal in their criticism, where allowed, of their leaders' apparent tolerance of Israel's 2008 raid on Gaza. These populations tend to accept more readily the Iranian version of what occurred, based on immediate availability of images, news, and commentary, rather than what their official, government-sanctioned media may report.[6] A significant marker may be whether the Obama administration backs aid to the Palestinian Authority even if Hamas and Fatah settle their differences and form a unitary government, and if the U.S. Congress would approve such a policy.

Finally, we see widespread concern regarding the long-term military implications of Israel's 2006 war with Hizbollah in southern Lebanon. Whereas Israel continues to retain a decided military advantage over any other Middle East state with respect to armor, aircraft, and technology, its ground forces were fought to a standstill by Hizbollah, whose troops proved to be formidable opponents. Their deployment and use of missiles, antitank weapons, and communications systems displayed a sophistication Israel did not expect of any rival state, let alone a nonstate faction. Military analysts, including those at the U.S. Army War College, believe that this 2006 campaign holds major implications for asymmetric warfare in the future.[7]

Whether the Israel-Hizbollah clash is the harbinger of Middle Eastern warfare generally remains open to question, but Hizbollah's display of military capability could portend a future where nonstate actors gain popular support by being more willing and capable to confront perceived aggressors than the state's armed forces. Lebanon's June 2009 elections, if conducted properly, will indicate the extent to which the broader Lebanese populace accepts Hizbollah within the Lebanese body politic. Reports indicate widespread buying of votes by foreign sources with Saudi Arabia leading the anti-Hizbollah camp as an anti-Iran measure.[8]

For the moment, Israel does not seem to have learned the lessons of its war with Hizbollah. Its military and political leaders have declared that their successful and mostly unopposed assault on Gaza restored Israel's military confidence after it had been neutralized in Lebanon.

This perception resurrects the traditional Iron Wall mantra that Arabs will only accept Israel's existence once they admit that they can never match Israel militarily. Although many Israelis continue to accept it, this doctrine has never worked. Israel's tactics in Gaza, designed mostly to avert its casualties by air force strikes and artillery shelling that did not commit major troops to combat, explain the large numbers of Palestinian civilian deaths, but the Gazan assault was in no way comparable to Israel's confrontation with Hizbollah. Hamas had no freedom of movement in Gaza, whereas Hizbollah was well implanted in the wider terrain of south Lebanon.

The development of new weapons systems accessible to nonstate actors, as well as to Arab and Middle Eastern states generally, suggests that Israel's security will decline over time if it continues to rely on force to impel submission to maximal terms. Some regional links have already altered. Whereas Turkey formerly held military exercises with Israel, in April 2009 it held a joint drill with Syrian forces. And some Arab leaders are clearly alarmed at the implications of ongoing stalemate and the threat it might pose to their own regimes as well as regional stability. Jordan's King Abdullah said in Washington the same month that if Israel accepted the Arab League plan, it could "integrate itself into the region." But to reject the offer would mean Israel "would remain fortress Israel, isolated, holding itself and the region hostage to continued confrontation" with the greater likelihood of radicalization of Arab politics.[9]

As many observers have argued, including Israel's leading military historian, Martin van Creveld, Israel's security lies in peace treaties that include a withdrawal to the 1967 borders with appropriate, mutually agreed modifications.[10] Insistence on military dominance as the path to national security threatens rather than strengthens not only Israel's long-term security but that of Palestinians and the region as a whole.

Notes

1. I draw my data from Motti Bassick, "Israel at 61: Population Stands at 7.4 million, 75.5% Jewish," *Haaretz*, <www.haaretz.com>, April 27, 2009; "Regrettable Statistical Error: B. Michael Says Independence Day Report That Jews Comprise 75% of Israel's Population Inaccurate," <www.ynetnews.com>, May 2, 2009; the *CIA World Fact Book* country list of statistics for Israel, Gaza Strip, and the West Bank, <www.cia.gov/library/publications/the-world-factbook>; and "Population in Israel and West Bank Settlements, 1995–2005," Foundation for Middle East Peace, <www.fmep.org/settlement_info/settlement-info-and-tables>. Nearly 5 percent of Israel's current population, 32 million, is counted as "foreigners," neither Israeli Jews nor Arabs, meaning Jews are already a minority in Israel and the occupied territories.

2. Ibid., and Linda Gradstein, "If We Could, We'd Be Building Like Crazy: Why Jewish Settlers in the West Bank Are Looking forward to Benjamin Netanyahu's Premiership," *Slate*, <www.slate.com>, March 4, 2009, which notes that settlements averaged 5 percent growth during Ehud Olmert's premiership.

3. "Poll: Most Israelis Oppose Leaving West Bank for Arab World's Recognition," *Haaretz*, <www.haaretz.com>, December 16, 2008.

4. Liliy Galili and Barak Ravid, "Lieberman: U.S. to Accept Any Israeli Policy Decision," *Haaretz*, <www.haaretz.com>, April 22, 2009.

5. Taghreed el-Khodary and Ethan Bronner, "Addressing U.S., Hamas Says It Grounded Rockets," *New York Times*, May 5, 2009, where Hamas leader Khaled Meshal declared that Hamas would not recognize Israel but would accept a Palestinian decision to do so.

6. For Iran, Hizbollah, and Shi'ite influence generally, see Augustus R. Norton, *Hezbollah: A Short History* (Princeton, N.J., 2007); Roschanack Shaery-Eisenlohr, *Shi'ite Lebanon: Transnational Religion and the Making of National Identities* (New York, 2008); and Barbara Slavin, *Mullahs, Money, and Militias: How Iran Exerts Its Influence in the Middle East* (Washington, D.C., 2008).

7. Stephen D. Biddle, *The 2006 Lebanon Campaign and the Future of Warfare: Implications for Army and Defense Policy* (Carlisle, Pa., 2008).

8. Robert F. Worth, "Foreign Money Seeks to Buy Lebanese Votes," *New York Times*, April 23, 2009.

9. "Turkey Brushes Off Israel Concern over Syrian Drill," <www.ynetnews.com>, April 25, 2009; "Jordan's King Abdullah: Israel Must Choose Integration or Isolation," *Haaretz*, <www.haaretz.com>, April 25, 2009.

10. Martin van Creveld, *Defending Israel: A Controversial Plan for Peace* (New York, 2004).

GLOSSARY

al-Aqsa intifada Denotes the Palestinian uprising against Israeli occupation that erupted in September 2000, following Ariel Sharon's visit to the Haram al-Sharif/ Temple Mount, the location of the al-Aqsa mosque.

al-Qaida Arabic for "the base." Militant Sunni Islamic terrorist organization, led by Usama Bin Ladin, responsible for numerous attacks worldwide including the September 11, 2001, attacks on the United States.

al-Quds Arabic for "the sanctuary." The Arabic name for Jerusalem.

aliyah Hebrew for "to ascend." Describes Jewish immigration to the Land of Israel, either individually or in collective waves. Often refers to specific waves of immigration to Palestine prior to Israeli independence.

American-Israel Public Affairs Committee (AIPAC) Pro-Israel activist group that lobbies the U.S. government to pursue favorable policies toward Israel and to foster a strong relationship between the two countries.

anti-Semitism Prejudice and hostility against Jews as either an ethnic or a religious group. Can be manifest as informal discrimination or, as was the case during the Holocaust, as institutionalized persecution.

Arab Higher Committee Palestinian Arab leadership committee formed in April 1936 that attempted to direct the uprising known as the Arab Revolt. Composed of diverse Palestinian factions, including the archrival al-Husayni and al-Nashashibi clans.

Arab National Fund Second World War–era organization that attempted to acquire Palestinian land in the hopes of safeguarding it from Zionist purchase. Dominated by members of the Palestinian Istiqlal Party.

Ashkenazim Jews from central and eastern Europe.

bantustans Apartheid-era districts created in South Africa and Namibia as autonomous homelands for black Africans; known for their poverty and dependence upon the white-controlled government. Term is used to describe Israeli proposals for a truncated and divided Palestinian state in the West Bank.

Betar Revisionist Zionist youth group formed by Vladimir Jabotinsky during the 1920s with chapters in Europe and Palestine. Merged into the Irgun faction in the 1930s.

Black September Palestinian reference to King Husayn's bloody September 1970 suppression of PLO groups in Jordan. PLO group with that name noted for taking eleven Israeli Olympic athletes hostage at the 1972 Munich games.

caliph Anglicized form of the Arabic word *khalifa*, which means "successor to the Prophet Muhammad as leader of the Islamic community (*umma*)." Used in Sunni Islam. First adopted CE 632. (See also **Sunni** and **Shi'i**.)

Caliphate   Refers to family-based dynasties of caliphs and their empires within Sunni Islam. Abolished by the Turkish secular leader Mustafa Kemal Ataturk in 1924.

casus belli   Latin for "occasion of war," interpreted to mean a legitimate justification for war.

dhimmi   From the Arabic for "protected," meaning in Islamic history the right to practice one's non-Muslim religion. Applied to Christians and Jews living in Islamic lands who in return were subject to certain social and religious restrictions and paid a tax (*jizya*).

diaspora   The often-forced emigration of a particular ethnic, religious, or cultural group from its indigenous territory. The place where the group relocates. For example, "Jews living in the diaspora."

Dome of the Rock   Golden-domed Islamic shrine on the Haram al-Sharif/Temple Mount in Jerusalem that marks the spot where Muslims believe Muhammad ascended to heaven during his night journey.

Druze   A religion and its community of believers with origins in Shi'ite traditions. Its doctrines are closely guarded secrets and considered separate from Islam. Druze communities exist in Lebanon, Syria, Israel, and Jordan.

dunam   Unit of land measurement in the Middle East. One *dunam* = one-quarter acre.

emir   Literally, one who commands, gives orders. Refers to a military commander, prince, or ruler of a principality such as Amir Abdullah, who was awarded Trans-jordan. Often spelled *amir*.

Eretz Israel   Hebrew for the historic and biblical "Land of Israel." Zion.

Fatah   Literally, Arabic for "opening," designating conquest. Nationalist Palestinian guerilla organization founded in Kuwait in 1958 by Yasir Arafat.

fedayeen   Arabic for "those who sacrifice themselves." Term applied to Palestinians, mostly from refugee camps, encouraged by Egypt to conduct raids against Israel in the 1950s. Later applied to Palestinian militants and their groups, such as Fatah.

Gahal   Hebrew acronym for "Herut-Liberal bloc." Israeli political party that advocated expansion to take the West Bank, formed in 1965 as a merger between Menachem Begin's Herut Party and the Liberal Party. Combined with Likud in 1973. (See also **Likud**.)

Gush Emunim   Hebrew for "bloc of the faithful." Religious Zionist organization, with messianic ideals, formed in 1974, that spearheaded the founding of settlements in the West Bank following the 1967 war.

Hagana   Hebrew for "defense." Jewish paramilitary defense organization formed in 1920 to protect Zionist settlers in British Mandatory Palestine. Following 1948 Israeli statehood, replaced by the Israeli Defense Forces (IDF).

Hajj   Annual pilgrimage to Mecca undertaken by Muslims. Can also be an honorific title referring to one who has made the pilgrimage, as in Hajj Amin al-Husayni.

Hamas   Arabic for "enthusiasm" or "zeal." Also the acronym for *Harakat al-Muqawama al-Islamiyya*, the Islamic Resistance Movement, formed in 1987. Largest Palestinian

Islamic political party with armed factions. Won Palestinian parliamentary elections in January 2006.

Haram al-Sharif Arabic for "the noble sanctuary." Site of the Dome of the Rock and the al-Aqsa mosque in Jerusalem. Third holiest site in Islam after Mecca and Medina. (See also **Temple Mount.**)

haskala From the Hebrew word for "reason." Mid- to late nineteenth-century Russian Jewish modernist movement that emulated the Western European enlightenment. Advocated Jewish equality and assimilation. Anti-Semitic reactions to the movement fostered modern Zionist ideals.

Hatti Sharif of Gulhane (1839) Ottoman edict that promised equal legal status to all subjects, whether Muslim, Christian, or Jew. Reversed the centuries-long *dhimmi* system. Marks the beginning of the reformist *Tanzimat* period of Ottoman history.

Herut Hebrew for "freedom." Right-wing Israeli political party advocating capitalism and expansion to take the West Bank and Jordan, formed in 1948 and led by Menachem Begin. Major opposition party to David Ben-Gurion's Labor Zionist Mapai Party. (See also **Gahal.**)

Histradrut Hebrew for "federation." Labor Zionist trade union founded in 1920.

Hizbollah Arabic for "party of God." Lebanese Shi'ite military and political organization formed in the 1980s.

Imam Literally "one in front of," a leader. Refers in Sunni Islam to a prayer leader at Friday prayers. In Shi'i Islam, the title Imam was given to the leaders of two rival branches to whom semidivine powers were attributed.

intifada Arabic for "shaking off" (of a condition). Term used to describe two major Palestinian uprisings against Israeli occupation from 1987 to 1993 and again from 2000 to the present.

Irgun Revisionist Zionist paramilitary group that opposed labor Zionism and broke from the Hagana. Led by Menachem Begin from 1942 until its dissolution in 1948.

Islamic Jihad First Islamic militant group in Palestine, established in the early 1980s. Offshoot of the Muslim Brotherhood in Gaza. Stated goals include the destruction of Israel and the establishment of an Islamic state in Palestine.

Istiqlal Arabic for "independence." Pan-Arab Palestinian political party formed in 1932 that called for the inclusion of Palestine in a greater Syria.

Izz al-Din al-Qassam brigade Military wing of Hamas established in the early 1990s. Named after Izz al-Din al-Qassam, a resistance fighter whose 1935 death in part sparked the Arab Revolt.

Jewish Agency (JA) Governing body of the Zionist movement in Palestine during the British mandate, founded in 1929.

Jewish National Fund Financial institution created by the World Zionist Organization in 1901 to purchase land for Jewish settlement in Palestine. Still funds settlements in the occupied territories.

jihad Arabic for "struggle." There are two forms of *jihad* in Islam. Greater *jihad*, an internal struggle against sin, and lesser *jihad*, external struggle, or fighting, to defend Islamic lands from non-Muslim aggression.

jizya   A poll tax paid by non-Muslims.

Judea and Samaria   Biblical names for the occupied West Bank, used primarily by Israeli settlers and their supporters. Refers to the ancient kingdoms of Judah and Israel.

Kach   Right-wing Israeli political party labeled a terrorist group by the Israeli Knesset and barred from politics. Its backers still dominate settlements in the Hebron region.

Kadima   Hebrew for "forward." Israeli political party formed by Ariel Sharon in November 2005.

Kahan Commission   Israeli commission of inquiry for the September 1982 Sabra and Shatila refugee camp massacres of Palestinians.

kharaj   A property tax originally paid by non-Muslims, later paid by Muslims as well.

kibbutzim   Hebrew for "gatherings." Collective agricultural communities steeped in labor Zionist ideology, first created before World War I.

Knesset   Hebrew for "assembly." Israel's parliament.

Labor Party   Center-left Israeli political party created in 1968. Dominant political party in Israel until 1977. Since then it has vied with its right-wing rival, Likud. (See also **Mapai**.)

Labor Zionism   Major Zionist movement founded on socialist principles.

Law of Return   The 1950 law that granted eligibility for Israeli citizenship to all Jews of good character and good health.

League of Arab States   An association formed in Cairo in 1945 to promote Arab unity and coordination of political and commercial interests.

LEHI   Zionist terrorist organization, spun off from Irgun, that conducted assassination campaigns against British officials and Palestinians in the 1940s. Leaders included Yitzhak Shamir, who later became prime minister of Israel. (See also **Irgun**.)

Likud   Hebrew for "consolidation." The dominant right-wing political party in Israel. Based on Revisionist Zionist ideology, Likud united followers of Irgun and LEHI and advocated the takeover of the West Bank (Judea and Samaria) in particular. (See also **Gahal**.)

Madrid talks   Middle East peace talks (1991–1993) sponsored by the United States after the 1991 Gulf War. First official negotiations where Israeli and Palestinian representatives met.

mandates   Post–World War I system sanctioned by the League of Nations to permit British and French takeover of former German and Ottoman lands. Premised on the assumption the two powers would prepare inhabitants of a mandate territory for self-government.

Mapai   Hebrew acronym for "Land of Worker's Party." Labor Zionist political party grounded in socialist ideals. Founded in 1930 by David Ben-Gurion, it remained the dominant party in Israeli politics from 1948 to 1968, when it entered the coalition known as the Labor Party.

Maronites   Lebanese Eastern Catholic Christians unified with the Roman Catholic Church. Given favored political status by the French during the mandate period.

Mossad   Hebrew for "institute." Israel's intelligence and covert operations agency.

mufti   An interpreter of Islamic law. In the past, often the supreme religious authority in a given country or region.

Muslim Brotherhood   Islamic political and social services organization founded in Egypt by Hassan al-Banna in 1928.

Nakba   Literally "disaster" or "catastrophe." Palestinian term for the 1948 war and creation of Palestinians as a refugee population.

neoconservatives   American political thinkers and officials who support an aggressive, unilateral foreign policy in order to advance and preserve U.S. interests around the globe. Advocates of Israel's retention of the West Bank and military dominance of the Middle East.

"New Zionist Organization"   Founded by Revisionist Zionist Vladimir Jabotinsky in 1935 as rival to the World Zionist Organization.

Palestine Liberation Organization (PLO)   Founded in 1964 as an Egyptian-backed Palestinian movement. Incorporated various factions after the 1967 war. Regarded as "the sole legitimate representative of the Palestinian People," it was superseded by the Palestinian Authority (PA) following the 1993 Oslo Accords.

Palestine National Council (PNC)   Legislative decision-making body of the Palestine Liberation Organization (PLO) created in 1964. Initially a parliament-in-exile, it declared Palestinian independence in 1988 during the first intifada.

Palestinian Authority (PA)   Quasi-autonomous Palestinian government created in 1994 to fulfill stipulations contained in the Oslo-brokered Interim Agreement. The Oslo Accords permitted the PA to have full civil control over and limited police powers in areas in the West Bank and in Gaza that were not under Israeli rule.

Palmach   Literally "assault companies," formed as special Zionist military cadres in 1941. Became an elite Zionist military force from 1945 to the 1948 war of independence.

Pan-Arab nationalism   Secular political ideology that advocated unifying all Arab nations into a single state. Powerful ideology during the 1950s and 1960s until the 1967 war.

pogrom   Russian for "destruction." Violent attacks against the people and property of a minority community. Most commonly refers to outbreaks of violence against Jews, particularly those in late nineteenth-century Russia.

Revisionist Zionism   Militant, expansionist form of Zionism articulated in the 1920s by the movement's leader, Vladimir Jabotinsky. Opposed Labor Zionism's socialist ideology, called for a Jewish state east and west of the Jordan River. (See also **Irgun** and **LEHI**.)

right of return   Generally refers to the right of displaced people to return to their homeland. In this context, it applies to Palestinians who became refugees after 1948 and their descendants, whereas "Law of Return" applies to Jews in diaspora returning to Israel. (See also **Law of Return**.)

sanjak   Turkish for "banner." A district within an Ottoman imperial province.

Sephardim   Specifically refers to Jews who left Spain and settled in the Ottoman Empire after 1492. More commonly used to denote all non-Ashkenazi Jews.

sharia   Islamic law.

sharif   Literally, "noble," "illustrious." In Islam, it denoted a descendant of the Prophet Muhammad and also, in the Ottoman era, the governor of Mecca (e.g., Sharif Husayn of Mecca).

shaykh   Literally, a "respected elder." Used as a title for a tribal leader, a learned religious scholar, or a ruler of a state or dynasty, especially today in the Arab Gulf states.

Shi'i   From the Arabic for "party" or "faction." Minority sect in Islam born out of a succession dispute following Muhammad's death. (See also **Sunni**.)

Shin Bet   Israel's internal counterintelligence and security agency.

sultan   From the Arabic for "power," originally a Turkish term. Title used by various Islamic rulers who governed independently from, or in the name of, the caliph. Eventually, the Ottomans acquired and used both titles of sultan and caliph.

sultanate   A political entity ruled by a sultan.

Sunni   From the Arabic for "tradition." Majority sect in Islam that claims to follow the traditions of Muhammad and of the early community of believers.

Supreme Muslim Council (SMC)   Governing body for internal Muslim affairs in the British Mandate of Palestine. Made appointments to religious offices and managed charitable foundations (*waqfs*) and religious courts.

Tanzim   Arabic for "organization." Military group within Fatah that emerged during the al-Aqsa intifada. Led in part by activist Marwan Barghouti and popular among younger Palestinians.

Tanzimat   Originally from the Arabic for "reorganization." Nineteenth-century series of Ottoman modernizing reforms aimed at strengthening the empire in the face of Europe's rising power.

Temple Mount   Site in Jerusalem believed to be the location of the historic Jewish Temples. (See also **Haram al-Sharif** and **Western Wall**.)

"Tunisians"   PLO leaders, led by Yasir Arafat, who were exiled to Tunisia after expulsion from Lebanon in 1982. After the Oslo Accords in 1993, they returned to the Occupied Territories to form the Palestinian Authority. Controlled power and patronage to the exclusion of younger Palestinians from the territories.

United Nations Emergency Forces (UNEF)   Multinational force stationed in Sinai to act as a buffer between Egypt and Israel following the 1956 Suez Crisis.

United Nations Relief and Works Agency (UNRWA)   United Nations agency founded in 1950 that administers Palestinian refugee camps.

United Nations Special Committee on Palestine (UNSCOP)   The 1947 U.N. special committee that investigated conditions in Palestine and made a recommendation of partition between Arabs and Jews, which the General Assembly approved in November 1947.

vilayet   Ottoman term from the Arabic word for "to govern." A province within the Ottoman Empire.

vizier   Turkish adaptation of the Arabic term for "minister" or "one who bears responsibility." Title of government ministers in the Ottoman Empire.

waqf   Islamic charitable foundations—orphanages, schools, hospitals, mosques, shrines, etc.—free of taxation and held in perpetuity.

Western Wall   Remnant of the Second Temple's retaining wall adjacent to the Temple Mount in Jerusalem. Holiest physically accessible site in Judaism where prayers are offered.

World Zionist Organization (WZO)   Formed in 1897 through the efforts of Theodor Herzl. A worldwide collective body of Jewish representatives advocating a secure homeland for Jews and presenting the Zionist cause to the rest of the world.

yishuv   Hebrew for "settlement." Refers to the Jewish community in Palestine prior to Israeli independence.

Zionism   A nationalist ideology that advocates the creation of a secure Jewish homeland in Palestine for the worldwide community of Jews in fulfillment of their historical and religious associations with the region.

SELECTED BIBLIOGRAPHY

This bibliography, arranged primarily by chapters and time periods, calls attention to notable publications of the past decade not cited in the footnotes. In separate sections, I list some sources of contemporary interest according to topics including gender; water; Jerusalem; legal, demographic, and economic questions; and a new section on ethnicity and identity. I also provide a separate section listing Web sites of special value for accessing information on countries and organizations linked to the conflict. Journals that deal specifically with these topics on both a contemporary and a historical basis are *Israel Studies, Journal of Palestine Studies*, and *The Middle East Journal*. Journals that include such material along with broader treatment of Middle Eastern and Islamic subjects are *British Journal of Middle East Studies, International Journal of Middle East Studies*, and *Middle Eastern Studies*, but see also journals that may include articles and reviews on the Middle East such as *The American Historical Review, Historical Journal, Journal of Imperial and Commonwealth History, Journal of Modern History*, and the *Journal of Contemporary History*.

Prologue: 1000 BCE to 1517 CE

The material covered in the prologue ranges from ancient Israel and Judaic/ Palestinian history to the Ottoman conquest of Palestine. For recent scholarship on ancient Israel, see the footnotes to the prologue and Jonathan Golden, *Ancient Canaan and Israel: New Perspectives* (Santa Barbara: ABC-CLIO, 2004). A book encompassing Egypt and Israel as part of the ancient world is Gary N. Knoppers and Antoine Hirsch, eds., *Egypt, Israel and the Ancient Mediterranean World: Studies in Honor of Donald Redford* (Leiden and Boston: E. J. Brill, 2004). On Palestine under Islam, there is Andrew Petersen, *The Towns of Palestine under Muslim Rule, AD 600–1600* (Oxford: Archaeopress, 2005). For the Ottoman Empire in the early modern period, recent works include Colin Imber, *The Ottoman Empire, 1300–1650: The Structure of Power* (New York: Palgrave, 2002), and Virginia H. Aksan and Daniel Goffman, eds, *The Early Modern Ottomans: Remapping the Empire* (New York: Cambridge University Press, 2007).

Chapter 1: 1517–1914

Important, wide-ranging studies that include Palestine and Muslim or Jewish communities in the Ottoman Empire are Itzchak Weisman and Fruma Zachs, eds., *Ottoman Reform and Muslim Regeneration: Studies in Honor of Butros Abu-Manneh* (New York: St. Martin's Press, 2005); Avigdor Levy, ed., *Jews, Turks, Ottomans: A Shared History, Fifteenth through the Twentieth Century* (Syracuse,

N.Y.: Syracuse University Press, 2002); and Mark Mazower's superb study of Salonica and its inhabitants, *Salonica, City of Ghosts: Christians, Muslims and Jews, 1430–1950* (New York: HarperCollins, 2004). A social and political history that includes the themes of law and the status of women, as well as the Ottoman Empire's efforts to expand its authority in the region is Amy Singer, *Constructing Ottoman Beneficence: An Imperial Soup Kitchen in Jerusalem* (Albany: State University of New York Press, 2002). A study of early, religious-inspired Jewish settlement in Palestine is Arie Morgernstern, *Hastening Redemption: Messianism and the Resettlement of the Land of Israel*, trans. Joel A. Linsider (New York: Oxford University Press, 2006). Several important studies consider Palestine and Zionism from the mid-nineteenth century to the mid-twentieth: Mark LeVine, *Overthrowing Geography: Jaffa, Tel Aviv, and the Struggle for Palestine, 1880–1948* (Berkeley: University of California Press, 2005); S. Ilan Troen, *Imagining Zion: Dreams, Designs, and Realities in a Century of Jewish Settlement* (New Haven, Conn.: Yale University Press, 2003); Gideon Biger, *The Boundaries of Modern Palestine, 1840–1947* (London: Routledge, 2004); and the book of documents, Beitullah Destani, ed., *The Zionist Movement and the Foundation of Israel, 1839–1972*, ten volumes (London: Archive Editions, 2004). Two major sources on Palestine and Palestinian identity that span this period and extend to 1948 are Haim Gerber, *Remembering and Imagining Palestine: Identity and Nationalism from the Crusades to the Present* (New York: Palgrave, 2008), and Gudrun Kramer, *A History of Palestine: From the Ottoman Conquest to the Founding of the State of Israel*, trans. Graham Harman and Gudrun Kramer (Princeton, N.J.: Princeton University Press, 2008). An important study of Zionism that extends to Israeli statehood is Jacqueline Rose, *The Question of Zion* (Princeton, N.J.: Princeton University Press, 2005). Equally important for Palestinian society from the later nineteenth century is Salim Tamari, *Mountain against the Sea: Essays on Palestinian Society and Culture* (Berkeley: University of California Press, 2009).

Chapter 2: 1914–1921

On World War I, the European powers, and the Middle East, a recent analysis of Zionist approaches to British officials is James Renton, *The Zionist Masquerade: The Birth of the Anglo-Zionist Alliance, 1914–1918* (New York: Palgrave, 2007). Two important studies of the peace conference and postwar solutions are Margaret MacMillan, *Peacemakers, Paris 1919: Six Months That Changed the World* (New York: Random House, 2002); and Timothy J. Paris, *Britain, the Hashemites and Arab Rule, 1920–1925* (Portland, Ore.: Frank Cass Publishers, 2003). Michael Stanislawski analyzes differing visions of Zionism in *Zionism and the Fin de Siècle: Cosmopolitanism and Nationalism from Nordau to Jabotinsky* (Berkeley: University of California Press, 2001). A recent investigation of the challenges faced by the Ottomans during this period, though not focusing on Palestine, is Ryan Gingeras, *Sorrowful Shores: Violence, Ethnicity, and the End of the Ottoman Empire, 1912–1923* (New York: Oxford University Press, 2009). A broader study of the Middle East based on the results of World War I is D. K. Fieldhouse, *Western Imperialism in the Middle East, 1914–1958* (New York: Oxford University Press, 2006).

Chapters 3 and 4: 1920–1948

Recent studies that cover the period of the British mandate are Weldon Matthews, *Confronting an Empire, Constructing a Nation: Arab Nationalists and Popular Politics in Mandate Palestine* (New York: I. B. Tauris, 2006); and Ronit Lentin, ed., *Thinking Palestine* (New York: Zed Books, 2008). Earlier works on the period include Naomi Shepherd, *Ploughing Sand: British Rule in Palestine, 1917–1948* (New Brunswick, N.J.: Rutgers University Press, 2000), and Lawrence Davidson, *America's Palestine: Popular and Official Perceptions from Balfour to Israeli Statehood* (Gainesville: University Press of Florida, 2001). A provocative study of Zionist and Israeli attitudes and assumptions regarding Palestinian Arabs is Gil Eyal, *The Disenchantment of the Orient: Expertise in Arab Affairs and the Israeli State* (Stanford, Calif.: Stanford University Press, 2006).

Chapters 5–10: 1949–1999

There are fewer sources cited for this section, either because of updating in footnotes or because no new material has appeared that supplants previous citations. Two important studies of King Husayn of Jordan have appeared: Nigel Ashton, *King Hussein of Jordan: A Political Life* (New Haven, Conn.: Yale University Press, 2008); and Avi Shlaim, *Lion of Jordan: The Life of King Hussein in War and Peace* (New York: Alfred A. Knopf, 2008). A recent work on the Kennedy era is Warren Bass, *Support Any Friend: Kennedy's Middle East and the Making of the U.S.-Israel Alliance* (New York: Oxford University Press, 2003). Julie Peteet, *Landscapes of Hope and Despair: Palestinian Refugee Camps* (Philadelphia: University of Pennsylvania Press, 2005) examines Palestinian refugees in Lebanon. A recent Palestinian memoir on living under British and then Israeli rule is Rajah Shehadeh, *Strangers in the House: Growing Up in Occupied Palestine* (New York: Penguin Books, 2003). Zvi Ganin examines the ties between American Jews and Israel in *An Uneasy Relationship: American Jewish Leadership and Israel, 1948–1957* (Syracuse, N.Y.: Syracuse University Press, 2005). A good analysis of Anglo-American approaches to the Middle East after World War II is James R. Vaughan, *The Failure of American and British Propaganda in the Arab Middle East, 1945–1957: Unconquerable Minds* (New York: Palgrave, 2005). For Israeli civil-military relations, see Yoram Peri, *Generals in the Cabinet Room: How the Military Shapes Israeli Policy* (Washington, D.C.: U.S. Institute of Peace, 2006).

For the Oslo process, Israel, the Palestinian Authority, and the U.S. approach to the problem, see Nigel Parsons, *The Politics of the Palestinian Authority from Oslo to al-Aqsa* (New York: Routledge, 2005); J. W. Wright, ed., *Structural Flaws in the Middle East Peace Process: Historical Contexts* (New York: Palgrave, 2002); Rex Brynen, *A Very Political Economy: Peacebuilding and Foreign Aid in the West Bank and Gaza* (Washington, D.C.: U.S. Institute of Peace, 2000); and Kathleen Christison, *Perceptions of Palestine: Their Influence on Middle East Policy* (Berkeley: University of California Press, 2001). There are two books and two electronic resources on Israeli and Palestinian responses to the Oslo process and questions raised by it. The two books on politics and educational matters are Elie J. Podeh,

The Arab-Israeli Conflict in Israeli History Textbooks (Westport, Conn.: Bergin and Garvey, 2001); and Nathan J. Brown, *Palestinian Politics after the Oslo Accords: Resuming Arab Palestine* (Berkeley: University of California Press, 2003). Brown corrects many misperceptions about Palestinian representation of Israelis and also addresses Israeli representations of Palestinians. The two electronic resources are Nathan J. Brown, *The Palestinian Reform Agenda* (Washington, D.C.: U.S. Institute of Peace, 2002) — Peaceworks 48, <www.usip.org/pubs/PeaceWorks/ pwks48.pdf>; and Yoram Peri, *The Israeli Military and Israel's Palestine Policy: From Oslo to the al-Aqsa Intifada* (Washington, D.C.: U.S. Institute of Peace, 2002) — Peaceworks 47, <www.usip.org/pubs/PeaceWorks/pwks47.pdf>.

Chapter 11: 1999–2009

Books on the al-Aqsa intifada and life in Israel and the occupied territories include Roane Carey, ed., *The New Intifada* (London: Verso, 2001); Joshua Hammer, *A Season in Bethlehem: Unholy War in a Sacred Place* (New York: Free Press, 2003); and Amira Hass, *Drinking the Sea in Gaza: Days and Nights in a Land under Siege* (New York: Owl Books, 2000). Books examining policies of states and organizations involved in the violence, or conflicted by it, include Khalid Hroub, *Hamas: Political Thought and Practice* (Washington, D.C.: Institute for Palestine Studies, 2000); Shaul Mishal and Avraham Sela, *The Palestinian Hamas: Vision, Violence, and Coexistence* (New York: Columbia University Press, 2006); Jeroen Gunning, *Hamas in Politics: Democracy, Religion, Violence* (New York: Columbia University Press, 2008); Azzam Tamimi, *Hamas: A History from Within* (Northampton, Mass.: Olive Branch Press, 2007); Baruch Kimmerling, *The Invention and Decline of Israeliness: State, Society, and the Military* (Berkeley: University of California Press, 2001); Milton Viorst, *What Shall I Do with These People? Jews and the Fractious Politics of Judaism* (New York: Free Press, 2002); and Bernard Wasserstein, *Israel and Palestine: Why They Fight and Can They Stop?* (London: Profile, 2003); a memoir by an Israeli long active in the peace process is Meron Benvenisti, *Son of Cypresses: Memories, Reflections and Regrets from a Political Life*, trans. Maxine Kaufman-Lacusta (Berkeley: University of California Press, 2006).

Special Topics and Web Sites

Gender

There is a considerable and growing body of literature that investigates questions of gender and either its role in the conflict or the impact of the conflict on gender issues. Some studies focus exclusively on Arab/Palestinian or Jewish/Israeli experiences; others examine Palestinian-Israeli interactions as well. Among these works are studies that extend to the period prior to World War II but nevertheless cover questions of contemporary interest. With respect to Palestinian women, scholars have treated subjects such as resistance, Islam, property rights, and rights of personal freedom. Nancy Stockdale, *Colonial Encounters among English and Palestinian Women, 1800–1948* (Gainesville: University Press of Florida, 2007), covers the broadest period. For the theme of Palestinian resistance, see the study on Israeli-Arab women, Rhoda Ann Kanaaneh, *Birthing the Nation: Strategies of Palestinian Women in Israel* (Berkeley: University of California Press, 2002), and Cheryl Rubenberg, *Palestinian Women: Patriarchy and Resistance in the West Bank* (Boulder, Colo.: Lynne Reiner, 2001). A book addressing the question of Palestinian and Israeli women and conflict is Nahla Abdo-Zubi and Ronit Lentin, eds., *Women and the Politics of Military Confrontation: Palestinian and Israeli Gendered Narratives of Dislocation* (New York: Berghahn Books, 2002). Two books on gender in the first half of the twentieth century are Sheila H. Katz, *Women and Gender in Early Jewish and Palestinian Nationalism* (Gainesville: University Press of Florida, 2003); and Ellen Fleischmann, *The Nation and Its "New" Women: The Palestinian Women's Movement, 1920–1948* (Berkeley: University of California Press, 2003). With respect to Israel, scholars have examined topics such as Israeli women and Israeli society, and Israeli-Palestinian interaction, in light of gender issues: see Kalpana Misra and Melanie Rich, *Jewish Feminism in Israel: Some Contemporary Perspectives* (Hanover, N.H.: University Press of New England, 2003). A book that engages the themes of women and water, a separate topic below, is Nefissa Neguib, *Women, Water, Memory: Recasting Lives in Palestine* (Boston: Brill, 2009). For a wider historical perspective that includes British imperialism and the Middle East, see the earlier but important Billie Melman, ed., *Borderlands: Genders and Identities in War and Peace, 1870–1930* (New York: Routledge, 1998).

Ethnicity and Identity

A number of recent studies address the topics of ethnicity, identity, and sociopolitical boundaries for Israelis and Palestinians, but especially regarding Israeli Arabs: see Loren Lybarger, *Identity and Religion in Palestine: The Struggle between Islamism and Secularism in the Occupied Territories* (Princeton, N.J.: Princeton University Press, 2007); Sandy Sufian and Mark LeVine, eds., *Reapproaching Borders: New Perspectives on the Study of Israel-Palestine* (Lanham, Md.: Rowman and Littlefield, 2007); Aziza Khazzoom, *Shifting Ethnic Boundaries and Inequality in Israel: Or How the Polish Peddler Became a German Intellectual* (Stanford, Calif.: Stanford University Press, 2008); Daniel Bar-Tal and Yona Teichman, *Stereotypes and Prejudice in Conflict: Representations of Arabs in Israeli Jewish Society* (New York: Cambridge University Press, 2005); Nessim Rejwan, *Outsider in the Promised Land: An Iraqi Jew in Israel* (Austin: University of Texas Press, 2006); Dan Rabinowitz and Khawla Abu-Bakr, *Coffins on Our Shoulders: The Experience of Palestinian Citizens of Israel* (Berkeley: University of California Press, 2005); Daniel Monterescu and Dan Rabinowitz, eds., *Mixed Towns, Trapped Communities: Historical Narratives, Spatial Dynamics, Gender Relations, and Cultural Encounters in Palestinian-Israeli Towns* (Burlington, Vt.: Ashgate, 2007); As'ad Ghanem, *The Palestinian-Arab Minority in Israel, 1948–2000* (Albany: State University of New York Press, 2001); Oren Yiftachel, *Ethnocracy: Land and Identity Politics in Israel/Palestine* (Philadelphia: University of Pennsylvania Press, 2006); Ra'anan Cohen, *Strangers in Their Homeland: A Critical Study of Israel's Arab Citizens* (Portland, Ore.: Sussex Academic Press, 2009); Anita Shapira, ed., *Israeli*

Identity in Transition (London: Praeger, 2004); Adriana Kemp, ed., *Israelis in Conflict: Hegemonies, Identities, and Challenges* (Portland, Ore.: Sussex Academic Press, 2004); Calvin Goldschieder, *Israel's Changing Society: Population, Ethnicity, and Development* (Cambridge, Mass.: Westview, 2002); Laurence Louer, *Israel's Arab Citizens*, trans. John King (London: C. Hurst & Co, 2007).

Jerusalem

Several studies on Jerusalem and its political importance, as well as related Israeli settlement policies, have appeared in recent years. They are (including some in the Chapter 11 footnotes) Michael Dumper, *The Politics of Space: The Old City of Jerusalem in the Middle East Conflict* (Boulder, Colo.: Lynne Reinner, 2002); Bernard Wasserstein, *Divided Jerusalem: The Struggle for the Holy City* (New Haven, Conn.: Yale University Press, 2001); Menachem Klein, *Jerusalem, the Contested City* (London: C. Hurst, 2000); and Shlomo Hasson, *The Struggle for Hegemony in Jerusalem: Secular and Ultra-Orthodox Urban Politics* (Jerusalem: Floersheimer Institute for Policy Studies, 2002).

Water

Important studies on the significance of water issues are Tony Allan, *The Middle East Water Question: Hydropolitics and the Global Economy* (New York: I. B. Tauris, 2000); Alwyn R. Rouyer, *Turning Water into Politics: The Water Issue in the Palestinian-Israeli Conflict* (New York: St. Martin's Press, 2000); Hussein A. Amery and Aaron T. Wolf, *Water in the Middle East: A Geography of Peace* (Austin: University of Texas Press, 2000); and the more recent Jeffery K. Sosland, *Cooperating Rivals: The Riparian Politics of the Jordan River Basin* (Albany: State University of New York Press, 2007), and Mark Zeitoun, *Power and Water in the Middle East: The Hidden Politics of the Palestinian-Israeli Water Conflict* (New York: I. B. Tauris, 2008).

Israeli-Palestinian Legal, Demographic, and Economic Questions

The al-Aqsa intifada has undermined progress in economic development. A significant earlier work that should be updated is Ian Lustick, *Arab-Israeli Relations, Volume 6: Economic, Legal, and Demographic Dimensions of Arab-Israeli Relations* (New York: Garland Press, 1994).

Recommended Web Sites

I have chosen these search engines for the variety of sources and access they provide beyond individual newspaper addresses listed in the Chapter 11 notes. They provide links to governmental, media, and institutional Web sites.

The Web site with the broadest array of links is:

- www.mideasti.org—This is the Web site of the Middle East Institute in Washington, D.C. Go to "Countries and Organizations" for links to official sites and printed sources; includes access to all Middle East countries.

Three other more specialized Web sites are:

- www.fmep.org—The site for the Foundation for Middle East Peace based in Washington, D.C. It focuses on Israeli-Palestinian issues. Follow the links for access to governmental and nongovernmental sources. Also contains valuable map updates and settlement information, which can be downloaded.
- www.cmep.org—The site of Churches for Middle East Peace, its links are not limited to church organizations but provide access to many government and nongovernmental sources, especially Israeli and Palestinian. Also contains documents not found in other collections.
- gulf2000.columbia.edu—The best site on the states of the Persian Gulf region. It is an unrivaled source for countries such as Saudi Arabia, Iraq, and Iran, as well as the oil sheikhdoms. Though not listing Israel or Arab states bordering it, it provides the views of Gulf states on Arab-Israeli questions in addition to coverage of questions such as U.S. activities in Iraq or oil.

ACKNOWLEDGMENTS

Documents

Document 1.2 Edited excerpts from *The Middle East and North Africa in World Politics: A Documentary Record, 2nd ed., Revised and Enlarged: volume 1, European Expansion, 1535–1914*. Compiled, Translated, and Edited by J. C. Hurewitz. Reprinted by permission of J. C. Hurewitz.

Document 1.3 Theodor Herzl, *Der Judenstaat* (The Jewish State). Reprinted from *The Zionist Idea: A Historical Analysis and Reader*, © 1960 by Arthur Hertzberg, published by The Jewish Publication Society with the permission of the publisher.

Document 1.4 Theodor Herzl, "Who Fears a State?" Edited excerpts from *Zionist Writings: Essays and Addresses*, Volume 1, January 1896–June 1898, translated from the German by Harry Zohn (New York, 1973), pp. 211–15. Reprinted by permission of Judith Zohn.

Document 2.1 The Husayn-McMahon Correspondence. Edited text from pages 413–27 in *The Arab Awakening: The Story of the Arab National Movement* by George Antonius (Hamish Hamilton, 1938; reprinted 1945). Copyright © George Antonius, 1938. Reprinted by permission of Penguin Books Ltd.

Document 2.2 Leonard Stein, Appendix to Successive Drafts and Final Text of the Balfour Declaration. Excerpted from *The Balfour Declaration* by Leonard Stein. Published by The Jewish Chronicle Publication (1961).

Document 2.3 The Faysal-Weizmann Agreement. Edited text from pages 437–39 in *The Arab Awakening: The Story of the Arab National Movement* by George Antonius (Hamish Hamilton, 1938; reprinted 1945). Copyright © George Antonius, 1938. Reprinted by permission of Penguin Books Ltd.

Document 2.4 Resolutions of the General Syrian Congress. Edited text from pages 440–42 in *The Arab Awakening: The Story of the Arab National Movement* by George Antonius (Hamish Hamilton, 1938; reprinted 1945). Copyright © George Antonius, 1938. Reprinted by permission of Penguin Books Ltd.

Document 3.1 The Churchill White Paper. Edited excerpts from *The Middle East and North Africa in World Politics: A Documentary Record, 2nd ed., Revised and Enlarged: volume 2, British-French Supremacy, 1914–1945*. Compiled, Translated, and Edited by J. C. Hurewitz. Reprinted by permission of J. C. Hurewitz.

Document 3.3 The 1939 White Paper. Edited excerpts from *The Middle East and North Africa in World Politics: A Documentary Record, 2nd ed., Revised and Enlarged: volume 2, British-French Supremacy, 1914–1945*. Compiled, Translated, and Edited by J. C. Hurewitz. Reprinted by permission of J. C. Hurewitz.

Document 4.2 UNSCOP's Plan of Partition with Economic Union. UNSCOP Report, vol. 1, chapter VI, part I, Plan of partition with economic union. Copyright © United Nations. Reprinted by permission.

Document 4.3 Jamal al-Husayni, Testimony on Palestinian Arab Reaction to the UNSCOP Proposals. Edited excerpts from *The Middle East 1914–1979* by T. G. Fraser. Edward Arnold Publishers Ltd.

Document 4.4 Rabbi Hillel Silver, Testimony on Zionist Reaction to the UNSCOP Proposals. Edited excerpts from *The Middle East 1914–1979* by T. G. Fraser. Edward Arnold Publishers Ltd.

Document 5.1 Letter on the Position of the Palestinian Refugees. Copyright © United Nations. Reprinted by permission.

Document 6.1 Communiqué No. 1 from Headquarters of Asifa Forces (Fatah). Edited text from *Documents on the Middle East* by Ralph H. Magnus, ed. Copyright © 1969 American Enterprise Institute. Reprinted with the permission of The American Enterprise Institute for Public Policy Research, Washington, D.C.

Document 6.2 Gamal Abd al-Nasser, Speech to Members of the Egyptian National Assembly, from *The Israel-Arab Reader*, edited by Walter Laqueur and Barry Rubin, copyright © 1969, 1970 by B. L. Mazel, Inc. Copyright © 1976 by Walter Laqueur. Copyright © 1984, 1995, 2001, 2008 by Walter Laqueur and Barry Rubin. Used by permission of Viking Penguin, a division of Penguin Group (USA) Inc.

Document 6.3 Abba Eban, Speech to U.N. Security Council on Israel's Reasons for Going to War. Edited excerpts from *The Middle East 1914–1979* by T. G. Fraser. Edward Arnold Publishers Ltd.

Document 7.1 U.N. Security Council Resolution 242. Copyright © United Nations. Reprinted by permission.

Document 7.2 The Palestinian National Charter, from *The Israel-Arab Reader*, edited by Walter Laqueur and Barry Rubin, copyright © 1969, 1970 by B. L. Mazel, Inc. Copyright © 1976 by Walter Laqueur. Copyright © 1984, 1995, 2001, 2008 by Walter Laqueur and Barry Rubin. Used by permission of Viking Penguin, a division of Penguin Group (USA) Inc.

Document 7.3 Adapted from U.N. Security Council Resolution 338. Copyright © United Nations. Reprinted by permission.

Document 7.4 Address to the U.N. General Assembly by Yasir Arafat, from *The Israel-Arab Reader*, edited by Walter Laqueur and Barry Rubin, copyright © 1969, 1970 by B. L. Mazel, Inc. Copyright © 1976 by Walter Laqueur. Copyright © 1984, 1995, 2001, 2008 by Walter Laqueur and Barry Rubin. Used by permission of Viking Penguin, a division of Penguin Group (USA) Inc.

Document 7.5 Yosef Tekoah, Response to Arafat's Address. Adapted from United Nations 2283rd General Plenary Meeting official records, November 13, 1974. Copyright © United Nations. Reprinted by permission.

Document 8.1 Platform of the Likud Coalition from *The Israel-Arab Reader*, edited by Walter Laqueur and Barry Rubin, copyright © 1969, 1970 by B. L. Mazel, Inc. Copyright © 1976 by Walter Laqueur. Copyright © 1984, 1995, 2001, 2008 by Walter Laqueur and Barry Rubin. Used by permission of Viking Penguin, a division of Penguin Group (USA) Inc.

Document 8.2 Anwar al-Sadat, Speech to the Israeli Knesset. Edited excerpts from *The Middle East 1914–1979* by T. G. Fraser. Edward Arnold Publishers Ltd.

Document 9.1 Adapted from Communiqué No. 1 of the Intifada Issued by the Unified National Leadership, January 8, 1988. Copyright © United Nations. Reprinted by permission.

Document 10.1 The Israeli-PLO Declaration of Principles, Washington, D.C. September 13, 1993, from *Journal of Palestine Studies*, vol. 23, no. 1. Copyright © 1993, The Institute for Palestine Studies. Reprinted by permission of University of California Press via Copyright Clearance Center.

Document 10.2 The Israeli-Palestinian Interim Agreement (Oslo 2) on the West Bank and the Gaza Strip, September 28, 1995, from *Journal of Palestine Studies*, vol. 25, no. 2 (Winter 1996): 123–37. Copyright © 1996, The Institute for Palestine Studies. Reprinted by permission of University of California Press via Copyright Clearance Center.

Document 11.1 Ben Caspit, interview with Marwan Barghouti, from *Ma'ariv* (Tel Aviv), Friday, November 9, 2001, which appeared in the book *The Middle East and Islamic World Reader*, edited and translated by Marvin E. Gettleman and Stuart Schaar, copyright © 2003 by Marvin Gettleman and Stuart Schaar. Used by permission of Grove/Atlantic, Inc.

Document 11.2 Ami Ayalon, "The Urgent Thing, It Is to Unconditionally Disengage Ourselves from the Territories." Interview with Ami Ayalon, *Le Monde*, December 24, 2001. Translated by Americans for Peace Now. Copyright © 2001 *Le Monde* and Americans for Free Peace Now. Reprinted by permission of Le Monde and Americans for Peace Now.

Maps

Map 4.1 Adapted from Map 4, p. 121, in *The Transformation of Palestine* edited by Abu-Lughod. Copyright © 1971. Reprinted by permission of Northwestern University Press.

Map 4.2 Adapted from *The Middle East: A History*, Fourth Edition, edited by Sydney Nettleton Fisher and William Ochsenwald. Copyright © 1990 The McGraw-Hill Companies. Reprinted by permission of The McGraw-Hill Companies, Inc.

Map 4.3 Adapted from *Origins and Evolution of the Arab-Zionist Conflict* by Michael Cohen. Copyright © 1987 The Regents of the University of California. Reprinted by permission of the University of California Press via Copyright Clearance Center.

Map 5.1 Adapted from *The Middle East: A History*, Fourth Edition, edited by Sydney Nettleton Fisher and William Ochsenwald. Copyright © 1990 The McGraw-Hill Companies. Reprinted by permission of The McGraw-Hill Companies, Inc.

Map 6.1 Adapted from *Water and Power: The Politics of a Scarce Resource in the Jordan River Basin* by Miriam R. Lowi. Copyright © 1993 Miriam R. Lowi. Reprinted with permission of Cambridge University Press.

Map 6.2 Adapted from *A History of the Modern Middle East* by William Cleveland. Copyright © 1993 by Westview Press. Reprinted by permission of Westview Press, a member of Perseus Books Group.

Map 7.1 Adapted from *The Middle East: A History*, Fourth Edition, edited by Sydney Nettleton Fisher and William Ochsenwald. Copyright © 1990 The McGraw-Hill Companies. Reprinted by permission of The McGraw-Hill Companies, Inc.

Map 8.1 Map adapted from Itamar Rabinovich, *The War for Lebanon, 1970–1985*, Revised Edition. Copyright © 1984, 1985 by Cornell University Press. Used by permission of the publisher, Cornell University Press.

Map 9.1 Adapted from *A History of the Modern Middle East* by William Cleveland. Copyright © 1993 by Westview Press. Reprinted by permission of Westview Press, a member of Perseus Books Group.

Map 9.2 Adapted from *A Concise History of the Arab-Israeli Conflict*, Third Edition, by Ian J. Bickerton and Carla L. Klauser. Copyright © 1998. Reprinted by permission of Pearson Education, Inc., Upper Saddle River, N.J.

Map 10.2 Adapted from "Dividing a Land: Who Gets Control" map published in the *New York Times*, November 17, 1995. Copyright © 2000 by the New York Times Company. Reprinted by permission. Insert map adapted from *Le Monde Diplomatique*, November 1999. Reprinted by permission of the publisher.

Map 11.1 Copyright © Foundation for Middle East Peace.

Map 11.2 Copyright © Foundation for Middle East Peace.

Map 11.3 Copyright © Jan de Jong. Reprinted by permission of Foundation for Middle East Peace.

Map 11.4 Copyright © 2009 United Nations. Reprinted by permission.

Photos

1.1 Reproduced from the Collections of the Library of Congress.

1.2 Reproduced from the Collections of the Library of Congress.

1.3 Central Zionist Archives.

1.4 Reproduced from the Collections of the Library of Congress.

1.5 Reproduced from the Collections of the Library of Congress.

2.1 With permission of the Trustees of the Imperial War Museum, London.

2.2 Reproduced from the Collections of the Library of Congress.

2.3 Reproduced from the Collections of the Library of Congress.

2.4 With permission of the Trustees of the Imperial War Museum, London.

3.1 Reproduced from the Collections of the Library of Congress.

3.2 Reproduced from the Collections of the Library of Congress.
3.3 Reproduced from the Collections of the Library of Congress.
3.4 Reproduced from the Collections of the Library of Congress.
3.5 Reproduced from the Collections of the Library of Congress.
3.6 Reproduced from the Collections of the Library of Congress.
4.1 Reproduced from the Collections of the Library of Congress.
4.2 Central Zionist Archives.
4.3 Reproduced from the Collections of the Library of Congress.
4.4 Central Zionist Archives.
4.5 © Bettmann/Corbis.
4.6 © Bettmann/Corbis.
5.1 *Before Their Diaspora: A Photographic History of the Palestinians, 1876–1948.* Walid Khalidi, 1991 (2nd Edition), Institute for Palestine Studies.
5.2 © Bettmann/Corbis.
6.1 Yoichi R. Okamoto/Courtesy LBJ Library Collection.
6.2 © Bettmann/Corbis.
7.1 AP Photo.
7.2 © Bettmann/Corbis.
7.3 AP Photo/Marty Lederhandler.
8.1 Claude Salhani/Sygma/Corbis.
8.2 AP Photo/Bob Daugherty.
8.3 Dan Haddani.
8.4 © Bettmann/Corbis.
9.1 Howard Davies/Corbis.
9.2 David H. Wells/Corbis.
9.3 Dick Doughty.
10.1 Clinton Presidential Materials Project, National Archives photo #P7291-10a.
10.2 Dan Dean/Gamma.
10.3 Langevin Jacques/Corbis Sygma.
11.1 © Goran Tomasevic/Reuters/Corbis.
11.2 © Mohammed Saber/epa/Corbis.
11.3 © Amir Cohen/Reuters/Corbis.

INDEX

Documents, figures, and notes are indicated with *d*, *f*, and *n* following the page number. Surnames beginning with *al-* are alphabetized by the remaining portion of name.

c. 850–725 BCE Kingdoms of Israel and Judah founded.

586–539 BCE Babylonian captivity.

140–63 BCE Independent Hasmonean dynasty of Israel.

63 BCE–638 CE Palestine under Roman and Byzantine rule.

638–1918 Palestine under Muslim rule with intervals of European crusader control, 1099–1244.

1453 Ottoman Turks take Constantinople.

1516–1918 Ottomans rule Palestine.

1854–1856 Crimean War.

1861–1920 Mount Lebanon autonomous within Ottoman Empire.

1869 Suez Canal opens.

1882 British occupation of Egypt.

1896 *Der Judenstaat* published.

1897 World Zionist Organization founded.

1901 Jewish National Fund created.

1908 First Palestinian newspaper founded.

August 1914–November 1918 World War I.

February–December 1915 Gallipoli campaign.

March 1915 Constantinople Agreement.

July 1915–January 1916 Husayn-McMahon correspondence.

May 1916 Sykes-Picot Agreement.

June 1916 Arab Revolt against Ottomans begins.

March 1917 First Russian Revolution. British forces take Baghdad.

November 1917 Balfour Declaration. Second Russian Revolution.

June 1918 Allied Declaration to the Seven.

October 1918 Allies take Damascus. Mudros Armistice. Ottomans surrender.

November 1918 Anglo-French Declaration to Arabs. Armistice in Europe, end of World War I.

January 1919 Faysal-Weizmann agreement. Paris Peace Conference begins.

March 1920 Faysal proclaimed king of Greater Syria.

April 1920 San Remo Conference.

July 1920 French take Damascus, oust Faysal. Herbert Samuel appointed first high commissioner of Palestine.

March 1921 Cairo Conference. British install Faysal as king of Iraq, divide mandated Palestine; eastern region becomes Transjordan.

August 1929 Western Wall riots.

October 1930 Passfield White Paper.

January 1933 Adolf Hitler becomes chancellor of Germany.

April 1936 Arab Revolt begins. Arab Higher Committee formed.

July 1937 Peel Commission report.

February–April 1939 St. James Conference.

March 1939 Nazi takeover of Czechoslovakia.

May 1939 British White Paper.

September 1–3, 1939 Germany invades Poland, starts World War II.

November 1940 Hagana blows up S.S. *Patria* in Haifa harbor.

June 1941 Germany invades Soviet Union.

December 7, 1941 Japan attacks Pearl Harbor.

May 1942 Biltmore Conference.

November 1944 LEHI terrorists assassinate Lord Moyne.

April 1945 U.S. President Franklin D. Roosevelt dies, succeeded by Harry S. Truman.

May 8, 1945 War ends in Europe.

August 14, 1945 Japan surrenders, ending World War II.

April 1946 Anglo-American Committee of Inquiry report issued. President Truman calls for admission of 100,000 Jewish refugees to Palestine.

July 1946 Irgun blows up King David Hotel.

February 1947 Britain submits Palestine question to U.N.

June–July 1947 UNSCOP visits Palestine, recommends partition.

November 1947 U.N. General Assembly approves partition of Palestine.

May 14, 1948 Proclamation of state of Israel. David Ben-Gurion becomes first prime minister.

May 15–July 19, 1948 Israel at war with Arab states.

January–July 1949 Armistice agreements reached between Israel and Arab states.

July 1952 Egyptian army officers take over government.

July–October 1954 Anglo-Egyptian accord for British troop withdrawal from Suez Canal zone. Israeli spy ring discovered.

February 1955 Iraq and Turkey sign Baghdad Pact. Israeli raid into Gaza.

September 1955 Czech arms deal with Egypt.

July 1956 U.S. and Britain withdraw Aswan Dam funding. Nasser nationalizes Suez Canal.

October–November 1956 Suez crisis. Israel, Britain, and France coordinate invasion of Egypt.

January–March 1957 Eisenhower Doctrine ratified by Congress. Israel withdraws from Sinai.

February 1958 Egypt and Syria form United Arab Republic; lasts until September 1961.

January 1964 Arab League summit in Cairo; Palestine Liberation Organization (PLO) formed.

Summer 1964 Israel inaugurates national water carrier system.

January 1965 Fatah begins raids against Israel.

May 1967 Egyptian forces enter Sinai, close Straits of Tiran.

June 5–10, 1967 Six-Day War.

August 1967 Khartoum Conference.

November 1967 U.N. Security Council Resolution 242 passed.

1969 Golda Meir becomes prime minister of Israel.

February 1969 Yasir Arafat elected head of PLO.

March 1969–August 1970 Egyptian-Israeli war of attrition.

September 1970 Jordanian civil war. Gamal Abd al-Nasser dies, succeeded by Anwar al-Sadat.

November 1970 Hafiz al-Assad takes power in Syria.

September 1972 Fatah's Black September terrorists take Israeli Olympic athletes hostage in Munich.

October 6–22, 1973 Yom Kippur War. U.N. Security Council passes Resolution 338.

January 1974 First Egyptian-Israeli disengagement of forces agreement.

May 1974 Syrian-Israeli disengagement pact in Golan Heights.

October 1974 Arab summit at Rabat declares PLO is "sole legitimate representative of the Palestinian people."

April 1975–October 1976 Lebanese Civil War.

September 1975 Second Egyptian-Israeli disengagement agreement.

June 1977 Menachem Begin becomes Israel's prime minister.

November 1977 Sadat addresses Knesset in Jerusalem.

September 1978 Camp David talks.

January–February 1979 Iranian revolution; shah goes into exile.

March 1979 Egyptian-Israeli peace treaty.

June 1980 Venice Declaration. European community calls for Palestinian right to self-determination.

September 1980–July 1988 Iraq-Iran War.

January 1981 Ronald Reagan becomes U.S. president; Iran releases American hostages.

October 6, 1981 Sadat assassinated; Husni Mubarak becomes president of Egypt.

April 1982 Israeli pullback from Sinai completed.

June 6–August 1982 Israeli invasion of Lebanon.

September 1, 1982 Reagan peace plan.

September 14, 1982 Bashir Gemayel assassinated.

September 16–19, 1982 Maronite massacres of Palestinians at Sabra and Shatila.

August 1983 Begin resigns as Israeli prime minister, succeeded by Yitzhak Shamir.

October 1983 Suicide bomber kills 241 U.S. marines in Beirut.

February 1984 U.S. forces leave Lebanon.

December 1987 Intifada begins.

January 1988 PLO-intifada leadership calls for a Palestinian state to coexist with Israel.

February 1988 Hamas founded.

July 1988 King Husayn renounces claims to West Bank.

December 1988 U.S. agrees to enter dialogue with PLO in Tunis.

June 1990 U.S. suspends dialogue with PLO.

August 2, 1990 Iraq invades Kuwait.

January 16–February 28, 1991 First Gulf War.

October 1991 Arab-Israeli talks in Madrid.

July 1992 Yitzhak Rabin elected Israeli prime minister.

September 13, 1993 Israeli-Palestinian Accord (Oslo 1 Accord) signed in Washington, D.C.

May 1994 Palestinian self-rule begins in Jericho, Gaza Strip.

October 1994 Israel-Jordan Peace Treaty.

September 28, 1995 Oslo 2 Accord signed in Washington, D.C.

November 4, 1995 Rabin assassinated; Shimon Peres becomes prime minister of Israel.

January 20, 1996 Palestinian Interim Self-Government Authority elected.

May 1996 Binyamin Netanyahu elected Israeli prime minister.

January 1997 Hebron Agreement.

October 1998 Wye Memorandum.

December 1998 Palestine National Council votes to remove 1968 charter clauses calling for Israel's destruction.

February 1999 Jordan's King Husayn dies, succeeded by son Abdullah II.

May 18, 1999 Ehud Barak elected prime minister of Israel.

December 1999–March 2000 Unsuccessful Syrian-Israeli talks.

July 2000 Palestinian-Israeli summit at Camp David.

September 28, 2000 Ariel Sharon Temple Mount visit sparks al-Aqsa, second intifada.

November 2000 George W. Bush elected U.S. president; reelected 2004.

February 6, 2001 Ariel Sharon elected Israeli prime minister; reelected January 2003.

September 11, 2001 Al-Qaida attacks on U.S.

February 2002 Saudi Arabian peace initiative.

June 24, 2002 President Bush's Rose Garden speech.

March 2003 U.S. occupies Iraq.

April 30, 2003 Quartet Road Map.

June 2003 Aqaba summit.

April 14, 2004 U.S. accepts Israel's Gaza Disengagement Plan.

November 2004 Yasir Arafat dies.

August 2005 Israel withdraws from Gaza Strip, dismantling settlements.

January 2006 Sharon suffers debilitating stroke. Hamas wins Palestinian parliamentary elections.

March 2006 Ehud Olmert elected Israeli prime minister.

June–July 2006 Israel-Hamas conflict in Gaza.

July 12–August 14, 2006 Hizbollah-Israel war.

November 2007 Annapolis Conference.

June–November 2008 Hamas-Israel truce, broken by Israel November 4.

December 2008–January 2009 Israeli assaults on Gaza.

January 2009 Barack Obama takes office as president of the United States.

March 2009 Netanyahu becomes prime minister of Israel.